COMPLETE

EU LAW

Text, Cases, and Materials

COMPLETE

EU LAW

Text, Cases, and Materials

FOURTH EDITION

Elspeth Berry

Matthew J. Homewood

Barbara Bogusz

Great Clarendon Street, Oxford, OX2 6DP,
United Kingdom

Oxford University Press is a department of the University of Oxford. It furthers the University's objective of excellence in research, scholarship, and education by publishing worldwide. Oxford is a registered trade mark of Oxford University Press in the UK and in certain other countries

First Edition 2013
Second Edition 2015
Third Edition 2017

Impression: 1

Published in the United States of America by Oxford University Press
198 Madison Avenue, New York, NY 10016, United States of America

British Library Cataloguing in Publication Data
Data available

Library of Congress Control Number: 2019940595

ISBN 978-0-19-883621-6

Printed in Great Britain by
Bell & Bain Ltd., Glasgow

Preface

EU law is an ever-changing area of the legal landscape. It cannot be fully understood without a sound knowledge of its economic and political underpinnings, particularly the aim of establishing a single market across the European Union, yet the central role played by economics and politics also means that EU law is under constant and often conflicting pressures from its Member States and citizens. Furthermore, the EU legal order requires constant interaction between the Court of Justice of the European Union and the national courts in the Member States—an interaction that produces many challenges both for the legal procedures involved and for the content of the law at issue. The result is a wealth of legislation and case law that is often different in style and substance from traditional domestic law, but which is a crucial and integral part of UK law.

The aim of *Complete EU Law: Text, Cases, and Materials* is to provide the reader with a comprehensive, engaging, and accessible book. As a cases-and-materials book, it provides the reader with clear and lively textual commentary, combined with extracts from cases, legislation, and other materials.

EU law is a subject that necessitates the incremental development of the reader's knowledge and understanding. To achieve this, we have organized the materials in a structured and logical manner. The opening chapters provide the reader with the foundations of EU law. This provides a solid base that equips the reader with the fundamental principles on which to build a complete understanding of EU law. The following chapters then explore a number of issues of constitutional importance to the European Union and the way in which its law functions, as well as a number of substantive aspects of the internal market. This format will enrich your understanding of EU law, and the academic text is supported by the use of diagrams, flow charts, comprehension questions, and case studies. Through this approach, it is our intention that the book will provide an understandable and relevant explanation of EU law.

We firmly believe that EU law can be fun, as well as challenging, and we hope that our enthusiasm for this subject is apparent in the pages of this book. A lot of the enjoyment of any legal subject develops in discussion of the more complex issues, and so we would like to thank all those colleagues and students (past and present) who, with their ideas and interest, have indirectly contributed to the content of this book.

Our thanks also go to Amy Chard, Emily Hoyland, and the rest of the team at Oxford University Press.

Finally, special thanks to Mark Hodgson, to Sam, Abigail, and Alistair Homewood, and to Adam.

New for this edition

- Chapter 1 includes a detailed discussion of the issues arising from the UK's triggering of the Article 50 TFEU mechanism, including the European Union (Withdrawal) Act 2018 and the Draft Agreement on the Withdrawal of the UK from the EU. It also discusses the Political Declaration setting out the framework for the future relationship between the EU and the UK, and the possibility of the so-called Ukraine option for that relationship.
- Chapter 4 includes extensive coverage of the recent judgment of the Court of Justice in *Farrell* and the potential impact on direct effect of the Draft Agreement on the Withdrawal of the United Kingdom from the European Union.
- Chapter 5 includes discussion of the impact of the European Union (Withdrawal) Act 2018 on *Francovich* liability.
- Chapter 6 includes detailed coverage of the recent judgments of the Court of Justice in *Achmea* and *Taricco*, and discusses the impact on the Court of Justice's jurisdiction to give preliminary rulings of the European Union (Withdrawal) Act 2018, as well as the potential impact of the Draft Agreement on the Withdrawal of the UK from the EU.
- Chapter 9 includes discussion of the recent judgment of the Court of Justice in *MA, SA and AZ*.
- The edition also includes detailed discussion of recent Brexit-related judgments, including those of the Court of Justice in *Wightman* and *MA, SA and AZ*, and of the UK's Supreme Court in *The UK Withdrawal from the European Union (Legal Continuity) (Scotland) Bill* and its Upper Tribunal (Tax and Chancery) in *Coal Staff Superannuation Scheme Trustees Ltd*.
- Increased analysis throughout.
- Fully updated to include other developments in EU law, including many recent cases.

Acknowledgements

Grateful acknowledgement is made to all the authors and publishers of copyright material that appears in this book, and in particular to the Incorporated Council of Law Reporting for England and Wales for extracts from The Weekly Law Reports.

Every effort has been made to trace and contact copyright holders prior to publication. If notified, the publisher will undertake to rectify any error or omissions at the earliest opportunity.

Guide to using the book

Complete EU Law: Text, Cases, and Materials includes a number of different features that have been carefully designed to enrich your learning and to provide additional support as you develop your understanding of EU law.

Case 20/88 *Roquette Frères v Commission* [1989

23. The Court has consistently held that the Community's [now cannot be incurred through the adoption of a legislative me nomic policy unless a sufficiently flagrant violation of a sup tion of the individual has occurred. In a legislative context

Key cases and materials Extracts from key cases, legislation, and reports are reproduced and explained by the authors, helping you to develop your understanding of EU law and to gain confidence reading primary sources.

KEY POINTS

By the end of this chapter, you should be able to:

- understand the procedural and judicial stage of enforcem
- explain what acts may be challenged and by whom for a c
- be thoroughly familiar with the test of 'direct and individu
- explain the effect of a successful action under Article 263

Learning objectives Each chapter begins with a set of learning objectives, helping you to plan your reading and acting as a useful checklist for revision ahead of exams.

acte clair
The term *acte clair* refers to a particular legislative provision, the meaning of which is clear. However, determining whether

EU law at issue are *acte clair*, since, i unnecessary. The other is whether the the court. If they are not, a reference

6.4.1 *Acte clair*

Note that, as will be seen later in thi

Definition boxes Key terms and principles are clearly defined throughout the text, ensuring complete understanding as you work through a topic.

leclare such an act invalid; any other J law and infringe the principle of legal icle 263 TFEU (see Chapter 7) gave the the coherence of the EU legal system rpreted accordingly. Finally, the Court y of EU laws because the EU legislative ose laws were entitled to participate in

→ CROSS-REFERENCE
On the exception relating to interim measures referred to in *Foto-Frost*, at para 19, see further 6.10.

Cross-references Important connections between topics are highlighted to provide a fully integrated understanding of the subject.

?! THINKING POINT

While reading the following extract, consider why the Cou that the time limit in this case was compatible with the prin

Thinking point boxes Critical questions are included throughout the text and introduce significant extracts, helping to guide your reading of key materials and to develop your own analytical skills when working with legal sources.

REVIEW QUESTION

Suppose that you are involved in litigation in the UK's Employm
dismissal from employment, which you allege is contrary to a (fic
law that provides protection against dismissal. The dispute cent
provision in the Directive that removes this protection if the emp
ate behaviour'. How would *acte clair* be important in this scenar

Review questions Review questions help you to check and consolidate your understanding of a topic as you move through each chapter. They also provide an opportunity to apply your learning to practical examples and situations, helping to develop your legal reasoning skills.

NOTE

According to the Court of Justice in Case C-54/96 *Dorsch Con Bundesbaugesellschaft Berlin mbH* [1997] ECR I-496, the factors determining whether a body is a 'court or tribunal' include:

- whether the body is established by law;

Notes Notes from the authors offer a quick recap of the most significant points and highlight common areas of confusion or difficulty.

SUMMARY

- Article 267 TFEU provides that preliminary references may be m national court or tribunal on a question of the interpretation of ary legislation. The case will be stayed in the national court unt preliminary ruling, which will then be used by the national cou
- The term 'court or tribunal' has an autonomous meaning in EU l
- A court or tribunal against whose decisions there is a judicial re

Chapter summaries Each chapter concludes with a summary section to help you to check your understanding of key topics. These bulleted lists are an ideal checklist for you to use when preparing for exams or assessments and will help you to identify areas for revision.

QUESTION

Discuss, with examples from case law, the role of national cour

To view an outline answer to this questio support your EU law studies, visit the Onlin **www.oup.com/uk/eulaw-complete4e**

Assessment questions These exam-style questions provide an opportunity to test your knowledge, and to practise applying EU cases and legislation to problem and essay questions, ahead of exams and assessments. Outline answers and guidance from the authors can be found in the Online Resources that accompany the book.

FURTHER READING

Articles

A Arnull, 'The Law Lords and the European Union: Swimming 35(1) EL Rev 57

Examines the practice of the UK courts in dealing with preliminary references.

C Barnard, 'The PPU: Is it Worth the Candle? An Early Assessm

Annotated further reading Selected further reading is included at the end of each chapter to support independent research. Each suggestion is accompanied by a brief note from the authors explaining its significance, to help you to plan and prioritize your reading.

The Online Resources that accompany this book provide ready-to-use learning resources to further support your studies. These resources are free to use, and they have been designed to complement the book and to maximize your learning.

www.oup.com/uk/eulaw-complete4e

Outline contents

Detailed contents

Table of abbreviations

CAP	Common Agricultural Policy
CCT	Common Customs Tariff
CFC	controlled foreign company
CFSP	Common Foreign and Security Policy
CHEE	Charge Having Equivalent Effect
COREPER	Committee of Permanent Representatives
CSDP	Common Security and Defence Policy
DMV	Double Majority Voting
EAT	Employment Appeal Tribunal
EC	European Community
ECB	European Central Bank
ECHR	European Convention on Human Rights
ECSC	European Coal and Steel Community
EDA	European Defence Agency
EEC	European Economic Community
EFTA	European Free Trade Area
EMU	Economic and Monetary Union
ESDP	European Security and Defence Policy
EU	European Union
EURATOM	European Atomic Energy Community
HRA	Human Rights Act 1998
JHA	Justice and Home Affairs
MEP	Member of the European Parliament
MEQR	Measure Having Equivalent Effect to Quantitative Restrictions
MIB	Motor Insurers' Bureau
NATO	North Atlantic Treaty Organization
NCA	National Competition Authority
OECD	Organisation for Economic Co-operation and Development
QMV	Qualified Majority Voting
RGM	Relevant Geographic Market
RPM	Relevant Product Market
RTM	Relevant Temporal Market
SEA	Single European Act (1986)
SSNIP	Small but Significant Non-transitory Increase in Price
TEU	Treaty on European Union
TFEU	Treaty on the Functioning of the European Union
WEU	Western European Union

Table of cases

European Union

Court of Justice

Alphabetical

Numerical

General Court/Court of First Instance

Alphabetical

Numerical

Commission

International

European Court of Human Rights

National

Denmark

Germany

United Kingdom

United States

Table of legislation

European Union

Treaties and Conventions

Secondary legislation

Decisions

Directives

Regulations

International

National

United Kingdom

The origins of the European Union and EU law

1

KEY POINTS

By the end of this chapter, you should be able to:

- describe the history of the European Union (EU);
- explain the basic principles of economic integration underlying the policies of the EU; and
- understand the legal development of the EU through its governing Treaties.

INTRODUCTION

The legal framework of the European Union (EU) has developed specifically in order to support and further its aims, and therefore an awareness of its aims and origins is essential in order to understand its institutions and legal structures (see Chapters 2 and 3), and the nature of its laws and their impact on UK law, business, and society (see Chapter 4 onwards).

One point on terminology needs to be noted at the start. The EU has changed its name and its legal structure over the years. It began life on 1 January 1958 as the European Economic Community (EEC), but was renamed the European Community (EC) from 1987. In 1992, certain new functions were introduced, but transferred to a new body, the European Union (see 1.13 on the Treaty on European Union (TEU), which created the EU), and the two bodies existed in parallel until they finally became a single body again under the EU name in 2009 (see 1.18 on the Treaty of Lisbon, which achieved this). It is not necessary to remember this chronology in detail, but it explains why certain older cases or documents refer to the EEC or EC rather than the EU. For most purposes, you can read references to the EEC or EC as references to the EU.

The rationale for the creation of the EU is examined in detail in this chapter, but, to start, it is instructive to read the Preamble to the Treaty of Rome establishing the European Economic Community (1957) (the EEC Treaty). A further point on terminology arises in relation to this Treaty. You may sometimes find it referred to as the Treaty of Rome (after the city in which it was signed), but there have been many other treaties concluded in Rome and so a reference to the Treaty of Rome does not necessarily refer to the EEC Treaty. It is therefore more accurate to refer to it as the EEC Treaty. In parallel with the changes of name of the EEC/EC/EU itself, referred to above, the EEC Treaty has been renamed and substantially amended on a number of occasions, as will be explained later in this chapter. In particular, it became the EC Treaty from 1993 and the Treaty on the Functioning of the European Union (TFEU) from 2009.

The Preamble to the EEC Treaty set out the aspirations of the founders of the EEC.

Treaty of Rome establishing the European Economic Community (1957)

Preamble

HIS MAJESTY THE KING OF THE BELGIANS,

THE PRESIDENT OF THE FEDERAL REPUBLIC OF GERMANY,

THE PRESIDENT OF THE FRENCH REPUBLIC,

THE PRESIDENT OF THE ITALIAN REPUBLIC,

HER ROYAL HIGHNESS THE GRAND DUCHESS OF LUXEMBOURG, HER MAJESTY THE QUEEN OF THE NETHERLANDS,

DETERMINED to lay the foundations of an ever closer union among the peoples of Europe,

RESOLVED to ensure the economic and social progress of their countries by common action to eliminate the barriers which divide Europe,

AFFIRMING as the essential objective of their efforts the constant improvements of the living and working conditions of their peoples,

RECOGNISING that the removal of existing obstacles calls for concerted action in order to guarantee steady expansion, balanced trade and fair competition,

ANXIOUS to strengthen the unity of their economies and to ensure their harmonious development by reducing the differences existing between the various regions and the backwardness of the less favoured regions,

DESIRING to contribute, by means of a common commercial policy, to the progressive abolition of restrictions on international trade,

INTENDING to confirm the solidarity which binds Europe and the overseas countries and desiring to ensure the development of their prosperity, in accordance with the principles of the Charter of the United Nations,

RESOLVED by thus pooling their resources to preserve and strengthen peace and liberty, and calling upon the other peoples of Europe who share their ideal to join in their efforts,

DETERMINED to promote the development of the highest possible level of knowledge for their peoples through a wide access to education and through its continuous updating,

HAVE DECIDED to create a European Economic Community and to this end have designated as their Plenipotentiaries:

[*List of plenipotentiaries omitted*]

Who, having exchanged their Full Powers, found in good and due form, HAVE AGREED as follows:

[*Then follows the text of the Treaty*]

The Preamble demonstrates that the founders had in mind both political and economic objectives.

?! THINKING POINT

The EEC Treaty was concluded in 1957 after negotiations that took place over a number of years. What significant world event immediately prior to this period might have led European politicians to call for greater cooperation between European countries in economic and political matters?

The event that, above all, led European politicians to seek greater cooperation was the Second World War, and the political and economic devastation that it caused across Europe.

1.1 The historical rationale for the European Union

Although ideas of European political and economic integration had existed prior to the Second World War, these ideas began to look realistic only in the post-war years. Across Europe, memories were scarred by two devastating world wars centred on Europe, successive severe winters led to a fuel crisis, there was a series of bad harvests, and foreign reserves were drained by the lack of exports. It seemed that political cooperation might be the way to a better future.

The military threat from the then Union of Soviet Socialist Republics (USSR) at this time, which marked the beginning of the Cold War, was perceived as particularly acute and, in order to promote post-war stability in Europe, the United States offered support to Western European countries in the form of the Marshall Plan (which gave aid to those countries for post-war reconstruction) and the Truman Doctrine (which pledged military support to countries resisting aggression). The founding members of the EEC felt that the likelihood of a third world war centred on Europe would be further decreased by constructing close economic and political ties between European countries. A cooperative effort, including the pooling of resources, was needed for Europe to recover from the war and cope with the economic problems of the post-war years. In addition, while as individual countries each was too small to compete economically or militarily with either the United States or the then USSR (or, nowadays, China), working together the European countries might have more global influence.

REVIEW QUESTION

What other, non-EU, European legal initiatives (which you may have learned about in studies of constitutional or public law) came about as a result of the desire amongst Europeans that the horrors of the Second World War should never happen again?

Answer: The European Convention on Human Rights (ECHR) (see further 9.1) was also signed in the post-war period. This Convention, which operates under the auspices of the Council of Europe (see further 9.1) and which applies across a much wider geographical area than the EU and its Treaties, focuses on political human rights rather than economic rights. The relationship between the ECHR and EU law, and between the Council of Europe and the EU institutions, is explained in greater detail at 9.1.

Despite these cogent reasons for a European union, its formation was delayed for over a decade after the war; the EEC Treaty, which ultimately led to the formation of the EU, was not signed until 1957 rather than a decade earlier. The problems of the immediate post-war era—depleted national reserves, decimated industries, and large numbers of unemployed ex-servicemen, together with a series of bad harvests—meant that national reconstruction took priority over more grandiose European plans. In addition, some of the most ardent supporters of the ideal of a European union were not in a position to influence events. The former West Germany (now part of a united Germany), which saw a European union as a way in which to gain re-acceptance by its neighbours, had, in the immediate post-war era, little political influence and Winston Churchill, the British prime minister who had argued for a United States of Europe, was no longer in power. However, during the late 1940s, a number of organizations were set up that involved the close cooperation of European and other states. These included the Organisation for European Co-operation (now the Organisation for Economic Co-operation and Development (OECD)), the North Atlantic Treaty Organization (NATO), and the Council of Europe (see further 9.1 on the Council of Europe). A European Defence Community was also proposed, but failed to materialize.

1.2 The EEC, ECSC, and EURATOM Treaties

A number of countries, particularly France, recognized that if West Germany's coal and steel industries were tied to those of other countries, that country would be seriously hampered in any future war effort. In addition, it was recognized that cooperation in this area could be economically advantageous. As a result, in 1951, Belgium, the Netherlands, and Luxembourg (sometimes known as the Benelux countries), together with France, Italy, and Germany, signed the Treaty of Paris establishing the European Coal and Steel Community (ECSC) (see also 3.4.1). The ECSC Treaty expired in July 2002, but by then the ECSC had been successful in removing trade restrictions on coal and steel between the 15 Member States of the ECSC, and in creating a supranational authority (ie with powers over the Member States) to oversee the expansion of production.

In the Preamble to the ECSC Treaty, the six signatory Member States declared it to be only the first step towards a federal Europe, and those States (particularly the Benelux countries, which were already closely linked economically by their own Benelux Union) became increasingly anxious to extend their fledgling alliance to other economic and political areas. In 1957, on the basis of the Report of the Spaak Committee on the feasibility of European integration, the EEC Treaty (see also 3.4.1) was signed. The Spaak Report proposed a common market (see further 1.4.3) and noted that the advantages of a common market could be achieved only if it included rules to prevent the distortion of competition between producers, and cooperation between states to ensure monetary stability, economic expansion, and social progress. This went much further than the brief of the UK representative on the Committee, which had the simpler aim of a free trade area (see 1.4.1 and 1.19).

As noted in the Introduction to this chapter, the EEC Treaty has been subject to renaming and to considerable revision and supplementation over the years, and it now exists in the form of two Treaties: the Treaty on European Union (TEU) and the Treaty on the Functioning of the European Union (TFEU). These will be considered in detail throughout this book, as they now constitute the legal foundation of the EU.

NOTE

Treaties are normally divided into Articles, just as UK Acts of Parliament are divided into sections. When you cite a particular Article of the TFEU, for example Article 267, the correct citation is 'Article 267 TFEU'. When you cite a particular Article of the TEU, for example Article 6, you should cite it as 'Article 6 TEU'.

Also in 1957, the six members of the ECSC and the EEC signed the Treaty establishing the European Atomic Energy Community (EURATOM) (see also 3.4.1), formally agreeing to cooperate in the development of the peaceful use of atomic energy. EURATOM now has the same Member States as the EU and shares its major institutions, as agreed in the Merger Treaty 1965 (see also 3.4.1). It continues to exist, but is a separate body to the EU and will not be considered further in this book. However, it should be noted that Article 106(a) of the EURATOM Treaty provides that the provisions of Article 50 TEU, which allow a Member State to give notice of withdrawal from the EU, apply to the EURATOM Treaty so as to allow a similar notice of withdrawal from EURATOM to be given. When the UK government gave notice under Article 50 TEU of its intention to withdraw from the EU (see further 1.19), it also invoked Article 106(a) of the EURATOM Treaty so as to give notice of its intention to leave EURATOM, and therefore the discussion at 1.19 is also relevant to EURATOM.

?! THINKING POINT

Do you think that EU law could be classed as international law?

EU law may be regarded as a type of international law in that it governs the relations between sovereign States (the Member States of the EU) and regulates cross-border activities. However, it has a number of features not normally seen in international law, including the possibility of direct enforcement of its laws by individuals and businesses before national courts (see further Chapter 4), and the sovereignty of EU law over national law (see further Chapter 3). The term 'supranational' is sometimes used to refer to EU law because rather than governing relations between (*inter*) States, it puts in place institutions that are above (*supra*) the States. It has been suggested that there are occasions when the approach of the EU's Court of Justice (see 2.4 for an explanation of this court) is that of an international court (see, for example, Jed Odermatt, 'The Court of Justice of the European Union: International or Domestic Court?' (2014) 3(3) CJICL 696, 717–18).

1.3 The aims of the EU

The original aims have been updated over the years; for example, the aim of economic and monetary union (EMU) was introduced only in 1992. The current formulation of the aims is to be found in Article 3 TEU.

Article 3 TEU

1. The Union's aim is to promote peace, its values and the well-being of its peoples.
2. The Union shall offer its citizens an area of freedom, security and justice without internal frontiers, in which the free movement of persons is ensured in conjunction with appropriate measures with respect to external border controls, asylum, immigration and the prevention and combating of crime.
3. The Union shall establish an internal market. It shall work for the sustainable development of Europe based on balanced economic growth and price stability, a highly competitive social market economy, aiming at full employment and social progress, and a high level of protection and improvement of the quality of the environment.

   It shall promote scientific and technological advance. It shall combat social exclusion and discrimination, and shall promote social justice and protection, equality between women and men, solidarity between generations and protection of the rights of the child.

   It shall promote economic, social and territorial cohesion, and solidarity among Member States.

   It shall respect its rich cultural and linguistic diversity, and shall ensure that Europe's cultural heritage is safeguarded and enhanced.
4. The Union shall establish an economic and monetary union whose currency is the euro.
5. In its relations with the wider world, the Union shall uphold and promote its values and interests and contribute to the protection of its citizens. It shall contribute to peace, security, the sustainable development of the Earth, solidarity and mutual respect among peoples, free and fair trade, eradication of poverty and the protection of human rights, in particular the rights of the child, as well as to the strict observance and the development of international law, including respect for the principles of the United Nations Charter.
6. The Union shall pursue its objectives by appropriate means commensurate with the competences which are conferred upon it in the Treaties.

Many of these aims have already been at least partially fulfilled. For example, the internal market has largely been achieved (see further 1.4.3 on this stage of economic integration and, more generally, Chapters 10, 11, and 12), and substantial moves towards equality between men and women have been made (see 1.12 on social policy more generally). Of course, the extent to which the EU and its policies have caused or contributed towards the fulfilment of its other aims is open to argument. For example, the Member States have enjoyed an unprecedented period of peace since the middle of the twentieth century, albeit with some conflicts on the fringes of the EU in the Balkans and further east, but the impact of the Cold War balance of power and the existence of NATO may have been at least as important as that of the EU in this respect. Similarly, Member States have, overall, enjoyed significant economic growth over this time, but this is also true of many other countries that are not members of the EU.

?! THINKING POINT

Article 3(1) and (5) TEU refers to the 'values' of the EU. While reading Article 2 TEU and in the light of what you have read about the historical rationale for the EU, what sort of 'values' do you think that the Member States might have agreed upon?

What the Member States actually agreed upon is set out in Article 2 TEU.

Article 2 TEU

The Union is founded on the values of respect for human dignity, freedom, democracy, equality, the rule of law and respect for human rights, including the rights of persons belonging to minorities.

These values are common to the Member States in a society in which pluralism, non-discrimination, tolerance, justice, solidarity and equality between women and men prevail.

The Treaties contain hundreds of Articles, providing further detail of how the aims listed in Article 3 TEU are to be fulfilled. There is also a wide range of secondary legislation (see 3.4.2) providing still more detail.

1.4 Economic integration

Article 3(3) TEU (see 1.3) refers to an 'internal market' as one of the aims of the EU (see further 10.1 on the internal market) and, as explained at 1.1, economic integration as a means of avoiding military conflict was central to the creation of the EU. Since this forms the basis of much of the law explained in this book and, of course, the legal system that underpins it, it is necessary to have some understanding of the relevant economic theories.

Prior to any economic integration between countries, each country trades as an independent entity. It makes most sense for each country to concentrate on the goods or services that it can produce most efficiently.

REVIEW QUESTION

Suppose that two countries each produce both wine and beer. Vinland produces wine much more efficiently, and therefore cheaply, than Beeria, but Beeria produces beer much more efficiently and cheaply than Vinland. What might people in these countries, at least in theory, gain from trading with each other?

Answer: Consumers in Vinland will be able to buy Beerian beer more cheaply than beer produced in their own country. Consumers in Beeria will benefit similarly from buying their wine from Vinland. This suggests that efficiency can be maximized if Vinland concentrates on wine production rather than beer and Beeria concentrates on beer production rather than wine. However, the two countries can only optimize their efficiency in this way if they trade with each other in order to meet demand for the product of which they now produce less.

?! THINKING POINT

Can you see any potential problems for the two countries in the review question scenario?

If there are no restrictions at all on this trade, then this may produce disadvantages. For instance, if Vinland produces less (or no) beer and Beeria produces less (or no) wine, there will be unemployed workers in those industries. Furthermore, few countries would wish to be totally dependent on a single country for supply if the commodity involved were an essential one, such as oil or grain. Of course, in the real world, free trade does not exist between all countries because of protectionist measures taken by some and economic integration between others.

The Member States of the EU have adopted the approach of economic integration, although they have retained some protectionist measures in relation to countries outside the EU.

Economic integration is a process in which the countries in question pass through several stages over time. These will now be examined.

1.4.1 A free trade area

The first stage of economic integration is a free trade area.

A free trade area exists when a number of countries agree to remove all customs duties (payments made to States where goods cross their borders) and quotas (numerical limits imposed by States on the amount of goods that may be imported or exported) between themselves, so that there are no restrictions on the movement of goods from one country to another *within* the free trade area, but each country keeps its own (ie different) duties and quotas on goods imported from, or exported to, countries *outside* the area.

The concepts of 'customs duties' and 'quotas' will be discussed further in Chapter 10. The economic boom experienced by the Member States of the EEC in the late 1950s and early 1960s made the then EEC's aim of economic integration easier to achieve, and many quotas and duties were removed.

REVIEW QUESTION

Suppose that Vinland and Beeria have established a free trade area between them, and that you are a winemaker in Beeria. You could either buy cheap grapes from Distillia, a country outside the free trade area, but pay a 40 per cent duty to import them, or slightly more expensive grapes from Vinland on which, of course, you do not have to pay duty. Which would you choose? Will this cause any problems?

Answer: Owing to the abolition of duties, it is cheaper for you to buy from the less-efficient producer in another country within the free trade area (ie Vinland) than from the more efficient producer in a country outside it on whose products you then have to pay import duties (ie Distillia).

One problem with a free trade area, from an economist's point of view, is that it can encourage inefficiency within the free trade area. Of course, from the point of view of an inefficient producer, being in a free trade area is not a problem at all. Another problem is that such integration can lead to international trade diversion, which may cause economic difficulties for countries outside the free trade area.

Fear about the resulting diversion of trade was a factor in the creation in 1960 of an alternative free trade area to the EU, the European Free Trade Area (EFTA). This was formed by a number of European countries who did not wish to join the EEC, in an attempt to counter the negative effects on their trade caused by the economic integration of their neighbouring countries. Some of EFTA's members subsequently joined the EU instead, but EFTA remains in existence and currently consists of Iceland, Liechtenstein, Norway, and Switzerland. It is discussed in more detail at 1.19 in the context of the variety of relationships that the EU operates with non-Member States.

REVIEW QUESTION

Suppose that Vinland levies a duty of 10 per cent on goods imported from countries outside the free trade area, whereas Beeria levies a duty of 25 per cent on such imports. If you wished to export goods from Distillia to Beeria, how might you avoid the 25 per cent duty?

Answer: If exporters in Distillia market their goods to the whole of the free trade area (Vinland and Beeria) through Vinland, duty will be charged on the goods at only 10 per cent when they enter Vinland and the free trade area means that those goods can then pass into Beeria without further payment. This can be seen in Figure 1.1.

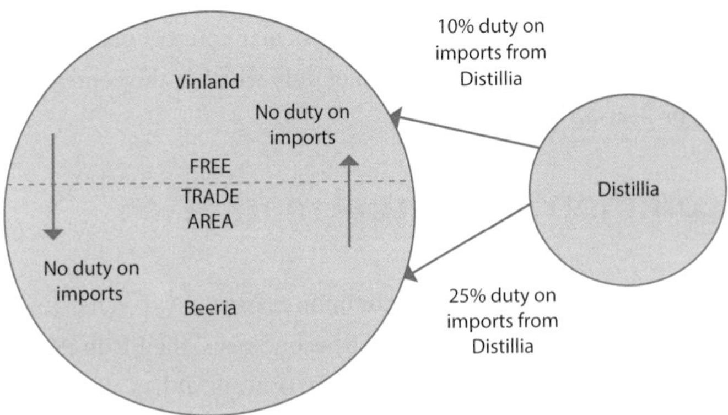

Figure 1.1 Impact of free trade area on third country imports

?! THINKING POINT

Who will benefit in the review question scenario? Who might suffer?

Clearly, exporters in Distillia will benefit from being able to avoid the higher rate of duty. Consumers in the free trade area will also benefit if the saving to exporters is passed on through cheaper prices for the goods. However, it may affect the relative competitiveness of industry in Beeria, because it now has to compete with goods from Distillia (and other countries outside the free trade area), which are cheaper than before. It may also affect the balance of trade, because Distillia's exports to Vinland will rise and its exports to Beeria will fall, while exports from Vinland to Beeria will also rise. Finally, it will reduce the amount of customs duties received by the government of Beeria on goods coming into it from countries outside the free trade area.

1.4.2 A customs union

The second stage of economic integration is a customs union.

A customs union consists of a free trade area (see 1.4.1) *plus* an agreement by countries in the area to impose a common level of duty on goods coming into the area from non-member countries.

In the EU, this common external duty is known as the Common Customs Tariff (CCT) (see further 10.1.2).

?! THINKING POINT

How might the addition of a common external duty solve some of the problems of a free trade area outlined in 1.4.1?

A customs union avoids a trade imbalance, such as that referred to earlier between Vinland, Beeria, and Distillia, because the same level of duty is charged by all the countries within the free trade area (ie Vinland and Beeria) to a particular country outside it (ie Distillia). So goods from Distillia would incur the same level of duty whether they enter the free trade area through Vinland or Beeria.

1.4.3 A common or internal market

The third stage of economic integration is a common market.

Although the term 'common market' is used by economists, the EU itself now uses a different term, the 'internal market', to describe the same concept. It has also sometimes used the term 'single market'.

?! THINKING POINT

Where have you already come across the use of the term 'internal market'?

Article 3 TFEU (see 1.3) states that one of the EU's aims is to achieve an internal market. A common, or internal, market consists of a customs union (see 1.4.2) *plus* an agreement by all member countries to remove restrictions on the free movement of goods, persons, services, and capital (sometimes collectively known as the factors of production or, in the EU context, the four freedoms) between themselves. Within the EU, steps were taken from the very beginning towards establishing the free movement of goods and workers between Member States, protecting the social security interests of such workers, regulating competition in goods, and establishing a Common Agricultural Policy (CAP)—and later a Common Fisheries Policy (CFP).

The definition of the EU's 'internal market' is contained in Article 26 TFEU.

Article 26 TFEU

1. The Union shall adopt measures with the aim of establishing or ensuring the functioning of the internal market, in accordance with the relevant provisions of the Treaties.
2. The internal market shall comprise an area without internal frontiers in which the free movement of goods, persons, services and capital is ensured in accordance with the provisions of the Treaties.
3. The Council, on a proposal from the Commission, shall determine the guidelines and conditions necessary to ensure balanced progress in all the sectors concerned.

?! THINKING POINT

What benefits might the 'free movement' referred to in Article 26 TFEU confer on individuals living in the EU?

The benefits conferred by the principle of free movement on individuals living in the EU include being able to move to a different Member State to take up employment opportunities, being able to travel abroad to receive services in tourism or health care, and, in either case, being able to take currency with them without restriction on the amount they can import and export. Even without leaving their own Member State, people can often buy goods from other Member States more easily or cheaply as compared to goods from outside the EU, and can buy them directly from those other Member States with consumer protection guarantees equal to those available in their home Member State.

1.4.4 Economic and monetary union

The fourth stage of economic integration, economic and monetary union (EMU), did not appear in the original EEC Treaty and was included only at a much later stage of the EU's history. It will therefore be considered (at 1.14) after discussing other developments that took place before EMU.

1.5 Economic and political difficulties

Despite the very many economic achievements of the EEC in its early years, there was a falling away of interest among its Member States from the mid-1960s until well into the 1980s. The economic boom of the early 1960s had not been sustained and EEC membership no longer appeared to guarantee economic success, particularly when oil prices rose sharply and a worldwide recession set in during the 1970s. The original 1969 deadline for the completion of the internal market came and went, scarcely noticed and certainly unfulfilled.

A further difficulty that came to the fore during this period was the decision-making process amongst the Member States. Initially, all decisions were taken by consensus—in other words, they required unanimity.

?! THINKING POINT

Why might consensus decision-making prove problematic?

Achieving agreement between several different countries, each with different economic and political priorities, on every decision necessary for the functioning of the EEC was often difficult and achieved only after protracted negotiations, and it was sometimes impossible. The same is true today of the EU.

However, during the 1960s, the EEC began to require certain decisions to be taken by a qualified majority vote. Qualified majority voting (QMV) requires a specific number of votes, rather than a simple majority, to be cast in favour of a measure in order for it to be passed (see further 1.15, 1.17, 1.18, and 2.2.2 on later reforms to QMV) and the number of votes given to each Member State is determined by the relative size of its population. Thus the larger States have greater power, but, crucially, no country has a veto. This means that decisions can be taken even if they are opposed by some Member States and these decisions will nonetheless bind all Member States.

Qualified majority decisions were due to include, from 1966, those concerning agricultural prices, an area of key importance to France. By refusing to exercise France's vote in the final period of consensus voting (which required unanimity), so that no decisions at all could be taken—sometimes referred to as the 'empty chair' approach—the French government succeeded in forcing the other countries to compromise on the issue of QMV. This was known as the Luxembourg Compromise (or the Luxembourg Accords) and it stated that where the Treaty provided for QMV and the vitally important interests of one or more Member States were involved, the EEC must try to find a unanimously agreed solution.

The extension of QMV in the Single European Act (1986) (see further 1.10 and 3.4.1 on the Single European Act) and subsequent Treaties (see further 1.13, 1.15, 1.17, 1.18, and 3.4.1 on these Treaties) led to further political difficulties and the adoption in 1994 of a further compromise, the Ioannina Compromise (see also 2.2.2). Although this was not limited to issues involving the vitally important interests of one or more Member States, it required the then EC to find a solution acceptable to only a majority—albeit a larger majority than was required by QMV. An amended version of the Ioannina Compromise now appears in Article 238(2) TFEU.

In addition to QMV, an additional and separate formula has since been introduced by the Treaty of Amsterdam (see 1.15) into both the EC Treaty and the TEU (1992) (now the TFEU and TEU), allowing for decision-making where the usual legislative procedures (explained at 3.5) cannot be used due to the objections of some Member States. This formula was originally known as closer cooperation, but it was amended by the Treaty of Nice (see 1.17) and renamed 'enhanced cooperation' (see also 1.15, 1.17, and 1.18 on its introduction and subsequent reforms). Although this term may sound rather imprecise, it has in fact a very particular meaning in the context of the EU and is a formal decision-making procedure with its own rules, as explained at 3.5.3. Effectively, the enhanced cooperation procedure allows a group of Member States to proceed with a particular course of action despite the absence of wider agreement within the EU.

Of course, difficulties for the EU have not been confined to this period of time, as demonstrated by the continuing arguments over whether the EU should be 'widened' (ie by expanding its membership—see 1.6) or 'deepened' (ie by closer integration—see 1.9), the political struggles over a European constitution (see 1.17), the economic difficulties and tensions between Member States caused, or at least exacerbated, by the single currency (see 1.14), and whether Turkey should be allowed to join the EU (see 1.6). Most recent is the challenge posed by the vote in the UK's 2016 referendum to withdraw from the EU ('Brexit'); the economic and political impact of any such exit on the EU itself may be considerable (see further 1.9, 3.2, and 3.3).

1.6 Expansion of membership

Despite the economic stagnation of the 1970s and early 1980s, and the apparent loss of momentum by the EEC, its membership began, and continued, to expand. In 1973, the UK, Denmark, and Ireland joined the original six members, followed by Greece in 1981.

Since then, the EU has experienced almost continual expansion, with Spain and Portugal joining in 1986, Austria, Finland, and Sweden in 1995, Cyprus, the Czech Republic, Estonia, Hungary, Latvia, Lithuania, Malta, Poland, Slovakia, and Slovenia in 2004, Bulgaria and Romania in 2007, and Croatia in 2013. Negotiations for the accession of a number of other States, including Albania, the former Yugoslav Republic of Macedonia, Montenegro, Serbia, and Turkey, are ongoing.

1.7 Institutional developments

There were also important developments in the 1960s and 1970s affecting the EEC institutions. The Budgetary Treaties of 1970 and 1975 introduced a special procedure for drafting and approving the EEC's budget, which gave the European Parliament greater powers (see 2.1.2). The 'own resources' concept was also introduced—that is, in addition to money contributed by the Member States, the EEC had its own resources coming from the levies under the CAP, the CCT, and other EEC-inspired taxes. A Court of Auditors was appointed as a financial watchdog over EEC spending (see Chapter 2).

NOTE

Do not be misled by the word 'Court' in the name of the Court of Auditors. It consists of a group of auditors and is not a court in the judicial sense, but more like a powerful committee.

Again, these developments continue and are discussed later in this chapter in the context of the various Treaties (see 1.10, 1.13, 1.15, 1.17, and 1.18).

1.8 Legal developments

The Court of Justice also pushed forward with the development of EEC law during the 1960s and 1970s. Some of the most significant judgments of this period included the following.

- **Case 22/70 *Commission v Council (ERTA)* [1971] ECR 263** In this case, the Court ruled that once EEC measures had been taken in a particular area of law, Member States could no longer act independently in that area, since this would prevent the uniform application of EEC law. This continues to have important consequences for the powers and competences of the EU.
- **Case 41/74 *Van Duyn v Home Office* [1974] ECR 1337** In this case, the Court ruled that, in certain circumstances, a type of EEC legislation called a Directive could be enforced in the national courts. As explained in 3.4.2, Directives are addressed to Member State governments, and the ruling that they could be enforced directly by ordinary individuals or businesses was controversial. (This case is discussed further at 4.1.1 and 4.1.4.)
- **Case 106/77 *Amministrazione delle Finanze dello Stato v Simmenthal SpA ('Simmenthal II')* [1978] ECR 629** The Court ruled that, since it had previously ruled that EEC law was supreme and took precedence over national law, any conflicting national legislation should be disapplied. Again, this was controversial—not least in the UK, where it could be argued that it detracted from the traditional doctrine of the supremacy of the Westminster Parliament. (This case is discussed further at 3.1.2 and 4.2.5.)

REVIEW QUESTION

Make a note of these cases, some of which are discussed in more detail in other chapters, as indicated. When you reach each of these cases in later chapters, think about the impact that they had on the development of EU law in those areas.

1.9 Closer integration

The momentum towards closer European integration was revived in the 1980s. First, in 1984, the draft EU Treaty, which was designed to create a federal Europe with a more powerful European Parliament (see 2.1), was proposed by the European Parliament. Although the draft Treaty was not accepted by the Council (see 2.2 on the Council), the Dooge Committee was set up to look into possible reforms of the original EEC Treaty.

Secondly, the long-running dispute over the UK's contribution to the EU's budget was resolved and the UK was pressured into accepting the work of the Dooge Committee.

Thirdly, in 1985, the Schengen Agreements were adopted by a majority of the Member States (although not the UK or Ireland), and have since been extended to some other Member States and a small number of non-EU European states. The Agreements abolished internal frontier controls and included a number of other measures to enhance the free movement of persons between these countries (see further Chapter 11 on the free movement of persons).

Finally, a new President of the European Commission (see 2.3.2) was appointed, Jacques Delors, who oversaw the drafting of the White Paper on European Union, which became the Single European Act.

The process of integration has continued, with temporary setbacks, but without significant loss of momentum, as will be seen in the rest of this chapter.

1.10 The Single European Act (1986)

Reference has already been made in this chapter to the earliest Treaty, the EEC Treaty (later renamed the EC Treaty) and to the current Treaties, the TEU and the TFEU (see Introduction).

The Single European Act (SEA) (see also 3.4.1) was the first Treaty to amend the EEC Treaty, which had, at that time, been in force for over 30 years. It was not the last: there have been a further four Treaties (and counting). The SEA was not a stand-alone Treaty, but consisted largely of provisions amending the EEC Treaty, the ECSC Treaty, and the EURATOM Treaty (see 1.2).

The key provisions of the SEA, which came into force on 1 July 1987, were as follows.

- **Amendments to the EEC Treaty to ensure completion of the internal market**
  The EEC Treaty had laid down a 12-year period for the establishment of an internal market, but, by the end of 1969, it was far from complete. The SEA therefore provided for:

- a deadline of the end of 1992 for the completion of the internal market;
- a specific obligation on the EEC to adopt the necessary measures to achieve this; and
- a new law-making power to be applied to such measures, known as the cooperation procedure (now replaced by other procedures—see further 3.5).

- **Amendments to the EEC Treaty to include new areas of EEC competence (in other words, EEC power), such as the environment**
- **Amendments to the EEC Treaty to introduce a second EEC court to supplement the role of the original EEC court, the Court of Justice** (see 2.4 on the Court of Justice) This second court was originally called the Court of First Instance, but is now called the General Court (see further 2.4.2). It was intended to reduce the workload of the Court of Justice and thereby to ease the problem of delays in the judicial process. However, it largely failed to do this and further reforms became necessary (see further 6.11.5 on these reforms).
- **Provisions (operating outside the EEC Treaty) formalizing the role of the European Council** (see further 2.5)
- **Provisions (operating outside the EEC Treaty) for European Political Cooperation** These set out principles to bring about closer and more systematic cooperation in the formulation and implementation of foreign policy. They were built upon by subsequent Treaties, becoming the Common Foreign and Security Policy (CFSP) (discussed at 1.13, 1.15, 1.17, and 1.18).

1.11 Regional development

In 1988, the European Regional Development Fund (ERDF) and the European Social Fund (ESF) were restructured to channel more EEC funds away from the CAP and towards regional development, as part of the EEC's commitment to the harmonization of development throughout the EEC, and to counter fears that the internal market would exacerbate regional inequalities.

The ERDF aims to strengthen economic and social cohesion in the EU by correcting imbalances between its regions through investment in priority activities, such as the low-carbon economy and support for small and medium-sized enterprises (SMEs) in less-developed regions.

The ESF supports employment-related projects to improve skills, provide training, and assist those from disadvantaged groups to get jobs.

1.12 Employment and social policy

In 1989, all of the Member States, except the UK, adopted the Charter of Fundamental Social Rights of Workers. This stated basic rights such as freedom of movement, fair remuneration, and adequate social protection, which were in addition to the provisions in the EEC Treaty on free movement, health and safety at work, and the prohibition of discrimination at work on grounds of sex. However, the Charter was not binding and conferred no new powers, but simply stated recommended standards of worker welfare, which were to be a goal for its signatories. It was the basis for the Social Protocol of the Treaty on European Union 1992 (the so-called Social Chapter), which extended the ambit and powers of EC social policy and into which the UK eventually opted. These provisions were eventually incorporated into the TFEU.

1.13 The Treaty on European Union (1992)

Although this Treaty is often known as the Treaty of Maastricht, its formal title is the Treaty on European Union (1992) (see also 3.4.1). Like the EEC Treaty (see 1.2), it has been amended several times, but unlike that Treaty it has not been renamed and so, in order to distinguish the current version, the Treaty on European Union 2009 (TEU), from the pre-2009 version, that pre-2009 version will be referred to as the 'TEU (1992)' in this book. Although some provisions of the TEU (1992) amended the EEC Treaty, others did not and instead formed part of a stand-alone Treaty. The two Treaties continue to exist in parallel today.

The key provisions of the TEU (1992), which came into force on 1 November 1993, were as follows.

- **A change of name of the European Economic Community (EEC) to the European Community (EC)** The word 'Economic' was dropped from the name to reflect the change of emphasis within the organization, from a purely economic and market-oriented body to one with competences in areas such as education, culture, and environmental and consumer protection.

?! THINKING POINT

What significance, if any, do you consider that this change of name might have?

- **Introduction of a new organization, the European Union (EU)** The EU had the same membership and institutions as the three European Communities (the EC, the ECSC, and EURATOM—see 1.2 on these bodies), but was effectively an umbrella organization, including not only those three Communities, but also two new policy areas—Cooperation on Justice and Home Affairs (JHA) (now Police and Judicial Cooperation in Criminal Matters) and a Common Foreign and Security Policy (CFSP). The reason for keeping these new areas of competence outside the structure of the Communities was to retain more decision-making power in the hands of national governments meeting in Council (see further 2.2 on the Council), and to allow less power to the European Parliament (see further 2.1 on the Parliament) and the two Community Courts (now EU Courts—the Court of Justice and the General Court, collectively known as the Court of Justice of the European Union (CJEU)—see further 2.4). However, the structure was complicated both in theory and in practice, as explained in the following extract, and was abolished by the Treaty of Lisbon (see further 1.18).

P Gragl, *The Accession of the European Union to the European Convention on Human Rights* (Oxford: Hart, 2013), p 11

It is a well-known fact that the legal construction of the European Union's predecessor organisations was, even for legal professionals, intricate and difficult to grasp. After the entry into force of the Treaty of Maastricht in 1993, the EU's three pillar structure was introduced which led to the distinction between the European Union itself (virtually as an 'umbrella organisation') and its three constituent pillars, among them the European Communities and the European Community (EC) itself. In fact, it was the Community which enjoyed legal personality and which was the main protagonist of European integration and legal communitarisation. However, the deconstruction of the Union's pillar structure via the Treaty of Lisbon and the EU's newly won international legal personality by virtue of Article 47 TEU left the European Union as a single international organisation, without the further need for temples, roofs, pillars or any other architectural metaphors. Today, the European Union is not merely the successor of the European Community, but rather it has absorbed both the Community and the former 'umbrella' or 'temple' construction of the EU.

- **The introduction of a new legislative procedure** Known originally as co-decision and now as the ordinary legislative procedure (OLP) (see 3.5.1), this gave greater power to the European Parliament in the decision-making process, so that certain decisions had to be taken jointly by it and the Council, instead of by the Council alone (see also 1.15, 1.17, and 1.18).
- **The principle of subsidiarity** (see also 1.15 on further reforms to subsidiarity) Subsidiarity is the principle of dealing with a particular issue at the most local level possible—for example by a city council rather than a national government or by a national government rather than the EU. It is discussed in more detail at 3.3.
- **The introduction of EU citizenship** (see further 11.2)
- **Policies on economic and social cohesion** (see further 1.12, 1.15, and 1.17 for the detail of, and subsequent reforms to, these policies)
- **Cooperation on Justice and Home Affairs (JHA)—now Police and Judicial Cooperation in Criminal Matters** The EU was given competence over the treatment of non-Member State nationals and aspects of law enforcement that fell outside EC competence, but which had the potential to affect the operation of the internal market. In particular, this included closer cooperation between police forces, customs authorities, and the judicial authorities in criminal matters.
- **The Common Foreign and Security Policy (CFSP)** (see further 1.15, 1.17, and 1.18 on the history and development of the CFSP) This built on European Political Cooperation, as introduced by the SEA (see also 1.10), and covers all areas of foreign and security

policy, 'including the eventual framing of a common defence policy, which might in time lead to a common defence' (Article 1(4) TEU 1992). The defence role was originally fulfilled by the existing Western European Union (WEU), of which the majority (but not all) of the EC Member States were members, but this was dissolved in 2011, its institutions largely having been transferred to the European Defence Agency (EDA), which is part of the EU.

- **Economic and Monetary Union (EMU)** (see further next)

1.14 Economic and monetary union

The final stage of the economic integration process discussed at 1.4 is an economic and monetary union.

REVIEW QUESTION

Can you recall the first three stages of economic integration?

Answer: The first three stages of economic integration are a free trade area, a customs union, and a common market (or 'single' or 'internal' market) (see 1.4.1, 1.4.2, and 1.4.3).

Economic and monetary union consists of a common market (explained at 1.4.3) *plus* unified monetary and fiscal policies. These include, inter alia, a single currency for all Member States, common policies on interest rates, and central control by the union of each country's budget.

The philosophy behind the economic policies of the EU was (and still is) that every individual and business based in the EU should be free to invest, produce, work, buy, sell, or supply services wherever in the EU this can be done most efficiently and without competition being artificially distorted. When the EEC was founded, it was decided that this policy was to be achieved through the establishment of an internal market (see 1.4.3), but, in the TEU (1992), the Member States added EMU to its aims. This is now set out in Article 119 TFEU:

Article 119 TFEU

1. For the purposes set out in Article 3 of the Treaty on European Union, the activities of the Member States and the Union shall include, as provided in the Treaties, the adoption of an economic policy which is based on the close coordination of Member States' economic policies, on the internal market and on the definition of common objectives, and conducted in accordance with the principle of an open market economy with free competition.
2. Concurrently with the foregoing, and as provided in the Treaties and in accordance with the procedures set out therein, these activities shall include a single currency, the euro, and the

definition and conduct of a single monetary policy and exchange-rate policy the primary objective of both of which shall be to maintain price stability and, without prejudice to this objective, to support the general economic policies in the Union, in accordance with the principle of an open market economy with free competition.

3. These activities of the Member States and the Union shall entail compliance with the following guiding principles: stable prices, sound public finances and monetary conditions and a sustainable balance of payments.

?! THINKING POINT

Do you consider that the EU has now achieved this final stage of economic integration?

The UK negotiated and exercised an opt-out from this final stage of economic integration, and thus has not adopted the euro as its currency, although it has adopted a number of other measures of integration belonging to this final stage. A number of other Member States have also remained outside this final stage of economic integration—some from choice, like the UK; others, because they have not yet satisfied the fiscal criteria laid down by the EU for entry into EMU.

If you have any difficulty in assessing whether the EU has now achieved this final stage of economic integration, look back at the definition of each stage and think about your own experience.

- Have you ever travelled to another EU country or bought goods there?
- What sort of restrictions or difficulties, if any, have you encountered (or do you think you might encounter)?

It is evident that the EU has *not* achieved full economic integration. For instance, there are still more restrictions on the trade in goods between Member States than within a single Member State (see further Chapter 10 on restrictions on the free movement of goods) and on the rights of, for instance, a Briton to work in Germany than for a German to work there (see further Chapter 11 on restrictions on the free movement of persons). There are also different rates of income and corporation tax in the Member States that can affect the movement of workers and businesses. These are not features that one would expect to see in a fully economically integrated area such as, for example, the United States.

1.15 The Treaty of Amsterdam (1997)

Substantial further enlargement of the EU was anticipated as a result of the fall of the Berlin Wall in 1989 and the disintegration of the USSR, leading to its dissolution at the end of 1991, and it was against this background that the Treaty of Amsterdam (see also 3.4.1) and the subsequent Treaty of Nice (see 1.17) were negotiated. Enlargement required both institutional reform to ensure that institutional structures designed for 6, 12 or 15 Member States would be administratively workable for 20 or 30 (see further 1.6 on expansion of membership) and greater flexibility to ensure that the smaller number of Member States that wished to proceed to greater integration could do so.

The key provisions of the Treaty of Amsterdam, which came into force on 1 May 1999, were as follows.

- **Renumbering of the EC Treaty and the TEU (1992).** For example, Article 177 EC became Article 234 EC as a result of the Treaty of Amsterdam, although its content was not changed. The Treaty of Lisbon caused a further renumbering (see 1.18) and so this is now Article 267 TFEU.
- **Institutional reform.** This included the reform and extension of co-decision (now the ordinary legislative procedure—see 3.5.1) (see also 1.13, 1.17, and 1.18), the extension of QMV (see also 1.5, 1.17, 1.18, and 2.2.2 on the history of QMV and later reforms to it), and amendments to subsidiarity (see also 1.13 on the introduction of subsidiarity and 3.3 for further detail of the principle).
- **The transfer of visas, asylum, immigration, and other policies relating to the free movement of persons from the TEU (1992) and thus to EU competence, to the EC Treaty and thus EC competence** (see 1.13). This was significant because, at the time, the EU was separate from the EC and largely under the control of the Member States acting in Council (see further 2.2 on the Council), rather than of the EC institutions. This transfer was part of a process known as communitization, and resulted in increased scrutiny of EC activities in these policy areas from the European Parliament and the EC Courts.
- **The renaming and amending of JHA to Police and Judicial Cooperation in Criminal Matters** (see 1.13, 1.17, and 1.18).
- **The introduction of the concept of 'an area of freedom, security and justice' (AFSJ),** to be established gradually through the provisions on the free movement of persons (including the newly communitized policy areas) and the provisions on Police and Judicial Cooperation in Criminal Matters.
- **Amendments to the CFSP** (see further 1.13, 1.17, and 1.18 on its history and development).
- **The creation of the role of EU High Representative for the CFSP,** to represent the EU overseas in this policy area (see also 1.18 on the subsequent development of this role).
- **Introduction of new provisions on employment and social policy** (see 1.12 on the origins of this policy, and 1.15 and 1.17 on later reforms to it).
- **Sanctions on Member States that breach EU fundamental principles.** A Member State that seriously breaches the fundamental principles of the EU—now set out in Article 2 TEU (see 1.3)—may have its Treaty rights, including voting rights, suspended (see

also 1.17 on subsequent reform of this provision, which is now contained in Article 7 TEU). These sanctions are supplemented by the Rule of Law Framework introduced in 2014, which formalizes a dialogue between the EU Commission (see 2.3 for an explanation of the Commission) and the Member State prior to the triggering of Article 7. The Commission first assesses whether there is a threat to the rule of law in the State. If the matter is not resolved, it addresses a Recommendation to the State, and finally it monitors the State's follow-up to the Recommendation. If there is no satisfactory follow-up by the time limit set, recourse can be had to Article 7. In January 2016, the Commission proceeded to the second stage of the Framework and addressed a Recommendation to Poland concerning reforms that Poland had made to its judicial system—in particular, the forced removal of senior court judges and the introduction of a discretionary presidential power, unfettered by any objective criteria, to prolong judges' terms in office. In December 2017, the Commission invoked the Article 7(1) procedure for the first time, by submitting to the Council a Reasoned Proposal for a Council Decision. The consent of the European Parliament to Council action, as required by Article 7(1), was given by Resolution in March 2018, but the Council has not yet taken action. In June 2018, the Commission launched enforcement proceedings against Poland for breach of EU law and earlier proceedings by it in relation to reforms to Poland's lower courts are ongoing.

- **Introduction of a new decision-making procedure known as closer cooperation**, subsequently amended and renamed the enhanced cooperation procedure, and now in Article 20 TEU and Articles 326–334 TFEU (see 1.5 for the context of this procedure, 1.17 and 1.18 on its reform, and 3.5.3 for further detail) This procedure is used to enable further integration between some, but not all, Member States where the other Member States do not wish to integrate, and measures taken in this way apply only to those Member States that agree to take part. It applies only where the EU's competence (ie its power to act) is shared with the Member States, for example in relation to the internal market (Article 3 TFEU) (see 1.4.3), and not where the EU has exclusive competence, for example in relation to competition law (Article 4 TFEU) (see further Chapters 13, 14, and 15). It has been used relatively infrequently; see, for example, Council Decision 2010/405/EU of 12 July 2010 authorizing enhanced cooperation in relation to the law applicable to divorce and separation, OJ 2010 L189/12, and Council Decision 2011/167/EU of 10 March 2011 authorizing enhanced cooperation in relation to unitary patent protection, OJ 2011 L76/53 (challenged unsuccessfully in C-274/11 and C-295/11 *Spain and Italy v Council* EU:C:2013:240).

acquis communautaire
The term *acquis communautaire* is used to refer to the accumulated body of EU law, including its objectives, policies, legislation, and case law. It is sometimes shortened simply to 'the *acquis*'. In relation to the Schengen Agreements, the term 'Schengen *acquis communautaire*' is used similarly to refer to the cumulative laws, conventions, and decisions passed under those Agreements (see 1.9).

- **Incorporation of the Schengen Agreements into the EC Treaty** (see 1.9 on the origin of these Agreements). The UK and Ireland are not automatically bound by the Agreements or the associated Schengen **acquis communautaire**, but may opt in to future developments. It is now, of course, unlikely that the UK will do so, given the outcome of its 2016 referendum on withdrawal from the EU. Denmark is bound by the Schengen Agreements and the existing *acquis*, but not by any further developments of the *acquis* unless it chooses to opt in to them.

1.16 The Charter of Fundamental Rights

Neither the EC nor the EU originally had a formal human rights competence, although the Court of Justice developed and applied principles of human rights (see further Chapter 9). However, in 2000, the EU proclaimed the Charter of Fundamental Rights of the European Union (see further 9.4), although this was not given full legal effect until the Treaty of Lisbon (see 1.18).

1.17 The Treaty of Nice (2001)

The reason for two Treaties in such short succession was predominantly that the Treaty of Amsterdam failed to make all of the necessary institutional reforms and so the Treaty of Nice was intended to achieve them. However, the lack of success of the Treaty of Nice itself in this respect was highlighted by the subsequent need for the Treaty of Lisbon (see 1.18).

The key provisions of the Treaty of Nice (see also 3.4.1), which came into force on 1 February 2003, were as follows.

- **Institutional and decision-making reforms**, including:
  - Further extension and reweighting of QMV (see also 1.5, 1.15, 1.18, and 2.2.2 on the history of QMV and later reforms to it) and the extension of the use of co-decision (now OLP—see 3.5.1) (see also 1.13, 1.15, 1.18, and 3.5.1 on co-decision)
  - Reforms to the procedures of the Court of Justice and extension of the jurisdiction of the Court of First Instance (now renamed the General Court—see further 2.4.2 on the General Court)
  - Alterations to the *locus standi* (standing) of the Parliament under Article 263 TFEU (discussed at 7.6.1 and 7.6.2)
  - Renaming and amending of the 'closer cooperation' procedure—now 'enhanced cooperation' (see also 1.5, 1.15, 1.18, and 3.5.3 on the history, development, and detail of this procedure)
- **Amendments to Police and Judicial Cooperation** (see also 1.13, 1.15, and 1.18 on the history and development of this policy), including:
  - Establishing the European Judicial Cooperation Unit (EuroJust), composed of national prosecutors, magistrates, or police officers of equivalent competence, which facilitates coordination between national prosecuting authorities, supports international criminal investigations, and cooperates with the European Judicial Network (an EU-wide network of national contact points created in 1998 to facilitate judicial cooperation and provide information to the public)
- **Amendments to the CFSP** (see further 1.13, 1.15, and 1.18 on the history and development of this policy), including reduction of the role of the WEU (now replaced by the EDA—see 1.13) and emphasis instead of that of NATO (see 1.1)

- **Amendments to social policy** (see 1.12, 1.13, and 1.15 on the history and detail of this policy)
- **Amendments to sanctions on Member States that breach fundamental EU principles** (see 1.15 on the introduction of these), which sanctions are now contained in Article 7 TEU and the associated Rule of Law Framework

1.18 The Treaty of Lisbon (2007)

As mentioned at 1.17, the anticipated expansion of the EU led to calls for reform of its procedures to make them fit for an organization of over 20 countries. At the same time, there were calls for further integration.

REVIEW QUESTION

List the original Member States. Which other Member States subsequently joined and when?

Answer: The original six Member States were Belgium, Netherlands, Luxembourg, France, Italy, and Germany.

Visit the Online Resources to see a timeline of the subsequent expansion of the EU, including accession dates for each of the newer Member States.

REVIEW QUESTION

By what terms are the contrasting processes of (a) enlarging the EU to spread the benefits of peace and prosperity more widely and (b) increasing its economic and political integration often referred to?

Answer: These two processes are often referred to, respectively, as 'widening' and 'deepening' the EU.

The processes of widening and deepening the EU are very often in conflict, both because of the increasing difficulty of reaching unanimous agreement amongst an increasing number of Member States and because deeper integration becomes more difficult until all of the new Member States—which, with the accession of ten States in 2004 and a further two in 2007, represented almost half the total number of Member States—have caught up with the level of economic and political integration achieved by the more established Member States. It also appears that existing Member States are less willing to provide the same financial support to new Member States than was provided to some of those that joined in the 1970s and 1980s.

These conflicts were apparent in the various attempts to produce a new Treaty for the EU in the first decade of the twenty-first century. A proposed EU Constitution (see also 3.4.1 on the draft Treaty Establishing a Constitution for Europe) was abandoned after it was rejected in referenda in the Netherlands and Ireland, and a subsequent proposal, the draft Reform Treaty, almost met the same fate after rejection by Irish voters. It was, however, amended and revived to become the Treaty of Lisbon amending the Treaty on European Union and the Treaty establishing the European Community (2007) (see also 3.4.1).

The main changes introduced by the Treaty of Lisbon, which came into force on 1 December 2009, were:

- a merger of the EC and the EU to form the EU (see also Introduction and 1.13);
- the renaming of the EC Treaty (now the TFEU) (see also 1.13);
- the renaming, and further extension of the use, of the OLP (see further 3.5.1), formerly known as co-decision (see also 1.13, 1.15, and 1.17 on its introduction and its reform by other Treaties);
- the further extension of the use of QMV and amendments to the weighting of votes (see 1.5, 1.15, 1.17, and 2.2.2 on the history of QMV and later reforms to it);
- the renaming of the Court of First Instance as the General Court (see further 2.4.2 on the General Court);
- an increased role for national parliaments (see Protocol No 1 to the Treaties for further details);
- the possibility for citizens to call on the Commission to bring forward legislation (see 2.3.2 and 11.2.3);
- a new role of President of the European Council (see further 2.5.2);
- a reduction in the number of Commissioners (see further 2.3.1);
- clarification of the 'enhanced cooperation' procedure (see also 1.5, 1.15, 1.17, and 3.5.3 on the history, reform, and detail of this procedure);
- amendments to the Charter of Fundamental Rights and recognition that it has the same legal effect as the Treaties (see 1.16 on the introduction of the Charter and 9.4 for further detail of its provisions);
- supplementing of the CFSP (see further 1.13, 1.15, and 1.17 on the history and development of the CFSP) by a Common Security and Defence Policy (CSDP), which grew out of an Anglo-French initiative in 1999, the European Security and Defence Policy (ESDP); and
- expansion of the powers of the High Representative of the EU for the CFSP (introduced by the Treaty of Amsterdam—see 1.15) and a renaming of the post as High Representative of the EU for Foreign Affairs and Security Policy.

The timeline of the EU, as discussed in 1.1–1.18, is summarized in Figure 1.2.

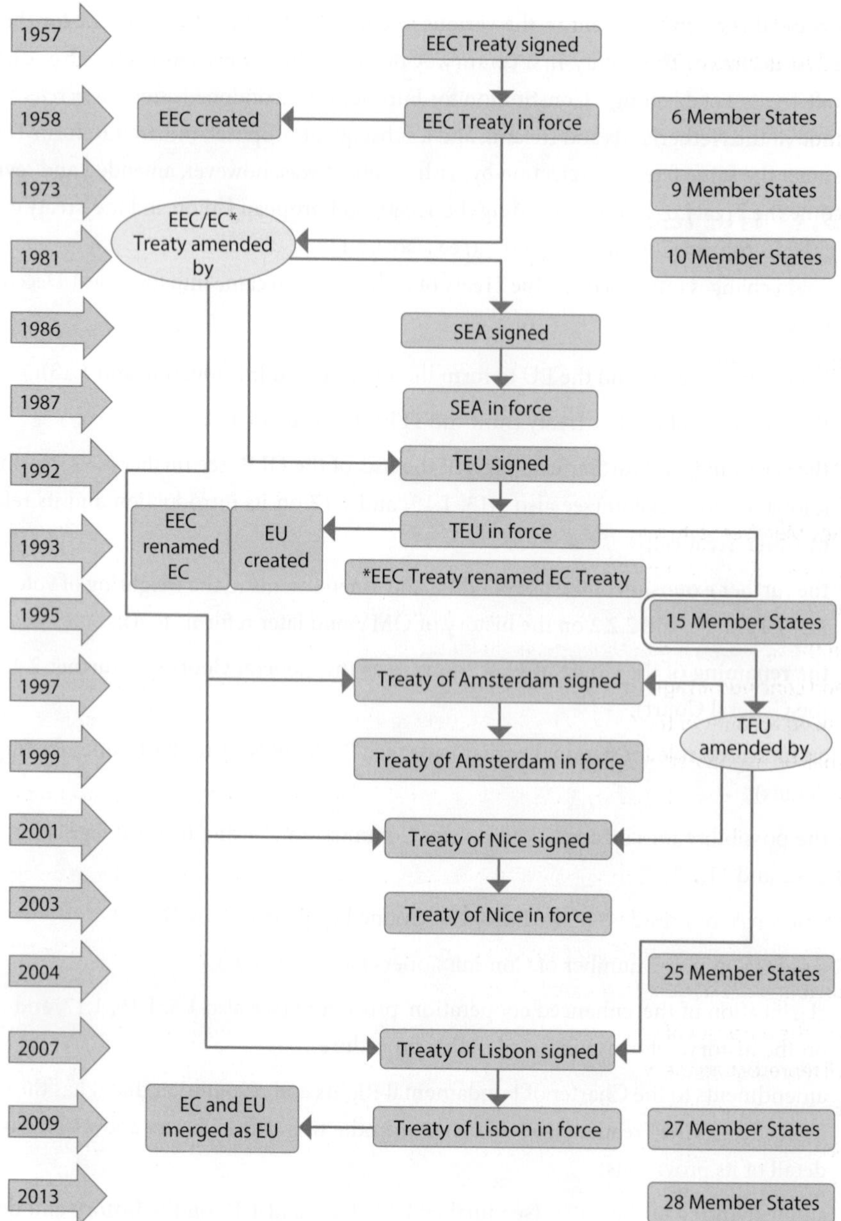

Figure 1.2 Summary of the development of the EU through its Treaties and its membership

1.19 The UK's referendum on EU membership ('Brexit')

In June 2016, the British people were asked, in a national referendum, whether they wished to 'Leave' or 'Remain' in the EU. By a small, but decisive, majority, they voted to 'Leave' (see further 3.1 on the events leading up to the decision to hold a referendum and the possible reasons for the result). The combination of the words 'Britain' and 'exit' has led to this commonly being referred to as 'Brexit'. The result of the referendum was not legally binding on the UK government as a matter of domestic law (see further 3.1), but it would be politically difficult for the government to ignore it.

1.19.1 The legal mechanism for a Member State to leave the EU

The legal mechanism for a Member State to leave the EU is provided by Article 50 TEU.

Article 50 TEU

1. Any Member State may decide to withdraw from the Union in accordance with its own constitutional requirements.
2. A Member State which decides to withdraw shall notify the European Council of its intention. In the light of the guidelines provided by the European Council, the Union shall negotiate and conclude an agreement with that State, setting out the arrangements for its withdrawal, taking account of the framework for its future relationship with the Union. That agreement shall be negotiated in accordance with Article 218(3) of the Treaty on the Functioning of the European Union. It shall be concluded on behalf of the Union by the Council, acting by a qualified majority, after obtaining the consent of the European Parliament.
3. The Treaties shall cease to apply to the State in question from the date of entry into force of the withdrawal agreement or, failing that, two years after the notification referred to in paragraph 2, unless the European Council, in agreement with the Member State concerned, unanimously decides to extend this period.
4. For the purposes of paragraphs 2 and 3, the member of the European Council or of the Council representing the withdrawing Member State shall not participate in the discussions of the European Council or Council or in decisions concerning it.

   A qualified majority shall be defined in accordance with Article 238(3)(b) of the Treaty on the Functioning of the European Union.
5. If a State which has withdrawn from the Union asks to rejoin, its request shall be subject to the procedure referred to in Article 49.

The first thing to note is that the procedure appears simple: the leaving Member State simply gives notice to the EU's European Council (see 2.5 for an explanation of this institution). The UK government gave notification of its withdrawal to the EU under Article 50 TFEU on 27 March 2017. However, it should be noted that, as explained in Article 50(1), Article 50 deals only with the former Member State's relationship with the EU and not its domestic constitutional arrangements or whether it will retain those of its national laws that are in place because they have been required as a result of its EU membership. In relation to the UK, these issues are considered at 3.1, but it should be noted that the UK's Supreme Court, in *R (on the application of Miller and another) v Secretary of State for Exiting the European Union* [2017] UKSC 5 (see also 6.13), ruled that the approval of the UK Parliament was required before the UK government could trigger Article 50 TEU, although the approval of the devolved parliaments of Northern Ireland, Scotland, and Wales was not.

Article 50 does not contain any express right for the withdrawing Member State to revoke its notice if it changes its mind, but, in C-621/18 *Wightman and others v Secretary of State for Exiting the European Union* EU:C:2018:999, the Court of Justice held that such a Member State may withdraw its notice of intention to withdraw and may do so unilaterally, without having to obtain the agreement of the EU or the other Member States. Its reasoning was as follows.

1. Although the terms of Article 50 TEU did not expressly address the possibility of revocation, it provided for notification of intention, which, by definition, could change, and it provided for that notification to be given unilaterally, subject only to the Member State's own constitutional requirements.
2. The purpose of Article 50 was to enshrine the sovereign right of a Member State to withdraw from the EU and to establish a procedure to enable this to take place in an orderly fashion. The sovereign nature of the right of withdrawal supported the conclusion that the Member State concerned had a right to revoke notification of its intention to withdraw for as long as a withdrawal agreement had not entered into force or, in the absence of such an agreement, the two-year negotiation period (possibly extended, in accordance with Article 50) had not expired. In the absence of an express provision on revocation, that revocation was subject to the rules laid down in Article 50 for the withdrawal itself and so could be given unilaterally.
3. The context of Article 50 included the EU's objective of 'ever closer union' (see the Preamble to the EEC Treaty, set out in the Introduction to this chapter), the values of liberty and democracy set out in the EU Charter (see further 9.4), the voluntary nature of EU membership, and the importance of EU citizenship, the rights attaching to which would be significantly impacted by the withdrawal of a Member State. In those circumstances, given that a State could not be forced to join the EU against its will, neither could it be forced to withdraw from it against its will as expressed in accordance with its constitutional requirements and following a democratic process through which it decided to revoke the notification of its intention to withdraw. The Advocate General in *Wightman* had earlier cited as examples of such a process a referendum, a parliamentary vote, or a general election, but the Court did not comment on these possibilities.
4. This interpretation of Article 50 was consistent with evidence about the drafting process leading to the adoption of Article 50.
5. It was consistent with the Vienna Convention on the Law of Treaties, which provided that revocation could be unilateral.
6. Notification of revocation could not be made conditional on the unanimous approval of the European Council, since that would be incompatible with the principle that a Member State could not be forced to leave the EU against its will.
7. Finally, the Court noted that any revocation must be submitted to the European Council before a withdrawal agreement had entered into force or, in the absence of such an agreement, before the expiry of the two-year negotiation period (possibly extended, in accordance with Article 50) and must be unequivocal in that its purpose must be 'to confirm

the EU membership of the Member State concerned *under terms that are unchanged as regards its status as a Member State*, and that revocation brings the withdrawal procedure to an end' (*Wightman*, at para 74, emphasis added). Thus, importantly for the EU, the UK's existing special arrangements with the EU, such as its budget rebate and its opt-outs from membership of the euro and the Schengen Agreements, would continue—arrangements that would cease to apply if the UK were to withdraw and, at a later date, decide to apply to rejoin.

The next thing to note is that Article 50 TEU does not specify the future relationship, if any, between the former Member State and the EU. The reference in Article 50(2) to the agreement 'taking account of the framework for the [Member State's] future relationship with the [EU]' suggests the possibility of two agreements:

- one on withdrawal (governed by Article 50 TEU); and
- one on the future relationship of the withdrawing Member State and the EU (governed by Article 218 TFEU).

Article 50(2) provides that there will be a negotiation between that State and the EU, and that the EU's position will be based on guidelines from the European Council (agreed on unanimously—Article 50(3) TEU). The withdrawing Member State may not participate in the discussions of the European Council or the Council (see further 2.2 for an explanation of the Council, which is different from the European Council) (Article 50(4)). An extension of the two-year time limit, which applies from the date of notification of withdrawal to the date on which the EU Treaties cease to apply to the withdrawing Member State, can be made only if all Member States agree. Article 50(2) also refers to Article 218(3) TFEU, which provides that the Commission shall submit Recommendations to the Council, which shall adopt a decision authorizing the opening of negotiations and nominating the EU's negotiator. The President of the EU Commission (see 2.3 for an explanation of this institution) has already appointed a Chief Negotiator of the Commission Taskforce for the Preparation and Conduct of the Negotiations with the UK under Article 50 TEU. Article 50(2) provides that any agreement must be approved by a qualified majority of the Council of the EU (see 1.5 on QMV and 2.2 for an explanation of the Council) and by the European Parliament (see 2.1 for an explanation of this institution).

Article 218 TFEU makes provision for the negotiation of agreements between the EU and third countries more generally.

Article 218 TFEU

1. Without prejudice to the specific provisions laid down in Article 207, agreements between the Union and third countries or international organisations shall be negotiated and concluded in accordance with the following procedure.
2. The Council shall authorise the opening of negotiations, adopt negotiating directives, authorise the signing of agreements and conclude them.

3. The Commission, or the High Representative of the Union for Foreign Affairs and Security Policy where the agreement envisaged relates exclusively or principally to the common foreign and security policy, shall submit recommendations to the Council, which shall adopt a decision authorising the opening of negotiations and, depending on the subject of the agreement envisaged, nominating the Union negotiator or the head of the Union's negotiating team.
4. The Council may address directives to the negotiator and designate a special committee in consultation with which the negotiations must be conducted.
5. The Council, on a proposal by the negotiator, shall adopt a decision authorising the signing of the agreement and, if necessary, its provisional application before entry into force.
6. The Council, on a proposal by the negotiator, shall adopt a decision concluding the agreement.

   Except where agreements relate exclusively to the common foreign and security policy, the Council shall adopt the decision concluding the agreement:

   (a) after obtaining the consent of the European Parliament in the following cases:

   (i) association agreements;

   (ii) agreement on Union accession to the European Convention for the Protection of Human Rights and Fundamental Freedoms;

   (iii) agreements establishing a specific institutional framework by organising cooperation procedures;

   (iv) agreements with important budgetary implications for the Union;

   (v) agreements covering fields to which either the ordinary legislative procedure applies, or the special legislative procedure where consent by the European Parliament is required.

   The European Parliament and the Council may, in an urgent situation, agree upon a time-limit for consent.

   (b) after consulting the European Parliament in other cases. The European Parliament shall deliver its opinion within a time-limit which the Council may set depending on the urgency of the matter. In the absence of an opinion within that time-limit, the Council may act.
7. When concluding an agreement, the Council may, by way of derogation from paragraphs 5, 6 and 9, authorise the negotiator to approve on the Union's behalf modifications to the agreement where it provides for them to be adopted by a simplified procedure or by a body set up by the agreement. The Council may attach specific conditions to such authorisation.
8. The Council shall act by a qualified majority throughout the procedure. However, it shall act unanimously when the agreement covers a field for which unanimity is required for the adoption of a Union act as well as for association agreements and the agreements referred to in Article 212 with the States which are candidates for accession. The Council shall also act unanimously for the agreement on accession of the Union to the European Convention for the Protection of Human Rights and Fundamental Freedoms; the decision concluding this agreement shall enter into force after it has been approved by the Member States in accordance with their respective constitutional requirements.

9. The Council, on a proposal from the Commission or the High Representative of the Union for Foreign Affairs and Security Policy, shall adopt a decision suspending application of an agreement and establishing the positions to be adopted on the Union's behalf in a body set up by an agreement, when that body is called upon to adopt acts having legal effects, with the exception of acts supplementing or amending the institutional framework of the agreement.
10. The European Parliament shall be immediately and fully informed at all stages of the procedure.
11. A Member State, the European Parliament, the Council or the Commission may obtain the opinion of the Court of Justice as to whether an agreement envisaged is compatible with the Treaties. Where the opinion of the Court is adverse, the agreement envisaged may not enter into force unless it is amended or the Treaties are revised.

Thus Article 218 TFEU provides that negotiations on any separate agreement on the future relationship between a withdrawing Member State and the EU will be opened by the Council, conducted by the Commission, and concluded by the Council after either obtaining the consent of the European Parliament or consulting it, depending on the content of the agreement (see Article 218(6) TFEU). The Council's decision is likely to be required to be taken unanimously, but it may be possible for it to be taken by QMV (see 1.5), again depending on the content of the agreement. It is also worth noting that Article 218(11) TFEU provides that a Member State, the European Parliament, the Council, or the Commission may obtain the opinion of the Court of Justice as to whether a proposed agreement is compatible with the EU Treaties and, if the Court's opinion is that it is not, the agreement may not enter into force.

The initial stance of the EU towards its future relationship with the UK was expressed in the following extract from the joint statement made by the leaders of the EU immediately after the result of the UK's referendum was announced.

Statement by the EU leaders and the Netherlands Presidency on the outcome of the UK referendum, 24 June 2016

Article 50 of the Treaty on European Union sets out the procedure to be followed if a Member State decides to leave the European Union. We stand ready to launch negotiations swiftly with the United Kingdom regarding the terms and conditions of its withdrawal from the European Union. Until this process of negotiations is over, the United Kingdom remains a member of the European Union, with all the rights and obligations that derive from this. According to the Treaties which the United Kingdom has ratified, EU law continues to apply to the full to and in the United Kingdom until it is no longer a Member.

[...]

As regards the United Kingdom, we hope to have it as a close partner of the European Union in the future. We expect the United Kingdom to formulate its proposals in this respect. Any agreement, which will be concluded with the United Kingdom as a third country, will have to reflect the interests of both sides and be balanced in terms of rights and obligations.

Some of the difficulties that will need to be resolved were noted by the UK's House of Lords European Union Committee, as set out in the following extract from its Report on the process of withdrawing the EU.

House of Lords European Union Committee, *The Process of Withdrawing from the European Union*, 11th Report of Session 2015–16, HL Paper 138 (London: HMSO, 2016), footnotes omitted

26. One of the most complex aspects of the negotiations would be deciding which rights would qualify as 'acquired rights', and putting in place transitional provisions for individuals and companies whose rights might be phased out over time. [Professor Derrick Wyatt QC] described this issue as follows: 'It is estimated that 2 million Brits live in other EU countries … Take elderly people who have lived for 10 years in Spain. After five years, they acquired a right of permanent residence as citizens of the Union and that includes access to the Spanish healthcare system. If we leave, what do we do about vested rights? Do we recognise rights to permanent residents that have arisen? What transitional rights do we give somebody who has been working for four years in the UK and has children at school and so forth? Let us not forget that for every example in the UK there is an example of a UK citizen elsewhere. We would want to tidy that up. My guess is that the inclination of Government and Parliament would be to be generous as regards those who had already made their lives in the UK, knowing that it would be likely to be reciprocated.'
27. Both witnesses thought that addressing these issues would be challenging. If the new relationship involved restrictions on the free movement of people, detailed arrangements would be necessary governing the rights of EU citizens resident in the UK and of UK citizens resident in the EU acquired prior to the UK's withdrawal. The arrangements would need to cover residence rights, rights to take up employment or self-employment, and rights to health care and social security. There would also have to be an agreement on the dates from which acquired rights would be recognised, and transitional arrangements for those not qualifying for acquired rights. On the other hand, if the new relationship preserved the free movement of persons, acquired rights could be maintained by a simple continuity clause.

[…]

49. [Sir David Edward, a former UK judge at the Court of Justice] gave the following illustrations of the complexity of the negotiations on acquired rights in the event of a unilateral withdrawal: 'A university has an EU research funding package with provision for cross-frontier movement of research scientists, and that has a life beyond two years. What happens to that? What happens to Erasmus students? When does participation in Erasmus end? A divorced couple live in the UK and another member state with special arrangements for access to children, and particularly cross-border payment of family maintenance. What happens to that? There are cross-border investments and tax treatment of capital and revenue. There are agricultural support payments and fishing quotas. Those are just examples.'
50. This led Sir David to conclude that: 'The long-term ghastliness of the legal complications is almost unimaginable.'

More detail on the UK's concerns as to what would need to be contained in both the withdrawal agreement—at time of writing, the Draft Agreement on the Withdrawal of the United Kingdom of Great Britain and Northern Ireland from the European Union and the European Atomic Energy Community, 14 November 2018, as amended on 11 April 2019 (by COM (2019) 194 final) (the Draft Withdrawal Agreement) in the light of the extension of the date of the UK's withdrawal from the EU—and the agreement on the UK's future relationship with the EU were contained in the UK government's 2017 paper *The Process for Withdrawing from the European Union* set out below.

HM Government, *The Process for Withdrawing from the European Union*, Cm 9216 (London: HMSO, February 2017), emphasis original, footnotes and case study omitted

4.1 The withdrawal negotiation would need to address a wide range of difficult issues related to withdrawal itself, and also to our future relationship with the EU. Article 50 does not set out explicitly what issues would need to be resolved and there is no precedent to draw on. The UK's relationship with the EU has built up over 40 years of membership and affects many aspects of life in the UK, and of UK citizens living across the EU; the terms of exit would have to cover the full extent of that relationship.

4.2 This would include the status and entitlements of the approximately 2 million UK citizens living, working and travelling in the other 27 Member States of the EU. They all currently enjoy a range of specific rights to live, to work and access to pensions, health care and public services that are only guaranteed because of EU law. There would be no requirement under EU law for these rights to be maintained if the UK left the EU. Should an agreement be reached to maintain these rights, the expectation must be that this would have to be reciprocated for EU citizens in the UK.

4.3 The negotiations would also have to cover the UK's access to the EU's Single Market, which currently rests on our membership of the EU, and related to that, the free movement of people. These negotiations would be complicated: the UK would want to disentangle regulatory frameworks and establish transitional arrangements across a wide number of areas; and secure preferential access to the EU market including in sectors like financial services and car manufacturing where the UK enjoys a trading surplus.

4.4 The impact of these negotiations would have a wide and profound impact across the UK and its economy. For instance, the UK's current access to the Single Market is important for the UK's manufacturing sector. Last year, the UK exported a record number of cars (1.23 million), with more than half going to the EU market. The industry directly employs 147,000 people and supports a further 300,000 jobs in the wider supply chain. The North-East of England has one of the highest shares of EU exports in the UK's regional economy and attracts high levels of foreign investment. Unless preferential access was agreed with the EU as part of the exit negotiations, UK car manufacturers would face a 10 per cent tariff when exporting to the EU. Moreover, over 40 per cent of components purchased by UK vehicle manufacturers are from the EU. These parts would become more expensive if the UK were forced to raise tariffs under WTO rules.

4.5 The UK's withdrawal from the EU would have a serious impact on UK farmers. In addition to the impact of withdrawing from the EU's Common Agricultural Policy and associated subsidy schemes, they would also lose their preferential access to the European market if the UK left the EU without a successor arrangement in place. The EU imposes an average tariff of 14 per cent [on] agricultural imports from non-EU countries (including countries that have their own special trading deals with the EU, like Norway and Switzerland), with higher rates on individual items, such as dairy products (average of 36 per cent). UK farmers would also no longer be able to benefit from preferential access to non-EU countries secured by the EU under trade agreements.

4.6 If the UK left the EU without an agreement in place, we would lose the security benefits of our participation in a range of EU Justice and Home Affairs measures that help the fight against crime and terrorism. For example, since 2004 the European Arrest Warrant has allowed 7000 people to be extradited from the UK to face trial and has resulted in just over 1000 people being returned to the UK to face justice here. The European Criminal Records Information System enables us to secure information about criminal records. The Schengen Information System II operates as a 'watch list' through which we have access to operational data on terrorist suspects and criminals. And from 2017 we will be part of the Prüm Decisions relating to information on fingerprints and DNA.

4.7 If we were outside the EU, this co-operation would be curtailed. Aside from those States that are not in the EU but are in the Schengen border-free area, there are no precedents for non-Members being able to cooperate within these mechanisms. Even Switzerland, for example, does not have an equivalent to the European Arrest Warrant. We would also lose our status as a full member of Europol, an agency that coordinates the fight against serious and organised crime among EU countries.

There would be serious implications for Gibraltar were the UK to withdraw from the EU. Inside the EU, Gibraltarians have the right to move freely to Spain, and the right to establish a business and provide services there. But, before Spain joined the EU in 1986, the border was closed from 1969–85. If the UK left the EU, there would be no certainty that the border would remain open. The Chief Minister of Gibraltar has said that this would pose 'an existential threat in economic terms' to the territory. The Channel Islands and the Isle of Man, which enjoy special arrangements for access to the EU, would face similar uncertainties.

Northern Ireland would be confronted with difficult issues about the relationship with Ireland. Outside the EU's Customs Union, it would be necessary to impose customs checks on the movement of goods across the border. Questions would also need to be answered about the Common Travel Area which covers the movement of people. This could have an impact on cross-border co-operation and trade. The withdrawal of structural funds, which have helped address economic challenges, would also have an impact.

4.8 Examples of other issues that negotiations would also need to cover in the context of managing the transition, fixing the terms of exit and, fixing any future arrangement, include:

- unspent EU funds due to UK regions and farmers;
- cross-border security arrangements including access to EU databases;
- co-operation on foreign policy, including sanctions;
- transfer of regulatory responsibilities;
- arrangements for contracts drawn up in accordance with EU law;
- access to EU agencies that play a role in UK domestic law, such as the European Medicines Agency;
- transition arrangements for UK exit from EU Free Trade Agreements with third countries;
- arrangements for the closure of EU agencies headquartered in the UK;
- departure from the Single European Sky arrangement;
- access for UK citizens to the European Health Insurance Card;
- the rights of UK fishermen to fish in traditional non-UK waters, including those in the North Sea;
- continued access to the EU's single energy and aviation markets; and
- the status of the UK's environmental commitments made as party to various UN environmental conventions and currently implemented through EU legislation.

Although the UK gave notification of its withdrawal to the EU under Article 50 TFEU on 27 March 2017, it still remains unclear at time of writing whether the Draft Withdrawal Agreement containing the terms of the UK's withdrawal from the UK will ultimately be ratified by the UK, given that the UK Parliament has rejected it on several occasions to date. It also remains unclear whether any agreement on the future relationship between the UK and the EU might be reached, and what the terms of any such agreement might be, although the Political declaration setting out the framework for the future relationship between the European Union and the United Kingdom of Great Britain and Northern Ireland, 22 November 2018 (the Political Declaration), which accompanies the Draft Withdrawal Agreement, provides an outline of a possible future relationship and is discussed shortly. No EU Member State has ever left the EU before (although Greenland, which is an autonomous part of Denmark, withdrew in 1995). However, the EU currently has a variety of agreements with different countries that are not Member States and it may be that one of these, or a combination of them, will form the template for any agreement with the UK. These agreements are sometimes referred to informally by reference to the countries involved and are discussed at 1.19.2. In any event, the UK's Constitutional Reform and Governance Act 2010 provides that although it is for the UK government on behalf of the UK to ratify any resulting Treaty with the EU, this is subject to the prior approval of both the House of Commons and the House of Lords (the lower and upper chambers of the UK Parliament). The High Court, although not the House of Lords, has the power to block ratification of the Treaty by the government.

It may also be noted that Article 50(5) TEU anticipates the possibility of a Member State that leaves subsequently applying to rejoin and states that this is governed by Article 49 TEU. Article 49 TEU lays down the procedure that must be followed in order for any candidate country to become a Member State of the EU; it does not differentiate between a country that used to be a Member State and a country that has never been a Member State.

The European Union (Withdrawal) Act 2018 is a piece of domestic UK legislation intended to fill the legislative gap that will be created when the UK leaves the EU and, potentially, EU law ceases to apply to the UK. It therefore does the following.

- Section 1 repeals the European Communities Act 1972, which was enacted by the UK when it joined the EU in order to enable EU law to take effect in the UK, either directly (as in the case of EU Treaties, Regulations and Decisions—see further 3.4.1 and 3.4.2) or through implementing provisions of UK law (as in the case of Directives—see further 3.4.2.2).
- Sections 2–7 convert the provisions of EU law at the time the UK exits into domestic UK law (referred to as 'retained EU law'—a process that has also been described as 're-importing' or 'onshoring') and preserve UK laws that were passed to implement EU law (referred to as 'EU-derived domestic legislation'). Thus the same laws will apply on the day after the UK leaves the EU as applied on the day before. These include those general principles of EU law which have been recognized as such by the Court of Justice in a case decided before 'exit day' (see further 3.4.5). However, they do not include the right to damages under the ruling in C-6 & 9/90 *Francovich v Italy* [1991] ECR I-5357 (discussed at 5.2 and 5.3) or the EU Charter of Fundamental Rights (discussed at 9.4).
- Section 8 gives the UK government the power to amend or repeal retained EU laws and EU-derived domestic legislation. However, this power is not unlimited; it lasts for only two years from 'exit day' and it can be used only if the law is 'deficient' as defined in the Act, for example if provisions are redundant or refer to EU entities or reciprocal arrangements with the EU that (depending on the terms of the withdrawal negotiated between the UK and the EU—see the next bullet point) no longer apply. This is the so-called Henry VIII clause because it gives power to the executive, as opposed to the legislature, to legislate.
- Section 13 provides that any withdrawal agreement approving the final terms of withdrawal from the EU (which are a matter for negotiation between the UK and the EU—negotiations that are still ongoing as at April 2019) must be approved by the UK Parliament. Section 9 gives the UK government limited powers to implement the agreement; it may take any action that is required on or before 'exit day' in order for the agreement to be effective from its first day in force.
- Sections 10–12 remove the restrictions that previously prohibited the devolved governments of Scotland, Wales, and Northern Ireland from acting incompatibly with EU law.
- 'Exit day' was originally due to be 29 March 2019, at 11 pm GMT (s 20 of the Act). This was subsequently extended in accordance with Council Decision (EU)

2019/476 taken in agreement with the United Kingdom of 22 March 2019 extending the period under Article 50(3)TEU, OJ 2019 L80/1, which provided that the UK would leave on 22 May 2019 if the Draft Withdrawal Agreement were approved by the House of Commons by 29 March 2019 (which it was not), or on 12 April 2019—in which case, the UK would 'indicate a way forward before 12 April 2019, for consideration by the European Council', with the possibility of a further extension if it did so. The date of 12 April was chosen because it was the latest date by which the UK would have to give notice of elections to the European Parliament, which it would be obliged to hold on 23–26 May 2019 if it were still a Member State. It was further extended to 31 October 2019 by an EU Council Decision of 11 April 2019 taken in agreement with the UK (EUCO XT 20013/19). However, this further extension may be reduced if the Draft Withdrawal Agreement is ratified by the UK and the EU before this date, in which case the UK's withdrawal will take place on the first day of the following month.

The European Union (Legal Continuity) (Scotland) Bill passed by the Scottish Parliament on 21 March 2018 purported to make provision in relation to the continued effect in Scotland of provisions of EU law upon the withdrawal of the UK from the EU. In large part, the Scottish Bill directly replicated the provisions and powers of the UK-wide European Union (Withdrawal) Act 2018, but with key powers under its provisions being exercised by the Scottish Parliament or the Scottish ministers. However, it purported to render of 'no effect' in Scots law any subordinate legislation—both of the kind provided for by the European Union (Withdrawal) Act (which was passed without Scottish consent for the devolution provisions) and that provided for under primary legislation in the future—to which the Scottish ministers had not consented. What Scottish ministers objected to under the European Union (Withdrawal) Act was that certain powers that are currently devolved, but which have always been exercised by the EU and EU-wide frameworks of law, will be used by the UK government to create similar UK-wide frameworks without the devolved governments having a say on those new laws. The Bill would retain EU law in devolved areas such as the environment and food standards, and creates powers for Scottish ministers to amend the law so it can operate effectively outside the European Union (Withdrawal) Act. The Attorney General and the Advocate General for Scotland therefore made a reference to the Supreme Court under s 33(1) of the Scotland Act 1998 on whether the Bill was within the competence of the Scottish Parliament.

In *The UK Withdrawal from the European Union (Legal Continuity) (Scotland) Bill—A Reference by the Attorney General and the Advocate General for Scotland* (UKSC 2018/0080), the UK's Supreme Court held that the Bill, as a whole, was within the competence of the Scottish Parliament because, although the relationship with the EU was not a devolved matter, the Bill did not relate to relations with the EU, but only regulated certain of the legislative consequences of the cessation of EU law as a source of domestic law (at para 33). However, it held that s 17 of the Bill was outside the legislative competence of the Scottish Parliament because it would impliedly amend the Scotland Act by making the legal effect of secondary legislation made by UK ministers in relation to retained EU law conditional on the consent of the Scottish ministers (at para 52). The Supreme Court also noted that the European Union (Withdrawal) Act 2018, which had been enacted after the date on which the Scottish Bill was passed, had been added to the list of legislation in the Scotland Act which was protected against modification by the Scottish Parliament. Those provisions of the Scotland Bill that amounted to modifications of the European Union (Withdrawal) Act 2018 were therefore outside the legislative competence of the Scottish Parliament. The Scottish government will now have to decide whether to amend the Bill in order to make it compatible with UK law or abandon the Bill entirely.

1.19.2 Possible options for the relationship between the EU and a former Member State

The Draft Withdrawal Agreement covers issues relating to the withdrawal itself and some limited issues relating to the future relationship.

In relation to the withdrawal, it covers:

- separation issues, such as the free movement of goods placed on the market before the end of the transition period, the protection of existing intellectual property rights including geographical indications, and the use of data and information already exchanged;
- a transition period until 31 December 2020 (draft Article 126), during which the UK will, in practice, enjoy continuing EU membership, but without certain institutional rights enjoyed by EU Member States, which period may be extended once by the Joint Committee (see below) before 1 July 2020, for up to one or two years (draft Article 132);
- the financial settlement between the UK and the EU; and
- the governance structure for implementing the Draft Withdrawal Agreement itself, including a Joint Committee of representatives of the EU and the UK to implement, apply, and interpret it.

In relation to the future relationship, it covers:

- the rights of UK and other EU citizens who have exercised their rights of free movement from the UK to the rest of the EU or vice versa (draft Articles 9–39);
- a Protocol on Northern Ireland, which provides for a 'backstop' (ie provisions that apply unless and until they are superseded by a subsequent agreement) to ensure that, whatever agreement is finally reached, there will be no hard border between Northern Ireland and Ireland; and
- a Protocol on Gibraltar, which provides for the rights of frontier workers (those who reside in Gibraltar or Spain and cross the border to work) and cooperation between the Gibraltarian and Spanish authorities to combat fraud, smuggling, and money laundering, and to resolve tax-residence conflicts.

In particular, the Protocol on Northern Ireland provides for a 'single customs territory' between the UK and the EU (Article 6 of the draft Protocol). It also provides for the Common Travel Area between Ireland and the UK (which predates the accession of those countries to the EU) and the Single Electricity Market in Ireland to continue. The UK government's own legal adviser, the Attorney General, has advised the government that 'despite statements in the Protocol that it is not intended to be permanent … in *international law* the Protocol would endure indefinitely until a superseding agreement took its place, [and] … the Withdrawal Agreement cannot provide a legal means of compelling the EU to conclude such an agreement … (Attorney General's Office, *Legal Effect of the Protocol on Ireland/Northern Ireland*, 13 November 2018, para 16).

The Draft Withdrawal Agreement also imposes a duty on both the UK and the EU to use their 'best endeavours' to reach an agreement on the future relationship between them that can apply from the end of the transition period.

Agreement on the withdrawal of the United Kingdom of Great Britain and Northern Ireland from the European Union and the European Atomic Energy Community, as endorsed by leaders at a special meeting of the European Council on 25 November 2018

Article 184

Negotiations on the future relationship

The Union and the United Kingdom shall use their best endeavours, in good faith and in full respect of their respective legal orders, to take the necessary steps to negotiate expeditiously the agreements governing their future relationship referred to in the political declaration of [DD/MM/2018] and to conduct the relevant procedures for the ratification or conclusion of those agreements, with a view to ensuring that those agreements apply, to the extent possible, as from the end of the transition period.

In addition to the limited provisions on the future relationship contained in the Draft Withdrawal Agreement itself, a second document agreed at the same time provides a more detailed basis for the future relationship. This is the Political Declaration, and its key provisions of particular relevance to the subjects covered in this book (including the free movement of goods (Chapter 10) and persons (Chapter 11), and arrangements for the resolution of disputes (Chapters 6, 7 and 8)) are set out below. It should be remembered that the Political Declaration has been rejected on several occasions by the UK Parliament and even if and when it is ratified by the UK and the EU, it will not be legally binding (unlike the Draft Withdrawal Agreement); formal negotiations on a legally binding document on the future relationship between the UK and the EU can take place, under the terms of Article 50 TEU, only after the UK has left the EU. This has led to concerns being expressed by those who agree with the content of the Political Declaration that it may, in the future, be rejected by the UK or the EU. It is also expressed in very general terms and even if the parties agree to adhere to it, there is considerable room for constructive interpretation.

Political declaration setting out the framework for the future relationship between the European Union and the United Kingdom of Great Britain and Northern Ireland, 22 November 2018

Introduction

[…]

2. The Union and United Kingdom are determined to work together to safeguard the rules-based international order, the rule of law and promotion of democracy, and high standards of free and fair trade and workers' rights, consumer and environmental protection, and cooperation against internal and external threats to their values and interests.

3. In that spirit, this declaration establishes the parameters of an ambitious, broad, deep and flexible partnership across trade and economic cooperation, law enforcement and criminal justice, foreign policy, security and defence and wider areas of cooperation. Where the Parties consider it to be in their mutual interest during the negotiations, the future relationship may encompass areas of cooperation beyond those described in this political declaration. This relationship will be rooted in the values and interests that the Union and the United Kingdom share. These arise from their geography, history and ideals anchored in their common European heritage. The Union and the United Kingdom agree that prosperity and security are enhanced by embracing free and fair trade, defending individual rights and the rule of law, protecting workers, consumers and the environment, and standing together against threats to rights and values from without or within.

4. The future relationship will be based on a balance of rights and obligations, taking into account the principles of each Party. This balance must ensure the autonomy of the Union's decision making and be consistent with the Union's principles, in particular with respect to the integrity of the Single Market and the Customs Union and the indivisibility of the four freedoms. It must also ensure the sovereignty of the United Kingdom and the protection of its internal market, while respecting the result of the 2016 referendum including with regard to the development of its independent trade policy and the ending of free movement of people between the Union and the United Kingdom.

[…]

Part I: Initial provisions

I. Basis for cooperation

A. Core values and rights

[…]

7. The future relationship should incorporate the United Kingdom's continued commitment to respect the framework of the European Convention on Human Rights (ECHR), while the Union and its Member States will remain bound by the Charter of Fundamental Rights of the European Union, which reaffirms the rights as they result in particular from the ECHR.

[…]

Part II: Economic partnership

I. Objectives and principles

[...]

17. Against this backdrop, the Parties agree to develop an ambitious, wide-ranging and balanced economic partnership. This partnership will be comprehensive, encompassing a free trade area as well as wider sectoral cooperation where it is in the mutual interest of both Parties. It will be underpinned by provisions ensuring a level playing field for open and fair competition, as set out in Section XIV of this Part. It should facilitate trade and investment between the Parties to the extent possible, while respecting the integrity of the Union's Single Market and the Customs Union as well as the United Kingdom's internal market, and recognising the development of an independent trade policy by the United Kingdom beyond this economic partnership.

[...]

19. The Parties recall their determination to replace the backstop solution on Northern Ireland by a subsequent agreement that establishes alternative arrangements for ensuring the absence of a hard border on the island of Ireland on a permanent footing.

II. Goods

A. Objectives and principles

[...]

22. However, with a view to facilitating the movement of goods across borders, the Parties envisage comprehensive arrangements that will create a free trade area, combining deep regulatory and customs cooperation, underpinned by provisions ensuring a level playing field for open and fair competition.

B. Tariffs

23. The economic partnership should ensure no tariffs, fees, charges or quantitative restrictions across all sectors, with ambitious customs arrangements that, in line with the Parties' objectives and principles above, build and improve on the single customs territory provided for in the Withdrawal Agreement which obviates the need for checks on rules of origin.

[...]

D. Customs

26. The Parties will put in place ambitious customs arrangements, in pursuit of their overall objectives ... .

[...]

IX. Mobility

50. Noting that the United Kingdom has decided that the principle of free movement of persons between the Union and the United Kingdom will no longer apply, the Parties should establish mobility arrangements, as set out below.

51. The mobility arrangements will be based on non-discrimination between the Union's Member States and full reciprocity.

52. In this context, the Parties aim to provide, through their domestic laws, for visa-free travel for short-term visits.

53. The Parties agree to consider conditions for entry and stay for purposes such as research, study, training and youth exchanges.

54. The Parties also agree to consider addressing social security coordination in the light of future movement of persons.

55. In line with their applicable laws, the Parties will explore the possibility to facilitate the crossing of their respective borders for legitimate travel.

56. Any provisions will be without prejudice to the Common Travel Area (CTA) arrangements as they apply between the United Kingdom and Ireland.

[...]

59. These arrangements would be in addition to commitments on temporary entry and stay of natural persons for business purposes in defined areas as referred to in Section III of this Part ...

Part IV: Institutional and other horizontal arrangements

[...]

II. Governance

[...]

D. Dispute settlement

132. The Parties will base the arrangements for dispute settlement and enforcement on those provided for in the Withdrawal Agreement. To that end, the Parties should first make every attempt to resolve any matter concerning the operation of the future relationship through discussion and consultation. If either Party deemed it necessary, it should be able to refer the matter to the Joint Committee for formal resolution.

[...]

134. Should a dispute raise a question of interpretation of Union law, which may also be indicated by either Party, the arbitration panel should refer the question to the CJEU as the sole arbiter of Union law, for a binding ruling. The arbitration panel should decide the dispute in accordance with the ruling given by the CJEU. Where a Party considers that the arbitration panel should have referred a question of interpretation of Union law to the CJEU, it may ask the panel to review and provide reasons for its assessment.

[...]

When discussing the possible future relationship between the UK and the EU, post-Brexit, it is also instructive to look at the EU's relationship with other third countries (ie countries that are not Member States of the EU). The first six of the following options have only ever applied to countries that have not been members of the EU (albeit including some countries that have later joined the EU) and have never applied to a former EU Member State. None of them therefore create a precedent for the treatment of such a country. However, they are often considered as providing possible templates for the relationship between the EU and a former Member State after it has left, and thus for the future relationship between the EU and the UK.

The seventh option is based on the position of Denmark, which is still a Member State, but part of which (Greenland) opted to leave the EU.

1.19.2.1 The European Free Trade Association (EFTA) and the European Economic Area (EEA): the 'Norway option'

The European Free Trade Association (EFTA) was founded by the EFTA Convention (sometimes referred to as the Stockholm Convention) in 1960 to establish a free trade area amongst those European countries that did not wish to integrate economically as fully as the then EEC (now the EU) countries. In the 1970s, the EFTA States concluded free trade agreements with the EEC and, from the 1990s onwards, with various other countries in all parts of the world. Many of the EFTA States, including the UK, subsequently left and joined the EU. The current EFTA Member States are Iceland, Liechtenstein, Norway, and Switzerland, all of which are party to the EFTA Convention, which regulates free trade between them in goods and services, and the free movement of persons.

The institutional structure of the EFTA is as follows.

- The EFTA Council decides on policy issues and is made up of ministers from the EFTA countries, who meet twice a year, and ambassadors, who meet more frequently.
- There are various committees that deal with particular issues such as relations with third countries.
- The EFTA Secretariat supports activities under the EFTA Convention and EFTA's agreements with free trade partners through its Geneva office, while its Brussels office supports the European Economic Area (EEA) Agreement with the EU Member States. It also has an office in Luxembourg.
- EFTA has a number of other institutions whose role relates only to the EEA Agreement and so these will be discussed in that context.

Three of the EFTA Member States—Iceland, Liechtenstein, and Norway—are also parties to the EEA Agreement with the Member States of the EU, which creates a single market (see 1.4.3) between those countries, applying EU legislation on the free movement of goods (see Chapter 10), services (see Chapter 12), and capital and persons (see Chapter 11), and establishing common rules on competition (see Chapters 14 and 15). It also covers cooperation in areas including research and development, the environment, and social policy. It does not cover EMU (see 1.14), the CAP, the CFP, the CFSP (see 1.13), or JHA (see 1.13). The EEA Agreement consists of Articles containing the primary legislation, annexes containing the *acquis communautaire* of EU law and certain non-binding measures, and protocols, which are generally not based on EU legislation and which contain provisions on specific issues. Unlike the EU Treaties, the EEA Agreement is updated with new legislation on a monthly basis.

REVIEW QUESTION

What does the term *acquis communautaire* mean?

Answer: If you have difficulty in remembering, look back at the definition in 1.15.

The institutional structure of the EEA is made up of joint EU–EFTA EEA bodies and bodies from the EFTA EEA structure. This is sometimes referred to as the two-pillar structure.

- **Joint bodies**
  - The EEA Council, composed of the foreign ministers of the EU and EEA EFTA States, provides political direction and guidance for the EEA Joint Committee.
  - The EEA Joint Committee is made up of representatives of those States, and it takes decisions by unanimity on the management of the EEA Agreement and the incorporation of further EU legislation.
  - The EEA Joint Parliamentary Committee comprises members of the national parliaments of the EEA EFTA States and members of the European Parliament (MEPs—see further 2.2), and it engages in dialogue and debate in areas covered by the EEA Agreement.
  - The EEA Consultative Committee comprises members of the EFTA Consultative Committee and the European Economic and Social Committee (EESC) of the EU (see 2.8), and it works to strengthen and develop cooperation in the economic and social aspects of the EEA Agreement.
- **EFTA EEA bodies**
  - The Standing Committee of the EFTA States provides a forum for the EFTA EEA States to consult and reach a common position before meeting with the EU in the EEA Joint Committee. It is made up of representatives from Norway, Iceland, and Liechtenstein, observers from Switzerland, and the EFTA Surveillance Authority.
  - The EFTA Court and EFTA Surveillance Authority are established by the Surveillance and Court Agreement of 1992.
    - The EFTA Surveillance Authority consists of three members, who are chosen on grounds of competence and appointed by agreement of the governments of the three EEA EFTA States. They must act independently, and their role (similarly, in part, to the role of the EU Commission—see 2.3) is to ensure that the EEA EFTA States fulfil their obligations under the EEA Agreement and that the competition rules are applied.
    - The EFTA Court consists of three judges appointed by the three EEA EFTA States. It adjudicates in matters relating to EFTA States, including enforcement actions brought by the Surveillance Authority against a State with regard to EFTA rules, the settlement of disputes between EFTA States, appeals from decisions of the EFTA Surveillance Authority, and advisory opinions to courts of the EFTA States on the interpretation of EFTA rules (see Chapter 6, Introduction).

The disadvantages of this relationship include the requirement to adopt much EU legislation despite having had no input in the decision-making procedure by which it was enacted and the need to contribute to the EU's budget. Whether the acceptance of free movement of persons is perceived to be an advantage or a disadvantage by a particular country depends on whether it hopes to enable migrants to fill jobs that its citizens are not prepared or able to do or to enable its own citizens to seek work abroad, or whether it fears increasing pressure on jobs, public services, and community cohesion.

It would also be necessary for the current EFTA States to agree to UK accession to EFTA and there are some indications that they might not agree, given the size of the UK and the potential impact of its membership on the balance of power within EFTA. Similarly, since the UK joined the EEA as part of the EU, it would presumably have to apply to rejoin it—although there has been some doubt expressed as to whether the UK will automatically leave the EEA when it leaves the EU and whether it should have given separate notice (under Article 127 of the EEA Agreement) had it wished to do so (see further the useful summary of arguments on this point in House of Commons, *The European Economic Area*, Briefing Paper No 8129, 21 December 2018).

Some British members of Parliament (MPs) have proposed an arrangement variously called 'Norway Plus' or 'Common Market 2.0', which would be similar to the Norway option, but whereas Norway is not a member of the EU customs union, the UK would have an additional customs arrangement with the EU in order to avoid a 'hard border' between Northern Ireland and the Republic of Ireland.

1.19.2.2 EFTA and bilateral arrangements: the 'Switzerland option'

Switzerland is not a member of the EEA, but, in addition to its membership of EFTA, it has a series of bilateral agreements with the EU. These relate to matters including the free movement of persons, technical trade barriers, public procurement, agriculture, transport, scientific research, participation in the Schengen Agreements on enhanced free movement of persons (see 1.9 and Chapter 11), and the Dublin Regulation on refugees (see further 9.5.2). However, in February 2014, the Swiss people voted in a referendum to reintroduce immigration quotas with the EU. Unlike the UK referendum on exit from the EU, this referendum was binding on that government, with a deadline of February 2017. However, the Swiss government and the EU are, at time of writing, still in negotiations on the free movement of persons as part of the draft Institutional Framework Agreement between the EU and the Swiss Confederation.

While this relationship avoids the wholesale application of large parts of EU law, it nonetheless has the disadvantages of applying much EU law on a sector-by-sector basis without Switzerland having had any input in the decision-making procedure by which it was enacted and of requiring a contribution to the EU's budget. It also requires the acceptance of free movement of persons.

1.19.2.3 The EU–Turkey Association Agreement: the 'Turkey option'

The Association Agreement between the then EEC (now EU) and Turkey, sometimes referred to as the Ankara Agreement, was signed in 1963 with the objectives of establishing a customs union (see 1.4.2) covering trade in goods and the free movement of workers (see Chapter 11).

In order to achieve these objectives and potentially pave the way for Turkish membership of the EU, Turkey had to adopt a considerable part of the *acquis communautaire* (see 1.5). This process is ongoing: restructuring of some economic sectors is still required and there are concerns on the part of the EU about Turkey's record on human rights.

As with the relationship with Switzerland outlined at 1.19.2.2, the EU's relationship with Turkey avoids the wholesale application of large parts of EU law, but it nonetheless has the disadvantage of applying some EU law on a sector-by-sector basis without Turkey having had any input in the decision-making procedure by which it was enacted. A further disadvantage, from the UK perspective, is that it applies only to free movement of goods; it does not apply to services, of which the UK is a leading exporter. As to the free movement of persons, while this is not yet in place, it is envisaged by the Association Agreement.

The EU has similar agreements for customs unions (but not the free movement of persons) with Andorra and San Marino.

1.19.2.4 Bilateral free trade agreements, including the 'Canada option'

The EU has a number of bilateral free trade agreements with countries with which it trades, including South Korea, Mexico, and South Africa. These bilateral agreements vary considerably in intensity and detail. Some of these are part of an association agreement with candidate countries for EU membership (for example with Albania).

The EU and Canada have negotiated the EU–Canada Comprehensive Economic and Trade Agreements (CETA) to remove customs duties (see 1.4.1 and Chapter 10), remove restrictions on bidding for public contracts, open up the market in services, and enhance protection of intellectual property rights. The EU and the United States are, at time of writing, negotiating the Transatlantic Trade Investment Partnership (TTIP) to remove trade barriers to the free movement of goods and services. There are, however, considerable concerns about these agreements and the following arguments (with which the EU disagrees) have been put forward.

- The negotiations were conducted in secret and with considerable input from business representatives, yet very little from elected representatives, consumer organizations, or trade unions.
- Proposals for regulatory cooperation may allow businesses to have considerable input into any new laws.
- New dispute resolution mechanisms may enable Canadian or US investors to sue EU Member States if they believe that EU or national laws, for example on environmental or consumer protection, have reduced their expected profits. It has been suggested that this could mean European countries being forced to allow technologies such as fracking or genetic modification (GM) technology.
- Workers' rights and job security, consumer protection, and food quality standards could be weakened because US standards in these areas are sometimes lower than those in the EU.

1.19.2.5 A deep and comprehensive free trade area: the 'Ukraine option'

The Deep and Comprehensive Free Trade Area (DCFTA) is part of the bilateral Association Agreement (AA) between the EU and Ukraine. It provides for the progressive removal of customs tariffs and quotas, and an extensive harmonization of laws in various trade-related sectors, in order to align key sectors of the Ukrainian economy to EU standards. Unlike classic free trade agreements, it provides for freedom of establishment and the expansion of the internal market for a set of key services, and it deals with trade-related energy issues.

Similar agreements have been concluded by the EU with Georgia and Moldova, countries that are not members of the EU's single market or customs union, but which are still granted 'deep and comprehensive' access to the EU market and customs cooperation in return for aligning their domestic laws to EU law. It has been estimated that Ukraine (whose agreement is the most advanced) will have to implement at least 80 per cent of the *acquis communautaire* (the existing body of EU law—see 1.5).

1.19.2.6 No formal agreement: the 'World Trade Organization (WTO) option'

If a Member State withdraws from the EU without having negotiated any special arrangements, either based on one of those outlined above or something different, it will simply be treated as any other state that is not a member of the EU or EFTA and which has no special agreement with the EU. Both it and the EU will remain part of the World Trade Organization (WTO) and subject to its rules. The WTO is an international organization of 164 countries, including all of the EU Member States and the EU itself, which facilitates the removal of trade barriers between countries through its rules and enforcement of those rules.

The potential disadvantages of a withdrawing Member State failing to conclude a withdrawal agreement with the EU are set out in the following extract.

House of Lords European Union Committee, *The Process of Withdrawing from the European Union*, 11th Report of Session 2015–16, HL Paper 138 (London: HMSO, 2016), footnotes omitted

46. [Sir David Edward, a former UK judge at the Court of Justice] confirmed that, should the UK be forced to withdraw unilaterally in this way, it would have no option but to fall back on the trading terms derived from its membership of the World Trade Organization (WTO). [Professor Derrick Wyatt QC] told us the following consequences would be likely to ensue:

> 'We would impose tariffs on goods almost certainly at the same level as the common external tariff. That is the tariff we impose to the outside world currently. We leave the EU; we impose those tariffs on goods coming to us. The EU would be a third country; the EU would be imposing those tariffs on us. Of course, that would cost customers; it would cost people in the shops. We cannot disarm in tariff terms, because that is our

ammunition in negotiating trade in goods. We also want to negotiate trade in services, where the WTO is not very good for us ... There would be tariffs between the UK and the EU, many of them not very high but some of them—as the Government pointed out—would be 10% on cars and 35% on dairy products.'

1.19.2.7 The 'reverse Greenland' option

The term 'Brexit' is normally used to refer to the UK leaving the EU. However, it has been suggested by some commentators that the UK could remain in the EU, but that those parts which voted to leave (England and Wales) could seek a territorial exemption from the continuing UK Member State and effectively leave the EU. UK membership would then continue to have effect only for those areas that voted to remain in the EU (Scotland, Northern Ireland, and Gibraltar), and its voting power in the European Parliament (see 2.1.1) and in QMV decisions in the EU Council (see 1.15 and 2.2.2) would be reduced because of the reduced size of the UK population remaining in the EU. The template for this option is Greenland, which, as mentioned earlier, is part of Denmark and joined what is now the EU along with the rest of Denmark in 1973 (see 1.6), but which subsequently left the EU (although it remains a part of Denmark). In the Danish referendum that preceded Denmark joining the EU, Greenland voted strongly against membership, whereas Denmark as a whole voted in favour, and in 1982 a non-binding consultative referendum held only in Greenland again resulted in a vote to leave. When Greenland finally left the EU in 1995, Denmark remained a Member State and Greenland joined the category of 'Overseas Countries and Territories' (OCTs), which are countries and territories that have special constitutional links to a Member State and have preferential trading relationships with the EU—governed by Council Decision 2013/755/EU of 25 November 2013 on the association of the overseas countries and territories with the European Union ('Overseas Association Decision'), OJ 2013 L344/1. However, it is by no means clear that this option is available to the UK or that England and Wales would be treated in the same way as Greenland: Article 50 TEU (discussed at 1.19.1) did not exist in 1995 when Greenland left and so there was no mechanism for a Member State to leave the EU, and Greenland is a small part of Denmark in terms of population and economy, whereas England and Wales account for the vast majority of the UK's population and economy.

?! THINKING POINT

Which of the above options do you think would be best for the UK? Can you foresee any disadvantages resulting from your choice?

1.20 Conclusions

The EU is a remarkable and unique organization. It has tied together the economies of almost 30 disparate countries to create an enormous internal market and contributed towards the raising of living standards, as well as developed a comprehensive legal system to support its activities. It has also been instrumental in creating and maintaining the unprecedented half-century of peace in Europe that has prevailed since its inception. Yet it continues to face significant challenges, not only economic and political, but also (as demonstrated in the rest of this book) legal. The most recent of these is 'Brexit', which poses challenges not only for the UK and its future relationship with the EU, but also for its impact on the economies of the remaining EU Member States and for the future direction of the EU—in particular, its relationship with its more Eurosceptic Member States.

SUMMARY

- In this chapter, you have learned about the history of the European Union (EU). This underlies the form and substance of EU law, and the EU's legislative and judicial structures.
- The EU, originally known as the European Economic Community (EEC) and then as the European Community (EC), was founded in 1957 and governed for much of its history by the EC Treaty (originally the EEC Treaty). Its origins lie in the desire of the original Member States to avoid another major war developing in Europe and to develop a trading bloc with global influence. It was preceded by the European Coal and Steel Community (ECSC), which attempted to integrate the traditional war industries, coal and steel, so that no Member State could engage in a war effort against another.
- Since then, the EU has proceeded along the path of economic integration (see further Chapter 10), and the Treaty on European Union 1992 (TEU 1992) established economic and monetary union (EMU) as an objective of the Member States.
- The TEU (1992)—and, to a lesser extent, the Single European Act (SEA) and the Treaties of Amsterdam and Nice—fundamentally changed the political, economic, and legal assumptions underlying the EU. The Treaty of Lisbon added a significant human rights dimension to the EU.
- However, there have been, and remain, difficulties. As the number of Member States increases, decision-making becomes more complex, not least because of the corresponding increase in the diversity of views as to what the EU should be about. How the tension between 'deepening' the level of integration and 'widening' the number of countries to be integrated will be resolved remains to be seen.
- The first major amending Treaty, the SEA, provided momentum to achieve the single market within the EC. It also extended the competences of the then EEC and set up the Court of First Instance (now the General Court) as part of the two-court structure of the Court of Justice of the European Union (CJEU).
- Perhaps the most important amending Treaty, the EU Treaty (1992) or TEU (1992), established a new aim of economic and monetary union, and provided new competences in foreign and defence policy, and justice and home affairs, under a new body, the EU. It also renamed the EEC as the EC.
- The Treaties of Amsterdam and Nice were primarily intended to streamline the institutional structures of the EC in anticipation of enlargement. However, they were not entirely successful in enabling the EC to function more efficiently.
- The Treaty of Lisbon merged the EC and the EU, so that there is now a single entity called the EU, although there are still two Treaties.

- The EU has 28 Member States (at time of writing), with accession negotiations continuing for further expansion (and one withdrawal).
- The economic, political, and legal impact of the likely withdrawal of the UK from the EU, and the future relationship between the UK and the EU, remain to be established.

FURTHER READING

Articles

M Aubelj, 'Theory of European Union' (2011) 36(6) EL Rev 818

Discusses the nature of European integration.

P Craig, 'The Treaty of Lisbon: Process, Architecture and Substance' (2008) 33(2) EL Rev 137

Discusses key provisions of the Treaty of Lisbon (2007).

B de Witte, 'An Undivided Union? Differentiated Integration in Post-Brexit Times' (2018) 55(2) Supp (Special Issue) CMLR 227

Considers whether the EU will still engage in differentiated integration projects after the UK leaves and the likelihood of a 'two-speed' EU.

J Odermatt, 'The Court of Justice of the European Union: International or Domestic Court?' (2014) 3(3) CJICL 696

Explores the possibility that there are occasions when the approach of the EU's Court of Justice is that of an international, rather than a supranational, court.

Books

I Bache, S Bulmer, S George, and O Parker, *Politics in the European Union*, 4th edn (Oxford: Oxford University Press, 2014)

See especially Chapter 1 on theories of economic integration and Chapters 5–11 on the history of the EU.

MJ Dedman, *The Origins and Development of the European Union 1945–95: A History of European Integration* (Oxford: Routledge, 1996)

Analyses the political and economic events leading up to the founding of the EEC and its subsequent progress.

R Gordon QC and R Moffatt, *Brexit: The Immediate Legal Consequences* (London: The Constitution Society, 2016)

Discusses the probable legal consequences of Brexit for the UK and its relationship with the EU and EU law.

Book chapters

J-C Piris, 'Which Options Would be Available for the United Kingdom in the Case of a Withdrawal from the EU?', in PJ Birkinshaw and A Biondi (eds), *Britain Alone! The Implications and Consequences of United Kingdom Exit from the EU* (Alpen aan den Rijn: Kluwer, 2016), ch 6

Considers the options for UK–EU relations after a UK exit from the EU.

Reports

European Commission

F Ilzkovitz, A Dierx, V Kovacs, and N Sousa, 'Steps towards a Deeper Economic Integration: The Internal Market in the 21st Century—A Contribution to the Single Market Review' (2007) European Commission, Directorate-General for Economic and Financial Affairs, Publication

No 291, available at http://ec.europa.eu/economy_finance/publications/publication_summary788_En.htm

Analyses progress towards achievement of the single market.

HM Government

The European Union (Withdrawal) Act 2018, Explanatory Notes

Explains the provisions of the Act and the background to those provisions.

***The future relationship between the United Kingdom and the European Union*, Cm 9593 (London: HMSO, July 2018)**

Outlines the UK government's plans for the post-Brexit relationship between the UK and the EU.

There are very many useful *House of Commons Briefing Papers*, including the following.

***Brexit: how does the Article 50 process work?*, Briefing Paper No 7551, 30 June 2016**

Explains the procedure for, and consequences of, triggering Article 50 TEU.

***Brexit: trade aspects*, Briefing Paper No 7694, 8 September 2016**

Considers which existing features of the UK's relationship with the EU should ideally be retained, which should be removed, and what other trade issues will need to be resolved.

***The status of 'retained EU law'*, Briefing Paper No 8375, 30 July 2018**

Discusses how the UK's concept of 'retained EU law' will work after Brexit.

House of Lords European Union Committee

***The Process of Withdrawing from the European Union*, 11th Report of Session 2015–16, HL Paper 138 (London: HMSO, 2016)**

Examines the Article 50 TEU process for withdrawal from the EU and the negotiation of a future relationship with the EU.

WEB LINKS

'The history of the European Union', available at https://europa.eu/european-union/about-eu/history_en

The EU's own account of its history.

Podcasts

Given the fast-moving nature of the Brexit-related material in this chapter, podcasts are particularly useful, and the following are highly recommended—especially *Brexitcast*.

'Brexit: A Guide for the Perplexed', available at https://www.bbc.co.uk/programmes/b08ffww9

This short Radio 4 podcast covers a variety of Brexit-related issues, particularly the possible practical consequences.

'Brexit: A Love Story?', available at https://www.bbc.co.uk/programmes/p062h50y

This BBC Radio 4 podcast covers not only the fascinating political history of the UK's relationship with the EU leading up to its withdrawal, but also more recent Brexit developments.

'Brexitcast', available at https://www.bbc.co.uk/programmes/p05299nl

This engaging and entertaining BBC Radio 5 podcast on Brexit-related legal and political developments in Westminster and Brussels is invaluable for two key reasons: first, it is produced weekly (and even more frequently when events so require); and secondly, expert commentary is provided by the BBC's political editor Laura Kuenssberg, Europe editor Katya Adler, and political correspondents Adam Fleming and Chris Mason.

Updating email services

As with the podcasts, updating email services are useful in relation to Brexit because of the fast-moving nature of developments. The UK Parliament itself provides two updating services in relation to Brexit, both of which are available for subscription at https://www.parliament.uk/brexit

Brexit email alerts

Updates released as soon as new research on Brexit is published by UK Parliament.

The Brexit Digest

An explainer of what is happening in the House of Commons to scrutinize Brexit, released every Monday morning.

QUESTIONS

1. Explain the reasons for the formation of the EEC in 1957.
2. What is the single market?
3. Why was the Single European Act (1986) necessary and how did it provide for achievement of its objectives?
4. What significant developments were introduced by the TEU (1992)?
5. What major changes were made by the Treaty of Lisbon (2007)?

To view outline answers to these questions plus further resources to support your EU law studies, visit the Online Resources for this book at www.oup.com/uk/eulaw-complete4e

The official institutions of the European Union

2

KEY POINTS

By the end of this chapter, you should be able to:

- describe the composition and functions of the key institutions of the European Union (EU);
- appreciate the relative importance and power of these institutions, including the extent of the so-called democratic deficit; and
- be familiar with the role of the Court of Justice within the framework of the European Union.

INTRODUCTION

Let us start by posing a question: what do you know about the institutions in the European Union (EU)? You may answer in the following way: 'The institutions are based in Brussels. They sometimes make laws that interfere with our lives. They have been known to make decisions that are ridiculous, for example the banning of abnormally shaped bananas.' 'Interfering' and 'remote' may be words that spring to mind and might indicate how the EU institutions have been or are perceived.

However you may view the EU, it is true to say that its institutions and policies have a direct impact on Member States, business both within the EU and outside it, EU citizens, and also those who are not citizens of the EU.

Good examples of policies that have emanated from the EU that could affect you can be found in the area of travel within the EU. If you are planning a trip abroad, for example to France or Spain, then you will have to obtain euros. At time of writing, 18 countries use the euro as their currency. Visa-free travel can be enjoyed across the whole EU and, indeed, there are no frontier controls at all between 22 EU countries thanks to the Schengen Agreements, of which all EU countries are full members except Bulgaria, Croatia, Cyprus, Ireland, Romania, and the UK. Furthermore, if you are unfortunate and find that your flight is delayed for two hours or more, then you can apply for compensation.

By looking more closely at the institutions, you will gain an appreciation of their composition and what functions they have. This in turn will help you to understand how much influence or power each institution has in relation to the decision-making process, which will be dealt with in Chapter 3.

THINKING POINT

Can you think of any policies that have emanated from the EU that could affect or have affected you?

The official EU institutions, which have been entrusted with carrying out the tasks of the EU, are listed under Article 13 of the EU Treaty (TEU).

Article 13 TEU

1. The Union shall have an institutional framework which shall aim to promote its values, advance its objectives, serve its interests, those of its citizens and those of the Member States, and ensure the consistency, effectiveness and continuity of its policies and actions.

   The Union's institutions shall be:

   — the European Parliament,

   — the European Council,

   — the Council,

   — the European Commission (hereinafter referred to as 'the Commission'),

   — the Court of Justice of the European Union,

   — the European Central Bank,

   — the Court of Auditors.

2. Each institution shall act within the limits of the powers conferred on it in the Treaties, and in conformity with the procedures, conditions and objectives set out in them. The institutions shall practice mutual sincere cooperation.

The EU does not strictly conform to the traditional separation-of-powers mode of State governance—that is, legislature, executive, and judiciary. The EU institutions have overlapping roles (see Figure 2.1 later in the chapter). For example, the Council of Ministers and the Commission have the role of executive, but only the Commission has the right to initiate legislation, whilst it is the European Parliament, together with the Council of Ministers, that has the primary role in the legislative decision-making process. Thus the institutions act as a collective, rather than independently, on behalf of the EU.

Each institution mentioned in Article 13 TEU must act within the scope of the powers conferred on it by the Treaties, and a system of checks and balances is in place to ensure that this has been done. This principle of institutional balance derives from Case 9/56 *Meroni & Co., Industrie Metallurgiche, SpA v High Authority of the European Coal and Steel Community* [1957–58] ECR 133 and effectively ensures that one institution does not encroach on the powers of another. It encompasses both a legal and a political dimension, with infringements falling under the jurisdiction of the Court of Justice.

?! THINKING POINT

Based upon your existing knowledge of the EU institutions, is it your impression that the institutions are on an equal footing and that the balance of power between the institutions is represented in a fair and balanced way?

The accusation that the EU lacks democratic legitimacy—the 'democratic deficit' argument—has been an ongoing issue for the EU. In the UK, we are familiar with the concept of a parliamentary democracy whereby dissatisfaction with those responsible for the direction of the country, its policies, and its laws can be expressed via the ballot box. The accusation is that, in the EU, the citizen is so far removed that little or no influence can be exerted. Of course, it is clear that the democratic deficit argument encapsulates more than simply which institutions have a right to engage in the legislative process and the accountability of those institutions. Other factors include the perceived lack of transparency, the spatial distance from the seats of power, and apathy in parliamentary elections. A greater understanding of the relationships between the institutions and the links to the Member States will assist you in judging to what extent you consider the accusation of a democratic deficit existing to be legitimate.

2.1 The European Parliament

2.1.1 Composition

The European Parliament has its official home in the French city of Strasbourg and its administrative offices in Luxembourg, with certain sessions and committee meetings taking place in Brussels. Members of the European Parliament (MEPs) are directly elected for a term of five years by European citizens in the Member States using proportional representation (PR). They represent some 500 million European citizens. Following the amendments made by the Treaty of Lisbon, the number of MEPs is fixed at a maximum of 750, plus the President. The European Council, with the Parliament's consent, determines the number of MEPs and the seats allocated to Member States on the basis of population size and 'degressive proportionality' (MEPs representing the larger Member States by population will represent more people than the smaller States), no one State having more than 96 or fewer than 6 MEPs (Article 14 TEU). The allocation is as represented in Table 2.1.

At the time of writing, it is unclear whether, and if so, when the UK will officially leave the EU. If and when it does leave, the UK will no longer have any MEPs and there will be a reduction in the overall number. Whilst some EU Member States will gain more (an example is Spain, which will gain 5 MEPs), no remaining Member State will lose seats. In the Europeaan elections of May 2019 the UK retained its 73 seats.

2.1.2 Functions and powers

As a parliament, the primary function of the European Parliament is that of a forum for discussion and debate. However, it enjoys additional functions and powers.

2.1.2.1 Legislative

The European Parliament's role within the decision-making institutional framework has changed dramatically through the amending Treaties. Originally, its participation in the

Table 2.1 Number of MEPs per Member State (from July 2014)

Member State	Number of MEPs
Germany	96
France	74
Italy; UK	73 (each)
Spain	54
Poland	51
Romania	32
Netherlands	26
Belgium; Czech Republic; Greece; Hungary; Portugal	21 (each)
Sweden	20
Austria	18
Bulgaria	17
Denmark; Finland; Slovakia	13 (each)
Croatia; Ireland; Lithuania	11 (each)
Latvia; Slovenia	8 (each)
Cyprus; Estonia; Luxembourg; Malta	6 (each)

→ CROSS-REFERENCE
See legislative procedures at 3.5.

legislative process was purely advisory and consultative. With the amending Treaties, the Parliament's powers in this regard have increased. Notably, where the ordinary legislative procedure (OLP) applies, as is now the case in most policy areas, the European Parliament's approval must be obtained before legislation can be adopted.

This greater involvement of the European Parliament in the legislative process has gone some way towards alleviating tensions of a democratic deficit in the EU. As the only directly elected body of the EU, it is important in both perception and reality that the European Parliament, and therefore 'the people', have a say.

?! THINKING POINT

Return to Chapter 1, which looks at the founding and amending Treaties. Can you chart the development of the greater involvement of the European Parliament in legislative matters? To what extent do you feel allegations of a democratic deficit are relevant in this regard?

2.1.2.2 Budgetary

Again, originally the European Parliament's role in the EU budget was one of consultation. Following the Treaty of Lisbon, the European Parliament has an equal right alongside the Council to adopt the EU budget (which will have been drafted by the European Commission). Article 314 of the Treaty on the Functioning of the European Union (TFEU) sets out the stages in the procedure. The importance of the Parliament's role is clear.

Article 314 TFEU

The European Parliament and the Council, acting in accordance with a special legislative procedure, shall establish the Union's annual budget in accordance with the following provisions.

1. With the exception of the European Central Bank, each institution shall, before 1 July, draw up estimates of its expenditure for the following financial year. The Commission shall consolidate these estimates in a draft budget, which may contain different estimates.

   The draft budget shall contain an estimate of revenue and an estimate of expenditure.

2. The Commission shall submit a proposal containing the draft budget to the European Parliament and to the Council not later than 1 September of the year preceding that in which the budget is to be implemented.

   The Commission may amend the draft budget during the procedure until such time as the Conciliation Committee, referred to in paragraph 5, is convened.

3. The Council shall adopt its position on the draft budget and forward it to the European Parliament not later than 1 October of the year preceding that in which the budget is to be implemented. The Council shall inform the European Parliament in full of the reasons which led it to adopt its position.

4. If, within forty-two days of such communication, the European Parliament:

   (a) approves the position of the Council, the budget shall be adopted;

   (b) has not taken a decision, the budget shall be deemed to have been adopted;

   (c) adopts amendments by a majority of its component members, the amended draft shall be forwarded to the Council and to the Commission. The President of the European Parliament, in agreement with the President of the Council, shall immediately convene a meeting of the Conciliation Committee. However, if within ten days of the draft being forwarded the Council informs the European Parliament that it has approved all its amendments, the Conciliation Committee shall not meet.

5. The Conciliation Committee, which shall be composed of the members of the Council or their representatives and an equal number of members representing the European Parliament, shall have the task of reaching agreement on a joint text, by a qualified majority of the members of the Council or their representatives and by a majority of the representatives of the European Parliament within twenty-one days of its being convened, on the basis of the positions of the European Parliament and the Council.

   The Commission shall take part in the Conciliation Committee's proceedings and shall take all the necessary initiatives with a view to reconciling the positions of the European Parliament and the Council.

6. If, within the twenty-one days referred to in paragraph 5, the Conciliation Committee agrees on a joint text, the European Parliament and the Council shall each have a period of fourteen days from the date of that agreement in which to approve the joint text.

7. If, within the period of fourteen days referred to in paragraph 6:
   (a) the European Parliament and the Council both approve the joint text or fail to take a decision, or if one of these institutions approves the joint text while the other one fails to take a decision, the budget shall be deemed to be definitively adopted in accordance with the joint text; or
   (b) the European Parliament, acting by a majority of its component members, and the Council both reject the joint text, or if one of these institutions rejects the joint text while the other one fails to take a decision, a new draft budget shall be submitted by the Commission; or
   (c) the European Parliament, acting by a majority of its component members, rejects the joint text while the Council approves it, a new draft budget shall be submitted by the Commission; or
   (d) the European Parliament approves the joint text whilst the Council rejects it, the European Parliament may, within fourteen days from the date of the rejection by the Council and acting by a majority of its component members and three-fifths of the votes cast, decide to confirm all or some of the amendments referred to in paragraph 4(c). Where a European Parliament amendment is not confirmed, the position agreed in the Conciliation Committee on the budget heading which is the subject of the amendment shall be retained. The budget shall be deemed to be definitively adopted on this basis.
8. If, within the twenty-one days referred to in paragraph 5, the Conciliation Committee does not agree on a joint text, a new draft budget shall be submitted by the Commission.
9. When the procedure provided for in this Article has been completed, the President of the European Parliament shall declare that the budget has been definitively adopted.
10. Each institution shall exercise the powers conferred upon it under this Article in compliance with the Treaties and the acts adopted thereunder, with particular regard to the Union's own resources and the balance between revenue and expenditure.

2.1.2.3 Supervisory

The European Parliament exerts control over the executive in a number of ways. An example can be found in the fact that appointments to the position of President of the Commission must first be approved by the European Parliament. Furthermore, the entire Commission is subject to approval by the European Parliament (Article 17(7) TFEU). Indeed, the Parliament has the power to require the whole Commission to resign from office. Such a motion is an exceptional sanction that could be quite damaging to the EU. As such, Article 234 TFEU sets out the conditions applicable.

Article 234 TFEU

If a motion of censure on the activities of the Commission is tabled before it, the European Parliament shall not vote thereon until at least three days after the motion has been tabled and only by open vote.

> If the motion of censure is carried by a two-thirds majority of the votes cast, representing a majority of the component Members of the European Parliament, the members of the Commission shall resign as a body and the High Representative of the Union for Foreign Affairs and Security Policy shall resign from duties that he or she carries out in the Commission. They shall remain in office and continue to deal with current business until they are replaced in accordance with Article 17 of the Treaty on European Union. In this case, the term of office of the members of the Commission appointed to replace them shall expire on the date on which the term of office of the members of the Commission obliged to resign as a body would have expired.

Note that this power does not extend to the removal of individual Commissioners or the President of the Commission.

The Parliament also has a power to question the Commission and the Council in writing or orally under Article 230 TFEU, and it has a right to discuss the Commission's annual general reports under Article 233 TFEU.

The Parliament may request the Commission to submit such legislative proposals as the European Parliament considers necessary.

The Parliament also exercises some political control over the Commission, the Council, the European Council, and the European Central Bank (ECB) through its right to examine the reports that must be submitted by these institutions.

?! THINKING POINT

How much control do you think the European Parliament has over the other institutions of the EU? Given that the Parliament is a directly elected body, do you think this impacts on the 'democratic legitimacy' of those institutions that are not directly elected or are appointed? (You may want to return to this point once you have worked through the chapter.)

2.2 The Council of the European Union

 **NOTE**

The Council of the European Union should not be confused with the European Council (see 2.5) or the Council of Europe (see 9.1).

2.2.1 Composition

The Council of the European Union is referred to by several different names. It used to be formally known as the Council of Ministers, but was referred to in the Treaties as merely 'the Council'. Although it has been officially renamed under TEU (1992) (see 1.13) and is now called the Council of the European Union, it is generally still referred to simply as 'the Council'. To add to the confusion a little more, you may also encounter it being referred to informally as the EU Council. The danger in this, of course, is that such inconsistency makes it likely to be confused with the European Council, which is, as noted earlier, a very different institution.

Such confusion of terminology could be argued to add to the public perception of unnecessary complexity within the EU institutions and does little to counter the 'democratic deficit' allegation that has been a constant accusation against the EU. Indeed, this particular aspect of EU terminology has proved to be a rich source of comedic material. (*Yes, Prime Minister*, a British comedy series in the early 1980s, provides an example of such.)

The Council itself comprises ministers of the Member States, its membership changing according to the matter under discussion. So, for instance, if agricultural matters are under consideration, the Council comprises national ministers of agriculture. Under the Treaty of Lisbon reforms (see 1.18), there are ten different configurations, with the General Affairs Council ensuring consistency in the work of the different Council configurations. Each configuration is chaired by the relevant minister of the Member State holding the Presidency—except for the Foreign Affairs Council, which, under Treaty of Lisbon amendments, is chaired by the High Representative of the Union for Foreign Affairs and Security Policy. Council members represent national interests, in contrast to members of the Commission, who are required to act independently of national governments. Thus it is within the Council that national interests are most strongly represented. For this reason, it lacks the cohesion of other EU institutions and could legitimately be said not to be as 'European' as the others.

In considering the 'democratic deficit' argument and the Council, it should be noted that the relevant ministers that compose the Council are actually elected by citizens in national elections. As such, they can be said to have a democratic mandate. However, arguably, their democratic legitimacy does not extend to their work in the Council, for they are not directly elected to this role. This position should be contrasted with Members of the European Parliament (MEPs).

2.2.2 Functions and powers

Article 16 TEU

1. The Council shall, jointly with the European Parliament, exercise legislative and budgetary functions. It shall carry out policy-making and coordinating functions as laid down in the Treaties.

[...]

The Council has final power of decision on the adoption of secondary legislation, exercised jointly with the European Parliament where the OLP applies. The Council can generally act only on a Commission proposal, but it can require the Commission to frame draft legislation in any specific area. The Council also has general powers to enact legislation in specific areas, for example the ability to adopt provisions for the harmonization of legislation concerning indirect taxes, under Article 113 TFEU. The Council also has a wide law-making power to attain the objectives of the EU, found in Article 352 TFEU. The Council can delegate power to the Commission to enact Regulations.

2.2.2.1 COREPER

Article 16 TEU

[...]

7. A Committee of Permanent Representatives of the Governments of the Member States shall be responsible for preparing the work of the Council.

   [...]

The Council's work is therefore prepared by the Committee of Permanent Representatives (COREPER). COREPER is composed of representatives from each Member State, who scrutinize legislative proposals drafted by the Commission and help to set the agenda for Council meetings. The Council Secretariat provides administrative support (Article 240 TFEU).

The Committee is hugely important in ensuring the smooth running of the work of the Council and ensuring that the important matters requiring Council discussion are identified, labelled 'category B', and scheduled accordingly, whilst other matters are labelled 'category A' and are adopted without further discussion. Of course, even if the Council can claim democratic legitimacy by way of ministers being elected, the question of 'democratic deficit' is raised once more in relation to COREPER, whose members are generally appointed. In sifting through issues that require the attention of the Council, COREPER effectively acts as a decision-maker for those issues that COREPER itself considers to be straightforward.

2.2.2.2 Voting

→ CROSS-REFERENCE
See 1.18 on the Treaty of Lisbon.

Voting in the Council is by unanimity, simple majority, or qualified majority, depending on the Treaty requirement for the particular matter. When unanimity is required, it can be difficult to press ahead with legislation, as any one State has power of veto (power to block the legislation). For that reason, the amending Treaties have continued to extend qualified majority voting (QMV) to more areas of EU activity.

The Treaty of Lisbon retained unanimous voting for certain areas, such as common foreign, security, and defence policy, taxation, and social security. Simple majority voting is rarely used, but Treaty amendments have gradually extended the use of QMV, which is required for the adoption of legislation in many areas, including most internal market measures and other areas such as the environment, agriculture, competition, consumer protection, asylum, immigration, and judicial cooperation in civil and criminal matters.

The system prior to 1 November 2014

Qualified majority voting used to operate simply as a system of weighted votes. The larger the Member State, the more votes it held, ranging from 29 (for Germany, France, and the UK) down to 3 (for Malta). Of a total of 352 votes distributed across the Member States, a qualified majority comprised 260 votes, provided that a majority of Member States had voted in favour (for Commission proposals) or two-thirds had voted in favour (in other cases). Additionally, a Member State could ask for confirmation that the votes in favour represented at least 62 per cent of the EU's total population. If not, the legislation could not be adopted.

The system from 1 November 2014

Under Lisbon Treaty amendments, the system was simplified significantly. Now, a qualified majority—known also as a double majority under a system of double majority voting (DMV)—is reached when at least 55 per cent of Member States agree to a proposal (15 out of 28 Member States, at time of writing) and when these States represent at least 65 per cent of the EU population. Where the proposal does not emanate from the Commission, a qualified majority is reached when at least 72 per cent of Member States agree to a proposal (again representing at least 65 per cent of the EU population). A blocking minority must include at least four Member States representing over 35 per cent of the EU's population, failing which a qualified majority will be deemed attained.

From 2014 and until 31 March 2017, a Member State was able to request that a vote by qualified majority be taken according to the method applied pre-2014 (Article 16 TEU). From 1 April 2017, this was no longer possible.

?! THINKING POINT

Does this system of QMV seem equitable to all? What problems can you see with such a system?

Where a group of Member States oppose the adoption of legislation, but are not large enough to reach a blocking minority, they may request the application of the 'Ioannina Compromise' (see 1.5). This enables a delay to the adoption of legislation by qualified majority, with the Council being required to undertake further discussion in an attempt to address their concerns.

Under the pre-2014 system, QMV was based on distributing votes according to the political, economic, and demographic 'weight' of each Member State. Over the years, the definition of qualified majority and the allocation of votes have been hotly disputed, the smaller States fearing domination by the larger States and the latter often claiming that the smaller States were overrepresented. The new post-Lisbon system is based more closely on the size of the population of a Member State, and in this way is both more equitable and more democratic.

The system of QMV has, however, been subject to much criticism. It means that it is, of course, possible for the Council to impose policy on Member States even where the representative from the Member State did not vote for it. Whilst accepting that there is pragmatism to the system, the UK certainly articulated such criticism in 1993 when it was overruled in relation to the imposition of a 48-hour maximum working week (Directive 2003/88/EC of the European Parliament and of the Council of 4 November 2003 concerning certain aspects of the organisation of working time, OJ 2003 L299/9).

Qualified majority voting therefore creates a particular dynamic in Council decision-making. Ministers representing different national interests across different policy areas frequently seek to 'trade' their agreement in one area in return for support from other Member States in other areas.

2.2.2.3 Presidency of the Council

The Presidency of the Council is held by each Member State, in rotation for six months, working closely together in groups of three (trios). The trio sets long-term goals and prepares a common agenda determining the topics and major issues that will be addressed over an 18-month period. Within this wider programme, each of the three Member States sets out its own programme and priorities for its Presidency. It is often an opportunity for the Member State concerned to make its mark on the direction of the EU, EU policy, and legislation. The Presidency plans and chairs most meetings of the Council and, in so doing, seeks to deliver results that often require compromise proposals and negotiating agreements. To this end, it is important that the Presidency acts as an honest, impartial broker.

The Presidency also represents the Council in its dealings with the other EU institutions, particularly the Commission and the Parliament.

However, to a large extent, its ability to do so is limited by existing projects and priorities. For example, the Romanian Presidency set out its core priorities of Presidency for the first six months of 2019 as follows:

Priorities of the Romanian Presidency of the Council of the European Union, 2019

The *priorities* of the Romanian Presidency are driven by this motto: cohesion, a common European value, understood as unity, equal treatment and convergence.

The presidency programme focuses on four main priorities: Europe of convergence, A safer Europe, Europe as a strong global actor and Europe of common values.

Europe of convergence

Main objectives:

- taking forward the negotiation process on the 2021–2027 Multiannual Financial Framework.
- developing the EU social dimension, through the enforcement of the European Pillar of Social Rights.
- advancing the EU agenda in the economic and financial fields, in order to stimulate growth and investment, to deepen the Economic and Monetary Union, as well as to support structural reforms.
- promoting research and innovation, digitalization and connectivity, in order to increase the competitiveness of the European economy and industry.

A safer Europe

Main objectives:

- strengthening the internal security, by boosting cooperation among Member States and increasing the interoperability of the EU security systems, protecting the safety of the citizens, companies and public institutions in the cyberspace and improving the overall resilience of the Union to cyber-attacks.
- continuing the fight against terrorism.
- facilitating the operationalization of the European Public Prosecutor's Office.
- giving further attention to migration issues, based on a comprehensive approach to action within the EU and on promoting cooperation with countries of origin and transit, as well as facilitating the dialogue among Member States with a view to finding solutions for an effective and sustainable EU migration and asylum policy.

Europe as a strong global actor

Main objectives:

- promoting the strengthening of EU's defence and security capabilities in strong connection with the similar processes within NATO, with a special emphasis on consolidating the Strategic EU-NATO Partnership.
- supporting further development of actions in the field of Common Security and Defence Policy, mainly by consolidating the current mechanisms while ensuring the synergy of the new instruments, such as: Coordinated Annual Review on Defence, European Defence Fund, and Permanent Structured Cooperation.
- advancing the enlargement process of the EU in order to ensure more internal and external security.
- promoting coordinated and coherent actions in the EU's neighbourhood, while celebrating 10 years since the launch of the Eastern Partnership, through reaffirming the importance of the Black Sea on EU agenda, including from the perspective of reinvigorating the Black Sea Synergy.
- promoting the European commercial interests through both the consolidation of multilateralism and the modernisation of the multilateral trade system and through the enlargement of the Economic and Free Trade Partnership Agreements.

Europe of common values

Main objectives:

- promoting the efficient countering of racism, intolerance, xenophobia, populism, antisemitism and discouraging hate speech.
- promoting the countering of online misinformation and fake news through better media literacy and the development of European mechanisms to share good practices in countering misinformation.
- promoting and supporting the legislative initiatives focusing on social progress and reducing development gaps, equal opportunities between men and women, as well as ensuring access to education and training for disadvantaged categories.
- countering gender discrimination in the labour market and business environment as well as the pay gaps between men and women.

2.2.2.4 *Brexit update*

The UK had been scheduled to host the rotating Presidency of the Council of the European Union in the second half of 2017.

However, on Tuesday 19 July 2016, the Prime Minister confirmed to President of the European Council Donald Tusk that the UK would be relinquishing the Presidency, noting 'that we would be prioritising the negotiations to leave the EU' (Written Statement by David Davis, Secretary of State for Exiting the European Union, 21 July 2016).

Subsequently, Council Decision (EU) 2016/1316 of 26 July 2016 amending Decision 2009/908/EU, laying down measures for the implementation of the European Council Decision on the exercise of Presidency of the Council, and on the chairmanship of preparatory bodies of the Council, OJ 2016 L208/42, had regard to the fact that a Member State had made it known publicly that it would withdraw from the EU and set out a revised table of presidencies up to 2030.

Table 2.2 sets out the Member States to hold the Presidency up to 2030.

Table 2.2 Presidency of the Council of the European Union (2019–30)

Member State	Period	Year
Romania	January–June	2019
Finland	July–December	2019
Croatia	January–June	2020
Germany	July–December	2020
Portugal	January–June	2021
Slovenia	July–December	2021
France	January–June	2022
Czech Republic	July–December	2022
Sweden	January—June	2023
Spain	July–December	2023
Belgium	January–June	2024
Hungary	July–December	2024
Poland	January–June	2025
Denmark	July–December	2025
Cyprus	January–June	2026
Ireland	July–December	2026
Lithuania	January–June	2027
Greece	July–December	2027
Italy	January–June	2028
Latvia	July–December	2028
Luxembourg	January–June	2029
Netherlands	July–December	2029
Slovakia	January–June	2030
Malta	July–December	2030

2.3 The Commission

Detailed rules on the operation and organization of the European Commission are set out in the Rules of Procedure of the Commission (C(2000) 3614), OJ 2000 L308/26.

2.3.1 Composition

The Commission is the most 'European' and least nationalistic of the principal institutions, and it represents the interests of the EU.

The Commission is made up of 28 individual Commissioners at time of writing, one from each Member State, each appointed for a five-year period of office.

2.3.1.1 The President of the Commission

The President of the Commission is elected as set out in Article 17(7) TEU.

Article 17 TEU

[...]

7. ... the European Council, acting by a qualified majority, shall propose to the European Parliament a candidate for President of the Commission. This candidate shall be elected by the European Parliament by a majority of its component members. If he does not obtain the required majority, the European Council, acting by a qualified majority, shall within one month propose a new candidate who shall be elected by the European Parliament following the same procedure.

[...]

In considering the candidate for President, the European Council (see 2.5) must take into account the elections to the European Parliament (Article 17(7) TEU).

The 'Spitzenkandidaten process'

The Spitzenkandidaten process establishes a direct link between European Parliament elections and the Commission President. It does this through European political parties appointing leading candidates for the role of Commission President ahead of the European elections. The candidate of the party with sufficient parliamentary support is then nominated by the European Council as the President of the Commission. The procedure is argued to address concerns of democratic deficit as, by electing MEPs, the electorate also has a direct say in who is appointed the head of the executive (the Commission). Further, it is argued that legitimacy is increased with anticipated increased voter turnout.

The process was first used in the 2014 election, under the slogan 'This time, it's different', and was be used again in the 2019 election.

The powers of the President are detailed in Article 17(6) TEU.

Article 17 TEU

[...]

6. The President of the Commission shall:

(a) lay down guidelines within which the Commission is to work;

(b) decide on the internal organisation of the Commission, ensuring that it acts consistently, efficiently and as a collegiate body;

(c) appoint Vice-Presidents, other than the High Representative of the Union for Foreign Affairs and Security Policy, from among the members of the Commission.

A member of the Commission shall resign if the President so requests. The High Representative of the Union for Foreign Affairs and Security Policy shall resign, in accordance with the procedure set out in Article 18(1), if the President so requests.

[...]

The President is therefore tasked with allocating the portfolios on particular policy areas to each of the Commissioners and can also reshuffle the portfolios during the Commission's term of office (Article 248 TFEU).

Commissioners' portfolios cover policy areas such as trade, competition, environment, and fisheries. The Commission is supported by a staff of around 25,000, based largely in Brussels, and organized into administrative departments known as Directorates-General (DGs)—for example the Directorate-General for Competition (DGCOMP)—each of which is headed by a Director-General.

The Commissioners themselves are usually senior politicians, who are nominated by their national governments in common accord with the nominee for President.

The Council appoints the Commissioners in agreement with the nominated President and this is followed by approval, as a body, by the European Parliament. The Commission is appointed for a renewable five-year term.

The Commissioners operate on the principle of collegiality. This principle was explained by the Court of Justice in Case 5/85 *AKZO Chemie v Commission* [1986] ECR 2585.

Case 5/85 *AKZO Chemie v Commission* [1986] ECR 2585

30. ... 'The Commission shall act by a majority of the number of members ... A meeting of the Commission shall be valid only if the number of members laid down in its rules of procedure is present' [ie a quorum equal to a majority of the number of Members specified in the Treaty, under Article 7 of the Rules of Procedure]. The principle of collegiate responsibility thus laid is founded on the equal participation of the members of the Commission

in the adoption of decisions and it follows from that principle, in particular, that decisions should be the subject of a collective deliberation and that all the members of the college of Commissioners bear collective responsibility on the political level for all decisions adopted.

According to this quotation, the Commissioners are equals, they will deliberate as a collective on an issue, and, as a college, they are jointly responsible for the Commission's decisions and actions. Once a collective decision has been reached, according to the principle of collegiality, all of the Commissioners must support this decision and have collective responsibility. From this, it can be seen that a decision made by the college must be supported by all the Commissioners and, according to the principle of collegiality, the Commissioners represent the college through a collective voice. Decisions are usually made during its weekly meetings or by written procedure whereby the proposal is circulated in writing to all the Commissioners. Any amendments or reservations may be noted within a specified period and if no amendments or reservations have been made, the proposal is tacitly adopted.

2.3.1.2 Conduct and removal

The Commissioners must have certain qualities—namely, they must possess general competence and their independence must be beyond reasonable doubt. This unelected college must act not as national representatives but independently, reflecting the interests of the EU during the course of their term in office. The independence of the Commissioners has been guaranteed by the Treaties, whereby the Commissioner is not to seek or take instructions from any government or from any other body, is to avoid activities that will be incompatible with their duties, and is not to engage in any other occupation during their term of office.

Article 245 TFEU

The Members of the Commission shall refrain from any action incompatible with their duties. Member States shall respect their independence and shall not seek to influence them in the performance of their tasks.

The Members of the Commission may not, during their term of office, engage in any other occupation, whether gainful or not. When entering upon their duties they shall give a solemn undertaking that, both during and after their term of office, they will respect the obligations arising therefrom and in particular their duty to behave with integrity and discretion as regards the acceptance, after they have ceased to hold office, of certain appointments or benefits. In the event of any breach of these obligations, the Court of Justice may, on application by the Council acting by a simple majority or the Commission, rule that the Member concerned be, according to the circumstances, either compulsorily retired in accordance with Article 247 or deprived of his right to a pension or other benefits in its stead.

Article 17 TEU

[...]

3. ... The members of the Commission shall be chosen on the ground of their general competence and European commitment from persons whose independence is beyond doubt.

   In carrying out its responsibilities, the Commission shall be completely independent. Without prejudice to Article 18(2), the members of the Commission shall neither seek nor take instructions from any Government or other institution, body, office or entity. They shall refrain from any action incompatible with their duties or the performance of their tasks.

   [...]

This requirement that a Commissioner be committed to the European project acts as a signal to the national parliaments to avoid putting forward a Commissioner who is Eurosceptic.

Upon entering their term of office, the Commissioner solemnly undertakes to respect the obligations and to behave with integrity and discretion. The Court of Justice may, on application by the Council or Commission, compulsorily retire a Commissioner for failure to perform their duties or for serious misconduct (Article 247 TFEU). Additionally, the President of the Commission can require a Commissioner to resign (Article 17(6) TEU).

The Commission, as a body, is responsible to the European Parliament. The European Parliament can remove the entire Commission by vote of censure, but has no power to remove individual Commissioners.

?! THINKING POINT

Does the fact that the Commission is responsible to the European Parliament adequately address concerns over the lack of democratic legitimacy of the most European of the principal institutions?

2.3.2 Functions and powers

Article 17 TEU, at the outset, stipulates the Commission's pivotal role in the integration process—namely, to 'promote the general interest of the Union'. In fulfilling its role, the Commission has distinct functions, which are set out as follows in Article 17 TEU.

Article 17 TEU

1. The Commission shall promote the general interest of the Union and take appropriate initiatives to that end. It shall ensure the application of the Treaties, and of measures adopted by the institutions pursuant to them. It shall oversee the application of Union law under the

> control of the Court of Justice of the European Union. It shall execute the budget and manage programmes. It shall exercise coordinating, executive and management functions, as laid down in the Treaties. With the exception of the common foreign and security policy, and other cases provided for in the Treaties, it shall ensure the Union's external representation. It shall initiate the Union's annual and multiannual programming with a view to achieving interinstitutional agreements.
>
> [...]

REVIEW QUESTION

Can you identify how each of the following four descriptions could correspond with the functions listed in Article 17(1) TEU?

- Guardian of the Treaties
- Policy initiator
- Legislative power
- Executive power

Answer: It is submitted that they can be categorized thus.

Guardian of the Treaties

- Ensure the application of the Treaties and of measures adopted by the institutions pursuant to them
- Oversee the application of EU law under the control of the Court of Justice of the European Union (CJEU)

Policy initiator

- Take appropriate initiatives to promote the general interest of the EU
- Initiate the EU's annual and multiannual programming with a view to achieving inter-institutional agreements

Legislative power

- Take appropriate initiatives to promote the general interest of the EU

Executive power

- Execute the budget and manage programmes
- Exercise coordinating, executive, and management functions
- External representation—with the exception of the Common Foreign and Security Policy (CFSP)

2.3.2.1 *Guardian of the Treaties*

Look back at the two functions listed in the answer to the review question under the heading 'Guardian of the Treaties'. Both reflect two distinct roles—namely, a supervisory role and one of enforcement.

→ CROSS-REFERENCE
For a discussion on Article 258 TFEU, see 7.1.

The supervisory nature of what the Commission does involves ensuring the correct implementation of EU law by Member States and taking enforcement proceedings where appropriate. For example, if a Member State has not transposed an EU Directive (see 3.4), the Commission can bring an enforcement action against that State under Article 258 TFEU.

The Commission also has the power to bring proceedings against the other EU institutions under Article 263 TFEU for a failure to comply with EU law. Supervision and compliance is not limited to Member States and the EU institutions, but also includes business undertakings and individuals. Proceedings could arise where undertakings or individuals are in breach of the competition provisions under the Treaty, for example where an agreement between undertakings has the effect of distorting trade (Article 101 TFEU) or an undertaking is abusing its dominant position in the market by charging a premium for its goods (Article 102 TFEU).

→ CROSS-REFERENCE
See Chapter 7 for a discussion on judicial review (Article 263 TFEU). See also Chapter 13 for a discussion of Article 101 TFEU and Chapter 14 for a discussion of Article 102 TFEU.

2.3.2.2 Policy initiator

The Commission plays an important role in devising and developing EU policy to forward the integrationist agenda. It can initiate and formulate policy in a number of ways. For example, the Commission has the right to initiate legislation and formulate proposals, and it has an annual work programme that contributes to the development of policy in general. It is not the only actor involved in agenda-setting in the EU, however, as Douglas-Scott observes.

S Douglas-Scott, *Constitutional Law of the European Union* (Harlow: Pearson, 2002), pp 62–3

[T]he Commission [has] considerable scope for developing new initiatives or pushing forward on-going debates. This can take a great variety of forms: the policy concerned might be general, spanning the whole framework of EC activity or quite detailed and sectoral in nature. Some important policy initiatives are taken as a result of decisions in the European Council and the high-profile nature of Council summits can be an important feature in supplying authority to Commission initiatives.

The Commission has described itself as 'the driving force behind European integration', but it might be thought that this is an inappropriate role for an unelected body. However, the Commission has the advantage of relatively long terms of office and the benefit of no direct political influence or constraints (unlike national government ministries) so, in fact, it can be quite well-placed to shape and manage policy. It also has better access to information than the Council or Parliament, being, as it has been described, 'at the hub of numerous highly specialised policy networks of technical experts designing detailed regulations'.

The development of policy can be influenced by a wide range of factors, and access to information is perhaps an important factor in devising a policy that would then lead to a legislative measure. In this sense, as Douglas-Scott notes in the previous extract, the Commission is well placed, since it has contact with a wide range of interest groups and the two advisory groups—namely, the European Economic and Social Committee (EESC) and the Committee of the Regions (CoR).

2.3.2.3 *Legislative power*

→ CROSS-REFERENCE
For a detailed discussion on the legislative procedures, see 3.5.

The Commission has almost a monopoly right to initiate draft legislation. It is excluded from a number of policy areas where the Treaty specifically requires the Council or Parliament to use the special legislative procedure, for example in relation to police and judicial cooperation on criminal and on civil matters, and taxation. The special legislative procedure allows the Council to initiate legislation and then adopt a measure, following consultation with the Parliament or with the consent of Parliament. Depending on the area concerned, the Treaty will stipulate which institution is involved and whether consultation or consent is required.

From 1 April 2012, EU citizens have had the right to participate directly in the development of EU policy, petitioning the Commission to make a legislative proposal. This is known as the European citizens' initiative and is found in Article 11(4) TEU.

Article 11 TEU

[...]

4. Not less than one million citizens who are nationals of a significant number of Member States may take the initiative of inviting the European Commission, within the framework of its powers, to submit any appropriate proposal on matters where citizens consider that a legal act of the Union is required for the purpose of implementing the Treaties.

[...]

Apart from having the right of initiative, the Commission will also amend draft legislation where either the European Parliament or Council, or both, have not agreed to the draft presented to them.

comitology
Comitology is a term used to describe the way in which the Commission exercises the implementing powers conferred on it by the Parliament and Council, with the assistance of committees of representatives from the EU Member States.

Under the Treaty of Lisbon, the system of **comitology** has been reformed. Comitology operated in a manner that allowed for specific or highly specialized legislation to be implemented by the Commission with the assistance of a committee of representatives from the Member States. These legislative powers were delegated by the Council to the Commission.

REVIEW QUESTION

How might the practice of comitology undermine the powers of the Commission?

Answer: The supervising committees were made up of representatives of the Member States and this gave Member States an indirect, but pervasive, influence over the work of the Commission in addition to the direct influence that they already have over the work of the Council.

The reform of comitology involves distinct changes to the procedures for implementing measures. Under Article 291 TFEU, the Commission will continue to implement measures adopted by the committee of representatives from Member States, but with an enhanced role for the European Parliament. In this case, the European Parliament, together with the Council, will set out rules and principles for the exercise of the Commission's powers in implementing measures. This effectively provides the European Parliament with a supervisory role in the comitology process.

In essence, the European Parliament's power has been extended to a law-making process that had previously escaped scrutiny. The criticism of democratic deficit existing in comitology at least has, it is submitted, been addressed.

2.3.2.4 Executive power

One role that we have already mentioned is the Commission's supervisory and monitoring role in the Member States' implementation of legislation and policy objectives.

The Commission has overall responsibility for the EU's budget, which includes revenue collection and expenditure of the budget. The Commission drafts the budget spending for the year, and this has to be agreed by the European Parliament and the Council. An annual report is produced by the Commission detailing how the budget is implemented.

?! THINKING POINT

As you read this and the following chapters, consider the extent to which you think the Commission fulfils its role and functions under Article 17 TEU.

Article 207 TFEU provides an external relations role for the Commission. Under the Common Commercial Policy (CCP), the Commission plays a central role in representing the EU and negotiating on its behalf in trade agreements. The Commission represents the EU in legal transactions within the Member States, for example in the acquisition or disposal of movable or immovable property (Article 335 TFEU).

2.3.2.5 The cabinet

Each Commissioner is assisted with advisory support by their private office, known as a cabinet. This supporting role includes being 'the eyes and ears' for the Commissioner, making sure that the Commissioner is properly informed about matters arising from within their portfolio, for example content and political policy priorities. The cabinet will also keep the Commissioner informed on other policy areas, and this is necessary since all Commissioners are collectively responsible for decision-making. The cabinet acts as a bridge between the Commissioner and the Directorate-General of the Commissioner's policy area, transmitting information to ensure that the Commissioner is kept up to date.

2.4 The Court of Justice of the European Union

The Court of Justice, the General Court (formerly known as the Court of First Instance), and the specialized courts (formerly the judicial panels) are now collectively referred to as the Court of Justice of the European Union (CJEU) (Article 19 TEU).

Judgment is drafted first in the language of the case. A full report includes a brief summary, the report of the hearing containing the facts and procedure, and a summary of the arguments of the parties. The next part is the Advocate General's Opinion, although this does not form an official part of the report. The final part comprises the reasons or grounds for judgment, presented in numbered paragraphs in a succinct single ruling.

Cases are reported in the European Court Reports, cited as ECR, and preceded by the year of publication. They are published in all official languages (24 at time of writing) and are equally authentic in each.

2.4.1 The Court of Justice

The Court of Justice's task is to ensure that, in the interpretation and application of the Treaties, the law is observed and to provide remedies sufficient to ensure effective legal protection in the fields covered by EU law. It has jurisdiction to give preliminary rulings on the interpretation of EU law under Article 267 TFEU (see Chapter 6) and to review the legality of acts of the institutions under Article 263 TFEU. The Court of Justice is not bound by its own decisions, but nevertheless seeks to maintain consistency in its judgments.

Article 19(1) TEU outlines the general function of the Court.

Article 19 TEU

1. The Court of Justice of the European Union shall include the Court of Justice, the General Court and specialised courts. It shall ensure that in the interpretation and application of the Treaties the law is observed.

   Member States shall provide remedies sufficient to ensure effective legal protection in the fields covered by Union law.

   [...]

The Court consists of one judge from each Member State and eight Advocates General, chosen 'by common accord' of Member State governments from among persons whose independence is beyond doubt and who possess the qualifications required for the highest judicial office in their respective jurisdictions. Appointments, which are scrutinized by a panel established under the Lisbon Treaty, including former judges of the Court of Justice and judges of national supreme courts, are for six years and are staggered to provide partial replacement every three years. Advocates General assist the Court by giving reasoned Opinions. Although these do not bind the Court or, as a consequence, national courts and are not always followed by the Court in the case, they carry considerable weight. Where no new points of law are raised, the Court's Statute permits it to reach a determination without an Advocate General's submission.

The Court sits in plenary session for cases of exceptional importance. It sits as a Grand Chamber of 13 judges when a Member State or institution that is a party to the proceedings so requests and, in the majority of cases, it sits in chambers of three or five judges.

The Court of Justice has played a key role in the development of EU law, using its jurisdiction creatively in ground-breaking decisions, for instance in establishing the principles of direct effect and State liability, upholding the fundamental principles of the free market, and furthering the rights of individuals.

2.4.2 The General Court

The General Court (previously known as the Court of First Instance) was set up under the Single European Act 1986 (SEA) to reduce the Court of Justice's workload. Since then, its jurisdiction has been extended to include most direct actions (such as annulment actions, actions for failure to act, and damages actions), the power to give preliminary rulings, and to hear appeals from the judicial panels. The General Court comprises at least one judge from each Member State and sits as a full court or in smaller chambers. In contrast to the Court of Justice, the General Court does not have permanent Advocates General. However, in exceptional circumstances, a judge may act as Advocate General to the General Court.

2.4.3 Specialized courts

Judicial panels, now known as specialized courts, were established by the Treaty of Nice. They may be set up by the Council to hear certain classes of action at first instance. Appeal lies to the General Court and, if there is a serious risk to the consistency of EU law, the Court of Justice may exceptionally review the General Court's decision.

An EU Civil Service Tribunal has been set up under these provisions to hear staff cases.

2.5 The European Council

NOTE

The European Council should not be confused with the Council of the European Union (see 2.2) or the Council of Europe (see 9.1).

2.5.1 Composition

The European Council began informally in 1974 as a forum for discussion between the heads of state and government of the Member States. This was outside the formal scope of the Treaties to provide direction for the EU or to act in response to international situations. It was given a developing formal role within the EU institutions by the SEA 1986 (see 1.10), and it rapidly developed into the body that fixed goals and priorities for the EU. It was the Treaty of Lisbon that afforded the European Council full official EU institution status.

The European Council comprises the heads of state or government of the Member States, together with its President and the President of the Commission. The High Representative of the Union for Foreign Affairs and Security Policy also takes part in its work. Its meetings, which take place twice every six months, usually in Brussels, are known as European summits. The President (see 2.5.2) can convene a special meeting if needed.

2.5.2 Functions and powers

Article 15 TEU

1. The European Council shall provide the Union with the necessary impetus for its development and shall define the general political directions and priorities thereof. It shall not exercise legislative functions.

[…]

The European Council therefore has a broad non-legislative role, consulting on topical political issues, setting the general political and policy direction and priorities of the EU, and dealing with complex or sensitive issues that cannot be resolved at a lower level of intergovernmental cooperation. Importantly, it gives the necessary political impetus for the development of the EU.

?! THINKING POINT

In light of all of this, to what extent would you expect the European Council to be involved in matters relating to Brexit?

2.5.2.1 Democratic legitimacy?

Since the members of the European Council are themselves usually elected individuals (as heads of state or government), it is an institution that can be considered to have democratic accountability at its source. However, the limited control that the European Parliament and indeed, it can be argued, national parliaments exercise over the European Council means that it is likely that the democratic legitimacy of the European Council will always be questioned. Indeed, the confidential and non-transparent nature of the deliberations of the European Council further exacerbate the issue. Given the supreme political power of the European Council, such accusations are likely to remain unless the supervisory powers of the Parliament are extended.

2.5.2.2 President of the European Council

The Treaty of Lisbon (see 1.18) created the new role of President of the European Council. Elected by the European Council by qualified majority (see 2.2.2) for a term of two-and-a-half years (renewable once), the President, who is not allowed to hold national office whilst holding the Presidency, ensures the preparation and continuity of the European Council's work, in cooperation with the President of the Commission (see 2.3.2), and reports to the European Parliament (see 2.1). European Council meetings are held four times a year. The President of the Commission is a full member of the European Council (Article 15 TEU).

The role of the President of the European Council is set out in Article 15(6) TEU.

Article 15 TEU

[...]

6. The President of the European Council:
   (a) shall chair it and drive forward its work;
   (b) shall ensure the preparation and continuity of the work of the European Council in cooperation with the President of the Commission, and on the basis of the work of the General Affairs Council;
   (c) shall endeavour to facilitate cohesion and consensus within the European Council;
   (d) shall present a report to the European Parliament after each of the meetings of the European Council.

   The President of the European Council shall, at his level and in that capacity, ensure the external representation of the Union on issues concerning its common foreign and security policy, without prejudice to the powers of the High Representative of the Union for Foreign Affairs and Security Policy.

   [...]

Herman Van Rompuy was the first President of the European Council.

2.5.2.3 High Representative of the Union for Foreign Affairs and Security Policy

The Treaty of Lisbon (see 1.18) created the new role of High Representative of the Union for Foreign Affairs and Security Policy. The post-holder, elected by the European Council by qualified majority, conducts the EU's Common Foreign and Security Policy (CFSP) and takes part in the work of the European Council. The role was created to ensure greater consistency, coherence, visibility, and effectiveness. It is often said to be a 'double-hatted', or indeed 'triple-hatted', post on the basis that it consolidates several previous roles into one. Thus it consolidates the roles of the former High Representative for Common Foreign and Security Policy, the European Commissioner for External Affairs, and the chair of the Foreign Affairs Council.

The role of the High Representative is set out in Article 18 TEU.

Article 18 TEU

1. The European Council, acting by a qualified majority, with the agreement of the President of the Commission, shall appoint the High Representative of the Union for Foreign Affairs and Security Policy. The European Council may end his term of office by the same procedure.
2. The High Representative shall conduct the Union's common foreign and security policy. He shall contribute by his proposals to the development of that policy, which he shall carry out as mandated by the Council. The same shall apply to the common security and defence policy.
3. The High Representative shall preside over the Foreign Affairs Council.
4. The High Representative shall be one of the Vice-Presidents of the Commission. He shall ensure the consistency of the Union's external action. He shall be responsible within the Commission for responsibilities incumbent on it in external relations and for coordinating other aspects of the Union's external action. In exercising these responsibilities within the Commission, and only for these responsibilities, the High Representative shall be bound by Commission procedures to the extent that this is consistent with paragraphs 2 and 3.

Following the entry into force of the Treaty of Lisbon, the European Council appointed former UK Commissioner Catherine Ashton as the first High Representative of the Union for Foreign Affairs and Security Policy.

2.5.2.4 Brexit update

The European Council plays a key role in the Brexit process. In order to withdraw from the EU, the UK was required to formally notify the European Council of its intention to do so—the 'triggering' of Article 50. This occurred shortly before 12.30 pm on 29 March 2017, enabling the European Council to unanimously agree the high-level guidelines for formal negotiations.

2.6 The European Central Bank

The European Central Bank (ECB) manages the EU's single currency—the euro—and safeguards price stability in the EU. It is responsible for the framing and implementation of the EU's economic and monetary policy. Its main purpose is to keep prices and the financial system stable. In regard to the latter, this requires assurance of the supervision of financial markets and institutions. In light of the outcome of the UK's 2016 referendum on EU membership, this role is increasingly important, with the ECB recognizing that heightened political uncertainty brings with it the risk of significant financial instability.

The ECB works with the central banks in all Member States, together forming the European System of Central Banks (ESCB), the primary objective of which is to maintain price stability.

Article 282 TFEU

1. The European Central Bank, together with the national central banks, shall constitute the European System of Central Banks (ESCB). The European Central Bank, together with the national central banks of the Member States whose currency is the euro, which constitute the Eurosystem, shall conduct the monetary policy of the Union.
2. The ESCB shall be governed by the decision-making bodies of the European Central Bank. The primary objective of the ESCB shall be to maintain price stability. Without prejudice to that objective, it shall support the general economic policies in the Union in order to contribute to the achievement of the latter's objectives.
3. The European Central Bank shall have legal personality. It alone may authorise the issue of the euro. It shall be independent in the exercise of its powers and in the management of its finances. Union institutions, bodies, offices and agencies and the governments of the Member States shall respect that independence.
4. The European Central Bank shall adopt such measures as are necessary to carry out its tasks in accordance with Articles 127 to 133, with Article 138, and with the conditions laid down in the Statute of the ESCB and of the ECB. In accordance with these same Articles, those Member States whose currency is not the euro, and their central banks, shall retain their powers in monetary matters.
5. Within the areas falling within its responsibilities, the European Central Bank shall be consulted on all proposed Union acts, and all proposals for regulation at national level, and may give an opinion.

Article 127 TFEU

1. The primary objective of the European System of Central Banks (hereinafter referred to as 'the ESCB') shall be to maintain price stability. Without prejudice to the objective of price stability, the ESCB shall support the general economic policies in the Union with a view to contributing to the achievement of the objectives of the Union as laid down in Article 3 of the Treaty on European Union. The ESCB shall act in accordance with the principle of an open market economy with free competition, favouring an efficient allocation of resources, and in compliance with the principles set out in Article 119.

   [...]

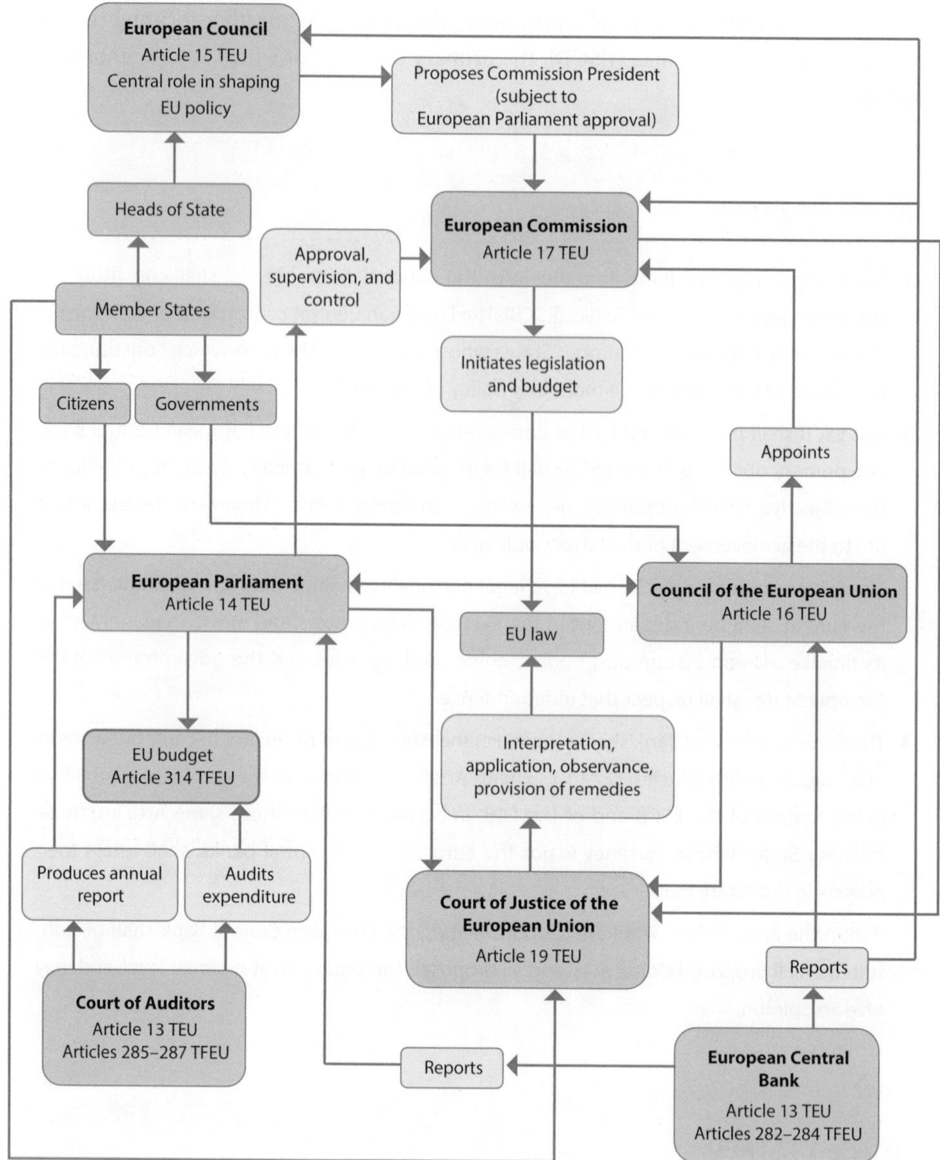

Figure 2.1

2.7 The Court of Auditors

2.7.1 Composition

The Court of Auditors is composed of one member from each Member State, each appointed by the Council for a renewable six-year term. To do its job properly, the Court of Auditors must stay completely independent of the other institutions, but remain in constant touch with them.

Article 286 TFEU

1. The Members of the Court of Auditors shall be chosen from among persons who belong or have belonged in their respective States to external audit bodies or who are especially qualified for this office. Their independence must be beyond doubt.
2. The Members of the Court of Auditors shall be appointed for a term of six years. The Council, after consulting the European Parliament, shall adopt the list of Members drawn up in accordance with the proposals made by each Member State. The term of office of the Members of the Court of Auditors shall be renewable.

   They shall elect the President of the Court of Auditors from among their number for a term of three years. The President may be re-elected.
3. In the performance of these duties, the Members of the Court of Auditors shall neither seek nor take instructions from any government or from any other body. The Members of the Court of Auditors shall refrain from any action incompatible with their duties.
4. The Members of the Court of Auditors may not, during their term of office, engage in any other occupation, whether gainful or not. When entering upon their duties they shall give a solemn undertaking that, both during and after their term of office, they will respect the obligations arising therefrom and in particular their duty to behave with integrity and discretion as regards the acceptance, after they have ceased to hold office, of certain appointments or benefits.
5. Apart from normal replacement, or death, the duties of a Member of the Court of Auditors shall end when he resigns, or is compulsorily retired by a ruling of the Court of Justice pursuant to paragraph 6.

   The vacancy thus caused shall be filled for the remainder of the Member's term of office.

   Save in the case of compulsory retirement, Members of the Court of Auditors shall remain in office until they have been replaced.
6. A Member of the Court of Auditors may be deprived of his office or of his right to a pension or other benefits in its stead only if the Court of Justice, at the request of the Court of Auditors, finds that he no longer fulfils the requisite conditions or meets the obligations arising from his office.
7. The Council shall determine the conditions of employment of the President and the Members of the Court of Auditors and in particular their salaries, allowances and pensions. It shall also determine any payment to be made instead of remuneration.
8. The provisions of the Protocol on the privileges and immunities of the European Union applicable to the Judges of the Court of Justice of the European Union shall also apply to the Members of the Court of Auditors.

2.7.2 Functions and powers

Article 285 TFEU

The Court of Auditors shall carry out the Union's audit.

The Court of Auditors therefore performs budgetary functions, auditing expenditure of the institutions for legality and sound financial management. To this end, it produces an annual report, which is debated by the European Parliament. The Court has the right to audit any person or organization handling EU funds.

Article 287 TFEU

1. The Court of Auditors shall examine the accounts of all revenue and expenditure of the Union. It shall also examine the accounts of all revenue and expenditure of all bodies, offices or agencies set up by the Union in so far as the relevant constituent instrument does not preclude such examination.

   The Court of Auditors shall provide the European Parliament and the Council with a statement of assurance as to the reliability of the accounts and the legality and regularity of the underlying transactions which shall be published in the Official Journal of the European Union. This statement may be supplemented by specific assessments for each major area of Union activity.
2. The Court of Auditors shall examine whether all revenue has been received and all expenditure incurred in a lawful and regular manner and whether the financial management has been sound. In doing so, it shall report in particular on any cases of irregularity.

   The audit of revenue shall be carried out on the basis both of the amounts established as due and the amounts actually paid to the Union.

   The audit of expenditure shall be carried out on the basis both of commitments undertaken and payments made.

   These audits may be carried out before the closure of accounts for the financial year in question.
3. The audit shall be based on records and, if necessary, performed on the spot in the other institutions of the Union, on the premises of any body, office or agency which manages revenue or expenditure on behalf of the Union and in the Member States, including on the premises of any natural or legal person in receipt of payments from the budget. In the Member States the audit shall be carried out in liaison with national audit bodies or, if these do not have the necessary powers, with the competent national departments. The Court of Auditors and the national audit bodies of the Member States shall cooperate in a spirit of trust while maintaining their independence. These bodies or departments shall inform the Court of Auditors whether they intend to take part in the audit.

   The other institutions of the Union, any bodies, offices or agencies managing revenue or expenditure on behalf of the Union, any natural or legal person in receipt of payments from the budget, and the national audit bodies or, if these do not have the necessary powers, the competent national departments, shall forward to the Court of Auditors, at its request, any document or information necessary to carry out its task.

In respect of the European Investment Bank's activity in managing Union expenditure and revenue, the Court's rights of access to information held by the Bank shall be governed by an agreement between the Court, the Bank and the Commission. In the absence of an agreement, the Court shall nevertheless have access to information necessary for the audit of Union expenditure and revenue managed by the Bank.

4. The Court of Auditors shall draw up an annual report after the close of each financial year. It shall be forwarded to the other institutions of the Union and shall be published, together with the replies of these institutions to the observations of the Court of Auditors, in the Official Journal of the European Union.

The Court of Auditors may also, at any time, submit observations, particularly in the form of special reports, on specific questions and deliver opinions at the request of one of the other institutions of the Union.

It shall adopt its annual reports, special reports or opinions by a majority of its Members. However, it may establish internal chambers in order to adopt certain categories of reports or opinions under the conditions laid down by its Rules of Procedure.

It shall assist the European Parliament and the Council in exercising their powers of control over the implementation of the budget.

The Court of Auditors shall draw up its Rules of Procedure. Those rules shall require the approval of the Council.

2.8 The European Economic and Social Committee and the Committee of the Regions

The European Economic and Social Committee (EESC) and the Committee of the Regions (CoR) are advisory bodies that must be consulted on proposed legislation concerning matters within their respective remits. The EESC represents Europe's employers, workers, and other interest groups. The CoR represents local and regional authorities within the EU. Both have 353 members.

?! THINKING POINT

Based upon your new knowledge of the EU institutions, has your impression changed as regards whether the institutions are on an equal footing and whether the balance of power between the institutions is represented in a fair and balanced way?

SUMMARY

- There are seven official EU institutions:
  - the European Parliament;
  - the European Council;
  - the Council;
  - the European Commission;
  - the Court of Justice of the European Union (CJEU);
  - the European Central Bank (ECB); and
  - the Court of Auditors.
- The European Parliament is the only directly elected body. Its primary function is that of a forum for discussion and debate. However, it enjoys legislative, budgetary, and supervisory powers.
- The Council of the European Union comprises ministers of the Member States, its membership changing according to the matter under discussion. Council members represent national interests. It exercises legislative and budgetary functions alongside the Parliament, and it has a general requirement to carry out policymaking and coordinating functions, as laid down in the Treaties.
- The Commission is the most European of the principal institutions and represents the interests of the EU. There are 28 Commissioners at time of writing (one from each Member State), including the President of the Commission and the High Representative of the Union for Foreign Affairs and Security Policy (who also acts as the Vice-President of the Commission). *Commissioners must possess general competence and their independence must be beyond reasonable doubt.* They must act not as national representatives but independently, reflecting the interests of the EU during the course of their term in office. The Commission's roles can be seen as falling within four areas:
  - as guardian of the Treaties;
  - policymaking;
  - legislative power; and
  - executive power.
- The CJEU combines the Court of Justice, the General Court (formerly known as the Court of First Instance), and the specialized courts (formerly the judicial panels). Its task is to ensure that, in the interpretation and application of the Treaties, the law is observed and to provide remedies sufficient to ensure effective legal protection in the fields covered by EU law. The Court of Justice consists of one judge from each Member State and eight Advocates General, chosen 'by common accord' of Member State governments from among persons whose independence is beyond doubt and who possess the qualifications required for the highest judicial office in their respective jurisdictions. Advocates General assist the Court by giving reasoned Opinions. The General Court comprises at least one judge from each Member State and sits as a full court or in smaller chambers. One judge may act as Advocate General in complex cases.
- The European Council comprises the heads of state or government of the Member States. It has a broad non-legislative role, consulting on topical political issues, setting the general political and policy direction, as well as the priorities, of the EU. The Treaty of Lisbon created two new roles: the President of the European Council; and the High Representative of the Union for Foreign Affairs and Security Policy.

- The ECB manages the EU's single currency and safeguards price stability in the EU. It is responsible for the framing and implementation of the EU's economic and monetary policy. Its main purpose is to keep prices and the financial system stable.
- The Court of Auditors performs budgetary functions, auditing expenditure of the institutions for legality and sound financial management. It is composed of one member from each Member State, appointed by the Council for a renewable six-year term.

FURTHER READING

Articles

M Dougan, 'The Treaty of Lisbon 2007: Winning Minds, Not Hearts' (2008) 45 CML Rev 617

A constructive account of the Treaty of Lisbon.

JT Lang, 'Checks and Balances in the European Union: The Institutional Structure and the "Community Method"' (2006) 12 EPL 127

A critical appraisal of the EU's institutional structure.

S Warntjen, 'Steering the Union: The Impact of the EU Presidency on Legislative Activity' (2007) 45 JCMS 1135

A consideration of the EU Presidency and its impact upon EU legislative activity.

Books

A Arnull, *The European Court of Justice*, 2nd edn (Oxford: Oxford University Press, 2006)

Leading text on the role of the Court of Justice.

R Corbett, F Jacobs, and M Shackleton, *The European Parliament*, 8th edn (London: Catermill, 2011)

Authoritative guide on the European Parliament, for academics and practitioners alike.

J Peterson and M Shackleton, *The Institutions of the European Union*, 2nd edn (Oxford: Oxford University Press, 2006)

A rigorous, but accessible, review of the key institutions of the EU.

WEB LINKS

https://curia.europa.eu/

The Court of Justice of the European Union

http://ec.europa.eu/

The European Commission

https://eca.europa.eu

The Court of Auditors

https://www.consilium.europa.eu/

The Council of the European Union

https://www.ecb.int

The European Central Bank

http://www.europarl.europa.eu/

The European Parliament

QUESTION

'The EU is, and always has been, characterized by its "democratic deficit".' Critically evaluate this statement, with reference to the composition and function of the EU institutions.

To view an outline answer to this question plus further resources to support your EU law studies, visit the Online Resources for this book at www.oup.com/uk/eulaw-complete4e

3 Sovereignty and sources of law

KEY POINTS

By the end of this chapter, you should be able to:

- explain the impact of membership of the European Union (EU) on the UK's sovereignty and the consequences of the UK's withdrawal from the EU;
- identify and describe the various sources of EU law;
- explain the concept of subsidiarity; and
- outline the main legislative processes of the EU.

INTRODUCTION

What has been the impact of the UK's accession to the European Union (EU) on national sovereignty? This is a much-debated topic and one that took centre stage during the campaigning for the 2016 UK referendum on membership of the EU. It was argued by opponents of continued UK membership of the EU that the UK has entirely ceded national sovereignty to 'Brussels', which prevents the UK from exercising control over important policies such as immigration or trade. The truth of the matter is not so simple, and the first part of this chapter considers to what extent EU law can be considered as a source of law that ranks above our national laws and what may be the status of EU law within the UK once the UK finally withdraws from the EU. In the second part of this chapter, the exact nature of these sources of law will be considered. The Treaty on European Union (TEU) and the Treaty on the Functioning of the European Union (TFEU) provide the starting point, but since 1957 a vast body of EU law has grown up that pervades virtually every aspect of UK law. It is vital for today's lawyer to be aware of these sources and to understand their potential importance as legal authorities.

3.1 The UK referendum

The decision taken on 23 June 2016 by a majority of UK voters to leave the EU after 43 years has significant constitutional and legal consequences. The withdrawal process, which is governed by Article 50 TEU, provides the only formal and legal route through which the UK can leave the EU. However, securing a withdrawal agreement within the two-year period provided for by Article 50 has proved challenging for the UK government, with Parliament rejecting the Draft Withdrawal Agreement that it had negotiated with the EU in January 2019.

The opportunity for a referendum to be held on the UK's continued membership of the EU was a commitment within the 2015 Conservative Party election manifesto. It was proposed that the referendum would be held after the UK had sought to 'renegotiate' its relationship with the EU, in order to bring certain decision-making powers back to the UK. In its renegotiation with the EU, the UK sought changes in a number of policy areas, but perhaps the two most important ones were a specific commitment that the UK would be excluded from the process of creating 'an ever-closer union' and that it could reduce the number of EU citizens coming to the UK, as well as limit their access to social welfare benefits.

Following the renegotiation, which was concluded at the February 2016 European Council, then Prime Minister David Cameron recommended the deal to Parliament and led the campaign in favour of a vote for the UK to remain in the EU. The referendum offered a clear choice for UK voters and asked the following question:

> Should the United Kingdom remain a member of the European Union or leave the European Union?

In response to this question, UK voters decided by a 52 per cent to 48 per cent margin to leave the EU. Notwithstanding this decision, it is not clear what the precise reasons were for UK citizens voting in the way they did, as the question was neutral in its wording. However, one reason commonly cited was the perceived effects of uncontrolled migration from the EU, as was the perception that the UK Parliament could no longer make its own laws (ie that Parliament was not sovereign). Although this latter point was addressed, to some extent, in the renegotiation through the UK not taking part in the process of ever-closer union, it was probably felt by UK citizens that this was insufficient to regain the sovereignty lost by Parliament through EU membership.

Thus, a concern about the loss of UK parliamentary sovereignty and the limits this places on the UK Parliament's ability to make its own laws can be considered as a general reason for the outcome of the vote. However, the question of sovereignty is one that has been an issue in many Member States and concerns about the effect of EU law on national law have not been exclusive to the UK. The next section considers how EU law has, through the principle of supremacy, challenged the sovereignty of the UK Parliament and especially its ability to pass laws that may conflict with the EU Treaties.

3.1.1 UK withdrawal from the EU

3.1.1.1 The European Union (Withdrawal) Act 2018

Leaving the EU under Article 50 TEU has required not only the negotiation of a withdrawal agreement with the EU, but also an end to the supremacy of EU law within the UK. This has been done through the enactment of the European Union (Withdrawal) Act 2018, which includes a specific provision that the UK would leave the EU on 29 March 2019 at 11 pm. This is known within the Act as exit day, but it has been extended to 31 October 2019 as a result of the UK Parliament's failure to ratify the Withdrawal Agreement that has been negotiated with the EU.

The primary objective of the 2018 Act is to repeal the European Communities Act 1972 (ECA 1972). The legal consequence of this will be to bring to an end the supremacy of EU law within the UK. The Act will keep most existing EU law as UK domestic law (retained EU law) after Brexit in order to ensure the continuity and completeness of the UK's legal system. It will also confer wide powers on the UK government to amend that retained EU law through the use of statutory instruments in order to remedy or mitigate any deficiencies arising from the UK's withdrawal from the EU.

The 2018 Act therefore does three principal things, as follows.

- Under s 1, it will repeal the ECA 1972 on exit day, bringing an end to the overriding role of EU law in the UK's legal system. This is both political and symbolic, as well as having an important legal impact.
- Under ss 2–6, it will bring into UK domestic law as 'retained EU law' most of the EU law that applies in the UK on the day immediately before exit day.
- Under s 8, it gives the UK government wide powers to amend this retained EU law in order to correct deficiencies in that law arising from the UK's withdrawal from the EU.

Retained EU law is wide-ranging. It covers 'EU-derived domestic legislation', which includes statutory instruments made under s 2(2) of the ECA 1972 to implement EU Directives, but also extends to 'any enactment so far as … relating otherwise to the EU or the EEA' (s 2(2)(d) of the 2018 Act). It therefore includes primary legislation passed to implement EU law, as well as implementing rules made by regulators under their statutory powers. There was no legal need for the 2018 Act to give continuing effect to primary legislation implementing EU law, but there is a need for the Act to authorize changes to that legislation in order to cope with the consequences of Brexit.

Retained EU law also includes 'direct EU legislation', which is any EU Regulation, EU Decision or EU tertiary legislation that is both in force and applies on the day immediately before exit day (s 3 of the 2018 Act). Legislation that has not yet completed the EU's legislative process on exit day will not form part of retained EU law. The UK government may have to use its powers under the 2018 Act to address any resulting gaps that might appear, in particular where EU legislation applies in stages, with some provisions taking effect before exit day, but some not doing so until afterwards.

The validity, meaning, and effect of retained EU law is to be interpreted in accordance with, amongst other matters, 'retained EU case law'. Retained EU case law means 'principles laid down by, and any decisions of, the European Court [ie the Court of Justice of the European Union, or CJEU, which comprises the General Court and the Court of Justice], as they have effect in EU law immediately before exit day' (s 6(3) of the 2018 Act). Only the UK's Supreme Court is excepted from this obligation placed on UK courts to apply pre-Brexit CJEU decisions to retained EU law. The Supreme Court can depart from a decision of the CJEU in the same way as it can depart from its own earlier case law (s 6(4) of the 2018 Act).

UK courts are not bound by decisions of the European Court made after exit day, but 'may have regard' to those decisions 'so far as relevant to any matter before the court' (s 6(1) and (2) of the 2018 Act). However, if the CJEU were to decide that a piece of EU legislation made prior to Brexit is invalid, the equivalent retained EU law would remain valid in the UK (para 1(1) of Sched 1 to the 2018 Act).

Retained EU law does not include the EU's Charter of Fundamental Rights (s 5(3) of the 2018 Act) nor does it include any right to damages in accordance with 'the rule in *Francovich*' (para 4 of Sched 1 to the 2018 Act). The rule decided in C-6 & 9/90 *Francovich v Italy* [1991] ECR I-5357 (see 5.2 and 5.3) allows people to claim damages from a Member State in certain circumstances if that Member State has wrongly implemented or failed to implement an EU Directive or has otherwise acted in breach of EU law. The UK has faced (and continues to face) numerous actions for enacting tax law in breach of EU law principles, requiring it to refund significant amounts. There will be no right in domestic law on or after exit day to damages in accordance with the rule in *Francovich*.

3.1.1.2 Amending retained EU law

The European Union (Withdrawal) Act 2018 gives the UK government wide powers to change retained EU law. These powers can be used for up to two years after exit day (s 8(8) of the 2018 Act), but the powers are not absolute. The UK government can use the powers in the Act to amend or repeal retained EU law only:

- if it considers that there is a failure of retained EU law to operate effectively or that there is another deficiency in retained EU law; and
- that failure or other deficiency arises from the UK's withdrawal from the EU (s 8(1) of the 2018 Act).

The UK government cannot, for example, change rights included within retained EU law just because it considers that the EU tipped the balance too far in one direction. In order to change retained EU law, it must first point to a deficiency in retained EU law arising from Brexit. Nor is retained EU law deficient merely because it does not include a change made by the EU to that law after Brexit (s 8(4) of the 2018 Act).

Section 8(2) of the 2018 Act sets out what constitutes a 'deficiency' in retained EU law (although the categories are capable of being expanded under s 8(3)(b)). These include anything that is of no practical application or which is otherwise redundant, which confers functions on EU entities, or which contains EU references that are no longer appropriate.

If there is a failure of retained EU law to operate effectively or any other deficiency arising from Brexit, the UK government can make 'such provision as [it] considers appropriate to prevent, remedy or mitigate' that deficiency (s 8(1) of the 2018 Act). This confers considerable latitude on the UK government. The changes required will not only be technical corrections, but also will involve policy choices and other complexities (for example even changing sums expressed in euro to sterling can raise significant issues). The UK government can, for example, provide for the functions of EU entities or public authorities (including making instruments 'of a legislative character') to be exercisable by UK public authorities (s 8(6) of the 2018 Act). The Act cannot, however, be used to create public authorities, to impose or increase taxation, or to make retrospective provision (s 8(7)).

3.1.2 Sovereignty

National courts across most, if not all, Member States have, since the early days of EU integration, been concerned with the reach of EU law, and in particular with the principle of supremacy and how this is to be accommodated within domestic constitutional orders. Each Member State has faced challenges with respect to how to give effect to EU law in the domestic legal order. The Court of Justice clearly stated in its judgment in Case 6/64 *Costa v ENEL* [1964] ECR 585 that all Member States have a legal obligation to ensure that the rights within the Treaty are equally available in all of the Member States and that no national rules can restrict those rights.

Throughout the UK's membership of the EU, its constitutional relationship with the EU and the principle of supremacy of EU law has been considered through the lens of parliamentary sovereignty and the extent to which membership of the EU limits the rights of Parliament to legislate. In particular, supporters of the UK's withdrawal from the EU made a 'sovereignty' argument that the principle of supremacy of EU law has prevented the UK Parliament from being able to pass legislation that may conflict with EU law and that, in circumstances in which it did so, the UK courts reacted by 'overturning' an Act of Parliament. For example, the judgments in *Factortame*—a series of cases starting with Case C-213/89 *R v Secretary of State for Transport, ex p Factortame Ltd* [1990] ECR I-2433—demonstrate how the UK courts sought to reconcile the constitutional principle of parliamentary sovereignty with the obligation laid out in s 2 of the ECA 1972. In particular, in *Factortame*, the UK courts recognized the obligation of the UK to give full effect to its Treaty obligations and, if necessary, disapply a UK Act of Parliament.

3.1.3 The political problem

The problem of 'sovereignty' has both a political and a legal dimension. By way of introduction, we will consider briefly the political dimension.

In the political arena, the term 'national sovereignty' is often used to mean the power of the British people, through their national government, to govern their own affairs as they see fit. There is little doubt that membership of the EU has limited the power of the UK government, since decisions in certain policy areas are taken by the EU. While it may have been theoretically open for the UK to repeal the ECA 1972 at any point during its membership and unilaterally declare that it had left the EU, this did not occur. Moreover, judgments such as *Factortame* were considered to provide an interpretation of the supremacy of EU law in the UK that, because of s 2 of the ECA 1972, entrenched EU law in the UK legal order and that meant that withdrawal from the EU would, for this reason, prove to be difficult.

However, the inclusion of Article 50 TEU in the Treaty of Lisbon has addressed procedural questions about EU withdrawal. Thus, once the UK decided to leave the EU, the process for leaving the EU could take effect only if the UK followed the procedure provided for in Article 50 TEU (as explained in 1.19.1).

In the case of *R (on the application of Miller and another) v Secretary of State for Exiting the European Union* [2017] UKSC 5, the UK's Supreme Court was asked to rule on how precisely Article 50 TEU should be triggered. Specifically, would an Act of Parliament be required to commence the process of withdrawal from the EU, or could the UK government commence the process without the need for parliamentary approval by using the royal prerogative? The use of the royal prerogative was controversial because it would bypass Parliament and challenge the principle of parliamentary sovereignty, which was a major political question in the referendum.

The Supreme Court identified the outer limits of the royal prerogative and acknowledged that although the UK government has the power to withdraw from the EU Treaties, the government cannot exercise this power without an Act of Parliament in circumstances in which the effect is to change UK law. Thus, whilst the ECA 1972 remains in force, its effect is to constitute EU law as an independent and overriding source of domestic law, and therefore to change the effect of the ECA 1972 requires an Act of Parliament.

On the question of the Act of Parliament being required to trigger Article 50 TEU, the Supreme Court anchored its judgment firmly in the argument that EU withdrawal will lead to UK citizens losing rights and that, because EU law is an independent source within the UK constitution, only an Act of Parliament can remove these rights (see also 1.19.1 and 6.13).

Crucially, the Supreme Court focused on the relationship between Parliament and government, and it held that where rights attached to UK membership of the EU were given by Parliament, they can be taken away only by Parliament. In particular, the Supreme Court considered the purpose and scope of the ECA 1972: when the EU institutions make new laws, these laws become part of UK law. The Supreme Court therefore concluded that EU law is, under s 2 of the ECA 1972, an independent source of UK law that provides rights to citizens. The Supreme Court held that an Act of Parliament is required, rather than merely a parliamentary vote, to authorize the executive to trigger Article 50 TEU.

In response to this judgment, the government presented before Parliament the European Union (Notification of Withdrawal) Act 2017, which was approved by Parliament by a majority of 498 to 114 votes and provided the necessary parliamentary authority for the government to trigger Article 50 TEU.

?! **THINKING POINT**

Does UK withdrawal from the EU mean that the UK will have fully regained its sovereignty and that it will no longer be bound by EU law?

Throughout the Article 50 TEU process, the UK has remained a Member State of the EU, which required its compliance with EU law in its entirety until the conclusion of the Article 50 EU withdrawal process.

The question, which is more a matter of politics than of law, is whether the obvious restrictions on UK parliamentary sovereignty that have accompanied the UK's membership of the EU are a price that has been worth paying for the benefits of EU membership. In 1992, in a Hamlyn Lecture titled 'Introducing a European Legal Order', Lord Slynn of Hadley contrasted the negative view of membership (that the EU endangers 'national sovereignty, national independence and national identity') with the positive view (that the situation is not one 'of surrendering sovereignty but of pooling sovereignty in certain areas for the good of all'). This analysis by Lord Slynn, which correctly captures the overall neo-functionalist objectives of EU integration, is one that was broadly rejected by the UK's referendum result. Moreover, the argument that the UK has now regained its sovereignty following the referendum was highlighted by Prime Minister Theresa May at the Conservative Party Conference on 2 October 2016 when she spoke about the effects of the then Great Repeal Bill on the ECA 1972: 'Its effect will be clear, our laws will be made not in Brussels but in Westminster. The judges interpreting those laws will sit not in Luxembourg but in courts in this country. The authority of EU law in Britain will end.'

3.1.4 The legal problem

The legal dimension to the question of sovereignty is more complex.

3.1.4.1 Parliamentary sovereignty

The UK's withdrawal will undoubtedly alter the UK's political and legal relationship with the EU. Central to this change will be the European Union (Withdrawal) Act 2018, which is intended to restore parliamentary sovereignty to the UK in the way that Prime Minister Theresa May highlighted. However, the extent to which the UK will have a 'clean break' with the EU and thus fully restore its parliamentary sovereignty is a moot point, and will be largely dependent upon the final version of what, if any, withdrawal agreement the UK agrees with the EU.

In January 2019, the UK Parliament rejected, by a majority of 230 votes, the withdrawal agreement that the UK government had negotiated with the EU. Members of Parliament (MPs) held the so-called Irish backstop, a provision of the agreement that guarantees no hard border between Northern Ireland and the Republic of Ireland, to be unacceptable, arguing that it would create a separate regulatory regime for Northern Ireland, which would remain within the single market—unlike the rest of the UK. Given this rejection so close to the 29 March 2019 deadline, one option for the government was to seek an extension to Article 50 TEU in line with the procedure set out therein, which requires the consent of all 27 EU Member States. Parliament did not approve the withdrawal agreement before the 29 March 2019 deadline, which led the prime minister to request an extension to the Article 50 period. Originally, only a short extension was granted, until 12 April 2019, in order for Parliament to vote again on the withdrawal agreement, but Parliament once again rejected the withdrawal agreement. This led the prime minister to request a further longer extension to Article 50 TEU, which the EU 27 agreed to, with a new date of 31 October 2019 being approved.

However, irrespective of on what date the UK actually leaves the EU, until exit day it remains fully obliged to continue to give effect to EU law, and with that comes a continued restriction on the doctrine of parliamentary sovereignty and the ongoing supremacy of EU law. In the UK, the long-established doctrine of parliamentary sovereignty means, first, that the courts may not question the validity of parliamentary legislation (*Pickin v BR Board* [1994] 4 All ER 609) and, secondly, that Parliament cannot bind its successors, so that a later Act of Parliament will impliedly repeal an earlier Act insofar as they are inconsistent (*Vauxhall Estates v Liverpool Corporation* [1932] 1 KB 733). In summary, this doctrine establishes the supremacy of parliamentary legislation.

The doctrine of parliamentary sovereignty has clearly been in conflict with the full recognition of EU law in the UK. First, if EU law is to be fully effective, the UK courts have, from time to time, had to question the validity of Acts of Parliament that conflict with, or inadequately transpose, EU law. Secondly, if UK legislation that is inconsistent with EU law were to have the effect of repealing it, this would destroy any possibility of EU law applying uniformly across the EU. Since the UK does not have a formal written constitutional document that could be amended to give effect to EU law, it has been the ECA 1972 that has provided the means by which priority of EU law could be incorporated into national law.

Section 2(1) of the ECA 1972 provides as follows.

European Communities Act 1972, s 2(1)

All such rights, powers, liabilities, obligations and restrictions from time to time created or arising by or under the Treaties, and all such remedies and procedures from time to time provided for by or under the Treaties, as in accordance with the Treaties are without further enactment to be given legal effect or used in the United Kingdom shall be recognised and available in law, and be enforced, allowed and followed accordingly; and the expression '[enforceable EU right]' and similar expressions shall be read as referring to one to which this subsection applies.

In relation to UK legislation, EU law is given direct effect. This applies in relation to the Treaties and those regulatory rules that are 'created or arising by or under the Treaties'.

Section 2(4) of the ECA 1972 cements the status of EU law in the UK:

European Communities Act 1972, s 2(4)

… any such provision (of any such extent) as might be made by Act of Parliament, and any enactment passed or to be passed … shall be construed and have effect subject to the foregoing provisions of this section; …

The status of 'any enactment' made or to be made by Parliament is subject to EU law and this includes directly effective EU law, as provided for under s 2(1) of the Act. This gives legal effect to the primacy of EU law over UK legislation. While it is too early, at the time of writing, to predict with any certainty what will be the final UK–EU agreement, should the UK choose to maintain some access to the single market, it will probably be necessary to maintain some form of statutory provision that continues to give effect to EU law in a similar way to s 2(1) of the ECA 1972, albeit to allow for the exercise of a much more narrowly defined list of competences.

The existing operation of s 2(1) of the ECA 1972 may be viewed as at odds with the doctrine of parliamentary sovereignty, which does not allow Parliament to bind its successors such that it limits its own powers. Rather than taking a restrictive approach towards s 2(4), the English courts view this provision as an interpretative rule whereby it is presumed that Parliament will not override EU law in future legislation. This interpretative approach was considered by Lord Denning MR in the Court of Appeal in *Macarthys Ltd v Smith* [1979] 3 All ER 325, where he explained the relationship between EU and UK legislation:

Macarthys Ltd v Smith [1979] 3 All ER 325, 329, Court of Appeal

In construing our statute, we are entitled to look to the Treaty as an aid to its construction; but not only as an aid but as an overriding force. If on close investigation it should appear that our legislation is deficient or is inconsistent with Community law by some oversight of our draftsmen then it is our bounden duty to give priority to Community law. Such is the result of s 2(1) and (4) of the European Communities Act 1972.

I pause here, however, to make one observation on a constitutional point. Thus far I have assumed that our Parliament, whenever it passes legislation, intends to fulfil its obligations under the Treaty. If the time should come when our Parliament deliberately passes an Act with the intention of repudiating the Treaty or any provision in it or intentionally of acting inconsistently with it and says so in express terms then I should have thought that it would be the duty of our courts to follow the statute of our Parliament. I do not however envisage any such situation ... Unless there is such an intentional and express repudiation of the Treaty, it is our duty to give priority to the Treaty.

The priority of EU law over UK national legislation has been acknowledged through the enactment of the ECA 1972. In Lord Denning's view, Parliament has not ceded sovereignty completely; rather, it is constrained in as far as priority is given to EU law. It was considered that Lord Denning was arguing that if Parliament were to deliberately repeal the ECA 1972, then EU law would no longer be applicable or bind the UK and Parliament would regain full sovereignty. However, it is now clear that, following the Treaty of Lisbon, in order for the UK to repeal the ECA 1972, it will first have to conclude its negotiations under Article 50 TEU. Moreover, it is the conclusion of negotiations under Article 50 TEU that will ultimately lead to the UK's departure from the EU. The repeal of the ECA 1972 through the European Union (Withdrawal) Act 2018 will be primarily for domestic purposes, in order to address the continued legal obligations that will exist once the UK has withdrawn from the EU.

Lord Denning's reasoning did leave scope for some uncertainty for the judiciary, especially on the question of Parliament passing legislation that may be at odds with obligations arising under the Treaties. In particular, what are the obligations of the judiciary when deciding whether to apply a UK Act of Parliament or EU law? In *Duke v GEC Reliance* [1988] AC 618, the House of Lords (now the Supreme Court) considered the compatibility of the Sex Discrimination Act 1975 with the Equal Treatment Directive (Council Directive 76/207/EEC of 9 February 1976 on the implementation of the principle of equal treatment for men and women as regards access to employment, vocational training and promotion, and working conditions, OJ 1976 L39/40). Their Lordships stated that because the UK Act was passed before the Directive, it would 'be most unfair to the respondent to distort the construction of the 1975 Sex Discrimination Act in order to accommodate the meaning of the Equal Treatment Directive' (*Duke v GEC Reliance*, at 627). Their Lordships were concerned that, through interpretative techniques, they would adopt the mantle of legislature and provide the Act with a meaning that Parliament had not intended.

The House of Lords subsequently showed greater willingness to apply a more purposive interpretation to equal treatment legislation. In *Webb v EMO Cargo* [1992] All ER 43, on similar facts to those of *Duke v GEC Reliance*, the House of Lords interpreted the Sex Discrimination Act 1975 to conform with the Equal Treatment Directive in a manner that the Court of

Appeal had previously rejected as a distortion of the statute. However, their Lordships accepted that there were limits to the extent to which the courts could interpret UK statutes so as to conform to EU law and held that this could not be done if the impact of such purposive interpretation was to alter the meaning of domestic legislation.

Unlike the political debate concerning the UK's relationships with the EU, which undoubtedly became more polarized, fulfilling EU obligations has been more readily accepted by the UK judiciary. In *Thoburn v Sunderland County Council* [2002] 3 WLR 247 (the *Metric Martyrs Case*), the applicant challenged a Directive requiring produce that was not prepacked to be sold in metric, not imperial, measurements. The High Court of England and Wales dismissed the applicant's defence, which was based on the argument that, as the Weights and Measures Act 1985 had entered into force after UK accession, this later statute impliedly repealed the ECA 1972. In such circumstances, the defendant argued, UK law takes precedence over EU law. The English court dismissed these arguments and held that the 1972 Act—the primary legislation that provides for the UK's accession to the EU—has a 'constitutional quality' that prevents implied repeal and thereby suggests a degree of entrenchment.

3.1.4.2 The role of the Court of Justice

There is no mention of supremacy of EU law in the founding Treaty of Rome (1957) or subsequent Treaties; rather, it is a judicial concept that has been developed through teleological (or purposive) reasoning. The Court of Justice, in developing supremacy, has given effect to the intention of those drafting the Treaties as found in Article 10 EC.

?! THINKING POINT

Compare and contrast the wording of Article 10 EC and post-Lisbon Article 4(3) TEU, as set out in Table 3.1.

Table 3.1 Article 10 EC and Article 4(3) TEU

Article 10 EC	Article 4(3) TEU
Member States shall take all appropriate measures, whether general or particular, to ensure fulfilment of the obligations arising out of this Treaty or resulting from action taken by the institutions of the Community. They shall facilitate the achievement of the Community's tasks.	Pursuant to the principle of sincere cooperation, the Union and the Member States shall, in full mutual respect, assist each other in carrying out tasks which flow from the Treaties.
They shall abstain from any measure which could jeopardize the attainment of the objectives of this Treaty.	The Member States shall take any appropriate measure, general or particular, to ensure fulfilment of the obligations arising out of the Treaties or resulting from the acts of the institutions of the Union.
	The Member States shall facilitate the achievement of the Union's tasks and refrain from any measure which could jeopardize the attainment of the Union's objectives.

It can be observed from Article 10 EC and the post-Lisbon Article 4(3) TEU (see Table 3.1) that neither of them mentions 'supremacy' or 'primacy' in relation to EU law and national legislation, although there is an implied obligation to give effect to the Treaty obligations even if this means disapplying national law. The essence of Article 10 EC has been replicated in Article 4(3) TEU, although the wording in the latter reflects a tone of solidarity and collaboration compared to the former. The only acknowledgement of supremacy made in the Treaty of Lisbon can be found in Declaration 17 of the Declarations annexed to the Treaty concerning primacy, which states as follows.

Declarations annexed to the Final Act of the Intergovernmental Conference which adopted the Treaty of Lisbon, signed on 13 December 2007, OJ 2012 C326/337

17. Declaration concerning primacy

The Conference recalls that, in accordance with well settled case law of the Court of Justice of the European Union, the Treaties and the law adopted by the Union on the basis of the Treaties have primacy over the law of Member States, under the conditions laid down by the said case law.

The Conference has also decided to attach as an Annex to this Final Act the Opinion of the Council Legal Service on the primacy of EC law as set out in 11197/07 (JUR 260):

> 'Opinion of the Council Legal Service of 22 June 2007
>
> It results from the case-law of the Court of Justice that primacy of EC law is a cornerstone principle of Community law. According to the Court, this principle is inherent to the specific nature of the European Community. At the time of the first judgment of this established case law (*Costa/ENEL*, 15 July 1964, Case 6/641) there was no mention of primacy in the treaty. It is still the case today. The fact that the principle of primacy will not be included in the future treaty shall not in any way change the existence of the principle and the existing case-law of the Court of Justice. The Court of Justice has, on a number of occasions, taken the view that the supremacy of Community law is implicit in the obligation imposed upon Member States by Article 10 (ex 5) EC [the substance of this provision can now be found in Art 4(3) TFEU].'

?! THINKING POINT

Does Declaration 17 help to guarantee the supremacy of EU law?

3.1.4.3 Developing the principle of supremacy

The Court of Justice was instrumental in the construction of a robust doctrine on the supremacy of EU law. In Case 26/62 *Van Gend en Loos v Nederlandse Administratie de Belastingen* [1963] ECR 1, the Court, in considering whether a litigant before the national court could rely directly upon a Treaty provision, stated that 'the Community [now Union] constitutes a new

→ CROSS-REFERENCE
See *Van Gend* at 4.1.1.

legal order of international law for the benefit of which the states have limited their sovereign rights, albeit within limited fields' (*Van Gend en Loos*, at 12).

The Court recognized that the EU Treaties were not simply new additions to international law, but rather 'a new legal order' in which Member States have limited their sovereignty and to which they are subject. The Court in Case 6/64 *Costa v Ente Nazionale per l'Energia Elettrica (ENEL)* [1964] ECR 585 went further, delivering the classic statement on supremacy of EU law.

→ CROSS-REFERENCE
See Chapter 6 for a discussion of Article 267 TFEU.

Costa argued that the nationalization of the Italian electricity industry was contrary to EU law. ENEL and the Italian government argued that this was irrelevant, since the Italian courts were obliged to apply the later Italian law under which nationalization was legal. The case was referred to the Court of Justice under the preliminary reference procedure set out in Article 267 TFEU for an interpretation of EU law.

The Court of Justice ruled that EU law was part of the legal systems of the Member States and had to be applied by national courts. There had been a transfer of sovereignty to the EU and it was integral to this new legal system that EU law took precedence over later, inconsistent, national law.

Case 6/64 *Costa v Ente Nazionale per l'Energia Elettrica (ENEL)* [1964] ECR 585, 593–4

By contrast with ordinary international treaties, the EEC Treaty has created its own legal system which, on the entry into force of the Treaty, became an integral part of the legal systems of the Member States and which their courts are bound to apply.

By creating a Community of unlimited duration, having its own institutions, its own personality, its own legal capacity and capacity of representation on the international plane and, more particularly, real powers stemming from a limitation of sovereignty or a transfer of powers from the States to the Community, the Member States have limited their sovereign rights, albeit within limited fields, and have thus created a body of law which binds both their nationals and themselves.

The integration into the laws of each Member State of provisions which derive from the Community [now Union], and more generally the terms and the spirit of the Treaty, make it impossible for the States, as a corollary, to accord precedence to a unilateral and subsequent measure over a legal system accepted by them on a basis of reciprocity. Such a measure cannot therefore be inconsistent with that legal system. The executive force of Community law [now EU law] cannot vary from one State to another in deference to subsequent domestic laws, without jeopardizing the attainment of the objectives of the Treaty set out in Article 5(2) [now Article 4(3) TEU] and giving rise to the discrimination prohibited by Article 7 [now Article 18 TFEU].

The obligations undertaken under the Treaty establishing the Community would not be unconditional, but merely contingent, if they could be called in question by subsequent legislative acts of the signatories. Wherever the Treaty grants the States the right to act unilaterally, it does this by clear and precise provisions … Applications, by Member States for authority to derogate from the Treaty are subject to a special authorization procedure … which would lose their purpose if the Member States could renounce their obligations by means of an ordinary law.

> The precedence of Community law is confirmed by Article 189 [now Article 288 TFEU], whereby a Regulation 'shall be binding' and 'directly applicable in all Member States'. This provision, which is subject to no reservation, would be quite meaningless if a State could unilaterally nullify its effects by means of a legislative measure which could prevail over Community law.
>
> It follows from all these observations that the law stemming from the Treaty, an independent source of law, could not, because of its special and original nature, be overridden by domestic legal provisions, however framed, without being deprived of its character as Community law and without the legal basis of the Community itself being called into question.
>
> The transfer by the States from their domestic legal system to the Community legal system of the rights and obligations arising under the Treaty carries with it a permanent limitation of their sovereign rights, against which a subsequent unilateral act incompatible with the concept of the Community cannot prevail. …

The Court reinforced its statement from *Van Gend en Loos* declaring that the EEC Treaty provides a 'new legal order' and went on to reaffirm the Member States' commitment to this legal order by their release of limited sovereignty powers to the EU. The Court also emphatically reinforced the principle of supremacy by declaring that 'the law stemming from the Treaty … could not, because of its special and original nature, be overridden by domestic legal provisions, however framed, without being deprived of its character as Community law and without the legal basis of the Community itself being called into question' (*Costa v ENEL*, at 594).

Crucially, the Court in *Costa v ENEL* adopted a dynamic mode of interpreting EU law, referring to '[t]he integration into the laws of each Member State of provisions which derive from the Community, and *more generally the terms and the spirit of the Treaty*' (*ENEL*, at 593, emphasis added). The Court has expressly reserved for itself the teleological mode of interpretation of EU law, which enables it to take a more dynamic approach so that it is aligned with the integrationist spirit of the Treaties.

Acceptance of the supremacy of EU law over national law has not been without some difficulties. In Case 106/77 *Amministrazione delle Finanze dello Stato v Simmenthal SpA ('Simmenthal II')* [1978] ECR 629, the Court of Justice had ruled in the earlier Case 35/76 *Simmenthal SpA v Italian Minister of Finance ('Simmenthal I')* [1976] ECR 1871 that a fee charged on Simmenthal's imports of beef into Italy was contrary to EU law on the free movement of goods. The Italian court ordered the fee to be repaid, but the Amministrazione delle Finanze appealed. Under Italian law, the constitutionality of the law imposing the fee had to be referred to the Constitutional Court. The case was referred to the Court of Justice.

→ CROSS-REFERENCE
See also *Simmenthal* at 1.8 and 4.3.3.

Case 106/77 *Amministrazione delle Finanze dello Stato v Simmenthal SpA ('Simmenthal II')* [1978] ECR 629

> 17. … in accordance with the principle of the precedence of Community law [now EU law], the relationship between provisions of the Treaty and directly applicable measures of the

institutions on the one hand and the national law of the Member States on the other is such that those provisions and measures not only by their entry into force render automatically inapplicable any conflicting provision of current national law but—in so far as they are an integral part of, and take precedence in, the legal order applicable in the territory of each of the Member States—also preclude the valid adoption of new national legislative measures to the extent to which they would be incompatible with Community [now Union] provisions.

18. Indeed any recognition that national legislative measures which encroach upon the field within which the Community exercises its legislative power or which are otherwise incompatible with the provisions of Community law had any legal effect would amount to a corresponding denial of the effectiveness of obligations undertaken unconditionally and irrevocably by Member States pursuant to the Treaty and would thus imperil the very foundations of the Community.

19. The same conclusion emerges from the structure of Article 177 of the Treaty [now Article 267 TFEU] which provides that any court or tribunal of a Member State is entitled to make a reference to the Court whenever it considers that a preliminary ruling on a question of interpretation or validity relating to Community law is necessary to enable it to give judgment.

20. The effectiveness of that provision would be impaired if the national court were prevented from forthwith applying Community law in accordance with the decision or the case-law of the Court.

21. It follows from the foregoing that every national court must, in a case within its jurisdiction, apply Community law in its entirety and protect rights which the latter confers on individuals and must accordingly set aside any provision of national law which may conflict with it, whether prior or subsequent to the Community rule.

22. Accordingly any provision of a national legal system and any legislative, administrative or judicial practice which might impair the effectiveness of Community law by withholding from the national court having jurisdiction to apply such law the power to do everything necessary at the moment of its application to set aside national legislative provisions which might prevent Community rules from having full force and effect are incompatible with those requirements which are the very essence of Community law.

23. This would be the case in the event of a conflict between a provision of Community law and a subsequent national law if the solution of the conflict were to be reserved for an authority with a discretion of its own, other than the court called upon to apply Community law, even if such an impediment to the full effectiveness of Community law were only temporary.

24. The first question should therefore be answered to the effect that a national court which is called upon, within the limits of its jurisdiction, to apply provisions of Community law is under a duty to give full effect to those provisions, if necessary refusing of its own motion to apply any conflicting provision of national legislation, even if adopted subsequently, and it is not necessary for the court to request or await the prior setting aside of such provision by legislative or other constitutional means.

The Court of Justice referred to the 'principle of the precedence of Community law' and stated expressly that a national court should 'disapply' national legislation that conflicts with EU law without waiting for it to be repealed by legislative or other means (such as a ruling by the Constitutional Court).

A different problem in according supremacy to EU law arose in the *Factortame* litigation, which involved a number of references to the Court of Justice. Case C-213/89 *R v Secretary of State for Transport, ex p Factortame Ltd ('Factortame I')* [1990] ECR I-2433 concerned the possibility of interim relief being granted, in the form of a suspension of the disputed parts of the national legislation, pending a final ruling on their validity from the Court of Justice. It was held by the House of Lords (now the Supreme Court) that the remedy was not available under the law of England and Wales, but, in the light of conflicting Court of Justice case law on an interim measure, a reference would be made to the Court of Justice under Article 267 TFEU concerning the award of interim protection.

→ CROSS-REFERENCE
See also *Factortame I* at 4.3.3 and 6.10.2, and *Factortame II* at 4.2.5, 5.4.1, and 6.10.2.

The Court of Justice stated as follows.

Case C-213/89 *R v Secretary of State for Transport, ex p Factortame Ltd ('Factortame I')* [1990] ECR I-2433

21. … the full effectiveness of Community law [now EU law] would be just as much impaired if a rule of national law could prevent a court seised of a dispute governed by Community law from granting interim relief in order to ensure the full effectiveness of the judgment to be given on the existence of the rights claimed under Community law. It follows that a court which in those circumstances would grant interim relief, if it were not for a rule of national law, is obliged to set aside that rule.

The Court of Justice ruled that, despite the provisions of national law, the national legislation could and should be suspended pending a conclusive ruling on its validity. Rights under EU law could not be truly effective if those who sought to enforce them were prejudiced by the operation of the allegedly conflicting national legislation while the issue was being resolved. Following *Factortame I*, Case C-221/89 *R v Secretary of State for Transport, ex p Factortame Ltd ('Factortame II')* [1991] ECR I-3905 concerned the validity of certain provisions of the Merchant Shipping Act 1988, which the applicants, a group of Spanish fishermen, claimed were in contravention of directly enforceable EU rights. The Court of Justice held the contested provisions of the 1988 Act to be contrary to EU law.

The UK—and, for that matter, all of the Member States—have surrendered, or pooled, their absolute national sovereignty. In terms of legal sovereignty, not only has the UK Parliament lost its exclusive right to legislate, but also EU law will prevail over national laws. This position is subject to two provisos: first, absolute sovereignty may be regained by withdrawing from the EU; and, secondly, in those areas in which the EU has no competence, such as defence and tax, sovereignty is, for the time being, intact (although, of course, many of these areas are affected indirectly by EU law).

3.2 Attribution of powers to the EU

→ CROSS-REFERENCE
See 3.3 for a discussion on subsidiarity.

The issues of sovereignty are concerned with the sharing of power. The fundamental rule is that the EU may act only if the Treaty has given it power to do so and the exercise of such power is subject to the principle of subsidiarity. Article 2 TFEU sets out in general terms the various levels of competence at both the EU and national levels.

Article 2 TFEU

1. When the Treaties confer on the Union exclusive competence in a specific area, only the Union may legislate and adopt legally binding acts, the Member States being able to do so themselves only if so empowered by the Union or for the implementation of Union acts.
2. When the Treaties confer on the Union a competence shared with the Member States in a specific area, the Union and the Member States may legislate and adopt legally binding acts in that area. The Member States shall exercise their competence to the extent that the Union has not exercised its competence. The Member States shall again exercise their competence to the extent that the Union has decided to cease exercising its competence.
3. The Member States shall coordinate their economic and employment policies within arrangements as determined by this Treaty, which the Union shall have competence to provide.
4. The Union shall have competence, in accordance with the provisions of the Treaty on European Union, to define and implement a common foreign and security policy, including the progressive framing of a common defence policy.
5. In certain areas and under the conditions laid down in the Treaties, the Union shall have competence to carry out actions to support, coordinate or supplement the actions of the Member States, without thereby superseding their competence in these areas.
6. Legally binding acts of the Union adopted on the basis of the provisions of the Treaties relating to these areas shall not entail harmonisation of Member States' laws or regulations.

→ CROSS-REFERENCE
See Chapter 1 for a discussion of the Treaty base.

The scope of the competence for certain policy areas is delineated in Articles 3–6 TFEU. These are expressed according to the level of competence granted to the EU, for example where the EU has exclusive powers, where the powers are shared with the Member States, and where the EU has a supportive role and the role of coordinator in specific areas. In addition to these provisions, more guidance is given in relation to particular policy areas in other parts of the Treaty and specific Treaty bases are provided for legislative measures. For example, Articles 151 and 153–155 TFEU provide a broad Treaty base for employment law measures. If the Treaty does not specifically give the EU power to act or where the Treaty has failed to provide the necessary power in another Treaty provision, Article 352 TFEU provides an alternative Treaty base for new measures. However, action under Article 352 TFEU requires unanimity among the Member States.

Article 352 TFEU

1. If action by the Union should prove necessary, within the framework of the policies defined in the Treaties, to attain one of the objectives set out in the Treaties, and the Treaties have not provided the necessary powers, the Council, acting unanimously on a proposal from the Commission and after obtaining the consent of the European Parliament, shall adopt the appropriate measures. Where the measures in question are adopted by the Council in accordance with a special legislative procedure, it shall also act unanimously on a proposal from the Commission and after obtaining the consent of the European Parliament.
2. Using the procedure for monitoring the subsidiarity principle referred to in Article 5(3) of the Treaty on European Union, the Commission shall draw national Parliaments' attention to proposals based on this Article.
3. Measures based on this Article shall not entail harmonisation of Member States' laws or regulations in cases where the Treaties exclude such harmonisation.
4. This Article cannot serve as a basis for attaining objectives pertaining to the common foreign and security policy and any acts adopted pursuant to this Article shall respect the limits set out in Article 40, second paragraph, of the Treaty on European Union.

Constraints on the scope of this provision are provided for in Article 352(2)–(4) TFEU and include, inter alia, drawing to the attention of national parliaments any proposals for new measures, to ensure compliance with the subsidiarity principle. Article 352 is not to be used for measures that are aimed at the harmonization of laws.

Article 352(1) TFEU limits the use of this provision specifically to the attainment of one of the objectives set out in the Treaties'. This reference to the objectives of the Treaties is further elaborated in Declaration 41 annexed to the Lisbon Treaty, which sets out which of the Treaty objectives this provision applies to—namely, Article 3(2), (3), and (5) TEU.

Article 3 TEU

[...]

2. The Union shall offer its citizens an area of freedom, security and justice without internal frontiers, in which the free movement of persons is ensured in conjunction with appropriate measures with respect to external border controls, asylum, immigration and the prevention and combating of crime.
3. The Union shall establish an internal market. It shall work for the sustainable development of Europe based on balanced economic growth and price stability, a highly competitive social market economy, aiming at full employment and social progress, and a high level of protection and improvement of the quality of the environment. It shall promote scientific and technological advance.

It shall combat social exclusion and discrimination, and shall promote social justice and protection, equality between women and men, solidarity between generations and protection of the rights of the child.

It shall promote economic, social and territorial cohesion, and solidarity among Member States.

It shall respect its rich cultural and linguistic diversity, and shall ensure that Europe's cultural heritage is safeguarded and enhanced.

[…]

5. In its relations with the wider world, the Union shall uphold and promote its values and interests and contribute to the protection of its citizens. It shall contribute to peace, security, the sustainable development of the Earth, solidarity and mutual respect among peoples, free and fair trade, eradication of poverty and the protection of human rights, in particular the rights of the child, as well as to the strict observance and the development of international law, including respect for the principles of the United Nations Charter.

From this extract, it can be noted that the objectives are broad and, so as to limit potential circumvention of the Treaty, Declaration 42 of the Lisbon Treaty places a strict limit on the application of Article 352 TFEU.

Declarations annexed to the Final Act of the Intergovernmental Conference which adopted the Treaty of Lisbon, signed on 13 December 2007, OJ 2012 C326/337

42. Declaration on Article 352 of the Treaty on the Functioning of the European Union

The Conference underlines that, in accordance with the settled case law of the Court of Justice of the European Union, Article 352 of the Treaty on the Functioning of the European Union, being an integral part of an institutional system based on the principle of conferred powers, cannot serve as a basis for widening the scope of Union powers beyond the general framework created by the provisions of the Treaties as a whole and, in particular, by those that define the tasks and the activities of the Union. In any event, this Article cannot be used as a basis for the adoption of provisions whose effect would, in substance, be to amend the Treaties without following the procedure which they provide for that purpose.

3.3 The principle of subsidiarity

EU competence arises from the Treaties, which provide a legal foundation for all EU action. As the EU has a multilevel governance structure, this requires that competences are allocated between the various levels. In some instances, the EU has exclusive competence to act, whereas in others, it shares competence with the Member States. In those circumstances in which the EU shares competence with the Member States, the principle of subsidiarity applies, which is used to determine whether legislative action should be taken at the EU or national level.

Article 5 TEU

1. The limits of Union competences are governed by the principle of conferral. The use of Union competences is governed by the principles of subsidiarity and proportionality.
2. Under the principle of conferral, the Union shall act only within the limits of the competences conferred upon it by the Member States in the Treaties to attain the objectives set out therein. Competences not conferred upon the Union in the Treaties remain with the Member States.
3. Under the principle of subsidiarity, in areas which do not fall within its exclusive competence, the Union shall act only if and in so far as the objectives of the proposed action cannot be sufficiently achieved by the Member States, either at central level or at regional and local level, but can rather, by reason of the scale or effects of the proposed action, be better achieved at Union level.

   The institutions of the Union shall apply the principle of subsidiarity as laid down in the Protocol on the application of the principles of subsidiarity and proportionality. National Parliaments ensure compliance with the principle of subsidiarity in accordance with the procedure set out in that Protocol.
4. Under the principle of proportionality, the content and form of Union action shall not exceed what is necessary to achieve the objectives of the Treaties.

   The institutions of the Union shall apply the principle of proportionality as laid down in the Protocol on the application of the principles of subsidiarity and proportionality.

Under Article 5(3) TEU, the principle of subsidiarity appears to suggest that the EU should take legislative action only if the Member States acting independently could not achieve the result. Although the presumption for action would, under Article 5 TEU, appear to lie with the Member States, it can be argued that the principle of subsidiarity conflicts with the objective of an 'ever-closer union', which presupposes action at the EU level to achieve integration. Protocol 2 of the Treaty of Lisbon, on the application of the subsidiarity principle, contains rules relating to the application of subsidiarity against which the Commission benchmarks legislative proposals.

In essence, subsidiarity is concerned with the complex issue of the allocation of competence between the Member States and the EU institutions. Academic journals in the field of EU law and policy have been filled in recent years with articles raising questions about the meaning of the principle of subsidiarity, its practical operation, its impact on the relationship between the EU and the Member States (including national parliaments), and the extent to which it is possible or appropriate for the Court of Justice to determine disputes that arise.

For example, Cygan has stated as follows.

A Cygan, 'The Parliamentarisation of EU Decision-Making? The Impact of the Treaty of Lisbon on National Parliaments' (2011) 36(4) EL Rev 480, 484

Under art. 5(3) TEU, in policy areas which do not come within the scope of exclusive EU competence the Union shall act only if, and, 'insofar as the objectives of the proposed action cannot be achieved by the Member States … but can rather by reason of scale or effects of the proposed action be better achieved at the EU level.'

This, prima facie, suggests a presumption against EU action, but, since the Treaty of Maastricht, the precise meaning of subsidiarity has been the subject of much debate. The Court has favoured a restrictive interpretation, shared by the Commission, in whose view art. 5 TEU raises a presumption that the measure satisfies the dual requirements of necessity and effectiveness for EU action to be justified.

The justification for EU action, and therefore for not applying the principle of subsidiarity, is that EU action is both necessary and efficient. This justification has proved very difficult to rebut, with the Court of Justice being unwilling to challenge the political judgement of the Commission that legislative action at the EU level is most appropriate.

In Case C-58/08 *Vodafone Ltd and others v Secretary of State for Business Enterprise and Regulatory Reform* [2010] ECR I-4999, for example, the Court considered whether legislation capping roaming charges for mobile phone users could be achieved only by means of an EU Regulation (then, Regulation (EC) No 717/2007 of the European Parliament and of the Council of 27 June 2007 on roaming on public mobile telephone networks within the Community …, OJ 2007 L171/32) and not by means of national legislation introduced by each individual Member State. The Court justified the need for EU legislative action on the basis that there was a genuine internal market in roaming services, which could be regulated only through harmonizing legislation. The Court stated as follows.

Case C-58/08 *Vodafone Ltd and others v Secretary of State for Business Enterprise and Regulatory Reform* [2010] ECR I-4999

72. It is appropriate to recall that the principle of subsidiarity is referred to in the second paragraph of Article 5 EC—and given actual definition by the Protocol on the application of the principles of subsidiarity and proportionality, annexed to the Treaty—, which provides that the Community, in areas which do not fall within its exclusive competence, is to take action only if and insofar as the objectives of the proposed action cannot be sufficiently achieved by the Member States and can therefore, by reason of the scale or effects of the proposed action, be better achieved by the Community. That protocol, in paragraph 5, also lays down guidelines for the purposes of determining whether those conditions are met.

73. As regards legislative acts, the protocol states, in paragraphs 6 and 7, that the Community is to legislate only to the extent necessary and that Community measures should leave as much scope for national decision as possible, consistent however with securing the aim of the measure and observing the requirements of the Treaty.

74. In addition, it states in its paragraph 3 that the principle of subsidiarity does not call into question the powers conferred on the European Community by the Treaty, as interpreted by the Court of Justice.

75. As regards Article 95 EC, the Court has held that the principle of subsidiarity applies where the Community legislature uses it as a legal basis, inasmuch as that provision does not give it exclusive competence to regulate economic activity on the internal market (*British American Tobacco (Investments) and Imperial Tobacco* [C-491/01 *The Queen v Secretary of State for Health, ex parte British American Tobacco (Investments) Ltd and Imperial Tobacco Ltd* [2002] ECR I-11453], paragraph 179).

76. In this respect, it must be pointed out that the Community legislature, wishing to maintain competition among mobile telephone network operators, has, in adopting Regulation No 717/2007, introduced a common approach, in order in particular to contribute to the smooth functioning of the internal market, allowing those operators to act within a single coherent regulatory framework.

77. As is clear from recital 14 in the preamble to the regulation, the interdependence of retail and wholesale charges for roaming services is considerable, so that any measure seeking to reduce retail charges alone without affecting the level of costs for the wholesale supply of Community-wide roaming services would have been liable to disrupt the smooth functioning of the Community-wide roaming market. For that reason, the Community legislature decided that any action would require a joint approach at the level of both wholesale charges and retail charges, in order to contribute to the smooth functioning of the internal market in those services.

78. That interdependence means that the Community legislature could legitimately take the view that it had to intervene at the level of retail charges as well. Thus, by reason of the effects of the common approach laid down in Regulation No 717/2007, the objective pursued by that regulation could best be achieved at Community level.

79. Therefore, the provisions of Articles 4 and 6(3) of Regulation No 717/2007 are not invalidated by any infringement of the principle of subsidiarity.

?! THINKING POINT

Are there any circumstances in which the subsidiarity principle could prevent the use of EU legislation when the EU is seeking to regulate the internal market?

In *Vodafone*, the Court made it very clear that when the operation of the internal market is at issue, then only through EU legislative action will its integrity be preserved. Based on this reasoning, it would appear to leave very little opportunity for Member States to legislate.

3.4 Sources of EU law

➔ CROSS-REFERENCE See 1.1 for a discussion on the rationale for the EU.

There are a number of sources of EU law and it is important to familiarize yourself with them.

3.4.1 The Treaties

➔ CROSS-REFERENCE The amending Treaties are discussed in Chapter 1.

➔ CROSS-REFERENCE Section 2(1) of the European Communities Act 1972 is discussed at 3.1.2. See also direct effect, which is considered at 4.1.

The TEU and the TFEU are of equal legal status and form the primary source of EU law. These are 'self-executing'—that is, they become law in a Member State immediately upon ratification by that State, which therefore need not pass national legislation in order to implement them. The UK, in fact, chose nonetheless to do so because of its approach to the status of non-national law. Unlike its European neighbours, the UK sees international law as separate from, rather than simply a superior part of, national law. In order for international law to become part of the UK's legal system, it must actually be written into national law. This was achieved in relation to EU law by s 2(1) of the ECA 1972. See Table 3.2 for an overview of the Treaties.

Table 3.2 An overview of the Treaties

Year	Title	Entry into force
1951	European Coal and Steel Community (ECSC) Treaty Signed: 18 April 1951	23 July 1952 Expired: 23 July 2002
1957	European Economic Community (EEC) Treaty Signed: 25 March 1957	1 January 1958
1957	European Atomic Energy Community (EURATOM) Treaty Signed: 25 March 1957	January 1958
1965	Merger Treaty Signed: 8 April 1965 (EEC, EURATOM, and ECSC share single Commission and Council)	1 July 1967 Repealed by Treaty of Amsterdam
1986	Single European Act Signed: 17 February 1986	1 July 1987
1992	Treaty on European Union—Treaty of Maastricht Signed: 7 February 1992 (European Community (EC) replaced European Economic Community (EEC))	1 November 1993
1997	Treaty of Amsterdam Signed: 2 October 1997	1 May 1999
2001	Treaty of Nice Signed: 26 February 2001	1 February 2003
2004	Treaty establishing a Constitution for Europe Signed: 29 October 2004	Not ratified
2007	Treaty of Lisbon Signed: 13 December 2007 Renamed and amended the European Community (EC) Treaty as the Treaty on the Functioning of the European Union (TFEU)	1 December 2009

A requirement of accession to the EU is that the Treaties must become part of the generally binding law of the Member State. EU law is also law having a special character, as made clear in Case 26/62 *Van Gend en Loos v Nederlandse Administratie de Belastingen* [1963] ECR 1.

Case 26/62 *Van Gend en Loos v Nederlandse Administratie de Belastingen* [1963] ECR 1, 2

3. [T]he European Economic Community [now European Union] constitutes a new legal order of international law for the benefit of which the States have limited their sovereign rights, albeit within limited fields, and the subjects of which comprise not only Member States but also their nationals.

   Independently of the legislation of Member States, Community law [now EU law] not only imposes obligations on individuals but is also intended to confer upon them rights which become part of their legal heritage. ...

As a result, these Treaties are directly applicable in the Member States, although they are not always directly enforceable in the national courts (ie they do not always have direct effect). Both the TEU and TFEU provide necessary frameworks, guidelines, and regulatory tools for the functioning of the EU. In some sense, the Treaties are similar to a constitution because they set out the competences of the EU and the EU institutions, and also, to some extent, the rights of the citizens. However, EU law is not solely dependent on Treaties: much of the detail implementing the objectives and policies of the EU is to be found in secondary legislation.

The TEU sets out the aims and values of the EU. Articles 2 and 3 TEU provide as follows.

Article 2 TEU

The Union is founded on the values of respect for human dignity, freedom, democracy, equality, the rule of law and respect for human rights, including the rights of persons belonging to minorities. These values are common to the Member States in a society in which pluralism, non-discrimination, tolerance, justice, solidarity, and equality between women and men prevail.

Article 3 TEU

1. The Union's aim is to promote peace, its values and the well-being of its peoples.
2. The Union shall offer its citizens an area of freedom, security and justice without internal frontiers, in which the free movement of persons is ensured in conjunction with appropriate measures with respect to external border controls, asylum, immigration and the prevention and combating of crime.
3. The Union shall establish an internal market. It shall work for the sustainable development of Europe based on balanced economic growth and price stability, a highly competitive social market economy, aiming at full employment and social progress, and a high level of protection and improvement of the quality of the environment. It shall promote scientific and technological advance.

It shall combat social exclusion and discrimination, and shall promote social justice and protection, equality between women and men, solidarity between generations and protection of the rights of the child.

It shall promote economic, social and territorial cohesion, and solidarity among Member States.

It shall respect its rich cultural and linguistic diversity, and shall ensure that Europe's cultural heritage is safeguarded and enhanced.

4. The Union shall establish an economic and monetary union whose currency is the euro.
5. In its relations with the wider world, the Union shall uphold and promote its values and interests and contribute to the protection of its citizens. It shall contribute to peace, security, the sustainable development of the Earth, solidarity and mutual respect among peoples, free and fair trade, eradication of poverty and the protection of human rights, in particular the rights of the child, as well as to the strict observance and the development of international law, including respect for the principles of the United Nations Charter.
6. The Union shall pursue its objectives by appropriate means commensurate with the competences which are conferred upon it in the Treaties.

The TEU also provides the principles by which the EU is governed, its institutional structure, provisions on enhanced cooperation and external action, including a common foreign and security policy, and new revision procedures for both Treaties.

The TFEU provides the detail on achieving the aims set out in the TEU and it sets out the explicit competences of the EU. External action has been excluded from the TFEU and is governed by the TEU. The TFEU provides the framework within which the EU can make laws and sets out the areas in which there has been an express transfer of law-making powers from the Member States to the EU.

Article 3 TFEU

1. The Union shall have exclusive competence in the following areas:
   (a) customs union;
   (b) the establishing of the competition rules necessary for the functioning of the internal market;
   (c) monetary policy for the Member States whose currency is the euro;
   (d) the conservation of marine biological resources under the common fisheries policy;
   (e) common commercial policy.
2. The Union shall also have exclusive competence for the conclusion of an international agreement when its conclusion is provided for in a legislative act of the Union or is necessary to enable the Union to exercise its internal competence, or in so far as its conclusion may affect common rules or alter their scope.

Article 4 TFEU

1. The Union shall share competence with the Member States where the Treaties confer on it a competence which does not relate to the areas referred to in Articles 3 and 6.
2. Shared competence between the Union and the Member States applies in the following principal areas:
   (a) internal market;
   (b) social policy, for the aspects defined in this Treaty;
   (c) economic, social and territorial cohesion;
   (d) agriculture and fisheries, excluding the conservation of marine biological resources;
   (e) environment;
   (f) consumer protection;
   (g) transport;
   (h) trans-European networks;
   (i) energy;
   (j) area of freedom, security and justice;
   (k) common safety concerns in public health matters, for the aspects defined in this Treaty.

   [...]
4. In the areas of research, technological development and space, the Union shall have competence to carry out activities, in particular to define and implement programmes; however, the exercise of that competence shall not result in Member States being prevented from exercising theirs.
5. In the areas of development cooperation and humanitarian aid, the Union shall have competence to carry out activities and conduct a common policy; however, the exercise of that competence shall not result in Member States being prevented from exercising theirs.

Article 5 TFEU

1. The Member States shall coordinate their economic policies within the Union. To this end, the Council shall adopt measures, in particular broad guidelines for these policies.

   Specific provisions shall apply to those Member States whose currency is the euro.
2. The Union shall take measures to ensure coordination of the employment policies of the Member States, in particular by defining guidelines for these policies.
3. The Union may take initiatives to ensure coordination of Member States' social policies.

Article 6 TFEU

The Union shall have competence to carry out actions to support, coordinate or supplement the actions of the Member States. The areas of such action shall, at European level, be:

(a) protection and improvement of human health;

(b) industry;

(c) culture;

(d) tourism;

(e) education, vocational training, youth and sport;

(f) civil protection;

(g) administrative cooperation.

→ CROSS-REFERENCE
See 3.2 for a discussion on Article 352 TFEU.

The EU has only those powers that are conferred on it by the Treaties, and any powers not so conferred remain with the Member States. However, not all Treaty provisions lay down clear limits on the powers they confer and so Article 352 TFEU can be used as a reserve power that enables the EU institutions to act where their action is necessary to attain one of objectives set out in the Treaties.

3.4.2 Secondary legislation

THINKING POINT

In the light of what you learned about the institutions in Chapter 2, can you identify the body/bodies responsible for making secondary legislation? Is it always the responsibility of the same body/bodies?

Article 288 TFEU provides a list of the five different kinds of legal acts of the EU.

Article 288 TFEU

To exercise the Union's competences, the institutions shall adopt regulations, directives, decisions, recommendations and opinions.

A regulation shall have general application. It shall be binding in its entirety and directly applicable in all Member States.

A directive shall be binding, as to the result to be achieved, upon each Member State to which it is addressed, but shall leave to the national authorities the choice of form and methods.

A decision shall be binding in its entirety. A decision which specifies those to whom it is addressed shall be binding only on them.

Recommendations and opinions shall have no binding force.

3.4.2.1 Regulations

Article 288 TFEU provides that Regulations 'shall have general application', such that they apply generally, rather than to specific groups or individuals. Regulations are binding in their entirety and directly applicable in all Member States. Regulations do not normally require implementing legislation (ie converting the Regulation into national law) because they will apply automatically. No further action is required by a Member State with regard to a Regulation because the Regulation applies in a uniform manner across the whole EU. If further action were required, it would deprive the measure of its uniform character as a measure of EU law. A Regulation becomes part of the national legislation in the Member State on the date specified within the Regulation or on the 20th day following that of its publication in the *Official Journal of the European Union* (Article 297 TFEU). Where a Regulation requires implementation measures to be adopted by the Member State, any failure to meet the requirements of the Regulation will amount to a breach of EU law.

3.4.2.2 Directives

Directives are binding as to the result to be achieved. Directives are not directly applicable and the Member State must transpose the Directive into national legislation. The Member State has discretion as to the form and method by which the implementation will be made. Directives are binding upon the Member State(s) to whom they are addressed.

All Directives provide a deadline for implementation, which will be specified in the Directive. In the event that a date of implementation has not been included in the Directive, Article 297 TFEU states that the date of implementation will be the 20th day following that of its publication in the *Official Journal of the European Union*. Sometimes, implementation of a Directive will not be necessary because the law in the Member State already conforms to the Directive. In this situation, the Member State must inform the Commission of the existing provision's conformity with the Directive.

3.4.2.3 Decisions

Decisions are binding in their entirety on those to whom they are addressed. Decisions may be addressed to all or some Member States, or to businesses, or to individuals. There is no requirement for implementing legislation. Article 297(2) TFEU provides that where Decisions specify to whom they are addressed, the addressee will be notified of that Decision, and the Decision will take effect only upon such notification. Where a Decision does not specify to whom it is addressed, the Decision will be published in the *Official Journal of the European Union*. In that case, the Decision will enter into force on the date specified in the Decision or, in the absence of a specified date, on the 20th day following that of its publication.

3.4.2.4 Recommendations or Opinions

Neither Recommendations nor Opinions have binding force. These are sometimes known as soft law. They cannot be altogether ignored, however, and it is wise to take note of them because they are often followed by binding measures along the same lines (Case 322/88 *Grimaldi v Fonds des Maladies Professionnelles* [1989] ECR 4407).

→ CROSS-REFERENCE
See also *Grimaldi* at 4.1.1.5 and 4.2.1.2.

3.4.3 Decisions of the Court of Justice

Acts that are not listed in Article 288 TFEU may have a legal effect. The rulings of the Court of Justice are authoritative on all aspects of the Treaties and other (secondary) legislation. The Court has also developed certain legal principles, some of which it has implied into the Treaties and others of which are part of the legal traditions of the Member States.

3.4.4 International agreements and Conventions

The EU, as an institution with international legal personality, is able to enter into international agreements with third countries (Article 47 TEU) and it does so quite frequently. The main fields relate to commercial and trade policy, relations with prospective Member States, and development policy.

3.4.5 General principles of EU law

Not all EU law is laid down in writing. Through its role, under Article 19 TEU, in ensuring that 'the law is observed' in the interpretation and application of the Treaties, the Court of Justice has developed principles known as general principles of law, which are the unwritten law of the EU.

The general principles of law have been derived from various principles of law found in the national legal orders of the Member States and are considered to be part of EU law with which the Court of Justice must ensure compliance. In the context of the primary legislation of the TFEU, these principles are used to inform interpretation—although TFEU provisions can override these principles. They are also used to interpret secondary legislation, such as Directives. In addition, secondary legislation must be consistent with these principles and may be challenged before the Court of Justice if it violates such principles.

The areas mainly affected by general principles of law include:

- fundamental rights;
- the development of a general principle of equality and non-discrimination, although this is now mainly addressed by legislative measures; and
- procedural fairness.

Under the category of procedural fairness, take note of the development of the following principles:

- the right to be heard;
- confidentiality and legal privilege;
- legal certainty;
- protection of legitimate expectations; and
- proportionality.

Legal certainty means that it should always be possible to ascertain the law applicable to the circumstances at the time and therefore that laws should neither be ambiguous nor apply retrospectively to the detriment of those who have fairly relied on them. The principle of legal certainty has been invoked, for example, to justify the possibility of placing time limits for bringing proceedings to challenge decisions that contravene EU law. Whilst the principle of effectiveness generally requires that remedies be available to challenge such decisions, the principle of legal certainty makes it permissible to place limits on those challenges.

Proportionality means that legislation should not go beyond that which is necessary to achieve the desired objective or deal with the problem. This requires that a measure must be both:

- *suitable* to promote the objective sought—that is, there must be a reasonable connection between the measure and its objective; and
- *necessary* to achieve that objective—that is, no more onerous than is required to achieve the objective and the least onerous approach by which that objective can be achieved.

These principles can be used by all courts to interpret EU law, and can be used by the Court of Justice to test the legality of EU acts and of implementing measures enacted by the Member States.

3.5 Legislative procedures

The law-making process enables policy objectives to be implemented. Article 17(2) TEU provides that 'Union legislative acts may only be adopted on the basis of a Commission proposal, except where the Treaties provide otherwise'. According to this provision, the Commission has the right of initiative such that legislative measures can be adopted on the basis of a Commission proposal only where the Treaties so provide. The usual procedure is for a measure to be proposed by the Commission and adopted jointly by the European Parliament and by the Council, but there are considerable variations on this procedure, the two most important of which are the ordinary legislative procedure (OLP)—formerly known as co-decision—and the special legislative procedure.

→ CROSS-REFERENCE
See more on co-decision at 1.13, 1.15, and 1.17.

The correct procedure in respect of a proposed piece of legislation is determined by the legal base of the proposed legislation—that is, the Treaty Article that gives the EU competence to act in that area.

It is also necessary to note that, in some cases, a completely different procedure may be used. For example, the Commission has direct legislative powers to make law in only two areas: under Article 106(3) TFEU in ensuring that public undertakings comply with the rules contained in the Treaty; and under Article 45(3)(d) TFEU in determining the conditions under which citizens of the EU may reside in another Member State after having worked there.

Article 289 TFEU provides for two legislative procedures.

Article 289 TFEU

1. The ordinary legislative procedure shall consist in the joint adoption by the European Parliament and the Council of a regulation, directive or decision on a proposal from the Commission. This procedure is defined in Article 294.
2. In the specific cases provided for by the Treaties, the adoption of a regulation, directive or decision by the European Parliament with the participation of the Council, or by the latter with the participation of the European Parliament, shall constitute a special legislative procedure.
3. Legal acts adopted by legislative procedure shall constitute legislative acts.
4. In the specific cases provided for by the Treaties, legislative acts may be adopted on the initiative of a group of Member States or of the European Parliament, on a recommendation from the European Central Bank or at the request of the Court of Justice or the European Investment Bank.

3.5.1 Ordinary legislative procedure

The OLP applies to the majority of areas of activity that fall within the competence of the EU. It is grounded in the adoption of legislation by both the European Parliament and Council, based on a proposal submitted by the Commission. Article 289 TFEU states that this procedure applies to legislative proposals submitted by the Commission. Article 289(4) TFEU provides that, in specific cases laid down in the Treaty, the legislative procedure will apply based on the initiative of a group of Member States, or the European Parliament, on a recommendation from the European Central Bank (ECB), or at the request of the Court of Justice. In these circumstances, the role and prerogatives of the Commission do not apply (Article 294(15) TFEU).

The OLP is set out in Article 294 TFEU (see Figure 3.1 for a summary):

Article 294 TFEU

1. Where reference is made in the Treaties to the ordinary legislative procedure for the adoption of an act, the following procedure shall apply.
2. The Commission shall submit a proposal to the European Parliament and the Council.

First reading

3. The European Parliament shall adopt its position at first reading and communicate it to the Council.
4. If the Council approves the European Parliament's position, the act concerned shall be adopted in the wording which corresponds to the position of the European Parliament.
5. If the Council does not approve the European Parliament's position, it shall adopt its position at first reading and communicate it to the European Parliament.

6. The Council shall inform the European Parliament fully of the reasons which led it to adopt its position at first reading. The Commission shall inform the European Parliament fully of its position.

Second reading

7. If, within three months of such communication, the European Parliament:
   (a) approves the Council's position at first reading or has not taken a decision, the act concerned shall be deemed to have been adopted in the wording which corresponds to the position of the Council;
   (b) rejects, by a majority of its component members, the Council's position at first reading, the proposed act shall be deemed not to have been adopted;
   (c) proposes, by a majority of its component members, amendments to the Council's position at first reading, the text thus amended shall be forwarded to the Council and to the Commission, which shall deliver an opinion on those amendments.
8. If, within three months of receiving the European Parliament's amendments, the Council, acting by a qualified majority:
   (a) approves all those amendments, the act in question shall be deemed to have been adopted;
   (b) does not approve all the amendments, the President of the Council, in agreement with the President of the European Parliament, shall within six weeks convene a meeting of the Conciliation Committee.
9. The Council shall act unanimously on the amendments on which the Commission has delivered a negative opinion.

Conciliation

10. The Conciliation Committee, which shall be composed of the members of the Council or their representatives and an equal number of members representing the European Parliament, shall have the task of reaching agreement on a joint text, by a qualified majority of the members of the Council or their representatives and by a majority of the members representing the European Parliament within six weeks of its being convened, on the basis of the positions of the European Parliament and the Council at second reading.
11. The Commission shall take part in the Conciliation Committee's proceedings and shall take all necessary initiatives with a view to reconciling the positions of the European Parliament and the Council.
12. If, within six weeks of its being convened, the Conciliation Committee does not approve the joint text, the proposed act shall be deemed not to have been adopted.

Third reading

13. If, within that period, the Conciliation Committee approves a joint text, the European Parliament, acting by a majority of the votes cast, and the Council, acting by a qualified majority, shall each have a period of six weeks from that approval in which to adopt the act in ques-

tion in accordance with the joint text. If they fail to do so, the proposed act shall be deemed not to have been adopted.

14. The periods of three months and six weeks referred to in this Article shall be extended by a maximum of one month and two weeks respectively at the initiative of the European Parliament or the Council.

Special provisions

15. Where, in the cases provided for in the Treaties, a legislative act is submitted to the ordinary legislative procedure on the initiative of a group of Member States, on a recommendation by the European Central Bank, or at the request of the Court of Justice, paragraph 2, the second sentence of paragraph 6, and paragraph 9 shall not apply.

    In such cases, the European Parliament and the Council shall communicate the proposed act to the Commission with their positions at first and second readings. The European Parliament or the Council may request the opinion of the Commission throughout the procedure, which the Commission may also deliver on its own initiative. It may also, if it deems it necessary, take part in the Conciliation Committee in accordance with paragraph 11.

3.5.2 Special legislative procedure

Article 289(2) TFEU refers to the special legislative procedure, which is used only in specific cases where the Treaties provide for the adoption of a Regulation, Directive, or Decision:

- by the European Parliament with the participation of the Council; or
- by the Council with the involvement of the European Parliament.

This procedure does not require the European Parliament and Council jointly to decide on the measure.

3.5.3 Enhanced cooperation

The Treaty of Amsterdam authorized 'closer cooperation' in the context of the EC Treaty generally and specifically Title VI TEU (on police and judicial cooperation under the Maastricht Treaty). This was a revolutionary concept, as it recognized the general principle that EU action could be taken by only some Members. Previously, this had been limited to opt-outs by particular Member States in specific areas.

→ CROSS-REFERENCE
See also enhanced cooperation at 1.5, 1.15, 1.17, and 1.18.

The Treaty of Nice renamed 'closer cooperation' as 'enhanced cooperation' and clarified the conditions under which such enhanced cooperation would operate. For example, it extended enhanced cooperation to the implementation of joint actions and common positions under the Common Foreign and Security Policy (CFSP). Such cooperation may not apply to matters with military or defence implications.

New provisions for enhanced cooperation can be found in the TEU and TFEU. Article 20 TEU provides that '[e]nhanced cooperation shall aim to further the objectives of the Union,

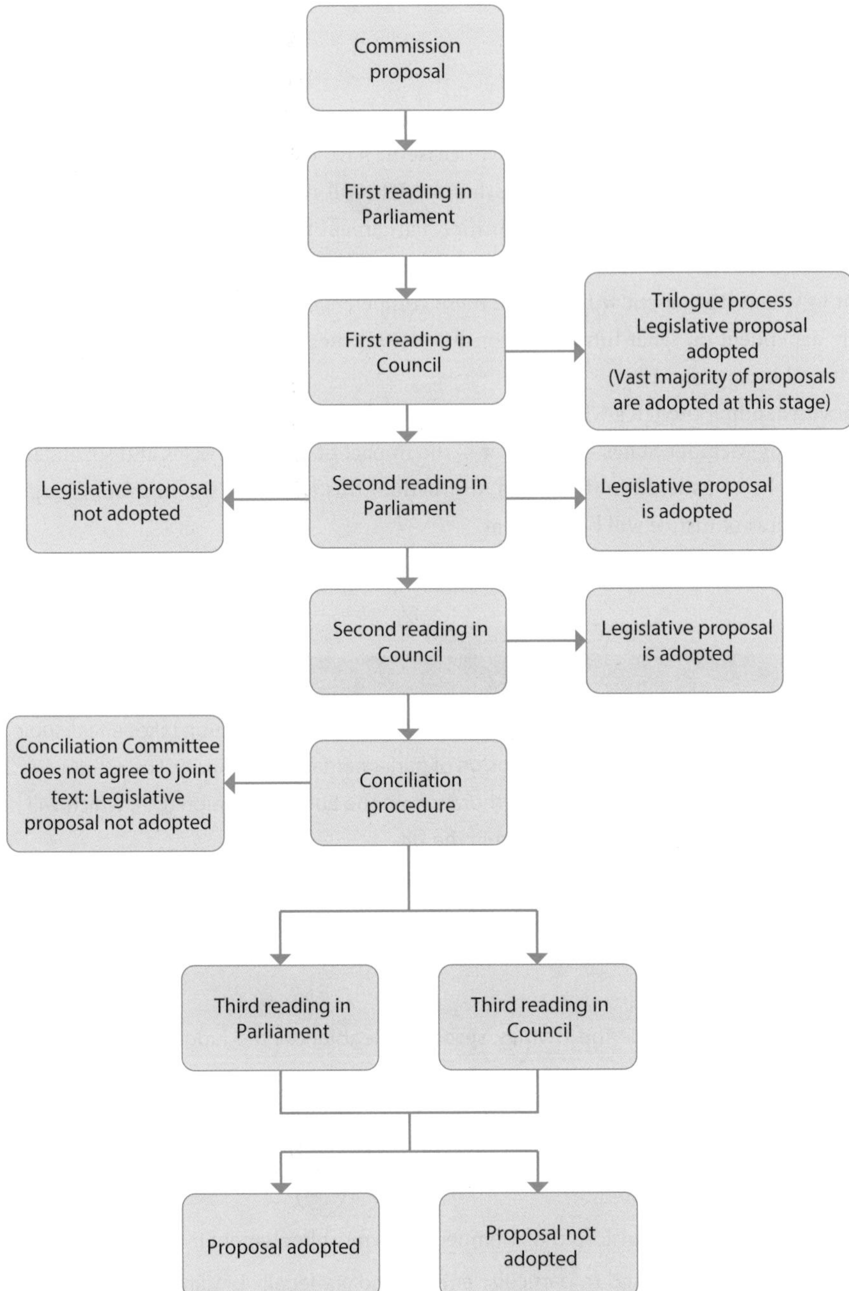

Figure 3.1 A summary of the ordinary legislative procedure

http://www.europarl.europa.eu/external/html/legislativeprocedure/default_en.htm © European Union, 2014 - Source: European Parliament, 2014. Responsibility for the adaptation lies entirely with the authors and publisher of the adapted figure.

protect its interests and reinforce its integration process'. Where Member States wish to engage in this cooperation, they may make use of the EU institutions. Articles 326–334 TFEU provide regulatory rules for the operation of enhanced cooperation, which will apply only to those participating Member States and not to all Member States.

3.6 Conclusions

Now that the UK has decided, by means of its 2016 referendum, to leave the EU, the key principle of the supremacy of EU law will cease to have effect once the withdrawal process is complete. In practice, this will mean that the UK will no longer be bound by EU legislation or the jurisdiction of the Court of Justice. Parliament will regain full legislative authority over those competences that were previously exercised at the EU level. However, the precise extent to which Parliament will exercise these competences independently of EU law will be largely dependent on what future relationship the UK negotiates with the EU as part of the withdrawal arrangements.

Notwithstanding the UK's withdrawal, EU law will continue to have the same effect within the remaining Member States. In Chapter 4, the impact of Treaty Articles and secondary legislation will be considered in detail and, throughout this textbook, the impact of judgments from the Court of Justice will be apparent.

SUMMARY

- The European Communities Act 1972 provides that future UK legislation takes effect subject to EU law. This represents a significant erosion of parliamentary sovereignty. The result of its 2016 referendum means that the UK will withdraw from the European Union (EU), which will bring to an end the supremacy of EU law within the UK.
- The powers of the EU are granted to it by the Member States in the Treaty on European Union (TEU) and the Treaty on the Functioning of the European Union (TFEU). These powers are subject to many limitations, including those laid down expressly in the Treaties and principles such as subsidiarity.
- Sources of EU law include the Treaties, secondary legislation, the judgments of the Court of Justice, and general principles laid down by the Court.
- Secondary legislation comprises Regulations, Directives, and Decisions.
  - Regulations are directly applicable, apply in a uniform manner, and have the force of law as soon as they are adopted.
  - Directives set out provisions that Member States must implement into national law.
  - Decisions are addressed to particular entities and are legally binding on them as soon as they are adopted.
- Law-making procedures in the EU include the ordinary legislative procedure (OLP) and the special legislative procedure.
- The OLP applies to the vast majority of activity areas. The decision on a legislative act must be made jointly by the European Parliament and Council.
- Enhanced cooperation allows a smaller group of Member States, as opposed to the entire EU membership, to take action within the framework of the EU.

FURTHER READING

Articles

A Cygan, 'The Parliamentarisation of EU Decision-Making? The Impact of the Treaty of Lisbon on National Parliaments' (2011) 36(4) EL Rev 480

Examines the role of national parliaments in monitoring subsidiarity post-Lisbon.

J Snell, ' "European Constitutional Settlement": An Ever Closer Union, and the Treaty of Lisbon—Democracy or Relevance?' (2008) 33 EL Rev 619

Examines whether a democratic deficit still exists within the EU.

QUESTION

Why has the supremacy of EU law proved so important for the process of EU integration?

To view an outline answer to this question plus further resources to support your EU law studies, visit the Online Resources for this book at www.oup.com/uk/eulaw-complete4e

4 Enforcing EU law rights in national courts

KEY POINTS

By the end of this chapter, you should be able to:

- understand and analyse the development and meaning of the concept of direct effect;
- explain the concept of indirect effect and the way in which it has been interpreted and applied by the courts;
- explain generally the rights of an individual or business to rely on a provision of EU law in their national courts;
- identify and explain the rules that apply to the grant of remedies for breach of EU law; and
- analyse (in conjunction with Chapter 5) the relationship between direct and indirect effect, and State liability.

INTRODUCTION

The ability of individuals and businesses to rely on their rights under EU law, and to enforce them in national courts, is an essential feature of the integrated legal system set up by the European Union (EU). Although the Court of Justice is the supreme authority on the interpretation of EU law, the national courts that form the lower tiers of the EU law system must also be able to apply EU law if the rights contained in it are to be effective in practice.

Whether it is possible for an applicant to enforce their EU rights depends primarily on whether either (or both) of two concepts developed by the Court of Justice apply: direct effect or indirect effect. Although both have limitations and neither guarantees an ultimate remedy, they do provide those intended to benefit from rights under EU law with the opportunity to make those rights real.

If an applicant is successful in the national courts in establishing a breach of EU law, whether through direct effect (see 4.1) or indirect effect (see 4.2)—or, indeed, through a separate action for State liability (see Chapter 5)—the remedy that will be awarded is governed principally by national law. However, the problem that this poses for the uniform application of EU law, and the effectiveness of rights granted by it, has led the Court of Justice to develop a number of principles with which national courts must comply when awarding a remedy (see 4.3).

4.1 Direct effect

direct effect
According to the Court of Justice, a measure that has direct effect is one that is capable of direct enforcement in national courts.

The Court of Justice ruled as early as 1963, in Case 26/62 *Van Gend en Loos v Nederlandse Administratie der Belastingen* [1963] ECR 1, that in order for rights under EU law to be effective, they must be capable of **direct effect**.

Before discussing direct effect in detail, it is important to distinguish between direct applicability (see Chapter 3) and direct effect.

?! THINKING POINT

What does 'directly applicable' mean in the context of EU law? If you cannot remember, look back at Chapter 3.

EU law is part of a Member State's legal system and some EU laws are said to be 'directly applicable' in the sense that they become part of a Member State's law without the need for them to be transposed into national law. For example, Treaties, Regulations, and Decisions are all directly applicable, whereas Directives are not (see further 3.4.2 on these different forms of EU law).

Although all of these measures have been held by the Court of Justice to be in principle capable of direct effect (see 4.1.1), this is subject to the fulfilment of certain conditions (see 4.1.2). It might seem odd that not every provision of EU law is capable of judicial enforcement, but in practice the same is true of national law: not every provision of every statute or statutory instrument is directly enforceable by a particular individual or business.

4.1.1 The measures that may have direct effect

Article 288 TFEU (see further 3.4.2) provides that, in addition to the EU Treaties (see Chapter 1), the EU may exercise its powers through various other types of legislation: Treaty Articles, Regulations, Decisions, Directives, Recommendations, and Opinions. However, not all of these can have direct effect.

4.1.1.1 Treaty Articles

The case that first established the principle of direct effect, Case 26/62 *Van Gend en Loos v Nederlandse Administratie der Belastingen* [1963] ECR 1, concerned a Treaty Article. Van Gend en Loos was required by Dutch law to pay an increased customs duty on imports. It argued in the Dutch courts that this was a violation of what is now Article 30 TFEU, which provided, inter alia, that Member States should not increase such charges. The Dutch court referred to the Court of Justice the question of whether a litigant before a national court could rely directly on the provisions of an EU Treaty and, in particular, on Article 30 TFEU.

?! THINKING POINT

While reading the following extract, consider why the Court of Justice concluded that Treaty Articles must be capable of having direct effect.

Case 26/62 *Van Gend en Loos v Nederlandse Administratie der Belastingen* [1963] ECR 1, 11–12

The first question of the Tariefcommissie is whether Article 12 of the [EEC] Treaty [now Article 30 TFEU] has direct application in national law in the sense that nationals of Member States may on the basis of this Article lay claim to rights which the national court must protect.

To ascertain whether the provisions of an international treaty extend so far in their effects, it is necessary to consider the spirit, the general scheme, and the wording of those provisions.

The objective of the EEC Treaty, which is to establish a Common Market, the functioning of which is of direct concern to interested parties in the Community [now Union], implies that this Treaty is more than an agreement which merely creates mutual obligations between the contracting states. This view is confirmed by the Preamble to the Treaty which refers not only to governments but to peoples. It is also confirmed more specifically by the establishment of institutions endowed with sovereign rights, the exercise of which affects Member States and also their citizens. Furthermore, it must be noted that the nationals of the states brought together in the Community are called upon to cooperate in the functioning of this Community through the intermediary of the European Parliament and the Economic and Social Committee.

In addition the task assigned to the Court of Justice under Article 177 [EEC, now Article 267 TFEU], the object of which is to secure uniform interpretation of the Treaty by national courts and tribunals, confirms that the states have acknowledged that Community law [now EU law] has an authority which can be invoked by their nationals before those courts and tribunals.

The conclusion to be drawn from this is that the Community constitutes a new legal order of international law for the benefit of which the states have limited their sovereign rights, albeit within limited fields, and the subjects of which comprise not only Member States but also their nationals. Independently of the legislation of Member States, Community law therefore not only imposes obligations on individuals but is also intended to confer upon them rights which become part of their legal heritage. These rights arise not only where they are expressly granted by the Treaty, but also by reason of obligations which the Treaty imposes in a clearly defined way upon individuals as well as upon the Member States and upon the institutions of the Community.

In *Van Gend en Loos*, the Court of Justice established the principle of direct effect on the basis that EU law was intended to confer rights on individuals and that these rights must therefore be enforceable. After its ruling in *Van Gend en Loos*, the Court of Justice went on in other cases to extend the principle of direct effect to other types of measure.

4.1.1.2 Regulations

In Case 43/71 *Politi SAS v Ministero delle Finanze* [1973] ECR 1039, Italy had levied import taxes on pork, contrary to the provisions of an EU Regulation. An importer, Politi, sought to rely on the Regulation to challenge the Italian taxes. The Italian court made a reference to the Court of Justice under what is now Article 267 TFEU (see further Chapter 6 on the preliminary reference procedure). The Court of Justice ruled that EU Regulations could be directly effective because, by reason of their nature and function within the EU legal system, they created individual rights that national courts must protect.

4.1.1.3 Decisions

The direct effect of EU Decisions was recognized by the Court of Justice in Case 9/70 *Grad v Finanzamt Traunstein* [1970] ECR 825 (see also 4.1.3). A Decision provided for the replacement of national freight taxes by a common EU freight tax. A freight transporter sought to rely on the Decision to challenge a German freight tax. The German court made a reference to the Court of Justice under what is now Article 267 TFEU (see further Chapter 6 on the preliminary reference procedure). The Court of Justice ruled that since Decisions had binding effect, they must be capable of enforcement by those who were affected by them. The Court also adduced the argument that since what is now Article 267 TFEU permitted national courts to refer to the Court of Justice questions concerning 'all acts' of the EU institutions (see further Chapter 6 on Article 267 TFEU), this presupposed that those courts could in the first place apply 'all acts'. On the facts of the case, however, Grad lost because (unusually) this Decision stated that it did not come into effect until the date specified in it, and since that date had not yet passed, the Decision had not yet become directly effective.

4.1.1.4 Directives

As discussed at 3.4.2, Article 288 TFEU provides that Regulations and Decisions are, like Treaty Articles, binding in their entirety and that Regulations are, like Treaty Articles, directly applicable in the Member States (as are Decisions, although this is not explicitly stated). However, in contrast, Directives are binding on Member States only as to the result to be achieved. The detail of their transposition into national law is therefore left to the discretion of the Member States. Direct effect should therefore not be necessary, since it should be possible to rely, in a national court, on the particular national law that transposed the provisions of the Directive in question. Unfortunately, the position is not so simple, as a Member State may have adopted national transposing legislation that does not accurately reflect the objectives of the Directive or, indeed, it may have failed to adopt any transposing legislation at all. The Court of Justice has therefore recognized that, in certain circumstances, a Directive may have direct effect.

The case in which the concept of direct effect was first established in relation to Directives is Case 41/74 *Van Duyn v Home Office* [1974] ECR 1337. Van Duyn, a Dutch national, applied for permission to enter the UK to work for the Church of Scientology. As the UK authorities officially disapproved of this organization, permission was refused under what is now Article 45 TFEU (see further 11.2.1), which allowed Member States to derogate on public policy grounds from the right to freedom of movement for workers. Van Duyn sought to enforce Council Directive 64/221/EEC of 25 February 1964 on the co-ordination of special measures concerning the movement and residence of foreign nationals which are justified on grounds of public policy, public security or public health, OJ 1964 56/850, which stated that such derogations could be based only on the personal conduct of the applicant.

?! **THINKING POINT**

While reading the following extract, consider why the Court of Justice considered that it should be possible to enforce a Directive directly.

Case 41/74 *Van Duyn v Home Office* [1974] ECR 1337

11. The United Kingdom observes that, since Article 189 of the [EEC] Treaty [now Article 288 TFEU] distinguishes between the effects ascribed to regulations, directives and decisions, it must therefore be presumed that the Council, in issuing a directive rather than making a regulation, must have intended that the directive should have an effect other than that of a regulation and accordingly that the former should not be directly applicable.
12. If, however, by virtue of the provisions of Article 189 regulations are directly applicable and, consequently, may by their very nature have direct effects, it does not follow from this that other categories of acts mentioned in that Article can never have similar effects. It would be incompatible with the binding effect attributed to a directive by Article 189 to exclude, in principle, the possibility that the obligation which it imposes may be invoked by those concerned. In particular, where the Community [now Union] authorities have, by directive, imposed on Member States the obligation to pursue a particular course of conduct, the useful effect of such an act would be weakened if individuals were prevented from relying on it before their national courts and if the latter were prevented from taking it into consideration as an element of Community law [now EU law]. Article 177 [EEC, now Article 267 TFEU], which empowers national courts to refer to the Court questions concerning the validity and interpretation of all acts of the Community institutions, without distinction, implies furthermore that these acts may be invoked by individuals in the national courts. It is necessary to examine, in every case, whether the nature, general scheme and wording of the provision in question are capable of having direct effects on the relations between Member States and individuals.

The Court of Justice held that it was possible to rely directly on a Directive to enforce rights contained in it. It reasoned that in order for Directives to have a useful effect, they must be capable of producing direct effects, subject to the nature and wording of the Directive in question.

On the facts, Van Duyn lost because the Court held that personal conduct could include membership of a particular organization (see 11.3.1).

4.1.1.5 Recommendations and Opinions

THINKING POINT

Given that Article 288 TFEU provides that neither Recommendations nor Opinions have binding legal force (see 3.4.2), do you think that they should be capable of having direct effect?

The key case on whether an EU Recommendation (or Opinion) can have direct effect is Case C-322/88 *Grimaldi v Fonds des Maladies Professionnelles* [1989] ECR 4407 (see also 4.2.1 and 3.4.2). Grimaldi suffered from a disease that was classified under an EU Recommendation as an occupational disease, thereby entitling him to compensation. Under French law, however, it was not so classified and therefore, under that law, Grimaldi was not entitled to any compensation. Grimaldi sought to rely directly on the provisions of the Recommendation. The French court made a preliminary reference to the Court of Justice under what is now Article 267 TFEU (see further Chapter 6 on the preliminary reference procedure).

The Court of Justice ruled in *Grimaldi* that since Recommendations were not intended to have binding legal effect, it would clearly be inappropriate for them to have direct effect. Grimaldi could therefore not rely directly on the Recommendation.

The same applies, *mutatis mutandis*, to Opinions.

4.1.2 The condition for the direct effect of Treaty Articles and Regulations

The conditions that must be satisfied in order for a particular piece of EU law to have direct effect vary according to the type of EU law at issue. The position in relation to Treaty Articles and Regulations is relatively simple: the only precondition for any of these measures to have direct effect is that the provision in question must be sufficiently clear, precise, and unconditional for reliance to be placed on it in the national courts.

A measure may be sufficiently clear even if its precise scope requires interpretation by the Court of Justice under the preliminary reference procedure (see further Chapter 6 on the preliminary reference procedure).

?! THINKING POINT

While reading the following extract, consider why the Court of Justice concluded that the particular Treaty Article at issue had direct effect.

Case 26/62 *Van Gend en Loos v Nederlandse Administratie der Belastingen* [1963] ECR 1, 12–13

With regard to the general scheme of the Treaty as it relates to customs duties and charges having equivalent effect it must be emphasized that Article 9 [EEC, now Article 28 TFEU], which bases the Community [now the Union] upon a customs union, includes as an essential provision the prohibition of these customs duties and charges. This provision is found at the beginning of the part of the Treaty which defines the 'Foundations of the Community'. It is applied and explained by Article 12 [EEC, now Article 30 TFEU].

The wording of Article 12 contains a clear and unconditional prohibition which is not a positive but a negative obligation. This obligation, moreover, is not qualified by any reservation on the part of states which would make its implementation conditional upon a positive legislative measure enacted under national law. The very nature of this prohibition makes it ideally adapted to produce direct effects in the legal relationship between Member States and their subjects. The implementation of Article 12 does not require any legislative intervention on the part of the states. The fact that under this Article it is the Member States who are made the subject of the negative obligation does not imply that their nationals cannot benefit from this obligation.

[...]

It follows from the foregoing considerations that, according to the spirit, the general scheme and the wording of the Treaty, Article 12 must be interpreted as producing direct effects and creating individual rights which national courts must protect.

In *Van Gend en Loos*, the Court of Justice ruled that the statement in the Treaty Article at issue, that 'Member States shall refrain from introducing any new customs duties ... and from increasing those which they already apply ... ', imposed a clear prohibition on such measures that was not conditional on Member States adopting national measures.

It is not necessary for an EU law to be clear in its entirety for direct effect to apply, but only the rights that are sufficiently clear are capable of having direct effect. An example of this is provided by Case 43/75 *Defrenne v SABENA* [1976] ECR 455, which involved a dispute over the policy of the Belgian airline SABENA to pay its female cabin crew less than its male crew and compulsorily retire them at a younger age. Defrenne, a female member of cabin crew employed by SABENA, claimed that this infringed the principle of equality contained in what is now Article 157 TFEU. The Belgian court made a preliminary reference to the Court of Justice under Article 267 TFEU (see further Chapter 6 on the preliminary reference procedure) as to the effect of what is now Article 157 TFEU.

?! THINKING POINT

While reading the following extract, consider which elements of what is now Article 157 TFEU the Court of Justice considered to be clear and which it did not.

Case 43/75 *Defrenne v SABENA* [1976] ECR 455

18. For the purposes of the implementation of these provisions a distinction must be drawn within the whole area of application of Article 119 [EEC, now Article 157 TFEU] between, first, direct and overt discrimination which may be identified solely with the aid of the criteria based on equal work and equal pay referred to by the article in question and, secondly, indirect and disguised discrimination which can only be identified by reference to more explicit implementing provisions of a Community [now Union] or national character.

[...]

> 21. Among the forms of direct discrimination which may be identified solely by reference to the criteria laid down by Article 119 must be included in particular those which have their origin in legislative provisions or in collective labour agreements and which may be detected on the basis of a purely legal analysis of the situation.
> 22. This applies even more in cases where men and women receive unequal pay for equal work carried out in the same establishment or service, whether public or private.
> 23. As is shown by the very findings of the judgment making the reference, in such a situation the court is in a position to establish all the facts which enable it to decide whether a woman worker is receiving lower pay than a male worker performing the same tasks.
> 24. In such situation, at least, Article 119 is directly applicable and may thus give rise to individual rights which the courts must protect.

The Court of Justice held that what is now Article 157 TFEU imposed a clear and unconditional prohibition on direct discrimination (discrimination based directly on grounds of sex) and was directly effective to this extent. It noted, however, that it was not sufficiently clear in respect of more indirect discrimination (discrimination that was purportedly based on factors other than sex, but which resulted in discrimination between men and women), since it did not identify what might constitute such discrimination.

It is worth mentioning that the final paragraph of the extract from *Defrenne* (para 24) provides an example of the confusion in terminology that has sometimes arisen in this area. The Court of Justice concluded that, in certain circumstances, Article 119 EEC (now Article 157 TFEU) is 'directly applicable'. In fact, that Article—like all other Articles of the EU Treaties—is *always* directly applicable, meaning that it automatically becomes part of national law. What the Court meant was that it was capable of having direct effect, at least insofar as direct discrimination was concerned.

In *R (on the application of Bancoult) v Secretary of State for Foreign and Commonwealth Affairs* [2014] EWCA Civ 708, [2014] 1 WLR 2921, the applicant, a member of the native population of the Chagos Archipelago in the British Indian Ocean Territory, challenged the UK government's decision to remove them from the islands and prohibit them from returning, in order for the UK to use the islands for defence purposes. He sought to rely on Articles 198 and 199 TFEU, under which Members States agreed to associate countries and territories with which they had special relationships (known as Overseas Countries and Territories, or OCTs) with the EU, in order to promote their development, further their interests, and apply the same treatment to trade with them as was applied to trade between Member States. The Court of Appeal of England and Wales held that Articles 198 and 199 TFEU were statements of aspiration about the attainment of the objectives of association between OCTs and the EU; they were not about the detailed ways in which those objectives could be fulfilled, so as to constitute directly effective provisions of EU law.

Just like Treaty Articles, Regulations must be sufficiently clear and unconditional if they are to have direct effect. As Advocate General Warner stated, in Case 131/79 *R v Secretary of State for Home Affairs, ex p Santillo* [1980] ECR 1585, 1608: 'Unquestionably every provision of every regulation is directly applicable, but not every provision of every regulation has direct effect, in the sense of conferring on private persons rights enforceable by them in national courts.'

REVIEW QUESTION

Suppose that you have recently suffered from a respiratory infection contracted while swimming in polluted seawater off a beach in Ireland. Tests indicate that the water contains 2.5 per cent blisterium, a chemical known to produce respiratory infections. (Fictitious) Regulation 00/00 provides that the presence of any amount over 2 per cent leads to the awarding of compensation to anyone contracting infection as a consequence. How, if at all, could direct effect apply in this scenario?

Answer: A Regulation will have direct effect and thus be directly enforceable in the national courts if the Regulation is sufficiently clear, precise, and unconditional (*Politi*). (Fictitious) Regulation 00/00 is clear as to the prohibition, as it specifies the level and the substance. It also appears to be clear that compensation must be provided to anyone contracting infection as a consequence. However, it is not clear as to the amount or source of the compensation, and it therefore cannot have direct effect.

4.1.3 The conditions for the direct effect of Decisions

In Case 9/20 *Grad v Finanzamt Traunstein* [1970] ECR 825, para 9 (see also 4.1.1), the Court of Justice ruled that a Decision could have direct effect if it was 'unconditional and sufficiently clear and precise to be capable of creating direct effects'—in other words, subject to the same condition as Treaty Articles and Regulations (see further 4.1.2).

At the time of the judgment in *Grad*, what is now Article 288 TFEU (see further 3.4.2) provided for only one type of Decision, a Decision that had one or more addressees, and stated that such Decisions were binding on their addressee(s). However, as a result of amendments introduced by the Treaty of Lisbon (2007) (see further 1.18), Article 288 TFEU now provides both for this type of Decision and for Decisions that do not have an addressee. Decisions that do not have an addressee are, in that respect, similar to Treaty Articles and Regulations, and are subject to the same condition for direct effect as those types of EU law and as laid down in *Grad*—that is, if they are sufficiently clear and precise (as explained in the context of Treaty Articles and Regulations at 4.1.2).

However, there is an exception to the rule that a Decision, like a Treaty Article or a Regulation, will be directly effective if it is sufficiently clear and precise. The exception is that a Decision which is addressed to the Member States (as opposed to a business or individual) will have direct effect only if a second condition is satisfied. In C-80/06 *Carp v Ecorad* [2007] ECR I-4473, the Court of Justice held that a Decision which was addressed to the Member States was binding only on them and could not be relied upon against an individual or a business. It justified this ruling by reference to the same arguments that it had previously developed in relation to Directives (discussed at 4.1.4), since Directives are always addressed to the Member States. A Decision addressed to the Member States therefore has direct effect only if the following conditions are satisfied:

- it is sufficiently clear and precise (as explained in the context of Treaty Articles and Regulations at 4.1.2); and

- the defendant against whom it is being enforced is a Member State or an emanation of the State (as explained in the context of Directives at 4.1.4).

4.1.4 The conditions for the direct effect of Directives

The position with regard to Directives is rather different because of their nature (see 4.1.1 and Chapter 3). There are three conditions that must be satisfied in order for a provision of a Directive to have direct effect, one of which is the same as that applicable to Treaty Articles, Regulations, and Decisions (see 4.1.2 and 4.1.3):

- the provision must be sufficiently clear, precise, and unconditional;
- the deadline for transposition into national law must have passed; and
- the defendant must be an emanation of the State.

4.1.4.1 The provision must be sufficiently clear, precise, and unconditional

The first condition is broadly the same as that applicable to Treaty Articles, Regulations, and Decisions, although the requirement of unconditionality has been relaxed, since, of course, Directives always require implementation by Member States. The discussion at 4.1.2 and 4.1.3 is therefore relevant here, although in practice Directives are rather more likely to be unclear or imprecise because they (unlike Treaty Articles, Regulations, and Decisions) are not intended to become law exactly as they are written.

In Joined Cases C-6 & 9/90 *Francovich and others v Italy* [1991] ECR I-5357 (see also 5.2 and 5.3), the applicant wished to rely on Council Directive 80/987/EEC of 20 October 1980 on the approximation of the laws of the Member States relating to the protection of employees in the event of the insolvency of their employer, OJ 1980 L283/23, which provided that employees whose employers had become insolvent must be able to obtain compensation for unpaid wages, holiday pay, and other money owed to them by their employers. The Court of Justice examined whether the Directive was sufficiently clear to have direct effect in three respects: the identity of the persons intended to benefit from the compensation; the scope of that compensation; and the identity of the person or entity liable to provide the compensation.

?! THINKING POINT

While reading the following extract, consider in what respect the Court of Justice held the Directive to be unclear (and therefore to be incapable of having direct effect).

Joined Cases C-6 & 9/90 *Francovich and others v Italy* [1991] ECR I-5357

13. With regard first of all to the identity of the persons entitled to the guarantee, it must be observed that according to Article 1(1) the directive applies to employees' claims arising from contracts of employment or employment relationships and existing against employers who are in a state of insolvency within the meaning of Article 2(1); the latter provision defines the circumstances in which an employer must be deemed to be in a state of insolvency. Article 2(2) refers to national law for the definition of the concepts of 'employee' and 'employer'. Finally, Article 1(2) provides that the member-States may, by way of exception and under certain circumstances, exclude claims by certain categories of employees listed in the annex to the directive.

14. Those provisions are sufficiently precise and unconditional to enable the national court to determine whether or not a person should be regarded as a person intended to benefit under the directive …

[…]

18. In this case the result required by the directive in question is a guarantee that the outstanding claims of employees will be paid in the event of the insolvency of their employer. The fact that Articles 3 and 4(1) and (2) give the member-States some discretion as regards the means of establishing that guarantee and the restriction of its amount do not affect the precise and unconditional nature of the result required.

19. That is to say, as the Commission and the applicants have pointed out, it is possible to determine the minimum guarantee provided for by the directive by taking the date whose choice entails the least liability for the guarantee institution. That date is that of the onset of the employer's insolvency, since the two other dates, that is to say that of the notice of dismissal issued to the employee and that on which the contract of employment or the employment relationship was discontinued are, according to the conditions laid down in Article 3, necessarily subsequent to the onset of the insolvency and thus define a longer period in respect of which the payment of claims must be ensured.

20. With regard to the possibility under Article 4(2) of limiting that guarantee, it should be observed that such a possibility does not make it impossible to determine the minimum guarantee. It follows from the wording of that Article that the member-States have the option of limiting the guarantees granted to employees to certain periods prior to the date referred to in Article 3. Those periods are fixed in relation to each of the three dates provided for in Article 3, so that it is possible in any event to determine what extent the member-State could have reduced the guarantee provided for by the directive depending on the date which it would have chosen if it had transposed the directive.

21. As regards Article 4(3), according to which the member-States may set a ceiling on liability in order to avoid the payment of sums going beyond the social objective of the directive, and Article 10, which states that the directive does not affect the option of member-States to take the measures necessary to avoid abuses, it should be observed that a member-State

which has failed to fulfil its obligations to transpose a directive cannot defeat the rights which the directive creates for the benefit of individuals by relying on the option of limiting the amount of the guarantee which it could have exercised if it had taken the measures necessary to implement the directive: see, in relation to an analogous option concerning the prevention of abuse in fiscal matters, Case 8/81, *Becker v. Finanzamt Münster-Innenstadt* [[1982] ECR 53].

22. It must therefore be held that the provisions in question are unconditional and sufficiently precise as regards the content of the guarantee.

[...]

25. ... It follows from the terms of the directive that the member-State is required to organise an appropriate institutional guarantee system. Under Article 5 the member-State has a broad discretion with regard to the organisation, operation and financing of the guarantee institutions. The fact, referred to by the Commission, that the directive envisages as one possibility among others that such a system may be financed entirely by the public authorities cannot mean that the State can be identified as the person liable for unpaid claims. The payment obligation lies with the guarantee institutions, and it is only in exercising its power to organise the guarantee system that the State may provide that the guarantee institutions are to be financed entirely by the public authorities. In those circumstances the State takes on an obligation which in principle is not its own.

26. Accordingly, even though the provisions of the directive in question are sufficiently precise and unconditional as regards the determination of the persons entitled to the guarantee and as regards the content of that guarantee, those elements are not sufficient to enable individuals to rely on those provisions before the national courts. Those provisions do not identify the person liable to provide the guarantee, and the State cannot be considered liable on the sole ground that it has failed to take transposition measures within the prescribed period.

It is noteworthy that the existence of a choice in Directive 80/987 as to the period in respect of which compensation was payable did not make the Directive unclear, because a minimum period could be identified. Nor did the option given to Member States to set a limit on the total compensation payable to an individual prevent the Directive from possessing sufficient clarity, since the State's failure to exercise this option by passing the necessary legislation by the deadline for the transposition of the Directive meant that it had lost the right to do so (see 4.1.4.2 in relation to the expiry of the deadline). However, the lack of clarity as to the source of the compensation was fatal to the claim that the Directive had direct effect.

→ CROSS-REFERENCE
The Court of Justice in *Francovich* developed an entirely new route for the claimant to enforce their rights: see further Chapter 5.

The Court reached a different conclusion as to the direct effect of Directive 80/987 in Case C-441/99 *Riksskatteverket v Gharehveran* [2001] ECR I-7687 because, in that case, the Member State (Sweden) had made provision for compensation to be provided from public funds. The Court concluded that since the identity of the person liable to provide the compensation was, on the facts, clear (in contrast to the situation in *Francovich*), the Directive could have direct effect.

In C-176/12 *Association de Mediation Sociale v Union Locale des Syndicats CGT and others* [2014] 2 CMLR 41 (see also 4.1.5), the applicant sought to enforce Directive 2002/14/EC of the

European Parliament and of the Council of 11 March 2002 establishing a general framework for informing and consulting employees in the European Community, OJ 2002 L80/29, which stated that Member States must provide for employee information and consultation rights in undertakings with at least 50 employees, or establishments employing at least 20 employees, in any one Member State. On a preliminary reference by the French court (see further Chapter 6 on the preliminary reference procedure), the Court of Justice held that the Directive did not prescribe exactly how these thresholds were to be calculated, but did contain a clear definition of employees, and so imposed a directly effective prohibition on Member States from excluding such persons when calculating whether the threshold was reached.

All Directives include an obligation on Member States to transpose the rights contained in them into national law (see 3.4.2). Directives are therefore never unconditional in the sense that Member States are not required to take further action to implement the obligations contained in them (unlike Treaty Articles, Regulations, and Decisions). This, however, has not been an obstacle to the Court of Justice ruling that Directives can be sufficiently clear to have direct effect. For example, in Case 152/84 *Marshall v Southampton and South West Area Health Authority (Teaching) (No 1)* [1986] ECR 723, Marshall, a dietician, sought to rely on the provisions of Council Directive 76/207/EEC of 9 February 1976 on the implementation of the principle of equal treatment for men and women as regards access to employment, vocational training and promotion, and working conditions, OJ 1976 L39/40 (the Equal Treatment Directive), in opposing her enforced retirement at the age of 62, which was three years earlier than her male colleagues. She sought to rely on the Directive, which had not been properly transposed by the UK and which prohibited discrimination at work on grounds of sex. The UK court made a preliminary reference to the Court of Justice under Article 267 TFEU (see further Chapter 6 on the preliminary reference procedure). The Court held that the Directive was sufficiently unconditional to have direct effect.

Case 152/84 *Marshall v Southampton and South West Area Health Authority (Teaching) (No 1)* [1986] ECR 723

52. Finally, with regard to the question whether the provision contained in Article 5(1) of Directive 76/207, which implements the principle of equality of treatment set out in Article 2(1) of the directive, may be considered, as far as its contents are concerned, to be unconditional and sufficiently precise to be relied upon by an individual as against the State, it must be stated that the provision, taken by itself, prohibits any discrimination on grounds of sex with regard to working conditions, including the conditions governing dismissal, in a general manner and in unequivocal terms. The provision is therefore sufficiently precise to be relied on by an individual and to be applied by the national courts.
53. It is necessary to consider next whether the prohibition of discrimination laid down by the directive may be regarded as unconditional, in the light of the exceptions contained therein and of the fact that according to Article 5(2) thereof the Member States are to take the measures necessary to ensure the application of the principle of equality of treatment in the context of national law.

54. With regard, in the first place, to the reservation contained in Article 1(2) of Directive 76/207 concerning the application of the principle of equality of treatment in matters of social security, it must be observed that, although the reservation limits the scope of the directive *ratione materiae*, it does not lay down any condition on the application of that principle in its field of operation and in particular in relation to Article 5 of the directive. Similarly, the exceptions to Directive 76/207 provided for in Article 2 thereof are not relevant to this case.

55. It follows that Article 5 of Directive 76/207 does not confer on the Member States the right to limit the application of the principle of equality of treatment in its field of operation or to subject it to conditions and that that provision is sufficiently precise and unconditional to be capable of being relied upon by an individual before a national court in order to avoid the application of any national provision which does not conform to Article 5(1).

Neither does the need to seek clarification of the correct interpretation of a provision of EU law from the national courts or from the Court of Justice through the preliminary reference procedure (see further Chapter 6 on the preliminary reference procedure) prevent such a provision from being held to be sufficiently clear to have direct effect. This was expressly acknowledged by the Court of Justice in Case 41/74 *Van Duyn v Home Office* [1974] ECR 1337 (see 4.1.1) when considering whether Directive 64/221 was sufficiently clear and unconditional to have direct effect, as the following extract demonstrates.

Case 41/74 *Van Duyn v Home Office* [1974] ECR 1337

13. By providing that measures taken on grounds of public policy shall be based exclusively on the personal conduct of the individual concerned, Article 3(1) of Directive No. 64/221 is intended to limit the discretionary power which national laws generally confer on the authorities responsible for the entry and expulsion of foreign nationals. First, the provision lays down an obligation which is not subject to any exception or condition and which, by its very nature, does not require the intervention of any act on the part either of the institutions of the Community [now Union] or of Member States. Secondly, because Member States are thereby obliged, in implementing a clause which derogates from one of the fundamental principles of the Treaty in favour of individuals, not to take account of factors extraneous to personal conduct, legal certainty for the persons concerned requires that they should be able to rely on this obligation even though it has been laid down in a legislative act which has no automatic direct effect in its entirety.

14. If the meaning and exact scope of the provision raise questions of interpretation, these questions can be resolved by the courts, taking into account also the procedure under Article 177 of the [EEC] Treaty [now Article 267 TFEU].

15. Accordingly, in reply to the second question, Article 3(1) of Council Directive No. 64/221 of 25 February 1964 confers on individuals rights which are enforceable by them in the courts of a Member State and which the national courts must protect.

4.1.4.2 The deadline for transposition of national law must have passed

?! THINKING POINT

Why might giving effect to a Directive that a Member State has failed to transpose by the deadline for it to do so or has transposed incorrectly be necessary in order to ensure the effectiveness of EU law?

In Case 148/78 *Pubblico Ministero v Ratti* [1979] ECR 1629, Ratti's company had complied with Council Directive 77/728/EEC of 7 November 1977 on the approximation of the laws, regulations and administrative provisions of the Member States relating to the classification, packaging and labelling of paints, varnishes, printing inks, adhesives and similar products, OJ 1977 L303/23, as to the information to be supplied on labels on chemicals. However, Italy had failed to transpose the Directive into national law and prosecuted Ratti under its own, stricter, laws. The Italian court made a preliminary reference to the Court of Justice (see further Chapter 6 on the preliminary reference procedure).

The Court of Justice ruled that the Directive had not become directly effective because the deadline for its transposition had not passed. Until that time, it was not intended to have legal effect and Ratti could not rely on it.

If a Member State wishes to take advantage of the discretion provided by a Directive, it must pass transposing legislation to set out how this discretion will be exercised. If it does not, it cannot rely on an option provided in the Directive, as the Court explained in Joined Cases C-6 & 9/90 *Francovich and others v Italy* [1991] ECR I-5357 (see 4.1.4.1). For example, in *East Riding of Yorkshire Council v Gibson* [2000] 3 CMLR 329, a swimming instructor employed by a local authority sought to rely directly on the Working Time Directive (Council Directive 93/104/EC of 23 November 1993 concerning certain aspects of the organization of working time, OJ 1993 L307/18), which provided for four weeks' annual paid leave and which the UK had not transposed into national law by the deadline contained in it. The House of Lords (now the Supreme Court) held that the provision on paid leave was not directly effective. However, it stated that had the provision been directly effective, the local authority could not have relied on the option in the Directive permitting Member States to specify a three-week leave period, rather than four, during a transitional period, because the UK had failed to pass transposing legislation. It was not open to the State, or an emanation of it, to rely upon an option that it had not exercised.

It is worth noting that the Court of Justice has, albeit rarely, recognized exceptions to the requirement that a Directive cannot have direct effect until the deadline has passed.

First, if it is a principle of law of the Member State in question that more favourable (to the accused) criminal laws should apply retroactively, and the provisions of a particular Directive are capable of having direct effect, that Directive may be applied retroactively by the courts of that Member State even where the cause of action arose before the date set for compliance with the Directive. For example, in Case C-230/97 *Criminal proceedings against Ibiyinka Awoyemi*

[1998] ECR I-6781, the Court of Justice ruled that Council Directive 91/439/EEC of 29 July 1991 on driving licences, OJ 1991 L237/1, was directly effective because it was clear and precise, and the deadline date had passed (albeit after the cause of action arose). The Member State in question, Belgium, recognized the principle that more favourable provisions of criminal law had retroactive effect and therefore Awoyemi could rely on the more favourable, directly effective, provisions of the Directive even before the deadline for transposition of that Directive into national law had passed.

Secondly, if the Directive enshrines a general principle of EU law (see 3.4.5), then that general principle must be respected even before the deadline for transposition of the Directive into national law has passed, and a Member State should not enact or maintain legislation which conflicts with that principle. The leading case here is Case C-144/04 *Mangold v Helm* [2005] ECR I-9981. Mangold had been employed by Helm on a fixed-term contract when he was 56 years old. Under German law, a fixed-term contract need not be objectively justified if the employee was aged 52 or older. The deadline for transposition of Council Directive 2000/78/EC of 27 November 2000 establishing a general framework for equal treatment in employment and occupation, OJ 2000 L303/16, which laid down a general framework for prohibiting discrimination and provided that differences in treatment did not constitute discrimination if they were objectively justified, had not yet passed. The Court of Justice held that the German legislation could not be justified under the Directive and the fact that the deadline for transposition had not yet passed at the time at which the facts of the case arose did not affect that finding. It was settled law that Member States were obliged, prior to the deadline for transposition of a Directive, to 'refrain from taking any measures liable seriously to compromise the attainment of the result prescribed' by that Directive (*Mangold*, at para 67), since a Directive was binding on Member States as to the result to be achieved under Article 288 TFEU (see further 3.4.2). Furthermore, the principle of equal treatment was not laid down by the Directive in question; the prohibition on discrimination was a general principle of EU law stemming from international law and the constitutional traditions common to the Member States.

Strictly speaking, this second 'exception' is not really an exception to the conditions for direct effect, because what is being given effect ahead of the deadline for transposition is not the Directive, but the underlying general principle of EU law.

→ CROSS-REFERENCE
See also Case C-555/07 *Kücüdeveci* [2010] ECR I-365, discussed at 9.4.3.

REVIEW QUESTION

Suppose that you have recently suffered from a respiratory infection contracted while swimming in polluted seawater off a beach in Ireland. Tests indicate that the water contains 2.5 per cent blisterium, a chemical known to produce respiratory infections. (Fictitious) Directive 00/00 provides that the presence of any amount over 2 per cent leads to the awarding of compensation to anyone contracting infection as a consequence. How, if at all, could direct effect apply in this scenario?

Answer: The comments made in the previous review question would apply equally here, but with the authority of, for example, *Van Duyn* rather than *Politi*, because a Directive rather than a Regulation is at issue.

However, there are two further conditions that must be satisfied in order for a Directive to have direct effect:

- the deadline set out in the Directive for its transposition must have passed (*Ratti*); and
- the defendant must be the State or an emanation thereof (see 4.1.4.3).

The deadline for transposition is not specified and it would be necessary to check the full text of the Directive to ascertain this, but, given that the (fictitious) Directive dates from 2000, it is highly likely that it has passed. If it has passed, then the Directive is capable of direct effect if the other two conditions are met. If it has not passed, then the Directive is not capable of direct effect. Ireland would still be under an obligation to refrain from measures liable to compromise the objectives of the Directive (*Mangold*), but the facts here do not disclose that it is acting in breach of this obligation.

4.1.4.3 The defendant must be the State or an emanation of the State

Directives can only have what is sometimes referred to as 'vertical' direct effect—in other words, they can have direct effect only in proceedings brought by an individual or business against the State (or an authority or 'emanation' of the State). This can be contrasted with the concept of 'horizontal' direct effect, which is where an EU measure has direct effect in proceedings brought by an individual or business against another individual or business. Treaty Articles, Regulations, and Decisions can have horizontal, as well as vertical, direct effect and therefore the distinction is not meaningful when discussing them.

?! THINKING POINT

What gap does this leave in the protection of rights under EU law?

The case that clearly established this principle was Case 152/84 *Marshall v Southampton and South West Area Health Authority (Teaching) (No 1)* [1986] ECR 723 (see 4.1.4.1 for the facts of *Marshall*), in which the Court of Justice ruled that the Equal Treatment Directive was directly effective against the defendant in the case (the employer health authority).

Case 152/84 *Marshall v Southampton and South West Area Health Authority (Teaching) (No 1)* [1986] ECR 723

46. It is necessary to recall that, according to a long line of decisions of the Court (in particular its judgment in Case 8/81, *Becker v Finanzamt Münster-Innenstadt* [1982] ECR 53), wherever the provisions of a directive appear, as far as their subject-matter is concerned, to be unconditional and sufficiently precise, those provisions may be relied upon by an individual against the State where that State fails to implement the directive in national law by the end of the period prescribed or where it fails to implement the directive correctly.
47. That view is based on the consideration that it would be incompatible with the binding nature which Article 189 [EEC, now Article 288 TFEU] confers on the directive to hold as a matter of principle that the obligation imposed thereby cannot be relied on by those concerned. From that the Court deduced that a Member State which has not adopted the implementing measures required by the directive within the prescribed

period may not plead, as against individuals, its own failure to perform the obligations which the directive entails.

48. With regard to the argument that a directive may not be relied upon against an individual, it must be emphasized that according to Article 189 of the EEC Treaty the binding nature of a directive, which constitutes the basis for the possibility of relying on the directive before a national court, exists only in relation to 'each Member State to which it is addressed'. It follows that a directive may not of itself impose obligations on an individual and that a provision of a directive may not be relied upon as such against such a person. It must therefore be examined whether, in this case, the respondent must be regarded as having acted as an individual.

49. In that respect it must be pointed out that where a person involved in legal proceedings is able to rely on a directive as against the State he may do so regardless of the capacity in which the latter is acting, whether as employer or public authority. In either case it is necessary to prevent the State from taking advantage of its own failure to comply with Community law [now EU law].

50. It is for the national court to apply those considerations to the circumstances of each case; the Court of Appeal has, however, stated in the order for reference that the respondent, Southampton and South West Hampshire Area Health Authority (Teaching), is a public authority.

51. The argument submitted by the United Kingdom that the possibility of relying on provisions of the directive against the respondent qua organ of the State would give rise to an arbitrary and unfair distinction between the rights of State employees and those of private employees does not justify any other conclusion. Such a distinction may easily be avoided if the Member State concerned has correctly implemented the directive in national law.

[...]

56. Consequently, the answer to the second question must be that Article 5(1) of Council Directive 76/207, which prohibits any discrimination on grounds of sex with regard to working conditions, including the conditions governing dismissal, may be relied upon as against a State authority acting in its capacity as employer, in order to avoid the application of any national provision which does not conform to Article 5(1).

The Court of Justice held that Directives were binding only against a Member State and its authorities, although the *capacity* in which the State or authority thereof acted, for example whether as public authority or employer, was irrelevant. The Court of Justice ruled out the possibility of horizontal direct effect on the grounds that the binding nature of a Directive applied only to its Member State addressee(s). A Directive could not impose obligations on an individual and should not be relied upon against them. However, since this defendant was 'a public authority' (*Marshall*, at para 50), *and* the Directive was sufficiently clear, precise, and unconditional to have direct effect, *and* its deadline for transposition had passed (*Marshall*, at para 46), Marshall succeeded in her claim.

The Court of Justice restated this position in Case C-91/92 *Faccini Dori v Recreb Srl* [1994] ECR I-3325, despite the Opinion of Advocate General Lenz in that case (see further 2.4.1 on Advocate Generals' Opinions) in which he persuasively argued that Directives should have horizontal direct effect.

?! **THINKING POINT**

While reading the following extract, consider which you find more compelling: the Advocate General's arguments in favour of the horizontal direct effect of Directives or the arguments that he acknowledges against it.

Case C-91/92 *Faccini Dori v Recreb Srl* [1994] ECR I-3325, Opinion of Advocate General Lenz

(2) Horizontal applicability of directives

43. The answer afforded by the court's consistent case law to the question as to the effects of an unimplemented directive on legal relations between private persons—also known as horizontal effect—is straightforward and clear: a directive may not of itself impose obligations on an individual.

[...]

47. However, such an approach appears unsatisfactory to me ...

48. Considerations favouring the horizontal effect of directives reflect a drive to do justice by the beneficiary of a provision which the Community [now Union] legislator intended to be binding and not to abandon his situation for an indefinite period to the whim of a member state in default of its obligations.

[...]

50. Foremost among the arguments in favour of directives having horizontal effect is that relating to equality of the conditions of competition. Moreover, in the absence of horizontal effect, persons in member states which comply with Community law [now EU law] are frequently placed at a disadvantage.

51. The principle of the prohibition of discrimination, which ranks as a fundamental right, also militates in favour of directives being given horizontal effect, from several points of view. First, it is unsatisfactory that individuals should be subject to different rules, depending on whether they have comparable legal relations with a body connected with the state or with a private individual. Secondly, it is contrary to the requirements of an internal market for individuals to be subject to different laws in the various member states even though harmonising measures have been adopted by the Community.

[...]

54. In the case of directives whose content is intended to have effects in relations between private persons and which embody provisions designed to protect the weaker party it

is obvious that the failure to transpose a directive deprives it of *effet utile*. Following the expiry of the period for transposition, the application of protective provisions with precise and unconditional content should be possible …

[…]

57. Although horizontal direct effect of directives appears desirable for the reasons given above, substantial arguments exist against such a change in the case law.

58. Reference is made regularly in those arguments to the wording of art 189 of the [EEC] Treaty [now Article 288 TFEU] and to the nature of directives, which are binding only on member states and then only as to the results to be achieved.

59. In my view, those arguments can be refuted. As regards in the first place the freedom given to the member states as to the choice of the form and methods for implementing directives, that freedom is completely unaffected until the transitional period expires. Even after that, the member states retain—also where individual provisions have direct effect—leeway wherever that is intended by the directive. Only a fraction of provisions of directives will lend themselves to horizontal applicability. For the rest, the member states are not entitled to invoke, after the expiry of the period for transposition, freedoms which were conferred on them only for the purposes of the due implementation of the directive within the time limit laid down.

[…]

67. The principle of legitimate expectations is invoked in favour of private individuals on whom a burden is imposed and against the horizontal effect of directives. Expectations deserving of protection certainly exist, in so far as a private individual does not have to reckon with the imposition of additional burdens provided that he acts lawfully within the context of his national legal system. On the other hand, once a directive has been published and the period for transposition has expired, the burden is foreseeable. I would ask whether the expectation that the national legislature will act contrary to Community law is worthy of protection.

68. An argument based on the democratic principle is put forward against the horizontal effect of directives. According to that argument, the democratic deficit, which is deplored in any event in the context of Community legislation, is increased where national parliaments are bypassed when directives are implemented.

[…]

70. The national legislature has every freedom during the period for transposition to choose the form and means of transposing the directive into national law (see *Grad* [Case 9/70 *Grad v Finanzamt Traunstein*] [1970] ECR 825 at 839 (para 13)). Even after the period for transposition has elapsed, the obligation on the national legislature to transpose the directive continues to exist, as well as leeway to fulfil that obligation in one way or another to the extent permitted by the directive (see *EC Commission v Belgium* Case 102/79 [1980] ECR 1473 at 1487 (para 12)). Only provisions of directives or protective rules which are sufficiently precise to be asserted without being fleshed out in any way and therefore have to be taken over by the national legislature would have legal effects as between the addressees of the legislation in question within the national legal system …

71. The objection that recognition of the horizontal direct effect of directives would increase member state's carelessness in transposing them does not convince me, since the national legislature remains responsible for their implementation in full. Recognition in principle of horizontal effect might possibly encourage member states to effect transposition within the prescribed period in order to forestall horizontal application by the authorities and courts of the Community and the member states. In my view, the arguments on the educative effect of horizontal applicability balance themselves out and hence do not tip the balance for or against.

[...]

73. ... horizontal effect seems to me to be necessary, subject to the limits mentioned, in the interests of the uniform, effective application of Community law. In my view, the resulting burdens on private individuals are reasonable, since they do not exceed the constraints which would have been applied to them if the member state concerned had acted in conformity with Community law. Lastly, it is the party relying on the unconditional and sufficiently precise provision of a directive who will have to bear the risk of the court proceedings.

The bodies that may be included in the definition of the State for this purpose have come to be known as 'emanations of the State'. The leading case on what constitutes an authority or emanation of the State for the purposes of the direct effect of Directives is Case C-188/89 *Foster v British Gas* [1990] ECR I-3313. British Gas employees were compulsorily retired at the age of 60 if female, but at 65 if male. In accordance with this retirement policy, Mrs Foster was compulsorily retired by British Gas at the age of 60. She alleged that this was contrary to the Equal Treatment Directive (see 4.1.4.1, in relation to *Marshall* and *Johnston*). A preliminary reference was made by the national court under Article 267 TFEU (see further Chapter 6 on the preliminary reference procedure).

The Court of Justice ruled that, as the deadline for transposition of the Directive had passed without appropriate measures having been taken by the UK, the Directive itself could be directly effective. It relied on *Marshall* as authority for the proposition that the State could not take advantage of its own failure to transpose a Directive.

?! THINKING POINT

While reading the following extract, consider:

(a) how the Court of Justice defined an authority or emanation of the State and how this prevents the State from taking advantage of its own failure to transpose a Directive; and

(b) what potential unfairness results from this principle and why the Court of Justice considered that the defendant State was not in a position to complain about this.

Case C-188/89 *Foster v British Gas plc* [1990] ECR I-3313

16. As the Court has consistently held (see *Becker v Finanzamt Münster-Innenstadt* (Case 8/81) [1982] ECR 53) where the Community [now the Union] authorities have, by means of a directive, placed Member States under a duty to adopt a certain course of action, the effectiveness of such a measure would be diminished if persons were prevented from relying upon it in proceedings before a court and national courts were prevented from taking it into consideration as an element of Community law [now EU law]. Consequently, a Member State which has not adopted the implementing measures required by the directive within the prescribed period may not plead, as against individuals, its own failure to perform the obligations which the directive entails. Thus, wherever the provisions of a directive appear, as far as their subject-matter is concerned, to be unconditional and sufficiently precise, those provisions may, in the absence of implementing measures adopted within the prescribed period, be relied upon as against any national provision which is incompatible with the directive or in so far as the provisions define rights which individuals are able to assert against the State.
17. The Court further held in *Marshall* [Case 152/84 *Marshall v Southampton and South West Area Health Authority (Teaching) (No 1)* [1986] ECR 723], at paragraph 49, that where a person is able to rely on a directive as against the State he may do so regardless of the capacity in which the latter is acting, whether as employer or as public authority. In either case it is necessary to prevent the State from taking advantage of its own failure to comply with Community law.
18. On the basis of those considerations, the Court has held in a series of cases that unconditional and sufficiently precise provisions of a directive could be relied on against organizations or bodies which were subject to the authority or control of the State or had special powers beyond those which result from the normal rules applicable to relations between individuals.
19. The Court has accordingly held that provisions of a directive could be relied on against tax authorities (Case 8/81, *Becker*, and Case C-221/88, *ECSC v Acciaierie E Ferriere Busseni* [1990] ECR I-495), local or regional authorities (Case 103/88, *Fratelli Costanzo v Comune Di Milano* [1989] ECR 1839), constitutionally independent authorities responsible for the maintenance of public order and safety (Case 222/84, *Johnston v Chief Constable of the Royal Ulster Constabulary* [1986] ECR 1651), and public authorities providing public health services (Case 152/84, *Marshall*).
20. It follows from the foregoing that a body, whatever its legal form, which has been made responsible, pursuant to a measure adopted by the State, for providing a public service under the control of the State and has for that purpose special powers beyond those which result from the normal rules applicable in relations between individuals is included in any event among the bodies against which the provisions of a directive capable of having direct effect may be relied upon.

21. With regard to Article 5(1) of Directive 76/207 it should be observed that in Case 152/84, *Marshall* at paragraph 52, the Court held that that provision was unconditional and sufficiently precise to be relied on by an individual and to be applied by the national courts.

22. The answer to the question referred by the House of Lords must therefore be that Article 5(1) of Council Directive 76/207 of 9 February 1976 may be relied upon in a claim for damages against a body, whatever its legal form, which has been made responsible, pursuant to a measure adopted by the State, for providing a public service under the control of the State and has for that purpose special powers beyond those which result from the normal rules applicable in relations between individuals.

The Court of Justice held that the Directive could be relied upon against British Gas because it was an emanation of the Member State. This was because it satisfied the following three criteria.

- It had been made responsible by the State for providing a public service.
- It provided that service under the control of the State.
- It had been given special powers to provide that service beyond those normally applicable in relations between individuals.

For many years, it was assumed—on the basis of para 20 of the judgment, which uses the word 'and' to connect the three parts of the test—that all three elements of the test in *Foster* must be proved. However, in the recent case C-413/15 *Farrell v Whitty and others* EU:C:2017:745, the Court of Justice stated that para 20 of *Foster* must be read in the light of para 18 of that judgment, in which the three parts of the test were connected by the word 'or', suggesting that they were alternatives. The Court in *Farrell* therefore concluded that the three parts of the test were not cumulative and that a Directive may be capable of having direct effect against a body that does not satisfy all three requirements.

Case C-413/15 *Farrell v Whitty and others* EU:C:2017:745

22 By its first question, the referring court seeks, in essence, to ascertain whether Article 288 TFEU must be interpreted as not precluding the possibility that the provisions of a directive that are capable of having direct effect may be relied upon against a body which does not display all the characteristics listed in paragraph 20 of the judgment of 12 July 1990, *Foster and Others* (C-188/89, EU:C:1990:313).

23 In paragraphs 3 to 5 of that judgment, the Court stated that the body concerned in the case that gave rise to that judgment, namely the British Gas Corporation, was a 'statutory corporation', 'responsible for developing and maintaining a system of gas supply in Great Britain, and had a monopoly of the supply of gas', and '[its] members … were appointed by the competent Secretary of State [who] also had the power to give [British Gas] directions

of a general character in relation to matters affecting the national interest and instructions concerning its management', and that British Gas had the right 'with the consent of the Secretary of State, to submit proposed legislation to Parliament'.

24 In that context, the Court stated in paragraph 18 of that judgment that it had 'held in a series of cases that unconditional and sufficiently precise provisions of a directive could be relied on against organisations or bodies which were subject to the authority or control of the State or had special powers beyond those which result from the normal rules applicable to relations between individuals'.

25 The Court concluded, in paragraph 20 of that judgment, that 'a body, whatever its legal form, which has been made responsible, pursuant to a measure adopted by the State, for providing a public service under the control of the State and has for that purpose special powers beyond those which result from the normal rules applicable in relations between individuals is included in any event among the bodies against which the provisions of a directive capable of having direct effect may be relied upon'.

26 As the Advocate General stated in point 50 of her Opinion, the fact that the Court chose in paragraph 20 of the judgment of 12 July 1990, *Foster and Others* (C-188/89, EU:C:1990:313) to use the words 'is included in any event among the bodies' confirms that the Court was not attempting to formulate a general test designed to cover all situations in which a body might be one against which the provisions of a directive capable of having direct effect might be relied upon, but rather was holding that a body such as that concerned in the case that gave rise to that judgment must, in any event, be considered to be such a body, since it displays all the characteristics listed in paragraph 20.

27 Paragraph 20 of that judgment must be read in the light of paragraph 18 of the same judgment, where the Court stated that such provisions can be relied on by an individual against organisations or bodies which are subject to the authority or control of the State or have special powers beyond those which result from the normal rules applicable to relations between individuals.

28 Accordingly, as stated, in essence, by the Advocate General in points 53 and 77 of her Opinion, the conditions that the organisation concerned must, respectively, be subject to the authority or control of the State, and must possess special powers beyond those which result from the normal rules applicable to relations between individuals cannot be conjunctive (see, to that effect, judgments of 4 December 1997, *Kampelmann and Others*, C-253/96 to C-258/96, EU:C:1997:585, paragraphs 46 and 47, and of 7 September 2006, *Vassallo*, C-180/04, EU:C:2006:518, paragraph 26).

29 In the light of the foregoing, the answer to the first question is that Article 288 TFEU must be interpreted as meaning that it does not, in itself, preclude the possibility that provisions of a directive that are capable of having direct effect may be relied on against a body that does not display all the characteristics listed in paragraph 20 of the judgment of 12 July 1990, *Foster and Others* (C-188/89, EU:C:1990:313), read together with those mentioned in paragraph 18 of that judgment.

Note the Court's assertion in para 26 of its judgment in *Farrell* that it had not, in *Foster*, been attempting to formulate a conclusive test for whether any particular body was an emanation of the State. It is perhaps a pity that the Court did not see fit to make this clearer at an earlier point in the almost 30 years that elapsed between its judgment in *Foster* and its judgment in *Farrell*.

The Court in *Farrell* went on to reiterate the general principles underlying direct effect.

?! **THINKING POINT**

Read the following extract from *Farrell* set out below and try to summarize these principles.

Case C-413/15 *Farrell v Whitty and others* EU:C:2017:745

30 By its second and third questions, which can be examined together, the referring court seeks, in essence, to ascertain whether there is a fundamental principle that should guide a court when examining the issue whether provisions of a directive that are capable of having direct effect may be relied upon against an organisation, and, in particular, whether such provisions may be relied upon against an organisation on which a Member State has conferred the task that is the subject of Article 1(4) of the Second Directive.

31 In that regard, it must be recalled that, in accordance with the Court's settled case-law, a directive cannot of itself impose obligations on an individual and cannot therefore be relied upon as such against an individual (judgments of 26 February 1986, *Marshall*, 152/84, EU:C:1986:84, paragraph 48; of 14 July 1994, *Faccini Dori*, C-91/92, EU:C:1994:292, paragraph 20; of 5 October 2004, *Pfeiffer and Others*, C-397/01 to C-403/01, EU:C:2004:584, paragraph 108, and of 19 April 2016, *DI*, C-441/14, EU:C:2016:278, paragraph 30). The effect of extending the possibility of relying on directives that are not transposed to the sphere of relations between individuals would be to recognize a power invested in the European Union to enact obligations for individuals with immediate effect, whereas it has competence to do so only where it is empowered to adopt regulations (judgment of 14 July 1994, *Faccini Dori*, C-91/92, EU:C:1994:292, paragraph 24).

32 Nonetheless, again in accordance with the Court's settled case-law, where a person is able to rely on a directive not against an individual but against the State, he may do so regardless of the capacity in which the latter is acting, whether as employer or as public authority. In either case it is necessary to prevent the State from taking advantage of its own failure to comply with EU law (judgments of 26 February 1986, *Marshall*, 152/84, EU:C:1986:84, paragraph 49; of 12 July 1990, *Foster and Others*, C-188/89, EU:C:1990:313, paragraph 17, and of 14 September 2000, *Collino and Chiappero*, C-343/98, EU:C:2000:441, paragraph 22).

33 On the basis of those considerations, the Court has held that provisions of a directive that are unconditional and sufficiently precise may be relied upon by individuals, not only against a Member State and all the organs of its administration, such as decentralised

authorities (see, to that effect, judgment of 22 June 1989, *Costanzo*, 103/88, EU:C:1989:256, paragraph 31), but also, as was stated in the answer to the first question, against organisations or bodies which are subject to the authority or control of the State or which possess special powers beyond those which result from the normal rules applicable to relations between individuals (judgments of 12 July 1990, *Foster and Others*, C-188/89, EU:C:1990:313, paragraph 18, and of 4 December 1997, *Kampelmann and Others*, C-253/96 to C-258/96, EU:C:1997:585, paragraph 46).

34 Such organisations or bodies can be distinguished from individuals and must be treated as comparable to the State, either because they are legal persons governed by public law that are part of the State in the broad sense, or because they are subject to the authority or control of a public body, or because they have been required, by such a body, to perform a task in the public interest and have been given, for that purpose, such special powers.

35 Accordingly, a body or an organisation, even one governed by private law, to which a Member State has delegated the performance of a task in the public interest and which possesses for that purpose special powers beyond those which result from the normal rules applicable to relations between individuals is one against which the provisions of a directive that have direct effect may be relied upon.

The Court here notes both the policy reasons for Directives being incapable of direct effect against *individuals* (*Farrell*, at para 31) and the policy reasons for Directives being capable of direct effect against *the State* (*Farrell*, at para 32)—and thus why 'the State' must be widely construed and include emanations of the State (*Farrell*, at paras 33–35). In particular, the Court notes that emanations of the State are *different from individuals* and *comparable to the State* because they:

- are legal persons governed by public law that are part of 'the State', as widely defined; or
- are subject to the authority or control of a public body; or
- have been required by such a body to perform a task in the public interest and have been given special powers for that purpose.

The facts of the *Farrell* case were that Ms Farrell had been injured in a motor vehicle accident while she was a passenger seated on the floor in the back of Mr Whitty's van. He was not insured for her injuries and so she sought compensation from the Motor Insurers Bureau of Ireland (MIBI). This was the body that Ireland had set up in response to the Second Council Directive 84/5/EEC of 30 December 1983 on the approximation of the laws of the Member States relating to insurance against civil liability in respect of the use of motor vehicles, OJ 1984 L8/17 (the Second Motor Insurance Directive), which required Member States to set up a body to provide compensation for property damage or personal injury caused by uninsured or unidentified vehicles. This Directive supplemented the First Motor Insurance Directive (Council Directive 72/166/EEC of 24 April 1972 on the approximation of the laws of Member States relating to insurance against civil liability in respect of the use of motor vehicles, and to the enforcement of the obligation to insure against such liability, OJ 1972 L103/1), which required motor insurance to be compulsory. Farrell's claim was based on the Third Motor Insurance Directive (Third Council Directive 90/232/EEC of 14 May 1990 on the approximation of the laws of the Member States relating to insurance against civil liability in respect of the use of motor vehicles, OJ 1990 L129/33), which extended the insurance and compensation obligation to all passengers. However, the MIBI rejected her claim on the grounds that Irish law did not require compensation for injuries caused to persons travelling in parts of vehicles that were not equipped to carry passengers.

The Court held that the body in question, the MIBI, was required to perform a task that contributed to the general objective of victim protection pursued by the EU legislation relating to compulsory motor vehicle liability insurance and that task must be regarded as being in the public interest. Further, Irish law made membership of the MIBI compulsory for all motor vehicle insurers and thereby conferred on the MIBI special powers in the form of the power to require all those insurers to become members of it and to contribute funds for the performance of the task conferred on it by the Irish State. The Court therefore concluded that the provisions of a Directive that were unconditional and sufficiently precise could have direct effect against the MIBI.

Other cases have given further guidance on which bodies may fall within the term 'emanation of the State'. For example, in Case 222/84 *Johnston v Chief Constable of the Royal Ulster Constabulary* [1986] ECR 1651, the Chief Constable of the Royal Ulster Constabulary (RUC) decided that, in view of the high numbers of police officers assassinated in Northern Ireland, it was not appropriate to continue with the existing policy that they should not carry firearms. He decided that male officers should carry firearms in the regular course of their duties, but that women police officers would not be equipped with firearms and would not receive training in firearms. As a result, fewer women police officers were required and the Chief Constable therefore refused to renew Mrs Johnston's contract as a police constable. Mrs Johnston challenged that refusal before an Industrial Tribunal. The Tribunal referred to the Court of Justice a number of questions on the interpretation of the Equal Treatment Directive (Directive 76/207) (see further Chapter 6 on the preliminary reference procedure). The Court of Justice ruled that a Directive could be relied upon directly against an 'emanation' of the State such as the Chief Constable of the RUC (*Johnston*, at para 56).

It is also likely that local government authorities will be regarded as emanations of the State. For example, in Case C-103/88 *Fratelli Costanzo SpA v Comune di Milano* [1989] ECR I-1839, Fratelli Costanzo submitted a tender to a municipal authority for a public works contract. The municipal authority eliminated this tender from the tendering procedure and Fratelli Costanzo sought the annulment of the decision to eliminate its tender. The national court referred to the Court of Justice a number of questions on the interpretation of Council Directive 71/305/EEC of 26 July 1971 concerning the co-ordination of procedures for the award of public works contracts, OJ 1971 L185/5 (see further Chapter 6 on the preliminary reference procedure). The Court of Justice ruled that Directives could be relied upon directly against 'all organs of the administration, including decentralized authorities such as municipalities' (*Fratelli Costanzo*, at para 32).

REVIEW QUESTION

Suppose that you have recently suffered from a respiratory infection contracted while swimming in polluted seawater off a beach in Ireland. Tests indicate that the water contains 2.5 per cent blisterium, a chemical known to produce respiratory infections. (Fictitious) Directive 00/00 provides that the presence of any amount over 2 per cent leads to the awarding of compensation to anyone contracting infection as a consequence. The (fictitious) Sea Watch Agency has the statutory duty under UK law of monitoring and enforcing environmental standards along the coast. How, if at all, could direct effect apply in this scenario?

Answer: The comments made in the previous review questions would apply equally here. In addition, the defendant here is not the State per se, but will constitute an 'emanation of the State' if it is a legal person governed by public law that is part of 'the State', as widely defined, or is subject to the authority or control of a public body, or has been required by such a body to perform a task in the public interest and been given special powers for that purpose (*Foster*, as interpreted by the Court in *Farrell*). The fact that the (fictitious) Agency has a statutory duty to monitor and enforce environmental standards can be argued to involve a degree of State control. Alternatively, the monitoring and enforcing of environmental standards can be argued to be a task in the public interest, particularly as these duties apply to publicly owned and accessible areas, and the enforcement of standards is likely to constitute a special power because it implies the imposition of sanctions and/or the ability to force a third-party polluter to take action or to refrain from taking action.

The judgment in *Farrell* means that it is now easier for applicants to prove that a body is an emanation of the State, because they need not prove all elements of the *Foster* test. This means that if the facts in *Doughty v Rolls Royce plc* [1992] 1 CMLR 1045 were to arise again, the result reached by the UK courts in that case might be different. In that case, not all elements of the *Foster* test were fulfilled and, on the interpretation of the test prevailing at that time, the claimant lost the case.

The facts of *Doughty* were similar to those of both *Marshall* and *Foster* (see 4.1.4.1 and earlier in this section), but the outcome was very different. Mrs Doughty was employed by Rolls Royce, which had a compulsory retirement policy similar to that of the health authority in *Marshall* and that of British Gas in *Foster*. She was compulsorily retired at the age of 60, in accordance with that retirement policy, whereas the policy applied a retirement age of 65 to her male colleagues. Like Marshall and Foster, Doughty sought to rely on the Equal Treatment Directive (Directive 76/207), which concerned discrimination at work on grounds of sex. The Court of Appeal held that the Directive could not be directly effective against Rolls Royce because it did not fulfil the test set out in *Foster* and so was not an emanation of the Member State. It was 100 per cent owned by the State and therefore any service it provided was under the control of the State. However, it was involved in a commercial undertaking and was not responsible for any public service, and it did not exercise any special powers (for example of the type enjoyed by British Gas). In the light of *Farrell*, the answer that would be given today on these facts might be that State ownership would be sufficient for Rolls Royce to be an emanation of the State, under the second limb of the test (ie that it is subject to the authority or control of a public body).

Nonetheless, the unfairness (criticized by the UK government in its submissions in Case 152/84 *Marshall v Southampton and South West Area Health Authority (Teaching) (No 1)*

[1986] ECR 723, at para 51) that can result from the Court of Justice's limitation of the direct effect of Directives to vertical (as opposed to vertical and horizontal) direct effect remains.

?! THINKING POINT

What is that unfairness?

The potential unfairness is that a claimant's success may depend solely on the accident of whether the defendant is, or is not, an emanation of the State and the claimant may be unable to enforce rights clearly granted to them by a Directive purely because the defendant in their case is not an emanation of the State.

REVIEW QUESTION

Would a woman employed by a private hospital, but otherwise in the same position as the applicant in Case 152/84 *Marshall v Southampton and South West Area Health Authority (Teaching) (No 1)* [1986] ECR 723, have been able to rely on the Equal Treatment Directive in the same way as Marshall?

Answer: In *Marshall*, the Court of Justice clearly stated that a Directive could not be relied upon against another individual. It would therefore be possible to rely on the Directive in this situation only if the private hospital could be shown to be an emanation of the Member State.

In the light of *Farrell*, it would be necessary for the hospital to be (1) a legal person governed by public law that is part of the State in the broad sense, or (2) subject to the authority or control of a public body, or (3) operating a public interest service under the control of the State, with special powers to do so. It is unlikely that any hospital would satisfy (1). As to (2), further information is required as to any State control over the provision of health care by the private hospital in question—for example there might be some State funding, regulation, and/or an inspection regime that might amount to sufficient 'control'. As to (3), it is established that health care is a public service (*Marshall*). It may be possible to argue that private health care is not, but if the private hospital provides public health care to the general public and recoups the cost from the government, this may be a service in the public interest. The hospital is likely to have the ability to dispense controlled medications to patients, which could be argued to be a special power. In those circumstances, an employee might be able to enforce the Directive against it.

The potential unfairness of the restriction of the direct effect of Directives to cases in which the defendant is an emanation of the State was again highlighted in Case C-91/92 *Faccini Dori v Recreb Srl* [1994] ECR I-3325. In that case, a consumer sought to cancel a contract with a business pursuant to Council Directive 85/577/EEC of 20 December 1985 to protect the consumer in respect of contracts negotiated away from business premises, OJ 1985 L372/31 (the Doorstep Selling Directive), which gave consumers the right of cancellation where the contract was concluded away from business premises and which Italy had not transposed into national law by the deadline date. On a preliminary reference under Article 267 TFEU (see further Chapter 6 on the preliminary reference procedure), the Court of Justice responded to the national court's criticism of the restriction on the direct effect of Directives to cases in which the defendant was an emanation of the State. It began by reiterating its reasoning for enforcing Directives directly against the State and its emanations.

Case C-91/92 *Faccini Dori v Recreb Srl* [1994] ECR I-3325

21. The national court observes that if the effects of unconditional and sufficiently precise but untransposed directives were to be limited to relations between State entities and individuals, this would mean that a legislative measure would operate as such only as between certain legal subjects, whereas, under Italian law as under the laws of all modern States founded on the rule of law, the State is subject to the law like any other person. If the directive could be relied on only as against the State, that would be tantamount to a penalty for failure to adopt legislative measures of transposition as if the relationship were a purely private one.
22. It need merely be noted here that, as is clear from the judgment in *Marshall*, cited above (paragraphs 48 and 49), the case-law on the possibility of relying on directives against State entities is based on the fact that under Article 189 [EEC, now Article 288 TFEU] a directive is binding only in relation to 'each Member State to which it is addressed'. That case-law seeks to prevent 'the State from taking advantage of its own failure to comply with Community law' [now EU law].
23. It would be unacceptable if a State, when required by the Community [now Union] legislature to adopt certain rules intended to govern the State's relations—or those of State entities—with individuals and to confer certain rights on individuals, were able to rely on its own failure to discharge its obligations so as to deprive individuals of the benefits of those rights. Thus the Court has recognized that certain provisions of directives on conclusion of public works contracts and of directives on harmonization of turnover taxes may be relied on against the State (or State entities) (see the judgment in Case 103/88 *Fratelli Costanzo v Comune di Milano* [1989] ECR 1839 and the judgment in Case 8/81 *Becker v Finanzamt Münster-Innenstadt* [1982] ECR 53).

The Court of Justice then reiterated its reasoning as to why the nature of Directives meant that they could not also be directly effective against private parties.

Case C-91/92 *Faccini Dori v Recreb Srl* [1994] ECR I-3325

24. The effect of extending that case-law to the sphere of relations between individuals would be to recognize a power in the Community [now Union] to enact obligations for individuals with immediate effect, whereas it has competence to do so only where it is empowered to adopt regulations.
25. It follows that, in the absence of measures transposing the directive within the prescribed time-limit, consumers cannot derive from the directive itself a right of cancellation as against traders with whom they have concluded a contract or enforce such a right in a national court.

The Court concluded that Faccini Dori might be able to enforce her rights through the doctrine of indirect effect (see 4.2) or a separate action for Member State liability (see Chapter 5).

In Case C-192/94 *El Corte Inglés SA v Blásquez Rivero* [1996] ECR I-1281, the Court of Justice repeated its reasoning in para 24 of *Faccini Dori*, but added to its reference to the horizontal effect of Regulations the words 'or Decisions' (*El Corte Inglés*, at para 17).

In Case C-201/02 *Wells v Secretary of State for Transport, Local Government and the Regions* [2004] ECR I-723 (see also 4.1.5 and 5.5.3), the Court of Justice additionally invoked the principle of **legal certainty** in support of its argument that Directives could not have direct effect against private parties.

legal certainty
Legal certainty is the principle that the law must be clear and foreseeable, so that persons subject to that law can foresee the legal consequence of their actions and regulate their conduct accordingly.

The Court held in *Wells*, at para 56, that 'the principle of legal certainty prevents directives from creating obligations for individuals. For them, the provisions of a directive can only create rights (see Case 152/84 *Marshall* [1986] ECR 723, paragraph 48) … '.

A further example of the application of the *Foster* test—now reformulated in *Farrell*—is provided by the judgment of the High Court of England and Wales in *Byrne and others v Motor Insurers Bureau* [2007] EWHC 1268 (QB), [2007] 3 CMLR 15, in which the claimants sought to rely on the Second Motor Insurance Directive (discussed earlier in this section in relation to the Court of Justice's judgment in *Farrell*), which provided for Member States to compensate the victims of road traffic accidents caused by uninsured or untraced drivers. In the UK, this role was performed by the Motor Insurers' Bureau (MIB). The High Court held that the MIB was not an emanation of the State and therefore the Directive could not be relied upon against it. The court considered that the provision of protection and compensation for victims of accidents involving uninsured or untraced drivers was a public service, but that there was no State control over this service—the fact that the Secretary of State had the power to appoint an arbitrator where a dissatisfied applicant sought to appeal against a decision of the MIB was insufficient—and a 'complete absence of "special powers" ' (*Byrne*, at para 60) since, contrary to the arguments of the claimant, the MIB did not have the power to exclude an insurer from membership with the effect that it would no longer be an authorized insurer and so could not issue insurance policies, and the relations between the MIB and its members were (as was to be expected from a corporate body) governed by its articles of association and not by statute.

?! THINKING POINT

Try to summarize the *Farrell* test in your own words without looking at the text. If you have difficulty in doing this, reread this section.

4.1.5 Incidental horizontal effect of Directives

Although the Court of Justice has made it clear that Directives cannot directly impose obligations on private parties, it has stated that Directives can, in certain circumstances, produce a degree of horizontal effect on such parties. Principally, this is through the doctrine of indirect effect, which is discussed in detail at 4.2. However, there are also other circumstances in which a horizontal effect, sometimes referred to as incidental horizontal effect, may be produced.

One is where the impact of a Directive is to invalidate an inconsistent national law on which a private party is seeking to rely as a defence to a claim and thereby expose that party to liability on that claim. For example, in Case C-194/94 *CIA Security International SA v Signalson SA and another* [1996] ECR I-2201, CIA sought an order requiring two rival firms to cease unfair trading practices. These practices took the form of alleging that CIA's products were not approved under national rules on technical equipment. The two rival firms counterclaimed for an order restraining CIA from carrying on business on the ground, inter alia, of that lack of approval. The Court held that Council Directive 83/189/EEC of 28 March 1983 laying down a procedure for the provision of information in the field of technical standards and regulations, OJ 1983 L109/8, required such national technical rules to be notified by the Member State to the EU Commission prior to adoption. As they had not been so notified, they could not be asserted against private individuals and therefore the counterclaims could not succeed, with the result that the two defendants were exposed to liability on the claim of unfair trading.

Similarly, in Case C-443/98 *Unilever Italia SpA v Central Food SpA* [2000] ECR I-7535, Directive 83/189 was again at issue. Goods supplied by Unilever to Central Food had been labelled in compliance with Council Directive 79/112/EEC of 18 December 1978 on the approximation of the laws of the Member States relating to the labelling, presentation and advertising of foodstuffs for sale to the ultimate consumer, OJ 1979 L33/1, but not in compliance with national rules, and Central Food consequently refused to pay for the goods. The national rules had not been notified to the EU Commission, as required by Directive 83/189. The Court of Justice again held that, as a result of the failure to notify, the national rules could not be applied by the national courts 'in civil proceedings between individuals concerning contractual rights and obligations' (*Unilever*, at para 52). The consequence was to deprive Central Food of its defence to the claim for non-payment.

In neither case was the Directive directly enforced against a private party in the sense of imposing an obligation on them, but in both the imposition of a detriment on a private party under national law was made possible only because the Directive was held to prevent their reliance on other national law that might have afforded a defence.

In Case C-201/02 *Wells v Secretary of State for Transport, Local Government and the Regions* [2004] ECR I-723 (see also 4.1.4 and 5.5.3), the applicant argued that the grant of a new mining permission to a quarry owner necessitated an environmental impact assessment (EIA) under Council Directive 85/337/EEC of 27 June 1985 on the assessment of the effects of certain public and private projects on the environment, OJ 1985 L175/40. Although her action was brought against the State authorities for their failure to carry out an assessment, the Court of Justice's preliminary ruling under Article 267 TFEU (see further Chapter 6 on the preliminary reference procedure)—that the Directive required an assessment to be made in this case—had an adverse impact on the quarry owner. The Court held that while the principle of legal certainty prevented a Directive from having direct effect against an individual (see 4.1.4) and thus from having direct effect against the State if the State's obligation were 'directly linked to the performance of another obligation falling, pursuant to that directive, on a third party' (*Wells*, at para 56), the obligation on the State in this case—to ensure that an assessment was carried out—was not directly linked to any obligation on the quarry owner. Although the halting of mining operations pending the outcome of the assessment was a consequence of the belated performance of the State's obligations, 'mere adverse repercussions on the rights of third parties, even if the repercussions are certain, do not justify preventing an individual from invoking the provisions of a directive against the Member State concerned' (*Wells*, at para 57).

Another situation in which a Directive may produce a horizontal effect is where a Regulation—which, of course, can have direct horizontal effect (see 4.1.2)—incorporates, by reference, certain provisions of a Directive. Joined Cases C-37 & 58/06 *Viamex Agrar Handels GmbH and another v Hauptzollamt Hamburg-Jonas* [2008] ECR I-69 concerned Commission Regulation (EC) No 615/98 of 18 March 1998 laying down specific detailed rules of application for the export refund arrangements as regards the welfare of live bovine animals during transport, OJ 1998 L82/19, which applied Regulation (EEC) No 805/68 of the Council of 27 June 1968 on the common organisation of the market in beef and veal, OJ 1968 L148/24, including making payment conditional on compliance with the animal welfare standards laid down in Council Directive 91/628/EEC of 19 November 1991 on the protection of animals during transport ... , OJ 1991 L340/17. The German authorities refused to pay the export refund on the ground that the applicant companies had not complied with the Directive. The applicants lodged formal objections to this and the national court made a preliminary reference to the Court of Justice under Article 267 TFEU (see further Chapter 6 on the preliminary reference procedure).

?! THINKING POINT

While reading the following extract, consider what requirements must be satisfied before a reference in a Regulation to a Directive will be sufficient for—effectively—horizontal effect to be given to the provisions of that Directive.

Joined Cases C-37 & 58/06 *Viamex Agrar Handels GmbH and another v Hauptzollamt Hamburg-Jonas* [2008] ECR I-69

27. It is true that, according to settled case-law, a directive cannot of itself impose obligations on an individual (see, inter alia, Case 152/84 *Marshall* [1986] ECR 723, paragraph 48; Joined Cases C-397/01 to C-403/01 *Pfeiffer and Others* [2004] ECR I-8835, paragraph 108; Joined Case C-387/02, C-391/02 and C-403/02 *Berlusconi and Others* [2005] ECR I-3565, paragraph 73; and Case C-80/06 *Carp* [2007] ECR I-0000, paragraph 20).

28. However, it cannot be precluded, in principle, that the provisions of a directive may be applicable by means of an express reference in a regulation to its provisions, provided that general principles of law and, in particular, the principle of legal certainty, are observed.

29. Moreover, the purpose of the general reference made by Regulation No 615/98 to Directive 91/628 is to ensure, for the purposes of the implementation of Article 13(9) of Regulation No 805/68, compliance with the relevant provisions of that directive on the welfare of

live animals and, in particular, the protection of animals during transport. That reference, which lays down the conditions for the grant of refunds, cannot therefore be interpreted as covering all the provisions in Directive 91/628 and, in particular, those provisions which have no connection with the principle objective pursued by that directive.

30. Consequently, it cannot properly be held, as was submitted by the applicant in the main proceedings in Case C-58/06, that that reference is contrary to the principle of legal certainty in so far as it covers all the provisions of Directive 91/628.

The Court of Justice held that the reference in the Regulation to the Directive must not be a general reference, but a reference to specific provisions of the Directive. Further, to comply with the principle of legal certainty, the Regulation must not refer to provisions of the Directive that did not relate to its principal objective.

However, in C-176/12 *Association de Mediation Sociale v Union Locale des Syndicats CGT and others* [2014] 2 CMLR 41 (see also 4.1.4), the Court held that the reference in Article 27 of the Charter of Fundamental Rights of the European Union (on the Charter, see further 9.4) to the right of employees to information and consultation required more specific detail to be provided in EU or national law in order to be fully effective, and therefore it could not be invoked to make the rights in Directive 2002/14/EC of the European Parliament and of the Council of 11 March 2002 establishing a general framework for informing and consulting employees in the European Community, OJ 2002 L80/29, directly effective in proceedings between an employer and a trade union, both of which were private parties.

?! THINKING POINT

What conditions must a Directive satisfy in order to have direct effect? In what way do these differ from the conditions applicable to Treaty Articles, Regulations, and Decisions?

4.1.6 Summary of direct effect

The key features of the concept of direct effect are summarized in Figure 4.1.

NOTE

Direct effect is one of the most important concepts in EU law. If you are having difficulty understanding this topic, review 4.1 in full before continuing on to the next topic, indirect effect.

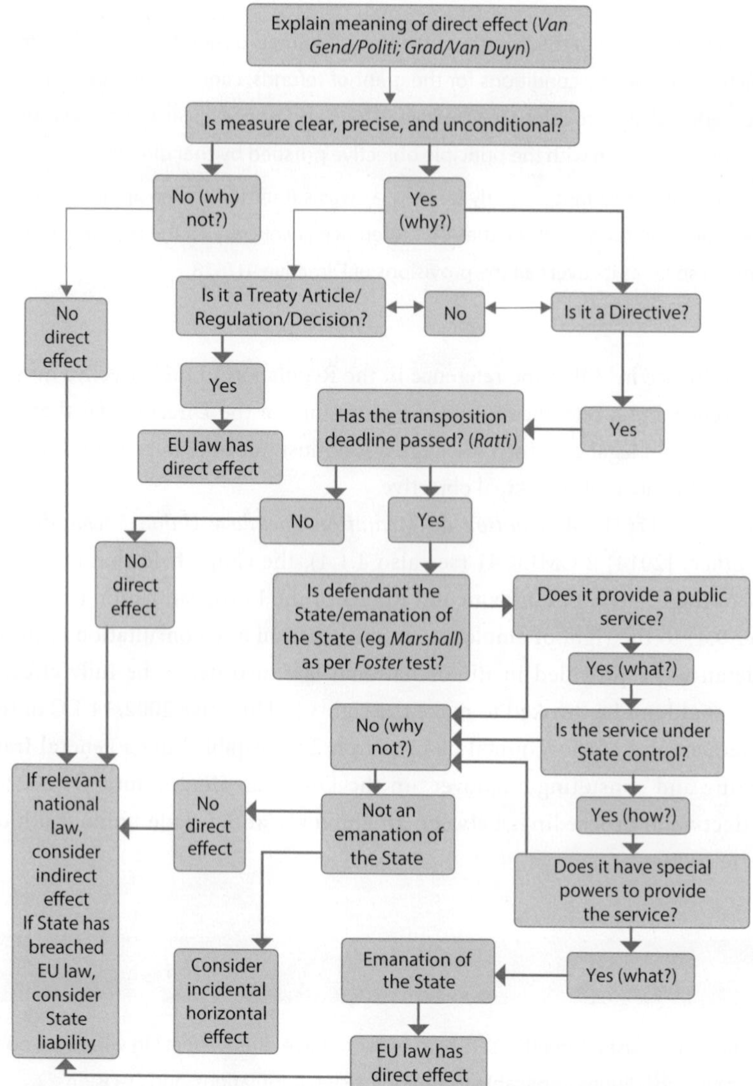

Figure 4.1 Summary of direct effect

4.2 Indirect effect

The discussion of direct effect at 4.1 included a number of points that are relevant to the related concept of indirect effect. First, direct effect was developed by the Court of Justice to make rights provided by EU law enforceable in the national courts. Secondly, not all provisions of EU law are directly effective in all circumstances. Thirdly, Directives pose particular problems in relation to direct effect. Given that the Court's attempts to make rights enforceable through direct effect were not successful in all cases, it was not surprising that it sought to develop an alternative method of making rights enforceable or that this alternative has been particularly valuable to applicants seeking to enforce Directives. This alternative method is known as indirect effect.

The term 'indirect effect' refers to the obligation on national courts to interpret national law consistently with EU law. EU law is then said to have an 'indirect effect' since it influences the interpretation of national law (as opposed to a direct effect where EU law is relied upon directly).

The obligation applies to both domestic legislation and domestic case law (see eg Case C-456/98 *Centrosteel v Adipol GmbH* [2000] ECR I-6007, para 17, quoted at 4.2.4).

4.2.1 The measures that may have indirect effect

4.2.1.1 Treaty Articles, Regulations, and Decisions

Although Treaty Articles, Regulations, and Decisions can in principle have indirect effect, it is a relatively unimportant concept in relation to them. This is because they will generally fail to have direct effect only if they are unclear or conditional, in which case they are unlikely to be of much assistance in interpreting national law.

4.2.1.2 Recommendations and Opinions

Although neither Recommendations nor Opinions can have direct effect (see 4.1.1), the Court of Justice ruled in Case C-322/88 *Grimaldi v Fonds des Maladies Professionnelles* [1989] ECR 4407 (see also 4.1.1 and 3.4.2) that Recommendations could have indirect effect. It reasoned that since Recommendations must have some legal effect, they should be taken into consideration when interpreting national implementing measures (ie have indirect effect) and also when interpreting EU measures that the particular Recommendation was designed to supplement. As with the Court's ruling on direct effect, this aspect of its ruling can be taken to apply equally to Opinions.

4.2.1.3 Directives

Indirect effect is of most importance in relation to Directives and so this topic will be examined in some detail. Since direct effect is restricted to those Directives that are sufficiently clear and unconditional, and may be relied upon only against the State or an emanation thereof (see 4.1.4), the doctrine of direct effect will not always be sufficient to make EU law rights contained in a Directive effective. However, the possibility exists that a Directive may have indirect effect—that is, it may be used in a national court in interpreting the relevant national legislation.

In Case 14/83 *Von Colson and Kamann v Land Nordrhein-Westfalen* [1984] ECR 1891 (see also 4.2.2 and 4.3.2), two men were appointed as social workers and two disappointed female applicants alleged that they had been discriminated against contrary to the Equal Treatment Directive (Directive 76/207), which prohibited discrimination at work on grounds of sex and required that alleged victims be able to pursue claims before the courts. The applicants sought an order that they be offered a contract of employment or payment of six months' salary.

Under German law, they were entitled only to recover their travel expenses by way of compensation. The German court made a preliminary reference to the Court of Justice under Article 267 TFEU (see further Chapter 6 on the preliminary reference procedure).

?! THINKING POINT

While reading the following extract, consider why the Equal Treatment Directive was held not to be directly effective and what the doctrine of indirect effect required the national court to do.

Case 14/83 *Von Colson and Kamann v Land Nordrhein-Westfalen* [1984] ECR 1891

26. However, the Member States' obligation arising from a directive to achieve the result envisaged by the directive and their duty under Article 5 of the [EC] Treaty [now Article 4(3) TEU] to take all appropriate measures, whether general or particular, to ensure the fulfilment of that obligation, is binding on all the authorities of Member States including, for matters within their jurisdiction, the courts. It follows that, in applying the national law and in particular the provisions of a national law specifically introduced in order to implement Directive No. 76/207, national courts are required to interpret their national law in the light of the wording and the purpose of the directive in order to achieve the result referred to in the third paragraph of Article 189 [EEC, now Article 288 TFEU].
27. On the other hand, as the above considerations show, the directive does not include any unconditional and sufficiently precise obligation as regards sanctions for discrimination which, in the absence of implementing measures adopted in good time may be relied on by individuals in order to obtain specific compensation under the directive, where that is not provided for or permitted under national law.

The Court of Justice held that the provisions of the Directive on the sanctions for discrimination were not sufficiently precise and unconditional to be directly effective. However, national law should be interpreted in the light of its provisions, which required that an effective remedy be available. A nominal remedy, such as the award of travel expenses, was not adequate.

4.2.2 The national law to which indirect effect can apply

The domestic legislation in Case 14/83 *Von Colson and Kamann v Land Nordrhein-Westfalen* [1984] ECR 1891 (see also 4.2.1 and 4.3.2) had been passed specifically in order to transpose the Equal Treatment Directive and it was perhaps unsurprising that the Court of Justice took the view that it should be interpreted consistently with the Directive that it was designed to implement. However, in its judgment, the Court referred to 'national law *and in particular* the provisions of a national law specifically introduced in order to transpose Directive 76/207' (*Von Colson*, at para 26, emphasis added). This implies that legislation *not* specifically passed to transpose a Directive could also fall to be construed in accordance with it.

Such an interpretation might prove particularly difficult where the national legislation predates the Directive, because such legislation would not have been drafted with the intention of reflecting the Directive and might even predate the State in question joining the EU—or indeed predate the existence of the EU itself. For example, one of the oldest pieces of legislation in the UK, the Statute of Marlborough 1267, would have to be interpreted consistently with any relevant EU law if indirect effect were to be applied to it. However, it could be argued that if indirect effect were to be limited to legislation transposing a Directive, an unscrupulous Member State could simply fail to pass any such legislation and thus prevent actions against it based on the indirect effect of a transposing law.

Nonetheless, the courts in the UK initially took this restrictive approach. In *Litster and others v Forth Dry Dock and Engineering Co Ltd* [1989] 2 CMLR 194, Litster and others were dismissed by their employer, a shipyard, one hour before it was sold to another company and new employees taken on. UK law designed to transpose Council Directive 77/187/EEC of 14 February 1977 on the approximation of the laws of the Member States relating to the safeguarding of employees' rights in the event of transfers of undertakings, businesses or parts of businesses, OJ 1977 L61/26, provided the employees with a remedy only if they had been employed immediately before such a transfer. Litster and other employees argued that 'immediately before' must be interpreted in the light of the Directive, which was clearly intended to protect all employees dismissed in the event of a transfer of employer. The House of Lords (now the Supreme Court) accepted the principle of indirect effect, but gave it a restricted scope. It took the view that the duty of consistent construction imposed on national courts by *Von Colson* applied only to legislation 'issued for the purpose of complying with directives'. Fortunately for the employees, the relevant UK law had been so intended and therefore they were entitled to compensation.

However, in Case C-106/89 *Marleasing SA v La Comercial Internacional de Alimentación SA* [1990] ECR I-4135, the Court of Justice clarified its position and confirmed an extended application of indirect effect. Spanish law laid down a number of grounds on which a company could be struck off the register, including lack of cause (meaning that the company had no real function). The Spanish law predated First Council Directive 68/151/EEC of 9 March 1968 on co-ordination of safeguards which, for the protection of the interests of members and others, are required by Member States of companies within the meaning of the second paragraph of Article 58 of the Treaty, with a view to making such safeguards equivalent throughout the Community, OJ 1968 L65/8 (the First Company Law Directive), which omitted this particular ground and which Spain had failed to transpose. When Marleasing attempted to have La Comercial struck off for lack of cause, La Comercial sought to rely on the Directive. The Court of Justice confirmed that a Directive could not have horizontal direct effect and thus that this Directive could not have direct effect against Marleasing (see 4.1.5 on the lack of horizontal direct effect of Directives). However, it held that it could have indirect effect and therefore, as the following extract demonstrates, that the Spanish law, even though it predated the Directive, must be interpreted in accordance with the Directive. This meant that the Spanish law must be interpreted as not including lack of cause as a ground for striking off and La Comercial could therefore not be struck off on this ground.

Case C-106/89 *Marleasing SA v La Comercial Internacional de Alimentación SA* [1990] ECR I-4135

7. However, it is apparent from the documents before the Court that the national court seeks in substance to ascertain whether a national court hearing a case which falls within the scope of Directive 68/151 is required to interpret its national law in the light of the wording and the purpose of that directive in order to preclude a declaration of nullity of a public limited company on a ground other than those listed in Article 11 of the directive.
8. In order to reply to that question, it should be observed that, as the Court pointed out in its judgment in Case 14/83 *Von Colson and Kamann v Land Nordrhein-Westfalen* [1984] ECR 1891, paragraph 26, the Member States' obligation arising from a directive to achieve the result envisaged by the directive and their duty under Article 5 of the [EC] Treaty [now Article 4(3) TEU] to take all appropriate measures, whether general or particular, to ensure the fulfilment of that obligation, is binding on all the authorities of Member States including, for matters within their jurisdiction, the courts. It follows that, in applying national law, whether the provisions in question were adopted before or after the directive, the national court called upon to interpret it is required to do so, as far as possible, in the light of the wording and the purpose of the directive in order to achieve the result pursued by the latter and thereby comply with the third paragraph of Article 189 of the [EEC] Treaty [now Article 288 TFEU].
9. It follows that the requirement that national law must be interpreted in conformity with Article 11 of Directive 68/151 precludes the interpretation of provisions of national law relating to public limited companies in such a manner that the nullity of a public limited company may be ordered on grounds other than those exhaustively listed in Article 11 of the directive in question.

It is essential to remember that the Court of Justice has consistently attempted to promote and expand the application of EU law, and for it to have given indirect effect a narrower application would have gone against this policy. In both Joined Cases C-397–403/01 *Pfeiffer and others v Deutsches Rotes Kreuz, Kreisverband Waldshut eV* [2004] ECR I-8835, at para 118, and Case C-212/04 *Adeneler and others v Ellinikos Organismos Galaklos (ELOG)* [2006] ECR I-6057, at para 111 (see also 4.2.3), the Court of Justice held that national courts were required 'to do whatever lies within their jurisdiction, taking the whole body of domestic law into consideration and applying the interpretative methods recognised by domestic law, with a view to ensuring that the Directive in question is fully effective and achieving an outcome consistent with the objective pursued by it' to give effect to the obligations contained in a Directive.

The first case involving indirect effect to come before the UK courts after Case C-106/89 *Marleasing SA v La Comercial Internacional de Alimentación SA* [1990] ECR I-4135 was *Webb v EMO Air Cargo (UK) Ltd* [1993] 1 CMLR 259. Ms Webb was employed for an unlimited period, but initially to cover the maternity leave of another colleague. Prior to taking up the employment, Webb discovered that she was pregnant and was dismissed as a result. In considering her argument that her dismissal was contrary to the Sex Discrimination Act 1975, the House of Lords (now the Supreme Court) accepted that *Marleasing* required it to interpret the Act consistently with the Equal Treatment Directive (Directive 76/207), even though the Act predated the Directive. This judgment clearly indicates that the UK has accepted the ruling of the Court of Justice in *Marleasing* that even national legislation that predates EU law must be interpreted consistently with it. However, where a contract is at issue, rather than legislation, it has held that this is not covered by the ruling in *Marleasing*. In *White (AP) v White and the Motor Insurers Bureau* [2001] 2 CMLR 1, the victim of a motor accident caused by an uninsured driver sought to rely on the agreement made between the Secretary of State for the Environment, Transport and the Regions and the Motor Insurers' Bureau (MIB) to implement the Second Motor Insurance Directive (discussed at 4.1.4.3 in relation to the Court of Justice judgment in C-413/15 *Farrell v Whitty and others* EU:C:2017:745 and also in relation to the decision of the domestic courts in *Byrne and others v Motor Insurers Bureau* [2007] EWHC 1268 (QB), [2007] 3 CMLR 15). This agreement provided, inter alia, for the compensation of any victim who had obtained judgment against an uninsured driver, unless that victim 'knew or ought to have known' that the driver was uninsured. The Directive excluded from compensation only victims who 'knew'.

In determining the meaning of the phrase in the agreement, the House of Lords ruled that there was no obligation to interpret it in line with the Directive pursuant to *Marleasing* since it was not legislation, but a contract between citizens. However, it ruled that, in accordance with the usual domestic rules of statutory interpretation, a purposive approach to the interpretation of the agreement should be taken. Account must therefore be taken of the Directive, since the purpose of the agreement was to give effect to the provisions of the Directive.

4.2.3 The time from which Directives can have indirect effect

?! THINKING POINT

What are the obligations of Member States in the period from the entry into force of the Directive to the deadline for its transposition into national law? If you cannot remember, look back at 3.4.2.

In Case C-212/04 *Adeneler and others v Ellinikos Organismos Galaklos (ELOG)* [2006] ECR I-6057 (see also 4.2.2 and 4.2.4), a number of applicants argued that ELOG's failure to renew their fixed-term employment contracts breached Council Directive 1999/70/EC of 28 June 1999 concerning the framework agreement on fixed-term work concluded by ETUC, UNICE and CEEP, OJ 1999 L175/43, which required the contracts to be interpreted as being of indefinite duration. The contracts were concluded after the entry into force of the Directive, but before expiry of the deadline for its transposition by Member States. The national court made a preliminary reference to the Court of Justice under Article 267 TFEU (see further Chapter 6 on the preliminary reference procedure) on, inter alia, whether the Directive had indirect effect prior to the expiry of the deadline.

?! **THINKING POINT**

While reading the following extract, consider what the Court of Justice ruled as to:

(a) the date from which a Directive had indirect effect; and

(b) why national courts were under an (almost) equivalent duty from an earlier date than this.

Case C-212/04 *Adeneler and others v Ellinikos Organismos Galaklos (ELOG)* [2006] ECR I-6057

113. With a view, more specifically, to determining the date from which national courts are to apply the principle that national law must be interpreted in conformity with Community law [now EU law], it should be noted that that obligation, arising from the second paragraph of Article 10 EC [now Article 4(3) TEU], the third paragraph of Article 249 EC [now Article 288 TFEU] and the directive in question itself, has been imposed in particular where a provision of a directive lacks direct effect, be it that the relevant provision is not sufficiently clear, precise and unconditional to produce direct effect or that the dispute is exclusively between individuals.

114. Also, before the period for transposition of a directive has expired, Member States cannot be reproached for not having yet adopted measures implementing it in national law (see Case C-129/96 *Inter-Environnement Wallonie* [1997] ECR I-7411, paragraph 43).

115. Accordingly, where a directive is transposed belatedly, the general obligation owed by national courts to interpret domestic law in conformity with the directive exists only once the period for its transposition has expired.

116. It necessarily follows from the foregoing that, where a directive is transposed belatedly, the date—envisaged by the referring court in Question 1(c)—on which the national implementing measures actually enter into force in the Member State concerned does not constitute the relevant point in time. Such a solution would be liable seriously to jeopardise the full effectiveness of Community law and its uniform application by means, in particular, of directives.

117. In addition, in light of the date envisaged in Question 1(a) and with a view to giving a complete ruling on the present question, it should be pointed out that it is already clear from the Court's case-law that the obligation on Member States, under the second paragraph of Article 10 EC, the third paragraph of Article 249 EC and the directive in question itself, to take all the measures necessary to achieve the result prescribed by the directive is binding on all national authorities, including, for matters within their jurisdiction, the courts (see, inter alia, *Inter-Environnement Wallonie*, paragraph 40, and *Pfeiffer and Others*

[Joined Cases C-397/01 to C-403/01 *Pfeiffer and Others* [2004] ECR I-8835], paragraph 110, and the case-law cited).

118. Also, directives are either (i) published in the Official Journal of the European Communities in accordance with Article 254(1) EC [now Article 297(1) TFEU] and, in that case, enter into force on the date specified in them or, in the absence thereof, on the 20th day following that of their publication, or (ii) notified to those to whom they are addressed, in which case they take effect upon such notification, in accordance with Article 254(3) EC [now Article 297(3) TFEU].

119. It follows that a directive produces legal effects for a Member State to which it is addressed—and, therefore, for all the national authorities—following its publication or from the date of its notification, as the case may be.

120. In the present instance, Directive 1999/70 states, in Article 3, that it was to enter into force on the day of its publication in the Official Journal of the European Communities, namely 10 July 1999.

121. In accordance with the Court's settled case-law, it follows from the second paragraph of Article 10 EC in conjunction with the third paragraph of Article 249 EC and the directive in question itself that, during the period prescribed for transposition of a directive, the Member States to which it is addressed must refrain from taking any measures liable seriously to compromise the attainment of the result prescribed by it (*Inter-Environnement Wallonie*, paragraph 45; Case C-14/02 *ATRAL* [2003] ECR I-4431, paragraph 58; and *Mangold* [Case C-144/04 *Mangold v Helm* [2005] ECR I-9981], paragraph 67). In this connection it is immaterial whether or not the provision of national law at issue which has been adopted after the directive in question entered into force is concerned with the transposition of the directive (*ATRAL*, paragraph 59 and *Mangold*, paragraph 68).

122. Given that all the authorities of the Member States are subject to the obligation to ensure that provisions of Community law take full effect (see *Francovich and Others* [Joined Cases C-6 & 9/90 *Francovich and others v Italy* [1991] ECR I-5357], paragraph 32; Case C-453/00 *Kühne & Heitz* [2004] ECR I-837, paragraph 20; and *Pfeiffer and Others*, paragraph 111), the obligation to refrain from taking measures, as set out in the previous paragraph, applies just as much to national courts.

123. It follows that, from the date upon which a directive has entered into force, the courts of the Member States must refrain as far as possible from interpreting domestic law in a manner which might seriously compromise, after the period for transposition has expired, attainment of the objective pursued by that directive.

124. In light of the foregoing reasoning, the answer to the first question must be that, where a directive is transposed belatedly into a Member State's domestic law and the relevant provisions of the directive do not have direct effect, the national courts are bound to interpret domestic law so far as possible, once the period for transposition has expired, in the light of the wording and the purpose of the directive concerned with a view to achieving the results sought by the directive, favouring the interpretation of the national rules which is the most consistent with that purpose in order thereby to achieve an outcome compatible with the provisions of the directive.

The Court of Justice held that the duty to interpret national law consistently with an EU Directive applied only after the expiry of the deadline for transposition of the Directive. However, it noted that the obligation on Member States to avoid measures liable to compromise the result prescribed by the Directive meant that national courts must try to avoid reaching an inconsistent interpretation from the (earlier) date on which the Directive entered into force.

4.2.4 The extent of the duty: 'as far as possible'

The Court of Justice has held that there is no duty to interpret national law *contra legem* (meaning 'against the law')—see eg Case C-212/04 *Adeneler and others v Ellinikos Organismos Galaklos (ELOG)* [2006] ECR I-6057, at para 110 (see 4.2.2) and Case C-105/03 *Pupino* [2005] ECR I-5285, at para 47 (see also later in this section)—and that the duty of consistent interpretation only applies 'as far as possible'—see eg Case C-106/89 *Marleasing SA v La Comercial Internacional de Alimentación SA* [1990] ECR I-4135, at para 8. This means that indirect effect will not always enable the rights contained in a Directive to be enforced.

The principle is therefore relatively clear and easily stated, as the Court of Appeal of England and Wales noted in *Google Inc v Vidal-Hall and others* [2015] EWCA Civ 311, [2015] 3 WLR 409.

Google Inc v Vidal-Hall and others [2015] EWCA Civ 311, [2015] 3 WLR 409

80. The *Marleasing* principle is not in doubt. It is that the courts of Member States should interpret national law enacted for the purpose of transposing an EU directive into its law, so far as possible, in the light of the wording and the purpose of the directive in order to achieve the result sought by the directive. The critical words (which have given rise to some difficulty) are 'so far as possible'. It is recognised that there are circumstances where it is not possible to interpret domestic legislation compatibly with the corresponding directive even where there is no doubt that the legislation was intended to implement the directive. If a national court is unable to rely on the *Marleasing* principle to interpret the national legislation so as to conform with the directive, the appropriate remedy for an aggrieved person is to claim *Francovich* damages against the state.

However, its application can be much more difficult, as can be seen in the following case.

?! THINKING POINT

While reading the following extract, compare the provisions of Spanish law and the Directive as to the grounds on which a company could be declared void and therefore struck off the register. Do you agree with the way in which the Court of Justice applied indirect effect?

Case C-106/89 *Marleasing SA v La Comercial Internacional de Alimentación SA* [1990] ECR I-4135

3. It is apparent from the grounds set out in the order for reference that Marleasing's primary claim, based on Articles 1261 and 1275 of the Spanish Civil Code, according to which contracts without cause or whose cause is unlawful have no legal effect, is for a declaration that the founders' contract establishing La Comercial is void on the ground that the establishment of the company lacked cause, was a sham transaction and was carried out in order to defraud the creditors of Barviesa SA, a co-founder of the defendant company. La Comercial contended that the action should be dismissed in its entirety on the ground, in particular, that Article 11 of Directive 68/151, which lists exhaustively the cases in which the nullity of a company may be ordered, does not include lack of cause amongst them.

   [...]

10. With regard to the interpretation to be given to Article 11 of the directive, in particular Article 11(2)(b), it should be observed that that provision prohibits the laws of the Member States from providing for a judicial declaration of nullity on grounds other than those exhaustively listed in the directive, amongst which is the ground that the objects of the company are unlawful or contrary to public policy.

11. According to the Commission, the expression 'objects of the company' must be interpreted as referring exclusively to the objects of the company as described in the instrument of incorporation or the articles of association. It follows, in the Commission's view, that a declaration of nullity of a company cannot be made on the basis of the activity actually pursued by it, for instance defrauding the founders' creditors.

12. That argument must be upheld. As is clear from the preamble to Directive 68/151, its purpose was to limit the cases in which nullity can arise and the retroactive effect of a declaration of nullity in order to ensure 'certainty in the law as regards relations between the company and third parties, and also between members' (sixth recital). Furthermore, the protection of third parties 'must be ensured by provisions which restrict to the greatest possible extent the grounds on which obligations entered into in the name of the company are not valid'. It follows, therefore, that each ground of nullity provided for in Article 11 of the directive must be interpreted strictly. In those circumstances the words 'objects of the company' must be understood as referring to the objects of the company as described in the instrument of incorporation or the articles of association.

Having held that the Spanish law must be interpreted 'as far as possible' in accordance with the Directive (*Marleasing*, at para 8), the Court of Justice ruled that since lack of cause was not a ground on which a company could be struck off under the Directive, La Comercial could not be struck off on this ground even though Spanish law quite clearly provided for this possibility.

The Court of Justice's application of the law in *Marleasing* may be contrasted with that in Case C-334/92 *Wagner Miret v Fondo de Garantía Salarial* [1993] ECR I-6911, in which, on comparable facts, the Court of Justice took a more restrictive approach to what was 'possible'. Wagner Miret was a senior manager in a company that became insolvent. Council Directive

80/987/EEC of 20 October 1980 on the approximation of the laws of the Member States relating to the protection of employees in the event of the insolvency of their employer, OJ 1980 L283/23—the same Directive that was at issue in Joined Cases C-6 & 9/90 *Francovich and others v Italy* [1991] ECR I-5357 (discussed at 4.1.4; see also 5.2 and 5.3)—obliged Member States to set up a fund to recompense employees whose employers became insolvent. Although Spain had set up such a fund, it did not cover payments to higher management staff. The Spanish court made a preliminary reference to the Court of Justice under Article 267 TFEU (see further Chapter 6 on the preliminary reference procedure). The Court of Justice ruled that Directive 80/897 was not sufficiently precise to be directly effective (see 4.1.4 on the conditions that must be met in order for Directives to have direct effect). It then considered whether the Directive could have *in*direct effect.

Case C-334/92 *Wagner Miret v Fondo de Garantía Salarial* [1993] ECR I-6911

14. The reply to the first two questions must therefore be that higher management staff may not be excluded from the scope of Council Directive 80/987/EEC on the approximation of the laws of the Member States relating to the protection of employees in the event of the insolvency of their employer, as amended by Council Directive 87/164/EEC of 2 March 1987, where they are classified under national law as employees and they are not listed in section I of the Annex to the directive.
15. By the third question, the national court in essence asks whether higher management staff are entitled, by virtue of the directive on the insolvency of employers, to request the payment of amounts owing to them by way of salary from the guarantee body established by national law for the other categories of employee or, if this is not the case, whether they are entitled to request the Member State concerned to make good the loss and damage sustained as a result of the failure to implement the directive in their respect.
16. It should first be observed that Spain has established no guarantee institution other than the Fondo de Garantía Salarial.
17. Secondly, in its judgment of 19 November 1991, (Cases C-6 & 9/90) *Francovich v Republic* [1991] 1 ECR 5357, the Court held that under Article 5 of the directive on the insolvency of employers, the Member States have a broad discretion with regard to the organization, operation, and financing of the guarantee institutions. The Court concluded that even though the provisions of the directive are sufficiently precise and unconditional as regards the determination of the persons entitled to the guarantee and as regards the content of that guarantee, those elements are not sufficient to enable individuals to rely, as against the State, on those provisions before the national courts.
18. With regard, more particularly, to the problem raised by the national court, it should be pointed out that the directive on the insolvency of employers does not oblige the Member States to set up a single guarantee institution for all categories of employee, and consequently to bring higher management staff within the ambit of the guarantee institution established for the other categories of employee. Article 3(1) leaves it to the Member

States to adopt the measures necessary to ensure that guarantee institutions guarantee payment of employees' outstanding claims.

19. From the discretion thus given to the Member States it must therefore be concluded that higher management staff cannot rely on the directive in order to request the payment of amounts owing by way of salary from the guarantee institution established for the other categories of employee.

20. Thirdly, it should be borne in mind that when it interprets and applies national law, every national court must presume that the State had the intention of fulfilling entirely the obligations arising from the directive concerned. As the Court held in *Marleasing SA v La Comercial Internacional de Alimentación SA* Case C-106/89, in applying national law, whether the provisions in question were adopted before or after the directive, the national court called upon to interpret it is required to do so, so far as possible, in the light of the wording and the purpose of the directive in order to achieve the result pursued by the latter and thereby comply with the third paragraph of Article 189 of the [EEC] Treaty [now Article 288 TFEU].

21. The principle of interpretation in conformity with directives must be followed in particular where a national court considers, as in the present case, that the pre-existing provisions of its national law satisfy the requirements of the directive concerned.

22. It would appear from the order for reference that the national provisions cannot be interpreted in a way which conforms with the directive on the insolvency of employers and therefore do not permit higher management staff to obtain the benefit of the guarantees for which it provides. If that is the case, it follows from the *Francovich* judgment, cited above, that the Member State concerned is obliged to make good the loss and damage sustained as a result of the failure to implement the directive in their respect.

23. The reply to the third question must therefore be that (a) higher management staff are not entitled, under Directive 80/987, to request payment of amounts owing to them by way of salary from the guarantee institution established by national law for the other categories of employee, and (b) in the event that, even when interpreted in the light of that directive, national law does not enable higher management staff to obtain the benefit of the guarantees for which it provides, such staff are entitled to request the State concerned to make good the loss and damage sustained as a result of the failure to implement the directive in their respect.

The relevant Spanish law quite clearly restricted the coverage of the existing fund by excluding higher management staff and the Court of Justice considered that it could therefore not be interpreted as permitting higher management employees to claim from it, despite the obligation in the Directive to establish a fund that covered *all* employees. The only possible remedy for Wagner Miret was that the State should recompense him for his losses, since its failure to transpose the Directive had caused his loss (see further Chapter 5 on the availability of actions against the State).

It is interesting to note, from a UK perspective, that the Court of Appeal in *Google Inc v Vidal-Hall and others* [2015] EWCA Civ 311, [2015] 3 WLR 409 (see also earlier), held that a consistent interpretation might be achievable even if part of a domestic law had to be disapplied, so long as this did not alter a key feature of the domestic legislation and was not inconsistent with its key principles.

Google Inc v Vidal-Hall and others [2015] EWCA Civ 311, [2015] 3 WLR 409

90. But it does not follow that it is never possible to interpret a measure by disapplying or striking down part of it in order to make it compatible with the Convention or a directive. Various interpretative techniques may be deployed in order to eliminate an incompatibility. The relevant question in each case is whether the change brought about by the interpretation alters a fundamental feature of the legislation or is inconsistent with its essential principles or goes against its grain, to use Lord Rodger's memorable phrase. In our view, there is no significance in the interpretative tool that is used. Reading in to a provision or reading it down may change a fundamental element of it. That is not permissible. But we do not see why, as a matter of principle, it is impermissible to disapply or strike down, say, a relatively minor incompatible provision in order to make the measure compatible. The question must always be whether the change that would result from the proposed interpretation (whichever interpretative technique is adopted) would alter a fundamental feature of the legislation. It will not be 'possible' to interpret domestic legislation, whether by reading in, reading down or disapplying a provision, if to do so would distort or undermine some important feature of the legislation.

Unsurprisingly, the duty to reach a consistent interpretation is greater if the national law at issue was intended to implement EU law. For example, in Case 80/86 *Kolpinghuis Nijmegen* [1987] ECR 3969, at para 12, the Court of Justice stated that 'in applying the national law *and in particular the provisions of a national law specifically introduced in order to implement the directive*, national courts are required to interpret their national law in the light of the wording and the purpose of the directive' (emphasis added) in order to achieve the result prescribed by the Directive. The duty is even greater—and indeed perhaps absolute—where the national law not only implements EU law, but also reproduces it word for word. In such circumstances, the Court of Justice held in C-306/12 *Spedition Welter GmbH v Avanssur SA* EU:C:2013:650, [2014] Lloyd's Rep IR 360, that the national court was required to interpret national law consistently with the Directive in question (Directive 2009/103/EC of the European Parliament and of the Council of 16 September 2009 relating to insurance against civil liability in respect of the use of motor vehicles, and the enforcement of the obligation to insure against such liability, OJ 2009 L263/11) and with the German law that transposed it. This was so even though the Directive (and the transposing law) authorized a claims representative to accept service of judicial documents, whereas German law on civil procedure required an agent to be authorized by formal act to accept service.

REVIEW QUESTION

Suppose that you have recently suffered from a respiratory infection contracted while swimming in polluted seawater off a beach in Ireland. Tests indicate that the water contains 2.5 per cent blisterium, a chemical known to produce respiratory infections. (Fictitious) Directive 00/00 provides that the presence of any amount over 2 per cent leads to the awarding of compensation to anyone contracting infection as a consequence. The (fictitious) Irish Sea Act 1827 provides that presence of any amount over 4 per cent triggers a mandatory procedure to reduce the proportion of blisterium to acceptable levels. The Act does not refer to compensation. How, if at all, could indirect effect apply in this scenario?

Answer: National courts are under a duty to interpret domestic legislation consistently with EU law (*Von Colson*) and thus to interpret the Act in line with the Directive. This is so regardless of whether the domestic law was intended to transpose the Directive and even where it predates the Directive (*Marleasing*), so the fact that the Act dates from 1927, long before the Directive was adopted, does not prevent the duty from arising. However, the duty applies only 'as far as possible' (per eg *Marleasing*). Two questions therefore arise.

(a) Is it possible to interpret 4 per cent as 2 per cent?

(b) Is it possible to interpret the Act as granting compensation even though its wording includes no such provision?

The answer is not clear-cut.

On one hand, in *Marleasing*, the Court of Justice held that it was possible to interpret a Spanish law that permitted a company to be declared void for lack of cause as not in fact permitting this, consistently with a Directive that contained no such provision, on the basis that the Directive's provisions were clear. Here, the Directive clearly specifies 2 per cent and the provision of compensation, and thus it could be argued that the Act must be interpreted accordingly, particularly since the Act actually contains broadly similar provisions—ie it does restrict blisterium to a minimum percentage and it does provide for serious consequences if this is exceeded.

On the other hand, in *Wagner Miret*, the Court of Justice concluded that it was not possible to interpret a national law that excluded higher management employees from compensation consistently with a Directive that did not. On this basis, it could be argued that 4 per cent is quite clear and cannot be interpreted as 2 per cent. The position as to compensation may be different—and while it could similarly be argued that the lack of provision in the Act is also clear and cannot be interpreted as meaning that compensation should be provided, it could alternatively be argued that this omission creates a neutral position on compensation under the Act and that, since indirect effect imposes a positive duty on national courts where 'possible', the Act must be interpreted so as to provide compensation.

Although it can be difficult to decide when a consistent interpretation is 'possible' and when it is not, it should always be remembered that it is not necessary for a consistent interpretation to be the only, or even the most obvious, interpretation. If there are several 'possible' interpretations, one of which is consistent with EU law, it is this consistent interpretation that must be adopted.

For example, in *Webb v EMO Air Cargo (UK) Ltd* [1993] 1 CMLR 259 (see 4.2.2 for the facts of *Webb*), the applicant claimed that she had been discriminated against. Section 5(3) of the Sex Discrimination Act 1975 provides that, in order to show discrimination, any comparison between the treatment of women and that of men must be made on the basis of similar 'relevant circumstances'. The House of Lords (now the Supreme Court) initially interpreted 'relevant circumstances' to mean Webb's unavailability for work and concluded that, since a male employee who was unavailable to work would have been treated in the same way, there was no discrimination. However, it made a preliminary reference to the Court of Justice as to whether the applicant's dismissal was contrary to the Equal Treatment Directive (Directive 76/207) (see further Chapter 6 on the preliminary reference procedure). The Court of Justice ruled that the Directive precluded the dismissal of an employee recruited for an unlimited term with a view, initially, to replacing another employee during the latter's maternity leave and who could not do so due to pregnancy. In the light of this ruling, the House of Lords reached a different interpretation of the term 'relevant circumstances' in the Sex Discrimination Act 1975 to that which it had adopted prior to the ruling. It held that the 'relevant circumstances' were Webb's unavailability for work due to pregnancy and concluded that, since a male employee could not have been dismissed for this reason, the dismissal was discriminatory (*Webb v EMO Air Cargo (UK) Ltd* [1996] 2 CMLR 990).

Although, in the cases just discussed, the applicants sought to establish the indirect effect of EU law in order to enforce their rights under it, an interpretation of national law that is consistent with an EU Directive can, in some circumstances, have adverse consequences for an individual. This is a logical consequence of the horizontal application of indirect effect: whereas Directives can have direct effect only against the State or an emanation of the State (see 4.1.4), they (and all other types of EU law) can have indirect effect against any potential defendant because it is national law that is being enforced directly, not the Directive itself.

There is, however, a restriction on the indirect effect of Directives. In Case 14/86 *Pretore di Salò v Persons unknown* [1987] ECR 2545, the defendant was prosecuted for an offence under Council Directive 78/659/EEC of 18 July 1978 on the quality of fresh waters needing protection or improvement in order to support fish life, OJ 1978 L222/1. The national court made a preliminary reference under Article 267 TFEU (see further Chapter 6 on the preliminary reference procedure) on whether, in the absence of specific transposing measures, national law must be interpreted so as to support such a prosecution. The Court of Justice concluded that a Directive 'cannot, of itself and independently of a national law adopted by a Member State for its implementation, have the effect of determining or aggravating the liability in criminal law of persons who act in contravention of the provisions of that directive' (*Pretore di Salò*, at para 20). As the following extract demonstrates, the Court took a similar approach in Case 80/86 *Kolpinghuis Nijmegen* [1987] ECR 3969, in which the defendant was prosecuted for an offence under Council Directive 80/777/EEC of 15 July 1980 on the approximation of the laws of the Member States relating to the exploitation and marketing of natural mineral waters, OJ 1980 L229/1. The alleged offence took place after the deadline for transposition of the Directive had passed, but before the Netherlands had amended its national legislation to comply with the provisions of the Directive.

Case 80/86 *Kolpinghuis Nijmegen* [1987] ECR 3969

13. However, that obligation on the national court to refer to the content of the directive when interpreting the relevant rules of its national law is limited by the general principles of law which form part of Community law [now EU law] and in particular the principles of legal

> certainty and non-retroactivity. Thus the Court ruled in its judgment of 11 June 1987 in Case 14/86 *Pretore di Salò v X* [1987] ECR 2545 that a directive cannot, of itself and independently of a national law adopted by a Member State for its implementation, have the effect of determining or aggravating the liability in criminal law of persons who act in contravention of the provisions of that directive.

In *Kolpinghuis Nijmegen*, the Court of Justice invoked not only the principle of legal certainty in support of its argument that Directives could not have the indirect effect of imposing criminal liability, but also the principle of **non-retroactivity**.

non-retroactivity The principle of the non-retroactive application of the criminal law means that an individual can only be prosecuted for an offence if it was an offence at the date they committed the act or omission constituting the offence and not if it only became an offence after that date. This principle is now enshrined in Article 47 of the EU Charter of Fundamental Rights of the European Union (see further 9.4 on the Charter).

?! THINKING POINT

What is the principle of legal certainty? If you have difficulty in answering this question, review 3.4.5.

However, in Case C-105/03 *Pupino* [2005] ECR I-5285 (see also earlier in this section), the Court of Justice held that this exception to the duty to give indirect effect to EU law wherever possible was limited to criminal liability and did not apply to the conduct of criminal proceedings. In that case, criminal proceedings were brought against a teacher, alleging ill-treatment of a number of pupils who were under 5 years old. The prosecution asked the judge to take the testimony of the children prior to the trial and in special facilities, on account of their extreme youth and psychological state. However, the case did not fall within the category of those for which such special arrangements were made available under national law and so the national court made a preliminary reference to the Court of Justice under Article 267 TFEU (see further Chapter 6 on the preliminary reference procedure) on the correct interpretation of Directive 2012/29/EU of the European Parliament and of the Council of 25 October 2012 establishing minimum standards on the rights, support and protection of victims of crime, and replacing Council Framework Decision 2001/220/JHA, OJ 2012 L315/57—a measure equivalent to a Directive under Article 34 TEU (1992), now repealed—on the status of victims in criminal proceedings. The Court of Justice held that although legal certainty and non-retroactivity prevented the doctrine of indirect effect from leading to the imposition or increase of criminal liability on the basis of EU law alone, independently of national implementing measures, the issue before it did not involve the imposition of such liability, but merely a procedural issue (*Pupino*, at para 46). The national court must therefore interpret the national law at issue, as far as possible, in the light of the wording and purpose of the Framework Directive, which required that young children claiming to be victims of ill-treatment be able to give their evidence with an appropriate level of protection.

In Case C-168/95 *Arcaro* [1996] ECR I-4705, a case involving criminal proceedings brought under Council Directive 76/464/EEC of 4 May 1976 on pollution caused by certain dangerous substances discharged into the aquatic environment of the Community, OJ 1976 L129/23, the Court of Justice similarly ruled that a Directive could not be used to interpret national law so as to give rise to the imposition of criminal liability. However, certain of the Court's comments in that case appear to apply also to civil liability, as the following extract demonstrates.

Case C-168/95 *Arcaro* [1996] ECR I-4705

41. It should be added that the Member States' obligation, arising under a directive, to achieve the result envisaged by the directive and their duty, under Article 5 of the [EC] Treaty [now Article 4(3) TEU], to take all appropriate measures, whether general or particular, to ensure fulfilment of that obligation, are binding on all the authorities of Member States including, for matters within their jurisdiction, the courts. It follows that, in applying national law, the national court called upon to interpret that law is required to do so, as far as possible, in the light of the wording and purpose of the directive in order to achieve the result pursued by the directive and thereby comply with the third paragraph of Article 189 of the [EEC] Treaty [now Article 288 TFEU] (see the judgments in Case C-106/89 *Marleasing* [1990] ECR I-4135, paragraph 8, and Case C-334/92 *Wagner Miret* [1993] ECR I-6911, paragraph 20).
42. However, that obligation of the national court to refer to the content of the directive when interpreting the relevant rules of its own national law reaches a limit where such an interpretation leads to the imposition on an individual of an obligation laid down by a directive which has not been transposed or, more especially, where it has the effect of determining or aggravating, on the basis of the directive and in the absence of a law enacted for its implementation, the liability in criminal law of persons who act in contravention of that directive's provisions (see the judgment in *Kolpinghuis Nijmegen*, [Case 80/86 *Kolpinghuis Nijmegen* [1987] ECR 3969], paragraphs 13 and 14).

Thus the Court refers to the limit on the application of indirect effect 'especially' (and therefore presumably not only) in cases of criminal liability, while the earlier part of the same sentence provides that the duty to apply indirect effect 'reaches a limit where such an interpretation leads to the imposition on an individual of *an obligation* laid down by a directive which has not been transposed' (*Arcaro*, para 42, emphasis added). The reference to 'an obligation' is apt to include civil obligations, as well as criminal liability. However, in Case C-456/98 *Centrosteel v Adipol GmbH* [2000] ECR I-6007, a case involving civil liability, Advocate General Jacobs argued at para 35 of his Opinion (see 2.4.1 on Advocate Generals' Opinions) that although a Directive could not, without transposing legislation, impose criminal liability, 'it may well lead to the imposition upon an individual of civil liability or a civil obligation which would not otherwise have existed'. In that case, Centrosteel, which had acted as commercial agent for Adipol, claimed against it for payment of commission. Under Italian law, Centrosteel was prohibited from recovering sums due to it under the agency contract because it was not registered as a commercial agent. However, Council Directive 86/653/EEC of 18 December 1986 on the coordination of the laws of the Member States relating to self-employed commercial agents, OJ 1986 L382/17, had previously been interpreted by the Court of Justice as precluding such a law. In *Centrosteel*, the Court of Justice's reasoning (set out in the following extract) did not explicitly address the principle of whether an untransposed Directive could impose civil liability on an individual or business, but its ruling had the result that such liability was imposed on Adipol.

Case C-456/98 *Centrosteel v Adipol GmbH* [2000] ECR I-6007

15. It is true that, according to settled case-law of the Court, in the absence of proper transposition into national law, a directive cannot of itself impose obligations on individuals (Case 152/84 *Marshall v Southampton and South-West Hampshire Health Authority* [1986] ECR 723, paragraph 48, and Case C-91/92 *Faccini Dori v Recreb* [1994] ECR I-3325, paragraph 20).
16. However, it is also apparent from the case-law of the Court (Case C-106/89 *Marleasing v La Comercial Internacional de Alimentación* [1990] ECR I-4135, paragraph 8; Case C-334/92 *Wagner Miret v Fondo de Garantía Salarial* [1993] ECR I-6911, paragraph 20; *Faccini Dori*, paragraph 26; and Joined Cases C-240/98 to C-244/98 *Ocèano Grupo Editorial v Salvat Editores* [2000] ECR I-4941, paragraph 30) that, when applying national law, whether adopted before or after the directive, the national court that has to interpret that law must do so, as far as possible, in the light of the wording and the purpose of the directive so as to achieve the result it has in view and thereby comply with the third paragraph of Article 189 of the EC Treaty (now the third paragraph of Article 249 EC) [now Article 288 TFEU].
17. Where it is seised of a dispute falling within the scope of the Directive and arising from facts postdating the expiry of the period for transposing the Directive, the national court, in applying provisions of domestic law or settled domestic case-law, as seems to be the case in the main proceedings, must therefore interpret that law in such a way that it is applied in conformity with the aims of the Directive. As the Advocate General points out in paragraph 36 of his Opinion, it seems in that regard that the Corte Suprema di Cassazione (Supreme Court of Cassation), following the judgment in *Bellone*, has changed its case-law so that a failure to comply with the obligation prescribed by Law No 204 to be entered in the register of commercial agents and representatives no longer entails the nullity of an agency contract in Italian law.

The Court of Justice held that the national court must interpret national law in line with the Directive and that the Directive precluded national legislation that made the validity of an agency contract conditional upon the registration of the agent. The result of this ruling was that Adipol was obliged to pay the amount due to Centrosteel under the contract, whereas, under Italian law interpreted without reference to the Directive, the contract would have been unenforceable and Adipol would not have been obliged to pay. This suggests that the limit on indirect effect in cases of criminal liability (ie to prevent national law from being interpreted consistently with a Directive where this would result in the imposition of criminal liability) may not apply to prevent the imposition of civil liability.

4.2.5 The relationship between indirect effect and the supremacy of EU law

THINKING POINT

How does the concept of indirect effect relate to what you learned about the sovereignty of EU law? If you have difficulty in answering this, look back at 3.1.

First, indirect effect is a practical manifestation of the sovereignty of EU law (see further 3.1.2), because an interpretation of national law that is consistent with EU law takes precedence over an interpretation that does not. Secondly, where national law clearly conflicts with EU law and cannot be interpreted consistently with it, the national court is under a duty to refuse to apply the conflicting elements of national law.

The duty on national courts to disapply national law that conflicts with EU law was established in Case 106/77 *Amministrazione delle Finanze dello Stato v Simmenthal ('Simmenthal II')* [1978] ECR 629 (see also 3.1.2), in which the applicants sought repayment of a fee on their imports that the Court had earlier ruled, in Case 35/76 *Amministrazione delle Finanze dello Stato v Simmenthal ('Simmenthal I')* [1976] ECR 1871, to be contrary to EU law on the free movement of goods (see Chapter 10).

?! THINKING POINT

While reading the following extract, consider why the Court of Justice considered that Italian law that was contrary to EU law must be disapplied.

Case 106/77 *Amministrazione delle Finanze dello Stato v Simmenthal ('Simmenthal II')* [1978] ECR 629

14. Direct applicability in such circumstances means that rules of Community law [now EU law] must be fully and uniformly applied in all the Member States from the date of their entry into force and for so long as they continue in force.
15. These provisions are therefore a direct source of rights and duties for all those affected thereby, whether Member States or individuals, who are parties to legal relationships under Community law.
16. This consequence also concerns any national court whose task it is as an organ of a Member State to protect, in a case within its jurisdiction, the rights conferred upon individuals by Community law.
17. Furthermore, in accordance with the principle of the precedence of Community law, the relationship between provisions of the Treaty and directly applicable measures of the institutions on the one hand and the national law of the Member States on the other is such that those provisions and measures not only by their entry into force render automatically inapplicable any conflicting provision of current national law but—in so far as they are an integral part of, and take precedence in, the legal order applicable in the territory of each of the Member States—also preclude the valid adoption of new national legislative measures to the extent to which they would be incompatible with Community [now Union] provisions.
18. Indeed any recognition that national legislative measures which encroach upon the field within which the Community exercises its legislative power or which are otherwise incompatible with the provisions of Community law had any legal effect would amount to a corresponding denial of the effectiveness of obligations undertaken unconditionally and irrevocably by Member States pursuant to the Treaty and would thus imperil the very foundations of the Community.

19. The same conclusion emerges from the structure of Article 177 of the [EEC] Treaty [now Article 267 TFEU] which provides that any court or tribunal of a Member State is entitled to make a reference to the Court whenever it considers that a preliminary ruling on a question of interpretation or validity relating to Community law is necessary to enable it to give judgment.
20. The effectiveness of that provision would be impaired if the national court were prevented from forthwith applying Community law in accordance with the decision or the case-law of the Court.
21. It follows from the foregoing that every national court must, in a case within its jurisdiction, apply Community law in its entirety and protect rights which the latter confers on individuals and must accordingly set aside any provision of national law which may conflict with it, whether prior or subsequent to the Community rule.
22. Accordingly any provision of a national legal system and any legislative, administrative or judicial practice which might impair the effectiveness of Community law by withholding from the national court having jurisdiction to apply such law the power to do everything necessary at the moment of its application to set aside national legislative provisions which might prevent Community rules from having full force and effect are incompatible with those requirements which are the very essence of Community law.
23. This would be the case in the event of a conflict between a provision of Community law and a subsequent national law if the solution of the conflict were to be reserved for an authority with a discretion of its own, other than the court called upon to apply Community law, even if such an impediment to the full effectiveness of community law were only temporary.
24. The first question should therefore be answered to the effect that a national court which is called upon, within the limits of its jurisdiction, to apply provisions of Community law is under a duty to give full effect to those provisions, if necessary refusing of its own motion to apply any conflicting provision of national legislation, even if adopted subsequently, and it is not necessary for the court to request or await the prior setting aside of such provision by legislative or other constitutional means.

The Court of Justice based its ruling on the requirement to disapply national law on the basis of 'the precedence of [EU] law' (*Simmenthal II*, at para 17) and the need to ensure the effectiveness of what is now Article 267 TFEU (see further Chapter 6). In subsequent cases, the Court has made it clear that the obligation on national courts to disapply conflicting national law arises only where that national law cannot be interpreted consistently with EU law (see, for example, C-306/12 *Spedition Welter GmbH v Avanssur SA* EU:C:2013:650, [2014] Lloyd's Rep IR 360, at para 28).

Where the conflicting national law imposes a duty or prohibition on an applicant that is contrary to EU law, the applicant could benefit from it being disapplied. For example, in Case C-221/89 *R v Secretary of State for Transport, ex p Factortame Ltd ('Factortame II')* [1991] ECR I-3905 (see further 3.1.2, 5.4.1, and 6.10.2), the applicants were Spanish fishermen who were prohibited from fishing in British waters by the provisions of the Merchant Shipping Act 1988. They therefore sought (successfully) to have the Act disapplied so that they could legally resume fishing.

This situation of direct conflict should be distinguished from the contrasting situation in which national law gives the applicant rights that are not as favourable as those granted by EU law. In this latter situation, the applicant could be worse off if the national law is disapplied. This is because if the EU measure in question has no direct or indirect effect, the applicant's only rights are under national law. In these circumstances, national law would not be disapplied.

NOTE

The indirect effect of EU law is of considerable practical importance. If you have difficulty in understanding indirect effect or its application by the UK courts (and most students do!), you should review 4.2 before going on to the next topic.

4.2.6 Summary of indirect effect

The key features of the concept of indirect effect are summarized in Figure 4.2.

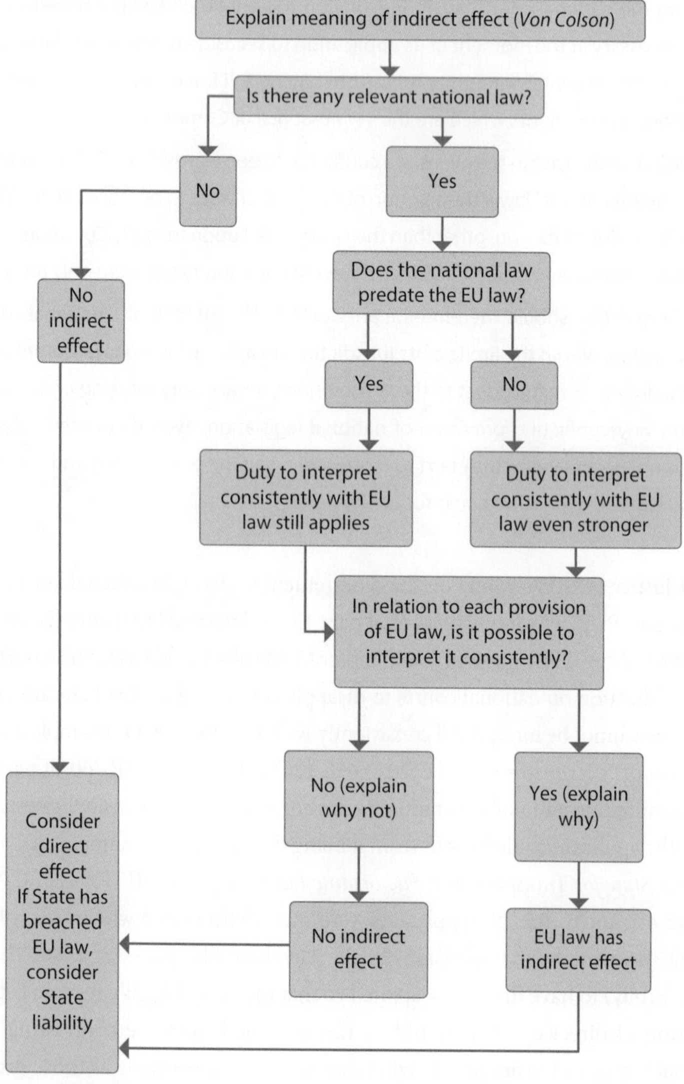

Figure 4.2 Summary of indirect effect

4.3 Remedies

The obligation on Member States to ensure that a remedy is available in the national courts for breaches of EU law is enshrined both in Article 19(1) TEU and Article 47 of the Charter of Fundamental Rights of the European Union (on the Charter, see further 9.4).

Article 19 TEU

1. Member States shall provide remedies sufficient to ensure effective legal protection in the fields covered by Union law.

Charter of Fundamental Rights of the European Union

Article 47

Right to an effective remedy and to a fair trial

Everyone whose rights and freedoms guaranteed by the law of the Union are violated has the right to an effective remedy before a tribunal in compliance with the conditions laid down in this Article.

A remedy may be awarded in the national courts for a breach of EU law where:

- the EU measure is directly effective and has been breached by the defendant;
- the EU measure is indirectly effective and national law, interpreted consistently with it, has been breached by the defendant; or
- a Member State has breached its obligations under EU law and is liable in damages as a result (see further Chapter 5).

Damages or the annulment of a provision of EU law may also be awarded for breaches of EU law committed by the EU itself, but actions against the EU must be brought before the EU Courts, which will apply the relevant remedy under EU law (see Chapters 7 and 8).

In an action in the national courts, the award of any remedy for breach of EU law is governed by national law (see eg Case 33/76 *Rewe-Zentralfinanz eG and Rewe-Zentral AG v Landwirtschaftskammer für das Saarland* [1976] ECR 1989). This is perhaps surprising, given that the cause of action is based directly or indirectly on EU law and given the Court of Justice's enthusiasm for making EU law rights enforceable.

?! THINKING POINT

While reading the following extract, consider why the Court of Justice held that the award of a remedy is governed by national law.

Case 33/76 *Rewe-Zentralfinanz eG and Rewe-Zentral AG v Landwirtschaftskammer für das Saarland* [1976] ECR 1989

5. Applying the principle of cooperation laid down in Article 5 of the [EC] Treaty [now Article 4(3) TEU], it is the national courts which are entrusted with ensuring the legal protection which citizens derive from the direct effect of the provisions of Community law [now EU law].

   Accordingly, in the absence of Community [now Union] rules on this subject, it is for the domestic legal system of each Member State to designate the courts having jurisdiction and to determine the procedural conditions governing actions at law intended to ensure the protection of the rights which citizens have from the direct effect of Community law, it being understood that such conditions cannot be less favourable than those relating to similar actions of a domestic nature.

   Where necessary, Articles 100 to 102 and 235 of the [EEC] Treaty [now Articles 115–117 and 352 TFEU] enable appropriate measures to be taken to remedy differences between the provisions laid down by law, regulation or administrative action in Member States if they are likely to distort or harm the functioning of the Common Market.

   In the absence of such measures of harmonization the right conferred by Community law must be exercised before the national courts in accordance with the conditions laid down by national rules.

   The position would be different only if the conditions and time-limits made it impossible in practice to exercise the rights which the national courts are obliged to protect …

However, this approach poses potential threats to the uniform application of EU law and even to the effective protection of rights granted by it. The Court of Justice has therefore attempted to mitigate these problems by laying down a number of principles with which the award of a remedy by the national courts must comply. These principles have been developed somewhat ad hoc by the Court over a number of years, and are not as clear and coherent as they might be; indeed, in some respects they appear to conflict.

4.3.1 Equivalence

The Court of Justice has held on many occasions that any remedy for breach of EU law must be available on conditions as favourable as those applicable to a remedy for breach of an equivalent national law. For example, in Case 33/76 *Rewe-Zentralfinanz eG and Rewe-Zentral AG v Landwirtschaftskammer für das Saarland* [1976] ECR 1989 (see 4.3), the applicants claimed for the repayment of certain customs duties that had been levied on them and which had been declared by the Court of Justice to be contrary to Article 30 TFEU (see 10.4). The action was dismissed for failure to bring it within the applicable time limits and the applicants alleged that this dismissal was contrary to EU law. The Court of Justice held that an action based on EU law could legitimately be dismissed on such a basis, because the procedure leading to the award of a remedy was governed by national law—but only as long as certain conditions were met. One of the conditions set by the Court in this case, the principle of effectiveness, is discussed at 4.3.2; the other is the principle of equivalence.

?! THINKING POINT

While reading the following extract, note the wording used by the Court of Justice to explain the principle—a formulation that appears in many of its judgments.

Case 33/76 *Rewe-Zentralfinanz eG and Rewe-Zentral AG v Landwirtschaftskammer für das Saarland* [1976] ECR 1989

5. ... The position would be different only if the conditions and time-limits made it impossible in practice to exercise the rights which the national courts are obliged to protect.
   This is not the case where reasonable periods of limitation of actions are fixed.
   The laying down of such time-limits with regard to actions of a fiscal nature is an application of the fundamental principle of legal certainty protecting both the tax-payer and the administration concerned.
6. The answer to be given to the first question is therefore that in the present state of Community law [now EU law] there is nothing to prevent a citizen who contests before a national court a decision of a national authority on the ground that it is incompatible with Community law from being confronted with the defence that limitation periods laid down by national law have expired, it being understood that the procedural conditions governing the action may not be less favourable than those relating to similar actions of a domestic nature.

In Case C-231/96 *Edilizia Industriale Siderurgica Srl (Edis) v Ministero delle Finanze* [1998] ECR I-4951 (see also 4.3.2), the Court of Justice re-examined this principle. In that case, the applicant had brought an action to recover charges levied in contravention of EU law. The action was dismissed because it was not brought within the three-year time limit applicable under national law to claims for repayment from the State. The applicant argued that the ten-year time limit applicable to claims between private parties should be applied and that the application of the three-year time limit discriminated against claims based on EU law.

?! THINKING POINT

While reading the following extract, consider why the Court of Justice reached the decision that the time limit in this case was compatible with the principle of equivalence.

Case C-231/96 *Edilizia Industriale Siderurgica Srl (Edis) v Ministero delle Finanze* [1998] ECR I-4951

24. It is clear from those judgments that a Member State may not adopt provisions making repayment of a tax held to be contrary to Community law [now EU law] by a judgment of the Court, or whose incompatibility with Community law is apparent from such a judgment,

subject to conditions relating specifically to that tax which are less favourable than those which would otherwise be applied to repayment of the tax in question.

[...]

36. Observance of the principle of equivalence implies, for its part, that the procedural rule at issue applies without distinction to actions alleging infringements of Community law and to those alleging infringements of national law, with respect to the same kind of charges or dues (see, to that effect, Joined Cases 66/79, 127/79, and 128/79 *Amministrazione delle Finanze dello Stato v Salumi* [1980] ECR 1237, paragraph 21). That principle cannot, however, be interpreted as obliging a Member State to extend its most favourable rules governing recovery under national law to all actions for repayment of charges or dues levied in breach of Community law.

37. Thus, Community law does not preclude the legislation of a Member State from laying down, alongside a limitation period applicable under the ordinary law to actions between private individuals for the recovery of sums paid but not due, special detailed rules, which are less favourable, governing claims and legal proceedings to challenge the imposition of charges and other levies. The position would be different only if those detailed rules applied solely to actions based on Community law for the repayment of such charges or levies.

The Court concluded that it was not contrary to EU law for national courts to apply a stricter time limit to an action based on EU law than to some other actions, so long as the stricter time limits were also applied to similar actions based on national law.

The Court of Justice provided guidance on how a national court should determine an appropriate comparative action under national law in Case C-326/96 *Levez v Jennings Ltd* [1998] ECR I-7835. Levez claimed arrears of pay that she had not received because of sex discrimination by her employer, in breach of the Equal Treatment Directive (Directive 76/207). The Employment Appeal Tribunal (EAT) made a preliminary reference to the Court of Justice under Article 267 TFEU (see further Chapter 6 on the preliminary reference procedure) on a number of issues, including which actions under national law should be treated as equivalent for the purposes of ensuring an equivalent remedy. The Court held that the UK could not claim that an action for breach of the Equal Pay Act 1970 was an appropriate comparison, because the Act was intended to transpose the Directive and therefore actions under each were effectively the same action, rather than two separate actions.

?! THINKING POINT

While reading the following extract, make a note of the guidance offered by the Court of Justice on whether actions can be regarded as equivalent.

Case C-326/96 *Levez v Jennings Ltd* [1998] ECR I-7835

43. In order to determine whether the principle of equivalence has been complied with in the present case, the national court—which alone has direct knowledge of the procedural rules governing actions in the field of employment law—must consider both the purpose

and the essential characteristics of allegedly similar domestic actions (see *Palmisani* [Case C-261/95 *Rosalba Palmisani v Istituto nazionale della previdenza sociale (INPS)* [1997] ECR I-4025], paragraphs 34 to 38).

44. Furthermore, whenever it falls to be determined whether a procedural rule of national law is less favourable than those governing similar domestic actions, the national court must take into account the role played by that provision in the procedure as a whole, as well as the operation and any special features of that procedure before the different national courts (see, *mutatis mutandis*, *Van Schijndel and Van Veen* [Joined Cases C-430/93 and C-431/93 *van Schijndel and van Veen v Stichting Pensioenfonds voor Fysiotherapeuten* [1995] ECR I-4705], paragraph 19).

4.3.2 Effectiveness

The Court of Justice has repeatedly stated that national laws on the award of a remedy for breach of EU law must not interfere with the 'effectiveness' of rights guaranteed under that law. However, the standard of effectiveness is not particularly high. In Case 33/76 *Rewe-Zentralfinanz eG and Rewe-Zentral AG v Landwirtschaftskammer für das Saarland* [1976] ECR 1989 (see also 4.3 and 4.3.1), the Court of Justice held that national law governed the award of a remedy subject only to the principles of equivalence (see 4.3.1) and effectiveness. It explained that the latter would be breached only where 'the conditions and time-limits made it impossible in practice to exercise the rights which the national courts are obliged to protect' (*Rewe-Zentralfinanz eG and Rewe-Zentral AG*, at para 5). In subsequent cases such as Case C-231/96 *Edilizia Industriale Siderurgica Srl (Edis) v Ministero delle Finanze* [1998] ECR I-4951 (see also 4.3.1), the Court refined the phrase used to encapsulate the principle of equivalence.

?! THINKING POINT

While reading the following extract, make a note of the phrase used by the Court of Justice to summarize the principle of effectiveness—a formulation that has appeared in many of its subsequent judgments.

Case C-231/96 *Edilizia Industriale Siderurgica Srl (Edis) v Ministero delle Finanze* [1998] ECR I-4951

34. This diversity between national systems derives mainly from the lack of Community [now EU] rules on the refunding of national charges levied though not due. In such circumstances, as pointed out in paragraph 19 of this judgment, it is for the domestic legal system of each Member State to designate the courts and tribunals having jurisdiction and to lay down the detailed procedural rules governing actions for safeguarding rights which individuals derive from Community law [now EU law], provided, first, that such rules are not

less favourable than those governing similar domestic actions (principle of equivalence) and, second, that they do not render virtually impossible or excessively difficult the exercise of rights conferred by Community law (principle of effectiveness).

One type of remedy that has led to many allegations of breach of the principle of effectiveness is the award of damages, and national restrictions on the availability or amount of damages have been held to impair the effectiveness of EU law on a number of occasions. For example, in Case C-271/91 *Marshall v Southampton and South West Area Health Authority (No 2)* [1993] ECR I-4367 (for the facts, see *Marshall (No 1)*, discussed at 4.1.4), Marshall disputed the severe restrictions that the Sex Discrimination Act 1975 imposed on the amount of damages that could be awarded to her and argued that interest should also be awarded. The House of Lords (now the Supreme Court) made a preliminary reference to the Court of Justice under Article 267 TFEU (see further Chapter 6 on the preliminary reference procedure).

?! THINKING POINT

While reading the following extract, consider why the limit on damages and the lack of any award of interest on those damages was held by the Court of Justice to be contrary to EU law.

Case C-271/91 *Marshall v Southampton and South West Area Health Authority (No 2)* [1993] ECR I-4367

26. Where financial compensation is the measure adopted in order to achieve the objective indicated above, it must be adequate, in that it must enable the loss and damage actually sustained as a result of the discriminatory dismissal to be made good in full in accordance with the applicable national rules.

[…]

30. It also follows from that interpretation that the fixing of an upper limit of the kind at issue in the main proceedings cannot, by definition, constitute proper implementation of Article 6 of the Directive, since it limits the amount of compensation a priori to a level which is not necessarily consistent with the requirement of ensuring real equality of opportunity through adequate reparation for the loss and damage sustained as a result of discriminatory dismissal.
31. With regard to the second part of the second question relating to the award of interest, suffice it to say that full compensation for the loss and damage sustained as a result of discriminatory dismissal cannot leave out of account factors, such as the effluxion of time, which may in fact reduce its value. The award of interest, in accordance with the applicable national rules, must therefore be regarded as an essential component of compensation for the purposes of restoring real equality of treatment.

The Court of Justice ruled that the UK Act conflicted with the UK government's obligation under what is now Article 288 TFEU (see further 3.4.2) to ensure that the objectives of Directives were fulfilled. The objective of the Equal Treatment Directive was to achieve real equality of opportunity, which required that where such equality had not been achieved, the victim of discrimination could be reinstated or compensated in full for the loss and damage sustained.

Similarly, in Case 14/83 *Von Colson and Kamann v Land Nordrhein-Westfalen* [1984] ECR 1891 (see also 4.2.1 and 4.2.2), two women who had attended job interviews, but failed to secure the post, brought claims for damages on the grounds of sex discrimination. The Court of Justice ruled that the compensation must be adequate in relation to the damage sustained and that a German law that limited the amount of compensation to a 'purely nominal amount, such as, for example, the reimbursement of expenses incurred by them in submitting their application' (*Von Colson*, at para 24), did not effectively protect the applicants' rights under EU law.

However, limited damages may nonetheless provide an effective remedy for breaches considered to be minor. For example, in Case C-180/95 *Draehmpaehl v Urania Immobilienservice OHG* [1997] ECR I-2195, the Court of Justice ruled that a national law that prescribed an upper limit of three months' salary as compensation for sex discrimination in the appointment of candidates to a job was contrary to EU law. However, the Court qualified this ruling by stating that such a rule was only invalid insofar as it applied to applicants who would have obtained a post had it not been for the discriminatory selection process. Where an applicant would not have obtained the position anyway and therefore suffered little or no loss, the ceiling of three months' salary was compatible with EU law.

Similar problems occur in the context of business as well as personal losses. For example, in Joined Cases C-46 & 48/93 *Brasserie du Pêcheur SA v Germany; R v Secretary of State for Transport, ex p Factortame ('Factortame III')* [1996] ECR I-1029 (see also 4.3.4, 5.4.1, and 5.5), the Court of Justice ruled that the total exclusion of loss of profit as a head of damages that could be awarded for breach of EU law was incompatible with EU law.

?! THINKING POINT

While reading the following extract, consider why the Court reached this conclusion.

Joined Cases C-46 & 48/93 *Brasserie du Pêcheur SA v Germany; R v Secretary of State for Transport, ex p Factortame ('Factortame III')* [1996] ECR I-1029

87. Total exclusion of loss of profit as a head of damage for which reparation may be awarded in the case of a breach of Community law [now EU law] cannot be accepted. Especially in the context of economic or commercial litigation, such a total exclusion of loss of profit would be such as to make reparation of damage practically impossible.

[...]

90. ... National legislation which generally limits the damage for which reparation may be granted to damage done to certain, specifically protected individual interests not including loss of profit by individuals is not compatible with Community law ...

The Court held that, in the context of commercial litigation, the total exclusion of damages for loss of profit would make genuine reparation of losses suffered practically impossible.

In Case C-453/99 *Courage Ltd v Crehan* [2001] ECR I-6297 (see 15.10), Crehan refused to pay for deliveries of beer from a brewery on the ground that his agreement with the brewery breached what is now Article 101 TFEU (see further Chapter 13). On a preliminary reference by the Court of Appeal to the Court of Justice under Article 267 TFEU (see further Chapter 6 on the preliminary reference procedure), the Court of Justice held that the fact that Crehan had been a party to an anti-competitive agreement did not prevent him from subsequently relying on Treaty provisions that invalidated the agreement or from seeking damages for loss caused by the agreement.

?! THINKING POINT

While reading the following extract, consider why the Court reached this conclusion.

Case C-453/99 *Courage Ltd v Crehan* [2001] ECR I-6297

25. As regards the possibility of seeking compensation for loss caused by a contract or by conduct liable to restrict or distort competition, it should be remembered from the outset that, in accordance with settled case-law, the national courts whose task it is to apply the provisions of Community law [now EU law] in areas within their jurisdiction must ensure that those rules take full effect and must protect the rights which they confer on individuals (see inter alia the judgments in Case 106/77 *Simmenthal* [1978] ECR 629, paragraph 16, and in Case C-213/89 *Factortame* [1990] ECR I-2433, paragraph 19).
26. The full effectiveness of Article 85 of the [EEC] Treaty [now Article 101 TFEU] and, in particular, the practical effect of the prohibition laid down in Article 85(1) would be put at risk if it were not open to any individual to claim damages for loss caused to him by a contract or by conduct liable to restrict or distort competition.
27. Indeed, the existence of such a right strengthens the working of the Community [now Union] competition rules and discourages agreements or practices, which are frequently covert, which are liable to restrict or distort competition. From that point of view, actions for damages before the national courts can make a significant contribution to the maintenance of effective competition in the Community.

The Court held that the effectiveness of the prohibitions on anti-competitive agreements in what is now Article 101 TFEU would be impaired if some individuals, for example those party to the agreements, could not claim damages for losses caused by such agreements.

In Joined Cases C-295, 296, & 298/04 *Manfredi v Lloyd Adriatico Assicurazioni SpA* [2006] ECR I-6619, a number of policyholders claimed damages in respect of increased insurance premiums that had been payable pursuant to an agreement between certain insurance companies, which the Court of Justice had ruled to be in breach of what is now Article 101 TFEU (see Chapter 13). Italian law did not recognize a right to punitive damages. On a further reference under Article 267 TFEU to the Court of Justice (see further Chapter 6 on the preliminary reference procedure), the Court ruled that the principle of effectiveness required that the policyholders be able to seek compensation not only for their actual loss, but also for loss of profit (as in *Factortame III*) *plus* interest (as in *Marshall No 2*) (see earlier in this section).

Another procedural hurdle in respect of which claimants have sought to rely on the principle of effectiveness is that of time limits. As with the award of damages, any time limits on bringing an action are governed by national procedural rules (three years for most actions in the UK), but these will not apply if they make it 'virtually impossible or excessively difficult' to exercise EU law rights.

In Case C-208/90 *Emmott v Minister for Social Welfare and another* [1991] ECR I-4269, Ireland had failed to transpose a Directive equalizing disability benefits until two years after the deadline by which it should have been transposed (on the transposition of Directives, see 3.4.2). Emmott claimed compensation in respect of benefits underpaid during this two-year period, but the Irish authorities alleged that her claim was outside the three-month time limit set by Irish law. This time limit ran from when the grounds for the application arose. The national court made a preliminary reference to the Court of Justice under Article 267 TFEU (see further Chapter 6 on the preliminary reference procedure). The Court of Justice ruled that the time limit should not start to run until the Directive had been properly transposed and therefore the claim was admissible.

In contrast, in Case C-231/96 *Edilizia Industriale Siderurgica Srl (Edis) v Ministero delle Finanze* [1998] ECR I-4951 (see earlier in this section and 4.3.1), the Court of Justice ruled that a time limit of three years on the commencement of actions to recover charges that had been levied in contravention of EU law was compatible with EU law, even though the relevant Directive had not been properly transposed into national law at the time those charges were levied. The charges had been levied between 1986 and 1992, and the Directive was correctly transposed in 1993, so it was still possible to bring an action for recovery of some of the charges once the Directive had been transposed (albeit not for all of them).

REVIEW QUESTION

What was the key distinction between *Emmott* and *Edis*?

Answer: In both cases, the applicants were unaware of their EU law rights at the time those rights were infringed by the defendant Member States, because those Member States had failed to transpose the relevant Directive by the deadline date. However, whereas the time limit in *Emmott* made it impossible for Emmott to exercise her EU law rights, because the three-month time limit for her entire claim had expired long before the relevant Directive was transposed and therefore before she could have become aware of her rights, the time limit in *Edis* had expired only in relation to the earliest unlawful charges and an action in respect of later levied charges was still possible.

Thus where a time limit on the bringing of another action does not make the exercise of EU law rights *virtually impossible*, that time limit will not be in conflict with EU law and will therefore be valid. So, in other cases that were similar to *Edis*, such as Case C-410/92 *Johnson v Chief Adjudication Officer* [1994] ECR I-5493 and Case C-338/91 *Steenhorst-Neerings v Bestuur van de Bedrifsvereniging voor Detailhandel* [1993] ECR I-5475, the Court of Justice has made it clear that time limits that do not prevent the bringing of an action at all, but simply limit the arrears of benefit payable, do not breach the principle of effectiveness.

Although much of the case law on the principle of effectiveness relates to the issues of damages or time limits, the principle of effectiveness can impact on a variety of other aspects of national law on the award of a remedy.

For example, alternative dispute resolution (ADR) procedures were at issue in Joined Cases C-317–320/08 *Alassini and others v Telecom Italia SpA* [2010] ECR I-2213, in which the applicants alleged breaches of contracts concerning the provision of telephone services. Italian law imposed a mandatory out-of-court procedure as a condition for the admissibility of the action before the Italian courts. The applicants failed to initiate that out-of-court procedure and the Italian court made a preliminary reference to the Court of Justice under Article 267 TFEU (see further Chapter 6 on the preliminary reference procedure) as to the correct interpretation of Directive 2000/22/EC of the European Parliament and of the Council of 7 March 2002 on universal service and users' rights relating to electronic communications networks and services, OJ 2002 L108/51 (the Universal Services Directive) on the use of out-of-court procedures in disputes concerning the provision of communications services.

?! THINKING POINT

While reading the following extract, consider what reasons the Court of Justice gave for holding that the principle of effectiveness was not breached.

Joined Cases C-317–320/08 *Alassini and others v Telecom Italia SpA* [2010] ECR I-2213

47. First, the Court has consistently held that, in the absence of EU rules governing the matter, it is for the domestic legal system of each Member State to designate the courts and tribunals having jurisdiction and to lay down the detailed procedural rules governing actions for safeguarding rights which individuals derive from EU law, but the Member States are nevertheless responsible for ensuring that those rights are effectively protected in each case (see Case C-268/06 *Impact* [2008] ECR I-2483, paragraphs 44 and 45, and *Mono Car Styling* [Case C-12/08 *Mono Car Styling SA, in liquidation v Dervis Odemis and Others* [2009] ECR I-6653], paragraph 48).

[…]

52. As regards the principle of effectiveness, it is admittedly true that making the admissibility of legal proceedings conditional upon the prior implementation of an out-of-court settlement procedure affects the exercise of rights conferred on individuals by the Universal Service Directive.

53. However, various factors show that a mandatory settlement procedure, such as that at issue, is not such as to make it in practice impossible or excessively difficult to exercise the rights which individuals derive from that directive.

54. First, the outcome of the settlement procedure is not binding on the parties concerned and thus does not prejudice their right to bring legal proceedings.

55. Secondly, the settlement procedure does not, in normal circumstances, result in a substantial delay for the purposes of bringing legal proceedings. The time-limit for completion of the settlement procedure is 30 days as from the date of the request and, on expiry of the deadline, the parties may bring legal proceedings even if the procedure has not been completed.

56. Thirdly, for the duration of the settlement procedure, the period for the time-barring of claims is suspended.

57. Fourthly, there are no fees for the settlement procedure before the Co.re.com. In the case of the settlement procedures before other bodies, there is nothing in the documents before the Court to suggest that they entail significant costs.

58. However, the exercise of rights conferred by the Universal Service Directive might be rendered in practice impossible or excessively difficult for certain individuals—in particular, those without access to the Internet—if the settlement procedure could be accessed only by electronic means. It is for the referring court to ascertain whether that is the case, having especial regard to Article 13(1) of the dispute settlement rules.

59. By the same token, it is for the referring court to ascertain whether, in exceptional cases where interim measures are necessary, the settlement procedure allows, or does not preclude, the adoption of such measures.

60. In those circumstances, it must be held that the national legislation at issue in the present case complies with the principle of effectiveness in so far as electronic means is not the only means by which the settlement procedure may be accessed and in so far as interim measures are possible in exceptional cases where the urgency of the situation so requires.

61. Secondly, it should be borne in mind that the principle of effective judicial protection is a general principle of EU law stemming from the constitutional traditions common to the Member States, which has been enshrined in Articles 6 and 13 of the ECHR and which has also been reaffirmed by Article 47 of the Charter of Fundamental Rights of the European Union (see *Mono Car Styling*, paragraph 47 and the case-law cited).

62. In that regard, it is common ground in the cases before the referring court that, by making the admissibility of legal proceedings concerning electronic communications services conditional upon the implementation of a mandatory attempt at settlement, the national legislation introduces an additional step for access to the courts. That condition might prejudice implementation of the principle of effective judicial protection.

63. Nevertheless, it is settled case-law that fundamental rights do not constitute unfettered prerogatives and may be restricted, provided that the restrictions in fact correspond to objectives of general interest pursued by the measure in question and that they do not involve, with regard to the objectives pursued, a disproportionate and intolerable interference which infringes upon the very substance of the rights guaranteed (see, to that effect, Case C-28/05 [*Dokter and others*] [2006] ECR I-5431, paragraph 75 and the case-law cited, and the judgment of the ECHR in *Fogarty v United Kingdom*, no. 37112/97, §33, ECHR 2001-XI (extracts)).

64. However, as the Italian Government observed at the hearing, it must first be noted that the aim of the national provisions at issue is the quicker and less expensive settlement of disputes relating to electronic communications and a lightening of the burden on the court system, and they thus pursue legitimate objectives in the general interest.
65. Secondly, the imposition of an out-of-court settlement procedure such as that provided for under the national legislation at issue, does not seem—in the light of the detailed rules for the operation of that procedure, referred to in paragraphs 54 to 57 of this judgment—disproportionate in relation to the objectives pursued. In the first place, as the Advocate General stated in point 47 of her Opinion, no less restrictive alternative to the implementation of a mandatory procedure exists, since the introduction of an out-of-court settlement procedure which is merely optional is not as efficient a means of achieving those objectives. In the second place, it is not evident that any disadvantages caused by the mandatory nature of the out-of-court settlement procedure are disproportionate to those objectives.
66. In the light of the foregoing, it must be held that the national procedure at issue in the main proceedings also complies with the principle of effective judicial protection, subject to the conditions referred to in paragraphs 58 and 59 of this judgment.

The availability of legal aid was the issue in Case C-279/09 *DEB Deutsche Energiehandels- und Beratungsgesellschaft mbH* [2010] ECR I-3849 (see also 9.4.4), in which the applicant company applied for legal aid to pursue an action for Member State liability in damages (see Chapter 5). German law permitted proceedings to be brought only if the applicant paid court costs in advance, but this payment could be waived if the applicant was legally aided. However, a legal entity such as a company was eligible for legal aid only if, in addition to it being unable to pay the costs of the proceedings, failure to pursue the action would be contrary to the public interest. The applicant's claim for legal aid was rejected on the ground that discontinuance of the action was not contrary to the public interest. The German court made a preliminary reference to the Court of Justice under Article 267 TFEU (see further Chapter 6 on the preliminary reference procedure) as to the correct interpretation of the principle of effectiveness in these circumstances. The Court made extensive reference to the principle of effectiveness enshrined in Article 47 of the Charter of Fundamental Rights of the European Union (set out at 4.3; on the Charter generally, see further 9.4), to which it had also referred in Joined Cases C-317–320/08 *Alassini and others v Telecom Italia SpA* [2010] ECR I-2213, and ruled that the principle of effectiveness could be relied upon by legal persons. Whether legal aid was necessary in order to ensure the effectiveness of EU law rights in any particular case depended on the specific facts of that case.

?! THINKING POINT

While reading the following extract, note the factors that the Court laid down for a national court to consider when assessing whether an award of legal aid was necessary to ensure the effectiveness of EU law in relation to a particular applicant.

Case C-279/09 *DEB Deutsche Energiehandels- und Beratungsgesellschaft mbH* [2010] ECR I-3849

57. In the light of all of the foregoing, the answer to the question referred must be that the principle of effective judicial protection, as enshrined in Article 47 of the Charter, must be interpreted as meaning that it is not impossible for legal persons to rely on that principle and that aid granted pursuant to that principle may cover, inter alia, dispensation from advance payment of the costs of proceedings and/or the assistance of a lawyer.
58. In that connection, it is for the national court to ascertain whether the conditions for granting legal aid constitute a limitation on the right of access to the courts which undermines the very core of that right; whether they pursue a legitimate aim; and whether there is a reasonable relationship of proportionality between the means employed and the legitimate aim which it is sought to achieve.
59. In making that assessment, the national court must take into consideration the subject-matter of the litigation; whether the applicant has a reasonable prospect of success; the importance of what is at stake for the applicant in the proceedings; the complexity of the applicable law and procedure; and the applicant's capacity to represent himself effectively. In order to assess the proportionality, the national court may also take account of the amount of the costs of the proceedings in respect of which advance payment must be made and whether or not those costs might represent an insurmountable obstacle to access to the courts.
60. With regard more specifically to legal persons, the national court may take account of their situation. The court may therefore take into consideration, inter alia, the form of the legal person in question and whether it is profit-making or non-profit-making; the financial capacity of the partners or shareholders; and the ability of those partners or shareholders to obtain the sums necessary to institute legal proceedings.

4.3.3 New remedies need not be created

The principle that new remedies need not be created was stated by the Court of Justice in Case 158/80 *Rewe Handelsgesellschaft Nord mbH and Rewe-Markt Steffen v Hauptzollamt* [1981] ECR 1005. In that case, cruises that went beyond German territorial waters had been organized by certain retailers so that goods could be technically 'exported', traded, and 'imported' again, thus incurring certain customs and tax advantages. Land-based retailers claimed that this practice was in breach of a number of EU Regulations and Directives on exemptions from import duties. The German court made a reference to the Court of Justice under Article 267 TFEU (see further Chapter 6 on the preliminary reference procedure) on the interpretation and validity of the relevant EU laws, and on the remedies that should be available for any breach of them.

The Court held that all actions available to enforce national law must be available to enforce EU law, but acknowledged that national courts need not create new remedies to ensure that EU law is fully effective if those remedies do not exist in national law.

This principle may, on occasion, conflict with the principle of effectiveness, as the Court of Justice noted in Case C-432/05 *Unibet Ltd v Justitiekanslern* [2007] ECR I-2271. In that case, Unibet had been prevented by the Swedish authorities from advertising its betting services. It sought a declaration that it was entitled to promote its services and also an interim declaration that the prohibition on advertising did not apply to it. The Swedish courts initially rejected its claims on the ground that an action for a declaration was inadmissible as a matter of Swedish law, but, on appeal, made a reference to the Court of Justice under Article 267 TFEU (see further Chapter 6 on the preliminary reference procedure).

?! THINKING POINT

While reading the following extract, note how the Court attempted in this case to reconcile the principle that new remedies need not be created by Member States with the principle of effectiveness.

Case C-432/05 *Unibet Ltd v Justitiekanslern* [2007] ECR I-2271

40. Although the EC Treaty has made it possible in a number of instances for private persons to bring a direct action, where appropriate, before the Community [now EU] Court, it was not intended to create new remedies in the national courts to ensure the observance of Community law [now EU law] other than those already laid down by national law (Case 158/80 *Rewe* [1981] ECR 1805, paragraph 44).
41. It would be otherwise only if it were apparent from the overall scheme of the national legal system in question that no legal remedy existed which made it possible to ensure, even indirectly, respect for an individual's rights under Community law (see, to that effect, Case 33/76 *Rewe*, paragraph 5; *Comet* [Case 45/76 *Comet BV v Produktschap voor Siergewassen* [1976] ECR 2043], paragraph 16; and *Factortame and Others* [Case C-213/89 *R v Secretary of State for Transport, ex p Factortame Ltd ('Factortame I')* [1990] ECR I-2433], paragraphs 19 to 23).

The Court of Justice held that other forms of proceedings were available to Unibet as a matter of Swedish law that adequately enabled it to enforce EU law rights.

In Case C-213/89 *R v Secretary of State for Transport, ex p Factortame ('Factortame I')* [1990] ECR I-2433 (see also 3.1.2), in which the applicants alleged that the Merchant Shipping Act 1988, which restricted the right to fish in British waters to individuals and businesses with British nationality or residence, conflicted with certain provisions of EU law and, pending a preliminary ruling on this issue from the Court of Justice under Article 267 TFEU (see further Chapter 6 on the preliminary reference procedure), should be suspended. The House of Lords (now the Supreme Court) considered that it had no power under English law to order an interim suspension and made a further preliminary reference to the Court of Justice on this issue.

The Court of Justice referred to its judgment in Case 106/77 *Amministrazione delle Finanze dello Stato v Simmenthal ('Simmenthal II')* [1978] ECR 629 (see 4.2.5), in which it had ruled that national law that conflicted with EU law must be disapplied. It applied similar reasoning to the remedy of interim suspension, as the following extract demonstrates.

Case C-213/89 *R v Secretary of State for Transport, ex p Factortame ('Factortame I')* [1990] ECR I-2433

20. The Court has also held that any provision of a national legal system and any legislative, administrative or judicial practice which might impair the effectiveness of Community law [now EU law] by withholding from the national court having jurisdiction to apply such law the power to do everything necessary at the moment of its application to set aside national legislative provisions which might prevent, even temporarily, Community [now EU] rules from having full force and effect are incompatible with those requirements, which are the very essence of Community law (judgment of 9 March 1978 in *Simmenthal* [Case 106/77 *Amministrazione delle Finanze dello Stato v Simmenthal ('Simmenthal II')* [1978] ECR 629], paragraphs 22 and 23).
21. It must be added that the full effectiveness of Community law would be just as much impaired if a rule of national law could prevent a court seised of a dispute governed by Community law from granting interim relief in order to ensure the full effectiveness of the judgment to be given on the existence of the rights claimed under Community law. It follows that a court which in those circumstances would grant interim relief, if it were not for a rule of national law, is obliged to set aside that rule.
22. That interpretation is reinforced by the system established by Article 177 of the EEC Treaty [now Article 267 TFEU] whose effectiveness would be impaired if a national court, having stayed proceedings pending the reply by the Court of Justice to the question referred to it for a preliminary ruling, were not able to grant interim relief until it delivered its judgment following the reply given by the Court of Justice.
23. Consequently, the reply to the question raised should be that Community law must be interpreted as meaning that a national court which, in a case before it concerning Community law, considers that the sole obstacle which precludes it from granting interim relief is a rule of national law must set aside that rule.

4.3.4 No further substantive conditions

Where liability has arisen under EU law, no further substantive conditions may be imposed by national law prior to the award of a remedy. In the case that established this principle, Case C-177/88 *Dekker v Stichting VJV* [1990] ECR I-3941, Dekker's name had been put forward as the most suitable candidate for a job, but, after she informed the employer that she was pregnant, she was rejected because the employer's insurance would not cover the cost of a replacement worker during her maternity leave. Dekker sought to rely on the Equal Treatment Directive (Directive 76/207), which prohibited discrimination at work on grounds of sex. Under Dutch law, Dekker was required to prove not merely discrimination, but unjustified discrimination.

The employer claimed that his action was justified because his insurance would not cover the cost of her maternity leave in these circumstances. The Dutch court made a reference to the Court of Justice under Article 267 TFEU (see further Chapter 6 on the preliminary reference procedure). The Court of Justice held that since the Directive imposed liability purely on the basis of discrimination, regardless of any fault, national provisions requiring such fault to be proved could not be applied.

A further example of this principle is provided by the Court of Justice's statement in Joined Cases C-46 & 48/93 *Brasserie du Pêcheur SA v Germany; R v Secretary of State for Transport, ex p Factortame ('Factortame III')* [1996] ECR I-1029, at para 79 (see also 4.3.2, 5.4.1, and 5.5) that if the conditions for Member State liability are satisfied, no further requirement of proof of fault may be imposed by national law.

4.4 The possible impact of Brexit

When the UK leaves the EU (see further 1.19 and 3.1), EU law will cease to be directly or indirectly effective in the UK, subject to the provisions of the Draft Agreement on the withdrawal of the United Kingdom of Great Britain and Northern Ireland from the European Union and the European Atomic Energy Community, 14 November 2018 (the Draft Withdrawal Agreement). Article 4 of the Draft Withdrawal Agreement states that certain provisions of EU law will continue to have direct effect and that the UK must continue to disapply inconsistent provisions of national law. It also provides that the Draft Withdrawal Agreement itself will have direct effect.

Agreement on the withdrawal of the United Kingdom of Great Britain and Northern Ireland from the European Union and the European Atomic Energy Community, as endorsed by leaders at a special meeting of the European Council on 25 November 2018

Article 4

Methods and principles relating to the effect, the implementation and the application of this Agreement

1. The provisions of this Agreement and the provisions of Union law made applicable by this Agreement shall produce in respect of and in the United Kingdom the same legal effects as those which they produce within the Union and its Member States.

   Accordingly, legal or natural persons shall in particular be able to rely directly on the provisions contained or referred to in this Agreement which meet the conditions for direct effect under Union law.
2. The United Kingdom shall ensure compliance with paragraph 1, including as regards the required powers of its judicial and administrative authorities to disapply inconsistent or incompatible domestic provisions, through domestic primary legislation.

3. The provisions of this Agreement referring to Union law or to concepts or provisions thereof shall be interpreted and applied in accordance with the methods and general principles of Union law.
4. The provisions of this Agreement referring to Union law or to concepts or provisions thereof shall in their implementation and application be interpreted in conformity with the relevant case law of the Court of Justice of the European Union handed down before the end of the transition period.
5. In the interpretation and application of this Agreement, the United Kingdom's judicial and administrative authorities shall have due regard to relevant case law of the Court of Justice of the European Union handed down after the end of the transition period.

Article 4 of the Draft Withdrawal Agreement also provides that these provisions of EU law must be interpreted compatibly with the jurisprudence of the Court of Justice up until the end of the transition period. In contrast, s 6 of the UK's own European Union (Withdrawal) Act 2018 provides that UK courts are expected to determine cases in accordance with *pre-exit* Court of Justice case law and retained general principles of EU law (see 1.19.1 on retained law and 3.4.5 on general principles of EU law), but are not bound by judgments of the Court of Justice given on or after exit day—even if these are given before the end of the transition period.

Where primary UK legislation has been adopted in order to comply with the UK's obligations under EU law—particularly under Directives (see further 3.4.2)—it will remain part of UK law unless specifically repealed. However, where secondary UK legislation has been adopted in order to fulfil the UK's EU obligations, this will be automatically repealed as soon as the UK's European Communities Act 1972 (see further 3.1.2) is repealed, because it is only s 2(2) of that Act that has allowed the UK government to implement its EU obligations via secondary legislation; without that provision, such secondary legislation ceases to be valid.

Where EU law applies directly (see 4.1) without any UK legislation, this will cease to be the law in the UK once the UK leaves the EU. However, given the volume of such directly applicable EU law, it is possible that the UK will choose to incorporate some of this into UK law, in which case it will simply become part of ordinary national law. If and to the extent that the UK retains some elements of directly applicable EU law, for example by taking the European Economic Area (EEA) option outlined at 1.19.2, it is possible that those elements of EU law will have a direct or indirect effect in the UK, but the position in relation to EEA law is far from clear (see further eg Walter van Gerven, 'The Genesis of EEA Law and the Principles of Primacy and Direct Effect' (1992) 16(4) Fordham Int'l LJ 955 and Thomas Burri and Benedikt Pirker, 'Constitutionalization by Association? The Doubtful Case of the European Economic Area' (2013) YEL 1) and will depend on the UK's own constitutional principles (see further 3.1).

It is also possible that between now and the UK's withdrawal from the EU, the UK will cease to bother with transposing new EU Directives into its national law. However, while the UK is formally still a Member State, such Directives will continue to be capable of direct and indirect effect in the UK—and failure to transpose them may still give rise to a claim against the UK government for damages (see further Chapter 5).

4.5 Conclusions

It is essential to the supremacy and effectiveness of EU law that it should be capable of being enforced in national courts, as a matter both of principle and of practice. The Court of Justice therefore developed the doctrine of direct effect and, after this proved to have gaps in its protection, the doctrine of indirect effect. In the national courts, the most satisfactory course of action for a litigant is, of course, to rely directly on EU law (or on any national transposing legislation).

If the applicant is successful in enforcing EU law, whether directly or indirectly, the availability and nature of any remedy will be governed by national law, subject to a number of guidelines laid down by the Court of Justice. The primacy of national law in this area means that there is no guarantee of uniformity across the Member States of remedies for breaches of EU law. It also means that a remedy awarded may be insufficient to fully recompense the claimant for their loss or to deter future breaches.

As discussed in Chapter 5, the Court of Justice has developed an alternative cause of action for those whose EU law rights may not be sufficiently guaranteed by either direct effect or indirect effect—namely, an action for damages from the Member State.

SUMMARY

- Direct effect refers to a characteristic possessed by some EU legislation—that it may be enforced directly and produce legal effects. Treaty Articles, Regulations, Decisions, and Directives are all—in principle—capable of direct effect. However, a particular measure will have direct effect only if it is clear and precise (*Politi*; *Grad*; *Van Duyn*). In addition, if it is a Directive, the deadline for its transposition into national law must have passed (*Ratti*) and it may be enforced only against an emanation of the State (*Marshall*). An emanation of the State is an entity that provides a public service, under the control of the State, with special powers to do so (*Foster*).
- Indirect effect refers to another characteristic of some EU legislation—that it may be enforced indirectly through influencing the interpretation of national law. All national law, whatever its date or purpose, must be interpreted consistently with EU law (*Marleasing*). However, sometimes, the national law in question is so different from the relevant EU law that it is simply not possible to interpret it in that way (*Wagner Miret*).
- Remedies may be awarded for breach of directly effective EU law, or for breach of national law interpreted in accordance with EU law.
- In either event, remedies are governed by national law, both in substance and procedure.
- However, the Court of Justice has ruled that any remedy awarded for breach of EU law rights must be equivalent to that awarded for breach of national law and effective.

FURTHER READING

Articles

A Arnull, 'The Principle of Effective Judicial Protection in EU Law: An Unruly Horse?' (2011) 36(1) EL Rev 51

Examines the principle of effectiveness in the jurisprudence of the Court of Justice.

P Craig, 'The Legal Effect of Directives: Policy, Rules and Exceptions' (2009) 34(3) EL Rev 349
Analyses the effect given to Directives by the Court of Justice and the underlying policy reasons.

S Drake, 'Twenty Years after *Von Colson*: The Impact of "Indirect Effect" on the Protection of the Individual's Community Rights' (2005) 30(3) EL Rev 329
Discusses indirect effect and incidental horizontal effect.

CNK Franklin, 'Limits to the Limits of the Principle of Consistent Interpretation?' (2015) 40(6) EL Rev 910
Examines the possible impact of the *Spedition* case on the doctrine of indirect effect.

P Koutrakos, 'Is There More to Say about the Direct Effect of Directives?' (2018) 43(5) EL Rev 621
Critiques the judgment in *Farrell* as a useful clarification of direct effect, particularly the meaning of 'special powers'.

K Lenaerts, 'National Remedies for Private Parties in the Light of the EU Law Principles of Equivalence and Effectiveness' (2011) 46 Irish Jurist 13
Examines the extent to which the principles of effectiveness and equivalence have affected national procedural autonomy.

M Lenz, 'Horizontal What? Back to Basics' (2000) 25(5) EL Rev 509
Discusses direct effect, with particular reference to horizontal effects and the supremacy of EU law.

P Pescatore, 'The Doctrine of "Direct Effect": An Infant Disease of Community Law' (2014) 40(2) EL Rev 135
Discusses the rationale for, and workings of, direct effect.

K Sawyer, 'The Principle of "*interprétation conforme*": How Far Can or Should National Courts Go when Interpreting National Legislation Consistently with European Community Law?' (2007) 28(3) Stat LR 165
Evaluates the extent of the obligation to give indirect effect to EU law through a consistent interpretation of national law.

QUESTIONS

Alf works for Humber plc, a company created to build and operate a railway bridge across the Humber estuary. It is authorized to do so under s 1 of the (fictitious) Estuary Bridges Act 1990, which also gives it powers to regulate the connecting train service.

(Fictitious) Directive 2010/2010 requires Member States to take all measures necessary to ensure that bridge workers are provided with appropriate safety equipment, including hard hats. The Act merely provides that licence holders must ensure that their employees are aware of safety hazards and are advised to wear appropriate clothing.

Alf sustained a serious head injury when a cable fell on him during construction of the bridge and, as a result, he is unfit to work. He claims that his injury was caused by Humber plc's failure to provide workers with hard hats. Humber plc claims that it had made Alf aware of the risks and had advised him to wear a hard hat, although the company itself did not provide them. It argues that the Act only requires the provision of information and advice.

1. Advise Alf as to how he might enforce his rights under EU law against Humber plc.
2. How, if at all, would your answer to the first question differ if Humber did not have the power to regulate the train service, but was wholly owned by the State?
3. If Alf is successful in a claim based on the direct or indirect effect of the Directive, what remedy is he entitled to as a matter of EU law?

To view outline answers to these questions plus further resources to support your EU law studies, visit the Online Resources for this book at www.oup.com/uk/eulaw-complete4e

5 Member State liability in damages

KEY POINTS

By the end of this chapter, you should be able to:

- explain the reasoning of the Court of Justice for establishing the principle of State liability in damages in Joined Cases C-6 & 9/90 Francovich and others v Italy [1991] ECR I-5357;
- explain the (different) conditions for liability set out in *Francovich* and Joined Cases C-46 & 48/93 *Brasserie du Pêcheur SA v Germany; R v Secretary of State for Transport, ex p Factortame ('Factortame III')* [1996] ECR I-1029 and identify the differences between them;
- identify the different types of breach of EU law so far held by the Court of Justice to give rise to State liability and the conditions for liability applicable to each;
- apply the conditions laid down in *Francovich* and *Factortame III* to a range of factual situations;
- analyse (in conjunction with Chapter 4) the relationship between State liability and direct and indirect effect; and
- analyse (in conjunction with Chapter 8) the relationship between the Court's jurisprudence on Member State liability and its jurisprudence on EU liability.

INTRODUCTION

The EU Treaties make no provision for a Member State that breaches EU law to be liable in damages to individuals who have thereby suffered loss, although there is provision for the EU Commission (see 2.3 on the Commission) to take enforcement proceedings to end the breach (Article 258 TFEU; see further 7.1). However, in a series of judgments dating from the early 1990s, the Court of Justice ruled that, if certain conditions are fulfilled, such liability may arise.

Like the doctrines of direct and indirect effect considered in Chapter 4, the rationale underlying the development of Member State liability in damages for breaches of EU law is the need to make the rights enshrined in EU law real and effective. If a Member State that breaches EU law could do so with impunity, it would have little incentive to refrain from such breaches, and the wronged party would have no redress.

Another similarity with direct and indirect effect is that State liability has been developed by the Court of Justice without any direct foundation in the Treaties, although Article 340 TFEU makes express provision for the European Union (EU) itself to be liable for damage caused by its institutions (see further Chapter 8) and the Court has drawn on its own jurisprudence under Article 340 TFEU in developing State liability in parallel.

5.1 The meaning of 'Member State' for the purpose of damages claims

Before considering the circumstances in which Member State liability will arise, it is first necessary to give some guidance on the meaning of 'Member State' in this context. The jurisprudence of the Court of Justice indicates that breaches of EU law by any part of the State may give rise to liability. However, a Member State may require actions in respect of such liability to be brought against the particular part of the State which committed the breach. For example, in Case C-302/97 *Konle v Austria* [1999] ECR I-3099, Austrian law provided that damages claims arising out of infringements committed by part of the federal State could be brought only against that part of the State and not the State as a whole. The Court of Justice accepted that, in a federal State, reparation for damage caused by breaches of EU law committed by a federated local authority need not be provided by the federal State itself. However, the State must ensure that individuals could obtain reparation for damage caused to them by breaches of EU law, regardless of which public authority was responsible for the breach and which public authority was, in principle, under the law of that State, responsible for making reparation. A Member State could not therefore plead the separation of powers that existed in its national legal system in order to avoid liability. In Case C-424/97 *Haim v Kassenzahnärztliche Vereinigung Nordrhein* [2000] ECR I-5123, the Court gave a similar ruling in relation to damage caused by breaches of EU law committed by a public law body (in that case, an association of public dental practitioners).

5.2 The establishment of the principle of State liability: *Francovich*

The principle of State liability for breach of EU law was first established by the Court of Justice in Joined Cases C-6 & 9/90 *Francovich and others v Italy* [1991] ECR I-5357. Francovich was owed wages by his employer, a company that had become insolvent. Italian law provided no remedy in these circumstances, but Council Directive 80/987/EEC of 20 October 1980 on the approximation of the laws of the Member States relating to the protection of employees in the event of the insolvency of their employer, OJ 1980 L283/23, required each Member State to set up a scheme under which employees of insolvent companies would receive at least some of their outstanding wages. The problem for such employees in Italy was that the Italian government had failed to transpose the rights in the Directive into national law as it was legally obliged to do (see further 3.4.2). The Italian court made a reference to the Court of Justice under Article 267 TFEU (see further Chapter 6 on the preliminary reference procedure). The Court considered first whether the Directive could have direct effect.

?! **THINKING POINT**

What three conditions must be satisfied in order for a Directive to have direct effect? (If you have difficulty answering this question, review 4.1.4.)

The Court held that since one of the three conditions for a Directive to have direct effect was not satisfied in *Francovich*, Francovich could not enforce Directive 80/987 directly.

Joined Cases C-6 & 9/90 *Francovich and others v Italy* [1991] ECR I-5357

12. It is therefore necessary to see whether the provisions of Directive 80/987 which determine the rights of employees are unconditional and sufficiently precise. There are three points to be considered: the identity of the persons entitled to the guarantee provided, the content of that guarantee and the identity of the person liable to provide the guarantee …

[…]

26. Accordingly, even though the provisions of the directive in question are sufficiently precise and unconditional as regards the determination of the persons entitled to the guarantee and as regards the content of that guarantee, those elements are not sufficient to enable individuals to rely on those provisions before the national courts. Those provisions do not identify the person liable to provide the guarantee, and the State cannot be considered liable on the sole ground that it has failed to take transposition measures within the prescribed period.

REVIEW QUESTION

Why do you think that the Court did not consider the possibility of indirect effect in *Francovich*? (If you have difficulty with understanding the concept of 'indirect effect', review 4.2.)

Answer: The Directive at issue in *Francovich* could not have indirect effect on the facts of this particular case because there was no relevant Italian legislation in accordance with which it could be construed.

The Court was thus faced with a problem: the EU had intended employees to have rights under the Directive, yet neither of the doctrines that the Court had previously developed to make rights effective—direct effect and indirect effect—were of assistance here.

The Court's response was to develop an alternative solution to make those rights effective: it ruled that a Member State that breached its obligation to transpose a Directive by the deadline for its transposition could be held liable in damages to an individual who had suffered loss as a result. Its reasoning can be seen in the following extract.

Joined Cases C-6 & 9/90 *Francovich and others v Italy* [1991] ECR I-5357

Liability of the State for loss and damage resulting from breach of its obligations under Community law

28. In the second part of the first question the national court seeks to determine whether a Member State is obliged to make good loss and damage suffered by individuals as a result of the failure to transpose Directive 80/987.

29. The national court thus raises the issue of the existence and scope of a State's liability for loss and damage resulting from breach of its obligations under Community law [now EU law].

30. That issue must be considered in the light of the general system of the Treaty and its fundamental principles.

(a) The existence of State liability as a matter of principle

31. It should be borne in mind at the outset that the EEC Treaty has created its own legal system, which is integrated into the legal systems of the Member States and which their courts are bound to apply. The subjects of that legal system are not only the Member States but also their nationals. Just as it imposes burdens on individuals, Community law [now EU law] is also intended to give rise to rights which become part of their legal patrimony. Those rights arise not only where they are expressly granted by the Treaty but also by virtue of obligations which the Treaty imposes in a clearly defined manner both on individuals and on the Member States and the Community institutions (see the judgments in Case 26/62 *Van Gend en Loos* [1963] ECR 1 and Case 6/64 *Costa v ENEL* [1964] ECR 585).

32. Furthermore, it has been consistently held that the national courts whose task it is to apply the provisions of Community law in areas within their jurisdiction must ensure that those rules take full effect and must protect the rights which they confer on individuals (see in particular the judgments in Case 106/77 *Amministrazione delle Finanze dello Stato v Simmenthal* [1978] ECR 629, paragraph 16, and Case C-213/89 *Factortame* [1990] ECR I-2433, paragraph 19).

33. The full effectiveness of Community [now Union] rules would be impaired and the protection of the rights which they grant would be weakened if individuals were unable to obtain redress when their rights are infringed by a breach of Community law for which a Member State can be held responsible.

34. The possibility of obtaining redress from the Member State is particularly indispensable where, as in this case, the full effectiveness of Community [now Union] rules is subject to prior action on the part of the State and where, consequently, in the absence of such action, individuals cannot enforce before the national courts the rights conferred upon them by Community law.

35. It follows that the principle whereby a State must be liable for loss and damage caused to individuals as a result of breaches of Community law for which the State can be held responsible is inherent in the system of the Treaty.

36. A further basis for the obligation of Member States to make good such loss and damage is to be found in Article 5 of the [EC] Treaty [now Article 4(3) TEU], under which the Member States are required to take all appropriate measures, whether general or particular, to ensure fulfilment of their obligations under Community law. Among these is the obligation to nullify the unlawful consequences of a breach of Community law (see, in relation to the analogous provision of Article 86 of the ECSC Treaty, the judgment in Case 6/60 *Humblet v Belgium* [1990] ECR 559).

37. It follows from all the foregoing that it is a principle of Community law that the Member States are obliged to make good loss and damage caused to individuals by breaches of Community law for which they can be held responsible.

REVIEW QUESTION

What were the Court's arguments for establishing the principle of State liability in *Francovich* and what criticisms might be made of these arguments?

Answer: The Court held that the EU legal system was designed to give rights to individuals, that national courts must enforce these rights, and that the effectiveness of these rights would be impaired if there were no redress available from a State that breached those rights. It also cited the obligation of States under what is now Article 4(3) TEU (formerly Article 5 EC) to take all measures to ensure that they fulfilled their Treaty obligations and explained that this included making good the consequences of a breach of these obligations.

It might be argued that the doctrines of direct and indirect effect make rights under EU law enforceable against any part of the State that has acted in breach of the substantive provisions of EU law—for example a local council that discriminates against its female employees—and that it is not necessary for the State to be liable further than this. Article 4(3) TEU leaves it to the State to decide on the appropriate methods of fulfilment of EU obligations; had the States wanted to provide for State liability in damages, they could have done so, and indeed the inclusion of Treaty provisions for EU liability (Article 340 TFEU) might imply that the omission of parallel provisions for State liability was deliberate.

5.3 The *Francovich* conditions governing the imposition of State liability

Having established the principle of State liability, the Court of Justice in *Francovich* then proceeded to specify the conditions according to which such liability would arise in a particular case.

Joined Cases C-6 & 9/90 *Francovich and others v Italy* [1991] ECR I-5357

(b) The conditions for State liability

38. Although State liability is thus required by Community law [now EU law], the conditions under which that liability gives rise to a right to reparation depend on the nature of the breach of Community law giving rise to the loss and damage.

39. Where, as in this case, a Member State fails to fulfil its obligation under the third paragraph of Article 189 of the [EC] Treaty [now Article 288 TFEU] to take all the measures necessary to achieve the result prescribed by a directive, the full effectiveness of that rule of Community law requires that there should be a right to reparation provided that three conditions are fulfilled.
40. The first of those conditions is that the result prescribed by the directive should entail the grant of rights to individuals. The second condition is that it should be possible to identify the content of those rights on the basis of the provisions of the directive. Finally, the third condition is the existence of a causal link between the breach of the State's obligation and the loss and damage suffered by the injured parties.
41. Those conditions are sufficient to give rise to a right on the part of individuals to obtain reparation, a right founded directly on Community law.

   [...]
44. In this case, the breach of Community law by a Member State by virtue of its failure to transpose Directive 80/987 within the prescribed period has been confirmed by a judgment of the Court. The result required by that directive entails the grant to employees of a right to a guarantee of payment of their unpaid wage claims. As is clear from the examination of the first part of the first question, the content of that right can be identified on the basis of the provisions of the directive.
45. Consequently, the national court must, in accordance with the national rules on liability, uphold the right of employees to obtain reparation of loss and damage caused to them as a result of failure to transpose the directive.

The Court laid down three conditions that must be satisfied before a State can be held liable in damages to an individual for its failure to transpose a Directive.

REVIEW QUESTION

What were the three conditions laid down by the Court and how did the Court apply them in *Francovich*?

Answer: The three conditions are that:

(a) the result prescribed by the Directive must involve the grant of rights to individuals;

(b) the content of those rights must be clear from the Directive; and

(c) there must be a causal link between the breach of the State's obligation and the damage suffered by the individual.

On the facts of the case, the Court held that (1) the Directive gave rights to employees (to be paid their wages), and (2) the content of those rights (how much pay they were entitled to) was clear from the Directive. It left the referring national court to decide (3) the issue of causation—whether Francovich himself had suffered loss as a result of Italy's failure to transpose the Directive.

The application of the first two conditions is within the jurisdiction of the Court of Justice (see further 2.4) because they involve the interpretation of EU law (a particular Directive). In contrast, the third condition requires the establishment of the facts and the application of EU law to those facts, which are matters for the national courts.

The Italian court was therefore required to consider whether Francovich was among the employees who were given rights under the Directive (the content of those rights having been established by the Court of Justice) and, if he was, what loss he had suffered as a result of Italy's failure to transpose those rights into national law. This exercise necessitated a further reference by the Italian court to the Court of Justice, this time on the correct interpretation of the detail of the substantive provisions of the Directive. In Case C-479/93 *Francovich v Italy* ('*Francovich II*') [1993] ECR I-3843, the Court of Justice ruled that the Directive applied only to those employees whose employer had been made subject to specified types of insolvency proceeding. Since the Italian court had found that, as a matter of Italian law, Francovich's employer could not be subjected to such proceedings, Francovich was not entitled to the protection of the Directive and thus was unable to prove that he had suffered any loss as a result of Italy's failure to transpose the Directive.

NOTE

Before setting out the conditions for liability in *Francovich*, the Court stated that it was not laying down a single immutable set of conditions applicable to all possible breaches of EU law (*Francovich*, at para 38). Instead, the conditions to be applied would depend on the nature of the breach. In later cases involving different types of breaches from that at issue in *Francovich* (ie the failure to transpose a Directive), the Court has indeed laid down different conditions (see 5.5).

5.4 The development of the principle of State liability

5.4.1 Enactment of national legislation contrary to EU law: *Factortame III*

The judgment in *Francovich* may readily be seen as a logical development of the Court of Justice's previous jurisprudence establishing the principles of direct and indirect effect, in particular where the problem for the individual arises from the State's failure to transpose a Directive into national law. However, over subsequent years, the Court has developed the principle of State liability into a free-standing area of jurisprudence, often not involving Directives or indeed any explicit consideration of direct or indirect effect.

The Court's judgment in *Francovich* was, of course, based on the facts of that case. Although it established the principle of State liability in damages, it did so only in the context of a State's failure to transpose a Directive. After the judgment in *Francovich*, it was unclear whether Member States would incur liability in damages for any other sort of breach of EU law and, if so, what sort of breaches and under what conditions. However, the Court's comments in

Francovich that the conditions for liability would vary according to the nature of the breach of EU law suggested that other kinds of breach might give rise to liability.

In Joined Cases C-46 & 48/93 *Brasserie du Pêcheur SA v Germany; R v Secretary of State for Transport, ex p Factortame ('Factortame III')* [1996] ECR I-1029, the Court was called upon to consider whether a State could be liable in damages for a very different kind of breach of EU law from that at issue in *Francovich*. One of the arguments put by the German and other governments that intervened in the case (on the possibility of intervention in preliminary reference proceedings, see 6.11.4 and 6.11.5) was that State liability was a possibility only where the provisions of EU law that had been breached were not directly effective. The Court rejected this argument for the reasons which appear in the following extract.

?! THINKING POINT

While reading the following extract, make a note of these reasons.

Joined Cases C-46 & 48/93 *Brasserie du Pêcheur SA v Germany; R v Secretary of State for Transport, ex p Factortame ('Factortame III')* [1996] ECR I-1029

18. The German, Irish and Netherlands Governments contend that Member States are required to make good loss or damage caused to individuals only where the provisions breached are not directly effective: in *Francovich and Others* the Court simply sought to fill a lacuna in the system for safeguarding rights of individuals. In so far as national law affords individuals a right of action enabling them to assert their rights under directly effective provisions of Community law [now EU law], it is unnecessary, where such provisions are breached, also to grant them a right to reparation founded directly on Community law.
19. That argument cannot be accepted.
20. The Court has consistently held that the right of individuals to rely on the directly effective provisions of the Treaty before national courts is only a minimum guarantee and is not sufficient in itself to ensure the full and complete implementation of the Treaty (see, in particular, Case 168/85 *Commission v Italy* [1986] ECR 2945, [1988] 1 CMLR 580, paragraph 11, Case C-120/88 *Commission v Italy* [1991] ECR I-621, paragraph 10, and C-119/89 *Commission v Spain* [1991] ECR I-641, [1993] 1 CMLR 41, paragraph 9). The purpose of that right is to ensure that provisions of Community law prevail over national provisions. It cannot, in every case, secure for individuals the benefit of the rights conferred on them by Community law and, in particular, avoid their sustaining damage as a result of a breach of Community law attributable to a Member State. As appears from paragraph 33 of the judgment in *Francovich and Others*, the full effectiveness of Community law would be impaired if individuals were unable to obtain redress when their rights were infringed by a breach of Community law.
21. This will be so where an individual who is a victim of the non-transposition of a directive and is precluded from relying on certain of its provisions directly before the national court because they are insufficiently precise and unconditional, brings an action for damages against

> the defaulting Member State for breach of the third paragraph of Article 189 of the [EC] Treaty [now Article 288 TFEU]. In such circumstances, which obtained in the case of *Francovich and Others*, the purpose of reparation is to redress the injurious consequences of a Member State's failure to transpose a directive as far as beneficiaries of that directive are concerned.
>
> 22. It is all the more so in the event of infringement of a right directly conferred by a Community [now Union] provision upon which individuals are entitled to rely before the national courts. In that event, the right to reparation is the necessary corollary of the direct effect of the Community provision whose breach caused the damage sustained.
> 23. In this case, it is undisputed that the Community provisions at issue, namely Article 30 of the [EC] Treaty [now Article 34 TFEU] in Case C-46/93 and Article 52 [EC, now Article 49 TFEU] in Case C-48/93, have direct effect in the sense that they confer on individuals rights upon which they are entitled to rely directly before the national courts. Breach of such provisions may give rise to reparation.

The Court of Justice held that, in order to make EU law rights effective, it was essential that State liability in damages be available where direct effect did not afford a remedy (*Factortame III*, para 21). However, it considered that it was even more important to ensure that EU law rights that were directly effective in principle were also effective in practice, if necessary by making the State liable in damages (*Factortame III*, para 22).

In its judgment in *Factortame III*, the Court of Justice considered together two separate claims for damages: one brought by Spanish fishermen against the UK government and one brought by a French brewery against the German government. Both arose out of national legislation that conflicted with TEU provisions.

Factortame and other Spanish fishermen claimed damages from the UK government after the Merchant Shipping Act 1988, which had made it unlawful for them to fish in UK waters, was declared by the Court of Justice to be contrary to EU law (in Case C-221/89 *R v Secretary of State for Transport, ex p Factortame Ltd ('Factortame II')* [1991] ECR I-3905—see further 3.1.2 and 4.2.5). They alleged, in particular, that the provisions of the Act were contrary to what is now Article 49 TFEU (see further 12.1.1), which gives Member State nationals the right to establish themselves in another Member State as self-employed persons, and to set up and manage undertakings in another Member State. Brasserie du Pêcheur, a French brewery, claimed damages from the German government after a German prohibition on its exports was declared by the Court of Justice to be contrary to what is now Article 34 TFEU (see further 10.8).

In *Factortame III*, the Court of Justice held that the principle of Member State liability applied where a State had enacted legislation that was contrary to EU law.

?! NOTE

The *Factortame* litigation had already produced significant judgments concerning the supremacy of EU law. If you are unsure as to the importance of the judgments, review 3.1.2. This will help you to understand the nature of the claim for damages.

The Court's rationale for imposing liability in *Factortame III* shows some development from its reasoning in *Francovich*, as is apparent from the following extract.

?! THINKING POINT

While reading the following extract, consider what element of the Court's reasoning had already been seen in its judgment in *Francovich*.

Joined Cases C-46 & 48/93 *Brasserie du Pêcheur SA v Germany; R v Secretary of State for Transport, ex p Factortame ('Factortame III')* [1996] ECR I-1029

State Liability for Acts and Omissions of the National Legislature Contrary to Community Law (First Question in both Case C-46/93 and Case C-48/93)

[...]

27. Since the Treaty contains no provision expressly and specifically governing the consequences of breaches of Community law [now EU law] by Member States, it is for the Court, in pursuance of the task conferred on it by Article 164 of the [EC] Treaty [now Article 19 TEU] of ensuring that in the interpretation and application of the Treaty the law is observed, to rule on such a question in accordance with generally accepted methods of interpretation, in particular by reference to the fundamental principles of the Community [now Union] legal system and, where necessary, general principles common to the legal systems of the Member States.
28. Indeed, it is to the general principles common to the laws of the Member States that the second paragraph of Article 215 of the [EC] Treaty [now Article 340 TFEU] refers as the basis of the non-contractual liability of the Community for damage caused by its institutions or by its servants in the performance of their duties.
29. The principle of the non-contractual liability of the Community expressly laid down in Article 215 of the Treaty is simply an expression of the general principle familiar to the legal systems of the Member States that an unlawful act or omission gives rise to an obligation to make good the damage caused. That provision also reflects the obligation on public authorities to make good damage caused in the performance of their duties.

[...]

31. In view of the foregoing considerations, the Court held in *Francovich and Others*, at paragraph 35, that the principle of State liability for loss and damage caused to individuals as a result of breaches of Community law for which it can be held responsible is inherent in the system of the Treaty.
32. It follows that that principle holds good for any case in which a Member State breaches Community law, whatever be the organ of the State whose act or omission was responsible for the breach.

[...]

36. Consequently, the reply to the national courts must be that the principle that Member States are obliged to make good damage caused to individuals by breaches of Community law attributable to the State is applicable where the national legislature was responsible for the breach in question.

REVIEW QUESTION

How did the reasoning used by the Court of Justice to justify the principle of State liability in *Factortame III* differ from its reasoning in *Francovich*?

Answer: The Court referred in both cases to the Treaty obligation of Member States to ensure the fulfilment of EU law. However, whereas in *Francovich*—as also in much of its jurisprudence on direct and indirect effect (see further Chapter 4)—it stressed the need to make individual rights under EU law effective, in *Factortame III* it also argued that liability for breach of non-contractual obligations was a principle of EU law, as reflected in the express imposition of such liability on the EU itself in Article 340 TFEU (see further Chapter 8). The Court's assertion of a link between the liability of the EU and the liability of Member States has also had implications for the conditions governing State liability (see 5.5).

5.4.2 Incorrect transposition of Directives: *BT*

In Case C-392/93 *R v HM Treasury, ex p British Telecommunications plc* [1996] ECR I-1631, BT brought proceedings claiming that the UK had incorrectly transposed Council Directive 90/531/EEC of 17 September 1990 on the procurement procedures of entities operating in the water, energy, transport and telecommunications sectors, OJ 1990 L297/1, into national law. The national court referred to the Court of Justice a number of questions on the possibility of Member State liability (see further Chapter 6 on the preliminary reference procedure). The Court held that the principles enunciated in *Francovich* and *Factortame III* applied also where a Member State had failed to transpose a Directive into national law correctly. In such circumstances, the State could therefore be liable for damages, as explained in the following extract.

Case C-392/93 *R v HM Treasury, ex p British Telecommunications plc* [1996] ECR I-1631

Question 4

37. By its fourth question, the Divisional Court seeks to ascertain whether a Member State which, in transposing the directive into national law, has itself determined which services of a contracting entity are to be excluded from its scope pursuant to Article 8, is required by Community law [now EU law] to compensate that undertaking for any loss suffered by it as a result of the error committed by the State.

38. It should be recalled, as a preliminary point, that the principle of State liability for loss and damage caused to individuals as a result of breaches of Community law for which the State

can be held responsible is inherent in the system of the Treaty (judgments in *Francovich and Others* (Joined Cases C-6 & 9/90), [1993] 2 CMLR 66 and in *Brasserie du Pêcheur and Factortame* (Joined Cases C-46 & 48/93) [1996] 1 CMLR 889). It follows that that principle holds good for any case in which a Member State breaches Community law (*Brasserie du Pêcheur and Factortame*).

39. In the latter judgment the Court also ruled, with regard to a breach of Community law for which a Member State, acting in a field in which it has a wide discretion in taking legislative decisions, can be held responsible, that Community law confers a right to reparation where three conditions are met: the rule of law infringed must be intended to confer rights on individuals; the breach must be sufficiently serious; and there must be a direct causal link between the breach of the obligation resting on the State and the damage sustained by the injured parties.

40. Those same conditions must be applicable to the situation, taken as its hypothesis by the national court, in which a Member State incorrectly transposes a Community [now Union] directive into national law. A restrictive approach to State liability is justified in such a situation, for the reasons already given by the Court to justify the strict approach to non-contractual liability of Community institutions or Member States when exercising legislative functions in areas covered by Community law where the institution or State has a wide discretion—in particular, the concern to ensure that the exercise of legislative functions is not hindered by the prospect of actions for damages whenever the general interest requires the institutions or Member States to adopt measures which may adversely affect individual interests (see, in particular, the judgments in Joined Cases 83/76, 94/76, 4/77, 15/77 and 40/77 *HNL and Others v EC Council and EC Commission* [1978] ECR 1209, and in *Brasserie du Pêcheur and Factortame*).

?! THINKING POINT

How does the Court's judgment in *BT* enhance its existing jurisprudence on the direct and indirect effect of Directives? If you have difficulty in answering this question, you may need to review Chapter 4.

5.4.3 Administrative breaches: *Hedley Lomas*

In Case C-5/94 *R v Ministry of Agriculture, Fisheries and Food, ex p Hedley Lomas (Ireland) Ltd* [1996] ECR I-2553 (see also 5.5.2), the UK refused to grant licences for the export of live animals to Spain on the ground that Spanish slaughterhouses were not complying with Council Directive 74/577/EEC of 18 November 1974 on stunning of animals before slaughter, OJ 1974 L316/10. Hedley Lomas, a sheep exporter, sought damages from the British government on the basis of its breach of what is now Article 35 TFEU on the free movement of goods (see further 10.8). Even though the alleged breach consisted not of legislation, but of only an administrative practice, the Court of Justice held that the UK government could be liable in damages, as the Court explained in the following extract.

Case C-5/94 *R v Ministry of Agriculture, Fisheries and Food, ex p Hedley Lomas* [1996] ECR I-2553

24. The principle of State liability for loss and damage caused to individuals as a result of breaches of Community law [now EU law] for which the State can be held responsible is inherent in the system of the Treaty: *Francovich and Others* (Joined Cases C-6 & 9/90) [1993] 2 CMLR 66, and *Brasserie du Pêcheur and Factortame* (Joined Cases C-46 & 48/93) [1996] 1 CMLR 889. Furthermore, the conditions under which State liability gives rise to a right to reparation depend on the nature of the breach of Community law giving rise to the loss or damage (*Francovich and Others, Brasserie du Pêcheur and Factortame*).
25. In the case of a breach of Community law attributable to a Member State acting in a field in which it has a wide discretion to make legislative choices the Court has held, at paragraph [51] of its judgment in *Brasserie du Pêcheur and Factortame*, that such a right to reparation must be recognised where three conditions are met: the rule of law infringed must be intended to confer rights on individuals; the breach must be sufficiently serious; and there must be a direct causal link between the breach of the obligation resting on the State and the damage sustained by the injured parties.
26. Those three conditions are also applicable in the circumstances of this case.

[...]

32. The answer to the third question must therefore be that a Member State has an obligation to make reparation for the damage caused to an individual by a refusal to issue an export licence in breach of Article 34 of the [EC] Treaty [now Article 35 TFEU] where the rule of Community law infringed is intended to confer rights on individuals, the breach is sufficiently serious and there is a direct causal link between the breach and the damage sustained by the individuals. Subject to that reservation, the State must make good the consequences of the loss or damage caused by a breach of Community law attributable to it, in accordance with its domestic law on liability. However, the conditions laid down by the applicable domestic laws must not be less favourable than those relating to similar domestic claims or framed in such a way as in practice to make it impossible or excessively difficult to obtain reparation.

5.4.4 Judicial breaches: *Köbler*

The possibility of liability for acts of the judiciary had been signalled by the Court of Justice in *Factortame III*, as can be seen from the following extract.

Joined Cases C-46 & 48/93 *Brasserie du Pêcheur SA v Germany; R v Secretary of State for Transport, ex p Factortame ('Factortame III')* [1996] ECR I-1029

33. In addition, in view of the fundamental requirement of the Community [now Union] legal order that Community law be uniformly applied (see, in particular, Joined Cases C-143/88

and C-92/89 *Zuckerfabrik Süderdithmarschen* and *Zuckerfabrik Soest* [1991] ECR I-415, paragraph 26), the obligation to make good damage caused to individuals by breaches of Community law [now EU law] cannot depend on domestic rules as to the division of powers between constitutional authorities.

34. As the Advocate General points out in paragraph 38 of his Opinion, in international law a State whose liability for breach of an international commitment is in issue will be viewed as a single entity, irrespective of whether the breach which gave rise to the damage is attributable to the legislature, the judiciary or the executive. This must apply *a fortiori* in the Community legal order since all State authorities, including the legislature, are bound in performing their tasks to comply with the rules laid down by Community law directly governing the situation of individuals.

However, it was not until Case C-224/01 *Köbler v Austria* [2003] ECR I-10239 that the Court of Justice had the opportunity to rule directly on the issue. Köbler alleged that an increment payable to university professors with 15 years' service in Austrian universities was discriminatory, because no account was taken of periods of service in universities in other Member States. The Austrian Verwaltungsgerichtshof (its Supreme Administrative Court) dismissed his claim. Köbler then brought an action for damages against the Austrian State on the grounds that the Austrian court's judgment infringed EU law.

The Court of Justice noted in *Köbler* (at paras 48 and 49) that the principle of State liability for the judiciary was accepted in most Member States and had also been recognized by the Court of Human Rights (on the role of this court, see further 9.1, 9.5.2, and 9.6). The Court of Justice held that, as a matter of EU law, a Member State could, in certain circumstances, be liable in damages for the acts of its judiciary adjudicating at last instance. Its rationale appears in the following extract.

?! **THINKING POINT**

While reading the following extract, consider why the Court believed it to be so important that damages be available in respect of judicial breaches of EU law. Why did it argue that this applied specifically to the judgments of courts of last instance?

Case C-224/01 *Köbler v Austria* [2003] ECR I-10239

Principle of State liability

30. First, as the Court has repeatedly held, the principle of liability on the part of a Member State for damage caused to individuals as a result of breaches of Community law [now EU law] for which the State is responsible is inherent in the system of the Treaty (Joined Cases C-6/90 and C-9/90 *Francovich and Others* [1991] ECR I-5357, paragraph 35; *Brasserie du Pêcheur* and *Factortame* [Joined Cases C-46 & 48/93 *Brasserie du Pêcheur SA v Germany; R v Secretary of State*

for Transport, ex p Factortame ('Factortame III') [1996] ECR I-1029], paragraph 31; Case C-392/93 *British Telecommunications* [1996] ECR I-1631, paragraph 38; Case C-5/94 *Hedley Lomas* [1996] ECR I-2553, paragraph 24; Joined Cases C-178/94, C-179/94, C-188/94, C-189/94 and C-190/94 *Dillenkofer and Others* [1996] ECR I-4845, paragraph 20, Case C-127/95 *Norbrook Laboratories* [1998] ECR I-1531, paragraph 106 and *Haim* [Case C-424/97 *Haim v Kassenzahnärztliche Vereinigung Nordrhein* [2000] ECR I-5123], paragraph 26).

31. The Court has also held that that principle applies to any case in which a Member State breaches Community law, whichever is the authority of the Member State whose act or omission was responsible for the breach (*Brasserie du Pêcheur* and *Factortame*, cited above, paragraph 32; Case C-302/97 *Konle* [1999] ECR I-3099, paragraph 62 and *Haim*, cited above, paragraph 27).
32. In international law a State which incurs liability for breach of an international commitment is viewed as a single entity, irrespective of whether the breach which gave rise to the damage is attributable to the legislature, the judiciary or the executive. That principle must apply *a fortiori* in the Community [now Union] legal order since all State authorities, including the legislature, are bound in performing their tasks to comply with the rules laid down by Community law which directly govern the situation of individuals (*Brasserie du Pêcheur* and *Factortame*, cited above, paragraph 34).
33. In the light of the essential role played by the judiciary in the protection of the rights derived by individuals from Community rules, the full effectiveness of those rules would be called in question and the protection of those rights would be weakened if individuals were precluded from being able, under certain conditions, to obtain reparation when their rights are affected by an infringement of Community law attributable to a decision of a court of a Member State adjudicating at last instance.
34. It must be stressed, in that context, that a court adjudicating at last instance is by definition the last judicial body before which individuals may assert the rights conferred on them by Community law. Since an infringement of those rights by a final decision of such a court cannot thereafter normally be corrected, individuals cannot be deprived of the possibility of rendering the State liable in order in that way to obtain legal protection of their rights.
35. Moreover, it is, in particular, in order to prevent rights conferred on individuals by Community law from being infringed that under the third paragraph of Article 234 EC [now Article 267 TFEU] a court against whose decisions there is no judicial remedy under national law is required to make a reference to the Court of Justice.
36. Consequently, it follows from the requirements inherent in the protection of the rights of individuals relying on Community law that they must have the possibility of obtaining redress in the national courts for the damage caused by the infringement of those rights owing to a decision of a court adjudicating at last instance (see in that connection *Brasserie du Pêcheur* and *Factortame*, cited above, paragraph 35).

In *Köbler*, the Court of Justice held that the principle of State liability applied regardless of whether the breach was committed by the legislature, the executive or the judiciary. The essential role played by the judiciary in protecting rights under EU law meant that the effectiveness of EU law would be undermined if damages were not available to individuals whose rights were affected by breaches of EU law committed by the judiciary. Where such a breach was committed by a court of last instance, individuals would have no other remedy against the judgment.

In the course of its judgment in *Köbler,* the Court of Justice refuted a number of arguments put forward by the Austrian and other governments that intervened in the case (on the possibility of such interventions, see 6.11.4 and 6.11.5) to object to the extension of the principle of State liability to breaches of EU law committed by national courts.

First, the Court rejected the suggestion that the availability of an action in damages against the State in respect of the acts of its judiciary would interfere with the principle of *res judicata*.

res judicata

Res judicata is the principle that once a civil matter has been judicially decided and no further appeals are possible, the decision is final and the issue cannot be litigated again.

?! THINKING POINT

While reading the following extract, consider why the Court rejected this argument.

Case C-224/01 *Köbler v Austria* [2003] ECR I-10239

37. Certain of the governments which submitted observations in these proceedings claimed that the principle of State liability for damage caused to individuals by infringements of Community law [now EU law] could not be applied to decisions of a national court adjudicating at last instance. In that connection arguments were put forward based, in particular, on the principle of legal certainty and, more specifically, the principle of *res judicata*, the independence and authority of the judiciary and the absence of a court competent to determine disputes relating to State liability for such decisions.

38. In that regard the importance of the principle of *res judicata* cannot be disputed (see judgment in *Eco Swiss*, cited above, paragraph 46). In order to ensure both stability of the law and legal relations and the sound administration of justice, it is important that judicial decisions which have become definitive after all rights of appeal have been exhausted or after expiry of the time-limits provided for in that connection can no longer be called in question.

39. However, it should be borne in mind that recognition of the principle of State liability for a decision of a court adjudicating at last instance does not in itself have the consequence of calling in question that decision as *res judicata*. Proceedings seeking to render the State liable do not have the same purpose and do not necessarily involve the same parties as the proceedings resulting in the decision which has acquired the status of *res judicata*. The applicant in an action to establish the liability of the State will, if successful, secure an order against it for reparation of the damage incurred but not necessarily a declaration invalidating the status of *res judicata* of the judicial decision which was responsible for the damage. In any event, the principle of State liability inherent in the Community [now Union] legal order requires such reparation, but not revision of the judicial decision which was responsible for the damage.

40. It follows that the principle of *res judicata* does not preclude recognition of the principle of State liability for the decision of a court adjudicating at last instance.

The Court pointed out that imposing liability in damages in relation to an incorrect judgment did not directly impact on that judgment or its legal status. An action for damages was an entirely separate action.

A related argument was raised in the subsequent case of Case C-453/00 *Kühne & Heitz NV v Productschap voor Pluimvee en Eieren* [2004] ECR I-837, in which the Court of Justice was asked to rule on whether an administrative (rather than a judicial) decision could be reopened where it became evident that it had been based on a flawed interpretation of EU law. The Court held that the duty of cooperation between the Member States and the EU, as set out in what is now Article 4(3) TEU, imposed an obligation on a domestic administrative body to reopen its decision if:

- it had the power to do so as a matter of national law;
- its decision had become final as a result of a judgment of a national court ruling at final instance;
- that judgment was, in the light of a later Court of Justice ruling, based on a misinterpretation of EU law and had been given without a preliminary reference being made under Article 267 TFEU (see further Chapter 6 on the preliminary reference procedure); and
- the person concerned had complained to the administrative body immediately after becoming aware of the Court of Justice ruling.

Secondly, in *Köbler,* the Court also rejected the suggestion that State liability for the acts of the judiciary would weaken judicial independence. Indeed, according to the Court, judicial authority would be strengthened by the possibility of State liability, as explained in the following extract.

Case C-224/01 *Köbler v Austria* [2003] ECR I-10239

41. Nor can the arguments based on the independence and authority of the judiciary be upheld.
42. As to the independence of the judiciary, the principle of liability in question concerns not the personal liability of the judge but that of the State. The possibility that under certain conditions the State may be rendered liable for judicial decisions contrary to Community law [now EU law] does not appear to entail any particular risk that the independence of a court adjudicating at last instance will be called in question.
43. As to the argument based on the risk of a diminution of the authority of a court adjudicating at last instance owing to the fact that its final decisions could by implication be called in question in proceedings in which the State may be rendered liable for such decisions, the existence of a right of action that affords, under certain conditions, reparation of the injurious effects of an erroneous judicial decision could also be regarded as enhancing the quality of a legal system and thus in the long run the authority of the judiciary.

44. Several governments also argued that application of the principle of State liability to decisions of a national court adjudicating at last instance was precluded by the difficulty of designating a court competent to determine disputes concerning the reparation of damage resulting from such decisions.

45. In that connection, given that, for reasons essentially connected with the need to secure for individuals protection of the rights conferred on them by Community [now Union] rules, the principle of State liability inherent in the Community legal order must apply in regard to decisions of a national court adjudicating at last instance, it is for the Member States to enable those affected to rely on that principle by affording them an appropriate right of action. Application of that principle cannot be compromised by the absence of a competent court.

In C-160/14 *Ferreira da Silva e Brito and others v Portugal* EU:C:2015:565 (for the facts of this case, see later in this section), the defendant State raised a third objection to the principle of State liability for breaches of EU law by national courts—that of **legal certainty**.

As can be seen in the following extract, the Court of Justice rejected this argument on the basis that the need for legal certainty should not frustrate the operation of the principle of State liability or prevent an individual asserting their EU law rights, such as those based on that principle.

legal certainty
Legal certainty is the principle that the law must be clear and foreseeable, so that persons subject to that law can foresee the legal consequence of their actions and regulate their conduct accordingly.

C-160/14 *Ferreira da Silva e Brito and others v Portugal* EU:C:2015:565

56. As regards the argument concerning infringement of the principle of legal certainty, it must be stated that, even if this principle may be taken into account in a legal situation such as that at issue in the main proceedings, it cannot frustrate the principle that the State should be liable for loss and damage caused to individuals as a result of infringements of EU law which are attributable to it.

57. To take account of the principle of legal certainty would mean that, where a decision given by a court adjudicating at last instance is based on an interpretation of EU law that is manifestly incorrect, an individual would be prevented from asserting the rights that he may derive from the EU legal order and, in particular, those that stem from the principle of State liability.

The importance of the principle of State liability for acts of its judiciary, as established in *Köbler*, was emphasized by the Court of Justice in Case C-173/03 *Traghetti del Mediterraneo SpA v Italy* [2006] ECR I-5177. In that case, a dispute arose as to the legality of certain provisions of Italian law restricting State liability for damage caused by a decision of a national court adjudicating at last instance. The Court referred to its reasoning in *Köbler* (at paras 33–36) before applying that reasoning to the facts of *Traghetti*. It considered, first, the exclusion under Italian law of liability arising from an interpretation of the law by a court. Its reasoning appears in the following extract.

Case C-173/03 *Traghetti del Mediterraneo SpA v Italy* [2006] ECR I-5177

31. Basing its reasoning in that respect, inter alia, on the essential role played by the judiciary in the protection of the rights derived by individuals from Community [now Union] rules and on the fact that a court adjudicating at last instance is by definition the last judicial body before which individuals may assert the rights conferred on them by Community law [now EU law], the Court infers that the protection of those rights would be weakened—and the full effectiveness of the Community rules conferring such rights would be brought into question—if individuals were precluded from being able, under certain conditions, to obtain reparation when their rights are affected by an infringement of Community law attributable to a decision of a court of a Member State adjudicating at last instance (see *Köbler*, paragraphs 33 to 36).
32. It is true that, having regard to the specific nature of the judicial function and to the legitimate requirements of legal certainty, State liability in such a case is not unlimited. As the Court has held, State liability can be incurred only in the exceptional case where the national court adjudicating at last instance has manifestly infringed the applicable law. In order to determine whether that condition is satisfied, the national court hearing a claim for reparation must take account of all the factors which characterise the situation put before it, which include, in particular, the degree of clarity and precision of the rule infringed, whether the infringement was intentional, whether the error of law was excusable or inexcusable, the position taken, where applicable, by a Community institution and non-compliance by the court in question with its obligation to make a reference for a preliminary ruling under the third paragraph of Article 234 EC [now Article 267 TFEU] (*Köbler*, paragraphs 53 to 55).
33. Analogous considerations linked to the need to guarantee effective judicial protection to individuals of the rights conferred on them by Community law similarly preclude State liability not being incurred solely because an infringement of Community law attributable to a national court adjudicating at last instance arises from the interpretation of provisions of law made by that court.
34. On the one hand, interpretation of provisions of law forms part of the very essence of judicial activity since, whatever the sphere of activity considered, a court faced with divergent or conflicting arguments must normally interpret the relevant legal rules—of national and/or Community law—in order to resolve the dispute brought before it.
35. On the other hand, it is not inconceivable that a manifest infringement of Community law might be committed precisely in the exercise of such work of interpretation if, for example, the court gives a substantive or procedural rule of Community law a manifestly incorrect meaning, particularly in the light of the relevant case-law of the Court on the subject (see, in that regard, *Köbler*, paragraph 56), or where it interprets national law in such a way that in practice it leads to an infringement of the applicable Community law.
36. As the Advocate General observed in point 52 of his Opinion, to exclude all State liability in such circumstances on the ground that the infringement of Community law arises from an interpretation of provisions of law made by a court would be tantamount to rendering meaningless the principle laid down by the Court in the *Köbler* judgment.

That remark is even more apposite in the case of courts adjudicating at last instance, which are responsible, at national level, for ensuring that rules of law are given a uniform interpretation.

REVIEW QUESTION

Why did the Court rule that national restrictions on liability arising from an interpretation of law by a national court were contrary to EU law?

Answer: The Court held that the interpretation of law was an integral part of the work of the courts and that errors in such interpretation could constitute a serious breach of EU law. Given the importance of the judiciary in protecting individual rights and the fact that a court of last instance was the final judicial body able to provide such protection in a particular case, the exclusion of State liability for any infringement of an individual's rights by such a court would impair the effectiveness of EU law and would render the judgment in *Köbler* meaningless.

The Court in *Traghetti* next considered the exclusion under Italian law of liability arising from an assessment of the facts or evidence by a court.

?! THINKING POINT

While reading the following extract, consider in what respects the Court's reasoning on this issue was 'analogous' (*Traghetti*, at para 37) to its reasoning on the exclusion of liability for errors of interpretation.

Case C-173/03 *Traghetti del Mediterraneo SpA v Italy* [2006] ECR I-5177

37. An analogous conclusion must be drawn with regard to legislation which in a general manner excludes all State liability where the infringement attributable to a court of that State arises from its assessment of the facts and evidence.
38. On the one hand, such an assessment constitutes, like the interpretation of provisions of law, another essential aspect of the judicial function since, regardless of the interpretation adopted by the national court seised of a particular case, the application of those provisions to that case will often depend on the assessment which the court has made of the facts and the value and relevance of the evidence adduced for that purpose by the parties to the dispute.
39. On the other hand, such an assessment—which sometimes requires complex analysis—may also lead, in certain cases, to a manifest infringement of the applicable law, whether that assessment is made in the context of the application of specific provisions relating to the burden of proof or the weight or admissibility of the evidence, or in the context of the application of provisions which require a legal characterisation of the facts.

40. To exclude, in such circumstances, any possibility that State liability might be incurred where the infringement allegedly committed by the national court relates to the assessment which it made of facts or evidence would also amount to depriving the principle set out in the *Köbler* judgment of all practical effect with regard to manifest infringements of Community law [now EU law] for which courts adjudicating at last instance were responsible.

41. As the Advocate General observed in points 87 to 89 of his Opinion, that is especially the case in the State aid sector. To exclude, in that sector, all State liability on the ground that an infringement of Community law committed by a national court is the result of an assessment of the facts is likely to lead to a weakening of the procedural guarantees available to individuals, in that the protection of the rights which they derive from the relevant provisions of the Treaty depends, to a great extent, on successive operations of legal classification of the facts. Were State liability to be wholly excluded by reason of the assessments of facts carried out by a court, those individuals would have no judicial protection if a national court adjudicating at last instance committed a manifest error in its review of the above operations of legal classification of facts.

Finally, the Court considered the limitation of liability under Italian law to cases of intentional fault and serious misconduct by the court. Its reasoning appears in the following extract.

Case C-173/03 *Traghetti del Mediterraneo SpA v Italy* [2006] ECR I-5177

42. With regard, finally, to the limitation of State liability to cases of intentional fault and serious misconduct on the part of the court, it should be recalled, as was pointed out in paragraph 32 of this judgment, that the Court held, in the *Köbler* judgment, that State liability for damage caused to individuals by reason of an infringement of Community law [now EU law] attributable to a national court adjudicating at last instance could be incurred in the exceptional case where that court manifestly infringed the applicable law.

43. Such manifest infringement is to be assessed, inter alia, in the light of a number of criteria, such as the degree of clarity and precision of the rule infringed, whether the infringement was intentional, whether the error of law was excusable or inexcusable, and the non-compliance by the court in question with its obligation to make a reference for a preliminary ruling under the third paragraph of Article 234 EC [now Article 267 TFEU]; it is in any event presumed where the decision involved is made in manifest disregard of the case-law of the Court on the subject (*Köbler*, paragraphs 53 to 56).

44. Accordingly, although it remains possible for national law to define the criteria relating to the nature or degree of the infringement which must be met before State liability can be incurred for an infringement of Community law attributable to a national court adjudicating at last instance, under no circumstances may such criteria impose requirements stricter than that of a manifest infringement of the applicable law, as set out in paragraphs 53 to 56 of the *Köbler* judgment.

REVIEW QUESTION

To what extent, if any, did the Court of Justice in *Traghetti* permit a Member State to restrict its liability in damages in the event of a sufficiently serious breach of EU law by that State's supreme court?

Answer: The Court reiterated that the conditions governing such liability were those laid down in *Köbler*. Although a Member State, in its domestic law, could clarify the criteria for liability, 'under no circumstances' could it impose stricter conditions than those laid down in *Köbler* so as to make a successful claim for damages more difficult.

A different type of domestic restriction on State liability was at issue in C-160/14 *Ferreira da Silva e Brito and others v Portugal* EU:C:2015:565, in which the applicants were dismissed when their employer, an airline, was wound up. Another airline subsequently began to operate some of its flights, using its assets and employing some of its former employees. The applicants sought to enforce their rights under Council Directive 77/187/EEC of 14 February 1977 on the approximation of the laws of the Member States relating to the safeguarding of employees' rights in the event of transfers of undertakings, businesses or parts of businesses, OJ 1977 L61/26. The Portuguese Supreme Court of Justice dismissed their claim, having refused to make a preliminary reference to the Court of Justice (see further Chapter 6 on preliminary references). The applicants brought proceedings against the State for damages in relation to what they alleged was a serious breach of EU law by the national court, consisting of its incorrect interpretation of the Directive and its refusal to make a mandatory reference. Under Portuguese law, such a claim for damages could be made only if the court judgment causing the loss had been set aside. The national court made a reference to the Court of Justice, which ruled that where the conditions for State liability were satisfied—which was a matter for the national courts to determine—the remedy to be awarded was governed by national law so long as the requirements laid down by national law in relation to the remedy were not excessively difficult to obtain (the principle of effectiveness, discussed further at 4.3.2). The Portuguese law at issue was liable to make it excessively difficult to obtain reparation because the setting aside of the wrongful judgment was, in practice, impossible. That law was therefore contrary to EU law and should not be applied in the domestic proceedings against the State.

5.5 The development of the conditions governing the imposition of State liability: the *Factortame III* conditions

In *Francovich*, the Court of Justice had indicated that the conditions for liability could differ according to the nature of the breach. In *Factortame III*, having held that the principle of Member State liability applied in circumstances different from those in *Francovich*, the Court laid down a set of conditions that did indeed differ from those that it had applied in *Francovich* and which are set out in the following extract.

Joined Cases C-46 & 48/93 *Brasserie du Pêcheur SA v Germany; R v Secretary of State for Transport, ex p Factortame ('Factortame III')* [1996] ECR I-1029

51. In such circumstances, Community law [now EU law] confers a right to reparation where three conditions are met: the rule of law infringed must be intended to confer rights on individuals; the breach must be sufficiently serious; and there must be a direct causal link between the breach of the obligation resting on the State and the damage sustained by the injured parties.

This second set of conditions have been ruled by the Court of Justice to govern State liability for a number of different types of breach of EU law by a Member State: the enactment of national legislation which is contrary to EU law (for example, *Factortame III*), the incorrect transposition of a Directive (for example, *BT*), administrative breaches (for example, *Hedley Lomas*), and judicial breaches (for example, *Köbler*).

REVIEW QUESTION

What three conditions for liability were set out by the Court in *Factortame III*?

Answer: The conditions were that:

(a) the rule of EU law infringed must be intended to confer rights on individuals;

(b) the breach must be sufficiently serious; and

(c) there must be a causal link between the breach of the State's obligation and the damage suffered by the individual.

These three conditions will be examined in more detail at 5.5.1–5.5.3. However, before doing this, it is important to note that, in laying down those conditions, the Court of Justice drew explicitly on its existing jurisprudence on EU liability in damages under Article 340 TFEU (see Chapter 8).

THINKING POINT

While reading the following extract, consider which features of its existing jurisprudence under Article 340 TFEU the Court drew on when developing Member State liability in *Factortame III*.

Joined Cases C-46 & 48/93 *Brasserie du Pêcheur SA v Germany; R v Secretary of State for Transport, ex p Factortame ('Factortame III')* [1996] ECR I-1029

Conditions under which the State may Incur Liability for Acts and Omissions of the National Legislature Contrary to Community Law (Second Question in Case C-46/93 and First Question in Case C-48/93)

[...]

38. Although Community law [now EU law] imposes State liability, the conditions under which that liability gives rise to a right to reparation depend on the nature of the breach of Community law giving rise to the loss and damage (*Francovich and Others*, paragraph 38).

39. In order to determine those conditions, account should first be taken of the principles inherent in the Community [now Union] legal order which form the basis for State liability, namely, first, the full effectiveness of Community rules and the effective protection of the rights which they confer and, second, the obligation to cooperate imposed on Member States by Article 5 of the [EC] Treaty [now Article 4(3) TEU] (*Francovich and Others*, paragraphs 31 to 36).

40. In addition, as the Commission and the several governments which submitted observations have emphasized, it is pertinent to refer to the Court's case-law on non-contractual liability on the part of the Community.

41. First, the second paragraph of Article 215 of the [EC] Treaty [now Article 340 TFEU] refers, as regards the non-contractual liability of the Community, to the general principles common to the laws of the Member States, from which, in the absence of written rules, the Court also draws inspiration in other areas of Community law.

42. Second, the conditions under which the State may incur liability for damage caused to individuals by a breach of Community law cannot, in the absence of particular justification, differ from those governing the liability of the Community in like circumstances. The protection of the rights which individuals derive from Community law cannot vary depending on whether a national authority or a Community authority is responsible for the damage.

43. The system of rules which the Court has worked out with regard to Article 215 of the Treaty, particularly in relation to liability for legislative measures, takes into account, *inter alia*, the complexity of the situations to be regulated, difficulties in the application or interpretation of the texts and, more particularly, the margin of discretion available to the author of the act in question.

44. Thus, in developing its case-law on the non-contractual liability of the Community, in particular as regards legislative measures involving choices of economic policy, the Court has had regard to the wide discretion available to the institutions in implementing Community policies.

45. The strict approach taken towards the liability of the Community in the exercise of its legislative activities is due to two considerations. First, even where the legality of measures is subject to judicial review, exercise of the legislative function must not be hindered by the prospect of actions for damages whenever the general interest of the Community requires legislative measures to be adopted which may adversely affect individual interests. Second, in a legislative context characterized by the exercise of a wide discretion, which is essential for implementing a Community policy, the Community cannot incur liability unless the institution concerned has manifestly and gravely disregarded the limits on the exercise of its powers (Joined Cases 83, 94/76, and 4, 15, & 40/77) *HNL and Others v Council and Commission* [1978] ECR 1209, paragraphs 5 and 6).

46. That said, the national legislature—like the Community institutions—does not systematically have a wide discretion when it acts in a field governed by Community law. Community law may impose upon it obligations to achieve a particular result or obligations to act or refrain from acting which reduce its margin of discretion, sometimes to a considerable degree. This is so, for instance, where, as in the circumstances to which the judgment in *Francovich and Others* relates, Article 189 of the [EC] Treaty [now Article 288 TFEU] places the Member State under an obligation to take, within a given period, all the measures needed in order to achieve the result required by a directive. In such a case, the fact that it is for the national legislature to take the necessary measures has no bearing on the Member State's liability for failing to transpose the directive.

47. In contrast, where a Member State acts in a field where it has a wide discretion, comparable to that of the Community institutions in implementing Community policies, the conditions under which it may incur liability must, in principle, be the same as those under which the Community institutions incur liability in a comparable situation.

[…]

49. As regards the facts of Case C-48/93, the United Kingdom legislature also had a wide discretion. The legislation at issue was concerned, first, with the registration of vessels, a field which, in view of the state of development of Community law, falls within the jurisdiction of the Member States and, secondly, with regulating fishing, a sector in which implementation of the common fisheries policy leaves a margin of discretion to the Member States.

50. Consequently, in each case the German and United Kingdom legislatures were faced with situations involving choices comparable to those made by the Community institutions when they adopt legislative measures pursuant to a Community policy. …

51. Firstly, those conditions satisfy the requirements of the full effectiveness of the rules of Community law and of the effective protection of the rights which those rules confer.

52. Secondly, those conditions correspond in substance to those defined by the Court in relation to Article 215 in its case law on liability of the Community for damage caused to individuals by unlawful legislative measures adopted by its institutions.

In *Factortame III*, the Court of Justice considered that the conditions governing State liability in damages for breach of EU law should be the same as those governing the liability of the EU itself under Article 340 TFEU (see Chapter 8). Thus the clarity of the EU law breached and the extent of the State's discretion were relevant to whether it should be made liable in damages.

5.5.1 The EU law breached must be intended to confer rights on individuals

The *Factortame III* conditions require an applicant to prove that the EU law that has been breached confers rights on individuals. For example, in the *Factortame III* case itself, the Court of Justice accepted that what is now Article 49 TFEU (formerly Article 43 EC), which provides that Member State nationals may move to another Member State as self-employed persons or in order to manage a business, conferred rights on individuals that national courts must protect.

In Case C-5/94 *R v Ministry of Agriculture, Fisheries and Food, ex p Hedley Lomas* [1996] ECR I-2553, the Court of Justice reached a similar conclusion on Article 35 TFEU, which prohibits Member States from restricting exports (see further 10.8).

?! THINKING POINT

What 'rights' does Article 35 TFEU provide and for which 'individuals'?

Case C-5/94 *R v Ministry of Agriculture, Fisheries and Food, ex p Hedley Lomas* [1996] ECR I-2553

27. As regards the first condition, as is clear from the answer given to the first question, the United Kingdom's refusal to issue an export licence to Hedley Lomas constituted a quantitative restriction on exports contrary to Article 34 of the [EC] Treaty [now Article 35 TFEU] which could not be justified under Article 36 [EC, now Article 36 TFEU]. Whilst Article 34 imposes a prohibition on Member States, it also creates rights for individuals which the national courts must protect (*Pigs Marketing Board v Redmond* (Case 83/78) [1978] ECR 2347).

In *AD v Secretary of State for the Home Department* [2015] EWHC 663 (QB), [2016] 2 CMLR 37 (see also 5.5.2), the applicant's claim for asylum in the UK was rejected and he was deported back to Mongolia, where he was detained before trial, convicted, and imprisoned. He subsequently escaped and returned to the UK, where his second asylum claim was granted. He then claimed damages from the UK government for its failure to implement the Qualification Directive on the criteria for refugee status (Council Directive 2004/83/EC of 29 April 2004 on minimum standards for the qualification and status of third country nationals or stateless persons as refugees or as persons who otherwise need international protection and the content of the protection granted, OJ 2004 L304/12) and the Procedure Directive on the procedure for granting refugee status (Council Directive 2005/85/EC of 1 December 2005 on minimum standards on procedures in Member States for granting and withdrawing refugee status, OJ 2005 L326/13). The High Court of England and Wales held that the Qualification Directive granted rights to individuals to be granted refugee status if the criteria were met.

5.5.2 The breach must be sufficiently serious

In *Factortame III*, the Court of Justice stated that the decisive test for finding a breach of EU law to be sufficiently serious was whether the Member State had 'manifestly and gravely disregarded the limits on its discretion' (*Factortame III*, at para 55). The Court also provided in

Factortame III (at para 56) a list of factors that the national court should take into consideration in assessing whether the breach was sufficiently serious:

(a) the clarity and precision of the rule breached;

(b) the measure of discretion left by that rule to the national or EU authorities;

(c) whether the infringement and the damage caused were intentional or involuntary;

(d) whether any error of law was excusable or inexcusable;

(e) the fact that the position taken by an EU institution may have contributed towards the omission; and

(f) the adoption or retention of national measures or practices contrary to EU law.

The Court in *Köbler* laid down an additional criterion for establishing the existence of a sufficiently serious breach in cases involving judicial breaches:

(g) non-compliance by the court in question with its obligation to make a reference for a preliminary ruling under Article 267 TFEU (see further Chapter 6 on Article 267 TFEU).

It can readily be seen that the first factor on the list, the clarity and precision of the EU law that has been breached, is crucial. If it is clear, then it is likely that any infringement was intentional and that any error of law is inexcusable—and thus that the breach is sufficiently serious. If the law breached is unclear in its terms, then it may be easier to argue that the infringement was involuntary and that any error of law is excusable—and thus that the breach is not sufficiently serious. A lack of clarity may also give greater scope for arguing that the State has wide discretion, again supporting the conclusion that any breach by it is not sufficiently serious.

The Court's application of this list of factors in the *Factortame III* case itself, as set out in the following extract, provides a useful example of how they should be used to support an argument on a particular set of facts that there is—or is not—a sufficiently serious breach.

Joined Cases C-46 & 48/93 *Brasserie du Pêcheur SA v Germany; R v Secretary of State for Transport, ex p Factortame ('Factortame III')* [1996] ECR I-1029

54. The first condition is manifestly satisfied in the case of Article 30 of the [EC] Treaty [now Article 34 TFEU], the relevant provision in Case C-46/93, and in the case of Article 52 [EC, now Article 49 TFEU], the relevant provision in Case C-48/93. Whilst Article 30 imposes a prohibition on Member States, it nevertheless gives rise to rights for individuals which the national courts must protect (Case 74/76 *Iannelli & Volpi v Meroni* 1977] ECR 557, [1977] 2 CMLR 688, paragraph 13). Likewise, the essence of Article 52 is to confer rights on individuals (Case 2/74 *Reyners* [1974] ECR 631, [1974] 2 CMLR 305, paragraph 25).

55. As to the second condition, as regards both Community [now Union] liability under Article 215 [EC, now Article 340 TFEU] and Member State liability for breaches of Community law [now EU law], the decisive test for finding that a breach of Community law is sufficiently

serious is whether the Member State or the Community institution concerned manifestly and gravely disregarded the limits on its discretion.

[…]

58. While, in the present cases, the Court cannot substitute its assessment for that of the national courts, which have sole jurisdiction to find the facts in the main proceedings and decide how to characterize the breaches of Community law at issue, it will be helpful to indicate a number of circumstances which the national courts might take into account.

[…]

61. The decision of the United Kingdom legislature to introduce in the Merchant Shipping Act 1988 provisions relating to the conditions for the registration of fishing vessels has to be assessed differently in the case of the provisions making registration subject to a nationality condition, which constitute direct discrimination manifestly contrary to Community law, and in the case of the provisions laying down residence and domicile conditions for vessel owners and operators.

62. The latter conditions are prima facie incompatible with Article 52 of the Treaty in particular, but the United Kingdom sought to justify them in terms of the objectives of the common fisheries policy. In the judgment in *Factortame II*, cited above, the Court rejected that justification.

63. In order to determine whether the breach of Article 52 thus committed by the United Kingdom was sufficiently serious, the national court might take into account, *inter alia*, the legal disputes relating to particular features of the common fisheries policy, the attitude of the Commission, which made its position known to the United Kingdom in good time, and the assessments as to the state of certainty of Community law made by the national courts in the interim proceedings brought by individuals affected by the Merchant Shipping Act.

64. Lastly, consideration should be given to the assertion made by Rawlings (Trawling) Ltd, the 37th claimant in Case C-48/93, that the United Kingdom failed to adopt immediately the measures needed to comply with the Order of the President of the Court of 10 October 1989 in *EC Commission v United Kingdom* (cited above), and that this needlessly increased the loss it sustained. If this allegation—which was certainly contested by the United Kingdom at the hearing—should prove correct, it should be regarded by the national court as constituting in itself a manifest and, therefore, sufficiently serious breach of Community law.

65. As for the third condition, it is for the national courts to determine whether there is a direct causal link between the breach of the obligation borne by the State and the damage sustained by the injured parties.

REVIEW QUESTION

Why did the Court in *Factortame III* consider the UK's breach of Article 52 EC (now Article 49 TFEU) to be 'sufficiently serious'?

Answer: To summarize briefly, the Court took into account:

- the previous legal disputes concerning the Common Fisheries Policy (CFP), which had clarified the law;
- the fact that the EU Commission had made known to the UK at an early stage its view that the measures were in breach of EU law;
- the fact that the national courts hearing the case had considered EU law to be clear in this respect; and
- the allegation that the UK had failed to comply promptly with the judgment of the Court pursuant to Article 258 TFEU proceedings brought against the UK by the EU Commission (see further 7.1 on the enforcement procedure under Article 258 TFEU), which, if true, in itself indicated that the UK had breached EU law to a sufficiently serious extent.

In Case C-392/93 *R v HM Treasury, ex p British Telecommunications plc* [1996] ECR I-1631, the Court of Justice held that the breach was not sufficiently serious because the interpretation of the Directive on which the flawed national transposing measures were based was reasonable in the circumstances.

?! THINKING POINT

While reading the following extract, consider why the Court reached this conclusion.

Case C-392/93 *R v HM Treasury, ex p British Telecommunications plc* [1996] ECR I-1631

41. Whilst it is in principle for the national courts to verify whether or not the conditions governing State liability for a breach of Community law [now EU law] are fulfilled, in the present case the Court has all the necessary information to assess whether the facts amount to a sufficiently serious breach of Community law.
42. According to the case law of the Court, a breach is sufficiently serious where, in the exercise of its legislative powers, an institution or a Member State has manifestly and gravely disregarded the limits on the exercise of its powers (judgments in *HNL and Others v EC Council and EC Commission* [Joined Cases 83/76, 94/76, 4/77, 15/77 and 40/77 *HNL and Others v EC Council and EC Commission* [1978] ECR 1209], and in *Brasserie du Pêcheur* and *Factortame*). Factors which the competent court may take into consideration include the clarity and precision of the rule breached (*Brasserie du Pêcheur* and *Factortame*).
43. In the present case, Article 8(1) is imprecisely worded and was reasonably capable of bearing, as well as the construction applied to it by the Court in this judgment, the interpretation given to it by the United Kingdom in good faith and on the basis of arguments which are not entirely devoid of substance. That interpretation, which was also shared by other Member States, was not manifestly contrary to the wording of the directive or to the objective pursued by it.

44. Moreover, no guidance was available to the United Kingdom from case law of the Court as to the interpretation of the provision at issue, nor did the Commission raise the matter when the 1992 Regulations were adopted.
45. In those circumstances, the fact that a Member State, when transposing the directive into national law, thought it necessary itself to determine which services were to be excluded from its scope in implementation of Article 8, albeit in breach of that provision, cannot be regarded as a sufficiently serious breach of Community law of the kind intended by the Court in its judgment in *Brasserie du Pêcheur* and *Factortame*.
46. The answer to Question 4 must therefore be that Community law does not require a Member State which, in transposing the directive into national law, has itself determined which services of a contracting entity are to be excluded from its scope in implementation of Article 8, to compensate that entity for any loss suffered by it as a result of the error committed by the State.

The Court concluded in *BT* that the EU legislation at issue was unclear and that there was no appropriate case law for the UK to consult for clarification. Further, the Commission had not raised any objection when the UK adopted its transposing measures. The UK did not, therefore, incur liability in damages.

The Court came to a similar conclusion in Joined Cases C-283, 291, & 292/94 *Denkavit International BV and VITIC Amsterdam BV and Voormeer BV v Bundesamt für Finanzen* [1996] ECR I-5063 (see also 5.5.3). In that case, the German government had failed to transpose correctly Council Directive 90/435/EEC of 23 July 1990 on the common system of taxation applicable in the case of parent companies and subsidiaries of different Member States, OJ 1990 L225/6. The Court ruled that this breach of EU law was not sufficiently serious to give rise to liability in damages because the rule breached (the Directive) was not clear and precise. Almost all Member States had adopted the same, incorrect interpretation as Germany and there had been no case law from the Court of Justice giving guidance as to how this Directive was to be interpreted.

In *R v Secretary of State for the Home Department, ex p Gallagher* [1996] 2 CMLR 951, the Court of Appeal of England and Wales examined the seriousness of a breach of EU law by the UK government in the light of the Court of Justice's ruling earlier in the same proceedings (in Case C-175/94 *R v Secretary of State for the Home Department, ex p Gallagher* [1995] ECR I-4253) that the procedure laid down by the Prevention of Terrorism (Temporary Provisions) Act 1989 for the exclusion from the UK of suspected terrorists was contrary to Council Directive 64/221/EEC of 25 February 1964 on the co-ordination of special measures concerning the movement and residence of foreign nationals which are justified on grounds of public policy, public security or public health, OJ 1964 56/850 (repealed by Directive 2004/38/EC of the European Parliament and of the Council of 29 April 2004 on the right of citizens of the Union and their family members to move and reside freely within the territory of the Member States …, OJ 2004 L158/77—see Chapter 11). Gallagher had been arrested and excluded from the UK under the 1989 Act on the ground that he had been involved in acts of terrorism, but his subsequent claim for damages from the UK government was rejected by the Court of Appeal.

Applying the *Factortame III* test, it ruled that the UK's breach of EU law was not sufficiently serious and had not, in any event, caused loss to Gallagher (see 5.5.3). Its reasoning as to why the breach was not sufficiently serious appears in the following extract.

R v Secretary of State for the Home Department, ex p Gallagher [1996] 2 CMLR 951, Court of Appeal

26. If, as we have concluded, it is necessary for Mr Gallagher to show that the United Kingdom's breach in failing correctly to transpose the Directive into domestic law was 'sufficiently serious', we conclude that he has failed to do so. McCullough J at first instance and Hirst LJ in the Court of Appeal did not consider it arguable that Schedule 2 of the 1989 Act in its unamended form violated Community law [now EU law]. In the Court of Appeal Farquharson LJ regarded Mr Gallagher's complaint as technical, and Steyn LJ went no further than to say that he did not regard it as self-evident that the argument advanced on behalf of Mr Gallagher should necessarily be regarded as technical. There is nothing to suggest that the United Kingdom wilfully deprived suspects of rights which the Directive was intended to confer, and the original statutory procedure (if operated fairly and in good faith) was one which could well be thought to give effective protection. While the chronology in Schedule 2 departed from that prescribed in the Directive, and could thus be described as 'manifest', we do not think the departure can be described as 'grave': the subject of an order was not obviously worse off as a result, and might be better; although notified to the Commission no objection had been taken to the United Kingdom measure; and three judges held there was no violation of Community law. There was authority of the Court of Justice which showed that expulsion should not precede reference to the competent authority (*Pecastaing v Belgium* (Case 98/79) [1980] ECR 691), but under Schedule 2 in its unamended form the subject of an order could, if he exercised his statutory rights, avoid expulsion until his case had been duly reconsidered.
27. After the argument in this appeal had been concluded, the Court of Justice gave judgment in *R v Ministry of Agriculture, Fisheries and Food, ex parte Hedley Lomas (Ireland) Limited* (Case C-5/94) [1996] All ER (EC) 493. The background to the case was a Council directive prescribing minimum standards for the humane slaughter of cattle. The Ministry refused Hedley Lomas a licence to export sheep for slaughter in a named Spanish slaughterhouse, thereby admittedly imposing a quantitative restriction on exports, on the ground that some Spanish slaughterhouses did not comply with the standards required by the Directive. This was held to be a breach of Community law, and the question of compensation accordingly arose.
28. The Court held that the three conditions laid down in *Brasserie du Pêcheur* and *Factortame* applied in this case also. With reference to the second 'sufficiently serious' condition, the Court said:

    'As regards the second condition, where, at the time when it committed the infringement, the Member State in question was not called upon to make any legislative choices and had only considerably reduced, or even no, discretion, the mere infringe-

> ment of Community law may be sufficient to establish the existence of a sufficiently serious breach.'

With reference to the facts of that case, the Court continued:

> 'In that respect, in this particular case, the United Kingdom was not even in a position to produce any proof of non-compliance with the Directive by the slaughterhouse to which the animals for which the export licence was sought were destined.'

29. The contrast with the present case is in our view obvious. Here, the United Kingdom certainly was called upon to make a legislative choice, and certainly did enjoy a measure of discretion. The choice made, although wrong, was not obviously wrong in substance. It was not, as in *Hedley Lomas*, committing what was on its face a blatant breach of the Treaty, without any evidence on which it could rely to justify its conduct. The present case was not one of 'mere infringement'.

REVIEW QUESTION

What factors did the Court of Appeal take into account in ruling that the breach in *Gallagher* was not sufficiently serious?

Answer: The Court of Appeal noted that persons subject to the 1989 Act were not 'obviously worse off' as a result of the breach, the Commission had not objected to the Act when notified of it, and the UK had enjoyed a measure of discretion that it had not blatantly exceeded.

A further domestic example is provided by *AD v Secretary of State for the Home Department* [2015] EWHC 663 (QB), [2016] 2 CMLR 37 (for the facts of this case, see 5.5.1). The High Court of England and Wales held that the alleged breaches in relation to the rejection of the applicant's first claim for asylum were not sufficiently serious because, even if the decision had been wrong, the errors had been excusable, and the Secretary of State had not manifestly and grossly disregarded the limits on her powers. She had had regard to the applicant's principal claims, but also to the fact that he could reasonably relocate within Mongolia to places where his human rights would not be threatened, and to the fact that he could expect a fair trial; the applicant had, at that time, failed to highlight the poor conditions of pretrial detention that were relevant to the success of his second asylum claim.

There are, however, circumstances in which a careful application of the detailed criteria laid down by the Court of Justice in *Factortame III* is not necessary.

First, the Court of Justice in Case C-5/94 *R v Ministry of Agriculture, Fisheries and Food, ex p Hedley Lomas* [1996] ECR I-2553 (see 5.4.3 for the facts of this case) held that the Member States had no discretion as to whether to comply with what is now Article 35 TFEU on the free movement of goods (see 10.8) and so any infringement of that Article must automatically be a sufficiently serious breach. This is open to criticism both as a general principle and on the facts of the case. In principle, the whole idea of according the automatic status of a 'sufficiently serious breach' to certain breaches is problematic because the main element of the *Factortame III* test—and the feature that distinguishes it from *Francovich* (see further 5.6)—is the very examination of *whether* there has been a sufficiently serious breach, and yet the Court appears to be prepared to omit that examination on a rather arbitrary basis. In practice, it is problematic because Member States do, in fact, have a discretion over the implementation of Article 35, because they can restrict the free movement of goods if one of the exceptions contained in Article 36 TFEU applies (see further 10.8.11). In *Hedley Lomas*, the UK had argued that one of these exceptions did indeed apply. Admittedly, the Court of Justice did not accept this argument, but it seems a little unjust for the Court then to rule that since the UK had been wrong to consider that an exception under Article 36 applied, it had had no discretion in the application of Article 35 and must therefore be guilty of a sufficiently serious breach. There was no evidence that the UK could have known that its interpretation of Article 36 was incorrect until the Court of Justice gave judgment in the case itself. In *Köbler*, the Court of Justice noted that EU law did not expressly state whether discrimination such as that at issue on the facts could be justified, this point had not been dealt with previously by the Court, and the answer was not obvious. It therefore concluded that although the national court had reached an incorrect conclusion and refused to make a reference, its infringement of EU law on the free movement of persons (see further Chapter 11) was not a sufficiently serious breach to give rise to liability in damages. This seems to be a fairer approach by the Court than that taken by it in *Hedley Lomas*.

Secondly, in *Factortame III*, the Court noted that a breach of EU law would clearly be sufficiently serious if that breach had persisted despite either a judgment confirming the existence of a breach, or a preliminary ruling (see further Chapter 6 on the preliminary reference procedure) or settled case law of the Court from which it was clear that the conduct in question constituted a breach.

A rather different problem with the application of the 'sufficiently serious breach' requirement, at least in English law, was highlighted by the UK's Supreme Court in *R (Chester) v Secretary of State for Justice and another; McGeoch v The Lord President of the Council and another* [2013] UKSC 63, [2013] 3 WLR 1076. In these joined cases, two convicted prisoners challenged the ban under English law on prisoner voting and sought damages from the UK government. The Supreme Court held that the ban did not infringe EU law and that, even if it had done, damages would not be awarded. In relation to the seriousness of the breach, it made the following comments (*per* Lord Mance).

R (Chester) v Secretary of State for Justice and another; McGeoch v The Lord President of the Council and another [2013] UKSC 63, [2013] 3 WLR 1076

79. The second condition is that the breach was sufficiently serious. This in turn depends, under European law, on whether Parliament, the relevant United Kingdom authority, can be said manifestly and gravely to have disregarded the limits on its discretion. This must be judged taking into consideration

'the clarity and precision of the rule breached; the measure of discretion left by that rule to the national or Community authorities; whether the infringement and the damage caused was intentional or involuntary; whether any error of law was excusable or inexcusable': para 77 above.

In relation to voting by convicted prisoners, the United Kingdom legislature enjoyed a wide margin of discretion. Further, this is in a context where there has been and remains a considerable lack of certainty about what the parameters of that discretion may be. This is evident from a reading of the Strasbourg case law, particularly the two *Hirst* judgments, the chamber judgment in *Frodl* v *Austria* [Application No 20201/04 (2011)] 52 EHRR 267 and the Grand Chamber judgment overruling the chamber judgment in *Scoppola* [*Scoppola v Italy (No 3)* Application No 126/05 [2012] ECHR 868], in which the European Court of Human Rights has sought to identify the relevant considerations and to apply them to particular facts. Accordingly, it is clearly very arguable that this condition is not met.

80. I will not however say more about the application of the second condition in this case, in view of one further factor, which I prefer to leave open. The test stated in the European authorities postulates some degree of examination of the conduct of the relevant national authority. Since the relevant United Kingdom authority is here Parliament in enacting and continuing in force the relevant legislation, an assessment of some of these matters (particularly whether the infringement was intentional or involuntary, excusable or inexcusable) may threaten conflict with the constitutional principle enshrined in the Bill of Rights 1688 that domestic courts in the United Kingdom ought not to 'impeach or question' proceedings in Parliament. To avoid this, it may perhaps be necessary to approach a claim for damages in a case like the present on an objective basis, without regard to what has actually happened or been said in Parliament. The decision in *R v Secretary of State for Transport, Ex p Factortame (No 5)* [2000] 1 AC 524 does not appear to throw any light on this problem, because there does not seem there to have been any call to consider parliamentary debates. On any view, however, the fact of parliamentary activity, referred to in *Greens* [*and MT v UK* Application No 60041/08 (2010)] 53 EHRR 710 and continuing, can no doubt be taken into account.

REVIEW QUESTION

What concerns did the Supreme Court raise in *McGeoch* as to the impact of the *Factortame III* test on the supremacy of the UK Parliament?

Answer: The Supreme Court noted that the *Factortame III* test required a court to assess, inter alia, whether the UK Parliament had deliberately breached EU law and that this assessment might conflict with the constitutional principle under UK law that UK courts should not impugn parliamentary proceedings.

5.5.3 Causation of damage

The issue of causation is, in principle, for the national court to determine on the facts (although, on occasion, the Court of Justice has asserted that it has the necessary information to do this itself (see, for example, Joined Cases C-283, 291, & 292/94 *Denkavit International BV and VITIC Amsterdam BV and Voormeer BV v Bundesamt für Finanzen* [1996] ECR I-5063, at para 49). A good example of such a determination is provided by *Gallagher* (discussed at 5.5.2), in which the Court of Appeal of England and Wales ruled that, in addition to the fact that the breach of EU law was not sufficiently serious, there was no causal link between the breach and Gallagher's losses.

?! **THINKING POINT**

Why did the Court of Justice consider that even if the UK had properly transposed the Directive into national law, Gallagher could—and indeed would—have been lawfully excluded from the UK?

***R v Secretary of State for the Home Department, ex p Gallagher* [1996] 2 CMLR 951, Court of Appeal**

19. There is nothing whatever to suggest that the Home Secretary's decision would have been any different had he awaited receipt of Mr Gallagher's representations and the report of the nominated person before making an exclusion order. The evidence is clear that after receiving the report and learning the effect of the representations the Home Secretary considered the case *de novo*, which must be taken to mean that he had an open mind. It was because of the unlikelihood that the order of events could have made any substantial difference to the outcome that the members of the Court of Appeal in February 1994, with varying degrees of emphasis, regarded Mr Gallagher's complaint as being, or at least appearing, technical. Had the nominated person favoured revocation and the Home Secretary exclusion, it might be plausible to suggest that the nominated person's opinion would have been more influential if it had preceded the making of any decision; but here the nominated person and the Home Secretary were of one mind. It is in our view clear that even if the procedure prescribed in the current Regulations had been followed, the outcome would have been the same; it is, however, probable that in such event Mr Gallagher would have been detained longer.
20. This is not a case in which Mr Gallagher is entitled to be compensated for the loss of a chance of securing a favourable result. Causation, as Lord Ackner pointed out in *Hotson v East Berkshire Area Health Authority* [1987] AC 750, is an issue to be decided on the balance of probabilities. The plaintiff must show on the balance of probabilities that the injury for which he seeks compensation was caused by the unlawful conduct of which he complains. In *Hotson's* case, the defendant was negligent but such negligence was not shown on the balance of probabilities to have caused any but a minimal part of the plaintiff's injury. So here: Mr Gallagher has established a breach of Community law [now EU law], but he cannot show that that breach probably caused him to be excluded from the United Kingdom when he would not otherwise have been excluded.

Another helpful example of the application of the requirement of causation to the facts is provided by Case C-319/96 *Brinkmann Tabakfabriken GmbH v Skatteministeriet* [1998] ECR I-5255 (see also 5.6), in which the applicant argued that the Danish government was responsible for two related breaches of EU law. First, it had failed to transpose the relevant provisions of the Second VAT Directive (Second Council Directive 67/228/EEC of 11 April 1967 on the harmonization of legislation of Member States concerning turnover taxes, OJ 1967 L1303/67) into Danish law. Secondly, although the Danish tax authorities had immediately implemented those provisions in practice, they had done so incorrectly. The Court of Justice held, first, that the failure to transpose the Directive into Danish law had not caused Brinkmann's loss, because the Danish tax authorities had immediately implemented the provisions of the Directive in practice and therefore the lack of legislation had not caused the damage alleged by Brinkmann. It held, secondly, that the damage had indeed been caused by the tax authority's incorrect interpretation of the Directive, but that this interpretation was not manifestly contrary to the wording or the aim of the Directive and so the breach of EU law was not sufficiently serious to give rise to liability.

The Court of Justice has made it clear that the chain of causation will not be broken by the possibility of the applicant making an alternative claim via direct effect (see 4.1). In Case C-150/99 *Stockholm Lindöpark v Sweden* [2001] ECR I-493, the Court noted that the fact that the provisions of the Sixth VAT Directive (Sixth Council Directive 77/388/EEC of 17 May 1977 on the harmonization of the laws of the Member States relating to turnover taxes, OJ 1977 L145/1), which Sweden had failed to transpose correctly into national law, were sufficiently clear to be capable of having direct effect might '[a]t first sight' suggest that an action for State liability in damages 'does not seem necessary' (*Stockholm Lindöpark*, at para 35). However, the Court went on to point out that it had also established the possibility of an action against the State for damages to be inherent in the EU Treaties and that, on the facts, Sweden was guilty of a sufficiently serious breach of EU law.

As to the losses that can be claimed to have been caused by a breach of EU law, the Court of Justice in *Factortame III* stated that, in determining the extent of the loss or damage for which compensation would be awarded, the national court should have regard to 'whether the injured person showed reasonable diligence in order to avoid the loss or damage or limit its extent and whether, in particular, he availed himself in time of all the legal remedies available to him' (*Factortame III*, at para 84)—in other words, that the applicant must mitigate their loss.

5.6 Comparing the conditions for liability

Although the *Francovich* and *Factortame III* conditions for State liability are different, the differences are more apparent than real, as the Court of Justice itself concluded in Joined Cases C-178, 179, & 188–90/94 *Dillenkofer and others v Germany* [1996] 3 CMLR 469, a case involving the German government's failure to transpose the Package Travel Directive (Directive (EU) 2015/2302 of the European Parliament and of the Council of 25 November 2015 on package travel and linked travel arrangements . . . , OJ 2015 L326/1) into its national law.

?! THINKING POINT

While reading the following extract, consider what similarities and differences between the *Francovich* and *Factortame III* tests were noted by the Court of Justice.

Joined Cases C-178, 179, & 188–90/94 *Dillenkofer and others v Germany* [1996] ECR I-4845

22. Moreover, it is clear from the *Francovich* case which, like [*Brasserie du Pêcheur* and *Factortame, British Telecommunications*, and *Hedley Lomas*], concerned non-transposition of a directive within the prescribed period, that the full effectiveness of the third paragraph of Article 189 of the [EC] Treaty [now Article 288 TFEU] requires that there should be a right to reparation where the result prescribed by the directive entails the grant of rights to individuals, the content of those rights is identifiable on the basis of the provisions of the directive and a causal link exists between the breach of the State's obligation and the loss and damage suffered by the injured parties.
23. In substance, the conditions laid down in that group of judgments are the same, since the condition that there should be a sufficiently serious breach, although not expressly mentioned in *Francovich*, was nevertheless evident from the circumstances of that case.
24. When the court held that the conditions under which State liability gives rise to a right to reparation depended on the nature of the breach of Community law [now EU law] causing the damage, that meant that those conditions are to be applied according to each type of situation.
25. On the one hand, a breach of Community law is sufficiently serious if a Community [now Union] institution or a Member State, in the exercise of its rule-making powers, manifestly and gravely disregards the limits on those powers (see *HNL and Others v EC Council and EC Commission* (Joined Cases 83 & 94/76, 4, 15 & 40/77) [1978] ECR 1209; *Brasserie du Pêcheur and Factortame*; and *British Telecommunications*). On the other hand, if, at the time when it committed the infringement, the Member State in question was not called upon to make any legislative choices and had only considerably reduced, or even no, discretion, the mere infringement of Community law may be sufficient to establish the existence of a sufficiently serious breach (see *Hedley Lomas*).
26. So where, as in *Francovich*, a Member State fails, in breach of the third paragraph of Article 189 of the Treaty, to take any of the measures necessary to achieve the result prescribed by a directive within the period it lays down, that Member State manifestly and gravely disregards the limits on its discretion.
27. Consequently, such a breach gives rise to a right to reparation on the part of individuals if the result prescribed by the directive entails the grant of rights to them, the content of those rights is identifiable on the basis of the provisions of the directive and a causal link exists between the breach of the State's obligation and the loss and damage suffered by the injured parties: no other conditions need be taken into consideration.

28. In particular, reparation of that loss and damage cannot depend on a prior finding by the Court of an infringement of Community law attributable to the State (see *Brasserie du Pêcheur*, paragraphs 94 to 96), nor on the existence of intentional fault or negligence on the part of the organ of the State to which the infringement is attributable (see paragraphs 75 to 80 of the same judgment).
29. The reply to Questions 8, 9, 10, 11 and 12 must therefore be that failure to take any measure to transpose a directive in order to achieve the result it prescribes within the period laid down for that purpose constitutes per se a serious breach of Community law and consequently gives rise to a right of reparation for individuals suffering injury if the result prescribed by the directive entails the grant to individuals of rights whose content is identifiable and a causal link exists between the breach of the State's obligation and the loss and damage suffered.

In *Dillenkofer*, the Court of Justice observed that both sets of conditions effectively required (1) a sufficiently serious breach of (2) a rule of law that gave rights to individuals, which (3) caused loss to the applicant. The key difference between them, according to the Court, was that instead of expressly requiring a sufficiently serious breach as per the *Factortame III* test, the *Francovich* test required the total non-transposition of a Directive, which can be seen simply as an obvious example of a sufficiently serious breach. The requirement in *Francovich* that the Directive give rights to individuals is effectively the same as the requirement in *Factortame III* that the rule of law be for the protection of individuals. The *Francovich* test can thus be seen as a very particular example of the broader test that the Court of Justice subsequently developed in *Factortame III*.

Case C-319/96 *Brinkmann Tabakfabriken GmbH v Skatteministeriet* [1998] ECR I-5255 (see also 5.5.3) provides a further example of the interplay between the two tests. To recap, the Danish government was potentially responsible for two breaches: it had failed to transpose the Second VAT Directive into Danish law; and its tax authorities, which had nonetheless immediately implemented the provisions of the Directive in practice, had done so incorrectly. There was thus both a *Francovich*-type breach (the government's failure to transpose the Directive into national law) and a *Hedley Lomas*-type breach (the failure of the tax authorities to apply the Directive correctly in practice). The Court of Justice first cited *Dillenkofer* on the principle of liability for failure to transpose a Directive, noting that '[i]t is true that failure to take any measure to transpose a directive in order to achieve the result it prescribes within the period laid down for that purpose constitutes per se a serious breach of [EU] law' (*Brinkmann*, at para 28) and examining whether this breach had caused Brinkmann's loss (see 5.5.3). It then examined the issue of whether the subsequent incorrect interpretation of the Directive by the tax authorities was a sufficiently serious breach according to the *Factortame III* test (see further 5.5.2).

The key points of the development of the Court of Justice's jurisprudence in the area of State liability are summarized in Table 5.1.

The methodology of the Court of Justice in establishing whether liability exists in principle and then applying the appropriate test to establish whether it exists in practice is summarized in Figure 5.1.

Table 5.1 Summary of Court of Justice jurisprudence on State liability

Type of breach	Case establishing the principle of liability	Case setting out conditions governing liability
Failure to transpose a Directive (at all) (automatically regarded as a sufficiently serious breach)	*Francovich*	*Francovich* (but similar to *Factortame III*)
Enactment of domestic legislation that conflicts with EU law	*Factortame III*	*Factortame III*
Failure to transpose a Directive correctly	*BT*	*Factortame III*
Administrative policy that conflicts with EU law	*Hedley Lomas*	*Factortame III*
Judgment by a court of last instance that makes an error of EU law, having failed to make a preliminary reference	*Köbler*	*Factortame III*

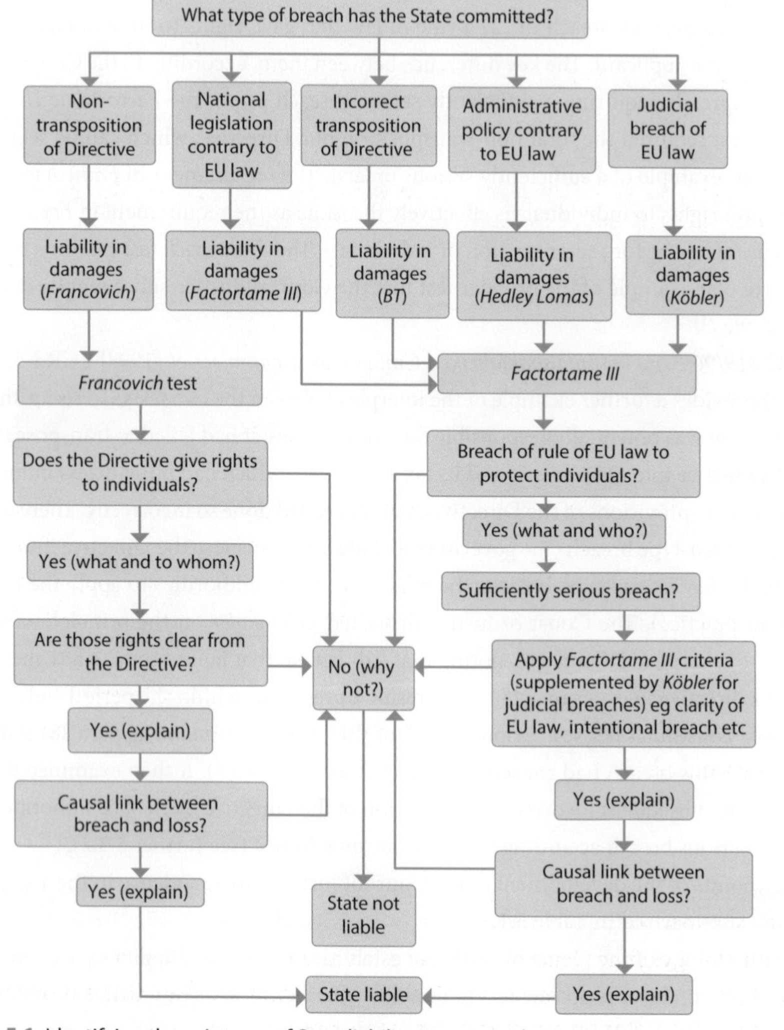

Figure 5.1 Identifying the existence of State liability in a particular scenario

5.7 Concurrent action against the EU

In some scenarios, individuals or businesses might potentially have not only a claim in damages against the Member State in the national courts, but also a claim in damages against the EU itself in the EU Courts (see Chapter 8 on damages claims against the EU). This possibility is discussed in detail at 8.9.2.

5.8 The possible impact of Brexit

When the UK leaves the EU (see further 1.19 and 3.1), the UK government will cease to be vulnerable to actions for EU Member State liability in damages. The European Union (Withdrawal) Act 2018 (see further 1.19.1) provides explicitly (at Sched 1, para 4) that 'there is no right in domestic law on or after exit day to damages in accordance with the rule in *Francovich*', with the exception of proceedings relating to anything that occurred before exit day and which were begun within two years from exit day (Sched 8, para 39(7)). In any event, since the UK would no longer be bound to implement EU Directives or otherwise to comply with EU law, the cause of action underlying a claim in damages for State liability would cease to exist. If the UK takes the European Economic Area (EEA) option outlined at 1.19.2, a form of State liability will apply to it, as this is an established principle under EEA law (see further eg Halvard Haukeland Fredriksen, 'State Liability in EU and EEA Law: The Same or Different?' (2013) 38(6) EL Rev 884), but it would differ considerably in substance from the principle of Member State liability in EU law that is discussed in this chapter.

5.9 Conclusions

The principle of State liability in damages for breach of EU law has been developed by the Court of Justice in order to make the rights granted by EU law effective, and as a response to the inadequacies of direct and indirect effect (see Chapter 4). It may thus be seen as a further step in the process begun by the Court when it developed the doctrine of direct effect and continued by it when it developed the doctrine of indirect effect. The principle of State liability developed by the Court also has some parallels to the principle of EU liability stated in Article 340 TFEU (see Chapter 8). However, it has now grown into its own separate, albeit related, area of jurisprudence.

SUMMARY

- Where the Member State's breach consists of a failure to transpose a Directive, it will incur liability if the Directive gives rights to individuals, the content of those rights is clear from the Directive, and the State's breach caused loss to the applicant (*Francovich*).

- Where the Member State's breach consists of the enactment of national legislation that is contrary to EU law (*Factortame III*), incorrect transposition of a Directive (*BT*), administrative practices that are contrary to EU law (*Hedley Lomas*), or a wrongful judgment on EU law by a court of last instance after a refusal to make a reference under Article 267 TFEU (*Köbler*), the State will incur liability if the law breached is for the protection of individuals, is sufficiently serious, and has caused loss to the applicant (*Factortame III*).

FURTHER READING

Articles

G Anagnostaras, 'The Allocation of Responsibility in State Liability Actions for Breach of Community Law: A Modern Gordian Knot?' (2001) 26(2) EL Rev 139

Comprehensively reviews and comments on the pre-*Köbler* jurisprudence on the range of public bodies whose acts can give rise to liability on the part of the State.

RW Davis, 'Liability in Damages for a Breach of Community Law: Some Reflections on the Question of Who to Sue and the Concept of "the State"' (2006) 31(1) EL Rev 69

Discusses the variety of public bodies whose acts can give rise to State liability.

M Dougan, 'Addressing Issues of Protective Scope within the *Francovich* Right to Reparation' (2017) 13(1) ECL Review 124

Examines the purpose and nature of the *Francovich* State liability claim.

D Nassimpian, '... And We Keep on Meeting: (De)Fragmenting State Liability' (2007) 32(6) EL Rev 819

Considers State liability in the context of the Court of Justice's wider commitment to ensuring effective judicial protection, for example under Article 263 TFEU.

S Prechal, 'Member State Liability and Direct Effect: What's the Difference After All?' (2006) 17(2) EBL Rev 299

Analyses the conditions for State liability and their relationship to direct effect.

J Steiner, 'From Direct Effects to *Francovich*: Shifting Means of Enforcement of Community Law' (1993) 18 EL Rev 3

Examines the relationship between direct effect, indirect effect, and State liability.

QUESTIONS

[*Note*: The following scenario is the same as that set out at the end of Chapter 4, but the questions are different.]

Alf works for Humber plc, a company created to build and operate a railway bridge across the Humber estuary. It is authorized to do so under s 1 of the (fictitious) Estuary Bridges Act 2002, which also gives it powers to regulate the connecting train service.

(Fictitious) Directive 2010/2010 requires Member States to take all measures necessary to ensure that bridge workers are provided with appropriate safety equipment, including hard hats. The Act merely provides that licence holders must ensure that their employees are aware of safety hazards and are advised to wear appropriate clothing.

Alf sustained a serious head injury when a cable fell on him during construction of the bridge and, as a result, is unfit to work. He claims that his injury was caused by Humber plc's failure to provide workers with hard hats. Humber plc claims that it had made Alf aware of the risks and had advised him to wear a hard hat, although the company itself did not provide them. It argues that the Act requires only the provision of information and advice.

1. Advise Alf as to whether he has any cause of action against the UK government.
2. How, if at all, would your answer to question 1 differ if the Estuary Bridges Act were dated 2012?

To view outline answers to these questions plus further resources to support your EU law studies, visit the Online Resources for this book at **www.oup.com/uk/eulaw-complete4e**

6 Preliminary references

KEY POINTS

By the end of this chapter, you should be able to:

- recognize the types of legal issue that may be the subject of a preliminary reference to the Court of Justice under Article 267 TFEU;
- explain the criteria that determine what constitutes a domestic court or tribunal for the purposes of Article 267 TFEU;
- explain the circumstances in which national courts or tribunals are mandated to make a reference and those in which they have a discretion as to whether to do so;
- identify and explain the judicial guidelines on when a discretionary reference should be made; and
- identify and explain the exceptions to the making of mandatory references.

INTRODUCTION

Although the European Union (EU) legal system purports to form part of the legal system of each Member State, the initiation and enactment of EU legislation, and its most authoritative interpretation, are performed by legislative and judicial entities entirely distinct, and indeed distanced, from those national courts that are, as is explained in Chapter 4, expected to apply EU law. Not only that, but those national courts apply EU law independently of one another, leading potentially to different interpretations in different Member States of the same piece of legislation or judgment of the Court of Justice. Since EU law is supreme across the Member States (see 3.1), it must have a uniform meaning and effect in all those Member States, but this cannot be achieved by national courts acting alone.

To overcome these problems, the Treaty on the Functioning of the European Union (TFEU) provides a procedure whereby national courts or tribunals may submit questions to the Court of Justice on particular issues of EU law (a 'preliminary reference'), and those questions are then answered by the Court of Justice (a 'preliminary ruling'). Finally, the national court or tribunal will deliver judgment in the case, with the benefit of clarification of the issues of EU law from the Court of Justice. This preliminary reference or preliminary ruling procedure is to be found in Article 267 TFEU. It is the national court or tribunal that makes a reference of its questions on EU law to the Court of Justice and the Court of Justice that gives a ruling providing answers to those questions. The term 'preliminary' reflects the fact that this procedure takes place prior to final judgment being given in a particular case by the national court.

Although the Treaty of Nice 2001 (see 1.17) provided for the transfer of some Article 267 TFEU jurisdiction over preliminary rulings to the General Court (see 2.4.2) in specific areas laid down by the Statute of the Court of Justice, this has yet to be implemented. The Court of Justice's Recommendations to national courts and tribunals in relation to the initiation of preliminary ruling proceedings, OJ 2012 C338/01, notes, at para 3, that no provisions have yet been introduced into the Statute in this regard and so the Court of Justice alone has jurisdiction to give preliminary rulings. Given that the problem of delays in the hearing of cases is greater in the General Court than in the Court of Justice, it is unlikely that jurisprudence over preliminary references will be transferred from the latter to the former in the near future.

The starting point for consideration of the law in this area is Article 267 TFEU.

Article 267 TFEU

The Court of Justice of the European Union shall have jurisdiction to give preliminary rulings concerning:

(a) the interpretation of the Treaties;

(b) the validity and interpretation of acts of the institutions, bodies, offices or agencies of the Union;

(c) the interpretation of the statutes of bodies established by an act of the Council, where those statutes so provide.

Where such a question is raised before any court or tribunal of a Member State, that court or tribunal may, if it considers that a decision on the question is necessary to enable it to give judgment, request the Court to give a ruling thereon.

Where any such question is raised in a case pending before a court or tribunal of a Member State against whose decisions there is no judicial remedy under national law, that court or tribunal shall bring the matter before the Court.

If such a question is raised in a case pending before a court or tribunal of a Member State with regard to a person in custody, the Court of Justice of the European Union shall act with the minimum of delay.

It can be seen that this Article makes provision as to three particular issues:

- references may only be made on the issues of EU law specified in (a), (b) or (c);
- references may only be made by a 'court or tribunal' of a Member State; and
- some such courts or tribunals have a discretion to make a reference, while others are mandated to do so.

However, there are two very important matters that are *not* dealt with by Article 267 TFEU:

- the guidelines that govern whether and when to make a discretionary reference; and
- the exceptions to the mandating of a reference.

In order to understand the law governing these last two areas, it is essential to become familiar with the relevant jurisprudence, as well as Article 267 TFEU, as will be seen throughout this chapter.

6.1 The questions of law that may be referred to the Court of Justice

6.1.1 Article 267 TFEU

Article 267 TFEU does not give the Court of Justice unlimited jurisdiction to give rulings. It provides that the Court of Justice may give rulings only on:

- the *interpretation* of the EU Treaties and secondary legislation; and
- the *validity* of secondary EU legislation.

National courts and tribunals must confine the questions that they refer to the Court of Justice to these issues and may only make a reference if they consider that a decision on the question is necessary to enable them to give judgment.

The majority of references in fact concern interpretation—in other words, questions as to the meaning of particular provisions of EU law. However, it is also possible to pose questions as to the validity of a provision of EU secondary legislation (but not of a provision of the Treaties), although relatively few references concern validity for the reasons explained in 6.6.

6.1.2 Exclusion of certain policy areas

In a number of sensitive EU policy areas, the Court of Justice's jurisdiction under Article 267 TFEU has been limited by the Member States.

First, Article 24 TEU and Article 275 TFEU exclude the jurisdiction of the Court of Justice over the Common Foreign and Security Policy (CFSP) (see further 1.13) (subject to some limited exceptions, but these do not apply to preliminary references).

Secondly, Article 276 TFEU provides that the Court has no jurisdiction to review the validity or proportionality of operations carried out by national police or law enforcement authorities, or of the exercise of Member States' responsibilities for the maintenance of law and order and internal security.

Prior to the Treaty of Lisbon (see further 1.18), the Court of Justice's jurisdiction to give preliminary rulings relating to police cooperation and judicial cooperation in criminal matters was subject to even more extensive limitations: only the courts of a Member State that had accepted the jurisdiction of the Court of Justice in this area were able to make a reference at all and a Member State could restrict this ability to its courts of last instance.

6.1.3 Questions of EU law only

It is important to note that jurisdiction is not only limited to certain issues of EU law, but does not extend to national law at all. Thus, in Joined Cases C-78–80/08 *Ministero dell'Economia e delle Finanze v Paint Graphos Sarl* [2011] ECR I-7611 (see also 6.4.2), the Court of Justice rejected one of the questions referred because it related to rights granted solely by Italian domestic law and, since it did not concern the interpretation of EU law, the Court had no jurisdiction to rule on it. However, if the national law in question incorporates provisions or principles of EU law so directly that an independent interpretation by the national court would threaten the uniformity of EU law itself, the Court of Justice may give a ruling on the interpretation of EU law in such disputes. In Joined Cases C-297/88 & 197/89 *Dzodzi v Belgian State* [1990] ECR I-3763, the Togolese widow of a Belgian national claimed residency in Belgium, under a Belgian law that treated all foreign spouses of Belgian nationals as EU nationals for the purposes of residency rights. The Belgian government argued that since the case turned on the meaning of Belgian law and not EU law, a reference to the Court of Justice—on the meaning of a number of provisions of EU law on the free movement of persons (see Chapter 11)—was unnecessary. The Court of Justice ruled that it had jurisdiction because Article 267 TFEU did not preclude jurisdiction in such circumstances and it would destroy the system of uniform interpretation of EU law envisaged by that Article if national courts could interpret EU law themselves in purely internal cases in order to determine the meaning of national law that made reference to EU law.

6.1.4 No jurisdiction over the application of EU law to the facts

Once the Court of Justice has provided an interpretation of EU law, or a ruling on its validity, it is for the national court to apply this to the facts of the case before it and, if appropriate, decide on the compatibility of national law with EU law. Despite this, it is not unknown for the Court of Justice to take the view that it has been supplied with sufficient information to apply its interpretation of EU law to the facts of the case before it. For example, in Joined Cases C-46 & 48/93 *Brasserie du Pêcheur SA v Germany; R v Secretary of State for Transport, ex p Factortame ('Factortame III')* [1996] ECR I-1029 (see 5.4.1 and 5.5), the Court of Justice strayed beyond interpreting EU law and asserted that, since it had sufficient information, it would apply its ruling on EU law to the facts. The national court subsequently accepted this application, although, as Lord Hope of Craighead noted in the following extract, it was not obliged to do so.

Brasserie du Pêcheur SA v Germany; R v Secretary of State for Transport, ex p Factortame ('Factortame III') [1999] 3 WLR 1062, House of Lords

64. ... In various passages elsewhere in the judgment the court expressed its opinion about the nature of the breach for the consequences of which the respondents are claiming damages. But I would not be inclined to attach much importance to these expressions of opinion, because in para. 58 of the judgment the court made it clear that it was for the national courts to assess the seriousness of the breach. The national courts have the sole jurisdiction to find the facts in the main proceedings. It is for them to decide how to characterise the breaches of Community law which are in issue.

REVIEW QUESTION

Suppose that you recently bought a laptop computer while on holiday in France, but the handle subsequently split, causing a minor injury to your hand. You are considering a claim for damages against the French manufacturer and your research suggests that you have some rights under a (fictitious) EU Regulation that lays down product safety standards. The French manufacturer denies negligence and asserts that the Regulation is, in fact, invalid, and that you therefore have no rights under it in any event. Your view is that the Regulation is valid and imposes strict liability for any breaches or the standards. If you take your case to a national court, which—if any—of these issues could it refer to the Court of Justice?

Answer: Article 267 TFEU permits references to be made on the interpretation of EU law, including the Treaties and secondary legislation (see further 3.4.1 and 3.4.2) and thus, if necessary, on the meaning of the EU Regulation at issue here. It also permits references to be made on the validity of secondary EU legislation, such as a Regulation (although not on the validity of a Treaty Article).

Article 267 TFEU does not give the Court of Justice jurisdiction over findings of fact, such as how the handle came to split, or the interpretation of national law, such as the English or French laws of negligence or product safety.

6.2 The meaning of 'court or tribunal'

The EU refers to national criminal and civil courts as 'ordinary courts', and recognizes that they have an important role in interpreting and enforcing EU law. More specifically, according to Article 267 TFEU, only a national 'court or tribunal' can make a reference to the Court of Justice. These terms have an autonomous meaning in EU law, and the fact that a body is classified as a court or tribunal under national law is not conclusive (Case 43/71 *Politi v Italy* [1971] ECR 1039).

NOTE

According to the Court of Justice in Case C-54/96 *Dorsch Consult Ingenieurgesellschaft mbH v Bundesbaugesellschaft Berlin mbH* [1997] ECR I-496, the factors to be taken into account when determining whether a body is a 'court or tribunal' include:

- whether the body is established by law;
- whether it is permanent;
- whether its jurisdiction is mandatory;
- whether its procedure is *inter partes*;
- whether it applies rules of law; and
- whether it is independent.

inter partes

An *inter partes* hearing is one at which all parties relevant to the application being heard are present and able to make representations to the court.

The Court's judgment in the *Dorsch Consult* case itself provides a good example of how these factors may be applied in a particular case. In that case, the referring body was the Federal Public Procurement Awards Supervisory Board, which was a body set up to review the procedures for awarding public supply contracts, and the question arose as to whether it was a 'court or tribunal' for the purposes of Article 267 TFEU and therefore whether it had competence to make a preliminary reference.

Case C-54/96 *Dorsch Consult Ingenieurgesellschaft mbH v Bundesbaugesellschaft Berlin mbH* [1997] ECR I-496

23. In order to determine whether a body making a reference is a court or tribunal for the purposes of Article 177 of the [EC] Treaty [now Article 267 TFEU], which is a question governed by Community law [now EU law] alone, the Court takes account of a number of factors, such as whether the body is established by law, whether it is permanent, whether its jurisdiction is compulsory, whether its procedure is inter partes, whether it applies rules of law and whether it is independent (see, in particular, the judgments in Case 61/65 *Vaassen (née Göbbels)* [1966] ECR 261; Case 14/86 *Pretore di Salò v Persons unknown* [1987] ECR 2545, paragraph 7; Case 109/88 *Danfoss* [1989] ECR 3199, paragraphs 7 and 8; Case C-393/92 *Almelo and Others* [1994] ECR 1-1477; and Case C-111/94 *Job Centre* [1995] ECR 1-3361, paragraph 9).
24. As regards the question of establishment by law, the Commission states that the HGrG [Haushaltsgrundsätzegesetz] is a framework budgetary law which does not give rise to rights or obligations for citizens as legal persons. It points out that the Federal Supervisory Board's action is confined to reviewing determinations made by review bodies. However, in the field of public service contracts, there is, as yet, no competent review body. The Commission therefore concludes that in such matters the Federal Supervisory Board has no basis in law on which it can act.
25. It is sufficient to note in this regard that the Federal Supervisory Board was established by Paragraph 57c(7) of the HGrG. Its establishment by law cannot therefore be disputed. In determining establishment by law, it is immaterial that domestic legislation has not conferred on the Federal Supervisory Board powers in the specific area of public service contracts.
26. Nor is there any doubt about the permanent existence of the Federal Supervisory Board.
27. The Commission also submits that the Federal Supervisory Board does not have compulsory jurisdiction, a condition which, in its view, may mean two things: either that the parties must be required to apply to the relevant review body for settlement of their dispute or that determinations of that body are to be binding. The Commission, adopting the second interpretation, concludes that German legislation does not provide for the determinations made by the Federal Supervisory Board to be enforceable.
28. It must be stated first of all that Paragraph 57c of the HGrG establishes the supervisory board as the only body for reviewing the legality of determinations made by review bodies. In order to establish a breach of the provisions governing public procurement, application must be made to the supervisory board.
29. Secondly, under Paragraph 57c(5) of the HGrG, when the supervisory board finds that determinations made by a review body are unlawful, it directs that body to make a fresh determination, in conformity with the supervisory board's findings on points of law. It follows that determinations of the supervisory board are binding.
30. The Commission also submits that since, according to the Federal Supervisory Board's own evidence, procedure before that body is not inter partes, it cannot be regarded as a court or tribunal within the meaning of Article 177 of the Treaty.

31. It must be reiterated that the requirement that the procedure before the hearing body concerned must be inter partes is not an absolute criterion. Besides, under Paragraph 3(3) of the Verordnung über das Nachprüfungsverfahren für öffentliche Aufträge, the parties to the procedure before the procurement review body must be heard before any determination is made by the chamber concerned.

32. According to the Commission, the criterion relating to the application of rules of law is not met either, because, under Paragraph 57c of the HGrG and Paragraph 3(1) of the Verordnung über das Nachprüfungsverfahren für öffentliche Aufträge, procedure before the Federal Supervisory Board is governed by rules of procedure which it itself adopts, which do not take effect in relation to third parties and which are not published.

33. It is, however, undisputed that the Federal Supervisory Board is required to apply provisions governing the award of public contracts which are laid down in Community [now Union] directives and in domestic regulations adopted to transpose them. Furthermore, general procedural requirements, such as the duty to hear the parties, to make determinations by an absolute majority of votes and to give reasons for them are laid down in Paragraph 3 of the Verordnung über das Nachprüfungsverfahren für öffentliche Aufträge, which is published in the Bundesgesetzblatt. Consequently, the Federal Supervisory Board applies rules of law.

34. Finally, both Dorsch Consult and the Commission consider that the Federal Supervisory Board is not independent. They point out that it is linked to the organizational structure of the Bundeskartellamt, which is itself subject to supervision by the Ministry for Economic Affairs, that the term of office of the chairman and the official assessors is not fixed and that the provisions for guaranteeing impartiality apply only to lay members.

35. It must be observed first of all that, according to Paragraph 57c(1) of the HGrG, the supervisory board carries out its task independently and under its own responsibility. According to Paragraph 57c(2) of the HGrG, the members of the chambers are independent and subject only to observance of the law.

36. Under Paragraph 57c(3) of the HGrG, the main provisions of the Richtergesetz concerning annulment or withdrawal of their appointments and concerning their independence and removal from office apply by analogy to official members of the chambers. In general, the provisions of the Richtergesetz concerning annulment and withdrawal of judges' appointments apply also to lay members. Furthermore, the impartiality of lay members is ensured by Paragraph 57c(2) of the HGrG, which provides that they must not hear cases in which they themselves were involved through participation in the decision-making process regarding the award of a contract or in which they are, or were, tenderers or representatives of tenderers.

37. It must also be pointed out that, in this particular instance, the Federal Supervisory Board exercises a judicial function, for it can find that a determination made by a review body is unlawful and it can direct the review body to make a fresh determination.

38. It follows from all the foregoing that the Federal Supervisory Board, in the procedure which led to this reference for a preliminary ruling, is to be regarded as a court or tribunal within the meaning of Article 177 of the Treaty, so that the question it has referred to the Court is admissible.

As the Court of Justice noted in *Dosrch Consult*, at para 31, an *inter partes* hearing is not essential in order for the referring body to be a court or tribunal within the meaning of Article 267 TFEU. For example, in Case C-18/93 *Corsica Ferries v Corpo dei Piloti del Porto di Genova* [1994] ECR I-1783, the applicant brought proceedings in the Italian courts using an **ex parte** summary procedure. The Italian court made a preliminary reference to the Court of Justice, which held that a national court adjudicating on an application in *ex parte* summary proceedings for which provision was made in its national law was performing a judicial function within the meaning of Article 267 TFEU. That Article did not require there to have been an *inter partes* hearing in the proceedings in which the reference was made (*Corsica Ferries*, para 14).

ex parte

An *ex parte* application, hearing or order is one that is made or takes place for the benefit of only some of the parties to a particular case and in the absence of the other parties. This is the opposite of an *inter partes* procedure.

References have been accepted by the Court of Justice from a variety of UK courts and tribunals, including the following, amongst others, and it is therefore clear that all of these will constitute a 'court or tribunal' for the purposes of Article 267 TFEU:

- the Supreme Court (eg in *Factortame III*—referred to at 6.1.4);
- the Court of Appeal (eg in *R v Pharmaceutical Society of Great Britain, ex p the Association of Pharmaceutical Importers* [1987] 3 CMLR 951—referred to at 6.3.1);
- the High Court (see eg *Magnavision v General Optical Council (No 1)* [1987] 1 CMLR 887—referred to at 6.3.1);
- the County Court (see eg Case 222/82 *Apple and Pear Development Council v KL Lewis Ltd and others* [1983] ECR 4083);
- the Crown Court (see eg C-23/89 *Quietlynn Ltd and Richards v Southern BC* [1990] ECR I-3059);
- magistrates' courts (see eg Case 157/79 *R v Pieck* [1980] ECR 2171);
- the Employment Appeal Tribunal (EAT) (see eg Case C-326/96 *Levez v Jennings Ltd* [1998] ECR I-7835—discussed at 4.3.1);
- employment tribunals (see eg Case C-539/12 *Lock v British Gas Trading Ltd and others* (2014) IRLR 648);
- the Upper Tribunal (Tax and Chancery Chamber) (see eg Case C-495/12 *Commissioners for HMRC v Bridport and West Dorset Golf Club Ltd* [2014] STC 663);
- the Upper Tribunal (Immigration and Asylum Chamber) (see eg Case C-400/12 *Secretary of State for the Home Department v MG* [2014] 2 CMLR 40);
- the Upper Tribunal (Administrative Appeals Chamber) (see eg Case C-279/12 *Fish Legal and Shirley v Information Commissioner and others* [2014] 2 CMLR 36); and
- the First-Tier Tribunal (Tax Chamber) (see eg Case C-288/09 *British Sky Broadcasting Group plc and Pace v Commissioners for HMRC* [2011] ECR I-2851).

REVIEW QUESTION

Suppose that you were employed in Spain for some time, but have now been dismissed. You consider that your dismissal was contrary to a number of (fictitious) EU Directives on employment law and would like to take your case to an employment adjudication body in Spain. Would you be able to ask this adjudication body to make a preliminary reference to the Court of Justice on the interpretation of relevant provisions of the Directives?

Answer: Article 267 TFEU permits reference to be made as to the interpretation of EU law such as Directives. Whether the adjudication body in Spain can make a reference depends on whether it is a court or tribunal for the purposes of Article 267 TFEU. This, in turn, depends on the extent to which the factors laid down by the Court of Justice in *Dorsch Consult* apply—namely, whether it is established by law, is permanent, has mandatory jurisdiction, has an *inter partes* procedure, applies rules of law, and/or is independent. In practice, you would need to research Spanish law on the nature of the adjudication body in order to decide.

It is important to note that a reference is made by the domestic court or tribunal, not by the parties to the case, although they may put forward arguments as to whether or not a reference should be made and they are normally consulted by the court or tribunal on the wording of any questions that are referred to the Court of Justice.

Before leaving this topic, it is worth noting the case of C-284/16 *Slovakia v Achmea BV* EU:C:2018:158, in which the issues of what constitutes a court or tribunal for the Article 267 TFEU purposes arose, somewhat unusually, not in relation to the referring court, but in relation to the substance of the dispute. The applicant was a Dutch company that had established a subsidiary in Slovakia to provide private sickness insurance. The applicant claimed that it had suffered damage for a period of time during which Slovakia had prohibited the distribution of profits from such businesses. A bilateral treaty between the Netherlands and the then Czech and Slovak Republic on the protection of investments provided that an investor from one of those States could bring a dispute against one of those States before an arbitral tribunal whose jurisdiction that State had undertaken to accept. The applicant therefore brought arbitration proceedings against Slovakia before an arbitral tribunal in Germany. That tribunal found in favour of the applicant and, on appeal, the German court made a reference to the Court of Justice. The Court of Justice noted that the German arbitral tribunal was not part of the legal systems of either Slovakia or the Netherlands and that its exceptional nature compared to the courts of those two countries meant that it was not a court or tribunal of a Member State; yet its rulings could include the interpretation or application of EU law, since EU law was part of the law of both the Netherlands and Slovakia. The Court of Justice therefore held that the possibility of submitting disputes to such a tribunal was contrary to Article 267 TFEU (and to Article 344 TFEU, which prohibited disputes concerning the application of the EU Treaties being brought before any method of dispute resolution other than those provided by the EU Treaties).

6.3 The status of the national court

The third key issue that is dealt with by Article 267 TFEU is whether a reference is discretionary or mandatory.

?! THINKING POINT

What other two key issues, already considered in this chapter, are dealt with by Article 267 TFEU?

Before deciding on whether a reference is discretionary or mandatory, it is necessary to establish whether a reference (of any kind) is even possible. In order to do this, it is necessary to determine:

(a) whether the question to be referred relates to the type of legal issue on which references are permitted by the Article—that is, the interpretation of EU law or the validity of secondary EU legislation; and

(b) whether the national body that is hearing the case is a 'court or tribunal' for the purposes of the Article and thus entitled to make a reference.

Once this is determined, Article 267 TFEU divides the courts and tribunals to which it applies into two categories. One category consists of those courts and tribunals 'against whose decisions there is no judicial remedy under national law', which 'shall' make a reference. In other words, such a court or tribunal has no choice but to make a reference and so this is known as a mandatory reference. The other category consists of courts and tribunals 'against whose decision there is a judicial remedy under national law', which 'may' make a reference. Such a court or tribunal has a choice as to whether to make a reference, and so this is known as a discretionary reference. The making of both types of reference will be discussed in more detail later in this chapter.

6.3.1 Courts and tribunals against whose decisions there is no judicial remedy under national law

?! THINKING POINT

What do you think might be meant by a court or tribunal 'against whose decisions there is no judicial remedy under national law'?

There is, in fact, only one possible judicial remedy against the decision of a court or tribunal and that is to appeal against it to a higher court or tribunal. So this phrase refers to a court or tribunal against whose decision no such appeal is possible. This clearly includes the highest court in a particular legal system (eg the Supreme Court in the UK, the Cour de Cassation in France, the Bundesgerichtshof in Germany, the Corte Suprema di Cassazione in Italy, and the Tribunal Supremo in Spain) because there is no higher court in the national system to which an appeal can be made.

However, the phrase does not only apply to the highest court in the land; it applies also to any court against whose decision in a particular case no appeal lies. For example, in Case 6/64 *Costa v ENEL* [1964] ECR 585, an Italian magistrates' court made a reference to the Court of Justice under Article 267 TFEU. Under the Italian legal system, certain categories of case could be appealed from the magistrates' court, while other categories could not. The proceedings in *Costa* fell into the latter category, so there was no possibility of appeal. The Court of Justice ruled that there was no judicial remedy under national law in this case and therefore the national court was obliged to make a reference.

In the English legal system, this phrase would include, for example, the Court of Appeal in certain probate or insolvency proceedings, since statute provides that its decisions in such actions are final (County Courts Act 1984, s 82, and Insolvency Act 1986, s 375(2), respectively) and thus there is no possibility in such cases of a judicial remedy in the form of an appeal to the Supreme Court. Generally, however, this phase would not apply to the Court of Appeal because generally it is possible to request leave to appeal against its decisions to the Supreme Court.

A further issue that has arisen is whether a court from which an appeal is possible in principle (for example the Court of Appeal in most proceedings in the UK), but from which leave to appeal is not in fact given (in this example, if leave is refused by both the Court of Appeal and the Supreme Court) should be treated as a court against whose decisions there is no judicial remedy under national law. In other words, does the 'judicial remedy' consist of the appeal itself, or of being able to apply for leave to appeal?

In Case C-99/00 *Lyckeskog* [2002] ECR I-4839, the Court of Justice held that a decision of a national court which could be appealed by the parties to a superior court could not constitute a decision against which there was no judicial remedy under national law, even if the bringing of the appeal was conditional upon the granting of leave to appeal, and therefore leave might be refused and no appeal allowed. Such a condition did not deprive the parties of a judicial remedy under national law (*Lyckeskog*, at para 16).

This approach is also supported by the wording of Article 267 TFEU itself, which refers to 'decisions' against which there is no remedy in the plural and thus to decisions generally of a particular court, rather than to a single decision by it in a specific case.

In *Magnavision v General Optical Council (No 1)* [1987] 1 CMLR 887, a Belgian company that had been fined by a magistrates' court for marketing spectacles in a way that was contrary to the Opticians Act 1958 argued that the Act breached EU law. The High Court of England and Wales declined to make a reference to the Court of Justice and upheld the ruling of the magistrates' court. It subsequently refused to give leave to appeal and, in *Magnavision v General Optical Council (No 2)* [1987] 2 CMLR 262, the company argued that the High Court had, as a result of that refusal, become a court against whose decisions there was no judicial remedy under national law, with the result that it must now make a reference to the Court of Justice. Watkins LJ, delivering the judgment of the High Court, dismissed this argument.

?! THINKING POINT

While reading the following extract, consider why the High Court rejected the submission of counsel for the company that, by refusing leave to appeal, the High Court had turned itself into a court against whose decisions there was no judicial remedy under national law.

Magnavision v General Optical Council (No 2) [1987] 2 CMLR 262, Queen's Bench Division

6. Now that judgments have been delivered, we are in this position. We were invited, at the conclusion of giving judgment, to certify points of law for consideration by the House of Lords. Having looked at the drafts of those points, we had no hesitation in coming to the conclusion that they did not call for certification by us. So we rejected the application therefore. There is no appeal against the refusal by this Court, in a criminal cause or matter, to certify a point of law for consideration by the House of Lords. There is, therefore, nothing a disappointed appellant, or respondent for that matter, can do if he applies for such a certificate and fails. It is, to put it in homely language, 'the end of the road' for him.
7. I am bound to say that when we announced that decision, I thought it was the end of the road for us. But my Lord and I were soon disabused of such a notion, for Mr Bellamy was once again on his feet, this time making what I regard as a most daring application. The purport of that was that although we had decided the appeal, and refused to certify points of law for the consideration of the House of Lords, we should, notwithstanding all that, refer the point which he had canvassed during argument in the course of the appeal to the European Court for the purpose of obtaining the opinion of that Court upon it.

   [...]

12. His second argument is that by refusing to certify a point or points of law, we have turned ourselves into a final court, that is a court of final decision. In a sense, I agree with that. There is no appeal now from our decision to any other court in this country or elsewhere. Consequently, he submits that the prospect looms, if we do not make a reference to the European Court now, of the matter of which he complains being taken up either by the Commission of the European Community [now Union], or by a Member State of it. That may happen. But such a prospect cannot be permitted to sway this Court away from considering the application now made to it otherwise than strictly in accordance with the law of this country. Likewise, when deciding to make a reference during the hearing of a case.

   [...]

16. I should, I think, add that even if nothing I have said so far properly and rightly answers the submissions made by Mr Bellamy, there remains the question of the common sense of the matter. Supposing we were now to send off to the European Court the question which we have been asked to refer, and supposing that Court were to accept that reference—I cannot envisage it doing so—and gave a ruling upon it, where, I ask rhetorically, would Mr Bellamy take it after he had carried it away from Luxembourg? If he brought it back here, there is nothing to which we could apply it. We are functus in every sense, in my judgment, no matter that our order has not yet been drawn up. It will in fact be drawn up any moment now. For these reasons, I would dismiss this application.

A decision by a party to a case on whether to seek leave to appeal against a judgment, and by the court(s) as to whether to grant leave to do so, can only be made after the judgment to be appealed has been given. As the High Court pointed out in the above extract from *Magnavision*, it is not possible after judgment has been given for a court to reopen the case in order to make a reference. The prospect of leave being refused could therefore not affect the status of the court for the purpose of Article 267 TFEU, or the consequent nature of a reference from it as being mandatory or discretionary. The assessment of whether there is or is not a judicial remedy must be capable of being made during the hearing, since this is when any decision to make a reference will be made, and thus can only be based on whether leave to appeal can be requested, not on whether such a request will be granted. As the Court of Appeal of England and Wales pointed out in *Chiron Corporation and others v Murex Diagnostics Ltd (No 8)* [1995] FSR 309, at 313 (emphasis added), '[t]he essence of a *preliminary* ruling is that it must *precede the judgment* of the referring court'.

In *R v Pharmaceutical Society of Great Britain, ex p Association of Pharmaceutical Importers* [1987] 3 CMLR 951, a pharmaceutical association alleged that the prohibition under UK law on the dispensing of products that were identical to those prescribed, but were of a different brand, was contrary to EU law. The Court of Appeal exercised its discretion to refer this issue to the Court of Justice, Kerr LJ remarking, *obiter*, that a judicial remedy from its decisions lay in the possibility of applying for leave to appeal and that a court or tribunal below the House of Lords (now the Supreme Court) could be a court against whose decisions there was no judicial remedy only if there were no possibility of appeal (eg the Court of Appeal in certain proceedings).

R v Pharmaceutical Society of Great Britain, ex p Association of Pharmaceutical Importers [1987] 3 CMLR 951, Court of Appeal

23. […]

(2) The present case falls within the penultimate paragraph of Article 177 [EC, now Article 267 TFEU], since it is not 'a case pending before a court … against whose decision there is no judicial remedy'. There is a judicial remedy against a decision of this Court by applying for leave to appeal to the House of Lords, first to this Court and then to the House of Lords itself if necessary. A court or tribunal below the House of Lords can only fall within the last paragraph where there is no possibility of any further appeal from it.

It is evident from these cases that a UK court below the Supreme Court in the domestic court hierarchy will constitute a court 'against whose decisions there is no judicial remedy under national law' only where, as a matter of procedure, there is no possibility of requesting leave to appeal. This approach may understandably be perceived as unfair by a losing party who has been denied both a preliminary ruling from the Court of Justice and leave to appeal to a higher national court, but it is preferable to the alternative, which would be to reopen decided cases in which leave to appeal is subsequently applied for and refused.

6.3.2 Courts and tribunals against whose decisions there is a judicial remedy under national law

REVIEW QUESTION

Try to think of as many examples as you can of English courts or tribunals against whose decisions there is generally a judicial remedy (that is, the possibility of requesting leave to appeal) under national law.

Answer: You might have listed, among others, the Court of Appeal, the High Court, the County Court, the Crown Court, the Magistrates' Court, and the Employment Tribunal.

If it is established that a particular court or tribunal is one against whose decisions there is a judicial remedy under national law, Article 267 TFEU provides that it has a discretion as to whether to refer a question to the Court of Justice. Despite the wording of the Article, which simply says that such a court 'may' make a reference, it is crucial to appreciate that there is a considerable body of jurisprudence which provides guidelines as to whether and when a national court in this position should, or should not, make a reference. The discretion to refer therefore cannot be exercised by a particular court on a whim, but must be exercised in accordance with the guidelines (see 6.4). It is thus impossible to make a legally authoritative and comprehensive argument as to whether a particular court should or should not make a discretionary reference without considering and applying these guidelines.

If, instead, it is established that a court or tribunal is one against whose decisions there is no judicial remedy under national law, Article 267 TFEU provides that it has an obligation to make a reference to the Court of Justice. However, yet again, the wording of the Article, which says that such a court 'shall' make a reference, needs to be read together with the relevant jurisprudence. The jurisprudence effectively provides a number of exceptions to this obligation, and, once again, it is impossible to make a full and authoritative argument as to whether a particular court against whose decisions there is no judicial remedy under national law is actually obliged to make a reference without considering these exceptions and whether they apply in the particular case.

REVIEW QUESTION

Suppose that you are advising a client on litigation in the UK, which involves EU law. The court of first instance for the particular matter is the High Court of England and Wales. An appeal from that court lies to the Court of Appeal and from there to the Supreme Court. Would any of these courts be able to make a preliminary reference to the Court of Justice and, if so, would a reference be discretionary or mandatory?

Answer: First, these bodies satisfy the criteria for a 'court or tribunal' set out in Case C-54/96 *Dorsch Consult Ingenieurgesellschaft mbH v Bundesbaugesellschaft Berlin mbH* [1997] ECR I-496 (see 6.2) and would thus be eligible to make a preliminary reference under Article 267 TFEU (assuming that the issue of EU law to be referred in this case falls within the matters listed in the Article).

Secondly, it is stated in the question that there is the possibility of an appeal from both the High Court and Court of Appeal in these particular proceedings, and therefore these are both courts against whose decisions there is a judicial remedy under national law and therefore from which the making of a reference is discretionary. In contrast, there is no possibility of an appeal from a decision of the Supreme Court and therefore the making of a reference by this court would be mandatory, subject to the limited exceptions established in the jurisprudence (see 6.5).

6.4 Discretionary references

Although the exercise of the discretion to refer is a matter for the national court or tribunal seised of a particular case, both the Court of Justice and the national courts have laid down guidelines as to how and when the discretion should be exercised. It is important to remember that, while the jurisprudence of the Court of Justice is binding on the courts of all Member States, judgments of UK courts apply only within the UK. Thus, for example, a French court would apply the guidelines laid down by the Court of Justice, but would not consider those laid down by the English courts. English courts, of course, would apply both sets of guidelines.

Although all of the guidelines should be taken into account when considering whether to make a reference, two are of particular importance because they go to the very heart of whether a reference is 'necessary' as required by Article 267 TFEU. One is whether the provisions of EU law at issue are *acte clair*, since, if they are, a reference as to their correct interpretation is unnecessary. The other is whether those provisions of EU law are relevant to the dispute before the court. If they are not, a reference is also unnecessary.

acte clair

The term *acte clair* refers to a particular legislative provision, the meaning of which is clear. However, determining whether that is so can be difficult, as explained in the next section.

6.4.1 *Acte clair*

Note that, as will be seen later in this chapter, this topic is also relevant to mandatory references. If a national court considers that the meaning of a particular provision of EU law is *acte clair*, it can apply that law to the dispute before it and will have no need to make a preliminary reference on the correct interpretation of the provision to the Court of Justice.

The chief problem in applying this guideline is that a measure which might appear to one judge to have a clear meaning might appear to have an equally clear, but different, meaning to another—and appear to still another judge to be quite unclear. This problem is magnified across the EU legal system, which incorporates many different Member States, each with its own laws and legal traditions that might produce a different understanding of the meaning of a particular EU law.

Of course, the system established by Article 267 TFEU is designed to solve the problem of courts in different Member States applying EU law in different ways, by enabling them to refer questions to the Court of Justice to obtain a single authoritative ruling on the meaning of a particular provision of EU law. However, it would cause excessive and unnecessary delays to the administration of justice were every single case involving an issue of EU law to be referred to the Court of Justice. A balance must therefore be struck when determining which issues are so unclear that they should be referred and which are sufficiently clear not to require a reference.

The factors to be considered when assessing where the balance lies were set out by the Court of Justice in Case 283/81 *CILFIT and Lanificio di Gavardo SpA v Ministry of Health*

[1982] ECR 3415, which is the leading case on *acte clair* (and on a number of other issues—see 6.4.2 and 6.5), in which a number of textile firms complained that an Italian levy on wool was in contravention of EU law. The Italian government claimed that a preliminary reference was unnecessary because the meaning of the EU law in question was clear. The Italian court referred to the Court of Justice the question of whether a national court against whose decisions there was no judicial remedy under national law could refuse to make a reference where there was no reasonable doubt about the interpretation of the EU law at issue. The Court of Justice ruled that there was no obligation to refer if the particular EU law was *acte clair* in the sense that its correct application is 'so obvious as to leave no scope for any reasonable doubt' and that, in order to determine whether this was so, three factors must be taken into account.

?! THINKING POINT

While reading the following extract, consider what three factors were stated by the Court of Justice in *CILFIT* as determining a national court's decision on whether a provision of EU law is 'so obvious as to leave no scope for any reasonable doubt', as to be *acte clair*.

Case 283/81 *CILFIT and Lanificio di Gavardo Spa v Ministry of Health* [1982] ECR 3415

16. Finally, the correct application of Community law [now EU law] may be so obvious as to leave no scope for any reasonable doubt as to the manner in which the question raised is to be resolved. Before it comes to the conclusion that such is the case, the national court or tribunal must be convinced that the matter is equally obvious to the courts of the other Member States and to the Court of Justice ...

    [...]

18. To begin with, it must be borne in mind that Community [now Union] legislation is drafted in several languages and that the different language versions are all equally authentic. An interpretation of a provision of Community law thus involves a comparison of the different language versions.
19. It must also be borne in mind, even where the different language versions are entirely in accord with one another, that Community law uses terminology which is peculiar to it. Furthermore, it must be emphasized that legal concepts do not necessarily have the same meaning in Community law and in the law of the various Member States.
20. Finally, every provision of Community law must be placed in its context and interpreted in the light of the provisions of Community law as a whole, regard being had to the objectives thereof and to its state of evolution at the date on which the provision in question is to be applied.

The three factors according to which *acte clair* is to be assessed are therefore as follows.

(a) Since EU legislation is drafted in a number of official EU languages, each version being equally authentic, it is possible to say that the meaning of the measure is clear only if it has the same meaning in all of the languages and is equally clear in all.

(b) The terminology and legal concepts used in EU law do not necessarily have the same meaning in all Member States.

(c) Measures must be interpreted in the context of EU law as a whole, with particular regard to the objectives and progress of EU law at the time the measure is to be applied.

In *R v International Stock Exchange of the UK and the Republic of Ireland Ltd, ex p Else (1982) Ltd and others* [1993] 2 CMLR 677 (see also 6.4.2, 6.4.5, 6.4.6, and 6.4.7), the Court of Appeal of England and Wales provided further guidance (for English courts) on how to decide whether a provision of EU law was *acte clair*. In that case, shareholders in a company whose London Stock Exchange listing was suspended sought to challenge the suspension. The High Court of England and Wales referred to the Court of Justice a number of questions on the interpretation of Council Directive 79/279/EEC of 5 March 1979 coordinating the conditions for the admission of securities to official stock exchange listing, OJ 1979 L66/21, and the Stock Exchange appealed against the making of that reference. In allowing the appeal, the Court of Appeal held that a national court considering whether a provision of EU law was *acte clair* should ask itself whether it could 'with complete confidence resolve the issue itself' or instead had 'any real doubt'. Sir Thomas Bingham MR delivered the Court's judgment.

?! THINKING POINT

While reading the following extract, note the factors that the Court of Appeal in *Else* held that a national court should take into account when asking itself this question.

R v International Stock Exchange of the United Kingdom and the Republic of Ireland Ltd, ex p Else (1982) Ltd and another [1993] 2 WLR 70, 76, Court of Appeal

... I understand the correct approach in principle of a national court (other than a final court of appeal) to be quite clear: if the facts have been found and the Community law [now EU law] issue is critical to the court's final decision, the appropriate course is ordinarily to refer the issue to the Court of Justice unless the national court can with complete confidence resolve the issue itself. In considering whether it can with complete confidence resolve the issue itself the national court must be fully mindful of the differences between national and Community [now Union] legislation, of the pitfalls which face a national court venturing into what may be an unfamiliar field, of the need for uniform interpretation throughout the Community and of the great advantages enjoyed by the Court of Justice in construing Community instruments. If the national court has any real doubt, it should ordinarily refer.

The factors to be taken into account in assessing whether a measure is *acte clair* are, according to the Court of Appeal in *Else*:

- the differences between national and EU legislation;
- the difficulties in dealing with what might be an unfamiliar field;
- the need for a uniform interpretation throughout the EU; and
- the advantages enjoyed by the Court of Justice in interpreting EU law (see further 6.4.5).

In *R v Henn and Darby* [1980] 1 CMLR 246 (which was decided prior to the ruling in *CILFIT*), importers of pornographic material argued that UK restrictions on such imports were in contravention of Article 34 TFEU (see further 10.8), which prohibited restrictions on imports, and were not covered by Article 36 TFEU, which permitted restrictions on imports on grounds of public policy (see further 10.8.11). The Court of Appeal of England and Wales refused to make a preliminary reference on the ground that the application of EU law was clear. The House of Lords (now the Supreme Court) reversed this decision and made a reference. In the judgment of the House, Lord Diplock warned that a court should not be too ready to apply *acte clair* and treat a reference as purely discretionary simply because the meaning of the English text was clear to that particular court. First, the English text was only one of six of equal authority (at that time, there were nine Member States and six official languages), any one of which might be unclear or capable of a different interpretation. Secondly, the possibility of judicial disagreement over the meaning of EU law was highlighted in this very case by the contrasting views on the correct interpretation of Articles 34 and 36 TFEU of the House of Lords, which considered that Article 34 had been breached, and the Court of Appeal, which considered that an exception under Article 36 applied and therefore that Article 34 had not been breached.

More recently, in *R (on the application of OJSC Rosneft Oil Co) v HM Treasury* [2015] EWHC 248 (Admin), Green J, delivering the judgment of the High Court of England and Wales, held as follows.

R (on the application of OJSC Rosneft Oil Co) v HM Treasury [2015] EWHC 248 (Admin)

30. The reason that we consider that a reference is necessary of all issues is that although, as we explain later, we have views as to the merits of a number of the Claimant's arguments, we cannot be confident that the same conclusions would be arrived at by all courts across the EU and we are conscious that already there are differences of view on some key issues between the competent authorities of the different Member States.

In *R v Secretary of State for the Environment, ex p RSPB* [1997] Env LR 431, the Royal Society for the Protection of Birds (RSPB) challenged the decision of the UK Secretary of State for the Environment to exclude an area known as Lappel Bank from a designated Special Protection Area (SPA) for birds, on the ground that Council Directive 79/409/EEC of 2 April 1979 on the conservation of wild birds, OJ 1979 L103/1, did not permit economic considerations to be taken into account when classifying an SPA. The Divisional Court (part of the High Court of

England and Wales) and the majority of the Court of Appeal held that the Directive was *acte clair* and that the Secretary of State was indeed entitled to take into account such considerations. The dissenting judge in the Court of Appeal also considered that the Directive was *acte clair*, but argued that it was clear that the Secretary of State could not take economic factors into account.

?! THINKING POINT

In the light of these differing judgments in the case, what conclusion do you consider that the House of Lords (now the Supreme Court) should have reached as to whether the relevant provisions of the Directive were *acte clair?* Why?

The House of Lords concluded in *RSPB* that if, as was the situation here, the judges hearing a single case within a single Member State had not agreed on the interpretation of the relevant EU law, it was not possible for them to conclude that that law was *acte clair*. A reference to the Court of Justice was therefore essential. The UK's Supreme Court took a similar view in *MB v Secretary of State for Work and Pensions* [2016] UKSC 53 on the question of whether Council Directive 79/7/EEC of 19 December 1978 on the progressive implementation of the principle of equal treatment for men and women in matters of social security, OJ 1979 L6/24, precluded a national law that required a transgender person to be unmarried in order to qualify for a State retirement pension on the basis of their new gender. The Supreme Court concluded that, because it was divided on the question and there was no Court of Justice authority directly on the question (see 6.4.3 on the impact of previous Court of Justice judgments), it could not resolve the dispute without making a preliminary reference (*MB*, at para 17).

In *Cadbury UK Ltd v Société des Produits Nestlé SA* [2013] EWHC 16 (Ch), [2014] ETMR 17, a dispute arose as to whether Nestlé could register a trademark over the shape of a product—in this case, the KitKat chocolate bar. Cadbury opposed the application for registration, arguing that it should be refused under the provisions of the Trade Marks Act 1994, which transposed Directive 2008/95/EC of the European Parliament and of the Council of 22 October 2008 to approximate the laws of the Member States relating to trade marks, OJ 2008 L299/25, into UK law (on the obligation to transpose Directives into national law, see 3.4.2). The High Court held that the correct interpretation of the Directive was not clear and should be referred to the Court of Justice. Its reasoning appears in the following extract from its judgment.

Cadbury UK Ltd v Société des Produits Nestlé SA [2013] EWHC 16 (Ch)

46. An issue which has been considered by English courts in a number of cases is whether, having regard to the propositions set out above, it is sufficient to establish that a trade mark has acquired a distinctive character that at the relevant date a significant proportion of the relevant class of persons recognise the mark and associate it with the applicant's goods in the sense that, if they were to be asked who marketed goods bearing that mark,

they would identify the applicant (whether expressly or impliedly e.g. by reference to some other trade mark used by the applicant)?

47. To date, the answer which has been given to this question by the English courts is that this is not sufficient, and that what the applicant must establish is that a significant proportion of the relevant class of persons rely upon the trade mark (as opposed to any other trade marks which may also be present) as indicating the origin of the goods. It is not essential for the applicant to have explicitly promoted the sign in question as a trade mark. It is sufficient for the applicant to have used the sign in such a way that consumers have in fact come to rely on it as indicating the origin of the goods. On the other hand, if the applicant has explicitly promoted the sign as a trade mark, it is more likely that consumers will have come to rely upon it as indicating the origin of the goods …

48. Nevertheless, the English courts have recognised that it is not clear that this analysis is correct. Accordingly, in *Unilever* Jacob J. referred questions to the Court of Justice, but the reference was withdrawn when the dispute between the parties was settled. In *Dyson* Patten J. also referred questions to the Court of Justice, but the Court dealt with the reference on other grounds. In *Vibe* I stated at [89] that, had it not been for the applicant's opposition, I would have referred questions once again. Despite the passage of more than five years since then, the position is no clearer now.

REVIEW QUESTION

Suppose that you are involved in litigation in the UK's Employment Appeal Tribunal (EAT) over your dismissal from employment, which you allege is contrary to a (fictitious) EU Directive on employment law that provides protection against dismissal. The dispute centres on the correct interpretation of a provision in the Directive that removes this protection if the employee is guilty of 'grossly inappropriate behaviour'. How would *acte clair* be important in this scenario?

Answer: If you were to research the role of the EAT in the English legal system, you would conclude that it is a court or tribunal because it satisfies the criteria set out in *Dorsch Consult* (discussed at 6.2) and that it is a court or tribunal against whose decisions there is a judicial remedy under national law because it is possible to apply for leave to appeal against its decisions (see further 6.3.2). It therefore has a discretion under Article 267 TFEU to refer the interpretation of the disputed provision of EU law—ie the Directive—to the Court of Justice. In deciding whether to exercise the discretion to refer or not, the EAT must take account of a number of judicial guidelines, one of which is *acte clair*. If a measure is *acte clair*, it is not necessary to refer; if it is not *acte clair*, it might be necessary to refer, but the other guidelines (discussed at 6.4.2–6.4.7) will need to be taken into account in making a final decision as to how the discretion should be exercised. In deciding whether a measure is *acte clair*, the Court of Justice in *CILFIT* suggested that a national court should consider whether its meaning would be equally clear to the judges in other Member States, taking into account possible discrepancies in translation, the potential for the same legal concepts to be given different meanings in different Member States, and the state of development of EU law. If there were 'any reasonable doubt' as to its correct interpretation, the measure could not be *acte clair*. The disputed phrase here could be argued to be inherently imprecise and so, assuming that the Directive provides no definition or guidance, it is not *acte clair* according to the *CILFIT* criteria, and the national court could not interpret it 'with complete confidence' and without 'any real doubt' (*per Else*). Of course, if the members of the EAT agree on the meaning of the Directive, both amongst themselves and with the Employment Tribunal (from which the case would have been appealed to the EAT, this would suggest to the contrary that the measure is *acte clair* (*per RSPB*)—although if they have not all agreed, this supports the argument that it is not *acte clair*.

6.4.2 Relevance

As will be seen later in this chapter, this topic is also relevant to mandatory references.

If a national court considers that the answer to a question of EU law is not relevant to the dispute before it, it will not be necessary or appropriate to refer it to the Court of Justice. Indeed, it might be said in relation to discretionary references that this is less a guideline than a statement of the obvious—ie that the reference of a particular question cannot be 'necessary', as required by Article 267 TFEU, if it is not relevant to the case. However, it can be difficult to decide whether a particular question is sufficiently relevant to the final disposal of the case by the national court to be considered relevant for the purposes of Article 267 TFEU.

In *CILFIT* (also discussed at 6.4.1 in relation to *acte clair* and 6.5 in relation to mandatory references), the Court of Justice held that a question of EU law would not be relevant 'if the answer to that question, regardless of what it may be, can in no way affect the outcome of the case' (*CILFIT*, at para 10). This gives a wide scope to the term 'relevant'. In *R v International Stock Exchange of the UK and the Republic of Ireland Ltd, ex p Else (1982) Ltd and others* [1993] 2 CMLR 677 (also discussed at 6.4.1, 6.4.5, 6.4.6, and 6.4.7 in relation to a number of other guidelines on the making of discretionary references), the Court of Appeal of England and Wales held that a question would be relevant for the purposes of Article 267 TFEU if the answer to it was 'critical' to the final decision. Since it may be impossible to know whether the answer is 'critical' until a ruling has been given on it, this must mean that it is sufficient that the answer to the question has the *potential* to be critical to the final decision. In other words, it is not necessary to prove that a ruling by the Court of Justice is essential, just that it might be, depending on what the Court actually rules.

In *Commissioners of Customs and Excise v Samex ApS* [1983] 3 CMLR 194 (discussed also at 6.4.5 in relation to the advantages of the Court of Justice in giving rulings on EU law), the High Court of England and Wales provided further guidance (to UK courts) on how to determine whether or not an issue of EU law was relevant for the purposes of Article 267 TFEU. The UK authorities had issued Samex with an import licence for textiles shipped on or before 31 December 1979. The goods were imported in January 1980 and were seized by the customs authorities. Samex argued that the time limit on the licence was contrary to Commission Regulation (EEC) No 2997/81 of 20 October 1981 amending the Annexes to Council Regulation (EEC) No 3059/78 on common rules for imports of certain textile products originating in certain third countries, OJ 1981 L300/8. In holding that a reference to the Court of Justice under Article 267 TFEU should be made, the High Court stated that the questions referred were 'substantially, if not quite totally, determinative of [the] litigation' (*Samex*, at para 26).

The Court of Justice has held on a number of occasions that questions on the interpretation of EU law referred by a national court benefit from a presumption that they are relevant (see eg Joined Cases C-188 & 189/10 *Melki and Abdeli* [2010] ECR I-5667, at para 27, and C-78–80/08 *Ministero dell'Economia e delle Finanze v Paint Graphos Sarl* [2011] ECR I-7611, at para 31) (discussed also at 6.1.3 in relation to the requirement that references relate to questions of EU law). The Court has explained this presumption as follows.

C-78–80/08 *Ministero dell'Economia e delle Finanze v Paint Graphos Sarl* [2011] ECR I-7611

31. According to settled case-law, questions on the interpretation of European Union law referred by a national court in the factual and legislative context which that court is responsible for defining and the accuracy of which is not a matter for the Court to determine, enjoy a presumption of relevance. The Court may refuse to rule on a question referred for a preliminary ruling from a national court only where it is quite obvious that the interpretation of European Union law that is sought bears no relation to the actual facts of the main action or its purpose, where the problem is hypothetical, or where the Court does not have before it the factual or legal material necessary to give a useful answer to the questions submitted to it (Joined Cases C-222/05 to C-225/05 *van der Weerd and Others* [2007] ECR I-4233, paragraph 22; Joined Cases C-188/10 and C-189/10 *Melki and Abdeli* [2010] ECR I-5667, paragraph 27; and *Bruno and Others* [Joined Cases C-395 & 396/08 *Istituto nazionale della previdenza sociale (INPS) v Bruno and others* [2010] ECR I-5119], paragraph 19).

However, despite this presumption, the Court of Justice in *Paint Graphos* rejected one of the questions referred because it concerned the compatibility with EU law (on State aid to businesses) of Italian law that had come into force after the facts in the case arose. The Court concluded that the question therefore had no relevance to the outcome of the dispute before the national court.

In some cases, the English courts have considered that, because of the delay caused by the lapse of time between the making by them of a preliminary reference and the giving of a preliminary ruling by the Court of Justice, a question that was relevant at the start of that period would have become irrelevant by the end and therefore that a reference should not be made. For example, in *R v Ministry of Agriculture, Fisheries and Food, ex p Portman Agrochemicals Ltd* [1994] 3 CMLR 18 (see also 6.4.7), the High Court of England and Wales noted that the delay involved in obtaining a preliminary ruling would render the questions to be referred academic and hence irrelevant, because although the dispute concerned the use of certain confidential data, the parties agreed that, by the time of the ruling, any right of confidentiality would have expired. Taking account of the impact of the delay, and the fact that neither party wished a reference to be made, the court concluded that the interests of justice would not be served by making a reference.

REVIEW QUESTION

Suppose that you are involved in litigation in the UK's EAT, as set out in the previous review question. How would the guideline concerning relevance be important in this scenario?

Answer: As explained in the answer to the previous review question, the EAT is a court or tribunal against whose decisions there is a judicial remedy under national law and therefore, under Article 267 TFEU, it has a discretion to make a reference as to the meaning of the disputed provision of the Directive. In deciding whether to exercise the discretion to refer or not to refer, the EAT must take account of a number of judicial guidelines, one of which is relevance. If the provisions of the Directive are not relevant to the outcome of the case, it is not necessary to refer questions about their meaning or validity. Even if the provisions are relevant in principle, not all possible questions about them will be relevant to the dispute.

In deciding whether the reference of a particular question is relevant, the Court of Appeal in *Else* held that it must be 'critical' to the final decision, and in *Samex* the High Court held that it must be 'substantially ... determinative' of the case. It is certainly possible that, in a case concerning dismissal, the extent of the protection under the Directive, as determined by the interpretation of 'grossly inappropriate behaviour', could impact on the outcome of the case. A reference on the correct interpretation of this term could therefore be regarded as relevant.

The other guidelines (including *acte clair* and the other guidelines discussed later in this chapter) will also need to be taken into account in making a final decision as to whether the discretion to refer should be exercised or not.

6.4.3 Previous Court of Justice rulings

As will be seen later in this chapter, the existence of a previous Court of Justice ruling on the same question of EU law is also relevant to mandatory references.

In principle, if the Court of Justice has already given a ruling on a particular question of EU law, it may not be necessary for a national court hearing a subsequent case to make another reference on the same issue. It can simply consult the previous ruling and apply it to the case before it, as the Court pointed out in Joined Cases 28–30/62 *Da Costa en Schaake NV and others v Nederlandse Belastingadministratie* [1963] ECR 31. In that case, a Dutch chemical exporter alleged that certain Dutch import taxes were contrary to what is now Article 30 TFEU (see 10.4). On a reference for a preliminary ruling under Article 267 TFEU as to the correct interpretation of the EU law at issue, the Court of Justice ruled that the existence of a prior ruling by it on a question that was 'materially identical' to that which a national court was proposing to refer could obviate the need to make a reference, although it did not preclude a reference being made if the national court considered it 'desirable' (*Da Costa*, at 38). The Court of Justice is not bound by its own decisions and a ruling could be considered desirable if, for example, new factors were to exist or where the national court considers that the Court of Justice was wrong in its earlier ruling and might be ready to correct its approach.

In Case C-338/95 *Wiener SI GmbH v Hauptzollamt Emmerich* [1997] ECR I-6495, Advocate General Jacobs went even further, arguing in his Opinion (see further 2.4 on Advocate Generals' Opinions) that a reference would be 'least appropriate' (*Wiener*, at para 20 of the

Opinion) where there was an established body of case law developed by the Court of Justice over the years that could easily be transposed to the facts of the particular case, or when the question turned on a narrow point considered in the light of a very specific set of facts and the ruling was unlikely to have any application beyond the particular case (see also 6.4.7). However, the Court of Justice did not accept this reasoning, and it is therefore not part of EU law on the exercise of the discretion under Article 267 TFEU.

6.4.4 The possibility of rejection of the reference

As will be seen later in this chapter, the possibility of rejection by the Court of Justice is also relevant in the context of mandatory references.

The Court of Justice has, on occasion, been prepared to reject a reference and refuse to give a ruling where it has felt that Article 267 TFEU is being misused.

?! **THINKING POINT**

How do you think that the possibility that the Court of Justice may reject a reference should affect the exercise by a national court of its discretion to make a preliminary reference to it?

National courts need to consider whether a ruling is likely to be rejected by the Court of Justice when considering whether to exercise their discretion to refer. If a rejection is likely, there is little point in the national court making a reference in the first place, because the result of a rejection for the parties is the worst of both worlds: a final decision by the national court is delayed by the making of a reference and additional expense is incurred, yet no ruling is given by the Court of Justice.

The grounds upon which the Court of Justice has based its rejection of questions referred for a preliminary ruling are that:

- there is no genuine dispute;
- the referring court has failed to explain the context of its questions;
- the questions referred are irrelevant to the dispute; or
- the questions do not concern EU law.

Each of these will be considered in turn, although it should be noted that there can be some overlap between the failure to explain the context and irrelevance, in circumstances in which a question is considered irrelevant *because* there is insufficient contextual information to explain its relevance.

6.4.4.1 No genuine dispute

The reason given for the Court of Justice's very first rejection of a reference from a national court, in Case 104/79 *Foglia v Novello (No 1)* [1980] ECR 745, was that there was no genuine dispute. Foglia, an Italian undertaking which traded in wine, contracted to sell wine to a buyer,

Mrs Novello, who was based in France. The contract between them provided that Novello would not be liable for any taxes that were unlawfully levied on the goods. The contract between Foglia and the carrier of the goods, Danzas, provided that Foglia would not be liable for such taxes. In the event, a tax was levied by the French authorities on the goods. Danzas paid the tax and Foglia reimbursed Danzas, but Novello refused to reimburse Foglia on the ground that the tax was contrary to EU law. Foglia sued Novello before an Italian court. The Italian court made a reference to the Court of Justice under Article 267 TFEU.

The Court of Justice refused to accept the reference, on the ground that it had no jurisdiction because there was no real dispute between the parties. A reference under Article 267 TFEU was designed to provide an interpretation of EU law that was required for the resolution of a genuine dispute. Article 267 TFEU did not confer jurisdiction on the Court of Justice in the context of a collusive action such as this, which disguised an attempt by the parties to have a foreign law struck down.

?! THINKING POINT

While reading the following extract, consider what facts suggested to the Court that the dispute was not genuine.

Case 104/79 *Foglia v Novello (No 1)* [1980] ECR 745

9. In their written observations submitted to the Court of Justice the two parties to the main action have provided an essentially identical description of the tax discrimination which is a feature of the French legislation concerning the taxation of liqueur wines; the two parties consider that that legislation is incompatible with Community law [now EU law]. In the course of the oral procedure before the Court, Foglia stated that he was participating in the procedure before the Court in view of the interest of his undertaking as such and as an undertaking belonging to a certain category of Italian trader in the outcome of the legal issues involved in the dispute.
10. It thus appears that the parties to the main action are concerned to obtain a ruling that the French tax system is invalid for liqueur wines by the expedient of proceedings before an Italian court between two private individuals who are in agreement as to the result to be attained and who have inserted a clause in their contract in order to induce the Italian court to give a ruling on the point. The artificial nature of this expedient is underlined by the fact that Danzas did not exercise its rights under French law to institute proceedings over the consumption tax although it undoubtedly had an interest in doing so in view of the clause in the contract by which it was also bound and moreover of the fact that Foglia paid without protest that undertaking's bill which included a sum paid in respect of that tax.
11. The duty of the Court of Justice under Article 177 of the EC Treaty [now Article 267 TFEU] is to supply all courts in the Community [now Union] with the information on the interpretation of Community law which is necessary to enable them to settle genuine disputes

which are brought before them. A situation in which the Court was obliged by the expedient of arrangements like those described above to give rulings would jeopardize the whole system of legal remedies available to private individuals to enable them to protect themselves against provisions which are contrary to the Treaty.

12. This means that the questions asked by the national court, having regard to the circumstances of this case, do not fall within the framework of the duties of the Court of Justice under Article 177 of the EC Treaty.
13. The Court of Justice accordingly has no jurisdiction to give a ruling on the questions asked by the national court.

The terms of the two contracts in question had the result that Foglia and Novello had the same interest in the outcome of the case (since, contractually, neither was liable to pay the tax if it was unlawful), and therefore there was no genuine dispute. The carrier, Danzas, had not appealed against the imposition of the tax, as it was entitled to do under French law, and Foglia had reimbursed it, despite the fact that he was not liable do so under the terms of their contract, which suggested that they expected the tax to be struck down. The two parties provided what the Court described as 'an essentially identical description' of the alleged tax discrimination under French law (*Foglia (No 1)*, at para 9), and Foglia stated that it was participating in the reference both as the representative of a category of Italian traders interested in the outcome of the dispute and in its own right. The Court concluded that it was therefore evident that the parties had the same interest in the outcome of the proceedings.

In Case 244/80 *Foglia v Novello (No 2)* [1981] ECR 3045, the Italian court made a further attempt to obtain a ruling from the Court of Justice. It repeated its request for a preliminary ruling, arguing that it was for the national court to exercise its discretion as to whether to refer. The Court of Justice accepted this argument, but nonetheless again refused to accept the reference on the basis that it retained the right to check its jurisdiction to hear a case and that, under Article 267 TFEU, the issue referred must be one on which a decision was necessary to the resolution of the case. Where, as here, there was no genuine dispute between the parties on a particular issue, it was clearly not susceptible to a reference under Article 267 TFEU.

In *Foglia*, the parties were, in effect, challenging the laws of one Member State in the courts of another.

?! THINKING POINT

Which country's tax laws were the subject of the dispute in *Foglia* and in which country was the court that made a reference to the Court of Justice in the course of the dispute?

However, this does not necessarily mean, as in *Foglia*, that there is no genuine dispute or that the reference will be rejected by the Court of Justice. This is evident from Case C-150/88 *Eau de Cologne v Provide* [1989] ECR I-3891, in which Provide, an Italian company, had ordered cosmetics from Eau de Cologne, a German company. The packaging complied with EU law, but not with Italian law, and therefore the goods could not be marketed in Italy. Provide refused to accept or pay for the goods and was sued by Eau de Cologne in the German courts. The German court made a reference to the Court of Justice on the interpretation of EU law, in order to enable it to determine whether the Italian law was compatible with EU law. The Italian government alleged that the reference was inadmissible.

The Court of Justice accepted the reference, despite the fact that the parties were questioning, in German courts, the compatibility of Italian law with EU law, because the case involved a genuine dispute. The Court of Justice held that, when giving a ruling on the interpretation of EU law in order to assist a national court in determining the compatibility of national law with EU law, it made no difference that the disputed law was that of a different Member State.

Whether there is a genuine dispute will turn very much on the facts of the individual case. In Case C-105/94 *Celestini v Saar-Sektkellerie Faber* [1997] ECR I-2971, certain of the facts paralleled those in *Foglia v Novello*. A German company bought wine from an Italian producer, but the German authorities impounded the wine and subsequently declared it unfit for human consumption. The German buyer sued the Italian producer in an Italian court, which made a reference to the Court of Justice. Although the buyer had not contested the actions of the German authorities and no case had been brought in the German courts, which had sole jurisdiction to rule on the validity of those actions, the Court accepted the reference. It expressly stated that there was nothing to indicate that the parties had jointly fabricated the dispute as a device to obtain a preliminary ruling (*Celestini*, at para 23).

Where it is alleged that there is no genuine dispute, the Court of Justice may exceptionally request further information before it decides whether or not to accept the reference, as happened in Case 46/80 *Vinal v Orbat* [1981] ECR 77 (see later).

6.4.4.2 Failure to explain the factual or legal context

The most common reason for the Court of Justice to refuse to provide a preliminary ruling is that the reference from the national court contains an inadequate explanation of the factual or legal context of the questions.

?! THINKING POINT

Why do you think it is so important that the Court of Justice has sufficient information about the facts and the national law?

As the Court has pointed out in a number of cases, such as Case C-458/93 *Saddik* [1995] ECR I-511 and Case C-167/94 *Grau Gomis and others* [1995] ECR I-1023, a lack of information may mean that the Court cannot give a meaningful answer to the questions referred.

In *Grau Gomis*, Grau Gomis and others were charged with smuggling tobacco contrary to Spanish law. The national court was uncertain as to the compatibility of the relevant national provisions with EU law and referred to the Court of Justice a number of questions on the interpretation of EU law. The Court of Justice ruled that the reference was inadmissible because the national court had supplied insufficient information.

?! **THINKING POINT**

While reading the following extract, consider what information should have been provided by the national court.

Case C-167/94 *Grau Gomis and others* [1995] ECR I-1023

7. As regards the other provisions mentioned in the order for reference, the Court observes that, apart from the parties to the main proceedings and the Commission, only the Spanish, French, and Italian Governments have submitted observations. The French and Italian Governments have referred to their difficulty in identifying the factual and legislative framework of the questions asked. In particular, the French Government notes that no details have been given of the monopolies in question in the main proceedings, while the Italian Government wonders whether the national court is considering an importation monopoly or a marketing monopoly and points out the complete lack of any statement of reasons as regards the possible incompatibility of those monopolies with Community law [now EU law]. Finally, neither the Commission nor some of the governments see the need for interpretation of several of the provisions referred to in order to resolve the dispute before the national court.

8. It must be pointed out that in view of the need to arrive at an interpretation of Community law which will be helpful to the national court, it is necessary for that court to define the factual and legislative context of the questions it is asking or, at the very least, explain the factual premisses on which those questions are based (see, in particular, the judgment in Joined Cases C-320/90, C-321/90 and C-322/90 *Telemarsicabruzzo v Circostel* [1993] ECR 1-393, paragraph 5, the order in Case C-157/92 *Pretore di Genova v Banchero* [1993] ECR 1-1085, paragraph 4, and the order in Case C-458/93 *Saddik* [1995] ECR 1-511, paragraph 12).

9. Furthermore, it is essential that the national court should give at the very least some explanation of the reasons for the choice of the Community [now Union] provisions of which it requests an interpretation and on the link it establishes between those provisions and the national legislation applicable to the dispute.

[...]

11. It must be stated that the order for reference does not contain sufficient information to comply with the abovementioned requirements. In particular, as the French and Italian Governments have rightly pointed out, the order contains insufficient details of the monopolies in question in the main proceedings and does not provide any indication of the reasons which led the national court to raise the question of the compatibility of the contested Spanish legislation with the various Community provisions which it asks the Court to interpret. One of the provisions, namely Article 8b of the EC Treaty [now Article 22 TFEU], even appears altogether irrelevant in view of the subject matter of the main proceedings. The order for reference does not therefore enable the Court to give a helpful interpretation of Community law.

12. In those circumstances it must be held, [that] ... the request from the national court is manifestly inadmissible.

The Court of Justice considered that, in order for it to provide an interpretation of EU law that would be helpful to the national court, it was necessary for the national court to define the factual and legislative context of its questions, or, at least, explain the factual basis for those questions. It was essential for the national court to give, at the very least, some explanation of the reasons for its choice of the provisions of EU law of which it was requesting an interpretation, and on the link between those provisions and the national legislation applicable to the dispute.

However, the Court considered that the provision of this information was essential not only to it, but also to other parties who might have a role to play in the preliminary ruling procedure (see further 6.11 on the procedure).

?! THINKING POINT

While reading the following extract, note who the Court considered could be prejudiced (other than the Court itself) by a national court's failure to provide adequate information in its reference.

Case C-167/94 *Grau Gomis and others* [1995] ECR I-1023

10. In that respect, it should be emphasized that the information provided in decisions making references to satisfy those requirements serves not only to enable the Court to give helpful answers but also to enable the Governments of the Member States and other interested parties to submit observations pursuant to Article 20 of the EC Statute of the Court. It is the Court's duty to ensure that the opportunity to submit observations is safeguarded, bearing in mind that, by virtue of the abovementioned provision, only the decision's main references are notified to the interested parties (see the judgment in Joined Cases 141/81, 142/81 and 143/81 *Holdijk and Others* [1982] ECR 1299, paragraph 6, and the order in *Saddik* [Case C-458/93 *Criminal Proceedings against Saddik* [1995] ECR I-511], paragraph 13).

The Court noted that the information given in the reference not only enabled it to give helpful answers, but also enabled the Member States and other interested parties to submit observations to the Court (see also the discussion at 6.4.5 of this procedural feature as an advantage of the Court of Justice when giving a ruling). It was therefore the Court's duty to ensure that the opportunity to submit observations was safeguarded.

In assessing whether it has sufficient information to provide answers to the questions referred, the Court of Justice may take into account any written and oral observations submitted to it by the parties (Case C-18/93 *Corsica Ferries v Corpo dei Piloti del Porto di Genova* [1994] ECR I-1783, para 13; see also 6.2 and later). In Case 46/80 *Vinal v Orbat* [1981] ECR 77, an Italian importer of synthetic alcohol, Vinal, contracted to supply French alcohol to another Italian company, Orbat. The Italian authorities imposed a duty on the goods, which Orbat refused to pay. The making of a preliminary reference was opposed by the Italian government on the grounds that there was no real dispute and that the parties simply wished to impugn the duty so as to avoid paying it. In the light of this opposition, the Court of Justice requested further information from the parties, which satisfied it that there was a genuine dispute and therefore valid grounds for an Article 267 TFEU ruling.

The Court also has a discretion under its Rules of Procedure to request further information from the national court.

Rules of Procedure of the Court of Justice, OJ 2012/L265/1

Article 101

Request for clarification

1. Without prejudice to the measures of organisation of procedure and measures of inquiry provided for in these Rules, the Court may, after hearing the Advocate General, request clarification from the referring court or tribunal within a time-limit prescribed by the Court.
2. The reply of the referring court or tribunal to that request shall be served on the interested persons referred to in Article 23 of the Statute.

However, the Court is not obliged to request additional information, either from the parties or the referring court, and may simply reject the reference if it considers the information contained in it to be inadequate.

Lack of factual or legal information may also mean that the questions referred are, or at least appear to be, irrelevant. This has been treated by the Court as a separate ground on which to reject a reference (see next section).

6.4.4.3 Questions that are irrelevant or hypothetical

This category concerns particular questions that the Court of Justice will refuse to answer because they are not relevant on the facts of the case or because the national court has failed to demonstrate that they are relevant because it has not provided sufficient information. The Court will not necessarily reject the entire reference: if there are relevant questions amongst the irrelevant ones, the Court will provide a ruling on those questions that are relevant.

The starting point for the Court is that questions relating to EU law which have been referred by a national court enjoy a presumption of relevance (see eg Case C-416/10 *Križan and others* [2013] Env LR 28). However, this presumption can be rebutted.

In Case C-343/90 *Lourenço Dias v Director da Alfândega do Porto* [1992] ECR I-4573, Lourenço Dias purchased a new van, which he subsequently modified. Prior to the purchase, the van had been imported into Portugal without paying the tax to which that modification would have given rise. The Portuguese authorities fined Lourenço Dias for failing to declare the changes to the van, which determined its tax classification. Lourenço Dias challenged this on the ground that the taxes were contrary to what is now Article 110 TFEU (see 10.7). The national court made a preliminary reference of a number of questions on the interpretation of what is now Article 110 TFEU, some (but not all) of which the Court of Justice rejected as hypothetical.

?! THINKING POINT

While reading the following extract, consider why the Court held that the questions referred by the national court on the interpretation of EU law were hypothetical.

Case C-343/90 *Lourenço Dias (Manuel José) v Director da Alfândega do Porto* [1992] ECR I-4675

The question concerning the different tax system for imported second-hand vehicles and second-hand vehicles registered in Portugal

24. In its first question, the national court asks whether the first paragraph of Article 95 [EC, now Article 110 TFEU] prohibits a Member State from imposing a motor-vehicle tax on second-hand vehicles imported from other Member States when it is not charged on second-hand vehicles which were new when they were imported or were originally assembled or manufactured in Portugal.

25. It is sufficient to recall in that connection that the motor vehicle which gave rise to the main proceedings was new when it was imported and purchased.

[…]

The question concerning the restriction of the period during which foreign-registered vehicles intended to be definitively imported may circulate

33. In its fifth question, the national court asks whether the second paragraph of Article 95 prohibits a Member State from restricting the circulation of imported vehicles to 48 hours from their entry into Portugal where vehicles assembled or manufactured in Portugal are not subject to any restriction.

34. According to the order for reference, that question relates to Article 5(1) of the Decree-Law. Under that provision foreign-registered motor vehicles intended for definitive importation whose owners are resident or have their registered office in the national territory may circulate only for a period of 48 hours following their entry into Portugal.

35. However, as the national court's order itself states, the vehicle at issue in this case was registered for the first time in Portugal. It was hence never subject to the restrictions on circulation laid down by Article 5(1) of the Decree-Law.

[…]

The question concerning the exemption for 'vintage' motor vehicles

39. In its seventh question, the national court asks whether Article 95 prohibits a Member State from exempting the importation of 'vintage' motor vehicles from a tax when other vehicles do not qualify for such exemption.

40. That question relates to Article 9 of the Decree-Law, which authorizes the importation free of motor-vehicle tax of motor vehicles manufactured no later than 1950, provided that they are of interest from the point of view of the national cultural heritage.

41. Suffice it to say that the motor vehicle in question in this case was manufactured in 1989.
42. In view of the foregoing considerations, there is no need to reply to [these] questions since they are manifestly unrelated to the actual nature of the main proceedings.

In Case C-2/97 *Società Italiana Petroli SpA (IP) v Borsana* [2001] 1 CMLR 27, the Court of Justice refused to answer a question on the compatibility with Council Directive 90/394/EEC of 28 June 1990 on the protection of workers from the risks related to exposure to carcinogens at work, OJ 1990 L196/1, and Council Directive 89/655/EEC of 30 November 1989 concerning the minimum safety and health requirements for the use of work equipment by workers at work, OJ 1989 L393/13, of certain criminal penalties laid down by national law because the dispute before the national court was a civil case. A question on criminal penalties was therefore irrelevant and 'a reply to that question cannot in any event be of any assistance to the national court when giving judgment' (*Borsana*, at para 52).

In Case C-18/93 *Corsica Ferries v Corpo dei Piloti del Porto di Genova* [1994] ECR I-1783 (see also 6.2 and earlier), the dispute related to whether a tariff paid by the applicant for pilot services in the port of Genoa was discriminatory. The Court of Justice therefore gave a ruling on the questions referred to it that related to the alleged discriminatory aspects of the tariff. However, it refused to answer questions on the compatibility with EU law of the compulsory nature of the pilot service or the fact that the tariff did not vary according to the ship's technical equipment, since the dispute did not relate to these issues (*Corsica Ferries*, paras 15–16).

More recently, in Case C-105/14 *Taricco and others* EU:C:2015:555, the defendants were accused of offences, some of which would become time-barred before the domestic courts were able to give final judgment. The national court referred to the Court of Justice a number of questions concerning the compatibility with EU law of Italian law on extending limitation periods in criminal cases. The Court had to first consider whether the questions were hypothetical, given that proceedings against the defendants were still ongoing and they had not yet been found guilty. The Court ruled, importantly, that questions concerning EU law enjoyed a presumption of relevance and it was not the case here that the interpretation of EU law was unrelated to the facts or purpose of the action before the domestic courts, or was otherwise hypothetical, or that the factual or legal material necessary to give judgment were not before the Court. Sufficient information had been provided to the Court, and the questions related to the actual facts and were in no way hypothetical, 'since they concern the interpretation of several provisions of EU law *that the referring court considers to be of crucial importance for its next decision in the main proceedings*, particularly as regards the committal of the accused for trial' (*Taricco*, para 32, emphasis added).

REVIEW QUESTION

Suppose that, in proceedings concerning a dispute over the transportation by air of live tigers, it is alleged that one of the parties has failed to provide the facilities required by a (fictitious) EU Directive on the protection of live animals such as cats and the following questions are referred to the Court of Justice under Article 267 TFEU:

(a) the meaning of the term 'air transport' in the Directive;

(b) the meaning of the term 'sea transport' in the Directive;

(c) whether the phrase 'live animals such as cats' in the Directive can be interpreted as including tigers; and

(d) whether the term 'animals' in the Directive could be interpreted as including elephants.

Which of these questions do you suspect that the Court of Justice might reject and why?

Answer: In this example, question (b) is clearly irrelevant since the case does not involve sea transport. Question (d) is also irrelevant as the case does not concern elephants. Questions (a) and (c) are relevant, and would therefore be accepted (unless, of course, the facts revealed that there was no genuine dispute, or the legal and factual context set out in the scenario has not been explained to the Court of Justice, in which case all of the questions would be rejected).

An example of a case in which the facts and legal context had either not been established by the national court, or at least had not been included in the reference sent to the Court, so that the questions referred were regarded by the Court as irrelevant, is Case C-83/91 *Meilicke v ADV/ORGA AG* [1992] ECR I-4871. In that case, a German shareholder in the company ADV/ORGA sought information from it concerning payment that it had received in return for a new issue of shares. When this was not forthcoming, he sought to rely on the Second Company Law Directive (Directive 2012/30/EU of the European Parliament and of the Council of 25 October 2012 … , OJ 2012 L315/74), which he alleged gave him greater rights to information than German law in circumstances in which the company had received payment for its shares otherwise than in cash. The national court referred to the Court of Justice a number of questions on the interpretation of the Second Company Law Directive.

The Court of Justice refused to answer the questions referred on the interpretation of the Second Company Law Directive on the ground that they were hypothetical.

?! THINKING POINT

While reading the following extract, consider what missing contextual information was identified by the Court, the absence of which caused it to regard the questions referred as hypothetical.

Case C-83/91 *Meilicke v ADV/ORGA* [1992] ECR I-4871

25. Nevertheless, in Case 244/80 *Foglia v Novello* [1981] ECR 3045, paragraph 21, the Court considered that, in order to determine whether it has jurisdiction, it is a matter for the Court of Justice to examine the conditions in which the case has been referred to it by the national court. The spirit of cooperation which must prevail in the preliminary-ruling procedure requires the national court to have regard to the function entrusted to the Court of Justice, which is to assist in the administration of justice in the Member States and not

to deliver advisory opinions on general or hypothetical questions (*Foglia v Novello*, cited above, paragraphs 18 and 20, and Case 149/82 *Robards v Insurance Officer* [1983] ECR 171, paragraph 19).

26. The Court has already made it clear that the need to provide an interpretation of Community law [now EU law] which will be of use to the national court makes it essential to define the legal context in which the interpretation requested should be placed and that, in that respect, it may be convenient, in certain circumstances, for the facts of the case to be established and for questions of purely national law to be settled at the time the reference is made to the Court, so as to enable the latter to take cognizance of all the features of fact and of law which may be relevant to the interpretation of Community law which it is called upon to give (Joined Cases 36 and 71/80 *Irish Creamery Milk Suppliers Association v Ireland* [1981] ECR 735, paragraph 6). Without such information, the Court may find it impossible to give a useful interpretation (see Case 52/76 *Benedetti v Munari* [1977] ECR 163, paragraphs 20, 21, and 22, and Joined Cases 205 to 215/82 *Deutsche Milchkontor v Germany* [1983] ECR 2633, paragraph 36).

27. In the light of those considerations, it must first be observed that the specific context of the dispute which gave rise to the reference for a preliminary ruling is defined by paragraphs 131 and 132 of the Aktiengesetz. Those articles concern the right of shareholders to receive information from the management.

28. The questions submitted do not relate directly to that right but essentially raise the problem of the compatibility with the Second Directive of the doctrine of disguised contributions in kind, as embodied in particular in the judgment of the Bundesgerichtshof of 15 January 1990, cited above. The national court considers that an answer to those questions is needed in order to enable it to adjudicate on the request for information made by Mr Meilicke. It states that the request would have to be rejected if it was found that the doctrine of disguised contributions in kind, as set out in the German case law, was incompatible with the Second Directive.

29. However, it is apparent from the documents before the Court that it has not been established that the conditions for the application of that doctrine have been satisfied in the main proceedings. Both in the proceedings before the national court and in its written observations to the Court of Justice, ADV/ORGA has rejected the view that the German case-law applies to the transactions entered into between it and Commerzbank. The national court's own reference to the issue is inconclusive, in that it states that Commerzbank's contribution may be contrary to the case law in question.

30. It follows that the problem of the compatibility of the doctrine of contributions in kind with the Second Directive is a hypothetical one.

31. Moreover, the hypothetical nature of the problem on which the Court is requested to give a ruling is confirmed by the fact that the documents forwarded by the national court do not identify the matters of fact and of law which might make it possible to define the context in which ADV/ORGA's increase of capital took place and to establish the links between the contribution made by Commerzbank and the doctrine of disguised contributions in

kind as set out in the German case law. The preliminary questions are specifically concerned with the compatibility of that doctrine with the Second Directive and therefore raise numerous problems, the answers to which largely depend on the circumstances in which the capital was increased.

32. The Court is thus being asked to give a ruling on a hypothetical problem, without having before it the matters of fact or law necessary to give a useful answer to the questions submitted to it.

33. Accordingly, the Court would be exceeding the limits of the function entrusted to it if it decided to answer the questions submitted to it.

34. It follows that it is not appropriate to answer the questions submitted by the Landgericht Hannover.

The Court of Justice considered that it had not been established on the facts whether the payment received by the company should be categorized as cash or not. It was therefore unclear how German law, which gave greater rights to information where payments other than cash were concerned, applied; and whether the Directive, which only applied to non-cash payments, applied at all.

In Case C-350/13 *Antonio Gramsci Shipping Corp and others v Aivars Lembergs* EU:C:2014:1516, the dispute before the referring Greek court had centred on the enforceability in Greece of a freezing injunction ordered by the High Court of England and Wales. However, the High Court had subsequently annulled the injunction and, as the Court of Appeal and Supreme Court had both dismissed appeals in the case, that annulment had become final. The Court of Justice therefore rejected the reference from the Greek court on the ground that the questions referred had become hypothetical because the Greek court was no longer dealing with a case that was pending before it. In response to the argument of one of the parties that, although the referred questions were no longer relevant, it would be useful to obtain answers to them because a similar case was pending before the referring court, the Court of Justice noted that if an interpretation of EU law were necessary to resolve a separate dispute, the referring court could make a separate reference.

6.4.4.4 The questions do not concern EU law

Since Article 267 TFEU only grants the Court of Justice jurisdiction to give preliminary rulings on the interpretation or validity of EU law, it is obvious that it has no jurisdiction to give rulings on questions that do not involve EU law at all. However, it is not always obvious whether a point of EU law can be said to be involved and thus whether a question on the interpretation of that law is relevant.

One common area of difficulty in this respect is where the dispute before the national court relates to national law. As discussed at 6.1.3, the Court of Justice may give a ruling on the interpretation of EU law in such disputes if the national law in question incorporates provisions or principles of EU law so directly that an independent interpretation by the national court would threaten the uniformity of EU law itself (see Joined Cases C-297/88 & 197/89 *Dzodzi v Belgian State* [1990] ECR I-3763). However, it must be established that this is indeed the case.

For example, in Case C-482/10 *Cicala v Regione Sicilia* [2011] ECR I-14139, a dispute arose as to the correct interpretation of a provision of Italian administrative law, which referred to 'principles derived from the EU legal order'. The Court of Justice held that such a general reference did not make specific provisions of the EU Treaty or the Charter of Fundamental Rights (see 9.4) applicable and therefore that it did not have jurisdiction to provide a ruling on their interpretation.

In Case C-310/10 *Agatfiței and others* [2011] ECR I-5989, a dispute arose as to the correct interpretation of a provision of Romanian anti-discrimination law that was intended to transpose a number of EU Directives. The Court of Justice ruled the reference made by the Romanian court inadmissible, because the disputed provision applied not only to discrimination prohibited by EU law, but also to discrimination prohibited by national law alone. In the latter situation, its interpretation was not necessarily contingent on the interpretation of the EU Directives and therefore the interpretation of this national law did not threaten the uniformity of EU law. Similarly, in Case C-583/10 *United States v Nolan* [2013] 1 CMLR 32, the Court of Justice held that it was not clear that provisions of the Trade Union and Labour Relations (Consolidation) Act 1992 in the UK applied the same solutions as those adopted by Council Directive 98/59/EC of 20 July 1998 on the approximation of the laws of the Member States relating to collective redundancies, OJ 1998 L225/16, to disputes such as that at issue, in which the employer of staff at a military base in the UK was the US government. It held further that, in any event, uniformity was not threatened since the Directive expressly excluded dismissal of staff at a military base.

In Case C-466/11 *Currà v Germany* EU:C:2012:465 (see also 9.4.2 on the human rights aspects of the case), the dispute concerned the interpretation of EU law as it related not only to national law, but also to international law. The Italian courts had ruled that Italian nationals could pursue, in the Italian courts, compensation claims against the German government for crimes that took place during the Second World War. However, the Italian government subsequently suspended the implementation of any decisions finding against the German government, pending a ruling by the International Court of Justice. The applicants, who were thereby prevented from pursuing their compensation claims, argued that this was contrary to EU law. The Italian court made a reference to the Court of Justice on the compatibility with EU law of (i) the Italian suspension of claims, (ii) a German law that restricted compensation, and (iii) State immunity from civil claims under international law. The Court of Justice held that it had no jurisdiction because the subject matter of the dispute did not fall within the ambit of EU law. Indeed, Italy and Germany had accepted the jurisdiction of the International Court of Justice over the dispute. In any event, the dispute concerned acts that took place before the EU Treaties had come into force and, in the absence of contrary intention expressed in those Treaties, the EU Treaties could not bind Member States in relation to predating acts. Accordingly, the reference was rejected in its entirety.

6.4.5 The advantages of the Court of Justice

In addition to the Court of Justice's supreme advantage in being able to give rulings that provide a uniform interpretation of EU law, it has a number of other advantages. The principle that the Court of Justice possesses certain advantages was acknowledged by the Court of

Appeal of England and Wales in *R v International Stock Exchange of the UK and the Republic of Ireland Ltd, ex p Else (1982) Ltd and others* [1993] 2 CMLR 677 (discussed also at 6.4.1, 6.4.2, 6.4.6, and 6.4.7 in relation to other guidelines on the exercise of the discretion to refer) and those advantages had previously been set out in detail by Bingham J, delivering the judgment of the High Court of England and Wales in *Commissioners of Customs and Excise v Samex ApS* [1983] 3 CMLR 194 (discussed also at 6.4.2 in relation to the relevance of a reference).

?! THINKING POINT

While reading the following extract, list the advantages that the Court of Justice was considered to have over national courts in providing rulings on EU law.

Commissioners of Customs and Excise v Samex ApS [1983] 3 CMLR 194, Queen's Bench Division

30. I therefore turn to the guidelines which the Master of the Rolls [Lord Denning, in *Bulmer Ltd and Another v Bollinger SA and Others* [1974] 2 CMLR 91] has indicated governing the exercise of discretion. He mentions, first, the time to get a ruling, second, the undesirability of overloading the Court of Justice, third, the need to formulate the question clearly, fourth, the difficulty and importance of the point …

31. In endeavouring to follow and respect these guidelines I find myself in some difficulty, because it was submitted by counsel on behalf of the defendant that the issues raised by his client should be resolved by the Court of Justice as the court best fitted to do so, and I find this a consideration which does give me some pause for thought. Sitting as a judge in a national court, asked to decide questions of Community law [now EU law], I am very conscious of the advantages enjoyed by the Court of Justice. It has a panoramic view of the Community [now Union] and its institutions, a detailed knowledge of the treaties and of much subordinate legislation made under them, and an intimate familiarity with the functioning of the Community market which no national judge denied the collective experience of the Court of Justice could hope to achieve. Where questions of administrative intention and practice arise the Court of Justice can receive submissions from the Community institutions, as also where relations between the Community and non-member states are in issue. Where the interests of member states are affected they can intervene to make their views known. That is a material consideration in this case since there is some slight evidence that the practice of different member states is divergent. Where comparison falls to be made between Community texts in different languages, all texts being equally authentic, the multinational Court of Justice is equipped to carry out the task in a way which no national judge, whatever his linguistic skills, could rival. The interpretation of Community instruments involves very often not the process familiar to common lawyers of laboriously extracting the meaning from words used but the more creative process of supplying flesh

> to a spare and loosely constructed skeleton. The choice between alternative submissions may turn not on purely legal considerations, but on a broader view of what the orderly development of the Community requires. These are matters which the Court of Justice is very much better placed to assess and determine than a national court.

According to the High Court in *Samex*, the advantages of the Court of Justice over national courts in interpreting EU law include:

- its ability to take a panoramic view of the EU and its institutions;
- its detailed knowledge of the EU Treaties and secondary legislation;
- its familiarity with the functioning of the internal market (see further 1.3 and 10.1);
- the opportunity for it to receive submissions from the other EU institutions and Member States, giving their views on the issue in question (see 6.11 on the procedure when a reference is made, and 6.4.4 on the importance to such submissions of a full explanation of the facts and national law);
- its ability to compare all of the authentic-language versions of the texts of the EU at issue; and
- its familiarity with the purposive and creative approach to interpretation required by EU law—which tends to be less detailed than English law.

?! THINKING POINT

If a national court takes into account all of the other guidelines and finds that the decision whether or not to refer is evenly balanced, what impact is taking into account the advantage of the Court of Justice likely to have on the ultimate exercise of the national court's discretion?

6.4.6 The impact of any binding domestic precedent

In many national legal systems, that of the UK included, national law provides that lower courts are, in certain circumstances, bound to follow the decision of a higher court within that national system. The existence of any such binding domestic precedent does not, however, prevent the lower court from making a reference to the Court of Justice in order to seek a preliminary ruling on the same issue. This was confirmed in Joined Cases 146 & 166/73 *Rheinmühlen-Dusseldorf v Einführ-und Vorratsstelle für Getreide und Futtermittel* [1974] ECR 33. In that case, a German appeal court had ruled that the withdrawal of export refunds from a barley exporter was contrary to EU law and the case had been sent back to the lower court, which had previously reached a different decision, to reconsider. As a matter of German law, the lower court was bound by the decision of the higher court. The lower court referred to the Court of

Justice the question of whether, in these circumstances, it was prevented from making a reference to the Court of Justice on the issues of EU law on which the higher court had already ruled. The Court of Justice held that the lower court could indeed exercise its discretion to refer in these circumstances. It confirmed that a national court was not precluded from making a reference by the existence of a domestic rule of law that required that court to follow the judgment of a higher court on points of law. The Court has more recently reached similar decisions in Case C-5/14 *Kernkraftwerke Lippe-Ems Gmbh v Kauptzollamt Osnabrück* EU:C:2015:354, [2015] 3 CMLR 41, and Case C-112/13 *A v B and others* EU:C:2014:2195.

In *Trent Taverns Ltd v Sykes* [1999] Eu LR 492, the Court of Appeal of England and Wales held that this principle applied equally to the English law doctrine of precedent, which required the Court of Appeal to follow its own judgments. However, on the facts, the Court of Appeal concluded that a reference was not necessary.

REVIEW QUESTION

Suppose that in a (fictitious) case last year the UK's Supreme Court ruled that the word 'workers' in Article 45 TFEU (see further 11.2.2) should be interpreted as meaning 'male workers' and that a subsequent case, which also involves a dispute as to the meaning of 'workers' in Article 45, is now before the High Court. Could the English law doctrine of precedent prevent the High Court from making a reference on the meaning of this term to the Court of Justice?

Answer: Even though the English doctrine of precedent obliges the High Court to apply the ruling of the Supreme Court on the meaning of Article 45 TFEU, the ruling of the Court of Justice in *Rheinmühlen* makes it clear that the High Court could still make a preliminary reference under Article 267 TFEU if appropriate (ie if the application of the other guidelines discussed in this section so indicated).

It should also be noted that the Court of Justice's ruling in *Rheinmühlen* applies similarly in circumstances in which a national court's decision to make a reference (rather than its decision on the substantive dispute) is appealed to a superior domestic court, which upholds the appeal and finds that a reference should not have been made—as was the case in *R v International Stock Exchange of the UK and the Republic of Ireland Ltd, ex p Else (1982) Ltd and others* [1993] 2 CMLR 677 (see also 6.4.1, 6.4.2, 6.4.5, and 6.4.7). Thus, as the Court held in Case C-210/06 *Cartesio Oktató és Szolgáltató bt* [2008] ECR I-9641, where a higher national court varies or sets aside a preliminary reference made by a lower court, the original reference remains in place unless revoked or amended by the court that originally made it; it is not automatically revoked or amended by the successful appeal. However, a national court whose decision to refer is successfully appealed is likely, in practice, to revoke or amend the reference rather than to maintain it.

6.4.7 Other factors influencing the exercise of the discretion

In *Bulmer Ltd and another v Bollinger SA and others* [1974] 2 CMLR 91, Lord Denning, in the Court of Appeal of England and Wales, indicated that a national court which is considering whether to exercise its discretion to refer should bear in mind the delay and expense involved in making a reference, the danger of overloading the Court of Justice, the difficulty and importance of the point to be referred, and the wishes of the parties. These guidelines are not as significant as those considered at 6.4.1–6.4.6, but, where the impact of the more significant guidelines is evenly balanced, they could be influential.

?! THINKING POINT

Which of these guidelines would, in principle, weigh against exercising the discretion to refer?

The delay and expense that making a reference would cause, and the increase in the Court of Justice's workload, would suggest that a national court should not exercise the discretion to refer. The other two factors are, in principle, neutral. It would depend on the facts and the law in a particular case whether the point of law that the national court is considering referring is sufficiently difficult and important to the outcome of the case to justify a reference. It would depend on the particular parties whether they want a reference to be made or not and, indeed, they may disagree, in which case their views will effectively cancel each other out.

The average time taken to obtain a preliminary ruling from the Court of Justice is 15 months (see 6.11.5) and has, in the past, been even longer. As previously discussed (at 6.4.2), this has on occasion led the English courts to refuse to make a reference on the grounds that questions that were relevant at the time the reference was being considered would have become irrelevant by the time a ruling was given (see eg *R v Ministry of Agriculture, Fisheries and Food, ex p Portman Agrochemicals Ltd* [1994] 3 CMLR 18, discussed at 6.4.2).

In Case C-338/95 *Wiener SI GmbH v Hauptzollamt Emmerich* [1997] ECR I-6495, Advocate General Jacobs in his Opinion (see further 2.4 on Advocate Generals' Opinions) examined the division of competence between the national courts and the Court of Justice under Article 267 TFEU. He argued that the Court of Justice could not cope with the workload which would result from the making of a reference in all cases in which a point of EU law was at issue, particularly in view of the expanding volume of EU legislation. Since the Court could not rule inadmissible questions on interpretation that had been properly referred, he considered that the national courts should exercise self-restraint in deciding whether to refer them in the first place. Where the Court had already established a body of principles as a result of previous references, national courts were in a position to apply these principles to new questions of law without making a reference (see also 6.4.3). The Advocate General concluded that the Article 267 TFEU procedure should instead focus on the reference of general questions in areas of law in which there was no comprehensive body of principles and rulings on these questions would then enable national courts to deal with more detailed questions themselves.

The Court of Justice subsequently answered the questions referred in *Wiener* without addressing these issues and the Advocate General's comments do not represent the law. Despite that, Advocate General Jacobs's comments have been cited by the Court of Appeal of England and Wales in a number of cases. In *Trinity Mirror plc v Commissioners of Customs and Excise* [2001] EWCA Civ 65, [2001] 2 CMLR 33, the Court of Appeal refused to make a reference, citing Advocate General Jacobs's comments on the need for self-restraint, as well as *R v*

International Stock Exchange of the UK and the Republic of Ireland Ltd, ex p Else (1982) Ltd and others [1993] 2 CMLR 677 on the need to refer where the national court had any real doubt (see 6.4.1). It concluded that since there was ample guidance from the Court of Justice on the question of principle in the area of law at issue, it was confident in applying that principle to the facts of the case. A similar approach was taken by the courts of England and Wales in *Littlewoods Organisation plc and others v Commissioners of Custom and Excise and others* [2001] EWCA Civ 1542, [2001] STC 1568, and *Professional Contractors' Group and others v Commissioners of Inland Revenue* [2001] EWCA Civ 1945, [2002] STC 165. Although an Opinion of an Advocate General is not binding on the national courts (see further 2.4.1), the Court of Appeal's approach indicates that the English courts may now be prepared to refuse to refer where they feel that the Court of Justice has established general principles that they themselves can apply to new situations.

One final point to add is that the European Court of Human Rights (ECtHR) (see further 9.1) has suggested, in *Ullens de Schooten and Rezabek v Belgium* Application Nos 3989/07 & 39353/07, judgment of 20 September 2011, not reported (also discussed at 6.8 in relation to the provision of reasons by the national court), albeit without ruling definitively, that a refusal to exercise the discretion to refer where a party has requested it may breach the right to a fair trial under Article 6 of the European Convention on Human Rights (ECHR), which all EU Member States have guaranteed (see further 9.1 on the ECHR).

6.4.8 Summary of the discretion to refer

The discretion to make a reference under Article 267 TFEU will arise only in certain circumstances.

- A reference can be made only by a body that constitutes a '*court or tribunal*', according to the criteria in Case C-54/96 *Dorsch Consult Ingenieurgesellschaft mbH v Bundesbaugesellschaft Berlin mbH* [1997] ECR I-496.
- A reference will be discretionary only if that court or tribunal is one against whose decisions there *is a judicial remedy under national law*—in other words, where it is possible to apply for leave to appeal against its decisions.
- A reference (discretionary or mandatory) can be made only on the *interpretation of EU law or the validity of secondary EU legislation.*

The guidelines that UK courts should take into account when exercising the discretion to refer and, in respect of each, whether it weighs in favour of making a reference or against or is neutral may be summarized as follows.

(1) Is the measure so clear (*acte clair*) that there is no room for doubt by any national court as to its meaning? If it is, then there is no need to make a reference; if it is not, then this favours making a reference to establish its meaning.

(2) In all of the circumstances of the case, is the question *relevant*, in the sense that an answer to it could be essential in order for the court to give judgment in the case? If it is, this favours making a reference; if it is not, then a reference is unnecessary.

(3) Is there *already a preliminary ruling from the Court of Justice on a similar point* that can assist the national court with the issue before it? If there is, then there is no need to make a reference—although it may still be desirable to do so.

(4) Does the case involve a *genuine dispute*? If not, there is little point in making a reference as it is likely to be rejected by the Court of Justice.

(5) Has the *factual and legal context been established*? If it has, then it must be included in the reference sent to the Court of Justice. If not (or if it is not included in the order for reference), there is little point in making a reference as it is likely to be rejected by the Court.

(6) Do the *particular questions to be referred relate directly to the dispute* before the national court? If not (or if their relevance is not explained by the national court in its order for reference), there is little point in referring them as the Court of Justice is unlikely to answer them.

In addition, the national court should also consider:

(a) the need for a *uniform interpretation* of EU law, which is, after all, the purpose of Article 267 TFEU (and which suggests that a reference should be made);

(b) the *advantages possessed by the Court of Justice* in interpreting EU law (which suggest that a reference should be made);

(c) the *delay and expense* involved in making a reference (both of which suggest that a reference should not be made);

(d) the *wishes of the parties* (the impact of which depends on what those wishes are in a particular case); and

(e) the fact that the existence of *domestic precedent on the issue of EU law cannot prevent* a national court from making a reference.

If the reference involves a question as to the *validity* of EU law rather than its interpretation, the national court also needs to consider the fact that it cannot itself declare EU law invalid (see further 6.6).

6.5 Mandatory references

Article 267 TFEU provides that where there is no judicial remedy under national law against the decision of a particular court or tribunal, that court 'shall' make a reference to the Court of Justice, provided that it is a 'court or tribunal' for the purposes of the Article (see 6.2) and that the issue to be referred concerns the interpretation of EU law or the validity of EU secondary legislation (see 6.1.1). This may sound simple enough, but, as will be seen, mandatory references have provoked almost as much dispute as discretionary references.

THINKING POINT

According to Article 267 TFEU, when will a reference be mandatory?

Although the text of Article 267 TFEU makes it appear that a reference is absolutely mandatory from a court against whose decisions there is no judicial remedy under national law—ie no possibility of requesting leave to appeal (see further 6.3.1)—the Court of Justice has ruled that there are in fact situations in which this obligation does not arise. The leading case is Case 283/81 *CILFIT and Lanificio di Gavardo SpA v Ministry of Health* [1982] ECR 3415, which has already been discussed at 6.4.1 in relation to the *acte clair* guideline. In that case, the Italian government claimed that a reference was unnecessary because the meaning of the EU law in question was clear. The Italian court made a reference to the Court of Justice on the obligations of a court from whose decisions there was no judicial remedy under national law. The Court of Justice ruled that there was no obligation to refer, even from a court whose decision was not subject to the possibility of appeal, if one of three conditions was fulfilled. It also noted, however, that even if no such obligation existed, the national court nonetheless had a discretion to make a reference if it considered it to be necessary.

?! THINKING POINT

While reading the following extract, note the three separate situations in which a court against whose decisions there is no judicial remedy under national law will not be obliged to make a reference.

Case 283/81 *CILFIT and Lanificio di Gavardo Spa v Ministry of Health* [1982] ECR 3415

7. That obligation to refer a matter to the Court of Justice is based on cooperation, established with a view to ensuring the proper application and uniform interpretation of Community law [now EU law] in all the Member States, between national courts, in their capacity as courts responsible for the application of Community law, and the Court of Justice. More particularly, the third paragraph of Article 177 [EC, now Article 267 TFEU] seeks to prevent the occurrence within the Community [now Union] of divergences in judicial decisions on questions of Community law. The scope of that obligation must therefore be assessed, in view of those objectives, by reference to the powers of the national courts, on the one hand, and those of the Court of Justice, on the other, where such a question of interpretation is raised within the meaning of Article 177.
8. In this connection, it is necessary to define the meaning for the purposes of Community law of the expression 'where any such question is raised' in order to determine the circumstances in which a national court or tribunal against whose decisions there is no judicial remedy under national law is obliged to bring a matter before the Court of Justice.
9. In this regard, it must in the first place be pointed out that Article 177 does not constitute a means of redress available to the parties to a case pending before a national court or tribunal. Therefore the mere fact that a party contends that the dispute gives rise to a question

concerning the interpretation of Community law does not mean that the court or tribunal concerned is compelled to consider that a question has been raised within the meaning of Article 177. On the other hand, a national court or tribunal may, in an appropriate case, refer a matter to the Court of Justice of its own motion.

10. Secondly, it follows from the relationship between the second and third paragraphs of Article 177 that the courts or tribunals referred to in the third paragraph have the same discretion as any other national court or tribunal to ascertain whether a decision on a question of Community law is necessary to enable them to give judgment. Accordingly, those courts or tribunals are not obliged to refer to the Court of Justice a question concerning the interpretation of Community law raised before them if that question is not relevant, that is to say, if the answer to that question, regardless of what it may be, can in no way affect the outcome of the case.

11. If, however, those courts or tribunals consider that recourse to Community law is necessary to enable them to decide a case, Article 177 imposes an obligation on them to refer to the Court of Justice any question of interpretation which may arise.

12. The question submitted by the Corte di Cassazione seeks to ascertain whether, in certain circumstances, the obligation laid down by the third paragraph of Article 177 might none the less be subject to certain restrictions.

13. It must be remembered in this connection that in its judgment of 27 March 1963 in Joined Cases 28 to 30/62 (*Da Costa v Nederlandse Belastingadministratie* [1963] ECR 31) the Court ruled that: 'Although the third paragraph of Article 177 unreservedly requires courts or tribunals of a Member State against whose decisions there is no judicial remedy under national law … to refer to the Court every question of interpretation raised before them, the authority of an interpretation under Article 177 already given by the Court may deprive the obligation of its purpose and thus empty it of its substance. Such is the case especially when the question raised is materially identical with a question which has already been the subject of a preliminary ruling in a similar case.'

14. The same effect, as regards the limits set to the obligation laid down by the third paragraph of Article 177, may be produced where previous decisions of the Court have already dealt with the point of law in question, irrespective of the nature of the proceedings which led to those decisions, even though the questions at issue are not strictly identical.

15. However, it must not be forgotten that in all such circumstances national courts and tribunals, including those referred to in the third paragraph of Article 177, remain entirely at liberty to bring a matter before the Court of Justice if they consider it appropriate to do so.

16. Finally, the correct application of Community law may be so obvious as to leave no scope for any reasonable doubt as to the manner in which the question raised is to be resolved. Before it comes to the conclusion that such is the case, the national court or tribunal must be convinced that the matter is equally obvious to the courts of the other Member States and to the Court of Justice. Only if those conditions are satisfied may the national court or tribunal refrain from submitting the question to the Court of Justice and take upon itself the responsibility for resolving it.

The three situations in which a court against whose decisions there is no judicial remedy under national law is nonetheless not obliged to make a reference will now be discussed.

6.5.1 *Acte clair*

The Court of Justice in *CILFIT* noted that the interpretation of an EU measure which was *acte clair* need not be referred to the Court of Justice even by a national court against whose decisions there is no judicial remedy under national law.

?! THINKING POINT

What does the term *'acte clair'* mean? If you have difficulty in answering this question, review 6.4.1.

The meaning of *acte clair* is discussed at 6.4.1 in relation to discretionary references. The only differences in relation to mandatory references are that a court from which a reference is mandatory is—as compared to a court from which a reference is discretionary—both much less likely to be a court of first instance and also much more likely to consist of more than one judge. As a result, it is much more likely that more than one judge has been seised of the case by the time the making of a reference is being considered and therefore that there has already been judicial agreement or disagreement at national level on the meaning of the particular EU law at issue, and this agreement or disagreement should be taken into account in determining whether the measure is *acte clair* (see further 6.4.1).

6.5.2 Relevance

The Court of Justice in *CILFIT* noted that the interpretation of an EU measure which was not relevant to the dispute before the national court should not be referred to the Court of Justice, even when that national court was a court against whose decisions there is no judicial remedy under national law.

The meaning of 'relevance' in the context of Article 267 TFEU is discussed at 6.4.2 in relation to discretionary references. It has exactly the same meaning in relation to mandatory references.

?! THINKING POINT

What does the term 'relevant' mean in the context of preliminary references? If you have difficulty in answering this question, review 6.4.2.

6.5.3 Previous Court of Justice rulings

The Court of Justice in *CILFIT* cited Joined Cases 28–30/62 *Da Costa En Schaake NV and others v Nederlandse Belastingadministratie* [1963] ECR 31 (see 6.4.3) as authority that the existence of a ruling by the Court of Justice on the interpretation of the EU measure at issue in the case could obviate the need to make a reference to it. This is so whether reference is discretionary or mandatory and therefore the discussion of this issue at 6.4.2 in relation to discretionary references is also relevant here. In both cases, however, it remains open to the national court to make a reference on the issue if it considers that it is 'desirable' to do so (*Da Costa*, at para 38).

?! THINKING POINT

In what particular circumstances might a national court consider it to be 'desirable' to refer a question that has already been decided by the Court of Justice? If you have difficulty in answering this question, review 6.4.3.

REVIEW QUESTION

What problems might be caused if courts against whose decisions there is no judicial remedy under national law habitually make use of the grounds given in *CILFIT* in order to avoid making a reference?

Answer: Among the problems that may result are the inconsistent interpretation and application of EU law across the Member States, injustice to particular applicants in whose cases no reference is made and a mistake is made as to EU law, and a diminution of the role of the Court of Justice. If such a court refuses to refer, an applicant has no possibility of appeal against the refusal but may, however, have an independent claim in damages against the State on the basis of the national court's wrongful refusal to refer, if the court also made an error of EU law in its judgment (see 5.4.4).

6.5.4 The possibility of rejection of the reference

The discussion at 6.4.4 of the possibility of the Court rejecting a reference in the context of discretionary references is equally applicable to mandatory references. Thus a court against whose decisions there is no judicial remedy under national law should not make a reference if one or more grounds exist on which the Court of Justice is likely to reject the reference. These grounds are discussed at 6.4.4.

?! THINKING POINT

On what grounds may the Court of Justice reject a reference? If you have difficulty in answering this question, review 6.4.4.

6.5.5 Refusal to make a mandatory reference in breach of the ECHR

The ECtHR (see further 9.1) has ruled that a refusal by a national court of last instance to make a reference to the Court of Justice will breach the right to a fair trial in Article 6 ECHR if that national court provides no reasoning to justify its refusal (see eg *Dhahbi v Italy* Application No 17120/09 [2014] ECHR 719, and *Schipani v Italy* Application No 38369/09 [2015] ECHR 735. In *Dhahbi*, at para 33, the ECtHR stated that '[i]t is therefore not clear from the reasoning of the impugned judgment [of the national court] whether [the question of EU law] was not considered to be relevant or to relate to a provision which was clear or had already been interpreted by the [Court of Justice], or whether it was simply ignored'. It is interesting to note, however, that one of the judges of the ECtHR in *Schipani* (Judge Wojtyczek) gave a separate judgment (which does not form part of the majority judgment of the Court and therefore does not represent the law) in which he argued that lack of reasoning should not automatically constitute a breach of Article 6 ECHR, but should be considered in the context of the seriousness of the interference with human rights in the case.

6.5.6 Summary of the obligation to refer

The circumstances in which the obligation to make a reference under Article 267 TFEU will arise are as follows.

- A reference can only be made by a body that constitutes a '*court or tribunal*' according to the criteria in Case C-54/96 *Dorsch Consult Ingenieurgesellschaft mbH v Bundesbaugesellschaft Berlin mbH* [1997] ECR I-496.
- A reference will only be mandatory if that court or tribunal is one against whose decisions there is *no judicial remedy under national law*—in other words, where it is not possible to apply for leave to appeal.
- A reference (discretionary or mandatory) can only be made on the *interpretation of EU law or the validity of secondary EU legislation.*

By way of exception, the national court is not obliged to refer if any one of the *CILFIT exceptions* are satisfied, that is to say:

(1) the EU measure that would be the subject of the reference is *acte clair*;

(2) the EU measure that would be the subject of the reference is *not relevant* to the outcome of the case;

(3) the Court of Justice has already given a ruling on the EU measure at issue; or

(4) the reference is likely to be *rejected* by the Court of Justice because:

  - the case does not involve a *genuine dispute*;
  - the *factual and legal context has not been established*; or
  - the *particular questions to be referred do not relate directly to the dispute* before the national court.

If the reference involves a question as to the *validity* of EU law, rather than its interpretation, the national court also needs to consider the fact that it cannot itself declare EU law invalid (see further 6.6).

6.6 References concerning the validity of EU law

In this chapter, discussion of preliminary references has so far largely been concerned with references on the interpretation of EU law (either Treaties or secondary legislation). Such references constitute the majority of all preliminary references made to the Court of Justice. However, Article 267 TFEU also permits preliminary references to be made concerning the validity of EU secondary legislation (see 6.1.1).

?! THINKING POINT

What measures of EU law may not be the subject of a reference as to their validity?

Article 267 TFEU only permits questions to be referred on the validity of EU secondary legislation and thus the validity of the EU Treaties may not be questioned.

Whereas a national court may often be able to interpret EU law itself, either because it is *acte clair* or because the Court of Justice has previously given a ruling as to the correct interpretation, it is much less likely that it will be competent to resolve questions as to the validity of an EU measure. This was explained in the Court's ruling in Case 314/85 *Firma Foto-Frost v Hauptzollamt Lübeck-Ost* [1987] ECR 4199, in which an EU levy was payable on imports of binoculars into Germany by Foto-Frost. The levy was subject to a waiver in certain circumstances, but the EU Commission (see further 2.3 on the Commission) adopted a Decision (see further 3.4.3 on Decisions) stating that, in this instance, the waiver could not apply. Foto-Frost applied to the German courts to have the Decision set aside. The German court requested a preliminary ruling on a number of questions, including whether it could declare an EU Decision invalid. The Court of Justice ruled that no national court could declare the act of an EU institution invalid, although a national court could make a declaration of validity; only the Court of Justice could declare such an act invalid.

?! THINKING POINT

When reading the following extract, note the reasons given by the Court for ruling that a national court could not declare EU law invalid.

Case 314/85 *Firma Foto-Frost v Hauptzollamt Lübeck-Ost* [1987] ECR 4199

13. In enabling national courts, against those decisions where there is a judicial remedy under national law, to refer to the Court for a preliminary ruling questions on interpretation or validity, Article 177 [EC, now Article 267 TFEU] did not settle the question whether those courts themselves may declare that acts of Community [now Union] institutions are invalid.
14. Those courts may consider the validity of a Community act and, if they consider that the grounds put forward before them by the parties in support of invalidity are unfounded, they may reject them, concluding that the measure is completely valid. By taking that action they are not calling into question the existence of the Community measure.
15. On the other hand, those courts do not have the power to declare acts of the Community institutions invalid. As the Court emphasized in the judgment of 13 May 1981 in Case 66/80 *International Chemical Corporation v Amministrazione delle Finanze* [1981] ECR 1191, the main purpose of the powers accorded to the Court by Article 177 is to ensure that Community law [now EU law] is applied uniformly by national courts. That requirement of uniformity is particularly imperative when the validity of a Community act is in question. Divergences between courts in the Member States as to the validity of Community acts would be liable to place in jeopardy the very unity of the Community legal order and detract from the fundamental requirement of legal certainty.
16. The same conclusion is dictated by consideration of the necessary coherence of the system of judicial protection established by the Treaty. In that regard it must be observed that requests for preliminary rulings, like actions for annulment, constitute means for reviewing the legality of acts of the Community institutions. As the Court pointed out in its judgment of 23 April 1986 in Case 294/83 *Parti Ecologiste 'les Verts' v European Parliament* [1986] ECR 1339, 'in Articles 173 and 184, on the one hand, and in Article 177, on the other, the Treaty established a complete system of legal remedies and procedures designed to permit the Court of Justice to review the legality of measures adopted by the institutions'.
17. Since Article 173 [EC, now Article 263 TFEU] gives the Court exclusive jurisdiction to declare void an act of a Community institution, the coherence of the system requires that where the validity of a Community act is challenged before a national court the power to declare the act invalid must also be reserved to the Court of Justice.
18. It must also be emphasized that the Court of Justice is in the best position to decide on the validity of Community acts. Under Article 20 of the Protocol on the Statute of the Court of Justice of the EEC, Community institutions whose acts are challenged are entitled to participate in the proceedings in order to defend the validity of the acts in question. Furthermore, under the second paragraph of Article 21 of that Protocol the Court may require the Member States and institutions which are not participating in the proceedings to supply all information which it considers necessary for the purposes of the case before it.

19. It should be added that the rule that national courts may not themselves declare Community acts invalid may have to be qualified in certain circumstances in the case of proceedings relating to an application for interim measures; however, that case is not referred to in the national court's question.
20. The answer to the first question must therefore be that the national courts have no jurisdiction themselves to declare that acts of Community institutions are invalid.

The Court in *Foto-Frost* explained that only it could declare such an act invalid; any other conclusion would destroy the uniform application of EU law and infringe the principle of legal certainty (see 5.4.4 on this principle). Further, since Article 263 TFEU (see Chapter 7) gave the Court exclusive competence to declare EU law invalid, the coherence of the EU legal system required that the power under Article 267 TFEU be interpreted accordingly. Finally, the Court held that it was in the best position to rule on the validity of EU laws because the EU legislative institutions (see further Chapter 2) that had adopted those laws were entitled to participate in the proceedings before it, and it could ask for further information from the EU institutions or Member States (see further Figure 6.2, at 6.11.4).

→ CROSS-REFERENCE
On the exception relating to interim measures referred to in *Foto-Frost*, at para 19, see further 6.10.

The ruling in *Foto-Frost* is now enshrined in the formal guidance published by the Court of Justice on this and many other issues concerned with Article 267 TFEU references, in its Recommendations to national courts and tribunals in relation to the initiation of preliminary ruling proceedings, OJ 2012 C338/01. The key statements on validity are set out in the following extract.

Court of Justice, Recommendations to national courts and tribunals in relation to the initiation of preliminary ruling proceedings, OJ 2012 C338/01

[...]

5. Since the preliminary ruling procedure is based on cooperation between the Court of Justice and the courts and tribunals of the Member States, it may be helpful, in order to ensure that that procedure is fully effective, to provide those courts and tribunals with the following recommendations.
6. While in no way binding, these recommendations are intended to supplement Title III of the Rules of Procedure of the Court of Justice (Articles 93 to 118) and to provide guidance to the courts and tribunals of the Member States as to whether it is appropriate to make a reference for a preliminary ruling, as well as practical information concerning the form and effect of such a reference.

[...]

References on determination of validity

15. Although the courts and tribunals of the Member States may reject pleas raised before them challenging the validity of acts of an institution, body, office or agency of the Union, the Court of Justice has exclusive jurisdiction to declare such an act invalid.

16. All national courts or tribunals must therefore submit a request for a preliminary ruling to the Court when they have doubts about the validity of such an act, stating the reasons for which they consider that the act may be invalid.
17. However, if a national court or tribunal has serious doubts about the validity of an act of an institution, body, office or agency of the Union on which a national measure is based, it may exceptionally suspend application of that measure temporarily or grant other interim relief with respect to it. It must then refer the question of validity to the Court of Justice, stating the reasons for which it considers the act to be invalid.

To summarize, a national court should make a reference to the Court of Justice whenever there is some doubt as to the validity of an EU measure that is relevant to the outcome of the case.

There is, however, an alternative route to challenging the validity of a piece of EU law if its validity is the only issue in dispute. That route is set out in Article 263 TFEU (see Chapter 7), and the Court of First Instance (now the General Court) in Case T-177/01 *Jégo Quéré & Cie SA v Commission* [2002] ECR II-2365 (see 7.9.1 and 9.5.1) and Advocate General Jacobs in that case and in Case C-50/00 P *Unión de Pequeños Agricultores v Council, Commission intervening* (*UPA*) [2002] 3 CMLR 1 (see 7.9.1 and 9.5.1) both criticized the use of Article 267 TFEU as a method for an individual or business to obtain a declaration that an EU measure was unlawful. The reasoning of the Advocate General appears in the following extract.

?! THINKING POINT

While reading the following extract, note the criticisms of Article 267 TFEU as a route to obtaining a ruling on the invalidity of EU law which were made by the Advocate General.

Case C-50/00 P *Unión de Pequeños Agricultores v Council, Commission intervening (UPA)* [2002] 3 CMLR 1, Opinion of Advocate General Jacobs

Proceedings before national courts may not provide effective judicial protection of individual applicants

38. As is common ground in the present case, the case-law of the Court of Justice acknowledges the principle that an individual who considers himself wronged by a measure which deprives him of a right or advantage under Community law [now EU law] must have access to a remedy against that measure and be able to obtain complete judicial protection.
39. That principle is, as the Court has repeatedly stated, grounded in the constitutional traditions common to the Member States and in Articles 6 and 13 of the European Convention on Human Rights. Moreover, the Charter of fundamental rights of the European Union, while itself not legally binding, proclaims a generally recognised principle in stating in Article 47 that [e]veryone whose rights and freedoms guaranteed by the law of the Union are violated has the right to an effective remedy before a tribunal.

40. In my view, proceedings before national courts are not, however, capable of guaranteeing that individuals seeking to challenge the validity of Community [now Union] measures are granted fully effective judicial protection.

41. It may be recalled, first of all, that the national courts are not competent to declare measures of Community law invalid. In a case concerning the validity of a Community measure, the competence of the national court is limited to assessing whether the applicant's arguments raise sufficient doubts about the validity of the impugned measure to justify a request for a preliminary ruling from the Court of Justice. It seems to me, therefore, artificial to argue that the national courts are the correct forum for such cases. The strictly limited competence of national courts in cases concerning the validity of Community measures may be contrasted with the important role which they play in cases concerning the interpretation, application and enforcement of Community law. In such cases, the national courts may, as the Commission stated at the hearing, be described as the ordinary courts of Community law. That description is, however, not appropriate for cases which do not involve questions of interpretation, but raise only issues of the validity of Community measures, since in such cases the national courts do not have power to decide what is at issue.

42. Second, the principle of effective judicial protection requires that applicants have access to a court which is competent to grant remedies capable of protecting them against the effects of unlawful measures. Access to the Court of Justice via Article 234 EC [now Article 267 TFEU] is however not a remedy available to individual applicants as a matter of right. National courts may refuse to refer questions, and although courts of last instance are obliged to refer under the third paragraph of Article 234 EC, appeals within the national judicial systems are liable to entail long delays which may themselves be incompatible with the principle of effective judicial protection and with the need for legal certainty. National courts—even at the highest level—might also err in their preliminary assessment of the validity of general Community measures and decline to refer questions of validity to the Court of Justice on that basis. Moreover, where a reference is made, it is in principle for the national court to formulate the questions to be answered by the Court of Justice. Individual applicants might thus find their claims redefined by the questions referred. Questions formulated by national courts might, for example, limit the range of Community measures which an applicant has sought to challenge or the grounds of invalidity on which he has sought to rely.

43. Third, it may be difficult, and in some cases perhaps impossible, for individual applicants to challenge Community measures which—as appears to be the case for the contested regulation—do not require any acts of implementation by national authorities. In that situation, there may be no measure which is capable of forming the basis of an action before national courts. The fact that an individual affected by a Community measure might, in some instances, be able to bring the validity of a Community measure before the national courts by violating the rules laid down by the measures and rely on the invalidity of those rules as a defence in criminal or civil proceedings directed against him does not offer the individual an adequate means of judicial protection. Individuals clearly cannot be required to breach the law in order to gain access to justice.

44. Finally, compared to a direct action before the Court of First Instance, proceedings before the national courts present serious disadvantages for individual applicants. Proceedings in

the national courts, with the additional stage of a reference under Article 234 EC, are likely to involve substantial extra delays and costs. The potential for delay inherent in proceedings brought before domestic courts, with the possibility of appeals within the national system, makes it likely that interim measures will be necessary in many cases. However, although national courts have jurisdiction to suspend a national measure based on a Community measure or otherwise to grant interim relief pending a ruling from the Court of Justice, the exercise of that jurisdiction is subject to a number of conditions and is—despite the Court's attempts to provide guidance as to the application of those conditions—to some extent dependent on the discretion of national courts. In any event, interim measures awarded by a national court would be confined to the Member State in question, and applicants might therefore have to bring proceedings in more than one Member State. That would, given the possibility of conflicting decisions by courts in different Member States, prejudice the uniform application of Community law, and in extreme cases could totally subvert it.

Proceedings before the Court of First Instance under Article 230 EC are generally more appropriate for determining issues of validity than reference proceedings under Article 234 EC

45. I consider, moreover, that proceedings before the Court of First Instance under Article 230 EC [now Article 263 TFEU] are generally more appropriate for determining issues of validity than reference proceedings under Article 234 EC.

46. The procedure is more appropriate because the institution which adopted the impugned measure is a party to the proceedings from beginning to end and because a direct action involves a full exchange of pleadings, as opposed to a single round of observations followed by oral observations before the Court. The availability of interim relief under Articles 242 and 243 EC [now Articles 278 and 279 TFEU], effective in all Member States, is also a major advantage for individual applicants and for the uniformity of Community law.

47. Moreover, where a direct action is brought, the public is informed of the existence of the action by means of a notice published in the Official Journal and third parties may, if they are able to establish a sufficient interest, intervene in accordance with Article 37 of the Statute of the Court. In reference proceedings interested individuals cannot submit observations under Article 20 of the Statute unless they have intervened in the action before the national court. That may be difficult, for although information about reference proceedings is published in the Official Journal, individuals may not be aware of actions in the national courts at a sufficiently early stage to intervene.

48. Of even greater importance is the point that it is manifestly desirable for reasons of legal certainty that challenges to the validity of Community acts be brought as soon as possible after their adoption. While direct actions must be brought within the time-limit of two months laid down in the fifth paragraph of Article 230 EC, the validity of Community measures may, in principle, be questioned before the national courts at any point in time. The strict criteria for standing for individual applicants under the existing case-law on Article 230 EC make it necessary for such applicants to bring issues of validity before the Court via Article 234 EC, and may thus have the effect of reducing legal certainty.

The Advocate General's criticisms in *Jégo-Quéré* of Article 267 TFEU as a route to obtaining a ruling of invalidity may be summarized as follows.

- National courts are not competent to declare EU law invalid.
- An applicant has no right to decide whether a reference is made by the national court or which questions it refers.
- Where there is no national measure implementing the EU law at issue (as was the case in *Jégo-Quéré*), there is no measure to form the basis of an action before a national court, and the applicant's only option would be to breach the EU law and then assert the illegality of that law in proceedings brought against it in respect of its breach. Individuals should not be required to breach the law in order to gain access to justice.
- A reference under Article 267 TFEU involves substantial extra costs and delays (see also 6.4.7 on these considerations).
- Those delays may necessitate the granting of interim measures by a national court pending a ruling from the Court of Justice. This would be up to the discretion of the national court and, even if granted, the impact of the measures would be confined to that Member State, which, in some cases, might mean that separate applications would have to be brought in each Member State where interim measures were required, thus prejudicing the uniform application of EU law.

The Advocate General also criticized Article 267 TFEU in comparison to Article 263 TFEU (see further 7.9.1), arguing that it had the following comparative disadvantages.

- The institution which adopted the allegedly invalid act is not a party to the proceedings from start to finish.
- The procedure (see 6.10) only involves a single round of observations followed by oral observations from the Court rather than a full exchange of pleadings.
- Interim relief is not available from the Court of Justice itself, but only from the national court.
- Only Member States, EU institutions, and those who had intervened in the national proceedings can intervene in the proceedings before the Court of Justice, rather than all third parties who can establish a sufficient interest.
- The absence of any time limit (unlike the time limit on the bringing of an application under Article 263 TFEU—see 7.13) on the making of a reference was prejudicial to the interests of legal certainty in relation to the validity of a particular measure.

6.7 Summary of the national courts' decision-making process in preliminary references

Figure 6.1 provides a summary of the national courts' decision-making process in preliminary references.

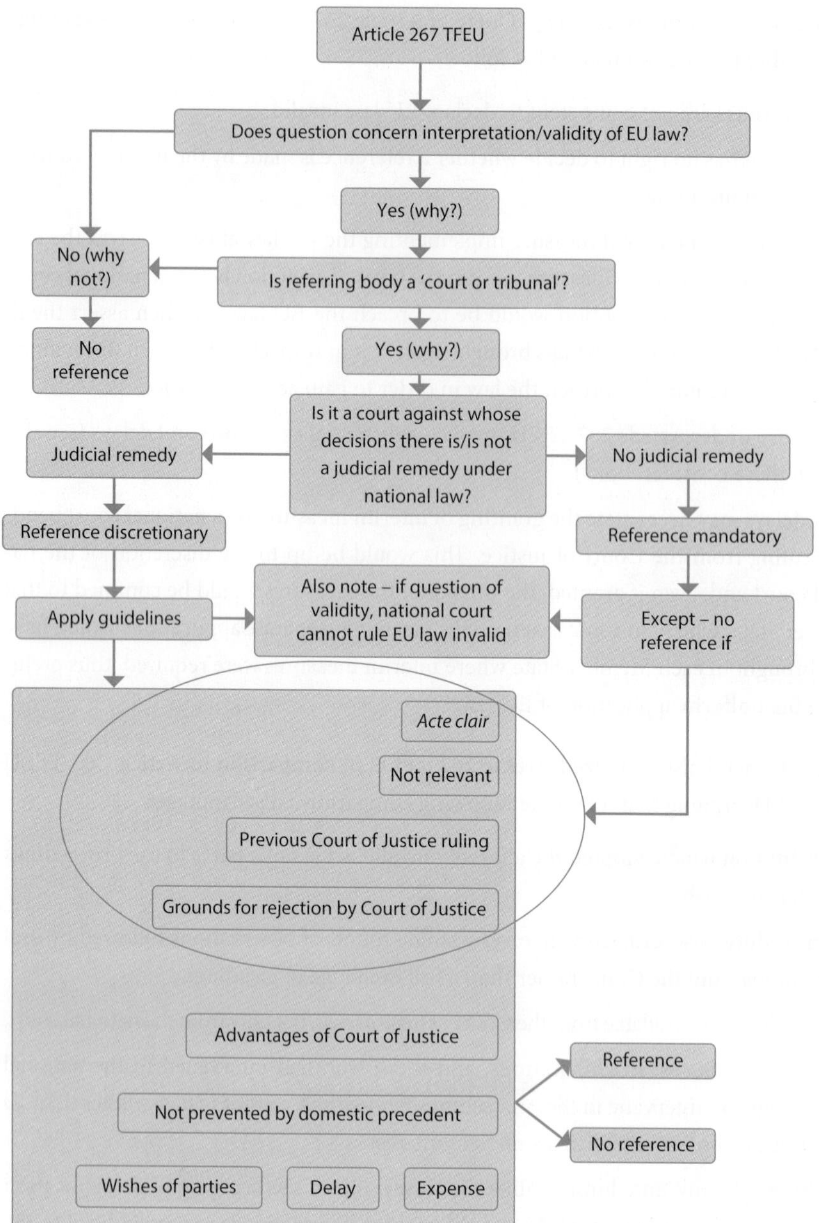

Figure 6.1 The decision as to whether to make a preliminary reference

6.8 The provision of reasons by the national court for not making a reference

The ECtHR (see further 9.1) ruled, in *Ullens de Schooten and Rezabek v Belgium* Application Nos 3989/07 & 39353/07, judgment of 20 September 2011, not reported (also discussed at 6.4.7 in relation to refusals to refer where a party has requested a reference), that the right to a fair trial under Article 6 ECHR, which all EU Member States have guaranteed (see further 9.1 on the ECHR), obliged national courts to give reasons for refusing to make a reference, whether the reference was discretionary or mandatory. This is essential in order for the parties and the public to understand the judgment, and for the parties to know whether and on what grounds to appeal against the refusal (where the national court is a court against whose decisions there is the possibility of appeal).

6.9 The timing of the reference

The timing of the reference is not about *whether* a reference should be made in a particular case, but about *when* any reference should be made—in other words, at what point during the hearing before the national court. It is, however, connected with one of the same issues that influence whether a reference should be made at all.

In Joined Cases 36 & 71/80 *Irish Creamery Milk Suppliers Association v Ireland* [1981] ECR 735, agricultural producers argued that an Irish levy on certain agricultural products was contrary to a number of EU Regulations and Treaty provisions. The Irish government wished to delay the Article 267 TFEU reference until the facts had been established. In its reference to the Court of Justice, the Irish court asked not only for an interpretation of the EU laws at issue, but also for clarification as to the correct timing of the reference.

?! THINKING POINT

What might be the consequence of making a reference before the national court has established the relevant facts and law?

The Court of Justice ruled that it was for the national court to decide on the most appropriate time to make a reference, but that it might be more convenient to make a reference *after* the facts of the case and questions of national law had been determined (see eg the approach of the UK's Upper Tribunal (Tax and Chancery Chamber) in *Coal Staff Superannuation Scheme Trustees Ltd v Commissioners for HMRC* [2017] UKUT 137 (TCC), discussed at 6.13). The Court of Justice would then have a clear legal context in which to give its ruling and so the ruling would be more likely to assist the national court.

The Court of Justice has now enshrined its guidance on this and many other issues concerned with Article 267 TFEU in its Recommendations to national courts and tribunals in relation to the initiation of preliminary ruling proceedings, OJ 2012 C338/01. The key statements on the timing of the reference are set out in the following extract.

Court of Justice, Recommendations to national courts and tribunals in relation to the initiation of preliminary ruling proceedings, OJ 2012 C338/01

The appropriate stage at which to make a reference for a preliminary ruling

18. A national court or tribunal may submit a request for a preliminary ruling to the Court as soon as it finds that a ruling on the interpretation or validity of European Union law is necessary to enable it to give judgment. It is that court or tribunal which is in fact in the best position to decide at what stage of the proceedings such a request should be made.
19. It is, however, desirable that a decision to make a reference for a preliminary ruling should be taken when the national proceedings have reached a stage at which the referring court or tribunal is able to define the legal and factual context of the case, so that the Court of Justice has available to it all the information necessary to check, where appropriate, that European Union law applies to the main proceedings. In the interests of the proper administration of justice, it may also be desirable for the reference to be made only after both sides have been heard.

6.10 Interim measures

As has already been discussed, it is not uncommon for 15 months to elapse between the making of a reference by a national court and the giving of a ruling by the Court of Justice, and thus, in some circumstances, one party may wish to request interim relief in the form of the suspension of national law, either because it is alleged to be inconsistent with EU law, as interpreted by the Court of Justice, or because it implements allegedly invalid EU law.

6.10.1 Suspension of national measures based on allegedly invalid EU law

In Case C-465/93 *Atlanta Fruchthandelsgesellschaft mbH and others v Bundesamt für Ernahrung und Forstwirtschaft* [1995] ECR I-3761, the Court of Justice laid down conditions to be applied by national courts when granting interim relief in the form of the suspension of national law implementing the disputed EU law, pending the outcome of a reference to the Court of Justice on the validity of that EU law. These conditions are that:

(a) the national court seriously doubts the validity of the EU law and the issue has already been referred to the Court of Justice;

(b) interim relief is necessary as a matter of urgency to avoid serious and irreparable damage to the applicant;

(c) due account of the effect of any suspension on the whole regime of EU law has been taken; and

(d) due account of any decisions of the Court of Justice or the General Court on the validity of the EU law (see further Chapter 7 on obtaining a ruling on validity), or on any similar application for interim relief, has been taken.

6.10.2 Suspension of national measures that may be incompatible with EU law as it is correctly interpreted

In *R v Secretary of State for Transport, ex p Factortame Ltd* (judgment of 10 March 1989, unreported) (see further 3.1.2, 4.2.5, and 5.4.1) the High Court of England and Wales referred to the Court of Justice a number of questions concerning the interpretation of EU law. The answers to those questions (subsequently given in Case C-221/89 *R v Secretary of State for Transport, ex p Factortame Ltd ('Factortame II')* [1991] ECR I-3905) were required in order to determine whether certain provisions of the Merchant Shipping Act 1988 contravened EU law and were therefore invalid. Pending receipt of the preliminary ruling from the Court of Justice, the High Court granted interim relief in the form of the suspension of the disputed provisions of the 1988 Act. The Secretary of State appealed against the granting of interim relief and the Court of Appeal upheld the appeal. During the hearing of the appeal, the House of Lords (now the Supreme Court) made a further reference to the Court of Justice as to whether, given that there was no power to grant such relief as a matter of national law, any such power or obligation arose as a matter of EU law ([1989] 3 CMLR 1).

The Court of Justice ruled, in Case C-213/89 *R v Secretary of State for Transport, ex p Factortame Ltd ('Factortame I')* [1990] ECR I-2433 (see further 3.1.2 and 4.3.3), that if the only obstacle to the granting of interim relief suspending the operation of the Act was a rule of national law, the national court must set aside that rule. Rights under EU law could not be truly effective if those who sought to enforce them were prejudiced by the operation of the allegedly conflicting national legislation while the issue was being resolved. In *Factortame II*, the contested provisions of the Merchant Shipping Act 1988 were found to be contrary to EU law and therefore invalid under s 2(4) of the European Communities Act 1972 (see further 3.1.2).

Although the Court of Justice ruled in *Factortame I* that suspension of national law must be possible in these circumstances, it was left for the House of Lords, on receipt of this ruling, to lay down guidelines for the award of this remedy. The House of Lords ruled, in *R v Secretary of State for Transport, ex p Factortame Ltd* [1990] 3 CMLR 375, that the applicants must demonstrate:

(1) a strong prima facie case that the national law was incompatible with EU law; and

(2) that the balance of convenience favoured the granting of an injunction suspending the Act.

The House of Lords concluded that a strong prima facie case had been shown by the Spanish fishermen that the Merchant Shipping Act 1988 was incompatible with EU law. It also concluded that the balance of convenience favoured the granting of an injunction, since the damage likely to be caused (to the British fishing industry) by the injunction was outweighed by that likely to be caused (to the Spanish fishermen) by the continued application of the Act.

6.11 The procedure

There are four procedures in the Court of Justice for dealing with preliminary references under Article 267 TFEU: one standard and three special. The standard procedure is discussed in detail at 6.11.4, and the special procedures at 6.11.5. However, certain elements are common to all procedures: the drafting of the reference; pleadings before the Court of Justice; and the position as to costs and legal aid.

6.11.1 The drafting of the reference

Once a national court has made a decision to make a reference to the Court of Justice under Article 267 TFEU, that national court must draft the reference. The parties are normally consulted by it on the wording of the questions to be referred.

?! **THINKING POINT**

The importance of the national court giving the Court of Justice sufficient information about the facts and the national law in the order for reference, and the possible consequences of failing to do so, has been explained at 6.4.4 and 6.4.5. Whose role(s) could be prejudiced by the absence of this information?

The following extract from the Court of Justice's Recommendations to national courts and tribunals in relation to the initiation of preliminary ruling proceedings, OJ 2012 C338/01, sets out the considerations that should be taken into account when drafting a reference to the Court of Justice under Article 267 TFEU.

Court of Justice, Recommendations to national courts and tribunals in relation to the initiation of preliminary ruling proceedings, OJ 2012 C338/01

The form and content of the request for a preliminary ruling

20. The decision by which a court or tribunal of a Member State refers one or more questions to the Court of Justice for a preliminary ruling may be in any form allowed by national law as regards procedural steps. However, it must be borne in mind that it is that document which will serve as the basis of the proceedings before the Court and that it must therefore contain such information as will enable the Court to give a reply which is of assistance to the referring court or tribunal. Moreover, it is only the request for a preliminary ruling which is notified to the parties to the main proceedings and to the other interested persons referred to in Article 23 of the Statute, including the Member States, in order to obtain any written observations.
21. Owing to the need to translate it into all the official languages of the European Union, the request for a preliminary ruling should therefore be drafted simply, clearly and precisely, avoiding superfluous detail.

22. About 10 pages is often sufficient to set out in a proper manner the context of a request for a preliminary ruling. That request must be succinct but sufficiently complete and must contain all the relevant information to give the Court and the interested persons entitled to submit observations a clear understanding of the factual and legal context of the main proceedings. In accordance with Article 94 of the Rules of Procedure, the request for a preliminary ruling must contain, in addition to the text of the questions referred to the Court for a preliminary ruling:
   - a summary of the subject-matter of the dispute and the relevant findings of fact as determined by the referring court or tribunal, or, at least, an account of the facts on which the questions referred are based;
   - the tenor of any national provisions applicable in the case and, where appropriate, the relevant national case-law;
   - a statement of the reasons which prompted the referring court or tribunal to inquire about the interpretation or validity of certain provisions of European Union law, and the relationship between those provisions and the national legislation applicable to the main proceedings.
23. The European Union law provisions relevant to the case should be identified as accurately as possible in the request for a preliminary ruling, which should include, if need be, a brief summary of the relevant arguments of the parties to the main proceedings.
24. If it considers itself able to do so, the referring court or tribunal may, finally, briefly state its view on the answer to be given to the questions referred for a preliminary ruling. That information may be useful to the Court, particularly where it is called upon to give a preliminary ruling in an expedited or urgent procedure.
25. In order to make the request for a preliminary ruling easier to read, it is essential that the Court receive it in typewritten form. To enable the Court to refer to the request it is also very helpful if the pages and paragraphs of the order for reference—which must be dated and signed—are numbered.
26. The questions themselves should appear in a separate and clearly identified section of the order for reference, preferably at the beginning or the end. It must be possible to understand them on their own terms, without referring to the statement of the grounds for the request, which will however provide the necessary background for a proper understanding of the implications of the case.
27. Under the preliminary ruling procedure, the Court will, as a rule, use the information contained in the order for reference, including nominative or personal data. It is therefore for the referring court or tribunal itself, if it considers it necessary, to delete certain details in its request for a preliminary ruling or to render anonymous one or more persons or entities concerned by the dispute in the main proceedings.
28. After the request for a preliminary ruling has been lodged, the Court may also render such persons or entities anonymous of its own motion, or at the request of the referring court or tribunal or of a party to the main proceedings. In order to maintain its effectiveness, such a request for anonymity must, however, be made at the earliest possible stage of the proceedings, and in any event prior to publication in the Official Journal of the European Union of the notice relating to the case concerned, and to service of the request for a preliminary ruling on the interested persons referred to in Article 23 of the Statute.

   […]

Communication between the Court of Justice, the referring court or tribunal and the parties to the main proceedings

45. In order to expedite and facilitate communication with the referring court or tribunal and the parties before it, a court or tribunal submitting a request for the expedited procedure or the urgent procedure to be applied is asked to state the e-mail address and any fax number which may be used by the Court of Justice, together with the e-mail addresses and any fax numbers of the representatives of the parties to the proceedings.
46. A copy of the signed order for reference together with a request for the expedited procedure or the urgent procedure to be applied can initially be sent to the Court by e-mail (ECJ-Registry@curia.europa.eu) or by fax (+352 43 37 66). Processing of the reference and of the request can then begin upon receipt of the e-mailed or faxed copy. The originals of those documents must, however, be sent to the Court Registry as soon as possible.

6.11.2 Pleadings before the Court of Justice

An oral hearing is not always granted and, in any event, written pleadings generally have more impact on the Court than oral pleadings. All pleadings will have to be translated, and therefore they should be kept as short and simple as possible, and propose answers to the questions referred.

6.11.3 Costs and legal aid

There are no Court of Justice fees for any of the preliminary reference procedures, but the parties may wish to instruct lawyers. Legal aid granted under a national system may include (or be extended to include) references to the Court of Justice, but where national legal aid is not available or is insufficient, it is possible to apply to the Court of Justice for legal aid, as set out under Articles 115–118 of the Court's Rules of Procedure, OJ 2012 L265/1, and summarized in its Recommendations to national courts and tribunals in relation to the initiation of preliminary ruling proceedings, OJ 2012 C338/01.

Court of Justice, Recommendations to national courts and tribunals in relation to the initiation of preliminary ruling proceedings, OJ 2012 C338/01

Costs and legal aid

31. Preliminary ruling proceedings before the Court of Justice are free of charge and the Court does not rule on the costs of the parties to the proceedings pending before the referring court or tribunal; it is for the referring court or tribunal to rule on those costs.
32. If a party to the main proceedings has insufficient means and where it is possible under national rules, the referring court or tribunal may grant that party legal aid to cover the costs,

including those of lawyers' fees, which it incurs before the Court. The Court itself may also grant legal aid where the party in question is not already in receipt of aid under national rules or to the extent to which that aid does not cover, or covers only partly, costs incurred before the Court.

6.11.4 The standard procedure

The standard procedure is the default procedure that applies unless there is reason to apply one of the other two procedures. It is set out in the Court of Justice's Rules of Procedure, OJ 2012 L265/1, and may be summarized in the form of Figure 6.2.

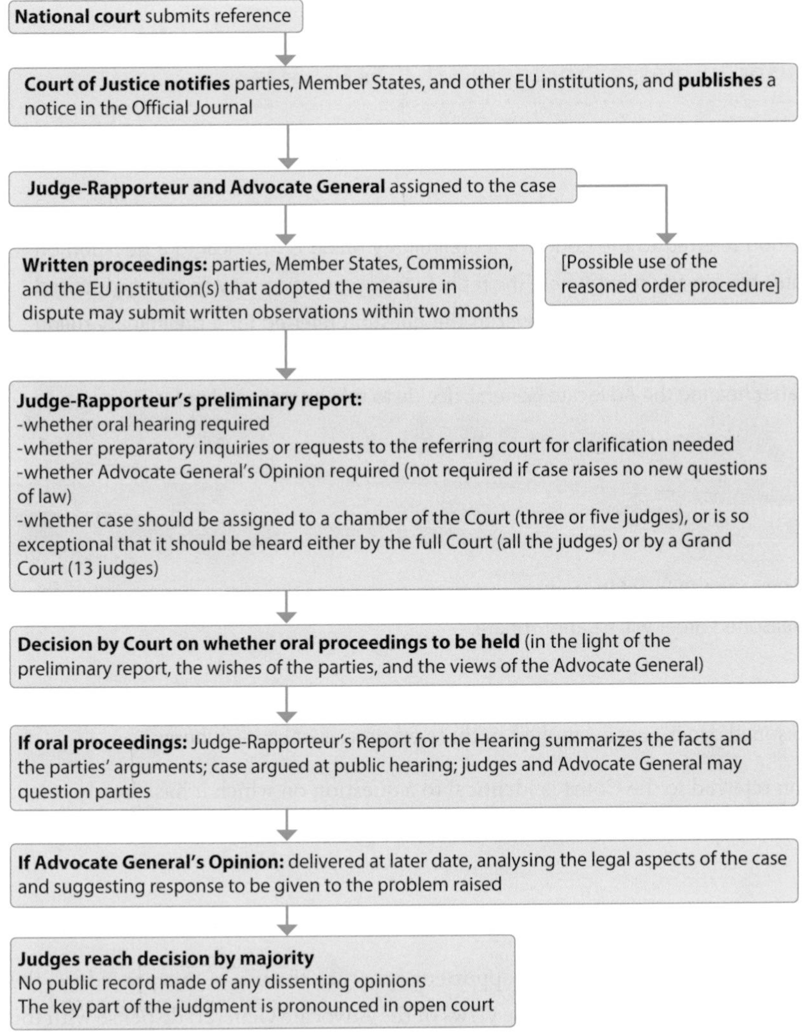

Figure 6.2 The standard procedure in Article 267 TFEU proceedings

6.11.5 Special procedures under Article 267 TFEU

The workload of the Court of Justice has led to delays in the Article 267 TFEU procedure of typically 15 months, and these are problematic for all references made under that Article. However, the Court has identified certain categories of case that are either so simple that they can easily be dealt with more quickly than usual or are so urgent that they must be dealt with more quickly. It has developed a special procedure for simple cases (decisions by reasoned order) and two alternative special procedures for urgent cases (the expedited procedure and the urgent, or PPU, procedure). These will now be examined.

6.11.5.1 Decision by reasoned order

The special procedure for certain categories of simple cases is set out in Article 99 of the Court of Justice's Rules of Procedure, OJ 2012 L265/1.

Court of Justice, Rules of Procedure, OJ 2012 L265/1

Article 99

Reply by reasoned order

Where a question referred to the Court for a preliminary ruling is identical to a question on which the Court has already ruled, where the reply to such a question may be clearly deduced from existing case-law or where the answer to the question referred for a preliminary ruling admits of no reasonable doubt, the Court may at any time, on a proposal from the Judge-Rapporteur and after hearing the Advocate General, decide to rule by reasoned order.

?! THINKING POINT

Read Article 99 of the Rules of Procedure and try to summarize the circumstances in which decision by reasoned order will be appropriate.

Decision by reasoned order may be applied in three categories of case—where:

- a question referred to the Court is identical to a question on which it has already ruled;
- the answer to a question referred to the Court may be clearly deduced from existing case law; or
- the answer to a question referred to the Court admits of no reasonable doubt.

The procedure is as follows: if the Judge-Rapporteur proposes the use of this procedure, the Court may at any time (and after hearing the views of the Advocate General) dispense with the standard procedure and give a reasoned decision.

6.11.5.2 *The expedited procedure*

The expedited procedure is set out in Articles 105–106 of the Court of Justice's Rules of Procedure, OJ 2010 L265/1, in Ch 2, titled 'Expedited preliminary ruling procedure'.

Court of Justice, Rules of Procedure, OJ 2012 L265/1

Article 105

Expedited procedure

1. At the request of the referring court or tribunal or, exceptionally, of his own motion, the President of the Court may, where the nature of the case requires that it be dealt with within a short time, after hearing the Judge-Rapporteur and the Advocate General, decide that a reference for a preliminary ruling is to be determined pursuant to an expedited procedure derogating from the provisions of these Rules.
2. In that event, the President shall immediately fix the date for the hearing, which shall be communicated to the interested persons referred to in Article 23 of the Statute when the request for a preliminary ruling is served.
3. The interested persons referred to in the preceding paragraph may lodge statements of case or written observations within a time-limit prescribed by the President, which shall not be less than 15 days. The President may request those interested persons to restrict the matters addressed in their statement of case or written observations to the essential points of law raised by the request for a preliminary ruling.
4. The statements of case or written observations, if any, shall be communicated to all the interested persons referred to in Article 23 of the Statute prior to the hearing.
5. The Court shall rule after hearing the Advocate General.

Article 106

Transmission of procedural documents

1. The procedural documents referred to in the preceding Article shall be deemed to have been lodged on the transmission to the Registry, by telefax or any other technical means of communication available to the Court, of a copy of the signed original and the items and documents relied on in support of it, together with the schedule referred to in Article 57(4). The original of the document and the annexes referred to above shall be sent to the Registry immediately.
2. Where the preceding Article requires that a document be served on or communicated to a person, such service or communication may be effected by transmission of a copy of the document by telefax or any other technical means of communication available to the Court and the addressee.

?! **THINKING POINT**

Read Articles 105–106 of the Rules of Procedure and try to summarize the circumstances in which this procedure will be appropriate.

Thus, if the national court requests the application of this procedure because the nature of the case requires a ruling within a short time or, exceptionally, the Court so decides, the Court is empowered to reduce the time limits that would normally apply under the standard procedure and give the case priority. All documents can be served electronically.

6.11.5.3 The urgent procedure/PPU

The urgent procedure is set out in Articles 107–114 of the Court of Justice's Rules of Procedure, OJ 2010 L265/1, in Ch 3, titled 'Urgent preliminary ruling procedure'. The urgent procedure is often known as PPU, which corresponds to its full title in French. Although its title might sound similar to the expedited procedure, it is in fact a separate procedure.

Court of Justice, Rules of Procedure, OJ 2012 L265/1

Article 107

Scope of the urgent preliminary ruling procedure

1. A reference for a preliminary ruling which raises one or more questions in the areas covered by Title V of Part Three of the Treaty on the Functioning of the European Union may, at the request of the referring court or tribunal or, exceptionally, of the Court's own motion, be dealt with under an urgent procedure derogating from the provisions of these Rules.
2. The referring court or tribunal shall set out the matters of fact and law which establish the urgency and justify the application of that exceptional procedure and shall, in so far as possible, indicate the answer that it proposes to the questions referred.
3. If the referring court or tribunal has not submitted a request for the urgent procedure to be applied, the President of the Court may, if the application of that procedure appears, prima facie, to be required, ask the Chamber referred to in Article 108 to consider whether it is necessary to deal with the reference under that procedure.

Article 108

Decision as to urgency

1. The decision to deal with a reference for a preliminary ruling under the urgent procedure shall be taken by the designated Chamber, acting on a proposal from the Judge-Rapporteur and after hearing the Advocate General. The composition of that Chamber shall be determined in accordance with Article 28(2) on the day on which the case is assigned to the Judge-Rapporteur if the application of the urgent procedure is requested by the referring

court or tribunal, or, if the application of that procedure is considered at the request of the President of the Court, on the day on which that request is made.

2. If the case is connected with a pending case assigned to a Judge-Rapporteur who is not a member of the designated Chamber, that Chamber may propose to the President of the Court that the case be assigned to that Judge-Rapporteur. Where the case is reassigned to that Judge-Rapporteur, the Chamber of five Judges which includes him shall carry out the duties of the designated Chamber in respect of that case. Article 29(1) shall apply.

Article 109

Written part of the urgent procedure

1. A request for a preliminary ruling shall, where the referring court or tribunal has requested the application of the urgent procedure or where the President has requested the designated Chamber to consider whether it is necessary to deal with the reference under that procedure, be served forthwith by the Registrar on the parties to the main proceedings, on the Member State from which the reference is made, on the European Commission and on the institution which adopted the act the validity or interpretation of which is in dispute.
2. The decision as to whether or not to deal with the reference for a preliminary ruling under the urgent procedure shall be served immediately on the referring court or tribunal and on the parties, Member State and institutions referred to in the preceding paragraph. The decision to deal with the reference under the urgent procedure shall prescribe the time-limit within which those parties or entities may lodge statements of case or written observations. The decision may specify the matters of law to which such statements of case or written observations must relate and may specify the maximum length of those documents.
3. Where a request for a preliminary ruling refers to an administrative procedure or judicial proceedings conducted in a Member State other than that from which the reference is made, the Court may invite that first Member State to provide all relevant information in writing or at the hearing.
4. As soon as the service referred to in paragraph 1 above has been effected, the request for a preliminary ruling shall also be communicated to the interested persons referred to in Article 23 of the Statute, other than the persons served, and the decision whether or not to deal with the reference for a preliminary ruling under the urgent procedure shall be communicated to those interested persons as soon as the service referred to in paragraph 2 has been effected.
5. The interested persons referred to in Article 23 of the Statute shall be informed as soon as possible of the likely date of the hearing.
6. Where the reference is not to be dealt with under the urgent procedure, the proceedings shall continue in accordance with the provisions of Article 23 of the Statute and the applicable provisions of these Rules.

Article 110

Service and information following the close of the written part of the procedure

1. Where a reference for a preliminary ruling is to be dealt with under the urgent procedure, the request for a preliminary ruling and the statements of case or written observations which

have been lodged shall be served on the interested persons referred to in Article 23 of the Statute other than the parties and entities referred to in Article 109(1). The request for a preliminary ruling shall be accompanied by a translation, where appropriate of a summary, in accordance with Article 98.

2. The statements of case or written observations which have been lodged shall also be served on the parties and other interested persons referred to in Article 109(1).
3. The date of the hearing shall be communicated to the interested persons referred to in Article 23 of the Statute at the same time as the documents referred to in the preceding paragraphs are served.

Article 111

Omission of the written part of the procedure

The designated Chamber may, in cases of extreme urgency, decide to omit the written part of the procedure referred to in Article 109(2).

Article 112

Decision on the substance

The designated Chamber shall rule after hearing the Advocate General.

Article 113

Formation of the Court

1. The designated Chamber may decide to sit in a formation of three Judges. In that event, it shall be composed of the President of the designated Chamber, the Judge-Rapporteur and the first Judge or, as the case may be, the first two Judges designated from the list referred to in Article 28(2) on the date on which the composition of the designated Chamber is determined in accordance with Article 108(1).
2. The designated Chamber may also request the Court to assign the case to a formation composed of a greater number of Judges. The urgent procedure shall continue before the new formation of the Court, where necessary after the reopening of the oral part of the procedure.

Article 114

Transmission of procedural documents

Procedural documents shall be transmitted in accordance with Article 106.

?! THINKING POINT

Read Articles 107–114 of the Rules and try to summarize the circumstances in which this procedure will be appropriate.

Rather than simply reducing time limits and prioritizing the case, as occurs in the expedited procedure, the urgent/PPU procedure reduces or omits certain of the procedural stages, so that the total duration of the case is much reduced. It is only applicable in the areas covered by Title V of Part 3 of the TFEU—in other words, the establishment of an area of freedom, security, and justice (see 1.15). As with the expedited procedure, a decision on whether to invoke it is normally made by the Court of Justice in response to a request by the referring court, but the Court can exceptionally make a decision to do so on its own initiative. References dealt with under the urgent/PPU procedure are completed in an average of 66 days (as compared to 15 months for the standard procedure) (see Court of Justice, *Report on the Use of the Urgent Preliminary Ruling Procedure*, 31 January 2012).

In Case C-195/08 PPU *Rinau* [2008] ECR I-5271, the Court of Justice granted the national court's request that the preliminary reference be dealt with under the urgent procedure, because the case involved a child custody dispute and the relevant EU legislation required the national court to issue judgment within six weeks of an application to it for the return of the child.

In C-211/10 PPU *Povse v Alpago* [2010] ECR I-6673 (see also the proceedings in the same matter brought before the ECtHR, discussed at 9.5.2), the Court of Justice granted a request from an Austrian court that the matter be dealt with under the urgent procedure. It did so on the grounds that the contact between a child and her father had been broken, and a delayed decision on whether the Austrian court should enforce an order of an Italian court ordering the return of the child to Italy, where her father lived, would exacerbate the deterioration of the relationship between the father and the child, and increase the risk of psychological harm if the child were sent back to Italy.

REVIEW QUESTION

What are the main differences between the urgent/PPU procedure and the expedited procedure?

Answer: First, the urgent/PPU procedure actually removes some elements of the standard process, unlike the expedited procedure, which simply speeds the process up.

Secondly, the urgent/PPU procedure is applicable only in the area covered by Title V of Part 3 of the TFEU, which relates to the area of freedom, security, and justice—in other words, judicial cooperation in civil matters.

6.12 The effects of a preliminary ruling

A ruling by the Court of Justice on the interpretation or validity of a measure provides a binding precedent for national courts. It is thus a further example of the way in which EU law (in this instance, a decision of the Court of Justice) takes precedence over national law (in this instance, the decision that the national court would otherwise have taken) (see further 3.1).

In the case of an interpretative ruling or a ruling that a particular EU measure is valid, national courts are not precluded from making further references on the point, but generally they will do so only where new evidence has come to light or where there is reason to believe that the Court of Justice may have changed its mind. In the case of a ruling of invalidity, the measure is void—that is to say, of no effect—and so a further reference on it in a future case would be redundant.

In general, the effect of a ruling is retrospective, but the Court of Justice may place a limitation on this, as in Case 43/75 *Defrenne v SABENA* [1976] 2 ECR 455 (see also 4.1.2). In that case, the Court had ruled that EU Treaty provisions on equal pay had direct effect (see further 4.1 on the concept of direct effect)—in other words, they could be enforced by employees who had suffered from discrimination in employment.

?! THINKING POINT

While reading the following extract, consider why the Court of Justice held that it was not appropriate to apply its ruling retrospectively.

Case 43/75 *Defrenne v SABENA* [1976] 2 ECR 455

The temporal effect of this judgment

69. The Governments of Ireland and the United Kingdom have drawn the Court's attention to the possible economic consequences of attributing direct effect to the provisions of Article 119 [EEC, now Article 157 TFEU], on the ground that such a decision might, in many branches of economic life, result in the introduction of claims dating back to the time at which such effect came into existence.
70. In view of the large number of people concerned, such claims, which undertakings could not have foreseen, might seriously affect the financial situation of such undertakings and even drive some of them to bankruptcy.
71. Although the practical consequences of any judicial decision must be carefully taken into account, it would be impossible to go so far as to diminish the objectivity of the law and compromise its future application on the ground of the possible repercussions which might result, as regards the past, from such a judicial decision.
72. However, in the light of the conduct of several of the Member States and the views adopted by the Commission and repeatedly brought to the notice of the circles concerned, it is appropriate to take exceptionally into account the fact that, over a prolonged period, the parties concerned have been led to continue with practices which were contrary to Article 119, although not yet prohibited under their national law.
73. The fact that, in spite of the warnings given, the Commission did not initiate proceedings under Article 169 [EEC, now Article 258 TFEU] against the Member States concerned on grounds of failure to fulfil an obligation was likely to consolidate the incorrect impression as to the effects of Article 119.
74. In these circumstances, it is appropriate to hold that, as the general level at which pay would have been fixed cannot be known, important considerations of legal certainty affecting all the interests involved, both public and private, make it impossible in principle to reopen the question as regards the past.
75. Therefore, the direct effect of Article 119 cannot be relied on in order to support claims concerning pay periods prior to the date of this judgment, except as regards those workers who have already brought legal proceedings or made an equivalent claim.

In *Defrenne*, the Court of Justice took account of the fact that although several Member States had failed to comply with what is now Article 157 TFEU by the deadline laid down in that Article as it was originally (but not currently) drafted, the Commission had failed to take enforcement proceedings under what is now Article 258 TFEU against them (see 2.3.2 and 7.1). It therefore held that, in the interests of legal certainty, its ruling that Article 157 TFEU was directly effective should not be applied retrospectively except in the case of proceedings already issued.

6.13 The possible impact of Brexit

The imminency of Brexit has been held by the Court of Justice not to justify the application of the expedited procedure (explained at 6.11.5.2), at least in the circumstances of C-661/17 *MA, SA and AZ v International Protection Appeals Tribunal, Minister for Justice and Equality, Attorney General, Ireland* EU:C:2017:1024. In that case, the Court refused to apply the expedited procedure (explained at 6.11.5.2) despite the national court's argument that the anticipated withdrawal of the UK from the EU required an urgent decision on whether EU asylum law under the Dublin Regulation (see further 9.4.2) should be enforced in circumstances in which it required asylum seekers who had first arrived in the EU in the UK, but who had only sought asylum subsequently, in Ireland, to be transferred back to the UK for a decision on their asylum status. When the case was finally heard (C-661/17 EU:C:2019:53), the Court accepted that the possible impact of Brexit on this system meant that the question was relevant and a ruling should be given (see further 6.4.2), but held that the UK's impending departure from the EU did not mean that Ireland should instead deal with the asylum claim (see further 9.4.2).

The Court has also held that questions about possible options for the Brexit process itself should not necessarily be rejected as hypothetical and theoretical. In C-621/18 *Wightman and others v Secretary of State for Exiting the European Union* EU:C:2018:999, it held that a Member State may withdraw its notification of withdrawal under Article 50 TFEU and may do so unilaterally, without having to obtain the agreement of the EU or the other Member States. The Court noted that it was for the national court to decide on the need for a preliminary reference and the relevance of the questions referred, and that a question relating to EU law enjoyed a presumption of relevance. On the facts, there was a genuine dispute on whether unilateral revocation was possible; an answer to the question was essential to resolve the dispute in the main proceedings, which concerned the UK Parliament's vote on the Draft Agreement on the Withdrawal of the United Kingdom of Great Britain and Northern Ireland from the European Union and the European Atomic Energy Community, 14 November 2018 (the Draft Withdrawal Agreement) and whether the UK's Article 50 notice could be withdrawn if the alternative was an unsatisfactory or no agreement on Brexit, since it would clarify the options open to members of Parliament (MPs) when voting; and the Court was not involved in giving an advisory opinion, but was enabling the domestic court to resolve a genuine dispute.

As to the position when the UK leaves the EU (see further 1.19 and 3.1), s 6(1) of the UK's European Union (Withdrawal) Act 2018 provides that '[a] court or tribunal ... cannot refer any matter to the European Court on or after exit day', and the UK government has stated on many occasions that it will not accept Court of Justice jurisdiction after the transitional period. However, the draft Withdrawal Agreement makes provision for the Court to have jurisdiction to give preliminary references in cases already pending at the end of the transition period (draft Article 86), cases in which the relevant facts arose before the end of the transitional period (draft Article 87), and cases that commence in the UK courts within eight years after the end of the transition period and which relate to Part Two of the draft Withdrawal Agreement on citizens' rights (draft Article 158). The draft Withdrawal Agreement also contains a separate Protocol on Northern Ireland and Ireland, which makes provision for the Court of Justice to have jurisdiction over its application (draft Article 14(4) of the Protocol).

In *Coal Staff Superannuation Scheme Trustees Ltd v Commissioners for HMRC* [2017] UKUT 137 (TCC), the UK's Upper Tribunal (Tax and Chancery Chamber) rejected the appellant's argument that it should make a reference before hearing the appeal in order to avoid the appellant being deprived of its ability to seek the assistance of the Court of Justice at a later stage owing to the UK's exit from the EU and the likely cessation of the Court's jurisdiction in the UK. The Tribunal held that, in the light of the case law on whether and when to make a reference, it made sense for it to hear the appeal first before deciding whether a reference was necessary, and that were it ultimately to decide that a reference was necessary, but this was superseded by legal developments consequent on Brexit, then so be it.

Disputes that may arise as a result of Brexit and which may then give rise to questions over the jurisdiction of the Court of Justice to give preliminary rulings include the interpretation and enforcement of any withdrawal agreement and/or agreement on the future relationship of the UK and the EU, and the arrangements during the transitional period (see further 1.19.1). These were discussed at some length by the House of Lords European Union Committee in its *Dispute resolution and enforcement after Brexit* (15th Report of Session 2017–19, 3 May 2018, HL Paper 130) and more recently in the light of the provisions of the Draft Withdrawal Agreement in its *Brexit: the Withdrawal Agreement and Political Declaration* (24th Report of Session 2017–19, 5 December 2018, HL Paper 245). The House of Lords considered that the most promising alternatives were joining the European Free Trade Area (EFTA) Court (see further 1.19.2.1 on EFTA), an arbitration agreement, or using the World Trade Organization (WTO) dispute system (see further 1.19.2.6 on the WTO). It noted that the creation of a special UK-based court to supervise agreements with the UK was unlikely to be acceptable to the UK, a joint UK–EU court was unlikely to be acceptable to the Court of Justice, and a Swiss-style approach (see further 1.19.2.2 on the Swiss arrangements with the EU) was unlikely to be acceptable to the EU given that it was already attempting to reform that system.

If the UK takes the 'Norway option' (see 1.19.2.1 on this option), a somewhat similar procedure will apply in relation to the EFTA Court, although the making of a reference is always discretionary and not mandatory, its opinion is only advisory in preliminary references (as opposed to direct actions), and a State may limit the courts that can request such an opinion to be given to those against whose decisions there is no judicial remedy (see 6.3.1).

Agreement between the EFTA States on the Establishment of a Surveillance Authority and a Court of Justice, OJ 1994 L344/3

Article 34

The EFTA Court shall have jurisdiction to give advisory opinions on the interpretation of the EEA Agreement. Where such a question is raised before any court or tribunal in an EFTA State, that court or tribunal may, if it considers it necessary to enable it to give judgment, request the EFTA Court to give such an opinion.

An EFTA State may in its internal legislation limit the right to request such an advisory opinion to courts and tribunals against whose decisions there is no judicial remedy under national law.

6.14 Conclusions

It is essential to the uniformity and effectiveness of EU law that a system exists whereby national courts, faced with a dispute as to the interpretation or validity of EU law in a case before them, may ask the Court of Justice for a ruling. This system is outlined in Article 267 TFEU, which provides that references may only be made by a 'court or tribunal', on questions of the interpretation of EU law or the validity of secondary EU legislation, and that the making of a reference may be either discretionary or mandatory. However, the Article itself gives no hint of the guidelines on the making of discretionary references, which have been established in the jurisprudence, nor of the exceptions that exist to otherwise mandatory references, which have also been established in the jurisprudence. The result of the existence of discretion and the guidelines affecting its use, and the exceptions to mandatory references, is some lack of uniformity in the making of references and thus, in some cases, a lack of uniformity in the way in which EU law is applied across the Member States. However, a less flexible approach to the making of references would increase the workload of the overstretched Court of Justice and result in increased delays (and thus expense) for the parties.

SUMMARY

- Article 267 TFEU provides that preliminary references may be made to the Court of Justice by any national court or tribunal on a question of the interpretation of EU law or the validity of EU secondary legislation. The case will be stayed in the national court until the Court of Justice provides a preliminary ruling, which will then be used by the national court in giving judgment.
- The term 'court or tribunal' has an autonomous meaning in EU law (*Dorsch Consult*).
- A court or tribunal against whose decisions there is a judicial remedy under national law—in other words, from which an appeal at national level is automatic or may be requested in the case in question—has a discretion to refer (Article 267 TFEU). In exercising this discretion, it must take account of a number of guidelines, including *acte clair* (*CILFIT*), the relevance of the issue to be referred

(*Else*), the existence of any Court of Justice authority on the issue (*Da Costa*), whether the reference is likely to be rejected by the Court of Justice (*Foglia*), and the advantages of the Court of Justice in interpreting EU law (*Samex*).

- A court or tribunal against whose decisions there is no judicial remedy under national law—in other words, from which it is not possible to request leave to appeal in the case in question—has no discretion and a reference is mandatory (Article 267 TFEU). However, the Court of Justice has established four exceptions to this: a reference need not be made if the EU law at issue is *acte clair*, or irrelevant to the dispute, or if there is already Court of Justice authority on the issue (*CILFIT*), or if the reference is likely to be rejected (*Foglia*).
- Questions concerning the validity of EU law must be referred to the Court of Justice unless the national court is satisfied that the measure is valid, as national courts have no power to declare EU law invalid (*Foto-Frost*).

FURTHER READING

Articles

A Arnull, 'The Law Lords and the European Union: Swimming with the Incoming Tide' (2010) 35(1) EL Rev 57

Examines the practice of the UK courts in dealing with preliminary references.

C Barnard, 'The PPU: Is it Worth the Candle? An Early Assessment' (2009) 34(2) EL Rev 281

Examines the effectiveness of the urgent/PPU procedure.

M Broberg, '*Acte Clair* Revisited: Adapting the *Acte Clair* Criteria to the Demands of the Times' (2008) 45(5) CML Rev 1383

Discusses *acte clair* as it relates to the highest national courts.

M Broberg and N Fenger, 'Preliminary References as a Right—but for Whom? The Extent to which Preliminary Reference Decisions Can be Subject to Appeal' (2011) 36(3) EL Rev 276

Discusses the relationship between the preliminary reference procedure and domestic appeals.

M Broberg and N Fenger, 'Preliminary References to the Court of Justice of the European Union and the Right to a Fair Trial under Article 6 ECHR' (2016) 41(4) EL Rev 599

Considers the duty of national courts under Article 6 ECHR to give reasons for not making a reference under Article 267 TFEU.

X Groussot and T Minssen, '*Res Judicata* in the Court of Justice Case-Law: Balancing Legal Certainty with Legality?' (2007) 3(3) ECL Rev 385

Discusses the impact of preliminary references on the finality of decisions by national courts and administrative authorities.

A Hofmann, 'Resistance against the Court of Justice of the European Union' (2018) 14(2) Int JLC 258

Discusses the reactions of Member States to preliminary rulings given by the Court of Justice.

D O'Keefe, 'Is the Spirit of Article 177 under Attack? Preliminary References and Admissibility' (1998) 23 6 EL Rev 509

Comments on the rejection of preliminary references by the Court of Justice.

N Wahl and L Prete, 'The Gatekeepers of Article 267 TFEU: On jurisdiction and admissibility of references for preliminary rulings' (2018) 55(2) CML Rev 511

Discusses whether the Court of Justice has started to apply the procedural requirements of Article 267 TFEU more strictly, in order to keep its workload manageable.

Reports

House of Commons, *Brexit: Article 50 TEU and the EU Court*, Briefing Papers No 773, 14 November 2016

Examines the Brexit litigation in the UK and the possible role of the Court of Justice at a future date.

House of Lords European Union Committee, *Dispute resolution and enforcement after Brexit*, 15th Report of Session 2017–18, 3 May 2018, HL Paper 130

Discusses the options for dispute resolution procedures after the UK leaves the EU, including the enforcement of rights by individuals and businesses, and disputes between the UK and the EU.

House of Lords European Union Committee, *The Workload of the Court of Justice of the EU*, 14th Report of Session 2010–11, 6 April 2011, HL Paper 128

Examines the current and likely future problem of, and possible solutions to, delays in the preliminary reference procedure.

Working Party for the European Commission, *Report by the Working Party on the Future of the European Communities' Court System* ('Due Report'), January 2000

The report which led to a number of procedural reforms to the preliminary reference system, but which examined and rejected a number of others.

QUESTION

Discuss, with examples from case law, the role of national courts under Article 267 TFEU.

To view an outline answer to this question plus further resources to support your EU law studies, visit the Online Resources for this book at **www.oup.com/uk/eulaw-complete4e**

7 Challenging EU action or inaction

KEY POINTS

By the end of this chapter, you should be able to:

- understand the procedural and judicial stage of enforcement actions;
- explain what acts may be challenged and by whom for a direct action;
- be thoroughly familiar with the test of 'direct and individual concern';
- explain the effect of a successful action under Article 263 TFEU or Article 265 TFEU;
- identify the circumstances in which an action under Article 265 TFEU is likely to be successful; and
- identify the circumstances in which a plea of illegality under Article 277 TFEU may be made.

INTRODUCTION

The most significant power conferred on the institutions under the Treaty on the Functioning of the European Union (TFEU) is the power to legislate. The Commission is tasked as the 'guardian of the Treaties' to ensure that EU law has been implemented properly; in the event that a Member State fails to do so an enforcement action may be instigated by the Commission. To ensure that the institutions do not act beyond their powers and obligations that have been conferred on them by the Treaties, mechanisms have been embedded within the Treaty to allow for judicial review of legislation or an action by one of the institutions. This process of judicial review provides a mechanism for accountability by which actions of the EU institutions are subject to scrutiny by the Court of Justice and this, in turn, provides for judicial control over the political institutions of the European Union (EU).

An EU measure can be challenged on different grounds depending on the nature of the act and the party bringing the proceedings. Article 263 TFEU specifically deals with the review of the legality of a regulatory measure, for example alleging that the EU has done something that it should not have done.

Parties who can bring an action under Article 263 TFEU to challenge the measure include individuals and companies (private applicants), as well as the institutions themselves and the Member States. Although individuals and companies are entitled to challenge measures under this Article, their capacity to do so has been hampered by the wording of Article 263 TFEU and its interpretation by the Court of Justice, which has meant that only persons immediately concerned by the measure may challenge it. This test of 'direct and individual concern' involves a number of elements that combine to create a considerable hurdle for private applicants under Article 263 TFEU. The applicant in an action for judicial review is seeking an annulment of the measure adopted by an institution.

The partner to Article 263 TFEU is Article 265 TFEU, which may be relied on where there has been a failure to act by one of the institutions. This is far less commonly relied on than Article 263 TFEU, and there has been a particular difficulty in establishing whether it, or Article 263 TFEU, should be used to challenge a positive refusal to act. The third possible challenge to EU law is the so-called plea of illegality under Article 277 TFEU, whereby the Member States or institutions, not subject to time limitations, can question the legality of a general act.

7.1 The Commission's supervisory role

One of the Commission's core roles according to the Treaty on European Union (TEU) is to supervise Member States' compliance with EU law. The general EU infringement procedure constitutes the Commission's main tool of enforcement. It consists of two distinct procedures stipulated in Articles 258 and 260 TFEU (which are discussed at 7.2), each with its own subject matter. The procedure established under Article 258 TFEU is designed to obtain a declaration that the conduct of a Member State is in breach of EU law and that the conduct will be terminated.

The procedure provided for under Article 260 TFEU is designed to induce a defaulting Member State to comply with a judgment establishing a breach of obligations (ie repetitive infringements) and it has a much narrower ambit than Article 258 TFEU. The procedural construction thus distinguishes between compliance with Treaty obligations ('first order compliance') and compliance with judgments of the Treaty regime's dispute settlement body ('second order compliance'). The two procedures have, however, the same purpose: to ensure the effective application of EU law.

7.1.1 Article 258 TFEU: enforcement actions by the Commission

The Commission has a supervisory role that involves ensuring the correct implementation of EU law by Member States and taking enforcement proceedings where appropriate. For example, if a Member State has not transposed an EU Directive or where national rules have been applied, the Commission can bring an enforcement action against a Member State under Article 258 TFEU.

Both the Commission and a Member State (although this is rare) can bring an action under Article 258 TFEU before the Court of Justice. For the Commission, by initiating an action under this provision, it is fulfilling its primary task of 'guardian of the Treaty'.

Article 258 TFEU

If the Commission considers that a Member State has failed to fulfil an obligation under the Treaties, it shall deliver a reasoned opinion on the matter after giving the State concerned the opportunity to submit its observations.

If the State concerned does not comply with the opinion within the period laid down by the Commission, the latter may bring the matter before the Court of Justice of the European Union.

Having considered the facts of a dispute, if the Commission is of the opinion that a Member State has failed to fulfil an obligation that arises under the Treaties, it must contact the Member State about the alleged breach of the Treaty and offer the Member State an opportunity to submit any observations that it may have. If the response provided by the Member State is deemed, by the Commission, not to be a satisfactory explanation, then the Commission must formally deliver a reasoned opinion to the Member State, which unequivocally requests that the Member State fulfils its obligations within a specified time—usually two months. In circumstances in which the Member State does not comply with the Commission's request, the Commission may refer the matter to the Court of Justice.

The Commission can set the time period because it may depend on the nature of the violation. This was acknowledged by the Court of Justice in Case 7/71 *Commission v France* [1971] ECR 1003, in which it stated that, 'by reason of its nature and its purpose, this procedure involves a power on the part of the Commission to consider the most appropriate means and time-limits for the purposes of putting an end to any contravention of the Treaty'. Failure to comply with the reasoned opinion will result in the matter being brought before the Court of Justice.

The Commission retains discretion as to whether to refer the matter to the Court and, in reaching its decision, will consider the seriousness of the breach and whether any further remedial action on the part of the Member State would be sufficient.

In Case 7/71 *Commission v France* [1971] ECR 1003, Advocate General Roemer suggested the existence of a number of situations in which the Commission might choose not to proceed with an Article 258 TFEU action—namely:

- where an amicable settlement can be achieved if the formal procedure is not invoked;
- where the effects of the violation are minor;
- where the Article 258 TFEU action might aggravate a sensitive political situation and the violation concerns matters of secondary importance; and
- where the EU provision is likely to be altered in the near future.

The time limit specified by the Commission for compliance must have passed and the Member State must have failed to comply. The judicial stage permits the Commission to bring a defaulting Member State before the Court of Justice. Where the Member States have defended their position, the Court of Justice has not been sympathetic and so Member States have rarely succeeded with their defence.

Where one Member State holds the opinion that another Member State has failed to fulfil an obligation arising under the Treaty, it must first bring the matter before the Commission. The Commission will then follow a process that gives each State an opportunity to submit its own views on the dispute, including comments on the observations of the other Member State. The Commission must then deliver a reasoned opinion within three months from the date on which the matter was first formally brought to its attention. However, the absence of the reasoned opinion from the Commission may not prevent the complaining Member State from bringing the matter before the Court.

In circumstances in which one Member State commences an action against another Member State, it is important to note the requirements of Article 344 TFEU. This provides as follows.

Article 344 TFEU

Member States undertake not to submit a dispute concerning the interpretation or application of the Treaties to any method of settlement other than those provided for therein.

The reason for Article 344 TFEU is that it ensures a uniform application of the law by the Court of Justice and that all disputes concerning the application of the Treaty are determined solely by the Court of Justice.

The outstanding question that relates to the procedure within Article 258 TFEU is how the Commission can enforce a decision against a Member State when it fails to comply with a decision of the Court of Justice that a breach of EU law has been committed.

7.2 Article 260 TFEU: judicial remedies against the Member State

Article 258 TFEU is silent on the legal effect of the judgment of the Court. Article 260 TFEU provides further guidance.

Article 260 TFEU

1. If the Court of Justice of the European Union finds that a Member State has failed to fulfil an obligation under the Treaties, the State shall be required to take the necessary measures to comply with the judgment of the Court.
2. If the Commission considers that the Member State concerned has not taken the necessary measures to comply with the judgment of the Court, it may bring the case before the Court after giving that State the opportunity to submit its observations. It shall specify the amount of the lump sum or penalty payment to be paid by the Member State concerned which it considers appropriate in the circumstances.

   If the Court finds that the Member State concerned has not complied with its judgment it may impose a lump sum or penalty payment on it.

   This procedure shall be without prejudice to Article 259.
3. When the Commission brings a case before the Court pursuant to Article 258 on the grounds that the Member State concerned has failed to fulfil its obligation to notify measures transposing a directive adopted under a legislative procedure, it may, when it deems appropriate, specify the amount of the lump sum or penalty payment to be paid by the Member State concerned which it considers appropriate in the circumstances.

   If the Court finds that there is an infringement it may impose a lump sum or penalty payment on the Member State concerned not exceeding the amount specified by the Commission. The payment obligation shall take effect on the date set by the Court in its judgment.

A finding by the Court of Justice under Article 260(1) TFEU is purely declaratory, but it gives rise to an independent obligation to rectify matters. This could involve a variety of actions, such as implementing a Directive and disapplying the national measure(s) that is incompatible with EU law. Where a Member State has failed to comply with the judgment of the Court, the

Commission can bring further proceedings under Article 260(2) TFEU and make a Recommendation relating to the financial sanction to be imposed on the Member State. Since this is a Recommendation, the Court of Justice can impose its own lump sum or penalty.

The sanction of a financial penalty against a Member State for failure to comply with a judgment of the Court was applied for the first time in July 2000 in Case C-387/97 *Commission v Greece* [2000] ECR I-5047. In this case, the Court of Justice held that Greece had failed to comply with a 1992 judgment in which the Court of Justice had held that Greece had failed to take the necessary measures for toxic and dangerous waste to be disposed of while ensuring that human health and the environment were protected, as required by two Directives of 1975 and 1978, which Greece should have applied from 1981. As a consequence of the failure of Greece to comply with the judgment, the Court of Justice imposed a penalty payment of €20,000 for each day the State delayed in complying with the 1992 judgment.

This judgment is significant because the purpose of the fine levied by the Court should not be considered only as a deterrent to other Member States, encouraging them to refrain from action that may call into question their obligations under the Treaties. The fine against a Member State is significant and should also be viewed as part of the overall principle of effective remedies against a Member State for any breach of EU law for which it may be responsible. This point has subsequently been developed by the Court through judgments in which it has focused on ensuring that an effective remedy is applied against a Member State. In doing so, the Court has the jurisdiction to impose a financial penalty that has not been suggested by the Commission.

The sanction under Article 260(2) TFEU provides for a lump sum *or* penalty, but, in consideration of the need for an *effective* remedy, the Court of Justice in Case C-304/02 *Commission v France* [2005] ECR I-6263 considered it could impose both a lump sum *and* a penalty.

Case C-304/02 *Commission v France* [2005] ECR I-6263

80. The procedure laid down in Article 228(2) EC [now Article 260(2) TFEU] has the objective of inducing a defaulting Member State to comply with a judgment establishing a breach of obligations and thereby of ensuring that Community law [now EU law] is in fact applied. The measures provided for by that provision, namely a lump sum and a penalty payment, are both intended to achieve this objective.

81. Application of each of those measures depends on their respective ability to meet the objective pursued according to the circumstances of the case. While the imposition of a penalty payment seems particularly suited to inducing a Member State to put an end as soon as possible to a breach of obligations which, in the absence of such a measure, would tend to persist, the imposition of a lump sum is based more on assessment of the effects on public and private interests of the failure of the Member State concerned to comply with its obligations, in particular where the breach has persisted for a long period since the judgment which initially established it.

82. That being so, recourse to both types of penalty provided for in Article 228(2) EC is not precluded, in particular where the breach of obligations both has continued for a long period and is inclined to persist.

83. This interpretation cannot be countered by reference to the use in Article 228(2) EC of the conjunction 'or' to link the financial penalties capable of being imposed. As the Commission and the Danish, Netherlands, Finnish and United Kingdom Governments have submitted, that conjunction may, linguistically, have an alternative or a cumulative sense and must therefore be read in the context in which it is used. In light of the objective pursued by Article 228 EC [now Article 260 TFEU], the conjunction 'or' in Article 228(2) EC must be understood as being used in a cumulative sense.

[...]

91. ... The procedure provided for in Article 228(2) EC is a special judicial procedure, peculiar to Community law, which cannot be equated with a civil procedure. The order imposing a penalty payment and/or a lump sum is not intended to compensate for damage caused by the Member State concerned, but to place it under economic pressure which induces it to put an end to the breach established. The financial penalties imposed must therefore be decided upon according to the degree of persuasion needed in order for the Member State in question to alter its conduct.

[...]

103. ... while it is clear that a penalty payment is likely to encourage the defaulting Member State to put an end as soon as possible to the breach that has been established (Case C-278/01 *Commission v Spain* [[2003] ECR I-14141], paragraph 42), it should be remembered that the Commission's suggestions cannot bind the Court and are only a useful point of reference (Case C-387/97 *Commission v Greece* [[2000] ECR I-5047], paragraph 89). In exercising its discretion, it is for the Court to set the penalty payment so that it is appropriate to the circumstances and proportionate both to the breach that has been established and to the ability to pay of the Member State concerned (see, to this effect, Case C-387/97 *Commission v Greece*, paragraph 90, and Case C-278/01 *Commission v Spain*, paragraph 41).

104. In that light, and as the Commission has suggested in its communication of 28 February 1997, the basic criteria which must be taken into account in order to ensure that penalty payments have coercive force and Community law is applied uniformly and effectively are, in principle, the duration of the infringement, its degree of seriousness and the ability of the Member State to pay. In applying those criteria, regard should be had in particular to the effects of failure to comply on private and public interests and to the urgency of getting the Member State concerned to fulfil its obligations (Case C-387/97 *Commission v Greece*, paragraph 92).

[...]

113. ... the French Republic should be ordered to pay to the Commission, into the account 'European Community own resources', a penalty payment of 182.5 × EUR 316 500, that is to say of EUR 57 761 250, for each period of six months from delivery of the present judgment at the end of which the judgment in Case C-64/88 *Commission v France* [[2005] ECR I-6263] has not yet been fully complied with.

Imposition of a lump sum

114. In a situation such as that which is the subject of the present judgment, in light of the fact that the breach of obligations has persisted for a long period since the judgment which initially established it and of the public and private interests at issue, it is essential to order payment of a lump sum (see paragraph 81 of the present judgment).

115. The specific circumstances of the case are fairly assessed by setting the amount of the lump sum which the French Republic will have to pay at EUR 20 000 000.

The Court held that it is therefore possible to impose both types of penalty (periodic payment and lump sum) at the same time, in particular where the breach of obligations has both continued for a long period and is inclined to persist.

In its judgment, the Court of Justice found that the persistence of the infringement by France (in the form of the practice of offering undersized fish for sale below the minimum size laid down in EU legislation) and the absence of effective action by the national authorities were such as to seriously prejudice the EU objectives of conserving and managing fishery resources. According to the Court, the French authorities neglected to carry out controls that were effective, proportionate, and dissuasive, as required by EU rules, and were not carrying out a sufficient number of proceedings, leading to penalties that were effective, proportionate, and dissuasive.

7.2.1 Interim measures: Articles 278 and 279 TFEU

As part of the enforcement process, Article 278 TFEU allows the Court of Justice, in exceptional circumstances, to suspend an act that is contested in the case before it. In addition, Article 279 TFEU enables the Court to grant interim measures where this is considered necessary and where, under the Court's Rules of Procedure, this is considered necessary on grounds of urgency.

Article 278 TFEU provides as follows.

Article 278 TFEU

Actions brought before the Court of Justice of the European Union shall not have suspensory effect. The Court may, however, if it considers that circumstances so require, order that application of the contested act be suspended.

This is supplemented by Article 279 TFEU, which provides as follows.

Article 279 TFEU

The Court of Justice of the European Union may in any cases before it prescribe any necessary interim measures.

The procedures within Articles 278 and 279 TFEU are rarely used. Intervention by the Court to grant an interim measure under Article 279 TFEU requires, following the judgment in Case C-76/08 *Commission v Malta* [2009] ECR I-8213, that there be a serious threat of harm to the applicant's interests and that these interests can be protected only through an interim measure. Thus the Court will need to be satisfied that there is a significant risk to the application of EU law before it can intervene.

7.3 Direct action: Article 263 TFEU

Article 263 TFEU

The Court of Justice of the European Union shall review the legality of legislative acts, of acts of the Council, of the Commission and of the European Central Bank, other than recommendations and opinions, and of acts of the European Parliament and of the European Council intended to produce legal effects vis-à-vis third parties. It shall also review the legality of acts of bodies, offices or agencies of the Union intended to produce legal effects vis-à-vis third parties.

It shall for this purpose have jurisdiction in actions brought by a Member State, the European Parliament, the Council or the Commission on grounds of lack of competence, infringement of an essential procedural requirement, infringement of the Treaties or of any rule of law relating to their application, or misuse of powers.

The Court shall have jurisdiction under the same conditions in actions brought by the Court of Auditors, by the European Central Bank and by the Committee of the Regions for the purpose of protecting their prerogatives.

Any natural or legal person may, under the conditions laid down in the first and second paragraphs, institute proceedings against an act addressed to that person or which is of direct and individual concern to them, and against a regulatory act which is of direct concern to them and does not entail implementing measures.

Acts setting up bodies, offices and agencies of the Union may lay down specific conditions and arrangements concerning actions brought by natural or legal persons against acts of these bodies, offices or agencies intended to produce legal effects in relation to them.

The proceedings provided for in this article shall be instituted within two months of the publication of the measure, or of its notification to the plaintiff, or, in the absence thereof, of the day on which it came to the knowledge of the latter, as the case may be.

There are a variety of factors that need to be addressed for a successful direct action challenge to a regulatory act that does not involve implementing measures, including:

- identifying the regulatory act that may be challenged;
- the *locus standi* (standing) of the applicant; and
- time limits.

7.4 Which acts may be challenged?

7.4.1 Acts of the legislative institutions

Article 263 TFEU permits challenges to be made to acts of:

- the Council, the Commission, and the European Central Bank (ECB), other than Recommendations and Opinions;
- the European Council and the European Parliament, insofar as those acts are intended to produce legal effects vis-à-vis third parties; and
- EU bodies, offices, or agencies of the EU intended to produce legal effects vis-à-vis third parties.

7.4.2 Acts with binding legal effects

The only acts that are reviewable by the Court of Justice are those that have been adopted by the EU institutions and EU bodies, offices, or agencies of the EU. The wording of Article 263 TFEU provides guidance on the types of legislative act that are subject to judicial review; these include Regulations, Directives, or Decisions, because they are explicitly intended to have legal effects. Not all acts by the legislative institutions can be challenged, however, and Article 263 TFEU expressly excludes from judicial review Recommendations and Opinions because they do not produce legal effects.

In Case 60/81 *IBM Corporation v Commission* [1981] ECR 2639, the Court of Justice considered what constitutes a legal act for the purposes of judicial review. The Commission notified IBM that it had commenced competition proceedings against the company on the basis that it was potentially abusing its dominant position in the market. IBM was offered the opportunity to submit its response to the Commission's statement of objections. IBM sought to challenge the statement of objections and the decision to initiate the Commission Decision on the basis that, in IBM's opinion, the Commission's procedure was defective. IBM had requested clarification from the Commission on the details of the basis for the Decision to initiate its statement of objections.

The Court of Justice held as follows.

Case 60/81 *IBM Corporation v Commission* [1981] ECR 2639

9. In order to ascertain whether the measures in question are acts within the meaning of Article 173 [now Article 263 TFEU] it is necessary, therefore, to look to their substance. According to the consistent case-law of the court any measure the legal effects of which are binding on, and capable of affecting the interests of, the applicant by bringing about a distinct change in his legal position is an act or decision which may be the subject of an

action under Article 173 for a declaration that it is void. However, the form in which such acts or decisions are cast is, in principle, immaterial as regards the question whether they are open to challenge under that article.

10. In the case of acts or decisions adopted by a procedure involving several stages, in particular where they are the culmination of an internal procedure, it is clear from the case-law that in principle an act is open to review only if it is a measure definitively laying down the position of the Commission or the Council on the conclusion of that procedure, and not a provisional measure intended to pave the way for the final decision.

[...]

20. An application for a declaration that the initiation of a procedure and a statement of objections are void might make it necessary for the Court to arrive at a decision on questions on which the Commission has not yet had an opportunity to state its position and would as a result anticipate the arguments on the substance of the case, confusing different procedural stages both administrative and judicial. It would thus be incompatible with the system of the division of powers between the Commission and the Court and of the remedies laid down by the Treaty, as well as the requirements of the sound administration of justice and the proper course of the administrative procedure to be followed in the Commission.

The Court of Justice applied the test of whether the act is intended to have legal effects. The letter from the Commission was only a preparatory measure notifying IBM of the Commission's position and not the Commission's definitive position. As a preliminary act, it was not subject to judicial review. The act to be challenged must be a final statement of an institution's position and not merely an interim position.

7.5 Who can bring an action under Article 263 TFEU?

All of the institutions of the EU referred to in Article 263 TFEU can seek an annulment of an EU measure, although there are restrictions as to the acts that may be challenged and these are dependent on the status of the applicant.

7.6 *Locus standi*: permissible applicants under Article 263 TFEU

What is meant by the term *locus standi*? It means the applicant's standing, or legal ability, to bring an action. The *locus standi* of each type of applicant considered at 7.5 is different, and we shall consider the position of each in turn (see Table 7.1).

Table 7.1
The type of applicant and which acts may be challenged

Applicant	Acts that may be challenged
Privileged applicants (Member States, European Parliament, Council, Commission)	Any act that constitutes the final statement of an institution's position and produces legal effects
'Semi-privileged' applicants (Court of Auditors, European Central Bank, Committee of the Regions)	Can protect only their own prerogatives
Non-privileged applicants (Companies, individuals)	Act which is addressed to the applicant. Legislative acts where they can establish that they are directly and individually concerned. Where the non-privileged applicant is directly concerned by a regulatory act that does not entail implementing measures

7.6.1 Privileged applicants

Privileged applicants include the institutions of the EU—namely, the Commission, the Council, the European Parliament, and Member States. They have *locus standi* to review any act under Article 263 TFEU.

7.6.2 'Semi-privileged' applicants

Semi-privileged applicants include the Court of Auditors, the ECB, and the Committee of the Regions (CoR). These bodies may challenge any act, but that challenge is restricted to the protection of their prerogatives.

The European Parliament, prior to the Treaty of Nice, was a semi-privileged applicant and could bring a direct action only as a means of protecting its prerogatives. One of the European Parliament's prerogatives, acknowledged in Case C-70/88 *Parliament v Council* [1970] ECR I-2041, was the right to influence the legislative process to the extent provided for in the EC Treaty. This prerogative would have been infringed if the European Parliament had been accorded less influence than it was entitled to because of the use of the wrong legislative base, and therefore the wrong legislative procedure, in passing a measure. In order for the European Parliament to bring an action on this ground, it had to identify the legal base that was used and then show that this was an incorrect base for the particular legislation. The legal base would normally have been a Treaty provision, but may have been secondary legislation.

7.6.3 Non-privileged applicants

The category of non-privileged applicants covers 'any natural or legal person'—in other words, individuals and other private parties, such as companies.

Following the entry into force of the Lisbon Treaty, Article 263 TFEU restricts the *locus standi* of non-privileged applicants to three specific actions:

- an act addressed to the applicant; or
- an act addressed to a third party that is of direct and individual concern to the applicant; or
- a regulatory act that is of direct concern to the applicant and which does not entail implementing measures.

The first category is fairly straightforward and existed prior to the Lisbon Treaty. Where an act is directly addressed to the applicant, they will have automatic standing to challenge the measure before the Court of Justice. This category is broad, and the acts that will come within it include Regulations, Directives, and Decisions.

→ CROSS-REFERENCE
For further discussion on non-privileged applicants, see 7.9.

Problems have arisen in the context of the second category and have been predominantly over the meaning of 'direct and individual concern', which will be considered further in the following sections. This category is sufficiently broad to include Regulations, Directives, and Decisions that are final reviewable acts. Under the former Article 230 EC, the scope of acts for review was considerably narrower in this category and limited to Decisions addressed to the applicant. A vast amount of case law developed in which the Court had to examine Decisions that were disguised as Regulations, and no doubt these cases will remain helpful in the future.

The final category was introduced by the Treaty of Lisbon and is in part somewhat vague in its actual scope. A challenge brought under this category applies only to an applicant who can demonstrate 'direct concern', as opposed to 'direct and individual concern', which is a condition in the previous category. The term 'direct concern' has been considered by the Court of Justice on numerous occasions and will be discussed further in 7.7. The term 'regulatory act' has not been defined either in Article 263 TFEU or elsewhere in the Treaties. It is thought that this provision was introduced as a means of addressing a potential lacuna in the law that the Court identified in Case C-50/00 P *Unión de Pequeños Agricultores v Council of the European Union* [2002] 3 CMLR 1.

7.7 Non-privileged applicants: direct concern

For a non-privileged applicant to bring a direct action under Article 263 TFEU, they must come within the scope of one of the categories listed earlier. Where the act is not directly addressed to the applicant, the applicant must establish that they are directly concerned by the act for which they are seeking annulment. This applies in the following circumstances: first, where the act complained of is of direct and individual concern to the applicant; or, secondly, where a regulatory act does not entail implementing measures and is of direct concern to the applicant.

→ CROSS-REFERENCE
See 7.6.3 for an explanation of non-privileged applicants.

The analysis of whether the applicant is directly concerned involves determining whether the act complained of has a direct causal link with the applicant. If there is an intervening act, this would break that causal link between the act and the applicant, and so eradicate the applicant's *locus standi* for judicial review.

Intervening acts may occur where a Member State has some discretion in the application of a measure. This can be illustrated by Case 123/77 *UNICME and others v Council* [1978] ECR

845. A Council Regulation made the importing of Japanese motorcycles subject to the issue of a licence from the Italian government. The applicants, Italian importers of such motorcycles, together with their trade association, UNICME, attempted to challenge the Regulation. As it was not an act addressed to them, the applicants had to show that they were directly and individually concerned by the Regulation. The Court of Justice held that the applicants were not directly concerned because the Italian government had discretion over the grant of import licences. It was not the Regulation that directly concerned the applicants, but any subsequent refusal by the Italian government to issue import licences to them.

REVIEW QUESTION

Can you think of an alternative action that the applicant importers might have been able to bring in *UNICME*?

Answer: The Court of Justice stated that if the Italian government did indeed refuse licences to the importers, they could bring an action in the national courts. A national court could then, if necessary, refer the question of the validity of the Regulation to the Court of Justice under Article 267 TFEU.

The applicant must ensure that the EU measure directly concerns them. In Case 62/70 *Bock v Commission* [1971] ECR 897, Bock had applied for a licence to import Chinese mushrooms. The German authorities had responded to this request by stating that they would refuse to grant the licence as soon as they were authorized by the Commission to do so. The Commission issued a Decision allowing Germany to refuse to issue import licences for Chinese mushrooms. Bock challenged the Decision. The Court of Justice held that Bock was directly concerned by the Decision. In this case, there was no intervening discretion, because the German authorities had already exercised their discretion when they expressly notified Bock of their intention to refuse his application as soon as they were able to do so. It was the Decision itself that actually affected Bock, who therefore had *locus standi* to challenge it. The Decision was annulled insofar as it applied to importers with licence applications pending at the time the Decision came into force. In contrast, in *UNICME*, the Regulation did not directly concern UNICME because the Member State involved had yet to exercise its discretion at the time the Regulation was issued.

In Case 11/82 *Piraiki-Patraiki v Commission* [1985] ECR 207, which was similar to *Bock*, the Commission Decision authorized France to impose quotas on imports of yarn from Greece. There was no obligation for France to implement this quota system—it was discretionary as to whether it would exercise its power under this Decision. However, at the time, France operated a very restrictive system of licences for imports. The Greek importers sought to challenge this Decision. The Court of Justice stated as follows.

Case 11/82 *Piraiki-Patraiki v Commission* [1985] ECR 207

6. With regard to the question of direct concern, the Commission and the Government of the French Republic argue that the applicants are not directly affected by the decision at issue since that decision merely authorizes the French Republic to institute a quota system on

imports of cotton yarn from Greece, and thus leaves the Member State which requested the authorization free to make use of it or not. The decision therefore does not itself establish a system limiting imports but, in order to have practical effect, requires implementing measures on the part of the French authorities.

7. It is true that without implementing measures adopted at the national level the Commission decision could not have affected the applicants. In this case, however, that fact does not in itself prevent the decision from being of direct concern to the applicants if other factors justify the conclusion that they have a direct interest in bringing the action.
8. In that respect it should be pointed out that, as the Commission itself admitted during the written procedure, even before being authorized to do so by the Commission the French Republic applied a very restrictive system of licences for imports of cotton yarn of Greek origin. It should moreover be observed that the request for protective measures not only came from the French authorities but sought to obtain the Commission's authorization for a system of import quotas more strict than that which was finally granted.
9. In those circumstances the possibility that the French Republic might decide not to make use of the authorization granted to it by the Commission decision was entirely theoretical, since there could be no doubt as to the intention of the French authorities to apply the decision.

The Court of Justice ruled that Greek importers with prior contracts had *locus standi* to challenge the Decision. The Decision would be annulled insofar as it applied to contracts entered into before the date of its notification and to be performed during the period of its application. The crucial distinction between this case and *UNICME* is that, on the facts, the possibility of an exercise of intervening discretion by the French government could be disregarded. France already severely restricted such imports and, in fact, had requested a quota that was stricter than that given, so the chance that it would not utilize the permission to impose quotas was 'entirely theoretical'.

By contrast, in *Bock* the German authorities had actually stated that the Decision would be applied directly to the applicant, whereas in *Piraiki-Patraiki* it was simply the opinion of the Court of Justice that the French authorities would apply the Decision directly to the applicants. The test would therefore seem to be whether the Member State has given a sufficiently clear indication of how it will use its discretion. In *Bock* and *Piraiki-Patraiki* the Court of Justice considered that the respective governments had given such an indication, whereas in *UNICME* it was clear that the Italian government had not.

7.8 Non-privileged applicants: individual concern

The requirement for determining individual concern forms the second condition for the applicant to satisfy where they are seeking an annulment of an act that is of 'direct and individual concern' under Article 263 TFEU. Prior to the Lisbon Treaty, *locus standi* for judicial review was limited to Decisions addressed to a third party or a decision in the form of a Regulation (ie a disguised Decision), whereas Article 263 TFEU is broader in its scope and applies to an act that includes Regulations, Directives, and Decisions.

The concept of individual concern, like direct concern, has acted as a filtering mechanism to eliminate cases in which the act did not directly affect the applicant. The concept of 'individual concern' was considered in the pre-Lisbon case law on judicial review and it is assumed that the Court of Justice will continue to adopt the existing line of case law on this issue.

The classic statement of the law in this area comes from Case 25/62 *Plaumann & Co v Commission* [1963] ECR 95. Plaumann was a German importer of clementines, who sought the annulment of a Commission Decision addressed to Germany, which refused permission to reduce the duty on imports of clementines. The Court of Justice held that Plaumann was not individually concerned by the Decision because it was a Decision that affected all German importers of clementines.

The *Plaumann* test provides as follows.

Case 25/62 *Plaumann & Co v Commission* [1963] ECR 95, 107 (emphasis added)

Persons other than those to whom a decision is addressed may only claim to be individually concerned if that decision affects them *by reason of certain attributes which are peculiar to them or by reason of circumstances in which they are differentiated from all other persons* and by virtue of these factors distinguishes them individually just as in the case of the person addressed. In the present case the applicant is affected by the disputed Decision as an importer of clementines, that is to say, by reason of a commercial activity which may at any time be practised by any person and is not therefore such as to distinguish the applicant in relation to the contested Decision as in the case of the addressee.

The text emphasized in the extract indicates the key parts of the test for individual concern. An applicant must show that they:

- were affected by reason of certain attributes or circumstances; and
- are differentiated from all others; and
- can be distinguished individually.

In applying this test to the facts, the Court held that Plaumann was not individually concerned by the Decision. The Decision applied to all importers of clementines and it could not be said that Plaumann was in any way differentiated from the others, or in a fixed or identifiable group, and therefore Plaumann did not have *locus standi*.

To summarize, individual concern requires that the applicant be singled out in some way by the measure. The applicant seeking an annulment must be a member of a closed class—that is, a fixed or identifiable group—as opposed to an open class. The open class would suggest that it is neither fixed nor a clearly identifiable group of persons. This means that it will be more difficult to prove individual concern where the measure challenged is a Regulation than where it is a Decision.

?! **THINKING POINT**

Why do you think this is so? If you have difficulty answering this question, look back at the difference between these types of legislative measure.

Unfortunately, for all concerned, the Court of Justice has not developed a consistent approach to the question of whether an applicant is sufficiently singled out by a measure. A number of approaches have been discernible for some years. First, the 'closed class' test often provides a starting point for establishing *locus standi*. Secondly, where an applicant fails to satisfy this test when strictly applied, the Court of Justice may consider whether it fulfils a more generous test based on the facts. Finally, where the measure in question has been issued as a result of proceedings, has been issued by the applicant, or is an anti-dumping measure, the Court has developed a special test.

7.8.1 The 'closed class' test

The 'closed class' test involves consideration of whether it was possible to identify all of the potential applicants at the time the measure allegedly affecting them was passed. In order to do this, the membership of the class must have been fixed at that time and it must have been possible to ascertain the identity of those members. Where is the burden of proof? It is for an applicant to show that it is a member of such a class (possibly the only member).

The test is a strict one, as can be seen from Case 231/82 *Spijker Kwasten BV v Commission* [1983] ECR 259. Spijker, a Dutch importer of Chinese brushes, applied for an import licence, which the Dutch authorities stated they would refuse if the Commission were to authorize them to do so. The Commission Decision authorized the Dutch government, for a period of six months, to ban imports of Chinese brushes. Not only had the Dutch request for such a Decision been made in response to Spijker's imports, but also Spijker was the only importer of such goods into the Netherlands at the time. Despite these facts, the Court of Justice concluded that Spijker was not individually concerned by the measure.

Case 231/82 *Spijker Kwasten BV v Commission* [1983] ECR 259

5. The Commission objects that the contested decision is addressed to the Benelux States alone and that it is neither of direct nor of individual concern to the applicant within the meaning of the second paragraph of Article 173 of the Treaty.
6. On the other hand the applicant contends in support of the admissibility of the action that the said decision is of direct and individual concern to it with regard to its legal position since it is the only trader-importer established in the Benelux States [Belgium, the Netherlands, and Luxembourg] which regularly imports into the Netherlands brushes originating

in the People's Republic of China and since, moreover, the contested decision was adopted on account of the importation with which the present case is concerned.

7. Under the second paragraph of Article 173 of the Treaty the admissibility of an action for a declaration that a decision is void brought by a natural or legal person to whom the decision was not addressed is subject to the requirements that the decision must be of direct and individual concern to the applicant. In this case since Spijker Kwasten BV is not one of the persons to whom the contested decision was addressed it is necessary to consider whether the decision is of direct or individual concern to it.
8. The Court has already stated in its judgment of 15 July 1963 in Case 25/62 Plaumann [1963] ECR 95 that persons other than those to whom a decision is addressed may claim to be individually concerned by that decision only if it affects them by reason of certain attributes which are peculiar to them or by reason of circumstances in which they are differentiated from all other persons and if by virtue of those factors it distinguishes them individually just as in the case of the person addressed.
9. That is not the case in the present proceedings. The contested decision concerns the applicant merely by virtue of its objective capacity as an importer of the goods in question in the same manner as any other trader who is, or might be in the future, in the same situation. In fact the purpose of the decision is to authorize the Benelux States not to apply Community treatment for a fixed period to all imports of brushes originating in the People's Republic of China and in free circulation in another Member State. With regard to the importers of such products it is therefore a measure of general application covering situations which are determined objectively and it entails legal effects for categories of persons envisaged in a general and abstract manner. Thus the contested decision is not of individual concern to the applicant.
10. That conclusion is not invalidated by the fact that the applicant, according to its statement which was not disputed by the Commission, is the only trader-importer established in the Benelux States regularly importing into the Netherlands brushes originating in the People's Republic of China and that it was one of its imports which led to the adoption of the contested decision. As the Court stated in its judgment of 6 October 1982 in Case 307/81 Alusuisse [1982] ECR 3463, a measure does not cease to be a regulation because it is possible to determine the number or even the identity of the persons to whom it applies at any given time as long as it is established that such application takes effect by virtue of an objective legal or factual situation defined by the measure in relation to its purpose.

The Court of Justice ruled that the class of those potentially affected was not closed (and therefore not ascertainable) at the time of the Decision because other importers might materialize during the six-month period, who would then be adversely affected by the Decision and form part of the class of potential applicants.

The next set of cases, Joined Cases 41–44/70 *International Fruit Co and Others v Commission* [1971] ECR 411, involved consideration of whether there was an identifiable closed class affected by two Regulations. The first Regulation provided that Member States were required to notify the Commission, on a weekly basis, of the quantity of apples for which import licences had been requested. This enabled the Commission to determine the percentage of licences that should be granted. The second Regulation provided that only 80 per cent of licence applications submitted by the applicants in the preceding week should be granted. Their applications were amongst those refused and they challenged the second Regulation. The Court of Justice held that the Regulation must be regarded as a conglomeration of individual decisions that individually concerned the applicant. It applied to a fixed and ascertainable class—that is, applicants in a particular week—and although it took account only of the total quantity of applications, the decision then had to be applied to each individual application. This necessarily involved a decision on each application. Despite the fact that the Commission named the measure a Regulation and it appeared to be a general measure, the Court acknowledged that in fact it was a set of disguised Decisions.

A similar approach was taken in one of the many '*Isoglucose* cases', a series of cases in the late 1970s and early 1980s involving the introduction of quotas and levies, and the abolition of subsidies, on the production of isoglucose, a liquid sugar substitute. In Case 138/79 *Roquette Frères v Council* [1980] ECR 3333, a Regulation had established quotas for the production of isoglucose and listed in an annex the companies to which these quotas applied. Roquette Frères, one of the companies listed, challenged the validity of the Regulation. The Court of Justice ruled that the Regulation was of individual concern to the applicants and other producers listed in the annex because specific quotas were allotted to them by name; therefore the Regulation was susceptible to challenge.

In 2010, the General Court in Case T-16/04 *Arcelor SA v Parliament and Council* [2010] Env LR D7 rejected an action for an annulment of Directive 2003/87/EC of the European Parliament and of the Council of 13 October 2003 establishing a scheme for greenhouse gas emission allowance trading within the Community … , OJ 2003 L275/32. Arcelor, which is the largest steel manufacturer in the world, claimed that the application of the Directive infringed several principles of EU law—in particular, the right of property, the freedom to pursue an economic activity, the principle of proportionality, the principle of equal treatment, freedom of establishment, and the principle of legal certainty. The General Court dismissed the action for annulment as inadmissible because Arcelor was neither individually nor directly concerned by the Directive. The General Court concluded that the legislation applies, in a general and abstract manner, to all of the operators listed in the annex to the Directive, including those in the steel production sector, and is therefore not capable of characterizing as different the factual and legal situation of Arcelor in comparison with those other operators.

7.8.2 A 'test' based on the facts and circumstances

In many cases, the Court of Justice has found that the contested measure potentially applies to a group of applicants that is neither fixed nor ascertainable, but has then gone on to accept that the applicant in the case before it is nonetheless individually concerned. This involves a careful examination of the particular facts of the case and an assessment as to whether the applicant

→ CROSS-REFERENCE
See 8.4.2.

is affected by the measure in a way that no other potential applicant is affected. There are a number of examples of this approach in the case law of the Court of Justice.

In Joined Cases 106 & 107/63 *Toepfer Getreide-Import Gesellschaft v Commission* [1965] ECR 405, the Court of Justice had to consider the facts and circumstances of the case to ascertain whether the applicant was in a 'closed class'. A zero levy was imposed on maize imports into Germany from 1 October 1963. A Commission Decision of 1 October then raised the levy with effect from 2 October, and a second Commission Decision, of 4 October, authorized Germany to refuse applications for import licences made between 1 and 4 October. Toepfer, a German maize importer who had made an application on 1 October, challenged the second Decision under Article 263 TFEU.

Joined Cases 106 & 107/63 *Toepfer Getreide-Import Gesellschaft v Commission* [1965] ECR 405, 410–12

Admissibility of the applications

As the contested decision was not addressed to the applicants the defendant argues that it was not of direct and individual concern to them within the meaning of Article 173 of the Treaty [now Article 263 TFEU]; it only concerns the applicants through the effect of the protective measure in question, and thus indirectly.

The defendant further argues that, since the protective measure was drawn up in general terms applicable to all importers in a position to ask for an import licence during the period between 1 and 4 October 1963, neither this measure nor the decision which upheld it is of individual concern to the applicants.

[…]

The expression 'of … individual concern'

It is clear from the fact that on 1 October 1963 the Commission took a decision fixing new free at-frontier prices for maize imported into the Federal Republic as from 2 October, that the danger which the protective measures retained by the Commission were to guard against no longer existed as from this latter date.

Therefore the only persons concerned by the said measures were importers who had applied for an import licence during the course of the day of 1 October 1963. The number and identity of these importers had already become fixed and ascertainable before 4 October, when the contested decision was made. The Commission was in a position to know that its decision affected the interests and the position of the said importers alone.

The factual situation thus created differentiates the said importers, including the applicants, from all other persons and distinguishes them individually just as in the case of the person addressed.

Therefore the objection of inadmissibility which has been raised is unfounded and the applications are admissible.

The Court of Justice held that Toepfer and other importers who had made applications on 1 October were individually concerned by the second Decision. The effect of the first Decision was that the 0 per cent levy was available only on 1 October and so only those importers which had applied for a licence on that day were adversely affected by the second Decision authorizing the refusal of their licences. Applications made on 2–4 October that were refused could be resubmitted thereafter without loss to the applicants, since the applicable levy would be the same. The class of potential applicants was therefore 'fixed and ascertainable' at the time the Decision was taken, and the factual situation differentiated them from all others in the same way that a Decision addressed to them would have done.

REVIEW QUESTION

Try to apply this 'factual' test to these facts. Do you think that Toepfer was individually concerned by this Decision?

Answer: In effect, Toepfer and the other 1 October applicants created a closed class within a larger class of 1–4 October applicants. This larger class was not closed at the date of the Decision because the Decision was issued on 4 October.

In *Bock* and *Piraiki-Patraiki*, the classes of potential applicant (all importers of Chinese mushrooms and all importers of Greek yarn into France, respectively) were not closed. However, the Court of Justice held that the applicant importers were individually concerned. In these cases, the Court of Justice adopted a similar test to that in *Toepfer* to find that the applicants were differentiated on the facts from all other potential applicants.

➔ CROSS-REFERENCE
See 7.7 for the facts in *Bock*.

In *Bock*, Bock did not challenge the Decision in its entirety, but only insofar as it applied to importers who had already applied for import licences. The Court of Justice considered that Bock was individually concerned by this part of the Decision because such importers constituted a fixed and ascertainable class. It therefore annulled the Decision insofar as it applied to existing licence applications.

➔ CROSS-REFERENCE
See 7.7 for the facts in *Piraiki-Patraiki*.

The reasoning in *Piraiki-Patraiki* was similar. The Decision applied to all potential importers of Greek yarn into France, but the Court of Justice accepted that importers already bound by contractual arrangements (and who would therefore be particularly prejudiced by the Decision when it was passed) could be distinguished from importers who were not so bound. The class of such importers was therefore fixed at the date of the Decision. The Commission could scarcely argue that it was not possible to identify the members of this class, since it was required to carry out precisely that task as part of the inquiry that the Greek Act of Accession to the EU obliged it to conduct into the effects of any proposed protective measure.

The Court of Justice adopted a similar line of reasoning in Case C-309/89 *Codorniu SA v Council* [1994] ECR I-1853. Significantly, the Court took a more liberal approach in its interpretation of individual concern by taking into account the impact and ability of the applicant to conduct its economic activity. Codorniu, a Spanish producer of quality sparkling wine, applied for an annulment of a Regulation that restricted the use of the word *crémant* to quality sparkling wines originating in France and Luxembourg. Codorniu had owned the registered trade mark 'Gran Cremant' since 1924 as an indication of the origin of its quality sparkling wines. The Court considered whether Codorniu had *locus standi*.

Case C-309/89 *Codorniu SA v Council* [1994] ECR I-1853

14. In support of its objection of inadmissibility the Council states that it did not adopt the contested provision on the basis of the circumstances peculiar to certain producers but on the basis of a choice of wine-marketing policy in relation to a particular product. The contested provision reserves the use of the term 'crémant' to quality sparkling wines psr ['produced in a specific region'] manufactured under specific conditions in certain Member States. It thus constitutes a measure applicable to an objectively determined situation which has legal effects in respect of categories of persons considered in a general and abstract manner.
15. According to the Council, Codorniu is concerned by the contested provision only in its capacity as a producer of quality sparkling wines psr using the term 'crémant', like any other producer in an identical situation. Even if when that provision was adopted the number or identity of producers of sparkling wines using the term 'crémant' could theoretically be determined, the measure in question remains essentially a regulation inasmuch as it applies on the basis of an objective situation of law or fact defined by the measure in relation to its objective.
16. Codorniu alleges that the contested provision is in reality a decision adopted in the guise of a regulation. It has no general scope but affects a well-determined class of producers which cannot be altered. Such producers are those who on 1 September 1989 traditionally designated their sparkling wines with the term 'crémant'. For that class the contested provision has no general scope. Furthermore, the direct result of the contested provision will be to prevent Codorniu from using the term 'Gran Cremant' which will involve a loss of 38 per cent of its turnover. The effect of that damage is to distinguish it, within the meaning of the second paragraph of Article 173 of the Treaty [now Article 263 TFEU], from any other trader. Codorniu alleges that the Court has already recognized the admissibility of an action for annulment brought by a natural or legal person against a regulation in such circumstances (see the judgment in Case C-358/89 *Extramet Industrie v Council* [1991] ECR I-2501).
17. Under the second paragraph of Article 173 of the Treaty the institution of proceedings by a natural or legal person for a declaration that a regulation is void is subject to the condition that the provisions of the regulation at issue in the proceedings constitute in reality a decision of direct and individual concern to that person.
18. As the Court has already held, the general applicability, and thus the legislative nature, of a measure is not called in question by the fact that it is possible to determine more or less exactly the number or even the identity of the persons to whom it applies at any given time, as long as it is established that it applies to them by virtue of an objective legal or factual situation defined by the measure in question in relation to its purpose (see most recently the judgment in Case C-298/89 *Gibraltar v Council* [1993] ECR I-3605, paragraph 17).
19. Although it is true that according to the criteria in the second paragraph of Article 173 of the Treaty the contested provision is, by nature and by virtue of its sphere of application, of a legislative nature in that it applies to the traders concerned in general, that does not prevent it from being of individual concern to some of them.

20. Natural or legal persons may claim that a contested provision is of individual concern to them only if it affects them by reason of certain attributes which are peculiar to them or by reason of circumstances in which they are differentiated from all other persons (see the judgment in Case 25/62 *Plaumann v Commission* [1963] ECR 95).
21. Codorniu registered the graphic trade mark 'Gran Cremant de Codorniu' in Spain in 1924 and traditionally used that mark both before and after registration. By reserving the right to use the term 'crémant' to French and Luxembourg producers, the contested provision prevents Codorniu from using its graphic trade mark.
22. It follows that Codorniu has established the existence of a situation which from the point of view of the contested provision differentiates it from all other traders.
23. It follows that the objection of inadmissibility put forward by the Council must be dismissed.

The Court ruled that Codorniu was differentiated from other producers who might be affected by the Regulation because it had registered and used the word *crémant* as part of its trade mark since 1924. Crucially, at para 21, the Court of Justice indicates a reluctance to interfere with the applicant's right to exploit its intellectual property right and affirms that the Court has to balance competing interests. Underlying the reasoning in this case, at para 19, the Court maintains the importance of ascertaining whether the act—in this particular case, in the form of a Regulation—was of individual concern to the applicant.

In Case C-152/88 *Sofrimport SARL v Commission* [1990] ECR I-2477, the Court of Justice took a relaxed approach towards individual concern where an EU institution is under a specific obligation to take into account specific circumstances when exercising its powers. Sofrimport had shipped apples from Chile prior to the issue of a Regulation that suspended import licences for Chilean apples. Sofrimport's subsequent application to the French authorities for an import licence was refused, and it then applied for annulment of the Regulation and damages under Article 340 TFEU.

The Court of Justice held that Sofrimport had *locus standi* to challenge the Regulation and that it should be annulled insofar as it applied to goods in transit. When taking protectionist measures, the Commission was required, under a previous Regulation, to take into account the position of importers with goods in transit, and since such importers constituted a fixed and ascertainable class, they could be said to be individually concerned. These importers therefore had *locus standi* to challenge the Regulation insofar as it applied to them.

The Court of First Instance (now the General Court) reached a different decision in Case T-489/93 *Unifruit Hellas v Commission* [1994] ECR II-1201—a case involving similar facts, but a different Regulation. Unifruit Hellas had shipped apples from Chile prior to the issue of a Regulation that imposed an import duty on Chilean apples. Unifruit Hellas applied for annulment of the Regulation and for damages. It was held that the action for annulment was inadmissible (but that the action under Article 340 TFEU was admissible). The Court of First Instance ruled that although importers whose goods were in transit to the EU when the Regulation introduced a charge on those goods constituted a fixed and identifiable class of persons, that was not sufficient. The Regulation in question did not require the Commission to take into account the special position of products in transit (unlike the Regulation in *Sofrimport*) and so there was no individual concern.

?! THINKING POINT

Do you agree with the reasoning of the Court of Justice in Unifruit Hellas?

7.8.3 Measures issued as a result of proceedings initiated by applicant

Where the measure complained of was adopted as a result of proceedings in which the applicant was involved, the Court of Justice has been prepared to rule that the applicant is individually concerned even though the act may not be specifically directed at the applicant. This is most likely to be the case where the measure concerns competition policy or is an anti-dumping measure (ie a measure designed to stop the import into the EU of goods priced below the normal price where this could cause economic harm within the EU).

For example, in Case 26/76 *Metro-SB-Grossmärkte GmbH & Co KG v Commission* [1977] ECR 1875, the applicant sought to challenge a Decision addressed to another company, SABA, regarding its distribution system. The Decision had been issued in response to a complaint made by the applicant to the Commission that SABA was in breach of EU competition policy. The Court ruled that since the applicant was entitled to request that the Commission investigate an infringement of competition rules, the applicant was equally entitled to institute annulment proceedings in order to protect its legitimate interests. The Court concluded that the applicant was individually concerned. Similarly, in Case 264/82 *Timex Corporation v Council* [1985] ECR 849, an applicant which had initiated the complaint and given evidence in the proceedings giving rise to the anti-dumping measure, and where the fixing of the anti-dumping duty was based on the effect of the dumping on the applicant, was held to be individually concerned by that measure.

7.8.4 Anti-dumping measures

As well as those who initiate the procedure leading to the adoption of an anti-dumping measure, the Court of Justice has also recognized that producers, exporters, or importers of the product at which the measure is directed may be individually concerned by it. This indicates a willingness on the part of the Court to take a more relaxed approach to individual concern in competition and anti-dumping cases.

In Joined Cases 239 & 275/82 *Allied Corporation v Commission* [1984] ECR 1005, the Court of Justice identified as relevant the fact that the producers and exporters had given undertakings pursuant to one of the contested Regulations, referred to in the other contested Regulation, and that their individual circumstances formed the subject matter of the two Regulations.

Where the applicant is not an exporter or a producer, but only an importer, it must prove that it is particularly singled out by the measure. For example, in Case C-358/89 *Extramet Industrie SA v Council* [1991] ECR I-2501, the Court of Justice ruled that an importer was individually concerned where it was the largest importer and end user of the product, its business was dependent to a large extent upon the product, and it was difficult to obtain supplies elsewhere.

7.9 Reforming *locus standi* for non-privileged applicants

7.9.1 A judicial debate

Prior to the Lisbon Treaty, the EU Courts considered several cases in which strong arguments were put forward for a relaxation of the rules of *locus standi*. In Case C-50/00 P *Unión de Pequeños Agricultores v Council, Commission intervening* (*UPA*) [2002] ECR I-6677, Advocate General Jacobs argued that a narrow interpretation of individual concern prevented the Court from fully protecting an applicant's fundamental rights—in particular, the right to obtain an effective remedy. The Court of First Instance (now the General Court) in Case T-177/01 *Jégo-Quéré SA v Commission* [2002] ECR II-2365 followed the reasoning of Advocate General Jacobs and found that, in the absence of an effective remedy in the national courts, an applicant could bring an action for annulment before the Court of Justice. The Court of First Instance concluded that there is no compelling reason to read into the notion of individual concern, within the meaning of the fourth paragraph of Article 230 EC (now Article 263 TFEU), a requirement that an individual applicant seeking to challenge a general measure must be differentiated from all others affected by it in the same way as an addressee.

Despite the Opinion of Advocate General Jacobs and the judgment of the Court of First Instance, the Court of Justice rejected any relaxation of the rules for *locus standi* within the Treaty, and held that any change to the Treaty was a matter for the Member States and that it was not for the Court to rewrite the Treaty. To this end, the Court of Justice, in *UPA*, reaffirmed that the understanding of individual concern in *Plaumann* remained the correct approach.

→ CROSS-REFERENCE
See 6.6 for a discussion on *UPA* and challenging the validity of EU law.

In Case C-50/00 P *UPA* [2002] ECR I-6677, UPA, a trade association representing small agricultural businesses in Spain, brought an action for the annulment of Council Regulation (EC) No 1638/98 of 20 July 1998 amending Regulation No 136/66/EEC on the establishment of a common organisation of the market in oils and fats, OJ 1998 L210/32. The Court of First Instance in Case T-173/98 *UPA v Council* [1999] ECR II-3357 held the action inadmissible on the grounds that the Regulation was neither a Decision nor of individual concern to UPA so as to constitute a Decision insofar as it applied to it. UPA appealed to the Court of Justice. In his Opinion, Advocate General Jacobs argued that the case law on the *locus standi* of natural and legal persons needed to be changed in order to provide adequate judicial protection of persons affected by EU measures, and that a person should be regarded as individually concerned where 'by reason of his particular circumstances, the measure has, or is liable to have, a substantial adverse effect on his interests'. The Advocate General therefore concluded that the judgment of the Court of First Instance should be annulled.

Case C-50/00 P *Unión de Pequeños Agricultores v Council, Commission intervening* (*UPA*) [2002] ECR I-6677, Opinion of Advocate General Jacobs

Suggested solution: a new interpretation of the notion of individual concern

59. The key to the problem of judicial protection against unlawful Community [now Union] acts lies therefore, in my view, in the notion of individual concern laid down in the fourth paragraph of Article 230 EC [now Article 263 TFEU]. There are no compelling reasons to read into that notion a requirement that an individual applicant seeking to challenge a general measure must be differentiated from all others affected by it in the same way as an addressee. On that reading, the greater the number of persons affected by a measure the less likely it is that judicial review under the fourth paragraph of Article 230 EC will be made available. The fact that a measure adversely affects a large number of individuals, causing wide-spread rather than limited harm, provides however to my mind a positive reason for accepting a direct challenge by one or more of those individuals.
60. In my opinion, it should therefore be accepted that a person is to be regarded as individually concerned by a Community measure where, by reason of his particular circumstances, the measure has, or is liable to have, a substantial adverse effect on his interests.

Advantages of the suggested interpretation of the notion of individual concern

61. A development along those lines of the case-law on the interpretation of Article 230 EC would have several very substantial advantages.
62. First … it seems the only way to avoid what may in some cases be a total lack of judicial protection—a *déni de justice*.
63. Second, the suggested interpretation of the notion of individual concern would considerably improve judicial protection. By laying down a more generous test for standing for individual applicants than that adopted by the Court in the existing case-law, it would not only ensure that individual applicants who are directly and adversely affected by Community measures are never left without a judicial remedy; it would also allow issues of validity of general measures to be addressed in the context of the procedure which is best suited to resolving them, and in which effective interim relief is available.
64. Third, it would also have the great advantage of providing clarity to a body of case-law which has often, and rightly in my view, been criticised for its complexity and lack of coherence, and which may make it difficult for practitioners to advise in what court to take proceedings, or even lead them to take parallel proceedings in the national courts and the Court of First Instance.

65. Fourth, by ruling that individual applicants are individually concerned by general measures which affect them adversely, the Court of Justice would encourage the use of direct actions to resolve issues of validity, thus limiting the number of challenges raised via Article 234 EC [now Article 237 TFEU]. That would, as explained above, be beneficial for legal certainty and the uniform application of Community law [now EU law] . . . Individuals who were adversely affected by general measures would therefore not be precluded by that case-law from challenging such measures before national courts. None the less, if the notion of individual concern were interpreted in the way I have suggested, and standing for individuals accordingly liberalised, it may be expected that many challenges would be brought by way of direct action before the Court of First Instance.

66. A point of equal, or even greater, importance is that the interpretation of Article 230 EC which I propose would shift the emphasis of judicial review from questions of admissibility to questions of substance. While it may be accepted that the Community legislative process should be protected against undue judicial intervention, such protection can be more properly achieved by the application of substantive standards of judicial review which allow the institutions an appropriate 'margin of appreciation' in the exercise of their powers than by the application of strict rules on admissibility which have the effect of 'blindly' excluding applicants without consideration of the merits of the arguments they put forward.

→ CROSS-REFERENCE
See 9.5.1 for a discussion on enforcement actions.

Subsequently, the Court of First Instance (now General Court) gave judgment in Case T-177/01 *Jégo-Quéré SA v Commission* [2002] ECR II-2365. Jégo-Quéré, a fishing company, applied for partial annulment of Commission Regulation (EC) No 1162/2001 of 14 June 2001 establishing measures for the recovery of the stock of hake in ICES sub-areas III, IV, V, VI and VII and ICES divisions VIII a, b, d, e and associated conditions for the control of activities of fishing vessels, OJ 2001 L159/4. The Regulation imposed minimizing mesh sizes on fishing vessels operating in certain areas and Jégo-Quéré alleged that its ability to carry on its business was adversely affected by the Regulation. In applying the *Plaumann* test, the Court of First Instance found that the applicant on the facts could not differentiate itself sufficiently to have individual concern. However, the Court was concerned that if Jégo-Quéré's action were to be held inadmissible, it would be denied any legal remedy enabling it to challenge the legality of the contested provisions. Access to the courts was an essential element of a union based on the rule of law, and was guaranteed by the establishment in the Treaties of a complete system of remedies and procedures enabling the Court to review the legality of acts of the institutions, as well as by the establishment by the Court of a right to an effective remedy. The latter had also been reaffirmed by Article 47 of the Charter of Fundamental Rights of the EU.

?! THINKING POINT

What other actions might have provided a remedy?

CROSS-REFERENCE
See Chapter 8 for actions under Article 340 TFEU; for a discussion on Article 267 TFEU, see Chapter 6.

There were two other routes by which an individual might obtain a declaration that an EU measure was unlawful: Article 267 TFEU and Article 340 TFEU. However, an Article 267 TFEU ruling was not possible in the present case because there were no acts of implementation capable of giving rise to an action in the national courts. Although Jégo-Quéré could breach the Regulation and then assert its illegality in proceedings against it, individuals could not be required to breach the law in order to gain access to justice. Neither could an Article 340 TFEU action provide a solution because it could not result in the annulment of an EU measure that was held to be unlawful.

The Court devised a test for individual concern.

Case T-177/01 *Jégo-Quéré SA v Commission* [2002] ECR II-2365

51. In the light of the foregoing, and in order to ensure effective judicial protection for individuals, a natural or legal person is to be regarded as individually concerned by a Community [now Union] measure of general application that concerns him directly if the measure in question affects his legal position, in a manner which is both definite and immediate, by restricting his rights or by imposing obligations on him. The number and position of other persons who are likewise affected by the measure, or who may be so, are of no relevance in that regard.

In Case C-50/00 P *UPA* [2002] ECR I-6677, the Court of Justice rejected the reasoning of the Court of First Instance in *Jégo-Quéré* and confirmed its judgment in Case C-321/95 P *Greenpeace* [1998] ECR I-1651 that a non-privileged applicant could challenge a Regulation only if it was, in fact, a Decision or if the applicant was individually concerned by it, so that it was a Decision in respect of that applicant. The Court of Justice made the following observation.

Case C-50/00 P *Unión de Pequeños Agricultores v Council, Commission intervening* (*UPA*) [2002] ECR I-6677

38. The European Community [now Union] is, however, a community based on the rule of law in which its institutions are subject to judicial review of the compatibility of their acts with the Treaty and with the general principles of law which include fundamental rights.

39. Individuals are therefore entitled to effective judicial protection of the rights they derive from the Community legal order, and the right to such protection is one of the general principles of law stemming from the constitutional traditions common to the Member States. That right has also been enshrined in Articles 6 and 13 of the European Convention for the Protection of Human Rights and Fundamental Freedoms …

40. … [T]he Treaty has established a complete system of legal remedies and procedures designed to ensure judicial review of the legality of acts of the institutions, and has entrusted such review to the Community Courts (see, to that effect, *Les Verts v Parliament* [Case 294/83

Parti Ecologiste 'les Verts' v European Parliament [1986] ECR 1339], paragraph 23). Under that system, where natural or legal persons cannot, by reason of the conditions for admissibility laid down in the fourth paragraph of Article 173 of the Treaty [now Article 263 TFEU], directly challenge Community measures of general application, they are able, depending on the case, either indirectly to plead the invalidity of such acts before the Community Courts ... or to do so before the national courts and ask them, since they have no jurisdiction themselves to declare those measures invalid (see Case 314/85 *Foto-Frost* [1987] ECR 4199, paragraph 20), to make a reference to the Court of Justice for a preliminary ruling on validity.

41. Thus it is for the Member States to establish a system of legal remedies and procedures which ensure respect for the right to effective judicial protection.

42. In that context, in accordance with the principle of sincere cooperation laid down in Article 5 of the Treaty [now repealed], national courts are required, so far as possible, to interpret and apply national procedural rules governing the exercise of rights of action in a way that enables natural and legal persons to challenge before the courts the legality of any decision or other national measure relative to the application to them of a Community act of general application, by pleading the invalidity of such an act.

43. As the Advocate General has pointed out in paragraphs 50 to 53 of his Opinion, it is not acceptable to adopt an interpretation of the system of remedies, such as that favoured by the appellant, to the effect that a direct action for annulment before the Community Court will be available where it can be shown, following an examination by that Court of the particular national procedural rules, that those rules do not allow the individual to bring proceedings to contest the validity of the Community measure at issue. Such an interpretation would require the Community Court, in each individual case, to examine and interpret national procedural law. That would go beyond its jurisdiction when reviewing the legality of Community measures.

44. Finally, it should be added that, according to the system for judicial review of legality established by the Treaty, a natural or legal person can bring an action challenging a regulation only if it is concerned both directly and individually. Although this last condition must be interpreted in the light of the principle of effective judicial protection by taking account of the various circumstances that may distinguish an applicant individually (see, for example, Joined Cases 67/85, 68/85, and 70/85 *Van der Kooy v Commission* [1988] ECR 219, paragraph 14; *Extramet Industrie v Council* [Case C-358/89 *Extramet Industrie v Council* [1991] ECR I-2501], paragraph 13; and *Codorniu v Council* [Case C-309/89 *Codorniu SA v Council* [1994] ECR I-1853], paragraph 19), such an interpretation cannot have the effect of setting aside the condition in question, expressly laid down in the Treaty, without going beyond the jurisdiction conferred by the Treaty on the Community Courts.

45. While it is, admittedly, possible to envisage a system of judicial review of the legality of Community measures of general application different from that established by the founding Treaty and never amended as to its principles, it is for the Member States, if necessary ... to reform the system currently in force.

The extract demonstrates a refusal on the part of the Court of Justice to follow the approach suggested in Advocate General Jacobs's Opinion in *UPA* or of the Court of First Instance (now General Court) in *Jégo-Quéré* to alter the orthodox criteria of the *Plaumann* test. The Court opined that it was more appropriate for a change in the Treaty to give effect to an alternative test and that inadequacies with the national procedural rules should be resolved by the Member States. The judgment of the Court of Justice in Case C-263/02 P *Jégo-Quéré* [2004] ECR I-3425 followed that in *UPA*.

?! THINKING POINT

Which of these arguments do you find most convincing?

→ CROSS-REFERENCE
See 7.15 for a discussion on Article 277 TFEU.

Even if you find the arguments of the Court of First Instance (now the General Court) convincing, remember that it is the judgment of the Court of Justice that is authoritative. Note that the Court of Justice accepted that applicants had rights of access to the courts and to an effective remedy, but concluded that Articles 263, 267, and 277 TFEU provided 'a complete system of legal remedies'.

7.10 Regulatory acts that do not entail implementing measures

In Case C-50/00 P *UPA v Council* [2002] ECR I-6677, at para 45, the Court of Justice considered that it would be possible to 'envisage a system of judicial review of the legality of Community [Union] measures of general application different from that established by the founding Treaty'. However, the Court concluded that any changes to the Treaty to broaden access to the Court for judicial review were a matter for the Member States and could be made only by a process of Treaty revision.

Following on from the Opinion of Advocate General Jacobs and the debate that took place within the Constitutional Convention with regard to the future operation of Article 230 EC (now Article 263 TFEU) (Secretariat of the Convention, CONV 7354/03, 12 May 2003), the Member States, in the Treaty of Lisbon, agreed a revised version of Article 230 EC (now Article 263 TFEU) that appears to have widened the scope of judicial review by an individual of 'a regulatory act which is of direct concern to them and which does not entail implementing measures'. This would appear to remove the need for an applicant to demonstrate individual concern and therefore avoids the difficulties that applicants face in establishing that a measure affects them in some unique way, as per *Plaumann*. Thus, where a regulatory act produces a legal effect, Article 263 TFEU would appear to grant *locus standi*. However, Article 263 TFEU represents only a partial reform and the changes do not go as far as those proposed by Advocate General Jacobs in *UPA*, in which he argued that an applicant should be able to seek judicial review of an act of general application in circumstances in which it had an effect upon the applicant's legal position.

Where regulatory acts are concerned, it is correct to assume that these are acts that concern all persons equally and are therefore not aimed at any specific individual. As a result, they would not normally be challenged by an individual unless, as discussed earlier, it is possible to demonstrate that the act includes a provision that has an 'individual', rather than a 'general', application. It may be suggested that the developments in Article 263 TFEU from previous versions of this provision are in recognition of the need for an effective remedy where an individual's rights are adversely affected by an EU act. However, there is an inherent risk that, by seeking to guarantee an effective remedy, a more relaxed interpretation of the *locus standi* criteria, which do not require that individual concern, may lead to increased litigation before an already overloaded Court.

Although what constitutes a regulatory act has not been defined by the Treaty and is subject to clarification by the Court, it is evident from judgments such as Case T-262/10 *Microban v Commission* [2011] ECR II-7697 that the EU Courts are distinguishing clearly between general legislative acts, such as Regulations, Directives, and Decisions, and regulatory acts. The latter appear to cover acts of general application, rather than legislative acts. In *Microban*, a Commission Decision amended Commission Directive 2002/72/EC of 6 August 2002 relating to plastic materials and articles intended to come into contact with foodstuffs, OJ 2002 L220/18, which regulated those chemicals that could be used in the manufacture of plastics. As a result of the Commission Decision, which amended the annex to the Directive to remove a chemical called triclosan from the list of permitted chemicals that could be used, Microban could no longer produce plastics.

In *Microban*, the regulatory act was in the form of a Decision that affected producers generally and thus there was no individual concern. But the Court permitted the action for judicial review, identifying that this was a clear regulatory act that required no further implementing measures. The General Court concluded that Microban should be able to seek judicial review because this was precisely the sort of regulatory act that was intended to be covered by the Treaty of Lisbon. It was an administrative act of the Commission to amend an existing legislative act and it required no further measures by a Member State or EU institution.

In Case T-18/10 *Inuit Tapiriit Kanatami ea v Parliament and Council* EU:T:2011:419, the General Court confirmed that a 'regulatory act' includes all acts of general application apart from legislative acts. The case concerned an action for judicial review brought by private traders of Regulation (EC) No 1007/2009 of the European Parliament and of the Council of 16 September 2009 on trade in seal products, OJ 2009 L286/36. In a very literal interpretation of 'regulatory act', the General Court held that this Regulation could not be considered as a 'regulatory act' because, as a Regulation, it was a general legislative measure. Furthermore, as it was a general legislative measure, the applicant would not be able to establish the necessary individual concern that would be required for judicial review, which therefore precluded the application from judicial review.

The judgment of the General Court was appealed to the Court of Justice in Case C-583/11 P *Inuit Tapiriit Kanatami v Parliament and Council* [2014] 1 CMLR 54, which followed the reasoning of the General Court. Advocate General Kokott endorsed the approach taken by the General Court regarding the notion of 'regulatory acts', as introduced by the Treaty of Lisbon. The Advocate General was therefore of the opinion that all 'regulatory acts' are acts of general application apart from legislative acts. Advocate General Kokott stated as follows.

Case C-583/11 P *Inuit Tapiriit Kanatami v Parliament and Council* [2014] 1 CMLR 54

38. The absence of easier direct legal remedies available to individuals against legislative acts can be explained principally by the particularly high democratic legitimation of parliamentary legislation. Accordingly, the distinction between legislative and non-legislative acts in respect of legal protection cannot be dismissed as merely formalistic; rather, it is attributable to a qualitative difference. In many national legal systems individuals have no direct legal remedies, or only limited remedies, against parliamentary laws.

In its judgment, the Court of Justice considered that, as a general rule and just as before the entry into force of the Treaty of Lisbon, any natural or legal person may institute proceedings against any EU act that produces binding legal effects where that act is addressed to that person or is of direct and individual concern to them. In that regard, the Court stated that those acts may be individual acts, such as a Decision addressed to a person, or acts of general application, which include both legislative acts, such as the basic Regulation, and regulatory acts.

The Court of Justice developed this point and held that, since the entry into force of the Treaty of Lisbon, some acts of general application *may* be challenged before the Court by natural and legal persons without their being obliged to satisfy the condition of individual concern. However, the Court was of the view that the Treaty states unequivocally that those less stringent admissibility rules apply only to a more restricted category of those acts—namely, regulatory acts. Thus, following the reasoning applied by the General Court, legislative acts, although they may also be of general application, are not covered by the concept of regulatory acts and therefore continue to be subject to more stringent admissibility rules.

Furthermore, the admissibility rules relating to actions brought against legislative acts, in particular the content of the condition of individual concern, were not altered by the Treaty of Lisbon. In that context, the General Court correctly ruled that the appellants involved did not satisfy at least one of the two conditions of admissibility applicable to them—namely, that of individual concern.

In C-274/12 P *Telefonica v Commission* EU:C:2013:852, the Court of Justice continued to define (and minimize) the scope of Article 263(4) TFEU along similar lines to that in *Inuit* and particularly with respect to the provision that '[a]ny natural or legal person may [...] institute proceedings against [...] a regulatory act which is of direct concern to them and does not entail implementing measures'.

The restrictive approach adopted in the interpretation of this provision is largely based on the potential reliance on requests for a preliminary ruling under Article 267 TFEU against the measures not susceptible to a direct challenge by 'non-qualified' applicants. Therefore, the Court of Justice could be said to have completed the reinterpretation of the post-Lisbon mechanisms for judicial review where it seems clear that Article 263(4) TFEU—and particularly its last limb—is bound to have (or to continue to have) a marginal role.

In *Inuit*, the Court of Justice made it clear that legislative measures are not covered by the concept of 'regulatory act'. However, that negative approach to the definition of 'regulatory act' left some questions unanswered, such as whether the definition excludes only those legislative measures derived from the ordinary legislative procedure (OLP), as the General Court had found, or all legislative measures, independently of their ultimate legal basis. The question of what 'implementing measures' meant was also not considered. This has now been addressed in *Telefonica*.

In its judgment in Case C-456/13 P *T & L Sugars Ltd, Sidul Açúcares, Unipessoal Lda v European Commission* EU:C:2015:284, the Court of Justice gave authoritative interpretation of the concept of 'implementing measures' for the determination of whether private parties have standing to challenge the legality of EU 'regulatory acts' under Article 263 TFEU. Arguably, this judgment, which broadly endorses the *Telefonica* judgment, would appear to have confirmed the restrictive application of Article 263(4) TFEU where there are 'implementing measures'. On an appeal from the General Court, the Court of Justice held that EU regulatory acts that require any type of implementing measure (no matter how mechanistic) under national law cannot be challenged under the third limb of Article 263(4) by direct action in the EU General Court by private parties who are not the addressee of the relevant regulatory act. Consequently, private parties' standing to seek the annulment of such acts by the General Court will depend on the claimant meeting the exacting standard of being 'directly and individually concerned' by the regulatory act under challenge.

The judgment of the Court of Justice in *T&L Sugars*, which follows the reasoning of the General Court, provides clarity on the concept of 'implementing measures' in Article 263(4) TFEU, which is a worthwhile development given the controversy that has dogged the Lisbon Treaty amendments to that Article. The Court of Justice's endorsement of the General Court's findings that any implementing measure, however minor and no matter how little discretion it requires from a Member State, is enough to deny standing narrows the scope—and therefore the usefulness to would-be claimants—of the test added to Article 263(4) by the Lisbon Treaty. This arguably excludes a wide variety of regulatory acts from the scope of Article 263(4) TFEU, contrary to the Lisbon Treaty's objective of facilitating direct access to the General Court for private parties whose interests are affected by non-legislative acts adopted by the EU institutions.

7.11 Directives

Directives have been subject to challenge by non-privileged applicants. It has been held that Directives are open to challenge if an applicant is directly and individually concerned by them (see eg Joined Cases T-172, 175, & 177/98 *Salamander AG v Parliament* [2000] ECR II-2487 and Case T-223/01 *Japan Tobacco Inc and JT International SA v Parliament and Council* [2002] ECR II-3259).

REVIEW QUESTION

What problems do you think might be encountered in relation to direct concern and Directives?

Answer: Since Directives leave some discretion to Member States and cannot produce direct legal effect until their implementation deadline has passed, it will be rare for a Directive to concern an applicant directly.

7.12 Grounds for annulment

Article 263 TFEU provides four grounds that may be relied upon by all applicants (subject to the fulfilment of the further requirements outlined earlier by non-privileged applicants and those in the intermediate category)—namely:

- lack of competence;
- infringement of an essential procedural requirement;
- infringement of the Treaties or of any rule of law relating to its application; and
- misuse of powers.

The grounds overlap and an applicant may rely on one or more in its challenge. The decision of the General Court need not identify the ground on which the challenge is successful. These grounds apply not only to direct actions, but also to indirect challenges under Article 277 TFEU.

7.12.1 Lack of competence

→ CROSS-REFERENCE
See 3.5 for a discussion on legal base.

If an institution acts beyond its powers, that act can be annulled. An example would be an act that had no legal base in the Treaty or in secondary legislation, and which the EU therefore had no power to take. This ground is rarely used because of the fallback power given by Articles 352–353 TFEU (see 3.2) and also because it can be difficult to establish that the institution adopting the measure in question lacked authority.

In Case C-84/94 *UK v Council (Working Time Directive)* [1996] ECR I-5755, the UK requested the annulment of a Directive imposing a maximum working week of 48 hours on the ground, inter alia, that the Council had no competence to adopt the Directive. The UK argued that the measure did not relate to health and safety at work, and therefore should not have been adopted under Article 154 TFEU; instead, its legal base should either have been Article 115 TFEU (as an internal market measure) or Articles 352 and 353 TFEU (as a measure not covered by any specific Treaty Article). In either case, the Council Decision adopting the measure would have had to be unanimous and, since the UK would have opposed the Directive, the Council would not have had the competence to adopt the Regulation. The Court of Justice ruled that Article 154 TFEU was the appropriate legislative base for the Directive and therefore that the Council was competent to adopt it.

In Joined Cases C-317 & 318/04 *Parliament v Council and Commission* [2006] ECR I-471, the European Parliament challenged two measures concerning the transfer of air passenger data from the EU to the US authorities. On the basis of Article 114 TFEU, which empowers the Council to take measures to approximate national law to further the single market, the Community had adopted Directive 95/46/EC of the European Parliament and of the Council of 24 October 1995 on the protection of individuals with regard to the processing of personal data and on the free movement of such data, OJ 1995 L281/31. The protection of this Directive was stated expressly not to apply to, inter alia, the processing of data in the course of an activity that fell outside EU law, including processing operations concerning public security or State activities in the area of criminal law. Where the protection of the Directive did apply, an exception was provided whereby data could be transferred to a third country if that country ensured an adequate level of data protection.

On the basis of Directive 95/46, the Commission adopted a Decision stating that the US authorities ensured an adequate level of protection for personal data contained in the passenger name records of air passengers arriving in the US ('the Decision on adequacy'). On the basis of Article 114 TFEU, the Council adopted a Decision approving an agreement between the Community and the United States allowing the US authorities to access the airlines' passenger name records for passengers travelling to the United States from the EU. The Parliament challenged both measures.

The Court of Justice held that the Decision on adequacy should be annulled because it concerned the processing of data for the purposes of national security and State activities in the area of criminal law—areas that were outside the scope of the Directive. It also ruled that the Decision on the agreement should be annulled because it concerned the processing of data for these purposes, rather than for the fulfilment of the single market, and was thus outside the scope of Article 114 TFEU.

7.12.2 Infringement of an essential procedural requirement

Although there are a number of possibilities here in relation to a breach of an essential procedural requirement, the most common infringements include a failure to give proper reasons for an act, as required by Article 296 TFEU, and use of the wrong legislative procedure (often because of use of the wrong legal base), in particular involving a failure to consult the Parliament.

The breach must relate to an 'essential' procedural requirement. The reason suggested by Hartley for a distinction between essential and non-essential requirements is as follows.

TC Hartley, *The Foundations of European Community Law*, 7th edn (Oxford: Oxford University Press, 2010), p 422

To invalidate an act for an insignificant procedural defect would unduly hamper administrative activity and would encourage excessive formalism and 'red tape', which in turn would stifle initiative and slow down the administrative process; on the other hand, not to annul for any formal defect at all would be detrimental to good administration and would prejudice the rights of individuals. The law therefore tries to achieve a compromise by restricting the rights of individuals. The law therefore tries to achieve a compromise by restricting the sanction of invalidity to those cases where an important provision has been violated.

This compromise has many advantages; but it has the disadvantage of uncertainty: how does one tell whether a requirement is to be regarded as essential or not? Union provision laying down procedural requirements do not normally state whether their infringement will lead to invalidity. Therefore, one must look to the function of the provision and to the likely consequences if it is not observed. Thus, if failure to observe it could affect the final content of the act, one would be justified in concluding that it was an essential requirement.

The infringement may, as suggested in the extract, affect the final content of the act, and this includes a failure to consult. In Case 138/79 *Roquette Frères v Council* [1980] ECR 3333, the measure challenged should have been adopted under the consultation procedure. The Council asked the Parliament for its opinion, but adopted the measure without waiting for that opinion to be given. The Court of Justice ruled that this amounted to an infringement of an essential procedural requirement, highlighting that the consultation procedure

Case 138/79 *Roquette Frères v Council* [1980] ECR 3333, 3334

… is the means which allows the Parliament to play an actual part in the legislative process of the Community [now Union]. Such power represents an essential factor in the institutional balance intended by the Treaty. Although limited, it reflects at Community level the fundamental democratic principle that the peoples should take part in the exercise of power through the intermediary of a representative assembly. Due consultation of the Parliament in the cases provided for by the Treaty therefore constitutes an essential formality disregard of which means that the measure concerned is void.

7.12.3 Infringement of the Treaties or of any rule of law relating to their application

The ground of infringement of the Treaties or of any rule of law relating to their application is commonly relied upon in Article 263 TFEU actions. It is broad in its scope, since it applies to any Treaty provision and any rule of law relating to the application of the Treaties. Under this heading, the word 'Treaties' not only covers the Treaties per se, but also encompasses secondary legislation. Specifically, this refers to binding legislative acts of the institutions. In Case 60/81 *IBM v Commission* [1981] ECR 2639, it was held that acts are binding where they lead to a distinctive change in the legal position of a party that is subject to EU law.

With respect to the phrase 'any rule of law relating to their application', this applies to the general principles of law that are common to all the Member States, for example the protection of fundamental rights and proportionality.

REVIEW QUESTION

Try to list as many 'rules of law' as possible.

Answer: You might have mentioned legal certainty, non-discrimination, proportionality, fundamental human rights, or any other general principle of law.

7.12.4 Misuse of powers

Where an institution has been given power to act, but only for a particular purpose or purposes, then if that power is used for an illegal end or in an illegal way, this may give grounds for a challenge. Review under this ground is very rare, but, in Case 92/78 *Simmenthal v Commission* [1979] ECR 777, the Court of Justice held that where the Commission had exceeded its powers, an individual applicant would have *locus standi* to challenge the act directly before the Court.

7.13 Time limits

Article 263 TFEU provides that proceedings by the applicant must be instituted within two months of:

- publication of the measure;
- notification of the measure to the applicant; or
- in the absence of notification of the measure to the applicant, the day on which the measure came to the applicant's knowledge.

There are strict rules on time limits that are provided for in Articles 49–52 of the Rules of Procedure of the Court of Justice. These must be adhered to, otherwise the application is deemed inadmissible.

7.14 Effect of annulment

If an Article 263 TFEU action is successful, the measure will be annulled, either in whole or in part.

Article 264 TFEU provides as follows.

Article 264 TFEU

If the action is well founded, the Court of Justice of the European Union shall declare the act concerned to be void.

However, the Court shall, if it considers this necessary, state which of the effects of the act which it has declared void shall be considered as definitive.

Accordingly, under this provision, the annulled measure (to the extent that it is annulled) is void—that is, has no legal effect. Paragraph 2 of this provision allows the Court to declare part of or the entirety of the act void and to state which parts of the act remain operative. This provides for legal certainty, for example in the application of the declaration whereby the Court may declare that the annulled act may remain operative until a new act has been adopted.

Article 266 TFEU states as follows.

Article 266 TFEU

The institution whose act has been declared void or whose failure to act has been declared contrary to the Treaties shall be required to take the necessary measures to comply with the judgment of the Court of Justice of the European Union.

This obligation shall not affect any obligation which may result from the application of the second paragraph of Article 340.

→ CROSS-REFERENCE See 7.12.1 for further discussion of Joined Cases C-317 & 318/04 *Parliament v Council and Commission* [2006] ECR I-4721.

The measure may not be reviewed or enforced and, according to Article 266 TFEU, the defendant institution must take such steps as are necessary to comply with the judgment of the Court of Justice. The Court will determine the time from which the annulment takes effect, which may be from the date of judgment, from the future date on which the measure is replaced, or retrospectively from an earlier date. For example, in Joined Cases C-317 & 318/04 *Parliament v Council and Commission* [2006] ECR I-4721, the Court held that annulment of the Decision on adequacy would not take effect until 30 September 2006, four months after the date of judgment. This was because the Decision approved an agreement between the EU and the United States that could be terminated only on 90 days' notice, and also because a period was required to adopt measures to comply with the annulment judgment.

7.15 The plea of illegality

Article 277 TFEU provides that, in proceedings in which an act of general application is at issue, an applicant may rely on the grounds for an Article 263 TFEU action (lack of competence and so forth) in order to allege that the act is inapplicable in that case. This form of indirect challenge is known as the plea of illegality. The act of general application refers to EU Regulations as opposed to other acts that have legal effects.

Article 277 TFEU

Notwithstanding the expiry of the period laid down in Article 263, sixth paragraph, any party may, in proceedings in which an act of general application adopted by an institution, body, office or agency of the Union is at issue, plead the grounds specified in Article 263, second paragraph, in order to invoke before the Court of Justice of the European Union the inapplicability of that act.

?! THINKING POINT

Can the plea of illegality give rise to an independent cause of action?

7.16 Failure to act

Where an institution has failed to carry out an obligation to act provided for under a Treaty or other measure that has legal effect, Article 265 TFEU provides that the Court of Justice may declare an institution's failure to act to be an infringement of the Treaty.

Article 265 TFEU

Should the European Parliament, the European Council, the Council, the Commission or the European Central Bank, in infringement of the Treaties, fail to act, the Member States and the other institutions of the Union may bring an action before the Court of Justice of the European Union to have the infringement established. This Article shall apply, under the same conditions, to bodies, offices and agencies of the Union which fail to act.

The action shall be admissible only if the institution, body, office or agency concerned has first been called upon to act. If, within two months of being so called upon, the institution, body, office or agency concerned has not defined its position, the action may be brought within a further period of two months.

Any natural or legal person may, under the conditions laid down in the preceding paragraphs, complain to the Court that an institution, body, office or agency of the Union has failed to address to that person any act other than a recommendation or an opinion.

This is an autonomous action, and not dependent on an action for annulment.

7.16.1 *Locus standi* (standing)

7.16.1.1 Privileged applicants

Privileged applicants, for the purpose of Article 265 TFEU, include Member States and 'other institutions of the Union'. These privileged applicants can bring an action against the European Parliament, the European Council, the Council, the Commission, and the European Central Bank (ECB) where there has been a failure to act.

7.16.1.2 Non-privileged applicants

Non-privileged applicants have limited entitlement to complain. The wording of Article 265 TFEU provides that the non-privileged applicants can 'complain to the Court that an institution, body, office or agency of the Union has failed to address to that person … '. This means that the non-privileged applicant cannot complain about all failures to act, but only about a failure by the institution to act in relation to an act that would be addressed to the non-privileged applicant. Since a non-privileged applicant cannot be the addressee of a Regulation or a Directive, they may challenge only a failure to adopt a Decision, which would be addressed directly to them. Furthermore, Article 265 TFEU specifically excludes a challenge relating to a failure to adopt a Recommendation or Opinion.

The scope of this provision appears to be very restrictive and makes it difficult for a non-privileged applicant to bring an action under Article 265 TFEU. The Court of Justice has interpreted this in a broad manner, such that an action for a failure to act lies only where there has been a failure to adopt a measure that the applicant was 'legally entitled to claim' under EU law. Furthermore, it is apparent from the case law that claims under Article 265 TFEU will be treated in the same manner as actions under Article 263 TFEU, whereby the non-privileged applicant will have *locus standi* if they can show individual and direct concern.

Case 246/81 *Lord Bethell v Commission* [1982] ECR 2277 illustrates this point. The applicant had notified the Commission of alleged anti-competitive practices by European airlines, contrary to EU law, and had requested an inquiry and a decision on the matter. When the Commission failed to take such action, Lord Bethell challenged this failure to act under Article 265 TFEU. The Court of Justice stated as follows.

Case 246/81 *Lord Bethell v Commission* [1982] ECR 2277

12. According to the third paragraph of Article 175 [now Article 265 TFEU], any natural or legal person may, under the conditions laid down in that article, complain to the Court that an institution of the Community [now Union] 'has failed to address to that person any act other than a recommendation or an opinion'.
13. It appears from the provisions quoted that the applicant, for his application to be admissible, must be in a position to establish either that he is the addressee of a measure of the Commission having specific legal effects with regard to him, which is, as such, capable of being declared void, or that the Commission, having been duly called upon to act in pursuance of the second paragraph of Article 175, has failed to adopt in relation to him a measure which he was legally entitled to claim by virtue of the rules of Community law.
14. In reply to a question from the Court the applicant stated that the measure to which he believed himself to be entitled was 'a response, an adequate answer to his complaint saying either that the Commission was going to act upon it or saying that it was not and, if not, giving reasons'.

    Alternatively the applicant took the view that the letter addressed to him on 17 July 1981 by the Director-General for Competition was to be described as an act against which proceedings may be instituted under the second paragraph of Article 173 [now Article 265 TFEU].
15. The principal question to be resolved in this case is whether the Commission had, under the rules of Community law [now EU law], the right and the duty to adopt in respect of the applicant a decision in the sense of the request made by the applicant to the Commission in his letter of 13 May 1981. It is apparent from the content of that letter and from the explanations given during the proceedings that the applicant is asking the Commission to undertake an investigation with regard to the airlines in the matter of the fixing of air fares with a view to a possible application to them of the provisions of the Treaty with regard to competition.
16. It is clear therefore that the applicant is asking the Commission, not to take a decision in respect of him, but to open an inquiry with regard to third parties and to take decisions

in respect of them. No doubt the applicant, in his double capacity as a user of the airlines and a leading member of an organization of users of air passenger services, has an indirect interest, as other users may have, in such proceedings and their possible outcome, but he is nevertheless not in the precise legal position of the actual addressee of a decision which may be declared void under the second paragraph of Article 173 or in that of the potential addressee of a legal measure which the Commission has a duty to adopt with regard to him, as is the position under the third paragraph of Article 175.

17. It follows that the application is inadmissible from the point of view of both Article 175 and Article 173.

REVIEW QUESTION

To whom do you think a Commission Decision in this case would have been addressed?

Answer: In this case, the potential addressees of any Decision on the anti-competitive behaviour of the airlines would have been the airlines themselves and not Lord Bethell (who would also have been unlikely to have been able to prove that any such Decision would have directly and individually concerned him). It was held that Lord Bethell had no locus standi to challenge the Commission's alleged failure to act.

In Case T-95/96 *Gestevisión Telecinco SA v Commission* [1998] ECR II-3407, the Court of Justice ruled that an undertaking would be directly concerned by a decision on State aid where the national authorities clearly intended to grant the aid and would be individually concerned where the decision would have affected them by reason of attributes or circumstances that differentiated them from all others. Where the Commission took a decision that a measure did not constitute aid, or constituted aid, but was nonetheless compatible with the common market, without initiating the procedure under Article 104 TFEU on the investigation of State aids, the beneficiaries of that procedure (in particular, competing companies) could secure compliance with the procedure only by challenging the decision to grant aid before the Court of Justice. A competing company whose interests would be affected by the grant of that aid was therefore directly and individually concerned by the Commission's failure to act.

7.16.2 Challengeable grounds

A failure to act on the part of the European Parliament, the European Council, the Council, or the European Commission is open to challenge only on the ground that:

- the defaulting institution has been called upon to act (as it would be inequitable to sue an institution before notifying it of the complaint and calling upon it to take the action required by the complainant); and
- the institution has failed to act.

?! **THINKING POINT**

Write down what you think 'fail to act' should mean in this context. Check, and if necessary correct, your definition when you have read the next sections of text.

In Case 48/65 *Alfons Lütticke v Commission* [1966] ECR 19, the applicants alleged that a German tax on imports of dried milk was contrary to EU law. They made a formal application requiring the Commission to take infringement proceedings against Germany under Article 226 EC (now Article 258 TFEU). The Commission responded that the tax was not contrary to EU law and that therefore it would not take such proceedings. The Court of Justice ruled that proceedings for a failure to act could be brought only if the institution had failed to define its position. The Commission had defined its position by taking the decision not to initiate proceedings against Germany and therefore it had not 'failed to act'. By making a decision not to initiate proceedings, the Commission had defined its position and had notified the applicant within the prescribed period. The institution is not obliged to take the action required by the complainant in order to avoid an Article 265 TFEU action; it is simply obliged to define its position and that will bring an end to the defendant institution's failure to act under Article 265 TFEU. As a result of this interpretation of 'fail to act', actions under Article 265 TFEU are rarely successful.

7.16.3 Procedure

Article 265(2) TFEU provides guidance on the procedure to be followed for an action for failure to act. The applicant must first make a formal request to the relevant institution to act. If the institution fails to define its position within two months, the applicant may apply directly to the Court of Justice within a further period of two months.

7.16.4 Effect

If the Court of Justice finds that a failure to act infringes the Treaty, it will order the institution concerned to take any necessary steps to remedy the omission. These steps are not necessarily those requested by the applicant.

7.17 The relationship between Article 263 TFEU and Article 265 TFEU

If the institution has not defined its position, Article 265 TFEU is the appropriate provision; if the position has been defined, Article 263 TFEU should be used, since the definition in itself amounts to an act that can be challenged. The two actions are often pleaded in the alternative, but a particular measure must amount either to an act or to a failure to act, and so only one action can be correct. If the requirements of the appropriate action are not fulfilled, for example because a challenge to an act under Article 263 TFEU is made by an individual lacking direct and individual concern, it is not open to that individual to bring an action under Article 265 TFEU instead.

In Joined Cases 10 & 18/68 *Eridania and others v Commission* [1969] ECR 459, a Commission Decision granted aid to three Italian sugar refineries. A number of other sugar producers asked the Commission to annul this Decision, which it refused to do. The other producers then made both Article 263 TFEU and Article 265 TFEU applications to the Court of Justice. The Court held that the Article 265 TFEU action could not succeed because the Commission's positive refusal to annul the Decision amounted to an act, rather than a failure to act. The Article 263 TFEU action could not succeed because there was no direct and individual concern. The Court of Justice stressed that Article 265 TFEU should not be used to circumvent the restrictions of Article 263 TFEU. If an institution refused to annul an act, recourse against that refusal was provided by the Treaty under Article 263 TFEU, and the refusal should not therefore be treated as a failure to act giving rise to an Article 265 TFEU action.

7.18 Conclusions

Although Articles 263, 265, and 277 TFEU permit actions taken by the EU to be challenged, these Articles will not provide a remedy in every case. Under Article 263 TFEU, both semi-privileged applicants and non-privileged applicants are extremely restricted, albeit in different ways, in their opportunities to challenge EU acts.

Under Article 265 TFEU, only total inaction may be challenged, rather than positive refusals to act, and non-privileged applicants must prove that the measure they are seeking would have been addressed to them. Given that Article 277 TFEU does not provide for an independent cause of action at all, it is evident that the EU is not overly anxious to encourage challenges to its measures. However, it should be remembered that the Member States are equally cautious about challenges to national law and that, under EU law (as discussed in Chapter 4), it is possible to claim damages in respect of an EU measure that has not been successfully challenged under Articles 263, 265, or 277 TFEU.

SUMMARY

Article 258 TFEU

- The Commission, in its supervisory capacity, can bring enforcement proceedings against a Member State for a failure to comply with its obligations under the Treaties.

Article 260 TFEU

- The Commission can recommend to the Court of Justice a lump sum or penalty payment for the Member State's breach.
- The Court of Justice can impose both a lump sum and a penalty payment.

Article 263 TFEU

- Legislative acts that may be challenged include Regulations, Directives, and Decisions. Recommendations, Opinions, and acts of preparatory character are not subject to review.
- Article 263 TFEU provides for the judicial review of EU measures.

Locus standi

- Privileged applicants (the Member States and the major EU institutions) have standing to bring a challenge to any measure.
- Semi-privileged applicants (certain other EU institutions) may challenge a measure only for the purpose of protecting their prerogatives.
- Non-privileged applicants (individuals and companies) may challenge only measures that are addressed to them, or which are of direct and individual concern to them, or where they are directly concerned by a regulatory act that does not entail implementing measures.

Direct and individual concern

- A measure will be of direct concern to an applicant if its impact on the applicant is direct at the time of its adoption and does not depend on the exercise of discretion by a Member State (*Bock*).
- A measure will be of individual concern to an applicant if, at the date on which the measure is adopted, it is part of a closed class of those affected by the measure, or is part of a group that is more seriously affected by the measure than others affected (*International Fruit*; *Toepfer*).
- Once the applicant has established its standing to bring the challenge, it must prove that at least one of the grounds listed in Article 263 TFEU is satisfied—namely, lack of competence, infringement of an essential procedural requirement, infringement of the Treaties or of a rule of law relating to its application, or misuse of powers.

Article 277 TFEU

- Article 277 TFEU allows an applicant to rely on one of the Article 263 TFEU grounds to avoid the application of a Regulation in legal proceedings. If successful, the Regulation is declared inapplicable in the proceedings, rather than invalid.

Article 265 TFEU

- Article 263 TFEU provides for the judicial review of the EU's failure to act. It is rarely used because any action by the EU, including a refusal to take measures, constitutes a positive act and is thus open to challenge under Article 263 TFEU rather than Article 265 TFEU.

FURTHER READING

Articles

A Arnull, 'Private Applicants and the Action for Annulment since *Codorniu*' (2001) 38 CML Rev 7

A comprehensive review of the developments in judicial review cases up to 2001.

S Balthasar, '*Locus Standi* Rules for Challenges to Regulatory Act by Private Applicants: The New Article 263(4) TFEU' (2010) 35 EL Rev 542

Contextual analysis of the changes made to Article 263 TFEU by the Treaty of Lisbon.

E Berry and S Boyes, 'Access to Justice in the Community Courts: A Limited Right?' (2005) 24 CJQ 224

Argues that the approach adopted by the Court of Justice to the standing of natural and legal persons under what is now Article 263 TFEU is both inconsistent and inappropriate.

A Cygan, 'Protecting the Interests of Civil Society in Community Decision-Making: The Limits of Article 230 EC' (2003) 52 ICLQ 995

Looks at the issue of the legal vacuum that exists when applicants do not fulfil the standing criteria.

J Usher, 'Direct and Individual Concern: An Effective Remedy or a Conventional Solution?' (2003) 28 EL Rev 575

Examines whether direct and individual concern provides an effective remedy for an applicant.

QUESTION

Imagine that the EU operates a system of production licences, administered by the Member States, in respect of soft toys, in order to avoid the development of a soft toy mountain. The Council has recently issued a Regulation, which has immediate effect, permitting Member States to prohibit the grant of production licences in respect of cuddly toy penguins.

The two EU producers of cuddly toy penguins wish to challenge the Regulation. Do they have *locus standi* (standing) to do so?

To view an outline answer to this question plus further resources to support your EU law studies, visit the Online Resources for this book at www.oup.com/uk/eulaw-complete4e

8 EU liability in damages

KEY POINTS

By the end of this chapter, you should be able to:

- explain the meaning of the phrase 'the general principles common to the laws of the Member States' in Article 340 TFEU;
- identify examples of rules of law that the Court of Justice of the European Union (CJEU), ie the Court of Justice and the General Court, are likely to regard as being for the protection of individuals;
- analyse the jurisprudence on what constitutes a wrongful act for the purposes of Article 340 TFEU;
- apply the criteria for assessing whether a wrongful act by the European Union (EU) is 'sufficiently serious';
- analyse (in conjunction with Chapter 5) the relationship between the Court's jurisprudence on EU liability and its jurisprudence on Member State liability; and
- analyse (in conjunction with Chapter 7) the relationship between an action under Article 340 TFEU and an action under Article 263 TFEU.

INTRODUCTION

The rules regarding the liability of the European Union (EU) in damages differ according to whether the claim is contractual or non-contractual. The primary rules governing both are set out in Article 340 TFEU.

Article 340 TFEU

The contractual liability of the Union shall be governed by the law applicable to the contract.

In the case of non-contractual liability, the Union shall, in accordance with the general principles common to the laws of the Member States, make good any damage caused by its institutions or by its servants in the performance of their duties.

Notwithstanding the second paragraph, the European Central Bank shall, in accordance with the general principles common to the laws of the Member States, make good any damage caused by it or by its servants in the performance of their duties.

The personal liability of its servants towards the Union shall be governed by the provisions laid down in their Staff Regulations or in the Conditions of Employment applicable to them.

This chapter, for reasons that will become apparent, will concentrate on the non-contractual liability of the EU, but, before doing so, brief mention should be made of its contractual liability. Article 340 TFEU provides that the EU will incur contractual liability according to 'the law applicable to the contract'. In the absence of a fully developed EU contract law, this 'law' will be the law of a particular country (either a Member State or a third country), and so EU liability for breach of contract will be determined by the content of that (contract) law and not by EU law.

In contrast, the non-contractual liability of the EU is governed by EU law, as provided for by Article 340 TFEU. Acts that may give rise to non-contractual claims for damages against the EU include the adoption of defective legislation, negligence, and unjust enrichment.

NOTE

If you have already studied actions for annulment under Article 263 TFEU (see Chapter 7), you may find that some of the applicants in Article 340 TFEU actions or factual scenarios giving rise to their claims are familiar to you. This is because damages are often claimed as an additional remedy to annulment, for instance to compensate for losses incurred prior to the annulment of the measure that caused these losses. For example, the same facts gave rise to an action for annulment under Article 263 TFEU in Case 48/65 *Alfons Lütticke v Commission* [1966] ECR 19 (see 7.16.2) and to an action for damages in Case 4/69 *Alfons Lütticke v Commission* [1971] ECR 325 (see 8.3).

8.1 Jurisdiction of the EU Courts

Jurisdiction to award damages under Article 340 TFEU is conferred by Articles 256(1) and 268 TFEU.

THINKING POINT

While reading the following two extracts, note which of the EU Courts have jurisdiction over such claims.

Article 256(1) TFEU

The General Court shall have jurisdiction to hear and determine at first instance actions or proceedings referred to in Articles 263, 265, 268, 270 and 272, with the exception of those assigned to a specialised court set up under Article 257 and those reserved in the Statute for the Court of Justice. The Statute may provide for the General Court to have jurisdiction for other classes of action or proceeding.

Decisions given by the General Court under this paragraph may be subject to a right of appeal to the Court of Justice on points of law only, under the conditions and within the limits laid down by the Statute.

Article 268 TFEU

The Court of Justice of the European Union shall have jurisdiction in disputes relating to compensation for damage provided for in the second and third paragraphs of Article 340.

Thus the General Court (see further 2.4.2 on the General Court) has jurisdiction over claims under Article 340 TFEU, subject to a right of appeal to the Court of Justice.

8.2 Parties to Article 340 TFEU actions

An action under Article 340 TFEU may be brought by a natural or legal person. In addition, the General Court has held that an association may bring proceedings, but only where it has an interest of its own to assert that is distinct from that of its members or a right to compensation that has been assigned to it by others (Case T-304/01 *Abad Pérez and others v Council and Commission* [2006] ECR II-4867, at para 52).

The appropriate defendant(s) will be the EU institution(s) against which the matter giving rise to liability is alleged. So where, as in Joined Cases 63–69/72 *Werhan and others v Council and Commission* [1973] ECR 1229, the Commission had proposed the legislation complained of and the Council had enacted it (see further 3.5 on legislative procedures), it was appropriate for the claim to be bought against both the Commission and the Council. The Court of Justice expressly rejected the Commission's claim that it was the Commission's role to represent the EU in all claims against it regardless of which institution was the subject of the allegation.

In T-479/14 *Kendrion v Court of Justice* EU:T:2015:2, Kendrion sought damages from the EU in respect of the General Court's failure to give judgment within a reasonable time (in the earlier case of T-54/06 *Kendrion v Commission* EU:T:2011:667). Kendrion brought the claim against the Court of Justice of the European Union (CJEU), on the basis that the General Court was part of the CJEU. The CJEU argued that it should be replaced as defendant by the EU Commission (see further 2.3 on this institution), but the General Court held that where the EU was liable for the wrongdoing of one its institutions, it must be represented by the institution which committed the act. Article 13 TEU provided that the CJEU was an EU institution, and Article 19 TEU provided that the CJEU comprised the General Court and the Court of Justice, and therefore it was for the CJEU to represent the EU in this case. The General Court confirmed that there was no general principle that the EU should always be represented by the EU Commission (see further 2.3 on the Commission) in cases before the CJEU and that it was not bound by Advocate General Sharpston's Opinion in C-58/12 P *Gascogne Group v Commission* EU:C:2013:360 (see further 2.4.1 on Advocate Generals' Opinions), which had indicated that there was such a principle, but which had not been followed by the Court of Justice in that case and which, in any event, conflicted with Advocate General Poiares Maduro's Opinion in Joined Cases C-120 & 121/06 P *FIAMM and another v Council and Commission* [2008] ECR I-6513 (see also 8.4.4). The General Court rejected the argument that the impartiality and independence of the CJEU would be compromised were it to be the defendant in this case, noting that the CJEU had appeared as a litigant before the General Court and the Court of Justice on many previous occasions without its independence or impartiality being called into question. The General Court therefore concluded that the claim against the CJEU was admissible, but it went on to rule against the applicant on the merits. An appeal against this judgment by the CJEU on the admissibility issue (C-71/15 P) was subsequently withdrawn.

8.3 The meaning of 'general principles common to the laws of the Member States'

Article 340 TFEU states that the non-contractual liability of the EU is to be determined 'in accordance with the general principles common to the laws of the Member States'. The meaning of this requirement was explained by the Court of Justice in its judgment in Case 4/69 *Alfons Lütticke GmbH v Commission* [1971] ECR 325.

Alfons Lütticke alleged that a German tax on its imports of milk and milk products was contrary to what is now Article 110 TFEU (see further 10.7), and requested that the Commission bring enforcement proceedings against the German government under Article 258 TFEU (see 2.3.2 and 7.1 on Commission enforcement actions). The Commission refused, and Alfons Lütticke brought an action under Articles 263 and 265 TFEU (see Chapter 7 on these Articles), seeking either annulment of the Commission's refusal to act or, in the alternative, a finding that it had wrongfully failed to act. When this claim was rejected by the Court of Justice in Case 48/65 *Alfons Lütticke GmbH v Commission* [1966] ECR 19 (see 7.16.2), it brought an action under Article 340 TFEU to recover damages for the losses caused to it by the Commission's inaction (Case 4/69 *Alfons Lütticke GmbH v Commission* [1971] ECR 325).

?! THINKING POINT

Remember that the 'general principles' referred to in Article 340 TFEU are those that are 'common to the laws of the Member States'. If you have already studied your domestic law of tort, you may be able to predict the elements that have to be proved before damages will be awarded under Article 340 TFEU.

In any event, while reading the following extract, note the elements which were specified by the Court of Justice.

Case 4/69 *Alfons Lütticke v Commission* [1971] ECR 325

10. By virtue of the second paragraph of Article 215 [EC, now Article 340 TFEU] and the general principles to which this provision refers, the liability of the Community [now Union] presupposes the existence of a set of circumstances comprising actual damage, a causal link between the damage claimed and the conduct alleged against the institution, and the illegality of such conduct.

So, according to the Court of Justice in *Alfons Lütticke*, the reference to 'the general principles common to the law of the Member States' in Article 340 TFEU means that the EU will be liable in damages if three elements are proved. Thus there must have been:

- actual damage to the applicant (personal or property damage);
- illegal conduct by a EU institution; and
- a causal link between the illegal conduct and the damage.

In *Alfons Lütticke*, the Court of Justice held that damages would not be awarded because, on the facts, the Commission's conduct had not been illegal. The Commission had previously required the German government to reduce the tax and had reasonably considered the reduced rate to be acceptable. It had therefore not failed in its task of supervising compliance with the EU rules on taxation.

Each of these three elements will now be examined in turn.

8.4 Wrongful acts by the EU institutions

8.4.1 An EU institution must be responsible for the act

Acts of the EU institutions include legislative acts such as Regulations, Directives, and Decisions, but not Treaties, because these are acts of the sovereign Member States and not of the EU (see further 3.4). Thus, in Case 169/73 *Compagnie Continentale France v Council* [1975] ECR 117, the Court of Justice ruled that where the act that allegedly caused harm to the applicant was in fact an Act of Accession, which was 'an integral part of the Treaty concluded between the original and the new Member States' (at para 16), this could not give rise to liability under Article 340 TFEU because no EU institutions were responsible. The General Court (see further 2.4.2 on the General Court) reiterated this point in Case T-113/96 *Dubois et Fils SA v Council and Commission* [1998] ECR II-125, in which it ruled that the EU Treaties were not acts of the institutions, but agreements by the Member States. They could not, therefore, give rise to liability on the part of the EU under Article 340 TFEU. (The Court of Justice subsequently dismissed the appeal in *Dubois* as unfounded: see Case C-95/98 *Dubois et Fils SA v Council and Commission* [1999] ECR I-4835.)

8.4.2 The act at issue must be wrongful

The distinction between an act that is wrongful and one that is not is crucial because only a wrongful act can give rise to liability in damages. However, as the jurisprudence demonstrates, it can be very difficult to identify where this distinction should be drawn. For example, in Joined Cases 19, 20, 25, & 30/69 *Richez-Parise and others v Commission* [1970] ECR 325 (see also 8.6 in relation to causation), a number of EU employees sought damages in respect of the impact of an incorrect calculation of their pension entitlement. The Court of Justice held that the provision of incorrect information to the applicants by the Commission did not itself constitute a wrongful act, but that the failure subsequently to correct it did.

The Court of Justice first laid down the test for what constitutes a 'wrongful' act for the purposes of Article 340 TFEU in Case 5/71 *Zuckerfabrik Schöppenstedt v Council* [1971] ECR 975, in which a number of German sugar producers alleged that Regulation 769/68 imposing minimum and maximum prices for raw sugar, OJ 1968 L143/14, was, in its detail, discriminatory.

?! THINKING POINT

While reading the following extract, note the conditions that the Court of Justice laid down in order for the act to be considered 'wrongful' for the purposes of Article 340 TFEU.

Case 5/71 *Zuckerfabrik Schöppenstedt v Council* [1971] ECR 975

11. In the present case the non-contractual liability of the Community [now Union] presupposes at the very least the unlawful nature of the act alleged to be the cause of the damage. Where legislative action involving measures of economic policy is concerned, the Community does not incur non-contractual liability for damage suffered by individuals as a consequence of that action, by virtue of the provisions contained in Article 215 [now Article 340 TFEU], second paragraph, of the [EC] Treaty, unless a sufficiently flagrant violation of a superior rule of law for the protection of the individual has occurred. For that reason the Court, in the present case, must first consider whether such a violation has occurred.

The Court of Justice held that the EU could not incur liability for legislative action involving measures of economic policy unless there had been a 'sufficiently flagrant violation of a superior rule of law for the protection of the individual' that had caused loss to the applicant.

On the facts of *Schöppenstedt*, the Court refused to award damages on the ground that the different prices for sugar varied according to the development of the market and therefore there had not been a 'sufficiently flagrant violation' by the EU of the principle of non-discrimination.

The Court has more often expressed the 'sufficiently flagrant violation' requirement as that of a 'sufficiently serious violation'. See, for example, the following extract from Joined Cases 83 & 94/76 and 4, 15, & 40/77 *Bayerische HNL and others v Council and Commission* [1978] ECR 120 (sometimes referred to as the *Second Skimmed Milk Powder* case).

Joined Cases 83 & 94/76 and 4, 15, & 40/77 *Bayerische HNL v Council and Commission* [1978] ECR 1209

4. The finding that a legislative measure such as the regulation in question is null and void is however insufficient by itself for the Community [now Union] to incur non-contractual liability for damage caused to individuals under the second paragraph of Article 215 of the EEC Treaty [now Article 340 TFEU]. The Court of Justice has consistently stated that

> the Community does not incur liability on account of a legislative measure which involves choices of economic policy unless a sufficiently serious breach of a superior rule of law for the protection of the individual has occurred.

Similarly, the Court of Justice used the 'sufficiently serious breach' wording in Joined Cases C-46 & 48/93 *Brasserie du Pêcheur SA v Germany; R v Secretary of State for Transport, ex p Factortame Ltd and others ('Factortame III')* [1994] ECR I-1593, at para 51, when laying down the conditions applicable to Member State liability in damages for breach of EU law (see 5.4.1 and 5.5).

The Court has also moved towards omitting the word 'superior' when referring to a rule of law for the protection of the individual (see eg Case C-352/98 P *Bergaderm v Commission* [2000] ECR I-5291, at para 42).

The test for imposing liability in damages on the EU may now be summarized as follows:

(1) the EU must have breached a rule of EU law which is for the protection of the individual;

(2) that breach must be sufficiently serious; and

(3) it must have caused loss to the applicant.

The key elements of the test will now be examined in greater detail.

8.4.2.1 The EU rule breached must be a rule of law for the protection of individuals

Such rules of law have been taken by the Court of Justice to include those general principles of law discussed at 3.4.5, such as legitimate expectation, legal certainty, equality and non-discrimination, and respect for fundamental rights.

For example, in Case 152/88 *Sofrimport SARL v Commission* [1990] ECR I-2477 (see also 7.8.2), which concerned the prohibition of import licences for Chilean apples by Commission Regulation (EEC) No 962/88 of 12 April 1988 suspending the issue of import licences for dessert apples originating in Chile, OJ 1988 L95/10, Commission Regulation (EEC) No 984/88 of 14 April 1988 amending Regulation (EEC) No 962/88 … , OJ 1988 L98/37, and Commission Regulation (EEC) No 1040/88 of 20 April 1988 fixing quantities of imports of dessert apples originating in third countries … , OJ 1988 L102/23, the Court of Justice imposed damages for breach of the legitimate expectation of the importers that goods in transit would be protected against the sudden introduction of such a prohibition. In Case 74/74 *CNTA v Commission* [1975] ECR 533, in which Regulation 189/72 of 26 January 1972 (published in the Official Journal on 28 January) abolished, without warning, compensation for the effect of exchange-rate fluctuations on trade in colza and rape seeds, the Court of Justice stated that there was a legitimate expectation that the compensation would not be withdrawn in relation to transactions that had already been entered into at the date of abolition of the compensation scheme and for which export licences fixing the amount of compensation in advance had already been obtained.

In Joined Cases 64 & 113/76 *Dumortier Frères SA and others v Council and Commission* [1979] ECR 309, at para 11, the Court of Justice ruled that the principle of equality was a superior rule of law for the protection of individuals, since it 'occupies a particularly important place among the rules of EU law intended to protect the interests of the individual'. The Court held that the principle had been breached by the abolition of refunds to maize gritz producers in circumstances in which producers of maize starch, which was in direct competition with maize gritz, continued to receive the refunds. In Joined Cases 83 & 94/76 and 4, 15, & 40/77 *Bayerische HNL and others v Council and Commission* [1978] ECR 120 (also discussed later in relation to the seriousness of the breach), the Court ruled that Council Regulation (EEC) No 563/76 of 15 March 1976 on the compulsory purchase of skimmed-milk powder held by intervention agencies for use in feedingstuffs, OJ 1976 L67/18, breached (albeit not sufficiently seriously) the principle of non-discrimination because it discriminated between different agricultural sectors (against non-dairy producers, who were obliged to purchase the stocks, and in favour of dairy producers, who were guaranteed sales at set prices), and that it was 'impossible to disregard the importance of this prohibition [on discrimination] in the system of the Treaty' (*Bayerische*, at para 5).

In addition to these general principles, particular Treaty Articles may constitute superior rules of law for the protection of individuals. For example, in Case 106/81 *Kind v EEC* [1982] ECR 2885, the Court of Justice held that, in principle, breach of Treaty Articles prohibiting charges having equivalent effect to customs duties (see further 10.4.1 on Article 30 TFEU) and establishing the common organization of the market in cereals could give rise to an award of damages against the EU although, on the facts, Council Regulation (EEC) No 1837/80 of 27 June 1980 on the common organization of the market in sheepmeat and goatmeat, OJ 1980 L183/1, which imposed an export levy on meat, was not in breach of any of these.

However, not all EU laws constitute rules of law for the protection of individuals for the purposes of Article 340 TFEU. For example, in *Kind*, the Court of Justice held that breach of Article 296 TFEU, which required the reasons for a measure to be given, could not give rise to an award of damages, even though that requirement was designed to enable the Court to exercise its powers of judicial review of EU legislation under Article 263 TFEU for the benefit of individuals to whom the Article 263 TFEU action was available (see further Chapter 7).

Similarly, in Case C-282/90 *Industrie- en Handelsonderneming Vreugdenhil BV v Commission* [1992] ECR I-1937, the applicant brought a claim for damages in respect of losses caused by the Commission's amendment of Commission Regulation (EEC) No 1687/76 of 30 June 1976 laying down common detailed rules for verifying the use and/or destination of products from intervention, OJ 1976 L190/1, which set out a waiver of import duties on certain goods. The amendment had already been declared illegal by the Court of Justice (in Case 22/88 *Vreugdenhil and another v Minister van Landbouw en Visserij* [1989] ECR 2049 on the grounds that the Commission had exceeded its powers. However, in *Industrie- en Handelsonderneming Vreugdenhil BV*, the Court held that the allocation of powers between the EU institutions did not constitute a rule of law for the protection of the individual.

Case C-282/90 *Industrie- en Handelsonderneming Vreugdenhil BV v Commission* [1992] ECR I-1937

20. In that context, it is sufficient to state that the aim of the system of the division of powers between the various Community [now Union] institutions is to ensure that the balance between the institutions provided for in the Treaty is maintained, and not to protect individuals.

21. Consequently, a failure to observe the balance between the institutions cannot be sufficient on its own to engage the Community's liability towards the traders concerned.
22. The position would be different if a Community measure were to be adopted which not only disregarded the division of powers between the institutions but also, in its substantive provisions, disregarded a superior rule of law protecting individuals.

In Joined Cases 5, 7, & 13–24/66 *Kampffmeyer and others v Commission* [1967] ECR 245 (see also 8.5.1 in relation to damage, 8.6 in relation to causation, and 8.9.2 on the possibility of a concurrent claim against the Member State), maize importers sought damages in respect of a Commission Decision of 3 October 1963 authorizing Germany to suspend import licences that had been annulled by the Court of Justice in Joined Cases 106–107/63 *Toepfer and another v Commission* [1965] ECR 405 (see 7.8.2). The Decision had been adopted in order to apply Regulation No 19/65/EEC of 2 March of the Council on application of Article 85(3) of the Treaty to certain categories of agreements and concerted practices, OJ 1965 36/533, which provided that the Commission must investigate protective measures imposed by Member States. The Court of Justice ruled that, in failing to investigate fully before adopting the Decision, the Commission had infringed the rule of law contained in the Regulation, which was for the protection of individuals. The fact that the interests protected were of a general nature (free trade, support for the relevant markets, and the establishment of a single market—see further 1.4 and 10.1 on the single market)—did not preclude their protection from being for the ultimate protection of individuals.

8.4.2.2 The breach must be sufficiently serious

In Joined Cases 83 & 94/76 and 4, 15, & 40/77 *Bayerische HNL v Council and Commission* [1978] ECR 1209, Regulation 563/76 (see 8.4.2.1) provided for the compulsory purchase of skimmed milk powder for use in animal feedstuffs in order to reduce EU milk stocks and poultry producers claimed damages against the EU for the resulting increases in the price of animal feed. Although the Court of Justice had already ruled, in Case 114/76 *Bela-Mühle v Grows-Farm* [1977] ECR 1211, that the Regulation was void because it imposed an obligation to purchase at a price that was disproportionate and constituted a discriminatory distribution of the burden of costs, the Court held that this breach of EU law was not sufficiently serious for the purposes of Article 340 TFEU, stating that individuals must accept 'within reasonable limits certain harmful effects on their economic interests'.

?! THINKING POINT

Before reading the following extract, consider the policy reasons that might have led the Court of Justice to restrict EU liability in damages to such a limited range of circumstances.

Joined Cases 83 & 94/76 and 4, 15, & 40/77 *Bayerische HNL v Council and Commission* [1978] ECR 1209

5. In the present case there is no doubt that the prohibition on discrimination laid down in the second subparagraph of the third paragraph of Article 40 of the [EEC] Treaty [now Article 40 TFEU] and infringed by Regulation No 563/76 is in fact designed for the protection of the individual, and that it is impossible to disregard the importance of this prohibition in the system of the Treaty. To determine what conditions must be present in addition to such breach for the Community [now Union] to incur liability in accordance with the criterion laid down in the case-law of the Court of Justice it is necessary to take into consideration the principles in the legal systems of the Member States governing the liability of public authorities for damage caused to individuals by legislative measures. Although these principles vary considerably from one Member State to another, it is however possible to state that the public authorities can only exceptionally and in special circumstances incur liability for legislative measures which are the result of choices of economic policy. This restrictive view is explained by the consideration that the legislative authority, even where the validity of its measures is subject to judicial review, cannot always be hindered in making its decisions by the prospect of applications for damages whenever it has occasion to adopt legislative measures in the public interest which may adversely affect the interests of individuals.
6. It follows from these considerations that individuals may be required, in the sectors coming within the economic policy of the Community, to accept within reasonable limits certain harmful effects on their economic interests as a result of a legislative measure without being able to obtain compensation from public funds even if that measure has been declared null and void. In a legislative field such as the one in question, in which one of the chief features is the exercise of a wide discretion essential for the implementation of the Common Agricultural Policy, the Community does not therefore incur liability unless the institution concerned has manifestly and gravely disregarded the limits on the exercise of its powers.

In *Bayerische*, the Court of Justice argued that it was essential for the EU to have a wide discretion in adopting economic legislation and that the EU should not be hindered, in making economic policy, by the prospect of continual applications for damages.

In Joined Cases 116, 124, & 143/77 *Amylum, Tunnel and KSH v Council and Commission* [1979] ECR 3497 (see also later in this section), at para 19, the Court of Justice emphasized the relatively high threshold for a finding of a sufficiently serious breach and held that the Commission's 'errors' were not sufficiently serious, because its conduct could not be said to have been 'verging on the arbitrary'.

However, while the public policy rationale for a conservative approach to the award of damages still exists, the Court of Justice has, in recent years, taken a slightly less restrictive approach to such action, by aligning the criteria for assessing whether the breach is sufficiently serious with that laid down in Joined Cases C-46 & 48/93 *Brasserie du Pêcheur SA v Germany; R v Secretary of State for Transport, ex p Factortame Ltd and others ('Factortame III')* [1994] ECR I-1593 (see 5.4.1 and 5.5), rather than focusing on previously considered criteria such as the number of persons affected and the seriousness of the impact on them.

This approach can be seen in Case C-352/98 P *Bergaderm v Commission* [2000] ECR I-5291, in which the Commission had adopted Council Directive 93/35/EEC of 14 June 1993 amending for the sixth time Directive 76/768/EEC on the approximation of the laws of the Member States relating to cosmetic products, OJ 1993 L151/32 (the Cosmetics Directive), to restrict the use of certain chemicals in cosmetics. Bergaderm was the producer of Bergasol, a product that contained one of the restricted chemicals. It subsequently went into liquidation and brought an action under Article 340 TFEU, claiming that Directive 93/35 had caused it significant financial loss and resulted in its liquidation. The Court of Justice had expressed the *Schöppenstedt* test as applying only to 'general' acts and so Bergaderm argued that, since the Directive exclusively concerned Bergasol and was therefore to be regarded as an individual administrative act rather than a general legislative act, the strict *Schöppenstedt* test did not apply. The Court rejected this argument for the reasons which appear in the following extract.

Case C-325/98 P *Bergaderm v Commission* [2000] ECR I-5291

41. The Court has stated that the conditions under which the State may incur liability for damage caused to individuals by a breach of Community law [now EU law] cannot, in the absence of particular justification, differ from those governing the liability of the Community [now Union] in like circumstances. The protection of the rights which individuals derive from Community law cannot vary depending on whether a national authority or a Community authority is responsible for the damage (*Brasserie du Pêcheur and Factortame* [Joined Cases C-46 & 48/93 *Brasserie du Pêcheur SA v Germany; R v Secretary of State for Transport, ex p Factortame Ltd and others ('Factortame III')* [1994] ECR I-1593], paragraph 42).

42. As regards Member State liability for damage caused to individuals, the Court has held that Community law confers a right to reparation where three conditions are met: the rule of law infringed must be intended to confer rights on individuals; the breach must be sufficiently serious; and there must be a direct causal link between the breach of the obligation resting on the State and the damage sustained by the injured parties (*Brasserie du Pêcheur and Factortame*, paragraph 51).

43. As to the second condition, as regards both Community liability under Article 215 of the [EC] Treaty [now Article 340 TFEU] and Member State liability for breaches of Community law, the decisive test for finding that a breach of Community law is sufficiently serious is whether the Member State or the Community institution concerned manifestly and gravely disregarded the limits on its discretion (*Brasserie du Pêcheur and Factortame*, paragraph

55; and Joined Cases C-178/94, C-179/94, C-188/94, C-189/94, C-190/94 *Dillenkofer and Others v Germany* [1996] ECR I-4845, paragraph 25).

44. Where the Member State or the institution in question has only considerably reduced, or even no, discretion, the mere infringement of Community law may be sufficient to establish the existence of a sufficiently serious breach (see, to that effect, Case C-5/94 *Hedley Lomas* [1996] ECR I-2553, paragraph 28).
45. It is therefore necessary to examine whether, in the present case, as the appellants assert, the Court of First Instance erred in law in its examination of the way in which the Commission exercised its discretion when it adopted the Adaptation Directive.
46. In that regard, the Court finds that the general or individual nature of a measure taken by an institution is not a decisive criterion for identifying the limits of the discretion enjoyed by the institution in question.
47. It follows that the first ground of appeal, which is based exclusively on the categorisation of the Adaptation Directive as an individual measure, has in any event no bearing on the issue and must be rejected.

The Court of Justice in *Bergaderm* ruled that whether the Directive could be categorized as a general or individual measure was, in fact, irrelevant. The key issue was the extent of the discretion permitted to the EU, and that discretion was not determined by the general or individual nature of the measure. The Court restated the *Schöppenstedt* test that a right to damages arose only if:

- a rule of law intended to confer rights on individuals had been breached;
- the breach was sufficiently serious; and
- there was a direct causal link between the breach by the EU and the damage sustained by the applicant.

Similarly, in Case C-390/95 P *Antillean Rice Mills NV v Commission* [199] ECR I-769, the Court held that the form of the alleged measure—in that case, a Decision—did not affect the EU's liability under Article 340 TFEU.

The decisive test for whether the breach is sufficiently serious is thus, as the Court of Justice has stated on many occasions, whether the institution concerned has 'manifestly and gravely disregarded the limits on the exercise of its powers' (eg in Joined Cases 83 & 94/76 and 4, 15, & 40/77 *Bayerische HNL and others v Council and Commission* [1978] ECR 120, at para 6) or 'manifestly and gravely disregarded the limits on its discretion' (eg in Case C-325/98 P *Bergaderm v Commission* [2000] ECR I-5291, at para 43). In *Bergaderm*, the Court of Justice noted a number of more specific factors that will be relevant to the assessment of whether a breach is sufficiently serious, including those laid down in the context of Member State liability in damages in Joined Cases C-46 & 48/93 *Brasserie du Pêcheur SA v Germany; R v Secretary of State for Transport, ex p Factortame Ltd and others ('Factortame III')* [1994] ECR I-1593 (see 5.4.1 and 5.5).

?! THINKING POINT

If you have already studied the topic of Member State liability in damages (see Chapter 5), try to recall the criteria laid down by the Court in *Factortame III* for assessing whether a breach of law by a Member State is 'sufficiently serious'.

In any event, while reading the following extract note the criteria that the Court of Justice laid down in *Bergaderm* for assessing whether a breach of law by the EU is sufficiently serious.

Case C-325/98 P *Bergaderm v Commission* [2000] ECR I-5291

39. The second paragraph of Article 215 of the [EC] Treaty [now Article 340 TFEU] provides that, in the case of non-contractual liability, the Community [now Union] is, in accordance with the general principles common to the laws of the Member States, to make good any damage caused by its institutions or by its servants in the performance of their duties.
40. The system of rules which the Court has worked out with regard to that provision takes into account, *inter alia*, the complexity of the situations to be regulated, difficulties in the application or interpretation of the texts and, more particularly, the margin of discretion available to the author of the act in question (Joined Cases C-46/93 and C-48/93 *Brasserie du Pêcheur and Factortame* [1996] ECR I-1029, paragraph 43).

In *Bergaderm*, the Court of Justice stated that the following criteria were indicative of the seriousness of any breach:

- the complexity of the factual situations to be regulated;
- the difficulties in the application or interpretation of the legal texts; and
- the margin of discretion available to the EU institution that adopted the act at issue.

In Joined Cases C-46 & 48/93 *Brasserie du Pêcheur SA v Germany; R v Secretary of State for Transport, ex p Factortame Ltd and others* ('*Factortame III*') [1994] ECR I-1593, cited in *Bergaderm*, the Court also referred to:

- whether the infringement and the damage caused was intentional or involuntary; and
- whether any error of law was excusable or inexcusable.

In T-343/13 *CN v European Parliament* EU:T:2015:926, the applicant, an official of the EU Council (see further 2.2 on the Council), had submitted a petition to the European Parliament (see 11.2.3 on such petitions) on the subject of the support given to disabled family members of EU officials, difficulties encountered by officials with health problems, and the mishandling of his case by the Council. The Parliament, which subsequently rejected the petition, published details of it on its website, including the official's name, the fact he was suffering from a serious illness, and the fact that his son had a severe disability. The applicant sought damages in respect of the Parliament's conduct, but the General Court dismissed his claim, holding that there had been no sufficiently serious breach of EU law by the Parliament (and no causal link between the Parliament's acts and the damage suffered by the applicant) (see further 8.5.1 on the damage suffered). The Court noted that the applicant had been given information as to the publication of petitions and the possibility of requesting anonymity, and that, when submitting his application, he had given consent to publication. The right to petition was an instrument of democratic participation that was intended to be transparent in order to generate public debate, and the applicant's illness and his son's disability were central to the petition and not incidental to it. The Court also held that there was no right to removal of the information, given that its publication was lawful and that the applicant had given his consent, and since the Parliament's decision to remove it was therefore merely a courtesy to the applicant, it had not been required to do so immediately, but only within a reasonable period, which it had done. The Court concluded that the Parliament had not been guilty of a sufficiently serious breach, noting, perhaps rather harshly, that the applicant could not invoke any unlawfulness in relation to his son's rights because there was no evidence that he was his son's legal representative or had been authorized to bring the claim on his behalf.

Where the EU institution has a wide discretion, it is unlikely that a breach will be sufficiently serious. For example, in Case T-212/03 *My Travel v Commission* [2008] ECR II-1967, at para 40, the General Court (see further 2.4.2 on the General Court) noted the 'complex' and 'delicate' nature of EU competition policy, and the correspondingly 'considerable degree of discretion' exercised by the EU, and concluded that the Commission's errors in exercising that discretion were not sufficiently serious. In Joined Cases 116 & 124/77 *Amylum NV and Tunnel Refineries Ltd v Council and Commission* [1979] ECR 3497 and Case 43/77 *KSH NV v Council and Commission* [1979] ECR 3583 (see also earlier), the Court of Justice noted, at para 13, that 'the exercise of a wide discretion [was] essential for the implementation of the Common Agricultural Policy', and concluded that the Council and the Commission had not seriously disregarded the limits on this discretion. Similarly, in Case T-16/04 *Arcelor Mittal v Parliament and Council* [2010] ECR II-211, the General Court noted, in relation to the EU's powers in environmental policy, the importance of it having a wide discretion, and concluded that this broad discretion had not been manifestly or gravely disregarded by the Commission. Its reasoning can be seen in the following extract.

Case T-16/04 *Arcelor v Parliament and Council* [2010] ECR II-211

143. In that regard, it must be pointed out, in the context of the present case, that a possible sufficiently serious breach of the rules of law at issue must be based on a manifest and serious failure to have regard for the limits of the broad discretion enjoyed by the Community [now Union] legislature when exercising its powers on environmental issues under Article 174 EC and 175 EC [now Articles 191 and 192 TFEU] ... The exercise of that discretionary power implies first, the need for the Community legislature to anticipate and evaluate ecological, scientific, technical and economic changes of a complex and uncertain nature and, second, the balancing and arbitration by that legislature of the various objectives, principles and interests set out in Article 174 EC ... In the contested directive, that is reflected in the establishment of a series of objectives and sub-objectives which are in part contradictory ...

In Case 120/86 *Mulder v Minister van Landbouw en Visserij* ('*Mulder I*') [1988] ECR 2321 and Case 170/86 *Von Deetzen v Hauptzollamt Hamburg-Jonas* [1988] ECR 2355, the Court of Justice awarded damages for losses resulting from the exclusion of certain producers from the milk quota system by Council Regulation (EEC) No 1078/77 of 17 May 1977 introducing a system of premiums for the non-marketing of milk and milk products and for the conversion of dairy herds, OJ 1977 L131/1 (for the facts of this case, see further 8.5.2). However, the Court refused to award damages for losses resulting from a subsequent Regulation, Council Regulation (EEC) No 857/84 of 31 March 1984 adopting general rules for the application of the levy referred to in Article 5c of Regulation (EEC) No 804/68 in the milk and milk products sector, OJ 1984 L90/13, which allocated quotas to the previously excluded producers, but on a less generous basis than those given to the other producers. It based its refusal on the fact that the Commission enjoyed a wide discretion in this area, which it had not exceeded, and so the breach of the producers' legitimate expectation was insufficiently serious.

In Case 20/88 *Roquette Frères v Commission* [1989] ECR 1553 (see also 8.9.2), Roquette Frères claimed damages for the effects of Commission Regulation (EEC) 652/76 of 24 March 1976 changing the monetary compensatory amounts following changes in exchange rates for the French franc, OJ 1976 L79/4, which had provided for compensation to be given for the effect of exchange-rate fluctuations and had been declared invalid by the Court of Justice in Case 145/79 *Roquette Frères SA v French Customs Administration* [1980] ECR 2917. Roquette Frères alleged that it had been required to make compensatory payments to the French authorities on the basis of the invalid Regulations and, further, that it had been placed at a disadvantage to its competitors as a result.

?! THINKING POINT

While reading the following extract, consider why the Court of Justice held that the breach of the rule of law (on compensation amounts) was insufficiently serious.

Case 20/88 *Roquette Frères v Commission* [1989] ECR 1553

23. The Court has consistently held that the Community's [now Union's] non-contractual liability cannot be incurred through the adoption of a legislative measure involving a choice of economic policy unless a sufficiently flagrant violation of a superior rule of law for the protection of the individual has occurred. In a legislative context characterized by a wide margin of discretion, which is essential for the implementation of the common agricultural policy, such liability can therefore be incurred only if the institution concerned has manifestly and gravely disregarded the limits on the exercise of its powers (judgment of 25 May 1978 in Joined Cases 83 and 94/76, 4, 15 and 40/77 *Bayerische HNL v Commission* [1978] ECR 1209).
24. It is therefore necessary to consider the nature of the rule which, according to the judgment in Case 145/79, was infringed by the fixing of the monetary compensatory amounts applicable to starch products. It is contained, for the most part, in Article 2(2) of Regulation

No 974/71 of the Council of 12 May 1971 on certain measures of conjunctural policy to be taken in agriculture following the temporary widening of the margins of fluctuation for the currencies of certain Member States (Official Journal, English Special Edition 1971 (I), p. 257), the basic regulation concerning monetary compensatory amounts. Under that provision, the monetary compensatory amounts applicable to products processed from maize or wheat must be equal to the incidence, on the product concerned, of the application of the compensatory amount to the price of the basic product.

25. The Court has admitted that the calculation of that incidence raised difficult technical and economic problems regarding products whose manufacturing process and composition might vary in different regions of the Community. However, it took the view that the Commission, in fixing the monetary compensatory amounts applicable to starch products, had made errors of calculation resulting in the fixing of amounts much higher than those corresponding to the incidence of the amounts applicable to the basic products and that it had thus exceeded the limits of its discretion. Those errors related in particular to the supply price of the maize and wheat used for the production of starch, the total of the amounts applicable to all the by-products obtained from the same quantity of maize or wheat in a specified manufacturing process, and the alignment of the amounts applicable to potato starch with those applicable to maize starch.

26. It is apparent from the foregoing considerations that the fixing of the contested monetary compensatory amounts resulted from a technical error which, even if it led de facto to unequal treatment for certain producers established in countries with weak currencies, cannot be considered to constitute a serious breach of a superior rule of law for the protection of the individual or a manifest and grave disregard by the Commission of the limits of its discretion.

Even though it had previously declared the Regulation to be invalid, the Court of Justice held that this did not constitute a sufficiently serious breach of a rule of law for the protection of individuals. The applicant's loss had been caused by the Commission's use in the Regulation of an incorrect basis for calculation, but this was merely a 'technical error' (*Roquette Frères*, at para 26), and did not amount to a manifest and grave disregard of the Commission's powers.

However, in policy areas in which the EU has little or no discretion, any infringement of the rule of law at issue will be regarded as sufficiently serious. This reflects the Court's approach to Member State liability as outlined in Joined Cases C-46 & 48/93 *Brasserie du Pêcheur SA v Germany; R v Secretary of State for Transport, ex p Factortame Ltd and others ('Factortame III')* [1994] ECR I-1593 and Case C-5/94 *R v Ministry of Agriculture, Fisheries and Food, ex p Hedley Lomas (Ireland) Ltd* [1996] ECR I-2553 (see 5.4.3 and 5.5.1).

A good example of this is Case C-472/00 *Commission v Fresh Marine Company A/S* [2003] ECR I-7541 (see also 8.5.2), in which the Commission had imposed **anti-dumping** duties on salmon imports.

Fresh Marine, a Norwegian salmon producer, brought an action for damages on the ground that it had given an undertaking not to import salmon into the EU at prices below a certain level and was therefore not engaged in dumping its products on the EU market contrary to EU law. It had supplied the Commission with a report demonstrating its compliance with its undertaking, but the Commission had then inaccurately amended the report.

anti-dumping
A non-EU producer is described as 'dumping' a product on the EU market if it exports it into the EU at prices lower than the product's normal value on the producer's domestic market. EU law permits the Commission to impose anti-dumping duties on such imports if they are causing injury to the EU industry concerned.

?! **THINKING POINT**

While reading the following extract, consider the limits that applied to the Commission's discretion in this area and why the Court of Justice considered these to have been exceeded.

Case C-472/00 *Commission v Fresh Marine Company A/S* [2003] ECR I-7541

25. According to settled case-law, Community law [now EU law] confers a right to reparation where three conditions are met: the rule of law infringed must be intended to confer rights on individuals; the breach must be sufficiently serious; and there must be a direct causal link between the breach of the obligation resting on the author of the act and the damage sustained by the injured parties (see *Brasserie du Pêcheur and Factortame* [Joined Cases C-46 & 48/93 *Brasserie du Pêcheur SA v Germany; R v Secretary of State for Transport, ex p Factortame Ltd and others ('Factortame III')* [1994] ECR I-1593], paragraph 51, *Bergaderm and Goupil* [Case C-325/98 P *Bergaderm v Commission* [2000] ECR I-5291], paragraphs 41 and 42, and Case C-312/00 P *Commission v Camar and Tico* [[2002] ECR I-11355], paragraph 53).
26. As regards the second condition, the decisive test for finding that a breach of Community law is sufficiently serious is whether the Community institution concerned manifestly and gravely disregarded the limits on its discretion. Where that institution has only considerably reduced, or even no, discretion, the mere infringement of Community law may be sufficient to establish the existence of a sufficiently serious breach (see, inter alia, *Bergaderm and Goupil*, paragraphs 43 and 44, and *Commission v Camar and Tico*, paragraph 54).
27. Therefore, the determining factor in deciding whether there has been such an infringement is not the general or individual nature of the act in question but the discretion available to the institution concerned (see, to that effect, *Bergaderm and Goupil*, paragraph 46, and *Commission v Camar and Tico*, paragraph 55).

In *Fresh Marine*, the Court of Justice noted that the Commission's power to impose anti-dumping duties was limited by the requirements that it must have grounds to believe that the undertaking given had been breached and that it must act on the basis of the best information available. Since the information available indicated that the undertaking had been complied with and the Commission had then amended that information without checking its amendment with the applicant, the Commission must be taken to have exceeded the limits on its discretion.

However, care must be taken in determining that the institution has indeed little or no discretion. In C-337/15 P *Staelen v European Ombudsman* EU:C:2017:256, the Court of Justice rejected the ruling by the General Court that the Ombudsman had no discretion as to whether to respect the principle of diligence in a particular case and therefore that mere breach of that principle amounted to a sufficiently serious breach of EU law. The Court of Justice held that the Ombudsman had a wide discretion and was merely under an obligation to use her best endeavours, and only in exceptional circumstances would a person be able to demonstrate that the Ombudsman had committed a sufficiently serious breach of EU law. It was therefore necessary to examine whether the Ombudsman had gravely and manifestly disregarded the limits on her discretion, taking into account whether she had shown an obvious lack of care in the conduct of the investigation, whether it was excusable or inexcusable, and whether the conclusions drawn from her examination were inappropriate and unreasonable.

REVIEW QUESTION

Suppose that Squirrel plc and Nutkin Ltd are UK producers of garden bird feeders and bird food. For many years, they received an EU subsidy pursuant to the (fictitious) Wildlife Regulation, but Nutkin's payments ceased without warning last week because the Regulation had been amended by the Commission to exclude producers with fewer than 100 employees. Nutkin has only 99 employees. Squirrel, which has 101 employees, is continuing to receive the subsidy. Advise Nutkin as to whether the Commission has committed a wrongful act for the purposes of Article 340 TFEU.

Answer: Article 340 TFEU provides that the EU may be liable in damages for the acts of its institutions, such as the Commission, according to the general principles common to the laws of the Member States. In Case 4/69 *Alfons Lütticke v Commission* [1971] ECR 325, the Court of Justice ruled that these principles required proof of a wrongful act, damage, and a causal link.

In Joined Cases 83 & 94/76 and 4, 15, & 40/77 *Bayerische HNL and others v Council and Commission* [1978] ECR 120, the Court of Justice held that an act was wrongful for the purposes of Article 340 TFEU only if there had been a sufficiently serious breach of a rule of law for the protection of individuals. Here, it is possible that there has been discrimination as between smaller and larger producers, given that no objective reason for such a difference of treatment is apparent. There may also be a breach of the principle of legitimate expectation, given that the subsidy was terminated without warning.

However, the breach of either principle must be sufficiently serious according to the factors laid down in Case C-352/98 P *Bergaderm v Commission* [2000] ECR I-5291 by reference to Joined Cases C-46 & 48/93 *Brasserie du Pêcheur SA v Germany; R v Secretary of State for Transport, ex p Factortame Ltd and others ('Factortame III')* [1994] ECR I-1593. These include the complexity of the situations to be regulated, the difficulties in the application or interpretation of the legal texts, the margin of discretion available to the EU institution that adopted the act at issue, whether the infringement was intentional or involuntary, and whether any error of law was excusable or inexcusable.

Although there is no evidence of complex law or factual situations here, the extent of the discretion regarding subsidies is likely to be wide, given that these come from public funds and are given to commercial producers. Further information is required about any reason for the difference in treatment of different producers, but the sudden withdrawal of the subsidy may go beyond even the Commission's wide discretion in this area.

In any event, Nutkin will also need to prove damage and causation.

8.4.3 Wrongful acts by EU servants

Article 340 TFEU (set out in the Introduction to this chapter) provides that the EU must make good any damage caused not only by the wrongful acts of its institutions, but also by those of its 'servants' (for example its employees or agents) in the performance of their duties.

The key issue here is whether the act is committed in the performance of the servant's EU duties; if it is not, the EU will not incur liability. This requirement has been interpreted strictly, as can been seen in Case 9/69 *Sayag v Leduc* [1969] ECR 329. In that case, Leduc was injured in a road traffic accident caused by an EU official, Sayag, who was driving his private car en route to a location where he was required to carry out work for the EU. EU law provided immunity against proceedings for its officials and servants in relation to acts performed by them in their official capacity, but the Court of Justice held that Sayag's wrongful act had not been committed in the performance of his duties because driving a car did not directly accomplish the EU's tasks.

8.4.4 Acts that are not wrongful

The possibility of EU liability in damages even in the absence of a wrongful act has been mooted, but not yet accepted, by the Court of Justice. The General Court (eg in Case T-383/00 *Beamglow v Parliament, Council and Commission* [2005] ECR II-5459, at para 174) (see further 2.4.2 on the General Court) and Advocate General Poiares Maduro (in his Opinion in Joined Cases C-120–121/06 P *FIAMM and another v Council and Commission* [2008] ECR I-6513) (see further 2.4 on Advocate Generals' Opinions), both argued that the EU could, in exceptional circumstances, be liable even in the absence of a wrongful act, albeit with the former concluding that the circumstances of the case were not in fact exceptional. However, although the Court of Justice, in Case C-237/98 *Dorsch Consult v Council and Commission* [2000] ECR I-4549, had discussed some of the conditions under which no-fault liability could be incurred, it subsequently held in *FIAMM*, at para 169, that it had done so solely 'in the event of the principle of [EU] liability for a lawful act being recognised in [EU] law' and rejected the existence of such liability at the current time.

8.5 Actual damage

8.5.1 Proof of loss

An applicant under Article 340 TFEU must be able to prove the existence and extent of the damage suffered. As the General Court noted in T-343/13 *CN v European Parliament* EU:T:2015:926 (see further 8.4.2), purely hypothetical and indeterminate damage does not give rise to a right to compensation; the damage suffered must be actual and certain. A good example of this requirement can be seen in Case 253/84 *GAEC v Council and Commission* [1987] ECR 123, in which subsidies had been provided to German farmers pursuant to Council Decision 84/361/EEC of 30 June 1984 concerning an aid granted to farmers in the Federal Republic of Germany, OJ 1984 L185/41. Aggrieved French farmers brought an action under Article 340 TFEU claiming damages for losses caused to them by competition from subsidized German milk, poultry, and cattle products.

?! THINKING POINT

While reading the following extract, consider why the Court of Justice rejected the claim in respect of sales of milk and poultry.

Case 253/84 *GAEC v Council and Commission* [1987] ECR 123

11. The preliminary observation may be made that GAEC maintains that the damage for which compensation is sought arose because the aid granted to German farmers by virtue of Decision 84/361 enabled those farmers to reduce their prices and hence to increase very substantially their exports to France of beef and veal, milk and poultry, triggering a fall in prices on the French market.
12. As regards the fact of the damage, although GAEC provisionally set an estimate of FF 60 000 on the damage which it allegedly suffered in respect of all of its products up to the date on which the application was brought, it has since provided no particulars of its losses on sales of milk and poultry, even though the Court asked it to provide figures, at least for the second half of 1984, for the damage suffered by it as a result of the discrimination caused by the contested aid.
13. In those circumstances it must be held that, as far as milk and poultry are concerned, GAEC has not proved that it has suffered damage.

The Court of Justice held that, in respect of sales of milk and poultry, actual damage was not proved because the farmers had produced no evidence of their losses. (The result of their claim for losses in respect of cattle products is discussed at 8.6.)

However, as the General Court noted in T-343/13 *CN v European Parliament* EU:T:2015:926 (see also 8.4.2), as long as the existence of the damage can be proved, compensation may be awarded even if there is uncertainty as to the exact quantification of the damage.

?! THINKING POINT

When reading the following extract, make a note of the Court's summary of the relevant principles and their application to the facts at issue.

T-343/13 *CN v European Parliament* EU:T:2015:926

118. It should first be recalled that, according to case-law, with regard to the condition that damage must have been suffered, such damage must be actual and certain. By contrast, purely hypothetical and indeterminate damage does not give a right to compensation (judgment of 28 April 2010 in *BST v Commission*, T-452/05, ECR, EU:T:2010:167, paragraph 165). However, the requirement relating to the existence of certain damage is met where the damage is imminent and foreseeable with sufficient certainty, even if the damage cannot yet be precisely assessed (judgment of 14 January 1987 in *Zuckerfabrik Bedburg and Others v Council and Commission*, 281/84, ECR, EU:C:1987:3, paragraph 14).
119. It is for the party seeking to establish the European Union's liability to adduce proof as to the existence or extent of the damage alleged and to establish a sufficiently direct causal

> link between that damage and the conduct complained of on the part of the institution concerned (judgment in *BST v Commission*, cited in paragraph 118 above, EU:T:2010:167, paragraph 167).
>
> 120. The Parliament does not dispute the existence of the material damage claimed by the applicant, namely the fees for his legal counsel, if unlawful conduct were to exist.
>
> 121. With regard to non-material damage, on the other hand, the applicant has not demonstrated the existence of such damage. He has merely claimed that the Parliament's dismissive and dilatory attitude hurt him deeply and caused him considerable stress, without providing any evidence in support of this claim. Consequently, it cannot be accepted.
>
> 122. Accordingly, the applicant's arguments relating to the existence of non-material damage must be rejected.

The General Court in *CN* held that the requirement that the damage must be actual and certain could be satisfied so long as the applicant was able to prove that the damage was imminent and foreseeable with sufficient certainty, even if it could not yet be assessed precisely. On the facts, the defendant European Parliament had accepted that the applicant had suffered material damage in the form of fees for legal counsel (who had been instructed to contact the Parliament to require it to remove the sensitive information about the applicant from its website). However, the applicant had failed to provide evidence of non-material damage; it was not enough merely to claim that the Parliament's dismissive and dilatory attitude had caused him emotional pain and stress.

The applicant in Case C-243/05 P *Agraz and others v Commission* [2006] ECR 10833, however, was more successful. In that case, the Commission had incorrectly calculated the production aid payable to EU tomato producers under Commission Regulation (EC) No 1519/2000 of 12 July 2000 setting for the 2000/01 marketing year the minimum price and the amount of production aid for processed tomato products, OJ 2000 L174/29, because it had failed to take account of Chinese tomato prices. The Court of Justice held that although the exact impact that taking those prices into account would have had was uncertain, it would inevitably have put the applicants in a better position. The Court concluded that, even though the damage could not be exactly quantified, it was possible to put an economic value on it for the purposes of awarding damages under Article 340 TFEU. Similarly, in C-611/12 P *Giordano v Commission* EU:C:2014:2282, the Court held that the damage caused to fishermen by the Commission's withdrawal of their quota for catching bluefin tuna was not hypothetical merely because they might have been unable to catch their quota for other reasons, although any such inability might have a bearing on the extent of the damage.

8.5.2 Reduction in damages

Even where an applicant is able to prove the loss that it claims to have sustained, the level of damages awarded may be less than the actual loss if the applicant has been guilty of contributory negligence or has failed to mitigate its loss.

These principles are both enshrined in English law.

?! **THINKING POINT**

From your own knowledge of domestic law, try to explain, or give an example of, one or both of these principles.

In the law of tort, it has been established that a claimant who has contributed through their own negligence to the tort, or to the resulting damage, may be expected to bear some or all of their own loss. For example, damages awarded to a claimant injured in a road traffic accident may be reduced if it is shown that they contributed to the accident by driving too fast, or contributed to the extent of the resulting damage by failing to wear a seat belt.

In both contract and tort, English law recognizes that a claimant should do their best to minimize the loss that they have suffered as a result of the tort or breach of contract. If the claimant does not do so, then in effect they have brought some of their loss upon themselves and should therefore bear a proportion of it. In the example of a claimant injured in a road traffic accident, damages awarded in respect of lost earnings while the claimant is unable to undertake their normal work may be reduced if they fail to take reasonable alternative work.

The use of both principles in EU law is similar.

8.5.2.1 The duty to mitigate any loss

The *Mulder* litigation (already discussed at 8.4.2 in relation to wrongful acts) involved a dispute concerning the allocation by the EU of milk quotas (the amount of milk that a particular undertaking could produce without incurring a levy). Council Regulation (EEC) No 857/84 of 31 March 1984 adopting general rules for the application of the levy referred to in Article 5c of Regulation (EEC) No 804/68 in the milk and milk products sector, OJ 1984 L90/13, did not allocate any milk quotas at all to those producers that had not produced any milk in the previous year as a result of an EU agreement aimed at reducing overproduction. They were therefore disadvantaged by the terms of the Regulation and they successfully applied for its partial annulment under Article 263 TFEU (see 7.3–7.14), on the ground of breach of their legitimate expectation that they would be able to resume milk production when the agreement came to an end (Case 120/86 *Mulder v Minister van Landbouw en Visserij* (*'Mulder I'*) [1988] ECR 2321; Case 170/86 *Von Deetzen v Hauptzollamt Hamburg-Jonas* [1988] ECR 2355).

In the light of this judgment, the EU introduced Council Regulation (EEC) No 764/89 of 20 March 1989 amending Regulation (EEC) No 857/84 adopting general rules for the application of the levy referred to in article 5c of Regulation (EEC) No 804/68 in the milk and milk products sector, OJ 1989 L84/2, to provide quotas for these producers, but at a lower rate than for other producers. This too was held to be invalid on the ground that it was discriminatory (Case C-189/89 *Spagl v Hauptzollamt Rosenheim* [1990] ECR I-4539; Case C-217/89 *Pastätter v Haupzollamt Bad Reichenhall* [1990] ECR I-4585).

The producers subsequently brought an action for damages under Article 340 TFEU. The Court held that reduced damages would be awarded in respect of Regulation 857/84 and none at all in relation to Regulation 764/89, because the breach was not sufficiently serious (see 8.4.2).

?! THINKING POINT

While reading the following extract, consider why the Court of Justice reduced the damages awarded.

Joined Cases C-104/89 & 37/90 *Mulder v Council and Commission* (*'Mulder II'*) [1992] ECR I-3061

33. As regards income from any replacement activities which is to be deducted from the hypothetical income referred to above, it must be noted that that income must be taken to include not only that which the applicants actually obtained from replacement activities, but also that income which they could have obtained had they reasonably engaged in such activities. This conclusion must be reached in the light of a general principle common to the legal systems of the Member States to the effect that the injured party must show reasonable diligence in limiting the extent of his loss or risk having to bear the damage himself. Any operating losses incurred by the applicants in carrying out such a replacement activity cannot be attributed to the Community [now Union], since the origin of such losses does not lie in the effects of the Community rules.

The Court of Justice reduced the damages awarded because the producers could reasonably be expected to have earned some profits by undertaking alternative activities. It therefore reduced the damages awarded by the amount of those notional profits.

8.5.2.2 Contributory negligence

In Case C-472/00 *Commission v Fresh Marine Company A/S* [2003] ECR I-7541 (already discussed at 8.4.2 in relation to wrongful acts), the applicant brought an action for damages on the ground that anti-dumping duties had been imposed on its products even though it had given an undertaking not to import products at prices below a certain level and was therefore not engaged in 'dumping' products in the EU market. It had supplied the Commission with a report indicating its compliance with its undertaking, but the Commission had then amended the report. The Court of Justice held that the amendment constituted a wrongful act (see 8.4.2), but reduced the damages awarded on account of Fresh Marine's contributory negligence.

THINKING POINT

While reading the following extract, consider what behaviour on the part of Fresh Marine was held by the Court to constitute contributory negligence.

Case C-472/00 *Commission v Fresh Marine Company A/S* [2003] ECR I-7541

135. It must therefore be held that, although, as is apparent from the grounds set out in paragraphs 73 to 92 above, [Fresh Marine] contributed to the same extent as the Commission in causing loss or damage to its business, continuation of that loss after the end of January 1998 is, on the other hand, exclusively due to a failure by the Commission to exercise due care; even though the explanations which it had obtained from [Fresh Marine] had definitely made it possible to correct their respective prior errors and removed any reason to continue to believe that the undertaking had been breached, the Commission delayed, for no apparent reason, in regularising [Fresh Marine]'s situation by withdrawing the provisional measures originally imposed against it.

136. It follows that the Commission must be held to be liable for one half of the loss of profit suffered by [Fresh Marine] between 18 December 1997 and 31 January 1998 and for all the loss caused to [Fresh Marine] from 1 February to 25 March 1998 …

[…]

The cross-appeal

66. As regards the substance, the Court of First Instance's reasoning, at paragraphs 91 and 92 of the contested judgment, is not contradictory. Having found that the Commission's reaction in unilaterally amending the October 1997 report was unlawful and that Fresh Marine's submission to the Commission of a report which did not contain the explanations necessary to understand it correctly was negligent, the Court of First Instance rightly held that, when determining the Commission's obligation to make reparation, account should be taken of the fact that each party bears half of the responsibility for the events.

The Court of Justice held that although the Commission had acted wrongfully in amending the report after it had been submitted, Fresh Marine itself had been negligent in submitting a report that did not contain the explanations necessary to understand it correctly. The fact that each party was equally responsible for the losses incurred by Fresh Marine prior to it providing the further explanations required led the Court to reduce by half the damages awarded in respect of losses incurred up to that point. (Damages in respect of losses incurred by Fresh Marine subsequent to its provision of further information were awarded in full.)

In Case 145/83 *Adams v Commission* [1985] ECR 3539, Adams had supplied the Commission with confidential information concerning breaches of EU competition law (see further Chapter 15 on the Commission's role in enforcing EU competition law) by his employer, Roche. In the course of proceedings against Roche, the Commission passed papers to it that enabled it to identify Adams as the source of the leaked information. The Commission then failed to warn Adams that Roche was planning to prosecute him and, when Adams returned to Switzerland, he was arrested and convicted of industrial espionage under Swiss law.

Adams brought a claim for damages under Article 340 TFEU, based on the Commission's wrongful acts in revealing sensitive documents and failing to warn him that it had done this. The Court of Justice awarded damages for Adams's loss of earnings and loss of reputation as a result of his conviction and imprisonment, which it attributed to the Commission's wrongful actions in allowing him to be identified and in failing to warn him that his identity was known by Roche. However, it reduced those damages on grounds of Adams's contributory negligence.

?! **THINKING POINT**

While reading the following extract, consider how the Court of Justice applied the principle of contributory negligence to the facts of the case.

Case 145/83 *Adams v Commission* [1985] ECR 3539

53. It must therefore be concluded that in principle the Community [now Union] is bound to make good the damage resulting from the discovery of the applicant's identity by means of the documents handed over to Roche by the Commission. It must however be recognised that the extent of the Commission's liability is diminished by reason of the applicant's own negligence. The applicant failed to inform the Commission that it was possible to infer his identity as the informant from the documents themselves, although he was in the best position to appreciate and to avert that risk. Nor did he ask the Commission to keep him informed of the progress of the investigation of Roche, and in particular of any use that might be made of the documents for that purpose. Lastly, he went back to Switzerland without attempting to make any inquiries in that respect, although he must have been aware of the risks to which his conduct towards his former employer had exposed him with regard to Swiss legislation.

54. Consequently, the applicant himself contributed significantly to the damage which he suffered. In assessing the conduct of the Commission on the one hand and that of the applicant on the other, the court considers it equitable to apportion responsibility for that damage equally between the two parties.

55. It follows from all the foregoing considerations that the Commission must be ordered to compensate the applicant to the extent of one half of the damage suffered by him as a result of the fact that he was identified as the source of information regarding Roche's anti-competitive practices. For the rest however, the application must be dismissed. The amount of the damages is to be determined by agreement between the parties or, failing such agreement, by the court.

The Court of Justice reduced the damages awarded by half as a result of Adams's contributory negligence. It ruled that Adams had been negligent in failing to warn the Commission that he could be identified from the documents, in failing to ask that he be kept informed of progress in the case, particularly with regard to the use of the documents, and in returning to

Switzerland without inquiring as to the current status of the proceedings and the use of the documentation. This judgment appears to be rather harsh, both in its finding of the existence of contributory negligence and in its decision on the impact of that contributory negligence. However, as discussed at 8.4.2 (see in particular Joined Cases 83 & 94/76 and 4, 15, & 40/77 *Bayerische HNL and others v Council and Commission* [1978] ECR 120), there are public policy reasons for taking a restrictive approach to the award of damages against the EU.

REVIEW QUESTION

Refer back to the previous review question. Suppose that Nutkin Ltd wishes to claim damages for the loss of subsidy, consequent loss of profit, and the cost of making all five members of staff employed in its garden bird feeder and bird food division redundant. Advise Nutkin as to whether these heads of damage are likely to be recoverable under Article 340 TFEU.

Note: The requirements of Article 340 TFEU and the application to the facts of the detailed requirements of a wrongful act are as outlined in the answer to the previous review question.

Answer: In relation to the issue of damage, the Court of Justice has held that existence of damage must be proved (Case 253/84 *GAEC v Council and Commission* [1987] ECR 123). This will be straightforward in relation to the loss of the subsidy that has been withdrawn by the Commission. The redundancies and associated costs should also be capable of proof. However, it is not clear from the facts that there has been any loss of profit as yet and any such losses would need to be proved in order for damages to be awarded in respect of them. It may not be necessary for the loss of profit to have occurred, but Nutkin must be able to prove that such loss is imminent and foreseeable with a reasonable degree of certainty.

There is also a duty to mitigate losses as far as reasonable. For example, given that Nutkin employs only a tiny fraction of its staff in the affected division of its business (5 out of 99), it might be possible to redeploy some of them.

Finally, if Nutkin itself has contributed to its damage (eg as in Case C-472/00 *Commission v Fresh Marine Company A/S* [2003] ECR I-7541), then the damages awarded may be reduced. However, there is no evidence of contributory negligence on the facts here.

In any event, Nutkin will also need to prove causation.

8.6 Causation

The applicant must prove that the wrongful act actually caused their loss. The EU Courts will not simply assume the existence of a causal link just because a wrongful act by the EU and loss to the applicant have been proved.

Although the French farmers in Case 253/84 *GAEC v Council and Commission* [1987] ECR 123 produced statistics to prove their damage in respect of beef and veal (unlike their losses in relation to milk and poultry—see 8.5.1), they failed to show causation because there was evidence that prices of these products had decreased prior to the subsidy to the competing German producers being provided, owing to increased levels of imports.

The test for causation is a strict one, as can be seen from Joined Cases 64 & 113/76 *Dumortier Frères SA and others v Council and Commission* [1979] ECR 309, in which refunds to maize gritz producers were abolished while producers of maize starch, which was in direct competition with maize gritz, continued to receive the refunds.

The maize gritz producers claimed compensation under Article 340 TFEU for:

(1) the loss of refunds

(2) lost sales

(3) the resulting factory closures by two producers and bankruptcy of one.

?! **THINKING POINT**

While reading the following extract, note whether claim 1 and/or claim 2 resulted in an award of damages by the Court of Justice and why. (The ruling in relation to claim 3 is discussed further later.)

Joined Cases 64 & 113/76 *Dumortier Frères SA and others v Council and Commission* [1979] ECR 309

14. This said, it is necessary to go on to examine the damage resulting from the discrimination to which the gritz producers were subjected. The origin of the damage complained of by the applicants lies in the abolition by the Council of the refunds which would have been paid to the gritz producers if equality of treatment with the producers of maize starch had been observed. Hence, the amount of those refunds must provide a yardstick for the assessment of the damage suffered.

[…]

17. The parties have put forward statistics and other data in support of their respective submissions. Those data do not permit the conclusion advanced by the Council to be accepted. The conclusion which emerges is rather that during the period in dispute the prices of gritz and starch developed along similar lines without reflecting the absence of refunds for gritz. The only exception concerns the period covering the last months of 1975 and the beginning of 1976, during which the prices of gritz were increased by amounts corresponding to the unpaid refunds. However, the applicants have explained that those increases were accepted by the breweries provisionally on condition that a clause was inserted in the contracts of sale guaranteeing the buyer the benefit, retroactively in the appropriate case, of any new refund granted by the Community [now Union].

18. It follows that the loss for which the applicants must be compensated has to be calculated on the basis of its being equivalent to the refunds which would have been paid to them if, during the period from 1 August 1975 to 19 October 1977 the use of maize for the manufacture of gritz used by the brewing industry had conferred a right to the same refunds as the use of maize for the manufacture of starch; an exception will have to be made for the quantities of maize used for the manufacture of gritz which was sold at prices increased by the amount of the unpaid refunds under contracts guaranteeing the buyer the benefit of any re-introduction of the refunds.

19. Some of the applicants have also submitted claims for compensation for certain additional items of damage which they claim to have suffered.
20. In the case of the two maize processors established in the north of France, the further damage lies particularly in a substantial fall in their sales to breweries. Although it is beyond dispute that the figures submitted by the applicants clearly show such a fall, that fact can hardly be ascribed to the absence of refunds. In fact, as has already been said, the applicants have insisted on the fact that the selling prices of gritz were not increased on account of the abolition of the refunds. On the contrary, as the Court recognised when examining the development of the prices, the gritz producers chose to sell at a loss in order to retain their markets, and not to increase their prices at the risk of losing those markets. Thus the inequality which existed between gritz and starch as regards the granting of refunds was not reflected in the selling prices. If in spite of that commercial policy the gritz producers' sales fell, the reason for this must be sought in something other than the inequality caused by the abolition of the refunds.

The Court of Justice ruled that damages should be awarded only in respect of the lost refunds. Contrary to the Council's argument, the maize gritz producers had not, apart from a short period, increased their prices to compensate for the loss of the refunds and so the abolition of the refunds had caused them loss. However, the reduction in sales could not be attributed to the withdrawal of the refunds, since the producers had not chosen to pass on the loss of refunds in increased prices.

In Joined Cases 19, 20, 25, & 30/69 *Richez-Parise and others v Commission* [1970] ECR 325 (see also 8.4.2 in relation to the existence of a wrongful act), a number of EU employees sought damages in respect of the impact of an incorrect calculation of their pension entitlement. The Court of Justice held that the applicants had failed to prove that they had relied on the uncorrected information when making their requests to retire and so were not entitled to reinstatement in their posts. However, it considered that the uncorrected information could have caused them to fail to apply for other benefits available to them and so the Court ordered that the limitation period on such applications be deemed not to have expired.

It can be observed from Joined Cases 64 & 113/76 *Dumortier Frères SA and others v Council and Commission* [1979] ECR 309 (just discussed) that not only must causation be proved, but also it must be sufficiently direct. As previously explained, the producers successfully claimed compensation for the lost refunds, but failed to prove that their lost sales had been caused by the Commission's action. They also claimed for the factory closures by two producers and the bankruptcy of one.

?! THINKING POINT

While reading the following extract, consider why the Court of Justice ruled that the factory closures and bankruptcy were insufficiently direct to be recoverable.

Joined Cases 64 & 113/76 *Dumortier Frères SA and others v Council and Commission* [1979] ECR 309

21. In the case of certain other applicants the further damage alleged is of a different nature. Two undertakings were forced to close their factories and a third had to commence insolvency proceedings. The Council argued that the origin of the difficulties experienced by those undertakings is to be found in the circumstances peculiar to each of them, such as the obsolescence of their plant and managerial or financial problems. The data supplied by the parties on that question in the course of the proceedings are not such as to establish the true causes of the further damage alleged. However, it is sufficient to state that even if it were assumed that the abolition of the refunds exacerbated the difficulties encountered by those applicants, those difficulties would not be a sufficiently direct consequence of the unlawful conduct of the Council to render the Community [now Union] liable to make good the damage. In the field of non-contractual liability of public authorities for legislative measures, the principles common to the laws of the Member States to which the second paragraph of Article 215 of the EEC Treaty [now Article 340 TFEU] refers cannot be relied on to deduce an obligation to make good every harmful consequence, even a remote one, of unlawful legislation.
22. It follows that the claims for compensation for the further damage alleged cannot be upheld.

The Court of Justice held that even if the abolition of refunds by the Commission had exacerbated the problems of certain producers, the factory closures and bankruptcy were not a sufficiently direct result of the loss of the refunds to render the EU liable in damages. There was no obligation to make good every unfortunate consequence, however remote, of unlawful legislation.

A further illustration of the difficulty of proving causation is provided by Joined Cases 5, 7, & 13–24/66 *Kampffmeyer v Commission* [1967] ECR 245, which concerned a Commission Decision of 3 October 1963 approving a German ban on maize imports, which had come into force on 1 October. The Decision was subsequently annulled by the Court of Justice (in Joined Cases 106–107/63 *Toepfer and another v Commission* [1965] ECR 405—see 7.8.2; see also 8.4.2 in relation to the existence of a wrongful act). Had imports been made on 1 October, they would—very unusually—have been subject to a zero-rate import levy (in other words, no levy at all) and importers who had applied for a licence on this date alleged that they had suffered damage as a result of the Decision because they had missed the opportunity to import maize without having to pay a levy. The Court held that only some of the alleged damage had been caused by the Decision.

First, importers which had entered into contracts after 1 October were aware of the German ban and could not claim that the resulting unavailability of the zero levy for their imports had caused any loss to them.

Secondly, importers which had entered into contracts to purchase maize on 1 October and chosen to fulfil them could be awarded damages in respect of the higher levies that they had

had to pay in order to do so, but only after they had proved that they had exhausted all possibilities for claiming reimbursement of the wrongfully charged levy from the German government (see further 8.9.2 on the possibility of a concurrent claim against the Member State).

Third, importers which had entered into contracts on 1 October but then chosen to repudiate them could be awarded damages in respect of penalties payable for breach of contract, since these were 'a direct consequence' (*Kampffmeyer*, at 265) of the Commission's wrongful act. However, since the alleged loss of profit on the repudiated contracts was 'based on facts of an essentially speculative nature' (*Kampffmeyer*, at 266), damages for loss of profit to this third category of importers would be limited (to an amount equivalent to 10 per cent of the sums that the importers would have paid by way of levy if they had carried out the contracts).

Finally, importers which had merely applied for import licences on 1 October and had proceeded no further with their proposed transactions could not claim compensation for loss of profits resulting from transactions that had never commenced because 'imports in which there was a mere intention to engage lack any substantial character capable of giving rise to compensation for loss of profits' (*Kampffmeyer*, at 267). In other words, such alleged losses could neither be proved (see further 8.5.1 on the requirement to prove damage) nor proved to have been caused by the Commission's wrongful act.

REVIEW QUESTION

Refer back to the previous review questions. Remember that Nutkin wishes to claim damages for the loss of subsidy, consequent loss of profit, and the cost of making all five members of staff employed in its garden bird feeders and bird food division redundant. Advise Nutkin:

(a) on whether it is likely to be able to satisfy the requirement of Article 340 TFEU as to causation; and

(b) in conclusion, on its likely chances of success in an action for damages against the Commission under Article 340 TFEU.

Note: The requirements of Article 340 TFEU and the application to the facts of the requirements of a wrongful act and damage are as outlined in the answers to the previous review questions.

Answer: In relation to the issue of causation, the Court of Justice has held that it must be proved (Case 253/84 *GAEC v Council and Commission* [1987] ECR 123). This will be straightforward in relation to the loss of the subsidy that has been withdrawn by the Commission. However, it is not clear from the facts whether the loss of profit (if any) and the redundancies have been caused by the allegedly wrongful act. In any event, it may be that the redundancies are too remote a consequence of the EU's actions, as in Joined Cases 64 & 113/76 *Dumortier Frères SA and others v Council and Commission* [1979] ECR 309.

In summary, it may be that the only loss that can be proved to have been suffered as a result of the Commission's act is the amount of the subsidy. If there has been a sufficiently serious breach of the principle of discrimination (see the answer to the first review question in this chapter), the full amount of the lost subsidy will be recoverable. However, if the only sufficiently serious breach is of the principle of legitimate expectation (see the answer to the first review question in this chapter), the amount recoverable will be limited to the subsidy that would have been payable during a reasonable notice period prior to its removal.

8.7 Unjust enrichment

Neither Article 340 nor Article 268 TFEU expressly refer to the possibility of an action against the EU for unjust enrichment, but the Court of Justice recognized the possibility in Case C-47/07 P *Masdar (UK) Ltd v Commission* [2008] ECR I-9761. In that case, the Court noted (at para 44) that 'the general principles common to the laws of the Member States' included the principle that 'a person who has suffered a loss which increases the wealth of another person without there being any legal basis for that enrichment has the right, as a general rule, to restitution from the person enriched, up to the amount of the loss'. The Court held that since such an action was, by definition, non-contractual, it was necessary to allow it to be pursued under Article 340 TFEU. However, the rules governing liability were not the same as those applicable to other non-contractual actions (see 8.3, 8.4, 8.5, and 8.6)—namely, unlawful conduct by the EU, damage, and a causal link between the conduct and the damage. Neither unlawful conduct nor, indeed, any conduct at all on the part of the EU, was required; instead, an applicant must prove enrichment on the part of the defendant, for which there was no valid legal basis, and impoverishment on the part of the applicant, which was linked to that enrichment.

However, the Court held that enrichment could not be categorized as unjust where it derived from contractual obligations. In *Masdar*, the Commission had contracted with a company, Helmico, for Helmico to provide services in relation to certain Moldovan and Russian projects. Helmico then entered into contracts with Masdar under which it subcontracted some of those services to Masdar. After finding Helmico guilty of fraud in the performance of the contracts, the Commission ceased to pay Helmico and requested the return of funds paid. Masdar brought an action for damages against the Commission under Article 340 TFEU. The Court of Justice upheld the ruling of the General Court (see further 2.4.2 on the General Court) that any enrichment of the Commission, or impoverishment of Masdar, arose from their contracts with Helmico and therefore could not be categorized as unjust. The Court noted, however, that Masdar was entitled to bring, and indeed had brought, an action against Helmico for breach of contract.

8.8 Time limits

Under Article 46 of the Statute of the Court of Justice, an applicant has five years from the event giving rise to the claim in which to bring an action under Article 340 TFEU, and this period will be suspended by any other Court of Justice proceedings.

Consolidated version of the Statute of the Court of Justice of the European Union

Article 46

Proceedings against the Union in matters arising from non-contractual liability shall be barred after a period of five years from the occurrence of the event giving rise thereto. The period of limitation shall be interrupted if proceedings are instituted before the Court of Justice or if prior to such proceedings an application is made by the aggrieved party to the relevant institution of the Union. In the latter event the proceedings must be instituted within the period of two months provided for in Article 263 of the Treaty on the Functioning of the European Union; the provisions of the second paragraph of Article 265 of the Treaty on the Functioning of the European Union shall apply where appropriate.

This Article shall also apply to proceedings against the European Central Bank regarding non-contractual liability.

The Court of Justice has interpreted this as meaning that an applicant may bring an action within five years from the day on which the damage materialized (Joined Cases 256, 257, 265, & 267/80 and 5/81 *Birra Wührer and others v Council and Commission* [1982] ECR 85), as explained in the following extract.

Joined Cases 256, 257, 265, & 267/80 and 5/81 *Birra Wührer and others v Council and Commission* [1982] ECR 85

10. The period of limitation which applies to proceedings in matters arising from the non-contractual liability of the Community [now Union] therefore cannot begin before all the requirements governing an obligation to provide compensation for damage are satisfied and in particular before the damage to be made good has materialized. Accordingly, since the situations concerned are those in which the liability of the Community has its origin in a legislative measure, the period of limitation cannot begin before the injurious effects of that measure have been produced, and consequently, in the circumstances of these cases, before the time at which the applicants after completing the transactions entitling them to the refunds, were bound to incur damage which was certain in character.

8.9 The relationship between Article 340 TFEU and other actions

8.9.1 Other actions against the EU

The success of an action under Article 340 TFEU is independent of any other action under EU law, for example under Article 263 TFEU (see 7.3–7.14), Article 265 TFEU (see 7.16), or Article 267 TFEU (see Chapter 6), so that it is irrelevant whether another action has been brought and whether any action brought has been successful. Indeed, Article 266 TFEU expressly provides that the EU's obligations resulting from a successful application for annulment under Article 263 TFEU, or from a declaration of failure to act under Article 265 TFEU, do not affect any obligation that it might also incur under Article 340 TFEU.

Article 266 TFEU

The institution whose act has been declared void or whose failure to act has been declared contrary to the Treaties shall be required to take the necessary measures to comply with the judgment of the Court of Justice of the European Union.

This obligation shall not affect any obligation which may result from the application of the second paragraph of Article 340.

In Case 175/84 *Krohn v Commission* [1986] ECR 753 (see also 8.9.2 in relation to concurrent actions against Member States), the Commission had, by Decisions of 23 November and 21 December 1982, authorized the German authorities to refuse to grant an import licence to Krohn for Thai manioc. Krohn brought an action for damages under Article 340 TFEU after it had become time barred from bringing an action for annulment of the individual Decisions under Article 263 TFEU (see further 7.3–7.14). The Court of Justice held that the action under Article 340 TFEU was nonetheless admissible because it was an autonomous form of action with a particular purpose to fulfil (*Krohn*, at para 32). The fact that the time limit for an action under Article 263 TFEU had passed and that the Decisions had thereby become definitively valid was irrelevant.

In Case 4/69 *Alfons Lütticke v Commission* [1971] ECR 325, the Court of Justice emphasized the independent nature of the action under Article 340 TFEU even in circumstances in which such an action, if successful, would have a similar result to that of a successful action under another Article.

Case 4/69 *Alfons Lütticke v Commission* [1971] ECR 325

6. The action for damages provided for by Article 178 [EC, now Article 268 TFEU] and the second paragraph of Article 215 [EC, now Article 340 TFEU] was established by the Treaty as an independent form of action with a particular purpose to fulfil within the system of actions and subject to conditions for its use, conceived with a view to its specific purpose. It would be contrary to the independent nature of this action as well as to the efficacy of the general system of forms of action created by the Treaty to regard as a ground of inadmissibility the fact that, in certain circumstances, an action for damages might lead to a result similar to that of an action for failure to act under Article 175 [EC, now Article 264 TFEU].

However, as noted in the Introduction to this chapter, it is nonetheless not uncommon for a measure that is the subject of Article 340 TFEU proceedings to have also been the subject of proceedings under Article 263 TFEU (see Chapter 7).

8.9.2 Concurrent action against a Member State

Where an EU measure is implemented by a Member State, the potential exists for the EU and the Member State each to be concurrently liable for damage caused to the applicant. In most cases, in fact, only the EU or the Member State, and not both, will be liable. For example, in Case 96/71 *Haegeman v Commission* [1972] ECR 1005, the Court of Justice ruled that where national authorities had imposed a levy on the applicant's imports pursuant to Regulation (EEC) No 816/70 of the Council of 28 April 1970 laying down additional provisions for the common organisation of the market in wine, OJ 1970 L99/1, the applicant should bring its claim for a refund of the levy and compensation for the consequential losses against the national authorities in the national courts. Similarly, in Case 126/76 *Dietz v Commission* [1977] ECR 2431, the Court of Justice accepted jurisdiction under Article 340 TFEU in respect of the applicant's losses resulting from the absence of transitional arrangements for contracts entered into before the coming into force of Regulation (EEC) No 2635/71 of the Commission of 30 December 1971 amending the compensatory amounts in agriculture following the temporary widening of the margins of fluctuation for the currencies of certain Member States, OJ 1971 L273/1. It did so because the action was directed at the absence of the transitional measures, for which the Commission was responsible, and not at Italy's reliance on the law pre-dating the Regulation.

However, in some cases, concurrent liability will arise. In such cases, the Court of Justice has ruled that if the primary liability appears to be that of the Member State, as in Joined Cases 5, 7, & 13–24/66 *Kampffmeyer v Commission* [1967] ECR 245 (see 8.4.2 on the existence of a wrongful act, 8.5.1 on damage, and 8.6 on causation), the applicant must exhaust its rights of action against the national authorities before the Court of Justice will issue final judgment as to any EU liability in damages. In its reasoning on this point, the Court in *Kampffmeyer* stated that '[i]t is necessary to avoid the applicants' being insufficiently or excessively compensated for the same damage by the different assessment of two different courts applying different rules of law' (*Kampffmeyer*, at 266). This concern has been repeated by the EU Courts on many occasions. However, as the Court of Justice has made clear in cases such as Case 20/88 *Roquette Frères v Commission* [1989] ECR 1553 (for the facts of this case, see 8.4.2) and Case 175/84 *Krohn v Commission* [1987] ECR 97 (see also 8.9.1), this applies only where the right of action against the national authorities could effectively compensate the applicant. This important qualification was stated clearly by the court in *Roquette Frères* in the following extract.

Case 20/88 *Roquette Frères v Commission* [1989] ECR 1553

5. The Court has consistently held that the action for compensation provided for in Article 178 [now Article 268 TFEU] and the second paragraph of Article 215 [now Article 340 TFEU] of the EEC Treaty was introduced as an autonomous form of action with a particular purpose to fulfil within the system of remedies. Although its admissibility may be conditional in certain

cases on the prior exhaustion of the remedies available under domestic law for obtaining satisfaction from the national authorities, it is essential, in order for that condition to apply, that those remedies under domestic law effectively ensure protection for individuals aggrieved by measures of Community [now Union] institutions (judgments of 12 April 1984 in Case 281/82 *Unifiex v Commission and Council* [1984] ECR 1969, and of 26 February 1986 in Case 175/84 *Krohn v Commission* [1986] ECR 753).

In *Roquette Frères*, the Court of Justice held that the potential remedies under French law to obtain reimbursement of overpaid compensatory amounts were not available to the applicant because the Court itself had previously ruled, in Case 145/79 *Roquette Frères SA v French Customs Administration* [1980] ECR 2917, that the invalidity of the EU Regulations fixing the compensatory amounts could not enable the charging of those amounts to be challenged in relation to the period prior to the date of its judgment. No national remedy could therefore effectively ensure reparation for the damage suffered by Roquette Frères. In *Krohn*, the Court held that the annulment by the German authorities of their decision to refuse Krohn an import licence would not adequately compensate it for its inability to import goods prior to the annulment and so an action under Article 340 TFEU should not be made dependent on first exhausting national remedies.

It is important to note that the possibility or existence of a claim in the national courts does not render a claim in the EU Courts inadmissible, or even prevent the EU Courts from commencing to hear the case, but only prevents them giving final judgment. The extent to which the EU Courts will examine the claim prior to the judgment of the national court being given was considered in T-317/12 *Holcim v Commission* EU:T:2014:782. In that case, the applicant company, Holcim, owned greenhouse gas emission allowances under an EU scheme for trading in such allowances. When these allowances were stolen, Holcim asked the EU Commission (see 2.3 on the Commission) to freeze the allowance, but the Commission refused to do so. Holcim then sought damages in relation to the Commission's conduct. The General Court noted that Holcim had also sought damages from the Romanian authorities in the Romanian courts, which gave rise to the risk of Holcim being compensated twice for the same damage. However, it also noted that the EU Courts had developed approaches to avoid such consequences, both at the admissibility stage (ie the decision as to whether the case can be heard at all) and at the merits stage (ie the decision, after the case is heard, as to whether the applicant's claim should be upheld) of the case.

?! THINKING POINT

When reading the following extract, consider what these approaches are.

Case T-317/12 *Holcim v Commission* EU:T:2014:782

A—Effect on the admissibility of the present action of bringing an action for damages before a Romanian court

73. By the judgment in Case 20/88 *Roquette frères v Commission* [1989] ECR 1553 (at paragraph 15), the Court held that the admissibility of an action for compensation provided for in Article 268 TFEU and the second paragraph of Article 340 TFEU may be conditional in certain cases on the prior exhaustion of the remedies available under domestic law for obtaining satisfaction from the national authorities, provided that those remedies under domestic law effectively ensure protection for the individuals concerned in that they are capable of resulting in compensation for the damage alleged.
74. In that formulation of the principle, the use of the verb 'may' shows that the non-exhaustion of 'remedies available under domestic law for obtaining satisfaction from the national authorities' must not automatically lead to a finding of inadmissibility by the EU judicature. It may result in the inadmissibility of an action only 'in certain cases'.
75. Admittedly, those cases were not defined in the judgment in *Roquette frères v Commission*, cited in paragraph 73 above (paragraph 15). However, the Court considers that there is only one situation in which the fact that a final ruling has not been given on the action for damages brought before the national court necessarily implies that the action for compensation brought before the EU judicature is inadmissible. This is where that fact precludes the latter from identifying the nature and quantum of the damage pleaded before it, with the result that the requirements of Article 44(1)(c) of the Rules of Procedure are not complied with (see the case-law set out in paragraph 55 above).
76. However, in the present case, notwithstanding the fact that nothing in the file leads to the conclusion that a Romanian court has ruled on the action for damages brought by the applicant, the General Court is able to ascertain the nature and quantum of the damage alleged (see paragraph 65 above).
77. Accordingly, the present action cannot be dismissed as inadmissible on the basis of the case-law resulting from the judgment in *Roquette frères v Commission*, cited in paragraph 73 above (paragraph 15).

B—Effect on the examination of the substance of the present action of bringing an action for damages before a Romanian court

78. Bringing an action before a national court seeking compensation for the same damage as that relied on before the EU judicature has a bearing not only on admissibility but also on the examination of the merits of the action for compensation before the EU judicature.
79. According to the case-law, where (i) a person has brought two actions before the EU judicature seeking compensation for the same damage, one against a national authority, before a national court, and the other against an EU institution or body, and (ii) there is a likelihood that, because of the different assessments of that damage by the two different

courts, the person in question may be insufficiently or excessively compensated, the EU judicature must, before deciding on the amount of the damage, wait until the national court has given final judgment on the action brought before it (see, to that effect, Joined Cases 5/66, 7/66 and 13/66 to 24/66 *Kampffmeyer and Others v Commission* [1967] 245, at p. 266; Case 30/66 *Becher v Commission* [1967] ECR 285, at p. 300, and Case T-138/03 *É.R. and Others v Council and Commission* [2006] ECR II-4923, paragraph 42).

80. Thus, in such a case, the EU judicature must wait until the national court has given judgment before ruling on the existence and the quantum of any damage. Nor can it adjudicate in the meantime on the causal link between the conduct alleged against the European Union and the damage invoked. On the other hand, it may, even before the national court has given its ruling, determine whether the conduct alleged is capable of giving rise to non-contractual liability on the part of the European Union. Moreover, in the judgment in *Kampffmeyer and Others v Commission* (at p. 262), cited in paragraph 79 above, before staying proceedings, the Court of Justice adjudicated on whether there was 'a wrongful act or omission capable of giving rise to liability on the part of the Community'.

81. In the present case, since the applicant has brought an action before a Romanian court which is still pending with a view to being compensated in respect of the same damage as that alleged in the context of the present proceedings, the examination of damage and causation must be reserved.

82. However, the Court finds that it is in a position to rule on the questions that are preliminary to that examination.

83. In particular, it is open to the Court to assess the lawfulness of the two forms of conduct alleged by the applicant in support of its claim for damages for fault-based liability. In addition, in the event that it dismisses that first claim, the Court would also be in a position to rule on whether conditions for engaging strict liability have been met, assuming that such a system of strict liability has a place in EU law.

On the admissibility point, the General Court held that a pending case in the national courts would make a claim for damages in the EU Courts inadmissible in only one situation—where the lack of a final domestic ruling made it impossible for the EU Courts to identify the nature and quantum of the damage alleged. That was not the case here. On the merits point, the General Court held that where there was a pending case in the national court, the EU Courts were obliged to wait for judgment before ruling on the nature and quantum of damage, and on the causal link between the allegedly wrongful conduct of the EU and the damage, because of the risk that the applicant would be insufficiently or excessively compensated as a result of different assessments of damage by the two courts. However, in contrast, the EU Courts could make a decision on whether there was a wrongful act capable of giving rise to non-contractual liability on the part of the EU even before the national court had adjudicated.

8.10 The possible impact of Brexit

Actions for damages against the EU institutions may be brought by individuals, businesses, or countries outside the EU and so such actions will continue to be available when the UK leaves the EU (see further 1.19 and 3.1), although, in practice, the likelihood of British businesses or individuals being adversely affected by EU law will be reduced. However, if the UK takes the 'Norway option' (see 1.19.2 on this option), a similar action will be available in the European Free Trade Area (EFTA) Court against the EFTA Surveillance Authority (see 1.19.2 on these institutions).

Agreement between the EFTA States on the Establishment of a Surveillance Authority and a Court of Justice, OJ 1994 L344/3

Article 46

The contractual liability of the EFTA Surveillance Authority shall be governed by the law applicable to the contract in question. In the case of non-contractual liability, the EFTA Surveillance Authority shall, in accordance with the general principles of law, make good any damage caused by it, or by its servants, in the performance of its duties.

8.11 Conclusions

In order for the EU to be liable in damages, an applicant must prove that it has suffered loss and that this is due to a wrongful act by an EU institution or servant. In the former scenario, the applicant must also prove that there has been a sufficiently serious breach of a rule of law for the protection of the individual. The Court of Justice has applied these requirements strictly and, as a result, there has been no opening of the floodgates to EU liability. There are, of course, policy reasons behind its narrow interpretation of Article 340 TFEU: the EU institutions should not be unduly restricted in their legislative activities by the threat of litigation, and indeed the cost to the EU—and therefore ultimately to the citizens of the Member States—would be too great were a wider interpretation to be adopted. Whether a correct balance has been achieved between policy considerations and providing justice for those adversely affected by EU measures is a matter of opinion, but this question has assumed greater importance with the development of Member State liability on principles similar to those in Article 340 TFEU (see further Chapter 5).

Although the rules on Member State liability (discussed in Chapter 5) have been developed from those applicable to EU liability, the former have also influenced the latter. This can be seen in the explicit adoption by the Court of Justice in Case C-352/98 P *Bergaderm v Commission* [2000] ECR I-5291 of the criteria laid down in Joined Cases C-46 & 48/93 *Brasserie du Pêcheur SA v Germany; R v Secretary of State for Transport, ex p Factortame Ltd and others ('Factortame III')* [1994] ECR I-1593 (discussed at 5.4.1, 5.5, and 5.5.2) as to what constitutes a sufficiently serious breach, and in the adoption in Case C-472/00 *Commission v Fresh Marine Company A/S* [2003] ECR I-7541 (see 8.4.2 on the existence of a wrongful act and 8.5.2 in relation to damage) of the principle outlined in *Factortame III* and in Case C-5/94 *R v Ministry of Agriculture, Fisheries and Food, ex p Hedley Lomas (Ireland) Ltd* [1996] ECR I-2553 (see 5.4.3 and 5.5.1) that where the defendant has little or no discretion, any breach of EU law will be sufficiently serious.

SUMMARY

- Article 340 TFEU provides that the European Union (EU) is liable for the acts of its institutions and servants according to the *general principles* common to the laws of the Member States.
- In *Alfons Lütticke*, the Court of Justice interpreted these general principles as requiring proof of a wrongful act that has caused damage to the applicant.
- Whether an act is wrongful depends on whether there has been a sufficiently serious breach of a rule of law for the protection of individuals (*Bayerische*; *Bergaderm*).
- Rules of law for the protection of individuals include most Treaty Articles and the general principles of EU law recognized by the Court of Justice, such as non-discrimination, legitimate expectation, and fundamental human rights.
- Whether a breach is sufficiently serious depends on the complexity of the situations being regulated, the clarity of the law, the margin of discretion available to the EU institution that adopted the act at issue, whether the infringement was intentional or involuntary, and whether any error of law was excusable or inexcusable (*Bergaderm*, applying *Factortame III*).

FURTHER READING

Articles

PL Athanassiou, 'Non-Contractual Liability under the Single Supervisory Mechanism: Key Features and Grey Areas' (2015) 30 (7) JIBLR 382

Critically analyses the law relating to the non-contractual liability of the European Central Bank (ECB), which is based on Article 340 TFEU.

T Tridimas, 'Liability for Breach of Community Law: Growing Up and Mellowing Down?' (2001) 38 CML Rev 301–32

Compares the development of EU and Member State liability in damages, with particular reference to *Bergaderm*.

N Vogiatzis, 'The EU's liability owing to the conduct of the European Ombudsman revisited: *European Ombudsman v Staelen*' (2018) 55 (4) CML Rev 1251, esp 1262–73

Discusses the *Staelen* judgment

Book chapters

A Biondi and M Farley, 'Article 288(2) EC: The Appropriate Forum and Concurrent Liability', in *The Right to Damages in European Law* (Alpen aan den Rijn: Kluwer, 2009), ch 4

Examines the interaction between EU and State liability.

A Biondi and M Farley, 'Non-Contractual Liability in Damages: Article 288(2) EC', in *The Right to Damages in European Law*, (Alpen aan den Rijn: Kluwer, 2009), ch 3

Thoroughly analyses the jurisprudence on EU liability.

AG Toth, 'The Concepts of Damage and Causality as Elements of Non-Contractual Liability', in T Heukels and AM McDonnell (eds), *The Action for Damages in Community Law* (Alpen aan den Rijn: Kluwer, 1997), ch 10

Discusses the requirements of damage and causation.

QUESTION

Critically discuss the development by the Court of Justice of the 'general principles' referred to in Article 340 TFEU.

To view an outline answer to this question plus further resources to support your EU law studies, visit the Online Resources for this book at **www.oup.com/uk/eulaw-complete4e**

9 Human rights in the European Union

KEY POINTS

By the end of this chapter, you should be able to:

- understand the historical development of human rights protection under EU law;
- explain the different sources of human rights protection under EU law and evaluate their relative importance;
- be familiar with the types of human rights that are part of EU law;
- understand the different enforcement mechanisms available, and be able to evaluate their strengths and weaknesses;
- distinguish between the EU Charter of Fundamental Rights and the European Convention of Human Rights (ECHR); and
- distinguish between the Court of Justice of the European Union (CJEU) and the European Court of Human Rights (ECtHR).

INTRODUCTION

Human rights is an area of law in which the European Union (EU) has been particularly active in recent years, and this chapter will discuss the key jurisprudence and legislation now in place, as well as developments likely to take place over the next few years.

A particular issue in relation to terminology should be noted at the outset. Throughout the legislation, case law, and policy documents, the various authorities involved in the protection of human rights use a variety of terms, including 'human rights', 'fundamental rights', and 'fundamental human rights'. There is no clear or agreed distinction between these terms, and they will be used interchangeably in this chapter.

9.1 A brief history of human rights protection in Europe: the EU and the Council of Europe compared

Given that the roots of what is now the EU lay primarily in a reaction to the horrors of the two world wars (see further 1.1), and that the Preamble to the original EEC Treaty 1957 included the aspiration to preserve and strengthen liberty, it might seem surprising that that Treaty did not include any reference to fundamental human rights. However, on a Europe-wide basis, the role of protecting human rights against nation states, in order to avoid a repeat of the abuses that had occurred in the years leading up to and during the Second World War, was taken on by the **Council of Europe** (which is *not* an EU institution), while the EU became responsible for economic integration between European countries as a device to prevent further wars (see further 1.3 on the aims of the EU).

Before considering the role of the EU and EU law in protecting human rights, it is therefore necessary to consider the role of the Council of Europe and its legal instruments.

In 1950, the Council of Europe agreed the text of the **European Convention on Human Rights** (ECHR).

The rights contained in the ECHR are largely civil and political rights (rather than social, economic, or cultural rights) and include, for example, the right to life, the right to a fair trial, and freedom of expression. The rights contained in the ECHR have not been formally amended since 1950, but they have been supplemented by additional rights contained in Protocols to the ECHR, which have been adopted on an ad hoc basis by the Council of Europe since 1950. Each State Party to the ECHR is free to adopt a particular Protocol or not.

The ECHR is enforceable in UK courts as a result of the Human Rights Act 1998 (HRA 1998), which permits victims of alleged human rights abuses for which the UK government is liable under the ECHR to bring their claims before the national courts.

The ECHR also has its own court, the **European Court of Human Rights** (ECtHR), based in Strasbourg. Cases can be brought directly in the ECtHR against one or more of the States Parties, by those claiming to be victims of human rights abuses contrary to the ECHR or, more rarely, by another State Party. However, victims must exhaust their remedies before their national courts before bringing a claim before the ECtHR. This means that they must exhaust all possible appeals in their domestic legal system or receive settled legal advice that further appeals would be bound to fail. The ECtHR's judgments do not form part of UK law, but s 2 of the HRA 1998 requires UK courts to 'take into account' such judgments when interpreting rights continued in the ECHR.

It is quite common for confusion to arise over these various 'European' bodies—but it is important to understand that, although they are all 'European' in some sense, the EU and the Council of Europe are two entirely separate organizations, with separate laws (see 3.4 on the different types of EU law) and separate legal systems (see in particular Chapters 2, 3, and 6 on the legal system of the EU).

Council of Europe
The Council of Europe is an international organization based in Strasbourg. It was founded in 1949 in order to promote democracy and protect human rights throughout Europe. It currently has 47 member countries, including all of the EU Member States.

The Council's decision-making body is the Committee of Ministers, which is formed of the ministers of foreign affairs from the member countries or their permanent representatives in Strasbourg.

European Convention on Human Rights
The ECHR is an international human rights treaty signed by all of the member countries of the Council of Europe. It provides that those countries, also known as States Parties or Contracting Parties to the ECHR, must secure to everyone within their jurisdiction (not only their own nationals) the rights set out in it.

European Court of Human Rights
The ECtHR is an international court set up by the Council of Europe to provide judicial enforcement of the ECHR. It has one judge from each of the States Parties (Article 20 ECHR).

?! THINKING POINT

What are the differences between the following?

- The Council of Europe and the EU
- The ECHR and EU law
- The ECtHR and the Court of Justice of the European Union (CJEU) (ie the General Court and the Court of Justice)

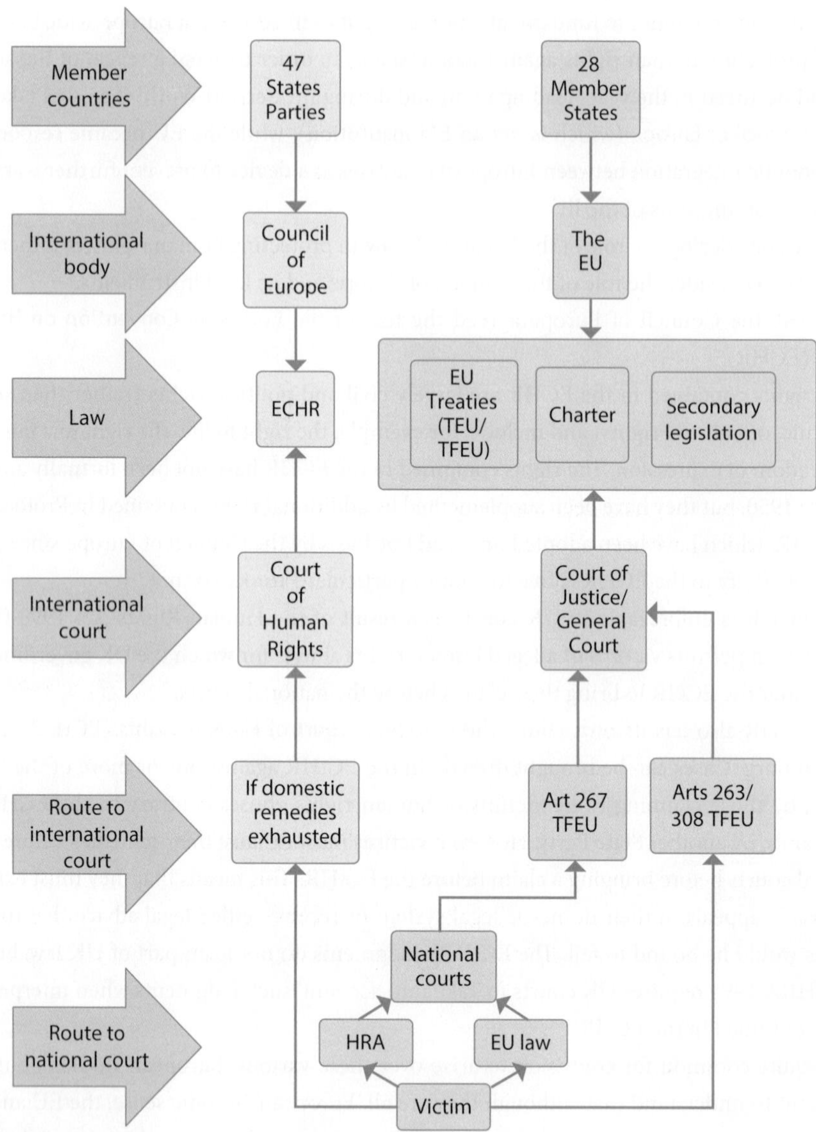

Figure 9.1 EU law and the ECHR compared

The key distinctions between the legal systems established by EU law and the ECHR are highlighted in Figure 9.1.

Some UK politicians, particularly in the Conservative Party, support the UK's withdrawal from the ECHR. If this were to take place, it is likely that a British Bill of Rights would be enacted to replace it. This would put in place different—and presumably lesser—rights and remove the role of the ECtHR as an enforcement body. However, on 17 May 2016, Michael Gove, then Secretary of State for Justice, wrote to the Chair of the Joint Committee on Human Rights in the House of Commons in the UK Parliament, stating that: 'The Bill of Rights will remain faithful to the principles in the ECHR. Whilst we cannot rule out withdrawal from the ECHR forever, our proposals for a Bill of Rights do not involve leaving.' It is noteworthy that the all-too-common confusion between the EU and the ECHR apparently extends to UK politicians, as highlighted in a pithy blog post by Professor Mark Elliott, 'Theresa May's case for withdrawal from the ECHR: Politically astute, legally dubious, constitutionally naive', 26 April 2016, available at https://publiclawforeveryone.com/2016/04/26/theresa-mays-case-for-withdrawal-from-the-echr-politically-astute-legally-dubious-constitutionally-naive/

9.2 The development of human rights protection by the EU

9.2.1 The EEC Treaty 1957

As mentioned earlier, the EU's founding Treaty—then known as the EEC Treaty, now the Treaty on the Functioning of the European Union (TFEU) (see further 1.2 and 3.4.1)—made no explicit provision for the protection of human rights, although a very few rights that might be regarded as human rights did appear, such as the right of free movement of workers (Article 48 EEC, now Article 45 TFEU), the freedom to establish a business (Article 52 EEC, now Article 49 TFEU), the freedom to provide services (Article 59 EEC, now Article 56 TFEU) (see further Chapters 11 and 12 on these rights), and the right to equal pay as between men and women (Article 119 EEC, now Article 157 TFEU).

While the complementary roles of the Council of Europe and the EU may explain the absence of human rights protection in EU law against EU Member States, because human rights obligations were imposed on States Parties to the ECHR before the EU existed and these States Parties included all of the Member States of the EU, it cannot account for the lack of protection in EU law against human rights abuses by the EU itself. The following extract, however, suggests the explanation for this omission.

House of Lords Select Committee on the European Union, *EU Charter of Fundamental Rights*, Eighth Report of Session 1999–2000, 16 May 2000

The European Convention on Human Rights

9. The objective of the Member States of the Council of Europe, under whose auspices the text of the ECHR was concluded in November 1950, was to secure the universal and effective recognition and observance of rights that had been proclaimed in the Universal Declaration of Human Rights on 10 December 1948 by the General Assembly of the United Nations. They 'resolved, as the Governments of European countries which are like-minded and have a common heritage of political traditions, ideals, freedom and the rule of law, to take the first step for the collective enforcement of certain of the rights stated in the Universal Declaration'. The rights chosen were civil and political in character. Economic and social

rights were left aside until later. The Articles of the convention not only proclaimed fundamental rights but also laid down limitations and balancing safeguards. A European Commission of Human Rights and a European Court of Human Rights (the 'Strasbourg Court') were set up. States could choose to accept the competence of the Human Rights Commission to examine petitions from individuals claiming that they were victims of a violation of their human rights. The rights proclaimed in the convention and the procedures for their enforcement have had a substantial impact on the relationship between the individual and the State. A human rights perspective has had to be introduced into the decision-making of public authorities for whose acts States may, ultimately, be held accountable before an international tribunal.

The Founding Treaties

10. The European Coal and Steel Community, established under the Treaty of Paris in April 1951, and the European Economic Community and European Atomic Energy Community which followed in 1957 were, like the Council of Europe, formed as part of the reaction to the Second World War. It is clear from the Preamble to the Treaty of Paris that the primary motive of the six original Member States was not narrowly economic. Their objectives were to safeguard world peace by creative efforts, to build Europe through practical achievements which would create real solidarity, and they 'resolved to substitute for age-old rivalries the merging of their essential interests; to create, by establishing an economic community, the basis for a broader and deeper community among peoples long divided by bloody conflicts; and to lay the foundations for institutions which will give direction to a destiny henceforward shared'.
11. Similarly, the Preamble to the Treaty of Rome set the goal of greater economic integration within a broader political and security context, referring to Member States 'pooling their resources to preserve and strengthen peace and liberty'. The Treaty itself prohibited discrimination on the grounds of nationality (Article 7 [now Article 18 TFEU]), and provided for free movement of workers and rights of establishment for nationals of Member States (Articles 48–58 [now Articles 45–55 TFEU]), for equal pay without discrimination on grounds of sex (Article 119 [now Article 157 TFEU]), and for improved working conditions and a better standard of living for workers (Articles 117–122 [now Articles 151–161 TFEU]). But the founding Treaties of the three Communities made no mention of fundamental rights.
12. This may not, initially, have been a matter of great concern. The focus on economic, rather than political, integration meant that the Communities were not seen to be operating in areas or through methods which were inherently likely to violate human rights. The Communities were not bound by the ECHR. They could not then, or now,* accede to that convention as it stands, since it is open only to Member States of the Council of Europe. All Member States of the Community became Contracting Parties to the ECHR (although not all initially accepted the right of individual petition and the compulsory jurisdiction of the Strasbourg Court—the UK accepted individual petition in 1966). When questions of fundamental rights did arise, incidentally, in matters involving the Communities, the European Court of Justice (ECJ or the 'Luxembourg Court') applied such rights as an integral part of

the 'general principles of Community law'. As the ECHR system developed a case law of increasing complexity, the ECJ came in practice to take into account and apply the details of the Strasbourg Court's case law ...

*The Treaty of Lisbon has subsequently changed the legal position in relation to accession to the ECHR (see further 9.6).

Unfortunately, as cases brought before the Court of Justice soon demonstrated, the assumption that the EU would not be operating in policy areas or by methods that were likely to violate human rights proved incorrect.

9.2.2 The role of the Court of Justice

In the absence of Treaty or, indeed, any legislative protection of human rights against the EU or its Member States as such, the Court of Justice took upon itself the responsibility of developing this protection.

Its first steps were tentative. In Case 29/69 *Stauder v City of Ulm-Sozialamt* [1969] ECR 419, Decision 69/71/EEC of the Commission of the European Communities of 12 February 1969 permitted the sale of butter at reduced prices to consumers who were in receipt of social assistance. The Court of Justice interpreted the Decision as not requiring the name of the consumer to be disclosed to the seller and concluded that, as so interpreted, the Decision contained nothing capable of prejudicing 'the fundamental human rights enshrined in the general principles of [EU] law and protected by the Court' (*Stauder*, at para 7).

9.2.2.1 The sources of human rights drawn upon by the Court of Justice

The Court of Justice gave more detail as to the rationale for protection and the nature of the rights protected in Case 11/70 *Internationale Handelsgesellschaft mbH v Einfuhr- und Vorratsstelle für Getreide und Futtermittel* [1970] ECR 1125. In that case, Regulation No 120/67/EEC of the Council of 13 June 1967 on the common organization of the market in cereals, OJ 1967 2269/33, provided that applications for import and export licences must be accompanied by a deposit, in order to guarantee that the underlying transactions would take place. The Court of Justice held that the system was justified by the need to have accurate information about the transactions and did not violate the applicant's fundamental rights.

?! THINKING POINT

While reading the following extract, consider what source(s) of fundamental protection of human rights the Court of Justice drew upon in this case.

Case 11/70 *Internationale Handelsgesellschaft mbH v Einfuhr- und Vorratsstelle für Getreide und Futtermittel* [1970] ECR 1125

The protection of fundamental rights in the Community legal system

3. Recourse to the legal rules or concepts of national law in order to judge the validity of measures adopted by the institutions of the Community [now Union] would have an adverse effect on the uniformity and efficacy of Community law [now EU law]. The validity of such measures can only be judged in the light of Community law. In fact, the law stemming from the Treaty, an independent source of law, cannot because of its very nature be overridden by rules of national law, however framed, without being deprived of its character as Community law and without the legal basis of the Community itself being called in question. Therefore the validity of a Community measure or its effect within a member state cannot be affected by allegations that it runs counter to either fundamental rights as formulated by the constitution of that state or the principles of a national constitutional structure.
4. However, an examination should be made as to whether or not any analogous guarantee inherent in Community law has been disregarded. In fact, respect for fundamental rights forms an integral part of the general principles of law protected by the Court of Justice. The protection of such rights, whilst inspired by the constitutional traditions common to the Member States, must be ensured within the framework of the structure and objectives of the Community. It must therefore be ascertained, in the light of the doubts expressed by the Verwaltungsgericht [the German court that made the reference to the Court of Justice], whether the system of deposits has infringed rights of a fundamental nature, respect for which must be ensured in the Community legal system.

In *Internationale Handelsgesellschaft*, the Court of Justice referred to the 'constitutional traditions common to the Member States' as the inspiration for its protection of fundamental rights in EU law. In Case 4-73 *Nold, Kohlen- und Baustoffgroßhandlung v Commission* [1974] ECR 491, it drew upon an additional source of fundamental rights.

?! THINKING POINT

While reading the following extract, consider what source(s) of fundamental protection of human rights the Court drew upon in this case in addition to that referred to in *Internationale Handelsgesellschaft*.

Case 4-73 *Nold, Kohlen- und Baustoffgroßhandlung v Commission* [1974] ECR 491

13. As the court has already stated, fundamental rights form an integral part of the general principles of law, the observance of which it ensures.

    In safeguarding these rights, the court is bound to draw inspiration from constitutional traditions common to the member states, and it cannot therefore uphold measures which are incompatible with fundamental rights recognized and protected by the constitutions of those states.

    Similarly, international treaties for the protection of human rights on which the member states have collaborated or of which they are signatories, can supply guidelines which should be followed within the framework of Community law [now EU law].

    The submissions of the applicant must be examined in the light of these principles.

In *Nold*, the Court of Justice drew inspiration for its protection of fundamental rights not only from the 'constitutional traditions common to the Member States', as in *Internationale Handelsgesellschaft*, but also from those international human rights treaties to which all Member States were party. However, on the facts of *Nold*, the Court dismissed the applicant's claim for annulment of an EU measure that allegedly restricted its right to the supply of certain goods, and thus its profitability and even its existence, ruling that the fundamental right to property could legitimately be restricted by reference to the objectives of the EU and that commercial opportunities were not guaranteed.

In Case 36/75 *Rutili v Ministre de l'intérieur* [1975] ECR 1219, the Court of Justice referred for the first time to the most important international human rights treaty signed by the Member States, the ECHR, as a source of human rights for EU law. In that case, the French authorities granted a residence permit to Rutili, who was a national of another Member State. The permit restricted residence to only certain regions of France, on the ground that Rutili was a threat to the interests of national security and public safety (see further 11.3 on the legal justifications for curtailing the right of free movement). On a preliminary reference to the Court of Justice under Article 267 TFEU (see further Chapter 6 on the preliminary reference procedure), the Court held that the limitations imposed by EU law on the ability of Member States to restrict the right of free movement of persons were 'a specific manifestation of the more general principle, enshrined in Arts 8, 9, 10 and 11 of the [ECHR]' and that derogations from such fundamental rights in the interests of national security or public safety were permissible only if they were strictly 'necessary for the protection of those interests in a democratic society' (*Rutili*, at para 32). Thus restrictions could be imposed on the free movement of a national of a Member State only if that individual's presence or conduct constituted a general and sufficiently serious threat to public policy.

The legitimacy of the two sources of law that the Court of Justice has drawn on as the inspiration for its protection of fundamental human rights has subsequently been enshrined in Article 6(3) TEU.

Article 6(3) TEU

Fundamental rights, as guaranteed by the European Convention for the Protection of Human Rights and Fundamental Freedoms and as they result from the constitutional traditions common to the Member States, shall constitute general principles of the Union's law.

However, the 'constitutional traditions common to the Member States' referred to in Article 6(3) TEU are not further defined. The UK has no written constitution and the HRA 1998 (see 9.1), which guarantees the enforcement of human rights in the UK (by incorporating the ECHR into UK law), was adopted many years after the UK joined the EU. However, most other Member States have constitutions guaranteeing fundamental rights, and their courts have, on occasion, indicated their reluctance to cede supremacy to the EU unless it protects human rights to the standard guaranteed in their national constitutions (see eg the German case of *Internationale Handelsgesellschaft mbH v Einfuhr- und Vorratsstelle für Getreide und Futtermittel ('Solange I')* [1974] 2 CMLR 540). In Case 44/79 *Hauer v Land Rheinland-Pfalz* [1979] ECR 3727, such concerns surfaced in an apparently innocuous dispute over the interpretation of Council Regulation (EEC) No 1162/76 of 17 May 1976 on measures designed to adjust wine-growing potential to market requirements, OJ 1976 L135/32.

?! THINKING POINT

While reading the following extract, consider how the Court of Justice addressed the concerns of the German court.

Case 44/79 *Hauer v Land Rheinland-Pfalz* [1979] ECR 3727

13. In its order making the reference, the Verwaltungsgericht states that if Regulation No 1162/76 must be interpreted as meaning that it lays down a prohibition of general application, so as to include even land appropriate for wine growing, that provision might have to be considered inapplicable in the Federal Republic of Germany owing to doubts existing with regard to its compatibility with the fundamental rights guaranteed by Articles 14 and 12 of the Grundgesetz concerning, respectively, the right to property and the right freely to pursue trade and professional activities.
14. As the Court declared in its judgment of 17 December 1970, *Internationale Handelsgesellschaft* [1970] ECR 1125, the question of a possible infringement of fundamental rights by a measure of the Community [now Union] institutions can only be judged in the light of Community law [now EU law] itself. The introduction of special criteria for assessment stemming from the legislation or constitutional law of a particular Member State would, by damaging the substantive unity and efficacy of Community law, lead inevitably to the

destruction of the unity of the Common Market and the jeopardizing of the cohesion of the Community.

15. The Court also emphasized in the judgment cited, and later in the judgment of 14 May 1974, *Nold* [1974] ECR 491, that fundamental rights form an integral part of the general principles of the law, the observance of which it ensures; that in safeguarding those rights, the Court is bound to draw inspiration from constitutional traditions common to the Member States, so that measures which are incompatible with the fundamental rights recognized by the constitutions of those States are unacceptable in the Community; and that, similarly, international treaties for the protection of human rights on which the Member States have collaborated or of which they are signatories, can supply guidelines which should be followed within the framework of Community law.

[...]

The question of the right to property

17. The right to property is guaranteed in the Community legal order in accordance with the ideas common to the constitutions of the Member States, which are also reflected in the first Protocol to the European Convention for the Protection of Human Rights.

[...]

27. It is in this context that Regulation No 1162/76 was adopted. It is apparent from the preamble to that regulation and from the economic circumstances in which it was adopted, a feature of which was the formation as from the 1974 harvest of permanent production surpluses, that that regulation fulfils a double function: on the one hand, it must enable an immediate brake to be put on the continued increase in the surpluses; on the other hand, it must win for the Community institutions the time necessary for the implementation of a structural policy designed to encourage high-quality production, whilst respecting the individual characteristics and needs of the different wine-producing regions of the Community, through the selection of land for grape growing and the selection of grape varieties, and through the regulation of production methods.

[...]

30. Therefore it is necessary to conclude that the restriction imposed upon the use of property by the prohibition on the new planting of vines introduced for a limited period by Regulation No 1162/76 is justified by the objectives of general interest pursued by the Community and does not infringe the substance of the right to property in the form in which it is recognized and protected in the Community legal order.

The question of the freedom to pursue trade or professional activities

31. The applicant in the main action also submits that the prohibition on new plantings imposed by Regulation No 1162/76 infringes her fundamental rights in so far as its effect is to restrict her freedom to pursue her occupation as a wine-grower.

32. As the Court has already stated in its judgment of 14 May 1974, *Nold*, referred to above, although it is true that guarantees are given by the constitutional law of several Member

States in respect of the freedom to pursue trade or professional activities, the right thereby guaranteed, far from constituting an unfettered prerogative, must likewise be viewed in the light of the social function of the activities protected thereunder. In this case, it must be observed that the disputed Community measure does not in any way affect access to the occupation of wine-growing, or the freedom to pursue that occupation on land at present devoted to wine-growing. To the extent to which the prohibition on new plantings affects the free pursuit of the occupation of wine-growing, that limitation is no more than the consequence of the restriction upon the exercise of the right to property, so that the two restrictions merge. Thus the restriction upon the free pursuit of the occupation of wine-growing, assuming that it exists, is justified by the same reasons which justify the restriction placed upon the use of property.

33. Thus it is apparent from the foregoing that consideration of Regulation No 1162/76, in the light of the doubts expressed by the Verwaltungsgericht, has disclosed no factor of such a kind as to affect the validity of that regulation on account of its being contrary to the requirements flowing from the protection of fundamental rights in the Community.

In *Hauer*, the Court of Justice held that the validity of a particular provision of EU law, such as Regulation 1162/76, could only be assessed by reference to EU law itself and not by reference to national law, but ruled that the rights to peaceful enjoyment of property and to pursue an occupation that were recognized by German law were also protected by EU law. However, on the facts, the Court concluded that the restrictions on those rights imposed by the Regulation were justified by the objective of reducing surplus production.

The Court of Justice's approach in cases such as *Hauer* was necessary in order to allay the concerns of national courts and to thereby preserve the supremacy of EU law (see further 3.1), as explained in the following the extract.

House of Lords Select Committee on the European Union, *EU Charter of Fundamental Rights*, Eighth Report of Session 1999–2000, 16 May 2000

The Court of Justice

13. The Luxembourg Court's assertion of a fundamental rights jurisdiction has been seen as a necessary expedient to ensure the supremacy of Community law [now EU law]. The objectives of the Community [now Union] could only be achieved by according primacy to Community rules interpreted and applied in a uniform manner in each Member State. The acceptance by Member States of the supremacy of Community law has not been unproblematic, particularly in those Member States where a written list of fundamental rights in the constitution is perceived as essential for the State's democratic legitimacy. The doctrine of the supremacy of Community law therefore carried with it the risk of displacing rights enshrined in national constitutions and safeguarded by the highest constitutional

> courts. To obviate this risk, the Court stated in the *Internationale Handelsgesellschaft* case that 'respect for fundamental rights forms an integral part of the general principles of Community law protected by the Court of Justice. The protection of such rights, whilst inspired by the constitutional traditions common to the Member States, must be ensured within the framework of the structures and objectives of the Community'. The Court has also found 'inspiration' in 'international treaties for the protection of human rights on which the Member States have collaborated or of which they are signatories'. In practice, a number of constitutional courts have only been prepared to accept the supremacy of Community law on the basis that Community law provides protection for fundamental rights equivalent to that afforded by national constitutions ...

In *Re Wünsche Handelsgesellschaft ('Solange II')* [1987] 3 CMLR 225, the German courts accepted that a sufficient measure of fundamental rights protection had been established by the EU, and national courts have also found reassurance in the limitation on the transfer of sovereign powers to the EU (see further 3.1) and the corresponding retention of a degree of domestic human rights protection by the national courts and legislative authorities (see the German case of *Brunner and others v The European Union Treaty* [1994] 1 CMLR 57 and the Danish case of *Carlsen and others v Prime Minister Rasmussen* (1999) 3 CMLR 854).

9.2.2.2 The Court of Justice's use of human rights to review the compatibility of national law with EU law

In Case 36/75 *Rutili v Ministre de l'intérieur* [1975] ECR 1219 (for the facts of this case, see 9.2.2.1) the Court of Justice's ruling on the correct interpretation of EU law had potential consequences for the validity of the national measures that implemented that EU law—in other words, the individual decisions taken by the French authorities restricting Rutili's free movement. However, although the Court interpreted EU law in the light of fundamental rights, it did not use these rights to review the national measures directly.

In Case 5/88 *Wachauf v Bundesamt für Ernährung und Forstwirtschaft* [1989] ECR 2609, however, it did. Wachauf was a tenant farmer who applied for compensation for discontinuing milk production. This was rejected pursuant to German legislation implementing Council Regulation (EEC) No 857/84 of 31 March 1984 adopting general rules for the application of the levy referred to in Article 5c of Regulation (EEC) No 804/68 in the milk and milk products sector, OJ 1984 L90/13, on the ground that the application was not accompanied by the landlord's written consent. Wachauf challenged this rejection and the German court made a preliminary reference to the Court of Justice under Article 267 TFEU (see further Chapter 6 on the preliminary reference procedure) of a number of questions on the interpretation of the Regulation.

?! THINKING POINT

While reading the following extract, consider what human rights obligation the Court imposed on the Member States and why.

Case 5/88 *Wachauf v Bundesamt für Ernährung und Forstwirtschaft* [1989] ECR 2609

17. The Court has consistently held, in particular in its judgment of 13 December 1979 in Case 44/79 *Hauer v Land Rheinland Pfalz* (1979) ECR 3727, that fundamental rights form an integral part of the general principles of the law, the observance of which is ensured by the Court. In safeguarding those rights, the Court has to look to the constitutional traditions common to the Member States, so that measures which are incompatible with the fundamental rights recognized by the constitutions of those States may not find acceptance in the Community [now Union]. International treaties concerning the protection of human rights on which the Member States have collaborated or to which they have acceded can also supply guidelines to which regard should be had in the context of Community law [now EU law].
18. The fundamental rights recognized by the Court are not absolute, however, but must be considered in relation to their social function. Consequently, restrictions may be imposed on the exercise of those rights, in particular in the context of a common organization of a market, provided that those restrictions in fact correspond to objectives of general interest pursued by the Community and do not constitute, with regard to the aim pursued, a disproportionate and intolerable interference, impairing the very substance of those rights.
19. Having regard to those criteria, it must be observed that Community rules which, upon the expiry of the lease, had the effect of depriving the lessee, without compensation, of the fruits of his labour and of his investments in the tenanted holding would be incompatible with the requirements of the protection of fundamental rights in the Community legal order. Since those requirements are also binding on the Member States when they implement Community rules, the Member States must, as far as possible, apply those rules in accordance with those requirements.

In *Wachauf*, the Court of Justice ruled that Member States must implement EU law in a way that was consistent with fundamental human rights as far as possible.

In Case 12/86 *Demirel v Stadt Schwäbisch Gmünd* [1987] ECR 3719, at para 28, the Court stated, unsurprisingly, that it would not examine the compatibility of national law with fundamental rights where the 'national legislation [lay] outside the scope of [EU] law'. As EU law did not confer the rights of family reunification claimed by the applicant—a Turkish national seeking to join her Turkish husband in Germany—the German immigration rules at issue were not adopted in order to implement EU law and the Court of Justice therefore had no jurisdiction to determine whether they were compatible with the fundamental right to family life.

In contrast, in Case C-260/89 *ERT* [1991] ECR I-2925, at para 42, the Court of Justice held that the national measures at issue in the case—the grant of an exclusive broadcasting licence to ERT—fell 'within the scope' of EU law. Although these national measures did not implement EU law, they nonetheless fell within its scope because they would constitute an illegal prohibition on the freedom to provide services unless they fell within the derogations from that freedom permitted by EU law (see further 11.3).

9.2.2.3 The margin of appreciation permitted to Member States by the Court of Justice

The ECtHR (see 9.1) has long accorded to the States Parties to the ECHR (see 9.1) a 'margin of appreciation'—in other words, a margin of discretion—in making public policy decisions that potentially impact on ECHR rights (see eg *Handyside v United Kingdom* Application No 5493/72 (1976) 1 EHRR 737). The extent of the margin permitted by the ECtHR varies according to the policy area in question. For example, it is usually wider in relation to economic or national security issues, where the Court is more inclined to defer to the choices made by States Parties, and narrower in the area of criminal justice, where the Court considers it appropriate for it to take a more activist role.

The Court of Justice has similarly allowed Member States some individual discretion in their decision-making, stating in Joined Cases 115 & 116/81 *Adoui and Cornuaille v Belgium* [1982] ECR 1665, at para 8 (see also 11.3.1), that EU law 'does not impose upon the Member States a uniform scale of values as regards the assessment of conduct which may be considered as contrary to public policy' (see also Case 249/86 *Commission v Germany* [1989] ECR 1263, at para 19). For example, other than requiring that any restrictions on the free movement of goods that are imposed in order to protect public morality must not discriminate (Case 34/79 *R v Henn and Darby* [1979] ECR 3795) (see 10.8.11), it has generally allowed Member States considerable discretion to determine the requirements of public morality in their countries (Case 121/85 *Conegate Ltd v Commissioners of Customs and Excise* [1986] ECR 1007) (see 10.8.11). However, although Advocate General Stix-Hackl, in Case C-60/00 *Carpenter v SSHD* [2002] ECR I-6279 (see 2.4.1 on Advocate Generals' Opinions), referred explicitly to a 'margin of appreciation' in relation to the States' obligations to respect private and family life (at para 88 of the Opinion), the Court of Justice's jurisprudence on this issue is relatively undeveloped compared to that of the ECtHR. As the ECtHR has recognized, the importance of fundamental human rights may often dictate that States are allowed only a narrow discretion to derogate from those rights. However, whereas the ECtHR has often justified the grant of a wider margin of discretion to States Parties by the fact that there is no European consensus on a particular issue (see eg *Evans v UK* Application No 6339/05 (2008) 46 EHRR 34 in relation to IVF treatment), the need to ensure that EU law is applied uniformly across the Member States of the EU may enable the Court of Justice to justify permitting them only a narrow discretion to derogate from fundamental rights under EU law.

9.2.2.4 The rights recognized by the EU Courts

The rights recognized by the Court of Justice and the General Court prior to the coming into force of the EU Charter of Fundamental Rights (see 9.4) include:

- the right to human dignity (Case C-36/02 *Omega Spielhallen- und Automatenaufstellungs-GmbH v Oberbür germeisterin der Bundesstadt Bonn* [2004] ECR I-9609);
- the right to physical integrity (Joined Cases T-121/89 & 13/90 *X v Commission* [1992] ECR II-2195);

- the right to marry (Case C-249/96 *Grant v South West Trains Ltd* [1998] ECR I-629);
- the right not to be discriminated against (Joined Cases 75 & 117/82 *Razzouk and Beydoun v Commission* [1984] ECR 1509);
- due process rights, such as:
  - the right to a fair hearing (Joined Cases 100–103/80 *Musique Diffusion Française v Commission* [1983] ECR 1825);
  - the right to a legal remedy (Case 222/84 *Johnston v Chief Constable of the Royal Ulster Constabulary* [1986] ECR 1651);
  - the right not to be convicted of an offence created retrospectively (Joined Cases 74 & 129/95 *X* [1996] ECR I-6639); and
  - the right to good administration (Case 173/82 R *Castille v Commission* [1982] ECR 4047);
- expressive rights, such as:
  - the right to respect for religion and belief (Case 30/75 *Prais v Council* [1976] ECR 589);
  - the right to freedom of expression (Case C-100/88 *Oyowe and Traore v Commission* [1989] ECR 4285); and
  - the right to freedom of assembly (Case C-235/92 P *Montecatini SpA v Commission* [1999] ECR I-4539); and
- economic rights, such as:
  - the right to peaceful enjoyment of property (Case 4/73 *Nold, Kohlen- und Baustoffgroßhandlung v Commission* [1974] ECR 491; Case 44/79 *Hauer v Land Rheinland-Pfalz* [1979] ECR 3727); and
  - the right to freedom to pursue a trade or profession (Case 234/85 *Staatsanwalt Freiburg v Keller* [1986] ECR 2879).

Although these rights did not include such crucial human rights as the right to life and the right not to be tortured, these would undoubtedly have been recognized by the Court of Justice had relevant cases been brought before it, and indeed the right to physical integrity has been recognized. As Takis Tridimas explained in *The General Principles of EC Law* (Oxford: Oxford University Press, 1998), at para 6.24, 'which rights are expressly recognised by the Court depends on the accidents of litigation'.

The disadvantage of the ad hoc nature of the development of EU human rights law, through the jurisprudence of the EU Courts, was that it was difficult for individuals or businesses to identify the existence and scope of their human rights when dealing with the EU or a Member State acting within the scope of its EU obligations.

9.2.3 Legislative developments and political statements

Eventually, the EU legislative institutions (see further 2.1, 2.2, and 2.3 on the European Parliament, the Council of the EU, and the EU Commission) began to adopt first political and then legislative measures in the area of human rights. The European Parliament (see 2.1) was particularly proactive in urging greater protection of human rights at EU level, as summarized in the following extract.

House of Commons, *Human Rights in the EU: The Charter of Fundamental Rights*, Research Paper 00/32, 20 March 2000

The European Parliament adopted a Resolution in 1973 'concerning the protection of the fundamental rights of Member States' citizens when Community law is drafted' and another in 1977 'on the granting of special rights to the citizens of the European Community'. The EP issued a declaration of political principle on the definition of fundamental rights on 10 February 1977, which was subsequently adopted by the Council and Commission. In a 1979 Resolution the EP urged EC accession to the European Convention and envisaged the drafting of a European Charter of Civil Rights. Further Resolutions in 1983 and 1984 emphasised the need to incorporate fundamental human rights in the EC in a constitutional manner and in 1989 the EP proposed the adoption of a declaration of fundamental rights as part of a 'Constitution' for the EU.

At the Copenhagen European Council in 1978 the Heads of State and Government issued the 'Declaration on Democracy' which confirmed their will:

> ... to ensure that the cherished values of their legal, political and moral order are respected and to safeguard the principles of representative democracy, of the rule of law, of social justice and of respect for human rights.

However, unfortunately, EU legislative measures were for many years adopted in a piecemeal fashion and, although often providing important rights, did little to address the problems of lack of transparency and accessibility.

The Preamble to the Single European Act 1986 (SEA) (see 1.10) stated that the Member States were 'determined to work together to promote democracy on the basis of the fundamental rights recognised in the constitutions and laws of the Member States, in the [ECHR] and the European Social Charter, notably freedom, equality and social justice'.

The Treaty on European Union 1992 (TEU 1992) (see 1.13) introduced the predecessor of what is now Article 6 TEU, stating that the EU 'shall respect fundamental rights, as guaranteed by the [ECHR] and as they result from the constitutional traditions common to the Member States, as general principles of [EU] law'. It also prohibited discrimination on grounds of nationality (now Article 18 TFEU) and introduced a number of rights for EU citizens (see further 11.2 on these rights and on the definition of EU citizens):

- the right of free movement, which had previously been limited to workers (now Articles 20 and 21 TFEU);
- rights to vote and stand in certain elections (now Articles 20 and 22 TFEU);
- the right to diplomatic representation abroad (now Articles 20 and 23 TFEU); and
- the right to petition the European Parliament and to access the European Ombudsman (now Articles 20 and 24 TFEU).

The Treaty of Amsterdam 1997 (see 1.15) further developed what is now Article 6 TEU, amending it to state that the EU was founded on principles that include respect for human rights, and introduced what are now Articles 7 TEU and 354 TFEU, which authorize the EU Council (see 2.2 on the Council) to take measures against Member States that have infringed the principles laid down in Article 6 TEU. The Treaty of Amsterdam also introduced the right of access to EU documents (now Article 15 TFEU) and empowered the EU to adopt legislation to combat discrimination on grounds of sex, racial or ethnic origin, religion or belief, disability, age, or sexual orientation (now Article 19 TFEU).

EU secondary legislation also provided a variety of human rights over this time, including:

- the protection of personal data (Directive 95/46/EC of the European Parliament and of the Council of 24 October 1995 on the protection of individuals with regard to the processing of personal data and on the free movement of such data, OJ 1995 L281/31; see also the Court of Justice's judgment in C-131/12 *Google Spain SL and another v Agencia Española de Protección de Datos (AEPD) and another* [2014] 3 WLR 659) (see further 9.5.3);
- the protection of certain workers' rights (for example Council Directive 94/45/EC of 22 September 1994 on the establishment of a European Works Council or a procedure in Community-scale undertakings and Community-scale groups of undertakings for the purposes of informing and consulting employees, OJ 1994 L254/64, Council Directive 89/391/EEC of 12 June 1989 on the introduction of measures to encourage improvements in the safety and health of workers at work, OJ 1989 L183/1, and Council Directive 92/85/EEC of 19 October 1992 on the introduction of measures to encourage improvements in the safety and health at work of pregnant workers and workers who have recently given birth or are breastfeeding, OJ 1992 L348/1); and
- the prohibition of discrimination in employment on grounds of religious belief, disability, age, or sexual orientation (Council Directive 2000/78/EC of 27 November 2000 establishing a general framework for equal treatment in employment and occupation, OJ 2000 L303/16).

Perhaps the most significant development in EU human rights legislation is the EU Charter of Fundamental Rights (see further 9.4). The Charter was proclaimed in 2000 and, although not initially legally binding, it was drafted 'as if' it were (Communication from the Commission on the Legal Nature of the Charter of Fundamental Rights of the EU, COM (2000) 644 final, points 7 and 8; see also Declaration 23 annexed to the Treaty of Nice 2001—see 1.17), with the expectation that it would become so in future. This expectation was realized in 2009 with the entry into force of the Treaty of Lisbon (see further 1.18), which made the Charter legally binding, but also made a number of changes to its Preamble and to its General Provisions concerning its scope and application. The legal effect of the Charter is now set out in Article 6(1) TEU: it has 'the same legal value as the Treaties'.

The Charter addresses the problem of the lack of transparency of EU human rights by effectively codifying the rights already recognized by the Court of Justice in the EU Treaties and in EU secondary legislation. However, a number of questions about the scope and impact of the Charter remain, and it is discussed in greater detail at 9.4.

9.2.4 Other developments

The European Monitoring Centre for Racism and Xenophobia was established by the EU in 1997 (see Regulation (EC) No 1035/97 of 2 June 1997 establishing a European Monitoring Centre on Racism and Xenophobia, OJ 1997 L151/1) in order to gather data to inform Member State action against racism and xenophobia, and it was subsequently incorporated into the EU Agency for Fundamental Rights (FRA), which was established in 2007 (see Council Regulation (EC) No 168/2007 of 15 February 2007 establishing a European Union Agency for Fundamental Rights, OJ 2007 L53/1) in order, primarily, to collect and disseminate data on the state of fundamental human rights in the EU Member States, but also to raise awareness of human rights. The European Institute for Gender Equality (EIGE) was also established by the EU in 2007 (see Regulation (EC) No 1922/2006 of the European Parliament and of the Council of 20 December 2006 on establishing a European Institute for Gender Equality, OJ 2006 L403/9) in order to contribute to the promotion of gender equality in EU policies and related national policies, and the combating of sex discrimination.

The next major development in EU human rights law is likely to be the accession of the EU to the ECHR. As discussed at 9.1, all EU Member States are also States Parties to the ECHR and so the ECHR can be enforced directly against any of them. However, the Treaty of Lisbon (see 1.18) provided for the accession of the EU itself to the ECHR, so that the ECHR will become enforceable against the EU and its institutions. Negotiations on the detail of accession, between the EU and the Council of Europe (see 9.1), which oversees the ECHR, were thought to have been concluded with a draft Accession Agreement in 2013, but the Court of Justice ruled in *Opinion 2/2013 pursuant to Article 218(11) TFEU* EU:C:2014:2454 that the Agreement was incompatible with EU law and so further negotiations are required before accession can take place. EU accession to the ECHR is discussed in greater detail at 9.6.

9.3 The need for human rights protection against the EU and its Member States

While it may not initially have been expected that the EU's competences and procedures would be likely to bring it into conflict with human rights (see further 9.1 and 9.2.1), this is exactly what has happened. The EU has competence in policy areas ranging from employment law, to police cooperation, to foreign affairs, in respect of half a billion people and across a geographical area of 4 million km^2. It is therefore inevitable that its activities will have a substantial impact on those living or trading in the Member States of the EU, both directly and through the acts of the Member States when they are required to implement EU law, and this impact can frequently have negative effects on human rights. For example, economic sanctions imposed by the EU pursuant to the Common Foreign and Security Policy (CFSP) (Title V TEU) have given rise to allegations of breaches of the rights to property and to pursue a trade or profession (see Case C-317/00 P(R) *'Invest' Import und Export GmbH and another v Commission*

[2000] ECR I-9541). Another example is the Member States' power under EU law to deport asylum seekers to another Member State, making the asylum seekers vulnerable to breaches of human rights by those States (see *MSS v Belgium and Greece* Application No 20696/09 (2011) 53 EHRR 2, discussed at 9.5.2). The EU has also increased its competence to act in the area of criminal justice, and the introduction of a **European arrest warrant (EAW)** (see Council Framework Decision 2002/584/JHA of 13 June 2002 on the European arrest warrant and the surrender procedures between Member States, OJ 2002 L190/1) has led to complaints from individuals who allege that their arrest was based on an unfair trial (see eg *Kostecki v Poland* Application No 14932/09, ECtHR, 4 June 2013, unreported) or resulted in them being unlawfully deprived of their liberty (see eg *Pianese v Italy and Netherlands* Application No 14929/08, ECtHR, 27 September 2011, unreported) or exposed to the risk of being subjected to inhuman or degrading treatment (C-404/15 & C-659/15 PPU *Aranyosi and Căldăru* EU:C:2016:198). In recent years, the EU has also legislated in relation to security at airports, including provision for body scanners (see Commission Regulation (EC) No 272/2009 of 2 April 2009 supplementing the common basic standards on civil aviation security laid down in the Annex to Regulation (EC) No 300/2008 of the European Parliament and of the Council, OJ 2009 L91/7, as amended by Commission Regulation (EU) No 1141/2011 of 10 November 2011 amending Regulation (EC) No 272/2009 supplementing the common basic standards on civil aviation security as regards the use of security scanners at EU airports, OJ 2011 L293/22), a measure that has implications for the right to privacy.

European arrest warrant (EAW)
An EAW is a request by a judicial authority in one EU Member State to arrest a person in another and surrender them for prosecution, or to execute a custodial sentence issued in the requesting State. The system is based on the principle of mutual recognition of judicial decisions and is operational in all EU countries. The governing legislation is Council Framework Decision 2002/584/JHA of 13 June 2002 on the European arrest warrant and the surrender procedures between Member States, OJ 2002 L190/1.

EU law has also extended into the realm of family law, where, if human rights are not observed, the consequences can be particularly serious. In Case C-578/08 *Chakroun* [2010] ECR I-1839, the Court of Justice noted that the Family Reunification Directive (Council Directive 2003/86/EC of 22 September 2003 on the right to family reunification, OJ 2003 L251/12) afforded no margin of appreciation (see 9.2.2) to a Member State to refuse to authorize the entry and residence of a family member of a non-EU national where that non-national was already lawfully resident in that State. It held that the Directive must be interpreted in the light of the right to respect for family life in the Charter, and thus precluded national rules that prevented reunification merely because the relationship arose after the lawful resident's entry into the Member State or because they failed to meet a minimum income requirement. In Case C-403/09 PPU *Detiček* [2009] ECR I-12193, the Court of Justice held that Council Regulation (EC) No 2201/2003 of 27 November 2003 concerning jurisdiction and the recognition and enforcement of judgments in matrimonial matters and the matters of parental responsibility . . . , OJ 2003 L338/1 (that is, jurisdiction in international child custody disputes), could not be interpreted as permitting a custody award made by the courts of one Member State to be overturned by those of another, where this would breach the child's fundamental right to maintain on a regular basis a personal relationship and direct contact with both parents (as provided for by Article 24(3) of the Charter).

The EU's own procedures, which can result in substantial adverse consequences for individuals and businesses, may involve breaches of human rights. Infringements of the rights of the defence—access to the courts, right to a fair hearing, and so on—are often alleged in relation to competition law proceedings by the EU (see, for example, Joined Cases 46/87 & 227/88 *Hoechst AG v Commission* [1989] ECR 2859). In Case C-407/08 P *Knauf Gips v Commission*

[2010] ECR I-6371, the Court of Justice held that the General Court (see 2.4.2) had infringed the applicant's rights to an effective remedy and of access to an impartial tribunal (as provided for by Article 47 of the Charter), by barring it from challenging matters of fact or law merely because it had failed to bring such a challenge during the administrative procedure that led to the Commission's adoption of a Decision finding it in breach of EU competition law and imposing a fine (see Chapter 13 on the enforcement of competition law).

EU human rights law can also be invoked by individuals or businesses in order to restrict the competing human rights of others. In Case C-70/10 *Scarlet Extended SA v Société Belge des Auteurs, Compositeurs et Éditeurs SCRL (SABAM)* [2012] ECDR 4, the Court of Justice held that drawing a fair balance between composers' rights to protection of their intellectual property (under Article 17 of the Charter) and the freedom of an Internet service provider (ISP) to conduct a business (under Article 16) and the rights of its customers to protection of their personal data (under Article 8) and to receive and impart information (under Article 11) required a number of Directives on the protection of intellectual property rights to be interpreted as prohibiting a national law that required the ISP to install a filtering system to prevent the sharing of music files. In Case C-112/00 *Schmidberger v Austria* [2003] ECR I-5659, the applicant sought to use EU law on the free movement of goods (see Chapter 10) so as to restrict the freedom of association and the freedom of expression of an environmental association whose demonstration blocked a motorway. On the facts, the Court of Justice upheld the national authorities' decision not to ban the demonstration, but cases such as *Scarlet* highlight the potential for EU law to be used to restrict human rights, as well as to protect them.

The key arguments that favour the protection of human rights by EU law are that it is necessary in order to protect against the risk of human rights abuses by the EU and to protect against the risk of abuses by Member States when implementing EU law. However, there are a number of other arguments in favour of EU law protection of human rights. First, as discussed at 9.2.2, adequate human rights protection by the EU is a precondition for the renunciation by the national courts of some Member States of their own jurisdiction over fundamental rights where EU law is at issue. Secondly, a failure to protect human rights against the EU itself would reduce the legitimacy of Article 49 TEU, which provides that any State wishing to join the EU must respect, inter alia, the values set out in Article 2 TEU (see 1.3), which include respect for human rights. Thirdly, the EU's attempts to promote human rights in countries outside the region would similarly lack credibility if it did not itself comply with a high standard of human rights protection.

9.4 The Charter of Fundamental Rights of the EU

9.4.1 The Charter rights

The rights contained in the Charter are not generally new to EU law; most have already been recognized in the Treaties, in secondary legislation, or by the Court of Justice (see 9.2.2).

However, their inclusion in the Charter makes them more transparent and accessible, and in some cases their scope has been made more generous, for example the right to marry provided for in Article 9 of the Charter, which is not confined to opposite-sex relationships.

The Charter is divided into Titles. Of those that contain substantive rights, Titles I (Dignity), II (Freedoms), and VI (Justice) largely reflect the same civil and political rights that are contained in the ECHR, but Title II also includes, for example, the right to data protection, the right to work, and the freedom to conduct a business, none of which appear in the ECHR. The content of Title III (Equality) is self-explanatory. Title IV (Solidarity) provides employment rights. Title V (Citizens' Rights) largely replicates rights found in the TFEU, such as the right of free movement and the right to vote and stand in elections (see Chapter 11), but also includes the right to good administration. Most of the rights in Title V are absent from the ECHR, although Article 3 of Protocol 1 to the ECHR provides certain electoral rights, and Article 3 of Protocol 4 to the ECHR provides the right of free movement within a State and the right to leave.

Title V is unusual for its restriction on the beneficiaries of the rights contained in it to EU citizens (see further 11.2.1 on the definition of EU citizens). Other Charter rights and EU human rights law more generally are not so restricted, and the ECHR applies to all those within the 'jurisdiction' of the States Parties (Article 1 ECHR) whether they are citizens of those States or not.

9.4.2 The legal effect of the Charter

The legal effect of the Charter is set out in Article 6(1) TEU; it has 'the same legal value as the Treaties'.

Article 6 TEU

1. The Union recognises the rights, freedoms and principles set out in the Charter of Fundamental Rights of the European Union of 7 December 2000, as adapted at Strasbourg, on 12 December 2007, which shall have the same legal value as the Treaties.

   The provisions of the Charter shall not extend in any way the competences of the Union as defined in the Treaties.

   The rights, freedoms and principles in the Charter shall be interpreted in accordance with the general provisions in Title VII of the Charter governing its interpretation and application and with due regard to the explanations referred to in the Charter, that set out the sources of those provisions.

   [...]

Thus, in Case C-236/09 *Association Belge des Consommateurs Test-Achats ASBL and others v Conseil des Ministres* [2011] ECR I-773, the Court of Justice ruled that Article 5(2) of Council Directive 2004/113/EC of 13 December 2004 implementing the principle of equal treatment between men and women in the access to and supply of goods and services, OJ 2004 L373/37, which permitted Member States to maintain national legislation allowing insurers to charge different premiums to men and women where gender was a determining factor in assessing risk, was incompatible with the rights in Articles 21 and 23 of the Charter to non-discrimination and equality of treatment between men and women, and must therefore be annulled.

However, there is a potential complication in relation to human rights claims based on EU law that might be brought against the UK, in the form of Protocol No 30, which makes special provision concerning the application of the Charter to the UK and Poland.

Protocol No 30 on the application of the Charter of Fundamental Rights of the European Union to Poland and to the United Kingdom

Article 1

1. The Charter does not extend the ability of the Court of Justice of the European Union, or any court or tribunal of Poland or of the United Kingdom, to find that the laws, regulations or administrative provisions, practices or action of Poland or of the United Kingdom are inconsistent with the fundamental rights, freedoms and principles that it reaffirms.
2. In particular, and for the avoidance of doubt, nothing in Title IV of the Charter creates justiciable rights applicable to Poland or the United Kingdom except in so far as Poland or the United Kingdom has provided for such rights in its national law.

Article 2

To the extent that a provision of the Charter refers to national laws and practices, it shall only apply to Poland or the United Kingdom to the extent that the rights or principles that it contains are recognised in the law or practices of Poland or of the United Kingdom.

Exactly what the Protocol means is, on the face of it, unclear. The statement in Article 1(1) to Protocol 30 that the Charter does not extend the powers of the Court of Justice or the national courts to find the UK (or Poland) in breach of fundamental rights is surely redundant. This is because, first, the Preamble to the Charter itself provides that it only 'reaffirms' existing rights.

Charter of Fundamental Rights of the European Union

Preamble

The peoples of Europe, in creating an ever closer union among them, are resolved to share a peaceful future based on common values.

Conscious of its spiritual and moral heritage, the Union is founded on the indivisible, universal values of human dignity, freedom, equality and solidarity; it is based on the principles of democracy and the rule of law. It places the individual at the heart of its activities, by establishing the citizenship of the Union and by creating an area of freedom, security and justice.

The Union contributes to the preservation and to the development of these common values while respecting the diversity of the cultures and traditions of the peoples of Europe as well as the national identities of the Member States and the organisation of their public authorities at national, regional and local levels; it seeks to promote balanced and sustainable development and ensures free movement of persons, services, goods and capital, and the freedom of establishment.

To this end, it is necessary to strengthen the protection of fundamental rights in the light of changes in society, social progress and scientific and technological developments by making those rights more visible in a Charter.

This Charter reaffirms, with due regard for the powers and tasks of the Union and for the principle of subsidiarity, the rights as they result, in particular, from the constitutional traditions and international obligations common to the Member States, the European Convention for the Protection of Human Rights and Fundamental Freedoms, the Social Charters adopted by the Union and by the Council of Europe and the case-law of the Court of Justice of the European Union and of the European Court of Human Rights. In this context the Charter will be interpreted by the courts of the Union and the Member States with due regard to the explanations prepared under the authority of the Praesidium of the Convention which drafted the Charter and updated under the responsibility of the Praesidium of the European Convention.

Enjoyment of these rights entails responsibilities and duties with regard to other persons, to the human community and to future generations.

The Union therefore recognises the rights, freedoms and principles set out hereafter.

A second argument for the redundancy of the statement in Article 1(1) of Protocol 30 that the Charter does not extend the powers of the Court of Justice or the national courts is that Article 51(2) of the Charter itself confirms that it does not extend the scope of EU law beyond the powers of the EU.

Charter of Fundamental Rights of the European Union

Article 51

Field of application

[…]

2. The Charter does not extend the field of application of Union law beyond the powers of the Union or establish any new power or task for the Union, or modify powers and tasks as defined in the Treaties.

The Preamble to the Charter states that the Charter will be interpreted 'with due regard to the Explanations', which were provided by the drafters of the Charter, and therefore the Explanation relating to Article 51(2) must also be taken into account when determining the meaning of the Protocol. (The earlier part of the Explanation on Article 51 is extracted at 9.4.3.)

Explanations relating to the Charter of Fundamental Rights, OJ 2007 C303/02

Explanation on Article 51—Field of application

[...]

Paragraph 2, together with the second sentence of paragraph 1, confirms that the Charter may not have the effect of extending the competences and tasks which the Treaties confer on the Union. Explicit mention is made here of the logical consequences of the principle of subsidiarity and of the fact that the Union only has those powers which have been conferred upon it. The fundamental rights as guaranteed in the Union do not have any effect other than in the context of the powers determined by the Treaties. Consequently, an obligation, pursuant to the second sentence of paragraph 1, for the Union's institutions to promote principles laid down in the Charter may arise only within the limits of these same powers.

Paragraph 2 also confirms that the Charter may not have the effect of extending the field of application of Union law beyond the powers of the Union as established in the Treaties. The Court of Justice has already established this rule with respect to the fundamental rights recognised as part of Union law (judgment of 17 February 1998, C-249/96 *Grant* [1998] ECR I-621, paragraph 45 of the grounds). In accordance with this rule, it goes without saying that the reference to the Charter in Article 6 of the Treaty on European Union cannot be understood as extending by itself the range of Member State action considered to be 'implementation of Union law' (within the meaning of paragraph 1 and the above-mentioned case-law).

A third argument for the redundancy of the statement in Article 1(1) of Protocol 30 that the Charter does not extend the powers of the Court of Justice or the national courts is that Article 6(1) TEU (see earlier in this section) states that the Charter does not 'extend in any way' EU competences. This was confirmed by the Court of Justice in Case C-466/11 *Currà v Germany* EU:C:2012:465, in which it held that compensation claims brought under international law by citizens of one Member State against another Member State in respect of events during the Second World War did not fall within the scope of EU law and that it therefore had no jurisdiction (see also 6.4.4). Neither Article 17 of the Charter (the right to property) nor Article 47 of the Charter (the right to an effective remedy and to a fair trial) could, in themselves, be relied on to form the basis of a new power that the EU did not otherwise have.

The meaning of Article 1(1) of Protocol 30 was examined by the Court of Justice in Joined Cases C-411 & 493/10 *NS v Secretary of State for the Home Department* [2012] 2 CMLR 9 (see also 9.4.3). The applicant, an Afghan asylum seeker who had entered the EU through Greece, sought to resist his deportation by the UK back to Greece on the grounds that it would breach his fundamental human rights. Under the Dublin Regulation—at that time, Council Regulation (EC) No 343/2003 of 18 February 2003 establishing the criteria and mechanisms for determining the Member State responsible for examining an asylum application lodged in one of the Member States by a third-country national, OJ 2003 L50/1 (the Dublin II Regulation)—the Member State of first entry into the EU by an asylum seeker had primary responsibility for considering his asylum application and the UK was therefore entitled to return NS to Greece (see further the judgment of the ECtHR in *MSS v Belgium and Greece* Application No 20696/09 (2011) 53 EHRR 2, discussed at 9.5.2).

NOTE

The Dublin Regulation establishes the criteria and mechanism for determining which Member State is responsible for examining an asylum claim that has been lodged in one of the Member States. The current Dublin Regulation is Regulation (EU) No 604/2013 of the European Parliament and of the Council of 26 June 2013 establishing the criteria and mechanisms for determining the Member State responsible for examining an application for international protection lodged in one of the Member States by a third-country national or a stateless person (the 'Dublin III Regulation'), OJ 2013 L180/31, which replaced Council Regulation (EC) No 343/2003 of 18 February 2003 establishing the criteria and mechanisms for determining the Member State responsible for examining an asylum application lodged in one of the Member States by a third-country national (the 'Dublin II Regulation'), OJ 2003 L50/1, which itself replaced the Convention determining the State responsible for examining applications for asylum lodged in one of the Member States of the European Communities (the 'Dublin Convention'), OJ 1997 C254/1.

The Court of Appeal of England and Wales made a preliminary reference to the Court of Justice under Article 267 TFEU (see further Chapter 6 on the preliminary reference procedure) as to, inter alia, the effect of Protocol No 30. The Court of Justice ruled that Article 1(1) of the Protocol did not affect the application of the Charter in the UK.

THINKING POINT

While reading the following extract, note the reasoning of the Court of Justice as to why the Protocol had no effect on the application of the Charter in the UK.

Joined Cases C-411 & 493/10 *NS v Secretary of State for the Home Department* [2012] 3 WLR 1374

116. By its seventh question in Case C-411/10, the Court of Appeal (England & Wales) (Civil Division) asks, in essence, whether, in so far as the preceding questions arise in respect of the obligations of the United Kingdom, the answers to the second to sixth questions should be qualified in any respect so as to take account of Protocol (No 30).

117. As noted by the EHRC [the Equality and Human Rights Commission, a body established by the UK government to promote human rights], that question arises because of the position taken by the Secretary of State before the High Court of Justice (England & Wales) (Administrative Court) that the provisions of the Charter do not apply in the United Kingdom.

118. Even if the Secretary of State no longer maintained that position before the Court of Appeal (England & Wales) (Civil Division), it must be noted that Protocol (No 30) provides, in Article 1(1), that the Charter is not to extend the ability of the Court of Justice or any court or tribunal of Poland or of the United Kingdom, to find that the laws, regulations administrative provisions, practices or action of Poland or of the United Kingdom are inconsistent with the fundamental rights, freedoms and principles that it affirms.

119. According to the wording of that provision, as noted by the Advocate General in points 169 and 170 of her Opinion in Case C-411/10, Protocol (No 30) does not call into question the applicability of the Charter in the United Kingdom or in Poland, a position which is confirmed by the recitals in the preamble to that protocol. Thus, according to the third recital in the preamble to Protocol (No 30), Article 6 TEU requires the Charter to be applied and interpreted by the courts of Poland and of the United Kingdom strictly in accordance with the explanations referred to in that article. In addition, according to the sixth recital in the preamble to that protocol, the Charter reaffirms the rights, freedoms and principles recognised in the Union and makes those rights more visible, but does not create new rights or principles.

120. In those circumstances, Article 1(1) of Protocol (No 30) explains Article 51 of the Charter with regard to the scope thereof and does not intend to exempt the Republic of Poland or the United Kingdom from the obligation to comply with the provisions of the Charter or to prevent a court of one of those Member States from ensuring compliance with those provisions.

121. Since the rights referred to in the cases in the main proceedings do not form part of Title IV of the Charter, there is no need to rule on the interpretation of Article 1(2) of Protocol (No 30).

122. The answer to the seventh question in Case C-411/10 is therefore that, in so far as the preceding questions arise in respect of the obligations of the United Kingdom, the answers to the second to sixth questions referred in Case C-411/10 do not require to be qualified in any respect so as to take account of Protocol (No 30).

The Court of Justice in *NS* noted that the Preamble to the Charter expressly stated that it did not create new rights and held that Protocol No 30 therefore did not affect the application of the Charter in the UK or Poland. As the High Court of England and Wales subsequently put it in *R (AB) v Secretary of State for the Home Department* [2013] EWHC 3453 (Admin), at para 14 (see also 9.4.4): 'Notwithstanding the endeavours of our political representatives at Lisbon it would seem that the … Charter of Rights is now part of our domestic law.'

Article 1(2) of the Protocol states that Title IV of the Charter (which is entitled 'Solidarity' and which provides a number of employment rights) creates no new justiciable rights beyond those already existing in national law. Like Article 1(1), Article 1(2) may also be redundant, as it may simply reflect the correct interpretation of Title IV. However, it is possible that Title IV does include at least some potentially justiciable new rights, in which case the Protocol may prevent the application of those rights in the UK (and in Poland). In *NS*, the Court of Justice held that, since the rights in Title IV were not at issue in that case, there was no need for it to rule on the interpretation of Article 1(2) of the Protocol.

The statement in Article 2 of the Protocol also appears to be redundant. It states that any Charter rights that refer to national laws and practices will only apply in the UK and Poland to the extent that the laws or practices of the UK and Poland recognize those rights. However, it seems unlikely that Charter rights which include such a reference would be interpreted other than as referring to the laws and practices of the particular State against which the right is being asserted.

9.4.3 The application of the Charter to Member States

Charter of Fundamental Rights of the European Union

Article 51

Field of application

1. The provisions of this Charter are addressed to the institutions, bodies, offices and agencies of the Union with due regard for the principle of subsidiarity and to the Member States only when they are implementing Union law. They shall therefore respect the rights, observe the principles and promote the application thereof in accordance with their respective powers and respecting the limits of the powers of the Union as conferred on it in the Treaties.

REVIEW QUESTION

Who or what is legally bound by the Charter?

Answer: Article 51(1) of the Charter provides that it applies to the EU and its institutions, and to the Member States, but 'only when they are implementing Union law'.

The determination of whether the Member State, when allegedly acting in violation of human rights, is 'implementing' EU law will often be difficult.

The Court of Justice has taken an expansive approach to the question of which national measures fall within the scope of EU law generally. For example, in Case C-117/01 *KB v National Health Service Pensions Agency and the Secretary of State for Health* [2004] ECR I-541 and Case C-423/04 *Richards v Secretary of State for Work and Pensions* [2006] ECR I-3585, both of which concerned UK law that prevented transgender persons from registering their change of sex, the Court of Justice held that although civil status was not a matter of EU law, equal treatment on grounds of sex was. It ruled that the UK's refusal to recognize the change of gender constituted discrimination because it prevented a trans man from marrying a woman and because it prevented that woman from inheriting pension rights as a widow, and because it prevented a trans woman from retiring at the lower retirement age then applicable to women. In Case C-555/07 *Kücüdeveci* [2010] ECR I-365 (see also 4.1.4), German law laid down minimum periods for notice of dismissal by reference to an employee's length of service, excluding employment before the age of 25. The Court of Justice held that this national provision was within the scope of EU discrimination law because it governed the conditions of dismissal and was adopted after the expiry of the deadline for the transposition (see further 3.4.2 on the obligation to transpose Directives into national law) of Council Directive 2000/78/EC of 27 November 2000 establishing a general framework for equal treatment in employment and occupation, OJ 2000 L303/16, including the conditions governing dismissal. (The Court concluded that the provision was discriminatory and thus prohibited by EU law.) However, even the Court's expansive approach has its limits. In Case C-328/04 *Vajnai* [2005] ECR I-8577, the Court of Justice held that a Hungarian prohibition on the wearing of symbols associated with totalitarian regimes, such as a swastika or hammer and sickle, was outside the scope of EU law and therefore the question of whether it was compatible with EU human rights law did not arise. The Court of Justice has also ruled that it has no jurisdiction to review national measures that were adopted before the Member State in question joined the EU (see eg Case C-302/04 *Ynos kft v Varga* [2006] ECR I-371).

Turning to the specific question of what national measures fall within the scope of EU law for the purposes of Article 51 of the Charter, the Explanation relating to Article 51(1) provides some limited guidance on this issue. (The later part of the Explanation on Article 51 is extracted at 9.4.2.)

Explanations relating to the Charter of Fundamental Rights, OJ 2007 C303/02

Explanation on Article 51—Field of application

The aim of Article 51 is to determine the scope of the Charter. It seeks to establish clearly that the Charter applies primarily to the institutions and bodies of the Union, in compliance with the principle of subsidiarity. This provision was drafted in keeping with Article 6(2) of the Treaty on European Union, which required the Union to respect fundamental rights, and with the mandate issued by the Cologne European Council. The term 'institutions' is enshrined in the Treaties. The expression 'bodies, offices and agencies' is commonly used in the Treaties to refer to all the authorities set up by the Treaties or by secondary legislation (see, e.g., Articles 15 or 16 of the Treaty on the Functioning of the European Union).

As regards the Member States, it follows unambiguously from the case-law of the Court of Justice that the requirement to respect fundamental rights defined in the context of the Union is only binding on the Member States when they act in the scope of Union law (judgment of 13 July 1989, Case 5/88 *Wachauf* [1989] ECR 2609; judgment of 18 June 1991, Case C-260/89 *ERT*

[1991] ECR I-2925; judgment of 18 December 1997, Case C-309/96 *Annibaldi* [1997] ECR I-7493). The Court of Justice confirmed this case-law in the following terms: 'In addition, it should be remembered that the requirements flowing from the protection of fundamental rights in the Community legal order are also binding on Member States when they implement Community rules … ' (judgment of 13 April 2000, Case C-292/97 [2000] ECR I-2737, paragraph 37 of the grounds). Of course this rule, as enshrined in this Charter, applies to the central authorities as well as to regional or local bodies, and to public organisations, when they are implementing Union law.

[…]

Although this Explanation provides some clarification as to which bodies within the Member States are included in the reference to 'the Member States' in Article 51 of the Charter, it provides little assistance on when a Member State will be regarded as 'implementing' EU law for the purposes of the application of the Charter. A claim brought in the national courts for breach of human rights might therefore have to be formulated both on the basis of the ECHR and, in the event that the human rights violation committed by a Member State is held to result from its action in 'implementing' EU law, on the basis of EU law. Of course, some claims may appropriately be based on the ECHR even if the violation results from measures implementing EU law (see eg *Matthews v United Kingdom* Application No 24833/94 (1999) 28 EHRR 361, discussed at 9.5.2). However, it will not be possible to base a claim on the ECHR if the right violated is granted only by EU law and not by the ECHR, and the question of whether the Member State has acted in the 'implementation' of EU law may then determine whether the victim is able to bring any claim at all.

The Court of Justice has held, in Case 36/75 *Rutili v Ministre de l'intérieur* [1975] ECR 1219 (see also 9.2.2), that even national measures that derogate from EU law are within the scope of EU law for the purpose of determining its jurisdiction to give a preliminary ruling under Article 267 TFEU (see further Chapter 6 on the preliminary ruling procedure) and has explicitly stated that such derogating measures, whether provided for by the Treaties (Case C-260/89 *ERT* [1991] ECR I-2925) or in its own jurisprudence (Case C-368/95 *Vereinigte Familiapress Zeitungsverlags- und vertreibs GmbH v Heinrich Bauer Verlag* [1997] ECR I-3689), will be assessed for their compliance with fundamental human rights.

In C-198/13 *Hernández and others v Reino de España and others* EU:C:2014:2055, the Court of Justice laid down a number of general principles on when a Member State should be considered to be implementing EU law for the purposes of Article 51 of the Charter.

?! THINKING POINT

When reading the following extract, make a note of these principles.

C-198/13 *Hernández and others v Reino de España and others* EU:C:2014:2055

34. In this regard, it should be borne in mind that the concept of 'implementing Union law', as referred to in Article 51 of the Charter, presupposes a degree of connection between the measure of EU law and the national measure at issue which goes beyond the matters covered being closely related or one of those matters having an indirect impact on the other (see, to that effect, the judgments delivered prior to the entry into force of the Charter in Case 149/77 *Defrenne* EU:C:1978:130, paragraphs 29 to 32; Case C-299/95 *Kremzow* EU:C:1997:254, paragraphs 16 and 17; Case C-144/04 *Mangold* EU:C:2005:709, paragraph 75; and [C-206/13] *Siragusa* EU:C:2014:126, paragraph 24).
35. In particular, the Court has found that fundamental European-Union rights could not be applied in relation to national legislation because the provisions of EU law in the area concerned did not impose any specific obligation on Member States with regard to the situation at issue in the main proceedings (see Case C-144/95 *Maurin* EU:C:1996:235, paragraphs 11 and 12, and [C-206/13] *Siragusa* EU:C:2014:126, paragraphs 26 and 27).
36. In the same vein, the Court has already held that Article 13 EC (now Article 19 TFEU) could not, as such, bring within the scope of EU law, for the purposes of the application of fundamental rights as general principles of EU law, a national measure which does not come within the framework of the measures adopted on the basis of that article (see, to that effect, Case C-427/06 *Bartsch* EU:C:2008:517, paragraph 18; Case C-555/07 *Kücükdeveci* EU:C:2010:21, paragraph 25; and Case C-147/08 *Römer* EU:C:2011:286, paragraph 61). Consequently, the mere fact that a national measure comes within an area in which the European Union has powers cannot bring it within the scope of EU law, and, therefore, cannot render the Charter applicable (see, to that effect, Joined Cases C-483/09 and C-1/10 *Gueye and Salmerón Sánchez* EU:C:2011:583, paragraphs 55, 69 and 70, and Case C-370/12 *Pringle* EU:C:2012:756, paragraphs 104, 105, 180 and 181).
37. In accordance with the Court's settled case-law, in order to determine whether a national measure involves the implementation of EU law for the purposes of Article 51(1) of the Charter, it is necessary to determine, inter alia, whether that national legislation is intended to implement a provision of EU law; the nature of the legislation at issue and whether it pursues objectives other than those covered by EU law, even if it is capable of indirectly affecting EU law; and also whether there are specific rules of EU law on the matter or rules which are capable of affecting it (see [C-309/96] *Annibaldi* EU:C:1997:631, paragraphs 21 to 23; Case C-40/11 *Iida* EU:C:2012:691, paragraph 79; Case C-87/12 *Ymeraga and Others* EU:C:2013:291, paragraph 41; and [C-206/13] *Siragusa* EU:C:2014:126, paragraph 25).

The Court in *Hernández* held that, in assessing whether a national measure implemented EU law, it was necessary to consider whether it was intended to implement EU law, whether it pursued other objectives, and whether there were EU rules that could affect it.

Some assistance on what will and will not constitute implementing measures for the purposes of Article 51 of the Charter can also be gleaned from the application of this requirement to the facts of some of the cases that have so far arisen. For example, in Joined Cases C-411 & 493/10 *NS v Secretary of State for the Home Department* [2012] 2 CMLR 9 (see also 9.4.2), the Court of Justice ruled that the decision of a Member State which was not responsible under Regulation 343/2003 (the Dublin II Regulation) for examining an asylum application, but which nonetheless chose to do so pursuant to an exception in that Regulation, had implemented EU law for the purpose of Article 51 of the Charter. In C-650/13 *Delvigne v Commune de Lesparre-Médoc and another* EU:C:2015:648, the Court of Justice held that French legislation which provided for EU citizens who had been convicted of a criminal offence to be excluded from the right to vote in elections to the European Parliament (see 2.1 on the Parliament) must be considered to be implementing the EU's 1976 Act concerning the election of members of the European Parliament (MEPs), annexed to EU Decision 76/787/ECSC, EEC, EURATOM of the representatives of the Member States meeting in the council relating to the Act concerning the election of the representatives of the Assembly by direct universal suffrage, OJ 1976 L278/1, and thus to be implementing EU law within the meaning of Article 51 of the Charter. In C-419/14 *WebMindLicenses Kft v Nemzeti Adó- és Vámhivatal Kiemelt Adó- és Vám Főigazgatóság* EU:C:2015:832, the Court held that an adjustment of VAT by the Hungarian tax authorities after they had found the applicant to have committed an abuse of rights aimed at circumventing Hungarian tax law constituted implementation of the VAT Directive (Council Directive 2006/112/EC of 28 November 2006 on the common system of value added tax, OJ 2006 L347/1) and Article 325 TFEU on combating fraud, and therefore constituted implementation of EU law for the purposes of Article 51 of the Charter.

In Case C-617/10 *Åklagaren v Åkerberg Fransson* [2013] 2 CMLR 36, tax penalties had been imposed on Åkerberg Fransson and criminal proceedings were then brought against him for providing false information to the Swedish tax authorities. He claimed that this was in breach of Article 50 of the Charter, which prohibited trial or punishment of a person for an offence for which they had already been finally acquitted or convicted. The Swedish court made a preliminary reference to the Court of Justice under Article 267 TFEU (see further Chapter 6 on the preliminary reference procedure), but the Swedish government claimed that the reference was inadmissible because neither the national legislation on the basis of which the tax penalties were ordered to be paid nor that upon which the criminal proceedings were founded arose from implementation of EU law. However, the Court of Justice noted that the tax penalties and criminal proceedings were connected in part to Åkerberg Fransson's breaches of his obligations to declare VAT, and held that those penalties and proceedings constituted implementation of the VAT Directive 2006/112, which obliged Member States to take all legislative and administrative measures appropriate to ensure collection of VAT due on their territory and prevent evasion, and of Article 325 TFEU, which obliged them to counter fraud affecting the financial interests of the EU (including VAT revenue, since this formed part of the EU's own resources). In response to the Swedish government's argument that its measures had not been adopted in order to implement EU law, the Court made the following clear statement.

Case C-617/10 *Åklagaren v Åkerberg Fransson* [2013] 2 CMLR 36

28. The fact that the national legislation upon which those tax penalties and criminal proceedings are founded has not been adopted to transpose Directive 2006/112 cannot call that conclusion into question, since its application is designed to penalise an infringement of that directive and is therefore intended to implement the obligation imposed on the Member States by the Treaty to impose effective penalties for conduct prejudicial to the financial interests of the European Union.

The Court of Justice therefore concluded that the reference in *Åkerberg Fransson* was admissible and the Charter applicable, although it held that Article 50 had not in fact been breached so long as the tax penalty was not criminal in nature.

However, a tenuous link between the Member State's action and EU law, as in *Åkerberg Fransson*, will not always be sufficient for that action to amount to implementing EU law. For example, in C-333/13 *Dano v Jobcentre Leipzig* EU:C:2014:2358, the Court of Justice held that the conditions laid down by German law for the grant of special non-contributory cash benefits and the extent of such benefits did not constitute implementation of Regulation (EC) No 883/2004 of the European Parliament and of the Council of 29 April 2004 on the coordination of social security systems, OJ 2004 L166/1, or of Directive 2004/38/EC of the European Parliament and of the Council of 29 April 2004 on the right of citizens of the Union and their family members to move and reside freely within the territory of the Member States … , OJ 2004 L258/77. The Court therefore had no jurisdiction to rule on whether that German law was compatible with the Charter. In C-446/12 *Willems v Burgemeester van Amsterdam* EU:C:2015:238, the applicants were denied passports or an identity card because they refused to provide their digital fingerprints, on the ground that this breached their right to privacy under the Charter. The Court of Justice held that the Dutch law requiring fingerprint data did not constitute implementation of Council Regulation (EC) No 2252/2004 of 13 December 2004 on standards for security features and biometrics in passports and travel documents issued by Member States, OJ 2004 L385/1, because the Regulation did not require a Member State to guarantee in its national legislation that biometric data would not be stored or used by it for purposes other than those specified in the Regulation and did not apply to identity cards at all. The Court therefore held that there was no need to examine whether the Dutch law complied with the Charter.

The UK's Supreme Court has noted that 'the rubric, "implementing EU law" is to be interpreted broadly and, in effect, means whenever a member state is acting "within the material scope of EU law" ' (*Rugby Football Union v Consolidated Information Services Ltd (formerly Viagogo Ltd) (in liquidation)* [2012] UKSC 55, [2013] 1 CMLR 56, at para 28). The Supreme Court in *Viagogo* cited in support the judgment of the High Court of England and Wales in *R (Zagorski and Baze) v Secretary of State for Business, Innovation and Skills* [2010] EWHC 3110 (Admin), [2011] HRLR 6 (see also 9.4.4). In that case, the claimants were US citizens sentenced to the death penalty in particular US states that carried out that penalty by lethal injection. They claimed that the UK had breached their right under Article 4 of the Charter not to be subjected to torture or inhuman or degrading treatment, because it had refused to prohibit the export of an anaesthetic (sodium thiopental), which was used in the lethal injection process. The High Court noted that Council Regulation (EC) No 1061/2009 of 19 October 2009 establishing common rules for exports, OJ 2009 L291/1, prohibited controls on exports to non-EU countries, subject to certain derogations, and the Torture Regulation (Council Regulation (EC) No 1236/2005 of 27 June 2005 concerning trade in certain goods which could be used for capital punishment, torture or other cruel, inhuman or degrading treatment or punishment, OJ 2005 L200/1) prohibited the export of specified goods (not including sodium thiopental) that had no practical use other than for the purpose of capital punishment, torture, or other cruel, inhuman, or degrading treatment or punishment. The prohibition of exports to third countries was thus subject to close and detailed regulation by the EU, and the power of Member States to act was greatly restricted. The UK authorities were therefore acting 'within the material scope of EU law' (*Zagorski and Baze*, at para 68), and so 'implementing' EU law within the meaning of Article 51(1) of the Charter, when deciding whether to impose an export ban. However, as will be discussed at 9.4.4, the claim fell outside the protection of the Charter on other grounds.

9.4.4 The scope and interpretation of the Charter

The key provision here is Article 52 of the Charter.

Charter of Fundamental Rights of the European Union

Article 52

Scope and interpretation of rights and principles

1. Any limitation on the exercise of the rights and freedoms recognised by this Charter must be provided for by law and respect the essence of those rights and freedoms. Subject to the principle of proportionality, limitations may be made only if they are necessary and genuinely meet objectives of general interest recognised by the Union or the need to protect the rights and freedoms of others.
2. Rights recognised by this Charter for which provision is made in the Treaties shall be exercised under the conditions and within the limits defined by those Treaties.
3. In so far as this Charter contains rights which correspond to rights guaranteed by the Convention for the Protection of Human Rights and Fundamental Freedoms, the meaning and scope of those rights shall be the same as those laid down by the said Convention. This provision shall not prevent Union law providing more extensive protection.
4. In so far as this Charter recognises fundamental rights as they result from the constitutional traditions common to the Member States, those rights shall be interpreted in harmony with those traditions.

5. The provisions of this Charter which contain principles may be implemented by legislative and executive acts taken by institutions, bodies, offices and agencies of the Union, and by acts of Member States when they are implementing Union law, in the exercise of their respective powers. They shall be judicially cognisable only in the interpretation of such acts and in the ruling on their legality.
6. Full account shall be taken of national laws and practices as specified in this Charter.
7. The explanations drawn up as a way of providing guidance in the interpretation of this Charter shall be given due regard by the courts of the Union and of the Member States.

REVIEW QUESTION

Summarize the rules set out in Article 52 of the Charter as to:

(1) the interpretation of the Charter generally;

(2) the interpretation of Charter rights that are also contained in other documents; and

(3) the conditions applicable to derogations from Charter rights.

Answer: As to question (1), Article 52(7) of the Charter expressly provides that the accompanying Explanations are to be 'given due regard' by the national and EU courts when interpreting the Charter.

As to question (2), Charter rights that are also laid down in the EU Treaties, the ECHR, or the constitutional traditions of the Member States are to be given an interpretation that is consistent with that other source. Thus, for example, the exceptions to the right to life set out in Article 2 ECHR, although not included in Article 2 of the Charter, which also provides for the right to life, are to be implied into it.

As to question (3), any limitation on Charter rights and freedoms must:

- be provided for by law;
- respect the essence of the rights and freedoms; and
- be proportionate to the aim of the limitation.

Although Article 52(3) provides that Charter rights derived from the ECHR must be interpreted consistently with the ECHR, it does not expressly require this interpretation to be consistent with the ECHR as it is interpreted by the ECtHR. This could have been a significant omission, as pre-Charter case law indicated that there was potential for the Court of Justice and the ECtHR to differ in their interpretation of human rights. For example, the Court of Justice ruled in Case C-159/90 *Society for the Protection of Unborn Children (Ireland) Ltd v Grogan* [1991] ECR I-4685 that a national law prohibiting the distribution of information about abortion clinics in another Member State did not constitute a restriction on the freedom to provide services because the information was not distributed by or on behalf of the service provider. In contrast, in *Open Door Counselling and Dublin Well Woman v Ireland* Application No 14234/88 (1993) 15 EHRR 244, the ECtHR declared the same prohibition to be in breach of the right to free expression.

However, the Preamble to the Charter states that '[t]he Charter reaffirms … the rights as they result, in particular, from … the caselaw of the … European Court of Human Rights', and in Case C-279/09 *DEB Deutsche Energiehandels- und Beratungsgesellschaft* [2010] ECR I-13849, at para 35 (see also 4.3.2), which concerned the right to legal aid in Article 47 of the Charter, the Court of Justice noted that the Explanation on Article 52(3) of the Charter required that 'the meaning and scope of the [Charter] rights are to be determined not only by reference to the text of the ECHR, but also, inter alia, by reference to the case-law of the European Court of Human Rights'.

Explanations relating to the Charter of Fundamental Rights, OJ 2007 C303/02

Explanation on Article 52—Scope and interpretation of rights and principles

[...]

Paragraph 3 is intended to ensure the necessary consistency between the Charter and the ECHR by establishing the rule that, in so far as the rights in the present Charter also correspond to rights guaranteed by the ECHR, the meaning and scope of those rights, including authorised limitations, are the same as those laid down by the ECHR. This means in particular that the legislator, in laying down limitations to those rights, must comply with the same standards as are fixed by the detailed limitation arrangements laid down in the ECHR, which are thus made applicable for the rights covered by this paragraph, without thereby adversely affecting the autonomy of Union law and of that of the Court of Justice of the European Union.

The reference to the ECHR covers both the Convention and the Protocols to it. The meaning and the scope of the guaranteed rights are determined not only by the text of those instruments, but also by the case-law of the European Court of Human Rights and by the Court of Justice of the European Union. The last sentence of the paragraph is designed to allow the Union to guarantee more extensive protection. In any event, the level of protection afforded by the Charter may never be lower than that guaranteed by the ECHR.

[...]

On this basis, the Court of Justice in *DEB Deutsche* proceeded to conduct a detailed review of the ECtHR's interpretation of the right to a fair trial in Article 6 ECHR, starting with the judgment of the latter Court expressly referred to in the Explanation on Article 47, *Airey v Ireland* Application No 6289/73 (1979) 2 EHRR 305. The Court of Justice concluded from the interpretation of Article 6 ECHR by the Court of Human Rights in *Airey* that the principle of effective judicial protection enshrined in Article 47 of the Charter could be relied on by legal, as well as natural, persons and could require exemption to be granted from the requirement of advance payment of the costs of the proceedings. A further example of a consistent interpretation in relation to Article 47 is provided by the Court of Justice's recognition of the principle of equality of arms in C-199/11 *Europese Gemeenschap v Otis NV and others* [2013] 4 CMLR 4, at para 71—a principle first adopted by the ECtHR in *Neumeister v Austria* Application No 1936/63 (1968) 1 EHRR 9. This principle requires that each party must be afforded a reasonable opportunity to present their case, including their evidence, under conditions that do not place them at a substantial disadvantage vis-à-vis their opponent.

In *R (Zagorski and Baze) v Secretary of State for Business, Innovation and Skills* [2010] EWHC 3110 (Admin), [2011] HRLR 6 (see also 9.4.3), the High Court of England and Wales held that although the UK was implementing EU law when it refused to impose an export ban on a drug that was used in the lethal injection process of execution to which the claimants had been sentenced by the US courts, and thus the Charter was in principle applicable, it did not confer any rights on the claimants. While the Charter rights were not expressly limited to persons within the jurisdiction of an EU Member State, such a restriction was to be implied. To read the Charter as guaranteeing rights without any such limitation would be very radical and, since Article 52(3) provided that Charter rights which corresponded to ECHR rights should have the same meaning and scope, Article 4 of the Charter should be interpreted in the light of Article 1 ECHR, which provided that rights were guaranteed to those within the jurisdiction of a defendant State. The Charter therefore conferred no rights on the claimants in this case.

The Explanation on Article 52 provides, by way of summary, two lists comparing the meaning and scope of the Charter Articles with those of the ECHR. The first list, set out at Table 9.1, compares rights that appear in both the Charter and the ECHR, and which are stated by the Explanation to have not only *the same meaning*, but also *the same scope*.

Thus, for example, in C-199–201/12 *Minister voor Immigratie en Asiel v X, Y and Z* [2014] 2 CMLR 16, the Court of Justice held that although the criminalization of homosexual acts did not constitute persecution within the meaning of Council Directive 2004/83/EC of 29 April 2004 on minimum standards for the qualification and status of third country nationals or stateless persons as refugees or as persons who otherwise need international protection and

Table 9.1

Charter Articles and ECHR Articles/Protocols with the same meaning and scope

Right	Charter Article	ECHR (or Protocol) Article
Right to life	Article 2	Article 2
Prohibition of torture/inhuman or degrading treatment	Article 4	Article 3
Prohibition of slavery	Article 5(1) and (2)	Article 4
Right to liberty	Article 6	Article 5
Right to respect for private and family life	Article 7	Article 8
Freedom of thought and religion	Article 10(1)	Article 9
Freedom of expression	Article 11	Article 10
Right to peaceful enjoyment of property	Article 17	Protocol 1, Article 1
Prohibition of collective expulsions of foreign nationals	Article 19(1)	Protocol 4, Article 4
Article 3 ECHR	Article 19(2)	Article 3 (as interpreted by the ECtHR in a particular series of cases)
Presumption of innocence and rights of the defence	Article 48	Article 6(2) and (3)
Right not to be convicted of an offence retrospectively or to be given a heavier penalty	Article 49(1) and (2)	Article 7

Table 9.2

Charter Articles with the same meaning as ECHR Articles/Protocols, but a wider scope

Right	Scope of Charter right	Charter Article	ECHR Article
Right to marry and found a family	May be extended to various forms of marriage if established by national legislation	Article 9	Article 12
Freedom of association and assembly	Applies to political parties at EU level	Article 12(1)	Article 11
Right to education	Includes vocational and continuing training	Article 14	Protocol 1, Article 2
Fair trial rights	Not limited to the determination of civil rights or criminal charges	Article 47(2) and (3)	Article 6(1)
Right not to be tried twice for the same offence	Applies at EU level between the courts of the Member States	Article 50	Protocol 7, Article 4
Political activity of aliens	Restrictions permissible only on non-EU nationals	Articles 11, 12, and 21	Articles 10, 11, 14, and 16

the content of the protection granted, OJ 2004 L304/12, the sanction of a term of imprisonment did, because it was disproportionate or discriminatory, contrary to Article 9(2)(c) of the Directive. In so ruling, the Court noted that '[s]uch a sanction infringes article 8 [ECHR], to which Article 7 of the Charter corresponds' (*X, Y and Z*, at para 54). Similarly, when ruling in Joined Cases C-71 & 99/11 *Germany v Y* and *Germany v Z* [2013] 1 CMLR 5 that the risk of persecution within the meaning of the Directive should be assessed without taking account of the possibility that the applicants could avoid the risk of persecution by abstaining from their religious practices, the Court of Justice noted, at para 56, that '[t]he right to religious freedom enshrined in art. 101(1) of the Charter corresponds to the right guaranteed by art. 9 of the ECHR'.

The second list in the Explanation on Article 52, set out at Table 9.2, compares rights that appear in the Charter and the ECHR, and which are stated by the Explanation to have the *same meaning*, but a *different scope*, the Charter rights having a *wider scope*.

Although the Explanation on Article 52 of the Charter does not contain a third list indicating which rights in the Charter have a *narrower scope* than the corresponding rights in the ECHR, there are nonetheless some rights in this category. For example, the voting rights granted by Articles 39 and 40 of the Charter (see further 11.2.3 on these rights) are restricted to EU citizens (see further 11.2.1 on the definition of EU citizens), and to European parliamentary and local elections, and do not bestow a right to vote as such, but only to do so 'under the same conditions as nationals' of the Member State where the election takes place. By contrast, Article 3 of Protocol 1 to the ECHR—at issue in *Matthews v United Kingdom* Application No 24833/94 (1999) 28 EHRR 361 (see further 9.5.2)—provides for the wider right to free elections by secret ballot. Thus, whereas the ECtHR has held that a complete ban on convicted prisoners voting breaches Article 3 of Protocol 1 to the ECHR (for example in *Hirst v UK (No 2)* Application No 74025/01 (2006) 42 EHRR 41), the UK's Supreme Court has held that the same ban does not breach EU law (*R (on the application of Chester) v Secretary of State for Justice* and *McGeoch (AP) v The Lord President of the Council and another (Scotland)* [2013] UKSC 63, [2014] 1 CMLR 45).

The Charter also contains a number of rights that are not explicitly included in the ECHR, such as the protection of personal data (Article 8), the freedom to choose an occupation (Article 15), and the rights of children (Article 24) and the elderly (Article 25). This point was emphasized by the High Court of England and Wales in *R (AB) v Secretary of State for the Home Department* [2013] EWHC 3453, (Admin) [2014] 2 CMLR 22.

R (AB) v Secretary of State for the Home Department [2013] EWHC 3453 (Admin) [2014] 2 CMLR 22

14. The Human Rights Act 1998 incorporated into our domestic law large parts, but by no means all, of the European Convention on Human Rights. Some parts were deliberately missed out by Parliament. The Charter of Fundamental Rights of the European Union contains, I believe, all of those missing parts and a great deal more. Notwithstanding the endeavours of our political representatives at Lisbon it would seem that the much wider Charter of Rights is now part of our domestic law. Moreover, that much wider Charter of Rights would remain part of our domestic law even if the Human Rights Act were repealed.

However, it should be noted that some rights which do not appear in the text of the ECHR (including the protection of personal data, for example) have been implied or interpreted into it by the ECtHR.

A further difficulty that arises when interpreting the Charter is that Article 52(5) of the Charter makes a distinction between 'rights' and 'principles'. This distinction is not particularly clear from the substantive provisions of the Charter, in which although most rights are expressed as such, those that are not so expressed are not explicitly stated to be principles. For example, Article 13 of the Charter provides that '[t]he arts and scientific research shall be free of constraint'. The only express statement that any particular substantive entitlements may be principles appears in the heading to Article 49, which is 'Principles of legality and proportionality of criminal offences and penalties'. However, the 'principles' set out in the text of Article 49 are expressed in mandatory terms similarly to the equivalent rights in Article 7 ECHR. The Court of Justice has so far provided little clarification of this issue. In C-356/12 *Glatzel v Freistaat Bayern* EU:C:2014:350, the applicant alleged that Directive 2006/126/EC of the European Parliament and of the Council of 20 December 2006 on driving licences (Recast), OJ 2006 L/403/18—ie on physical fitness to drive a motor vehicle—breached Article 20 of the Charter, which provides for equality before the law, Article 21 of the Charter, which prohibits discrimination on grounds of disability, and Article 26 of the Charter, which requires the EU to respect and recognize the right of persons with disabilities to benefit from integration measures. The Court of Justice emphasized that Article 26 (but apparently not Articles 20 or 21) was a principle, but did not clearly explain the grounds on which it reached that conclusion.

The distinction between rights and principles is potentially of considerable significance; Article 52(5) makes rights—but not principles—fully justiciable. In contrast, it provides that principles may be implemented by the EU institutions or the Member States and will only have judicial effect in the interpretation or judicial review of such implementing acts. In *Glatzel*, at para 78, the Court of Justice held that in order for Article 26 of the Charter to be fully effective, it must be given more specific expression in EU or national law, and therefore could not by itself confer a right on individuals that they could invoke. It has been argued (see P Craig and G de Búrca, *EU Law: Text, Cases, and Materials*, 6th edn (Oxford: Oxford University Press, 2015), pp 398–9) that this reflects a distinction between negative (ie requiring the State to refrain from interference) civil and political rights, and positive (ie obliging the State to act) social and economic rights, and this suggested distinction may be of assistance when interpreting the Charter provisions. Further guidance on Article 52(5) is provided by the related Explanation.

Explanations relating to the Charter of Fundamental Rights, OJ 2007 C303/02

Explanation on Article 52—Scope and interpretation of rights and principles

[...]

Paragraph 5 clarifies the distinction between 'rights' and 'principles' set out in the Charter. According to that distinction, subjective rights shall be respected, whereas principles shall be observed (Article 51(1)). Principles may be implemented through legislative or executive acts (adopted by the Union in accordance with its powers, and by the Member States only when they implement Union law); accordingly, they become significant for the Courts only when such acts are interpreted or reviewed. They do not however give rise to direct claims for positive action by the Union's institutions or Member States authorities. This is consistent both with case-law of the Court of Justice (cf. notably case-law on the 'precautionary principle' in Article 191(2) of the Treaty on the Functioning of the European Union: judgment of the CFI of 11 September 2002, Case T-13/99 *Pfizer v Council*, with numerous references to earlier case-law; and a series of judgments on Article 33 (ex-39) on the principles of agricultural law, e.g. judgment of the Court of Justice in Case 265/85 *Van den Berg* [1987] ECR 1155: scrutiny of the principle of market stabilisation and of reasonable expectations) and with the approach of the Member States' constitutional systems to 'principles', particularly in the field of social law. For illustration, examples for principles, recognised in the Charter include e.g. Articles 25, 26 and 37. In some cases, an Article of the Charter may contain both elements of a right and of a principle, e.g. Articles 23, 33 and 34.

Article 53 of the Charter is sometimes described as a minimum standard or non-regression clause, and provides that the Charter cannot be used to restrict human rights otherwise protected by EU law, international law and agreements (including the ECHR), and domestic law. It performs a broadly equivalent role to Article 53 ECHR, which provides that the ECHR cannot be used to limit any human rights which are protected by the domestic law of an ECHR State Party or protected by an agreement to which an ECHR State Party is a party.

Charter of Fundamental Rights of the European Union

Article 53

Level of protection

Nothing in this Charter shall be interpreted as restricting or adversely affecting human rights and fundamental freedoms as recognised, in their respective fields of application, by Union law and international law and by international agreements to which the Union or all the Member States are party, including the European Convention for the Protection of Human Rights and Fundamental Freedoms, and by the Member States' constitutions.

The impact of Article 53 of the Charter was clarified by the Court of Justice in Case C-399/11 *Melloni* [2013] 2 CMLR 43. In that case, the Italian authorities had issued a European arrest warrant (EAW) for the enforcement of a prison sentence imposed on Melloni following trial in his absence. The Court of Justice held that Article 4a(1) of Council Framework Decision 2002/584/JHA of 13 June 2002 on the European arrest warrant and the surrender procedures between Member States, OJ 2002 L190/1, did not permit a Member State to make execution of a warrant against a person who had been absent from the trial at which they had been convicted conditional on their conviction being subject to review, in circumstances in which they had been notified of the trial. As so interpreted, Article 4a(1) did not breach Articles 47 (the right to a fair trial) or 48 (the rights of the defence) of the Charter because these were not absolute rights; an accused could waive their rights provided that they did so freely and unequivocally, safeguards were in place, and it did not infringe any important public interest. Although Article 53 of the Charter permitted national authorities and courts to apply national standards of protection of fundamental rights, this was on condition that the level of protection of the Charter, as interpreted by the Court of Justice, and the primacy, unity, and effectiveness of EU law, were not thereby compromised. Permitting a State to use Article 53 to make enforcement of an EAW conditional on the reviewability of the underlying judgment, in order to avoid an adverse effect on the right to a fair trial and the rights of the defence guaranteed by that State's constitution, would compromise the effectiveness of the Framework Decision and the uniformity of the standard of protection.

9.5 The enforcement of human rights in EU law

Rights, of course, are only meaningful if they can be enforced.

9.5.1 Actions for enforcement against the EU

An action against the EU institutions for breach of fundamental rights may be brought in the EU Courts, either for annulment of the measure that resulted in the violation of rights (under

Article 263 TFEU—see Chapter 7) or for damages (under Article 340 TFEU—see Chapter 8). It may not be brought in the national courts or, until and unless the EU accedes to the ECHR (see 9.6), before the ECtHR.

One problem with bringing a claim in the EU Courts is that such claims are subject to considerable restrictions. In particular, the admissibility requirements that must be satisfied by an individual or business seeking to bring a claim under Article 263 TFEU before the EU General Court (see further 7.7–7.8) can prevent potential applicants from having their claims heard regardless of the substantive merits of that claim, and are much more demanding than the admissibility requirements in Articles 34 and 35 ECHR that must be satisfied in order for a case to be heard by the ECtHR. Additionally, although there are no admissibility restrictions on the bringing of a claim under Article 340 TFEU before the General Court, the substantive requirement that the breach of law be sufficiently serious (see further 8.4.2) significantly reduces the number of possible claims, and such an action can only result in the award of damages and not in the annulment of the EU measure that breached the applicant's human rights.

Examples of human rights claims against the EU that succeeded, at least in part, despite these obstacles include Joined Cases C-402/05 P and C-415/05 P *Kadi and Al Barakaat International Foundation v Council and Commission* [2008] ECR I-6351 and Case T-228/02 *Organisation des Modjahedines du peuple d'Iran v Council* [2006] ECR II-4665. In these cases, the Court of Justice and the General Court, respectively, ruled that a number of EU Regulations should be annulled for breach of human rights, including the right to a fair hearing, the obligation to state reasons, the right to effective judicial protection, and the right to respect for property, even though those Regulations had been designed to give effect to UN resolutions freezing the assets of suspected terrorists and terrorist organizations. However, the claim for damages in *Organisation des Modjahedines* was dismissed as inadmissible.

A further problem with bringing a claim against the EU in the EU Courts arises where the alleged breach of human rights arises not from EU secondary legislation, but from a Treaty, because Treaties are not subject to review, either under Article 263 TFEU (see further Chapter 7) or under Article 267 TFEU (see further Chapter 6). A limited solution exists in the form of a claim against the EU Member States (but not the EU itself) before the ECtHR, which has been prepared to hold Member States liable for breaches of the ECHR that are caused by their compliance with their EU Treaty obligations (see eg *Matthews v United Kingdom* Application No 24833/94 (1999) 28 EHRR 361, discussed at 9.5.2). The EU is not a party to the ECHR (see 9.1) and therefore cannot be held liable under it, but the planned accession by the EU to the ECHR (see 9.6) would permit the ECtHR to hear claims brought against the EU itself directly, including those resulting from provisions of the EU Treaties.

EU law (but again not the EU itself) may also be challenged, although only indirectly, in the national courts, either by challenging national law that implements EU law or, where a claim has been brought against an individual on the basis of EU law or national law that implements that EU law, by the individual then asserting by way of defence that the EU law infringes their human rights. For example, in Joined Cases C-92 & 93/09 *Volker und Markus Schecke GbR v and Hartmut Eifert Land Hessen* [2010] ECR I-11063 (see also 9.5.3), the Court of Justice upheld claims by applicants who had challenged in their national courts the implementation by the German authorities of EU Regulations requiring publication of the details of beneficiaries of certain agricultural funds and the amounts received by them, on the grounds that this breached their rights to respect for their private life (Article 7 of the Charter of Fundamental Rights of the EU) and protection of their personal data (Article 8 of the Charter).

However, there are also a number of difficulties with attempting to use EU law in the national courts. First, as Advocate General Jacobs in Case C-50/00 *UPA v Council* [2002] ECR I-6677 (see 2.4.1 on Advocate General's Opinions) and the General Court in Case T-177/01 *Jégo-Quéré et Cie SA v Commission* [2002] 2 CMLR 44 (see 6.6 and 7.9.1) noted, an individual should not be required to breach the law in order to gain access to justice where there are no domestic implementing measures for them to challenge. Secondly, EU acts can only be annulled by the Court of Justice and not by national courts (Case 314/86 *Foto-Frost v Hauptzollamt Lübeck-Ost* [1987] ECR 4199—see 6.6), and an applicant before a national court has no right to decide whether a reference from that court to the Court of Justice should be made, which EU measures are referred, and on what grounds their legality is questioned (see further Chapter 6 on the preliminary reference procedure). Finally, an action in the national courts with a reference to the Court of Justice during the course of the proceedings is likely to take much longer than a direct challenge in the EU Courts.

Of course, these difficulties apply to the enforcement of all EU rights, not only human rights, but, given the fundamental importance of human rights, such difficulties could have a particularly serious impact on potential applicants.

9.5.2 Actions for enforcement against Member States

9.5.2.1 The procedure

If a Member State has acted within the scope of EU law (see further 9.4.3), a claim by a victim against that Member State for a violation of EU human rights law must initially be brought before its national courts. Such proceedings are governed by national rules on the judicial review of government action, which may themselves impose restrictions on the bringing of an action. However, once an action is brought, the supremacy of EU law (see 3.1), the doctrines of direct and indirect effect, and the rules on the remedies available for breach of EU law (see further Chapter 4) may all support the enforcement of the victim's rights before the national court. The EU Commission (see 2.3) may also take enforcement proceedings against the Member State under Article 258 TFEU for its breach of EU law (see 2.3.2 and 7.1). In relation to Article 258 TFEU, it should be noted that although Article 35(2) ECHR prevents the ECtHR from hearing a case that 'has already been submitted to another procedure of international investigation or settlement', the ECtHR has held that the investigation of an individual complaint by the EU Commission under Article 258 TFEU does not constitute such a procedure (*Karoussiotis v Portugal* Application No 23205/08, ECtHR, 1 February 2011, unreported). An applicant who has submitted a complaint to the EU Commission may therefore still have their case heard by the ECtHR.

If a Member State has acted beyond the scope of EU law, an applicant may still be able to bring a claim against it under the ECHR. Again, the claim must initially be pursued in the national courts because Article 35(1) ECHR only permits a case to be brought before the ECtHR if the applicant has exhausted their domestic remedies in the national courts (see 9.1). However, s 3(1) of the HRA 1998 allows UK courts hearing a claim based on the ECHR to interpret national law compatibly with the ECHR only if it is possible for them to do so. If a UK court considers that this is not possible, the only alternative under the HRA 1998 is for it to make a declaration that national law is incompatible with the ECHR (s 4 of the HRA 1998) and it is then for the UK Parliament to amend or repeal the legislation if it chooses to do so. The enforcement mechanisms at national level in the UK are thus weaker in relation to the ECHR than in relation to EU law. An example of the contrast is provided by *Benkharbouche v Embassy of the Republic of Sudan* [2017] UKSC 62, in which members of staff at foreign embassies in London sought to bring various employment claims, and argued that the application of State immunity infringed their rights to a fair trial under both Article 6 ECHR and Article 47 of the EU Charter. The UK's Supreme Court held that it was not possible to interpret the State Immunity Act 1978 compatibly with the ECHR and therefore, under the HRA 1998, it was not possible to enforce the claimants' ECHR rights. In contrast, the claimants could rely directly upon their EU law rights and therefore national legislation that conflicted with those rights, such as the 1978 Act, had to be disapplied (see further Chapter 4).

At international level, however, it might be argued that the positions are reversed, since it is easier to bring a claim before the ECtHR than before the EU Courts.

Although both types of claim must be commenced initially in the national courts, if the case is to be pursued beyond those courts, it will be necessary to determine which law (EU law or the ECHR) applies and thus whether the appropriate court for further action is the Court of Justice in Luxembourg (EU law) or the ECtHR in Strasbourg (the ECHR). Such cases could also prove problematic for the UK courts, since while s 2(1)(a) of the HRA 1998 requires them to take account of the jurisprudence of the ECtHR when interpreting national law, they remain bound by the doctrine of supremacy (see 3.1) to uphold EU law in the event that such national law is inconsistent with it (Case 6/64 *Costa v ENEL* [1964] ECR 585 and Case 106/77 *Administrazione delle Finanze dello Stato v Simmenthal SpA* [1978] ECR 629; see further 3.1.2 on the judgments in both these cases).

9.5.2.2 The possibility of actions in the EU Courts

It is not possible for a victim to bring a claim against an EU Member State directly in either the Court of Justice or the General Court (see further 2.4 on these courts). It is possible for a victim to bring a claim in the national courts and, in the course of these proceedings, to request that a preliminary reference be made by the national court to the Court of Justice (see further Chapter 6), but there are a significant number of obstacles to this, as discussed at 9.5.1.

In contrast, victims have direct access to the ECtHR.

9.5.2.3 The possibility of actions in the ECtHR

A victim who considers that a Member State has breached the ECHR when acting within the scope of EU law may bring a claim against that Member State in the ECtHR, providing that the claimant has exhausted their domestic remedies in the national courts (see 9.1).

The ECtHR has been prepared to examine such claims on the basis that the transfer of powers to an international organization such as the EU is compatible with the obligations of a State Party to the ECHR only if fundamental rights continue to be protected (see eg *Matthews v United Kingdom* Application No 24833/94 (1999) 28 EHRR 361, at para 32, and *Bosphorus v Ireland* Application No 45036/98 (2006) 42 EHRR 1, at para 55).

In one of its earliest judgments on this point, *Cantoni v France* Application No 17862/91, ECtHR, 11 November 1996, unreported, the ECtHR ruled that the fact that a national measure was adopted in order to comply with an EU Directive, and indeed replicated that Directive almost exactly, did not affect the State's obligation to ensure that the measure complied with the ECHR (although it found no breach on the facts). However, in its landmark ruling in *Matthews v United Kingdom*, it held the UK liable for its breach of its obligations under Protocol 1 to the ECHR to hold free elections. Gibraltar had been excluded from direct elections to the European Parliament (see 2.1.1) pursuant to an EU Act of 1976 annexed to an EU Decision, a measure that was equivalent to a Treaty.

?! THINKING POINT

While reading the following extract, consider why the ECtHR was prepared to hold the UK liable for breaches of the ECHR caused by its compliance with its EU Treaty obligations.

Matthews v United Kingdom Application No 24833/94 (1999) 28 EHRR 361

34. In the present case, the alleged violation of the Convention flows from an annex to the 1976 Act, entered into by the United Kingdom, together with the extension to the European Parliament's competences brought about by the Maastricht Treaty. The Council Decision and the 1976 Act, and the Maastricht Treaty, with its changes to the EEC Treaty, all constituted international instruments which were freely entered into by the United Kingdom. Indeed, the 1976 Act cannot be challenged before the European Court of Justice for the very reason that it is not a 'normal' act of the Community [now Union], but is a treaty within the Community legal order. The Maastricht Treaty, too, is not an act of the Community, but a treaty by which a revision of the EEC Treaty was brought about. The United Kingdom, together with all the other parties to the Maastricht Treaty, is responsible *ratione materiae* under Article 1 of the Convention and, in particular, under Article 3 of Protocol No. 1, for the consequences of that Treaty.
35. In determining to what extent the United Kingdom is responsible for 'securing' the rights in Article 3 of Protocol No. 1 in respect of elections to the European Parliament in Gibraltar, the Court recalls that the Convention is intended to guarantee rights that are not theoretical or illusory, but practical and effective. It is uncontested that legislation emanating

from the legislative process of the European Community affects the population of Gibraltar in the same way as legislation which enters the domestic legal order exclusively via the House of Assembly. To this extent, there is no difference between European and domestic legislation, and no reason why the United Kingdom should not be required to 'secure' the rights in Article 3 of Protocol No. 1 in respect of European legislation, in the same way as those rights are required to be 'secured' in respect of purely domestic legislation. In particular, the suggestion that the United Kingdom may not have effective control over the state of affairs complained of cannot affect the position, as the United Kingdom's responsibility derives from its having entered into treaty commitments subsequent to the applicability of Article 3 of Protocol No. 1 to Gibraltar, namely the Maastricht Treaty taken together with its obligations under the Council Decision and the 1976 Act. Further, the Court notes that on acceding to the E.C. Treaty, the United Kingdom chose, by virtue of Article 227(4) of the Treaty, to have substantial areas of E.C. legislation applied to Gibraltar.

https://hudoc.echr.coe.int/eng#{%22itemid%22:[%22001-58910%22]}

In *Matthews*, the ECtHR held that since the provisions of an EU Treaty could not be challenged before the Court of Justice (see 9.5.1), the Member States remained responsible for any breaches of human rights that resulted from those Treaty provisions.

In *Bosphorus*, the ECtHR argued that the position in relation to the ECHR would be different where EU law left no discretion to Member States, so that a Member State was doing no more than implementing the legal obligations that flowed from its EU membership. In that case, the applicant company had leased two aircraft from the national airline of the former Yugoslavia. Pursuant to United Nations (UN) sanctions against the Federal Republic of Yugoslavia (Serbia and Montenegro) (the FYR) designed to address the armed conflict and human rights violations taking place in the FYR, the UN Security Council adopted a resolution that States should impound aircraft whose owners operated from the FYR, and Ireland impounded one of the applicant's aircraft when it landed in Dublin. The applicant argued that this was a breach of its right to peacefully enjoy its possessions and its freedom to pursue a commercial activity, and it brought judicial review proceedings in the Irish courts, which made a preliminary reference to the Court of Justice (see further Chapter 6 on the preliminary reference procedure). The Court of Justice held that these rights were not absolute, and that their infringement here was justified by the aim of restoring peace and security. The applicant then brought a claim before the ECtHR.

?! THINKING POINT

While reading the following extract, consider how the ECtHR reconciled the obligations of States Parties under the ECHR with their freedom to transfer their powers to international organizations such as the EU.

Bosphorus v Ireland Application No 45036/98 [2005] ECHR 440

152. The Convention does not, on the one hand, prohibit Contracting Parties from transferring sovereign power to an international (including a supranational) organisation in order to pursue cooperation in certain fields of activity (see *M. & Co.*, p. 144, and *Matthews*, § 32, both cited above). Moreover, even as the holder of such transferred sovereign power, that organisation is not itself held responsible under the Convention for proceedings before, or decisions of, its organs as long as it is not a Contracting Party (see *Confédération française démocratique du travail v. European Communities*, no. 8030/77, Commission decision of 10 July 1978, DR 13, p. 231; *Dufay v. European Communities*, no. 13539/88, Commission decision of 19 January 1989, unreported; and *M. & Co.*, p. 144, and *Matthews*, § 32, both cited above).

153. On the other hand, it has also been accepted that a Contracting Party is responsible under Article 1 of the Convention for all acts and omissions of its organs regardless of whether the act or omission in question was a consequence of domestic law or of the necessity to comply with international legal obligations. Article 1 makes no distinction as to the type of rule or measure concerned and does not exclude any part of a Contracting Party's 'jurisdiction' from scrutiny under the Convention (see *United Communist Party of Turkey and Others v. Turkey*, judgment of 30 January 1998, *Reports* 1998-I, pp. 17–18, § 29).

154. In reconciling both these positions and thereby establishing the extent to which a State's action can be justified by its compliance with obligations flowing from its membership of an international organisation to which it has transferred part of its sovereignty, the Court has recognised that absolving Contracting States completely from their Convention responsibility in the areas covered by such a transfer would be incompatible with the purpose and object of the Convention; the guarantees of the Convention could be limited or excluded at will, thereby depriving it of its peremptory character and undermining the practical and effective nature of its safeguards (see *M. & Co.*, p. 145, and *Waite and Kennedy*, § 67, both cited above). The State is considered to retain Convention liability in respect of treaty commitments subsequent to the entry into force of the Convention (see *mutatis mutandis*, *Matthews*, cited above, §§ 29 and 32–34, and *Prince Hans-Adam II of Liechtenstein v. Germany* [GC], no. 42527/98, § 47, ECHR 2001-VIII).

155. In the Court's view, State action taken in compliance with such legal obligations is justified as long as the relevant organisation is considered to protect fundamental rights, as regards both the substantive guarantees offered and the mechanisms controlling their observance, in a manner which can be considered at least equivalent to that for which the Convention provides (see *M. & Co.*, cited above, p. 145, an approach with which the parties and the European Commission agreed). By 'equivalent' the Court means 'comparable'; any requirement that the organisation's protection be 'identical' could run counter to the interest of international cooperation pursued ... However, any such finding of equivalence could not be final and would be susceptible to review in the light of any relevant change in fundamental rights protection.

156. If such equivalent protection is considered to be provided by the organisation, the presumption will be that a State has not departed from the requirements of the Convention when it does no more than implement legal obligations flowing from its membership of the organisation.

However, any such presumption can be rebutted if, in the circumstances of a particular case, it is considered that the protection of Convention rights was manifestly deficient. In such cases, the interest of international cooperation would be outweighed by the Convention's role as a 'constitutional instrument of European public order' in the field of human rights (see *Loizidou v. Turkey* (preliminary objections), judgment of 23 March 1995, Series A no. 310, pp. 27–28, § 75).

157. It remains the case that a State would be fully responsible under the Convention for all acts falling outside its strict international legal obligations …

https://hudoc.echr.coe.int/eng#{%22itemid%22:[%22001-69564%22]}

The ECtHR in *Bosphorus* held that so long as EU law provided protection of human rights that was equivalent to the ECHR, it would presume action by an EU Member State to be in compliance with that State's obligations under the ECHR if it was doing no more than implementing its legal obligations as a member of the EU. The Court then went on to examine whether EU law did provide such protection.

?! **THINKING POINT**

While reading the following extract, consider why the ECtHR held that EU law did provide protection equivalent to the ECHR. Do you agree with the Court?

Bosphorus v Ireland Application No 45036/98 [2005] ECHR 440

(b) Whether there was a presumption of Convention compliance at the relevant time

159. The Court has described above (see paragraphs 73–81) the fundamental rights guarantees of the European Community [now Union] which apply to member States, Community institutions and natural and legal persons ('individuals'). While the founding treaties of the European Communities did not initially contain express provisions for the protection of fundamental rights, the ECJ subsequently recognised that such rights were enshrined in the general principles of Community law [now EU law] protected by it, and that the Convention had a 'special significance' as a source of such rights. Respect for fundamental rights has become 'a condition of the legality of Community acts' (see paragraphs 73–75 above, together with the opinion of the Advocate General in the present case,

paragraphs 45–50 above) and in carrying out this assessment the ECJ refers extensively to Convention provisions and to this Court's jurisprudence. At the relevant time, these jurisprudential developments had been reflected in certain treaty amendments (notably those aspects of the Single European Act of 1986 and of the Treaty on European Union referred to in paragraphs 77–78 above).

This evolution has continued. The Treaty of Amsterdam of 1997 is referred to in paragraph 79 above. Although not fully binding, the provisions of the Charter of Fundamental Rights of the European Union were substantially inspired by those of the Convention, and the Charter recognises the Convention as establishing the minimum human rights standards. Article I-9 of the later Treaty establishing a Constitution for Europe (not in force) provides for the Charter to become primary law of the European Union and for the Union to accede to the Convention (see paragraphs 80–81 above).

160. However, the effectiveness of such substantive guarantees of fundamental rights depends on the mechanisms of control in place to ensure their observance.

161. The Court has referred (see paragraphs 86–90 above) to the jurisdiction of the ECJ in, inter alia, annulment actions (Article 173, now Article 230, of the EC Treaty [now Article 263 TFEU]), in actions against Community institutions for failure to perform Treaty obligations (Article 175, now Article 232 [now Article 265 TFEU]), to hear related pleas of illegality under Article 184 (now Article 241 [now Article 277 TFEU]) and in cases against member States for failure to fulfil Treaty obligations (Articles 169, 170, and 171, now Articles 226, 227, and 228 [now Articles 258–260 TFEU]).

162. It is true that access of individuals to the ECJ under these provisions is limited: they have no locus standi under Articles 169 and 170; their right to initiate actions under Articles 173 and 175 is restricted as is, consequently, their right under Article 184; and they have no right to bring an action against another individual.

163. It nevertheless remains the case that actions initiated before the ECJ by the Community institutions or a member State constitute important control of compliance with Community norms to the indirect benefit of individuals. Individuals can also bring an action for damages before the ECJ in respect of the non-contractual liability of the institutions (see paragraph 88 above).

164. Moreover, it is essentially through the national courts that the Community system provides a remedy to individuals against a member State or another individual for a breach of Community law (see paragraphs 85 and 91 above). Certain EC Treaty provisions envisaged a complementary role for the national courts in the Community control mechanisms from the outset, notably Article 189 (the notion of direct applicability, now Article 249 [now Article 288 TFEU]) and Article 177 (the preliminary reference procedure, now Article 234 [now Article 267 TFEU]). It was the development by the ECJ of important notions such as the supremacy of Community law, direct effect, indirect effect and State liability (see paragraphs 92–95 above) which greatly enlarged the role of the domestic courts in the enforcement of Community law and its fundamental rights guarantees.

The ECJ maintains its control on the application by national courts of Community law, including its fundamental rights guarantees, through the procedure for which Article 177 of the EC Treaty provides in the manner described in paragraphs 96 to 99 above. While the ECJ's role is limited to replying to the interpretative or validity question referred by the domestic court, the reply will often be determinative of the domestic proceedings (as, indeed, it was in the present case—see paragraph 147 above) and detailed guidelines on the timing and content of a preliminary reference have been laid down by the EC Treaty provision and developed by the ECJ in its case-law. The parties to the domestic proceedings have the right to put their case to the ECJ during the Article 177 process. It is further noted that national courts operate in legal systems into which the Convention has been incorporated, albeit to differing degrees.

165. In such circumstances, the Court finds that the protection of fundamental rights by Community law can be considered to be, and to have been at the relevant time, 'equivalent' (within the meaning of paragraph 155 above) to that of the Convention system. Consequently, the presumption arises that Ireland did not depart from the requirements of the Convention when it implemented legal obligations flowing from its membership of the European Community (see paragraph 156 above).

https://hudoc.echr.coe.int/eng#{%22itemid%22:[%22001-69564%22]}

The ECtHR in *Bosphorus* examined the EU legal system in detail, including the approach of the Court of Justice to human rights, the EU Charter (see 9.4), and the various actions available against Member States under the TFEU. It concluded that EU law did indeed offer protection of human rights that was equivalent to that of the ECHR. It was therefore to be presumed that Ireland had complied with the ECHR and this presumption had not been rebutted on the facts.

In contrast, the ECtHR did not apply the presumption of equivalent protection in *MSS v Belgium and Greece* Application No 20696/09 (2011) 53 EHRR 2. In that case, the applicant asylum seeker had entered the EU illegally through Greece, but claimed asylum in Belgium. Under the Dublin Regulation (see 9.4.2), Greece was responsible for dealing with his application for asylum and Belgium accordingly transferred him to Greece.

THINKING POINT

While reading the following extract, consider why the ECtHR did not apply the presumption of equivalent protection in this case.

MSS v Belgium and Greece Application No 30696/09 [2011] ECHR 108

338. The Court notes the reference to the *Bosphorus* judgment by the Government of the Netherlands in their observations lodged as third-party interveners …

The Court reiterated in that case that the Convention did not prevent the Contracting Parties from transferring sovereign powers to an international organisation for the purposes of cooperation in certain fields of activity (see *Bosphorus*, cited above, § 152). The States nevertheless remain responsible under the Convention for all actions and omissions of their bodies under their domestic law or under their international legal obligations (*ibid.*, § 153). State action taken in compliance with such legal obligations is justified as long as the relevant organisation is considered to protect fundamental rights in a manner which can be considered at least equivalent to that for which the Convention provides. However, a State would be fully responsible under the Convention for all acts falling outside its strict international legal obligations, notably where it exercised State discretion (*ibid.*, §§ 155–57).

The Court found that the protection of fundamental rights afforded by Community law was equivalent to that provided by the Convention system (*ibid.*, § 165). In reaching that conclusion it attached great importance to the role and powers of the ECJ—now the CJEU—in the matter, considering in practice that the effectiveness of the substantive guarantees of fundamental rights depended on the mechanisms of control set in place to ensure their observance (*ibid.*, § 160) …

339. The Court notes that Article 3 § 2 of the Dublin Regulation provides that, by derogation from the general rule set forth in Article 3 § 1, each Member State may examine an application for asylum lodged with it by a third-country national, even if such examination is not its responsibility under the criteria laid down in the Regulation. This is the so-called 'sovereignty' clause. In such a case the State concerned becomes the Member State responsible for the purposes of the Regulation and takes on the obligations associated with that responsibility.

340. The Court concludes that, under the Regulation, the Belgian authorities could have refrained from transferring the applicant if they had considered that the receiving country, namely Greece, was not fulfilling its obligations under the Convention. Consequently, the Court considers that the impugned measure taken by the Belgian authorities did not strictly fall within Belgium's international legal obligations. Accordingly, the presumption of equivalent protection does not apply in this case.

https://hudoc.echr.coe.int/eng#{%22itemid%22:[%22001-103050%22]}

The ECtHR in *MSS* noted that the Dublin Regulation (see further 9.4.2) allowed a Member State the discretion to examine an asylum claim even if it was not the responsible State and so Belgium could have refrained from transferring the applicant, and examined his asylum claim itself, if it considered that Greece was not complying with the ECHR. The transfer therefore did not fall strictly within Belgium's international obligations and so the presumption that protection of fundamental rights in EU law was equivalent to the ECHR was not applicable.

On the facts, the Court of Justice held that the applicant's treatment in Greece constituted inhuman treatment contrary to Article 3 ECHR. The behaviour of Belgium in exposing him to the risk of such ill-treatment also breached Article 3, since numerous reports on the deficiencies of the Greek asylum system were available to the Belgian authorities and the UN had directly requested them to suspend transfers to Greece.

The ECtHR also declined to apply the presumption of equivalent protection in *Michaud v France* Application No 47848/08 (2014) 59 EHRR 9, in response to a claim that EU Directives on money laundering breached Article 8 ECHR on the protection of correspondence. It held that the two conditions laid down in *Bosphorus* for the application of the presumption—the absence of any margin of manoeuvre on the part of the domestic authorities and the deployment of the full potential of the supervisory mechanism provided by EU law—were not satisfied. First, *Michaud* involved the implementation of Directives, over which the French authorities had a degree of discretion. Secondly, the control mechanism under EU law was not fully utilized; the French courts themselves had not examined the ECHR rights at issue and had not made a reference to the Court of Justice even though that Court had not yet had an opportunity to consider the particular question in the context of any previous case.

In contrast, in *Povse v Austria* Application No 3890/11 [2014] 1 FLR 944, the ECtHR held that the presumption of equivalent protection was applicable on the facts of the case because the Austrian courts, which had enforced an Italian court order for the return of a child to Italy where her father was living, pursuant to Council Regulation (EC) No 2201/2003 of 27 November 2003 concerning jurisdiction and the recognition and enforcement of judgments in matrimonial matters and the matters of parental responsibility … , OJ 2003 L338/1, had no discretion under the Regulation to refuse to enforce the Italian court order. Austria was therefore doing no more than fulfilling the strict obligations flowing from its membership of the EU. The Court concluded that, on the facts, the presumption of equivalent protection, and thus the presumption of ECHR compatibility, had not been rebutted. Indeed, it noted that the Court of Justice, which had given a preliminary ruling in the same matter (in C-211/10 PPU *Povse v Alpago* [2010] ECR I-6673, discussed at 6.11.5), had made it clear that, under the Regulation, it was for the Italian courts to protect the rights of the parties. In *Avotiņs v Latvia* Application No 150207/07, ECtHR, 23 May 2016, unreported, the ECtHR noted that the Latvian court had no margin of manoeuvre in giving effect to rights in Council Regulation (EC) No 44/2001 of 22 December 2000 on jurisdiction and the recognition and enforcement of judgments in civil and commercial matters (the 'Brussels I Regulation'), OJ 2001 L12/1, which was directly applicable, and the relevant provisions of which were precise and had been subject to extensive examination by the Court of Justice. Although the Latvian court had not made a preliminary reference, this was not essential where no genuine and serious issue arose with regard to the protection of fundamental rights by EU law or where the Court of Justice had already stated precisely how the applicable provisions of EU law should be interpreted in a manner compatible with fundamental rights. On the facts, the applicant had not advanced any argument as to the interpretation of the Regulation and its compatibility with fundamental rights, and had not requested a reference, and the Court of Justice had developed a considerable body of case law on the relevant provisions of the Regulation.

If a preliminary reference is made by a national court to the Court of Justice in the course of national proceedings (see further Chapter 6 on the preliminary reference procedure), then the reference procedure will form part of the Member State's actions, for which it can be held liable before the ECtHR. In *Cooperatieve Producentenorganisatie van de Nederlandse Kokkelvisserij UA v Netherlands* Application No 13645/05 (2009) 48 EHRR SE18, the ECtHR held that the presumption of equivalent protection applied not only to actions taken by a State Party in compliance with legal obligations flowing from its membership of an international organization, but also to the procedures followed within such an international organization and hence to the preliminary reference procedure.

9.5.3 Actions for enforcement against individuals or businesses

Although human rights are often thought of as primarily protecting individuals and businesses against the State—and, in the EU context, against the EU institutions—they can be infringed by other individuals or businesses, against whom claims can therefore be brought in the domestic courts. One of the leading examples in recent years is the so-called right to be forgotten, which has been most famously enforced not against a State or the EU, but against a business. The Court of Justice had previously held, in Joined Cases C-92/09 and C-93/09 *Volker und Markus Schecke GbR and Hartmut Eifert v Land Hessen v Bundesanstalt für Landwirtschaft und Ernährung* [2010] ECR I-11063 (discussed at 9.5.1), that although the rights to respect for private life and protection of personal data under Articles 7 and 8 of the Charter—in that case, to prevent disclosure of the amount of EU funds that the claimants had received—were not absolute rights and could be restricted in the interests of, inter alia, making the EU's actions transparent, such limitations could apply only insofar as was strictly necessary. In C-131/12 *Google Inc v Agencia Espanola de Proteccion de Datos, Mario Consteja González* EU:C:2014:317, the Court upheld the claimant's rights under Articles 7 and 8 of the Chapter against an Internet search engine operator, by interpreting Directive 95/46/EC of the European Parliament and of the Council of 24 October 1995 on the protection of individuals with regard to the processing of personal data and on the free movement of such data, OJ 1995 L281/31—now replaced by the General Data Protection Regulation (GDPR Regulation), Regulation (EU) 2016/679 of the European Parliament and of the Council of 27 April 2016 on the protection of natural persons with regard to the processing of personal data and on the free movement of such data … , OJ 2016 L119/1—as requiring it to remove data at the request of the data subject. The Court emphasized that, as a general rule, the rights in Articles 7 and 8 overrode the economic interest of the search engine operator and the interest of the general public in having access to that information unless there were 'particular reasons, such as the role played by the data subject in public life' (*Google Inc*, at para 97), which meant that the interference with the data subject's fundamental rights under Articles 7 and 8 was justified by the public interest in having access to that information. (Regulation 17 of the GDPR Regulation now expressly provides for 'the right to be forgotten', subject to restrictions that are 'necessary' in order to exercise the freedom of expression, comply with EU or Member State law, or exercise legal claims, or for public health reasons, archiving purposes in the public interest, scientific or historical research purposes or statistical purposes.)

9.6 Accession to the ECHR

The possibility of EU accession to the ECHR has been the subject of debate for several decades. However, in its *Opinion 2/94 pursuant to Article 228(6) of the EC Treaty* [1996] ECR I-1759, the Court of Justice ruled that the European Community (now the EU—see Chapter 1, Introduction) lacked competence to accede to the ECHR.

?! THINKING POINT

While reading the following extract, consider why the Court of Justice reached the conclusion that the EU lacked competence to accede to the ECHR.

Opinion 2/94 pursuant to Article 228(6) of the EC Treaty [1996] ECR I-1759

32. It should first be noted that the importance of respect for human rights has been emphasized in various declarations of the Member States and of the Community institutions (cited in point III.5 of the first part of this Opinion). Reference is also made to respect for human rights in the preamble to the Single European Act and in the preamble to, and in Article F(2), the fifth indent of Article J.1(2) and Article K.2(1) of, the Treaty on European Union. Article F provides that the Union is to respect fundamental rights, as guaranteed, in particular, by the Convention. Article 130u(2) of the EU Treaty provides that Community policy in the area of development cooperation is to contribute to the objective of respecting human rights and fundamental freedoms.
33. Furthermore, it is well settled that fundamental rights form an integral part of the general principles of law whose observance the Court ensures. For that purpose, the Court draws inspiration from the constitutional traditions common to the Member States and from the guidelines supplied by international treaties for the protection of human rights on which the Member States have collaborated or of which they are signatories. In that regard, the Court has stated that the Convention has special significance (see, in particular, the judgment in Case C-260/89 *ERT* [1991] ECR I-2925, paragraph 41).
34. Respect for human rights is therefore a condition of the lawfulness of Community acts. Accession to the Convention would, however, entail a substantial change in the present Community system for the protection of human rights in that it would entail the entry of the Community into a distinct international institutional system as well as integration of all the provisions of the Convention into the Community legal order.
35. Such a modification of the system for the protection of human rights in the Community, with equally fundamental institutional implications for the Community and for the Member States, would be of constitutional significance and would therefore be such as to go beyond the scope of Article 235. It could be brought about only by way of Treaty amendment.
36. It must therefore be held that, as Community law [now EU law] now stands, the Community has no competence to accede to the Convention.

The Court of Justice concluded that the EU's accession to the ECHR would be of constitutional significance and thus exceed the powers granted to the EU by the Member States.

However, with the introduction of the EU Charter (see 9.4), the President of the ECtHR, endorsed both by the Committee of Ministers of the Council of Europe (see 9.1) and its Parliamentary Assembly, warned that 'the Court's main concern … is to avoid a situation in which there are alternative, competing and potentially conflicting systems of human rights protection both within the Union and in the greater Europe. The duplication of protection systems runs the risk of weakening the overall protection offered and undermining legal certainty in this field' (Reply from the Committee of Ministers to Parliamentary Assembly Recommendation 1439 (2000) on the Charter of Fundamental Rights of the European Union, Adopted at the 711th meeting of the Ministers' Deputies, 31 May 2000).

Thus, in 2009, the Treaty of Lisbon (see further 1.18) amended the TEU (see further 1.3) to provide the EU with the necessary competence to accede to the ECHR and, indeed, Article 6(2) TEU not only empowers, but actually obliges, the EU to do so.

Article 6(2) TEU

The Union shall accede to the European Convention for the Protection of Human Rights and Fundamental Freedoms. Such accession shall not affect the Union's competences as defined in the Treaties.

A draft Accession Agreement was concluded in 2013 on the details of EU accession to the ECHR, including the relationship between the EU Courts and the ECtHR.

The key provisions of the draft Accession Agreement included the following.

- The EU would be a State Party and, as such, may be the respondent to an application before the ECtHR brought either by a victim or another State Party and may itself bring a claim against another State Party.
- The ECtHR would include one judge from the EU, in addition to (as at present) a judge from each of the other States Parties.
- The terms 'national law' and 'domestic' in the ECHR are to be interpreted as applying equally to the internal legal order of the EU.
- Terms in the ECHR such as 'national security', 'economic well-being of the country', and 'life of the nation', in proceedings brought against the EU or to which the EU is a co-respondent, are to be interpreted as applying to Member States of the EU, individually or collectively.
- Article 15 ECHR, which permits States Parties to derogate from certain of the ECHR rights where there is a threat to 'the life of the nation', is to be interpreted as permitting the EU to take derogating measures in support of action taken by one of its Member States, which asserts the existence of such circumstances.
- The co-respondent procedure (see later) would be introduced (as Article 36(4) ECHR).
- The EU would not become a member of the Council of Europe, but it would be able to participate and vote in certain meetings of the Council of Europe's Committee of Ministers that relate to the ECHR and its Protocols.
- A delegation of the European Parliament would be able to participate and vote in sittings of the Parliamentary Assembly of the Council of Europe whenever it exercises its functions in relation to the election of judges to the ECtHR.

The reason for introducing the co-respondent procedure is that the accession of the EU to the ECHR gives rise to the possibility of a scenario in which the State Party to the ECHR which enacted the legal measures that resulted in a violation of the ECHR is not the same State Party which implemented the measure. This is because measures enacted by the EU may be implemented by Member States and EU Treaties agreed upon by the Member States may be implemented by EU institutions. In such situations, in the absence of the co-respondent procedure, the application could be dismissed as inadmissible because the particular respondent is responsible only for the legal basis of the act or omission that gave rise to the alleged violation and not for the act or omission itself.

The co-respondent procedure would be as follows.

- Where an application is brought in the ECtHR against one or more Member States of the EU, the EU may be joined as co-respondent if the compatibility of EU law with the ECHR is at issue.
- Where an application is brought in the ECtHR against the EU, its Member States may be joined as co-respondents if the compatibility of a provision of the TEU or the TFEU with the ECHR is at issue.
- Where an application is brought in the ECtHR against the EU and one or more of its Member States, the status of any respondent may be changed to that of a co-respondent if either of the two preceding conditions is satisfied.
- The co-respondent procedure may be invoked either if the ECtHR so decides after a request by the proposed co-respondent or if the proposed co-respondent accepts an invitation by the Court.
- The admissibility of the application, including the requirement of exhaustion of domestic remedies (see 9.1), is examined only in relation to the claim against the respondent, without regard to the co-respondent.
- If the EU is a co-respondent and the Court of Justice has not yet assessed the compatibility with the ECHR of the EU law at issue, for example because the case has progressed through the national courts without those courts making a preliminary reference to the Court of Justice under Article 267 TFEU (see further Chapter 6 on the preliminary reference procedure), 'sufficient' time must be allowed for the Court of Justice to make such an assessment and thereafter for the parties to make observations on its assessment to the ECtHR.
- If the ECtHR finds a violation, the respondent and the co-respondent will be jointly liable unless, on the basis of reasons given by them and having sought the applicant's views, the Court decides that only one of them is liable.

However, Article 218 TFEU provides that the opinion of the Court of Justice may be sought (by a Member State, the European Parliament, the Council, or the Commission) on the compatibility with the EU Treaties of an agreement between the EU and an international organization or a third country. The EU Commission (see 2.3) made just such a request in relation to the compatibility of the draft Accession Agreement, and the Court of Justice's *Opinion 2/13 pursuant to Article 218(11) TFEU* EU:C:2014:2454 was that the Agreement was not compatible with EU law. It gave the following reasons.

(1) The Agreement would be liable to adversely affect 'the specific characteristics of EU law and its autonomy'.

In this respect, the Court noted, first, that the Agreement failed to limit Article 53 ECHR, which gives States Parties to the ECHR power to lay down higher standards of protection than those given by the ECHR, whereas Article 53 of the Charter, as interpreted by the Court of Justice in Case C-399/11 *Melloni* [2013] 2 CMLR 43 (see 9.4.4), which provides similarly for Charter rights, was subject to an exception because EU Member States could not give more protection to fundamental rights than that permitted by EU legislation which itself respected Charter standards.

In fact, Article 53 ECHR only provides that the ECHR itself does not prevent higher domestic standards; if these are prevented by EU legislation, this does not conflict with Article 53 ECHR (so long as the minimum ECHR standards are met). Further, Article 52(3) of the Charter states that Charter rights corresponding to those of the ECHR should be applied in accordance with the ECHR, which means that EU Member States could not give less protection than the minimum provided by the ECHR.

The Court noted, secondly, that the Agreement failed to allow for the application of mutual trust between EU Member States, which is a fundamental principle of EU law, because the Agreement would enable an EU Member State to check compliance by another Member State with the ECHR.

Thirdly, the Court noted that the Agreement failed to ensure the compatibility of Protocol No 16 to the ECHR—which, if and when it comes into force (as it has not yet been ratified by a sufficient number of States Parties) will allow the highest national courts to request advisory opinions from the ECtHR—with the Court of Justice's preliminary reference procedure (see further Chapter 6 on this procedure).

In fact, Protocol 16 would not exempt national courts from their obligations under Article 267 TFEU and so there is no incompatibility.

(2) The Agreement would be liable to affect Article 344 TFEU, which states that Member States may not submit a dispute over the interpretation or application of the EU Treaties to any method of settlement other than those provided by those Treaties, and this would be contrary to Protocol No 8 EU, which states that the Accession Agreement must not affect Article 344 TFEU.

In fact, since Article 55 ECHR vests exclusive jurisdiction over ECHR disputes in the ECtHR, it was necessary for the Agreement to contain a derogation from this to provide that disputes between EU Member States about the ECHR could be brought before the Court of Justice. It therefore seems unnecessary to state that if such a dispute were taken to the ECtHR, this would be inadmissible.

(3) The co-respondent mechanism was contrary to the EU law.

First, the Court of Justice considered that it would require the ECtHR to ascertain whether a party should become a co-respondent and whether the presumption of joint responsibility for a violation should be departed from, both of which would be liable to interfere with the division of powers between the EU and its Member States.

In fact, the decision as to whether a party should become a co-respondent would not be a binding ruling as to the division of powers as a matter of EU law.

The EU Council (see further 2.3 on the Council) has now proposed an amendment to the Agreement, so that where an application to the ECtHR is made against one or more Member States or the EU, the Member State(s) or the EU will have an unconditional right to become co-respondent(s) to the proceedings and to be informed of any applications notified to the other (Presidency of the Council of the European Union, *Technical Written Contribution from the Commission Services*, EU Council Meeting Document DS 1216/15, 14 April 2015).

The Court considered, secondly, that the mechanism failed to preclude a Member State from being held liable jointly with the EU in relation to a provision of the ECHR in respect of which that Member State had entered a reservation under Article 57 ECHR.

In fact, reservations are rare and given that the issue would arise only where a Member State was a party to proceedings, that State could draw it to the attention of the ECtHR, which would presumably not then give a ruling finding that State jointly liable.

The EU Council has now proposed an amendment to the Agreement to exclude the ECtHR's (draft) power to depart from the rule of joint responsibility in co-respondent proceedings except where the co-respondent has entered a formal reservation to the relevant ECHR right under Article 57 ECHR (see EU Council Meeting Document DS 1216/15).

(4) The procedure set out in the Agreement to ensure the prior involvement of the Court of Justice would require the ECtHR to examine whether the Court of Justice had given a ruling on the same question of law, whereas that should properly be for the EU to assess; the Explanatory Report accompanying the Agreement suggested that the procedure could be invoked only in relation to the interpretation of the Treaties and the validity of secondary legislation, thus adversely affecting the Court of Justice's power to provide an interpretation of EU secondary legislation.

In fact, as to the former, the EU would already be involved in the proceedings, and thus able to conduct such an assessment and inform the ECtHR accordingly. As to the latter, this relates to the wording of the Explanatory Report, rather than the Accession Agreement, which does not itself limit the prior involvement procedure in this way.

The EU Council has now proposed an amendment to the Agreement, so that where the EU is a co-respondent, its right to initiate the prior involvement procedure is unlimited (see EU Council Meeting Document DS 1216/15). The Council also proposes to amend the Explanatory Report, so that it is clear that the procedure applies where the interpretation of EU secondary legislation is at issue, not only its validity.

(5) Under the Agreement, the ECtHR would exclusively be empowered to rule on the compatibility with the ECHR of certain EU acts performed within the context of the Common Foreign and Security Policy (CFSP) (see further 1.13, 1.15, 1.17, and 1.18), which the Court of Justice itself, because of restrictions imposed on its jurisdiction in this area by EU law (see further 6.1.2), could not review for compliance with human rights.

> In fact, giving the ECtHR power to review acts and omissions on the part of the EU is the whole point of EU accession to the ECHR. Insofar as the objection is that this Court would have exclusive review powers, the problem lies in the restricted nature of the Court of Justice's powers in this area—something that the EU might be well advised to rectify in order to give it the opportunity to address such matters before its own EU Courts first.

While some of these criticisms could be addressed relatively easily, others are more fundamental. The prospect of EU accession to the ECHR in the short-to-medium term has therefore seemingly receded, although the EU Commission (see further 2.2 on the Commission) has stated that it will 'pursue the work towards the accession of the EU to the [ECHR], taking full account of the Opinion of the Court of Justice' (Communication from the Commission to the European Parliament, the Council, the European Economic and Social Committee and the Committee of the Regions, *Commission Work Programme 2016: No Time for Business as Usual*, COM (2015) 610 final, 27 October 2015), and the EU Council and Commission are working on addressing the Court of Justice's criticisms.

If and when these criticisms are addressed, Article 218 TFEU provides that the EU Council must act unanimously on the agreement for accession to the ECHR. Adoption of an accession agreement by the EU and the Council of Europe would have the effect of amending the ECHR and including the EU as a Party to the ECHR (and to Protocols 1 and 6, Protocols which all EU Member States have also ratified, while EU accession to other ECHR Protocols, which not all Member States have ratified, would require separate accession instruments). Judgments of the ECtHR would become binding on the EU's institutions, including on the Court of Justice.

9.7 The possible impact of Brexit

When the UK leaves the EU (see further 1.19 and 3.1), EU human rights law will cease to apply to it except insofar as the European Union (Withdrawal) Act 2018 retains it as part of UK law (see further 1.19.1)—although, of course, the ECHR as explained at 9.1, will continue to apply.

Section 5(4) of the European Union (Withdrawal) Act 2018 (see further 1.19.1) explicitly excludes the Charter from those EU laws that the UK will retain after it leaves the EU.

European Union (Withdrawal) Act 2018, s 5(4)

The Charter of Fundamental Rights is not part of domestic law on or after exit day.

?! THINKING POINT

What disadvantages can you see arising from the removal of the EU Charter as a source of rights in the UK?

As explained, the Charter contains many rights that are not present in the ECHR, although admittedly they apply only against the EU and Member States when they are implementing EU law.

However, s 5(5) of the 2018 Act states that the disapplication of the Charter in s 5(4) is not intended to deprive retained EU law of any fundamental rights or principles that exist irrespective of the Charter.

European Union (Withdrawal) Act 2018, s 5(5)

Subsection (4) does not affect the retention in domestic law on or after exit day in accordance with this Act of any fundamental rights or principles which exist irrespective of the Charter (and references to the Charter in any case law are, so far as necessary for this purpose, to be read as if they were references to any corresponding retained fundamental rights or principles).

Unfortunately, it is not entirely clear which Charter rights also exist as general principles and it may be difficult to separate the two, given that they have developed symbiotically.

The question of the effect of Brexit on human rights protection in the UK was raised in Case C-327/18 PPU *Minister for Justice and Equality v RO* EU:C:2018:733. The Court of Justice held that the European arrest warrant (EAW) system continued to apply to the UK while it remained a Member State and that the UK's formal notification under Article 50 TFEU of its intention to leave had no effect on this and therefore could not justify Ireland refusing to surrender RO to the UK pursuant to two EAWs that the UK had issued against him. Nor could such a refusal be made on the basis that RO's rights under the EU Charter would no longer be protected after the UK ceased to be a Member State, since it would remain a party to the ECHR and the 1957 European Convention on Extradition, and therefore equivalent rights would continue to apply.

The question of the effect of Brexit on human rights protection was also raised in C-661/17 *MA, SA and AZ v International Protection Appeals Tribunal, Minister for Justice and Equality, Attorney General, Ireland* EU:C:2019:53 (see also 6.13). In that case, the Court of Justice held that the anticipated withdrawal of the UK from the EU did not mean that Ireland should exercise its discretion under the Dublin Regulation (see further 9.4.2) to examine an asylum claim that was not its responsibility, in circumstances in which the asylum seekers had first arrived in the EU in the UK, but had only sought asylum subsequently, in Ireland, and therefore would ordinarily be transferred back to the UK for a decision on their asylum status.

Regardless of the application or otherwise of human rights contained in the Charter or other parts of EU law, the ECHR will continue to apply to the UK as this is unrelated to EU law.

9.8 Conclusions

Although it is likely that most complaints of human rights violations will continue to be made against the national authorities via the ECHR, rather than against the EU or against the national authorities via EU law, it is also likely that the right of redress against EU institutions will become increasingly important to individuals and business based on trading in the EU, particularly as the EU expands its competences in areas such as asylum, immigration, and closer police and judicial cooperation (see *Report by Mr Leo Tindemans, Prime Minister of Belgium, to the European Council*, Bull EC Supp 1976/1, at 26–7).

However, while the range of rights protected under EU law looks impressive, their real value can be assessed only by reference to their enforceability. There are a number of unresolved questions over how the Charter will be interpreted, in particular its relationship to the ECHR as interpreted by the ECtHR, and its application to the Member States. It also remains to be seen when EU accession to the ECHR will occur, and how it will work in substantive and procedural terms.

SUMMARY

- The European Union (EU) is a different and entirely separate organization from the Council of Europe, which oversees the European Convention on Human Rights (ECHR).
- EU law, including the Charter of Fundamental Rights of the European Union, is a separate body of law from the ECHR.
- The key source of EU human rights is now the Charter, but this is supplemented by provisions of the EU Treaties, the jurisprudence of the Court of Justice, and secondary legislation.
- The Charter makes EU human rights transparent, but the impact of it becoming legally enforceable remains to be seen.
- The accession of the EU to the ECHR would make the ECHR enforceable against the EU and ensure that there are no gaps in the ECHR protection guaranteed by Member States, but the adverse Opinion given by the Court of Justice makes accession unlikely in the immediate future.

FURTHER READING

Articles

J Callawaert, 'The European Convention on Human Rights and European Union Law: A Long Way to Harmony' (2009) 6 EHRLR 768

Comments on the relationship between the jurisprudence of the European Court of Human Rights (ECtHR) and that of the Court of Justice.

M Cartabia, 'Europe and Rights: Taking Dialogue Seriously' (2009) 5(1) ECL Rev 5

Analyses the role of the Court of Justice in protecting human rights.

P de Albuquerque and H-S Lim, 'The Cross-fertilisation between the Court of Justice of the European Union and the European Court of Human Rights: Reframing the Discussion on Brexit' (2018) 6 EHRLR 567

Discusses the potential impact of Brexit on the relationship between the UK and the ECHR, particularly given the influence of the jurisprudence of the ECtHR on that of the Court of Justice.

G de Búrca, 'After the EU Charter of Fundamental Rights: The Court of Justice as a Human Rights Adjudicator?' (2013) 20 Maastricht Journal of European and Comparative Law 168

Evaluates the Court of Justice's approach when applying the Charter.

B de Witte and Š Imanović, 'Opinion 2/13 on accession to the ECHR: defending the EU legal order against a foreign human rights court' (2015) 40(5) EL Rev 683

Critiques the Court of Justice's ruling in Opinion 2/2013 that the proposed terms of the EU's accession to the ECHR are incompatible with EU law.

D Denman, 'The Charter of Fundamental Rights' (2010) 4 EHRLR 349

Discusses the terms of the Charter and Protocol No 30.

C Dupré, ' "Human dignity is inviolable. It must be respected and protected": retaining the EU Charter of Fundamental Rights after Brexit' (2018) 2 EHRLR 101

Explores the importance of the Charter and the implications of it no longer applying in the UK as a result of Brexit.

J Krommendijk, 'Principled Silence or Mere Silence on Principles? The Role of the EU Charter's Principles in the Caselaw of the Court of Justice' (2015) 11(2) ECLR 321

Discusses the distinction drawn by the EU Courts between rights and principles in the EU Charter.

T Lock, 'Human Rights Law in the UK after Brexit' (2017) PL Nov Supp (Brexit Special Extra Issue 2017) 117

Assesses the possible impact of Brexit on human rights protection in the UK, according to the terms of the UK's withdrawal from the EU and the possible future UK–EU relationship.

P Mahoney, 'From Strasbourg to Luxembourg and Back: Speculating about Human Rights Protection in the European Union after the Treaty of Lisbon' (2011) 31(2) HRLJ 73

Considers the impact of access on the relationship between the courts and legal systems of the EU and the ECHR.

N Mole, 'The Complex and Evolving Relationship between the European Charter and the European Convention on Human Rights' (2012) 4 EHRLR 363

Highlights key cases on the relationship between EU law and the ECHR.

S Vessel and N Peart, 'Will the fundamental rights enshrined in the EU Charter survive Brexit?' (2018) 2 EHRLR 134

Considers whether disapplication of the Charter in the UK post-Brexit is possible in the light of the requirements of international law and how the UK can retain the general principles of EU law without the Charter.

A Weiss, 'EU Accession to the European Convention on Human Rights Process: The State of Play and the Added Value for Victims of Human Rights Violations in Europe' (2012) 4 EHRLR 391

Considers the potential advantages of EU accession to the ECHR.

W Weiss, 'Human Rights in the EU: Rethinking the Role of the European Convention on Human Rights After Lisbon' (2011) 7(1) ECL Rev 64

Examines the relationship between the ECHR and the Charter.

Books

V Kosta, N Skoutaris , and VP Tzevelekos , *The EU Accession to the ECHR* (Oxford: Hart, 2014)

Examines a comprehensive range of issues arising from the accession of the EU to the ECHR, including the role of the Court of Justice and the co-respondent mechanism.

J Nergelius and E Kristoffersson (eds), *Human Rights in Contemporary European Law* (Oxford: Hart, 2014)

Contains chapters by different authors on a variety of current issues, including key recent cases, the EU's human rights strategy in a number of areas, and EU accession to the ECHR.

S Peers, T Hervey, J Kenner, and A Ward (eds), *The EU Charter of Fundamental Rights: A Commentary* (Oxford: Hart, 2014)

Examines in detail each provision of the EU Charter, including substantive rights and provisions governing its interpretation and application, Protocol No 30, and the draft Accession Agreement.

M Varju, *European Union Human Rights Law: The Dynamics of Interpretation and Context* (Cheltenham: Edward Elgar, 2014)

Provides a detailed analysis of various aspects of the jurisprudence on EU human rights law.

Book chapters

P Craig and G de Búrca, 'Human Rights in the EU', in *EU Law: Text, Cases, and Materials*, 5th edn (Oxford: Oxford University Press, 2011), ch 11

Provides detailed analysis of the history and current status of human rights protection in the EU.

S Douglas Scott, 'The Relationship between the EU and the ECHR Five Years on from the Treaty of Lisbon', in S de Vries, U Bernitz, and S Weatherill (eds), *The EU Charter of Fundamental Rights as a Binding Instrument: Five Years Old and Growing* (Oxford: Hart, 2013), ch 2

Contains a particularly useful analysis of the development of the relationship and interaction between EU law and the ECHR.

P Gragl, 'Of Tangled and Truthful Hierarchies: EU Accession to the ECHR and its Possible Impact on the UK's Relationship with European Human Rights', in KS Ziegler, E Wicks, and L Hodson (eds), *The UK and European Human Rights: A Strained Relationship?* (Oxford: Hart 2015), ch 14

Analyses the advantages and disadvantages of EU accession to the ECHR in the light of Opinion 2/13, with a particular focus on the UK perspective.

Reports

House of Commons, 'Effects of the EU Charter of Rights in the UK', Note, 17 March 2014

Summarizes the impact of Protocol No 30 in the light of the Court of Justice's ruling in *NS v UK*.

House of Commons and House of Lords Joint Committee on Human Rights, *The Human Rights Implications of Brexit*, Fifth Report of Session 2016–17, HL Paper 88/HC 695, 19 December 2016

Examines the impact of Brexit on human rights protection in the UK.

House of Commons European Scrutiny Committee, *The Application of the EU Charter of Fundamental Rights in the UK: A State of Confusion*, 43rd Report of Session 2013–14, HC 979, 2 April 2014; Ministry of Justice, *Government Response to the House of Commons European Scrutiny Committee Report*, Cm 8915, July 2014

Discusses different views on the application of the EU Charter in the UK.

QUESTION

Critically analyse the protection of human rights by the EU.

To view an outline answer to this question plus further resources to support your EU law studies, visit the Online Resources for this book at www.oup.com/uk/eulaw-complete4e

10 Free movement of goods

KEY POINTS

By the end of this chapter, you should be able to:

- understand the principle of free movement of goods in the context of the internal market;
- be familiar with the relevant provisions of the Treaty on the Functioning of the European Union (TFEU);
- distinguish between the various barriers to trade with reference to relevant Treaty provisions; and
- understand the applicability and scope of the exceptions.

INTRODUCTION

The principle of the free movement of goods has been and continues to be of fundamental importance to the establishment and maintenance of the EU internal market. In essence, the principle implies that any unnecessary trade barriers must be removed by Member States. The principle's status and importance as one of the four fundamental freedoms of the European Union (EU) is clearly set out in Article 26 TFEU.

Article 26 TFEU

1. The Union shall adopt measures with the aim of establishing or ensuring the functioning of the internal market, in accordance with the relevant provisions of the Treaties.
2. The internal market shall comprise an area without internal frontiers in which the free movement of goods, persons, services and capital is ensured in accordance with the provisions of the Treaties.

However, whilst many trade barriers resulting from regulatory differences between Member States have been removed by EU-wide harmonizing procedures and trading rules, there remain areas that are still governed by differing national rules. It is the principle of the free movement of goods and the legislation in place to give effect to it that help to ensure that such non-harmonized rules do not amount to trade barriers.

10.1 Development

The concept of a common market was at the very heart of the Treaty of Rome 1957 establishing the European Economic Community (EEC). It has been referred to in many ways since, from the 'common market' at the outset, moving through a mixture of the 'common market' and 'internal market' following the Single European Act 1986 (SEA), to now be known, following the Lisbon Treaty, solely as the 'internal market'. Despite this, the term 'single market' is often used in political discussions. All three terms are taken to mean the same thing in practice, although strictly speaking there are differences between them. The subtle nuances between the various terms are outside the scope of this text.

→ CROSS-REFERENCE
See 1.4.1 on economic integration.

Whichever term is used, it essentially relates to a specific stage of economic integration between Member States. 'Economic integration' refers simply to an arrangement by which countries agree to coordinate their trade and monetary policies. In practice, such integration occurs over a number of different stages and these are set out below.

10.1.1 Free trade area

A free trade area involves Member States agreeing to remove all customs duties and quotas between themselves. Thus goods can move freely between the Member States without limitations on quantity and without being subjected to further **pecuniary charges** that may make non-national goods uncompetitive.

pecuniary charges
Pecuniary charges are charges relating to the payment of money.

However, each Member State may impose its own quotas and customs duties as regards countries outside the free trade area. These countries are referred to as third countries. Of course, should a producer in a third country wish to penetrate the market within the free trade area, they will inevitably do so by introducing goods through the country with the lowest import duty or tariff.

10.1.2 Customs union

A customs union develops this further by introducing an agreement between the Member States to impose a common level of duty on goods from non-member countries. This common level of duty is known as a common customs tariff.

Article 28 TFEU

The union shall comprise a customs union which shall cover all trade in goods and ... the adoption of a common customs tariff in their relations with third countries.

Article 31 TFEU

Common Customs Tariff duties shall be fixed by the Council on a proposal from the Commission.

→ CROSS-REFERENCE
See 2.2 on the Council of the European Union.

10.1.3 Internal market

An internal market develops this further still by introducing a further agreement between the Member States to remove restrictions on the factors of production. This is referred to as the free movement of goods, persons, services, and capital. A common market also introduces a competition policy. (See 10.1 on terms other than 'internal market' and their use in the EU context.)

10.1.4 Economic and monetary union

Economic and monetary union (EMU) develops this further still by introducing unified monetary and fiscal policies. Amongst other things, it includes a single currency and common policies on interest rates.

?! THINKING POINT

Which stage has the EU reached?

It can be argued that the EU is currently somewhere between the stages of an internal market and EMU. However, it can further be argued that a true internal market has yet to be achieved and the cases we will go on to consider in this chapter are evidence that a number of obstacles remain in place.

It should be noted that EMU was not one of the founding aims of the original European Communities and was not formally introduced until the TEU (1992). It remains a contentious political issue, especially given the current economic climate and difficulties faced in the eurozone (especially Greece and Italy, amongst others) as a result of the global economic crisis. However, currently over half of the Member States have established an EMU, with a central bank (the European Central Bank, or ECB) and a single currency (the euro).

Key to an understanding of the rules, both legislative and derived from case law, governing the free movement of goods is an appreciation of the principle of non-discrimination. This fundamental principle is enshrined in Article 18 TFEU and pervades this topic.

Article 18 TFEU

Within the scope of application of the Treaties, and without prejudice to any special provisions contained therein, any discrimination on grounds of nationality shall be prohibited.

The European Parliament and the Council, acting in accordance with the ordinary legislative procedure, may adopt rules designed to prohibit such discrimination.

This principle, in the context of free movement of goods, seeks to ensure that goods crossing borders are free from discriminatory internal rules. Of course, such discrimination can be both direct and indirect in form, and whilst Article 18 TFEU applies to both, there is a difference in how each are treated. Where direct discrimination exists, it can be justified only under the Treaty-provided exceptions, and even then will be subject to scrutiny to ensure such a rule goes no further than is necessary to achieve its aim (proportionality) and is indeed necessary. This contrasts with indirect discrimination, which may also be justified by exceptions developed within the case law.

10.2 Legislative provisions

The main Treaty provisions governing the free movement of goods are set out in Table 10.1.

THINKING POINT

To what extent, if at all, will these provisions apply if and when the UK leaves the EU?

Simply leaving the EU does not necessarily mean that a country no longer has access to the internal market. Indeed, it is entirely possible for a non-EU Member State to have full access to the internal market (and be subject to the rules that govern it) in much the same way as Norway currently has. Similarly, it is also possible to for a non-EU Member State to have partial, but not full, access to the internal market. Switzerland, for example, has access to the internal market for many of its industries, but the banking sector does not. Indeed, there are so many potential models that can be considered that it is dangerously simplistic to speak of a choice between a 'hard Brexit' and a 'soft Brexit', as has been commonplace following the UK's referendum on EU membership of 23 June 2016. A 'hard Brexit', in this sense, would likely be characterized by separate trade negotiations with individual countries, with the UK not having access to the internal market and therefore not being subject to the rules that govern it, whilst a 'soft Brexit', by contrast, would likely be characterized by the UK having full access to the

Table 10.1 Main Treaty provisions governing the free movement of goods

Treaty Article	Covers
Article 30 TFEU	Tariff barriers to trade prohibiting customs duties and charges having equivalent effect (CHEEs)
Articles 34 and 35 TFEU	Non-tariff barriers to trade prohibiting quantitative restrictions and measures having an equivalent effect on imports (Article 34) and exports (Article 35)
Article 36 TFEU	Derogations to Articles 34 and 35 TFEU justified upon certain grounds
Article 110 TFEU	Prohibition of discriminatory national taxation

internal market and therefore continuing to be subject to the rules ensuring free movement of goods.

At the time of writing, it remains unclear what relationship the UK will have with the internal market if and when it leaves the EU.

10.3 Meaning of 'goods'

As a starting point, it is logical that, when considering the principle of the free movement of goods, consideration should be given to the meaning of the term 'goods'.

In Case 7/68 *Commission v Italy* [1968] ECR 423, the Italian government had subjected exports of articles of an artistic, historical, archaeological, or ethnographic nature to a tax. The Commission argued that such articles fell under the provisions relating to the customs union. The Italian government disputed this, arguing that they were excluded, as the articles in question could not be compared to consumer goods or articles of general use. The Court of Justice held as follows.

Case 7/68 *Commission v Italy* [1968] ECR 423

[T]he Community is based on a customs union which shall cover all trade in goods. By goods, within the meaning of that provision, there must be understood products which can be valued in money and which are capable, as such, of forming the subject of commercial transactions. The Articles covered by the Italian law, whatever may be the characteristics which distinguish them from other types of merchandise, nevertheless resemble the latter, inasmuch as they can be valued in money and so be the subject of commercial transactions.

The scope of 'goods', for the purposes of the principle of free movement of goods, is therefore defined widely. However, subsequent case law has identified the outer edges of the scope of the concept.

Case C-97/98 *Jägerskiöld v Gustafsson* [1999] ECR I-7319

1. Are fishing rights or spinning licences 'goods' in accordance with the judgment in Case 7/68 *Commission v Italy* [1968] ECR 423?

30. Before this question is answered, it must be reiterated that, in its judgment in Case 7/68 *Commission v Italy*, cited above, which is expressly referred to by the national court, the Court defined goods, for the purposes of Article 9 of the EC Treaty (now, after amendment, Article 23 EC) [now Article 28 TFEU], which forms the first article of the third part of Title

I of the EC Treaty, entitled 'Free movement of goods', as products which can be valued in money and which are capable, as such, of forming the subject of commercial transactions.

31. Mr Jägerskiöld contends that fishing rights and fishing permits derived from them constitute 'goods' within the meaning of that judgment, in so far as they can be valued in money terms and may be transferred to other persons, as is expressly provided for by Article 5 of the Law on Fishing.

32. However, in *Commission v Italy* the Court was asked whether articles of artistic, historic, archaeological or ethnographic interest escaped the application of the Treaty provisions relating to the customs union on the ground that they could not be assimilated to 'consumer goods or articles of general use' and did not constitute 'ordinary merchandise'. As is clear from the actual definition given by the Court, the status of 'products' of the goods in question was not therefore contested, so that this definition cannot in itself serve to define fishing rights or permits as goods within the meaning of the Treaty provisions relating to the free movement of goods.

33. It must also be observed that anything which can be valued in money and which is capable, as such, of forming the subject of commercial transactions does not necessarily fall within the scope of application of those Treaty provisions.

34. As is clear from Council Directive 88/361/EEC of 24 June 1988 ... the Treaty provisions on the free movement of capital cover, in particular, operations relating to shares, bonds and other securities which, like fishing rights or fishing permits, can be valued in money and may be the subject of market transactions.

35. Similarly, as is clear from the judgment in Case C-275/92 *Schindler* [1994] ECR 1-1039, the organisation of lotteries does not constitute an activity relating to 'goods', even if such an activity is coupled with the distribution of advertising material and lottery tickets, but must be regarded as a provision of 'services' within the meaning of the Treaty. In that activity, the provisions of services in question are those provided by the lottery organiser in letting ticket buyers participate in the lottery against payment of the price of the lottery tickets.

36. The same applies to the grant of fishing rights and the issue of fishing permits. The activity consisting of making fishing waters available to third parties, for consideration and upon certain conditions, so that they can fish there constitutes a provision of services which is covered by Article 59 et seq. of the EC Treaty (now, after amendment, Article 49 EC et seq. [now Article 56 TFEU *et seq*]) if it has a cross-frontier character. The fact that those rights or those permits are set down in documents which, as such, may be the subject of trade is not sufficient to bring them within the scope of the provisions of the Treaty relating to the free movement of goods.

[...]

39. Consequently, the answer to be given to the first question must be that fishing rights or fishing permits do not constitute 'goods' within the meaning of the provisions of the Treaty relating to the free movement of goods but form a 'provision of a service' within the meaning of the Treaty provisions relating to the freedom to provide services.

In *Jägerskiöld*, it was concluded that the granting of fishing rights and the issue of fishing permits were not 'goods' within the meaning of Treaty provisions. Although seemingly within the *Commission v Italy* definition, the intangibility of the fishing rights and permits—that is, their lack of physicality and inability to be touched—resulted in them being excluded from classification as goods regardless of the fact that such rights could be set down in documents. It is therefore clear that whilst *Commission v Italy* provides a useful and practical first test for the classification of goods, one must be wary of assuming that simply being capable of being valued in money and being capable of forming the subject of commercial transactions will automatically result in such a classification.

10.4 Article 30 TFEU: the prohibition of customs duties and charges having equivalent effect

Article 30 TFEU

Customs duties on imports and exports and charges having equivalent effect shall be prohibited between Member States. This prohibition shall also apply to customs duties of a fiscal nature.

Two elements were identified by the Court of Justice in Joined Cases 2 & 3/69 *Sociaal Fonds voor de Diamantarbeiders v Chougol Diamond Co* [1969] ECR 211 in relation to customs duties.

?! THINKING POINT

As you read the following extract from the *Diamonds Case*, can you identify the two elements the Court referred to?

Joined Cases 2 & 3/69 *Sociaal Fonds voor de Diamantarbeiders v Chougol Diamond Co* [1969] ECR 211, 221–2

In prohibiting the imposition of customs duties, the Treaty does not distinguish between goods according to whether or not they enter into competition with the products of the importing country. Thus, the purpose of the abolition of customs barriers is not merely to eliminate their protective nature, as the Treaty sought on the contrary to give general scope and effect to the rule on the elimination of customs duties and charges having equivalent effect in order to ensure the free movement of goods. It follows from the system as a whole and from the general and absolute nature of the prohibition of any customs duty applicable to goods moving between Member States that customs duties are prohibited independently of any consideration of the purpose for which they were introduced and the destination of the revenue obtained therefrom. The justification for this prohibition is based on the fact that any pecuniary charge—however small—imposed on goods by reason of the fact that they cross a frontier constitutes an obstacle to the movement of such goods.

Thus the two elements considered in the identification of a customs duty were (a) a pecuniary charge (that is, a monetary charge) which is (b) imposed by reason of the fact that the goods have crossed a frontier.

10.4.1 Charges having an equivalent effect

?! THINKING POINT

Why is Article 30 TFEU drafted in such a way as to include not only customs duties, but also charges having equivalent effect (CHEEs)? If it were not drafted in this way, how might a Member State try to impose charges?

Whilst Joined Cases 2 & 3/69 *Sociaal Fonds voor de Diamantarbeiders v Chougol Diamond Co* [1969] ECR 211 (see 10.4) defined customs duties in a wide way, to prohibit only customs duties would not be enough to ensure the elimination of tariff-based trade barriers. A Member State could always argue that whilst a charge was imposed at the time goods crossed a frontier, the reason for the charge was something other than the mere fact that the goods entered the country, for example a charge imposed for an import licence or some kind of service provided for the importer. For this reason—that is, to prevent protectionist measures that have the same effect as a customs duty—Article 30 TFEU is drafted in a wider way and therefore encompasses not only customs duties, but also CHEEs.

It is therefore clear from the outset that the concept of a CHEE is necessarily wider than that of a customs duty.

The Court of Justice provided a definition of a CHEE in Joined Cases 2 & 3/62 *Commission v Luxembourg (Gingerbread)* [1962] ECR 425.

Joined Cases 2 & 3/62 *Commission v Luxembourg ('Gingerbread')* [1962] ECR 425

A duty, whatever it is called, and whatever its mode of application, may be considered a charge having equivalent effect to a customs duty, provided that it meets the following three criteria: (a) it must be imposed unilaterally at the time of importation or subsequently; (b) it must be imposed specifically upon a product imported from a member state to the exclusion of a similar national product; and (c) it must result in an alteration of price and thus have the same effect as a customs duty on the free movement of goods.

Thus the emphasis is not (as we might expect) upon the label attached to the charge, but rather attention is paid to the effect of the charge. This was developed further in Case 24/68 *Commission v Italy ('Statistical Levy Case')* [1969] ECR 193, in which the Court of Justice defined a CHEE in the following way.

Case 24/68 *Commission v Italy ('Statistical Levy Case')* [1969] ECR 193, 201

... any pecuniary charge, however small and whatever its designation and mode of application, which is imposed unilaterally on domestic or foreign goods by reason of the fact that they cross a frontier, and which is not a customs duty in the strict sense, constitutes a charge having equivalent effect ... even if it is not imposed for the benefit of the State, is not discriminatory or protective in effect or if the product on which the charge is imposed is not in competition with any domestic product.

This broad definition was a clear statement of the strict approach in which CHEEs were to be considered. A pecuniary charge imposed by reason of the fact that goods crossed a frontier would amount to a CHEE regardless of who was affected and irrespective of whether the measure was discriminatory or the importing country produced competing goods.

The Court of Justice continued (*Statistical Levy Case*, at 201): 'It follows ... that the prohibition of new customs duties or charges having equivalent effect, linked to the principle of the free movement of goods, constitutes a fundamental rule which, without prejudice to the other provisions of the Treaty, does not permit of any exceptions.'

However, whilst it is eminently clear that the Treaty itself does not allow for exceptions, the Court of Justice has considered circumstances in which such charges could be justified by reason of the fact that they constitute a charge for a service rendered. If categorized as such, the charge should not be regarded as a CHEE.

→ CROSS-REFERENCE
See 10.5 on charges for services rendered.

10.4.2 Examples of CHEEs

In Joined Cases 2 & 3/62 *Commission v Luxembourg and Belgium (Gingerbread)* [1962] ECR 425, Luxembourg and Belgium had increased and extended a special import duty levied upon the issue of import licences for gingerbread. The two governments argued that the charge concerned was in place to 'equate the price of the foreign product with the price of the Belgian product'. The Court pointed out that such an argument ignores the principle that the activities of the EU shall include the institution of a system ensuring that competition in the common market is not distorted. The Court of Justice was clear in determining that Article 30 TFEU was intended to prohibit not only measures in the classic form of a customs duty, but also measures that were presented under different names or which were introduced indirectly by virtue of other procedures that had the same discriminatory or protective results. The charge in this case therefore amounted to a CHEE.

In Joined Cases 2 & 3/69 *Sociaal Fonds voor de Diamantarbeiders v Chougol Diamond Co* [1969] ECR 211, a charge had been imposed upon diamonds imported into Belgium. Although the Court of Justice did not find the charge to be protectionist, it was held to be a CHEE. This causes us to refer back to the wide definition given in *Commission v Italy*. Thus it is the effect of the charge that is all-important and not its purpose.

In Case 24/68 *Commission v Italy ('Statistical Levy Case')* [1969] ECR 193, the Italian government had imposed a 10 lira levy on all imports and exports, with a view to financing the compilation of statistics that, it was argued, were of benefit to traders. However, the Court of Justice stressed that any charge hampers the interpenetration of goods into the market at which the Treaty aims and therefore has an effect upon the free circulation of goods. Further, the fact that the charge was in fact quite small did not preclude its being defined as a CHEE.

?! THINKING POINT

Why do you think the Court of Justice has chosen to interpret Article 30 TFEU in this way?

The Article 30 TFEU prohibition is a fundamental element of the customs union and the single market. As such, Article 30 TFEU has been applied strictly by the Court of Justice and an expansive interpretation has been given to CHEEs. This ensures that not only customs duties in the strict sense are prohibited, but also measures that create a similar barrier to trade, with an emphasis on the effect of the measure as opposed to its stated (or, indeed, actual) intent or purpose.

10.5 Charges for services rendered

In Case 24/68 *Commission v Italy ('Statistical Levy Case')* [1969] ECR 193, one argument advanced by the Italian government was that the charge constituted consideration for a service rendered and as such could not be designated as a CHEE. However, the Court of Justice determined that any alleged advantage was, in fact, so general and difficult to assess that the charge could not be classed as 'consideration for a specific benefit actually conferred'.

However, whilst the Court rejected the argument on the facts of the case before it, the Court did not appear to reject the potential for such justification out of hand.

In Joined Cases 2 & 3/69 *Sociaal Fonds voor de Diamantarbeiders v Chougol Diamond Co* [1969] ECR 211 (considered in 10.4), the Belgian government argued that the levy was imposed in order to contribute to a social fund for those working within the diamond industry. In this case, at 222–3, the Court of Justice openly acknowledged the 'charge for services rendered' argument: '[A]lthough it is not impossible that in certain circumstances a specific service actually rendered may form the consideration for a possible proportional payment for the service in question, this may only apply in specific cases which cannot lead to the circumvention of the provisions of Articles 9 and 12 of the Treaty.'

The argument of a charge for a service rendered has been raised in many cases. It is now clear that the following requirements must apply.

10.5.1 The service must be of direct benefit to the goods or traders concerned

In Case 132/82 *Commission v Belgium ('Customs Warehouses')* [1983] ECR 1649, EU rules allowed for customs formalities to be completed either at the frontier or within the territory at special public warehouses if the importer did not wish them to be placed immediately under a specific customs formality (a concept known as EU transit). Where goods were presented for completion of formalities at these special public warehouses, a storage charge was imposed on the goods whilst they awaited clearance. The Commission argued that the charge amounted to a CHEE as there was no service rendered to the importer, the charge being connected solely with completion of customs formalities. The Belgian government argued that it could not be a CHEE as it was imposed not by reason of crossing a frontier nor the completion of customs formalities, but for the use of the storage facilities. As such, the Belgian government argued, it amounted to a charge for a service rendered to the importer and was therefore justified. The Court was acceptant of the view that the placing of goods in temporary storage was a service rendered to the importer. Furthermore, the Court and the Commission accepted that such a service may legally give rise to a payment commensurate with the service provided. However, on the facts, the Court noted that the charge applied whether or not use was made of the temporary storage facility (ie where goods had been presented to the warehouses *solely* for the completion of customs formalities). As a result, the Court held that where payment of storage charges is demanded solely in connection with the completion of customs formalities, it could not be regarded as a charge for a service actually rendered to the importer.

?! THINKING POINT

What do you think is the purpose of this requirement?

Therefore, whilst the *principle* of a charge being in place for a service rendered was accepted by the Court of Justice, on the application of the facts, the charge in question was *not accepted* as a permitted charge.

In the absence of strict requirements and structured application, the scope for the imposition of tariff barriers to trade would be much greater, allowing Member States to justify protective measures in vague and uncertain terms. This, in turn, would severely hamper the free movement of goods.

In *Statistical Levy*, the Italian government's argument was set out as follows.

Case 24/68 *Commission v Italy ('Statistical Levy Case')* [1969] ECR 193

15. According to the Italian government the object of the statistics in question is to determine precisely the actual movements of goods and, consequently, changes in the state of the market. It claims that the exactness of the information thus supplied affords importers a better competitive position in the Italian market whilst exporters enjoy a similar advantage abroad and that the special advantages which dealers obtain from the survey justifies their paying for this public service and moreover demonstrates that the disputed charge is in the nature of a quid pro quo.
16. The statistical information in question is beneficial to the economy as a whole and inter alia to the relevant administrative authorities.

However, the Court decided that even if there was a particular advantage enjoyed, any direct benefit occasioned was still too general and difficult to assess. As such, the argument was rejected and the charge was held to be a CHEE.

In Case 87/75 *Bresciani v Amministrazione Italiana delle Finanze* [1976] ECR 129, a charge had been imposed on imported raw cowhides for veterinary and public health inspections. In determining whether the charge amounted to a CHEE, the Court of Justice focused upon who benefited from the alleged 'service' provided.

Case 87/75 *Bresciani v Amministrazione Italiana delle Finanze* [1976] ECR 129

10. ... The activity of the administration of the State intended to maintain a public health inspection system imposed in the general interest cannot be regarded as a service rendered to the importer such as to justify the imposition of a pecuniary charge. If, accordingly, public health inspections are still justified at the end of the transitional period, the costs which they occasion must be met by the general public which as a whole benefits from the free movement of Community goods.

The pecuniary charge imposed was therefore held to be a CHEE.

Thus it is clear that, in order to sustain the argument that a charge is justified on the basis of being in place for a service rendered, the service concerned must be of direct benefit to the goods or traders concerned. This is not satisfied where the service is merely in the 'general interest'. Furthermore, it is clear from *Statistical Levy* that the argument is a difficult one to sustain.

10.5.2 The charge must be proportionate to the services rendered

proportionate
A proportionate measure is suitable for its objective, but goes no further than is necessary to achieve it.

Many cases have been decided upon whether the charge is **proportionate**. It should be noted here that the important consideration is not the amount of the charge, but rather the extent to which the amount levied is commensurate with the service provided. Perhaps the clearest illustration of this is found in Case 170/88 *Ford España SA v Estado español* [1989] ECR 2305, in which a charge had been imposed relating to operations incidental to customs clearance when carried out at premises or places not open to the public. The charge concerned was calculated as a proportion of the declared value of the imported goods. The Court of Justice made it clear that even if the levying of a charge was allowed for a service rendered, the charge in the instant case amounted to a CHEE as the amount could not be *proportionate* to the service rendered, being based as it was on the value of the goods concerned rather than the costs related to the service.

In Case 87/75 *Bresciani v Amministrazione Italiana delle Finanze* [1976] ECR 129, the charge imposed was held to be a CHEE regardless of the fact that the charge was proportionate to the cost of the compulsory public health inspections and was calculated according to the quantity of imported goods rather than the value of the goods. Whilst proportionality will always be a vital consideration in determining the validity or otherwise of a charge for a service rendered, it will not in itself justify a charge. The same principle is applicable also to direct benefit to traders in the absence of proportionality. As was made clear by the Court of Justice in *Bresciani*:

Case 87/75 *Bresciani v Amministrazione Italiana delle Finanze* [1976] ECR 129

9. Consequently, any pecuniary charge, whatever its designation and mode of application, which is unilaterally imposed on goods imported from another Member State by reason of the fact that they cross a frontier, constitutes a charge having an effect equivalent to a customs duty. In appraising a duty of the type at issue it is, consequently, of no importance that it is proportionate to the quantity of the imported goods and not to their value.

NOTE

To justify a charge, that charge must be of direct benefit to the goods or traders concerned AND the charge must be proportionate to the services rendered.

10.5.3 'Services' permitted under EU law

In Case 314/82 *Commission v Belgium* [1984] ECR 1543, the Belgian government contended that the charges imposed for inspections were justified on the basis that Council Directive

71/118/EEC of 15 February 1971 on health problems affecting trade in fresh poultrymeat, OJ 1971 L55/23, permitted the inspections concerned. However, as the service provided was merely part of the administrative activity of the State intended to protect in the public interest, public health, and hygiene, it could not be regarded as a service that benefited the importer. As such, the fact that the health checks were permitted by EU law did not preclude them from classification as CHEEs.

10.5.4 'Services' mandated by EU law

?! THINKING POINT

While reading this section, consider why the conditions are different when the services or inspections are mandated by EU law. Which key principle (considered earlier) remains an integral element?

In Case 46/76 *Bauhuis v Netherlands State* [1977] ECR 5, the Dutch administrative authorities imposed fees on importers for veterinary and public health inspections on bovine animals and swine prescribed and provided for by Council Directive 64/432/EEC of 26 June 1964 on animal health problems affecting intra-Community trade in bovine animals and swine, OJ 1964 121/1977. One cattle dealer who had paid the fees claimed a refund on the basis that the charges amounted to a CHEE. The Court of Justice determined that where fees are charged for inspections that are prescribed by an EU provision, are uniform, and are required to be carried out before despatch within the exporting country, they do not constitute CHEEs, provided that they do not exceed the actual cost of the inspection for which they were charged.

In Case 18/87 *Commission v Germany* [1988] ECR 5427, the authorities charged a fee payable on the transit and importation of live animals from other Member States to cover the cost of veterinary inspections carried out under Council Directive 81/389/EEC of 12 May 1981 establishing measures necessary for the implementation of Directive 77/489/EEC on the protection of animals during international transport, OJ 1981 L150/1. Article 2 of the Directive required all Member States of transit and designation to carry out the inspections when animals were brought into the territory and, as such, the inspections were obligatory. The Court of Justice, applying and developing the principle established in Case 46/76 *Bauhuis v Netherlands* [1977] ECR 5, stated as follows.

Case 18/87 *Commission v Germany* [1988] ECR 5427

8. … [S]uch fees may not be classified as charges having an effect equivalent to a customs duty if the following conditions are satisfied:

   (a) they do not exceed the actual costs of the inspections in connection with which they are charged

(b) the inspections in question are obligatory and uniform for all the products concerned in the Community

(c) they are prescribed by Community law in the general interest of the Community

(d) they promote the free movement of goods, in particular by neutralizing obstacles which could arise from unilateral measures of inspection adopted in accordance with Article 36 of the Treaty.

It is useful to consider the application of the tests to the facts and the conclusion at which the Court arrived.

Case 18/87 *Commission v Germany* [1988] ECR 5427

9. In this instance these conditions are satisfied by the contested fee. In the first place it has not been contested that it does not exceed the real cost of the inspections in connection with which it is charged.

10. Moreover, all the Member States of transit and destination are required, under, inter alia, Article 2(1) of Directive 81/389/EEC, cited earlier, to carry out the veterinary inspections in question when the animals are brought into their territories, and therefore the inspections are obligatory and uniform for all the animals concerned in the Community.

11. Those inspections are prescribed by Directive 81/389/EEC, which establishes the measures necessary for the implementation of Council Directive 77/489/EEC of 18 July 1977 on the protection of animals during international transport, with a view to the protection of live animals, an objective which is pursued in the general interest of the Community and not a specific interest of individual States.

12. Finally, it appears from the preambles to the two above-mentioned directives that they are intended to harmonize the laws of the Member States regarding the protection of animals in international transport in order to eliminate technical barriers resulting from disparities in the national laws (see third, fourth, and fifth recitals in the preamble to Directive 77/489/EEC and third recital in the preamble to Directive 81/389/EEC). In addition, failing such harmonization, each Member State was entitled to maintain or introduce, under the conditions laid down in Article 36 of the Treaty, measures restricting trade which were justified on grounds of the protection of the health and life of animals. It follows that the standardization of the inspections in question is such as to promote the free movement of goods.

10.5.5 No other exceptions

Although the argument has certainly been advanced (see eg Case 7/68 *Commission v Italy* [1968] ECR 423), there are no other grounds upon which a Member State can seek to derogate from Article 30 TFEU. In particular, there is no applicable counterpart to Article 36 TFEU or the list of mandatory requirements laid down in *Cassis de Dijon* (see 10.8.6).

Case 7/68 *Commission v Italy* [1968] ECR 423, 430

The provisions of Title 1 of Part Two of the Treaty introduced the fundamental principle of the elimination of all obstacles to the free movements of goods between Member States by the abolition of, on the one hand, customs duties and charges having equivalent effect and, on the other hand, quantitative restrictions and measures having equivalent effect. Exceptions to this fundamental rule must be strictly construed.

Consequently, in view of the difference between the measures referred to in … Article 36, it is not possible to apply the exception laid down in the latter provision to measures which fall outside the scope of the prohibitions referred to in the chapter relating to the elimination of quantitative restrictions between Member States.

Finally, the fact that the provisions of Article 36 which have been mentioned do not relate to customs duties and charges having equivalent effect is explained by the fact that such measures have the sole effect of rendering more onerous the exportation of the products in question, without ensuring the attainment of the object referred to in that Article, which is to protect the artistic, historic or archaeological heritage.

REVIEW QUESTION

Do you think that the Court of Justice accepts the 'charge for a service rendered' argument in many cases or do you think it is a significant hurdle to overcome?

Answer: With consideration to jurisprudence in this regard, it is clear that the Court of Justice subjects such an argument to rigorous scrutiny, with strict adherence to narrowly defined conditions. As such, comparatively few cases result in the Court being willing to accept the justification.

10.6 Related considerations

10.6.1 Article 30 TFEU is inapplicable when dealing with internal taxation

When a charge relates not to the fact that a good has crossed a frontier and is instead imposed as part of a general system of internal taxation, it does not amount to a CHEE and should not be considered under Article 30 TFEU (see Figure 10.1). Such a charge amounts to a tax and, if challenged, should be considered under Article 110 TFEU.

→ CROSS-REFERENCE
See 10.7 on Article 110 TFEU.

10.6.2 Determining when the charge is a tax and when it is a CHEE

Before addressing the issue of categorization, it is worth taking time to consider why the distinction is important.

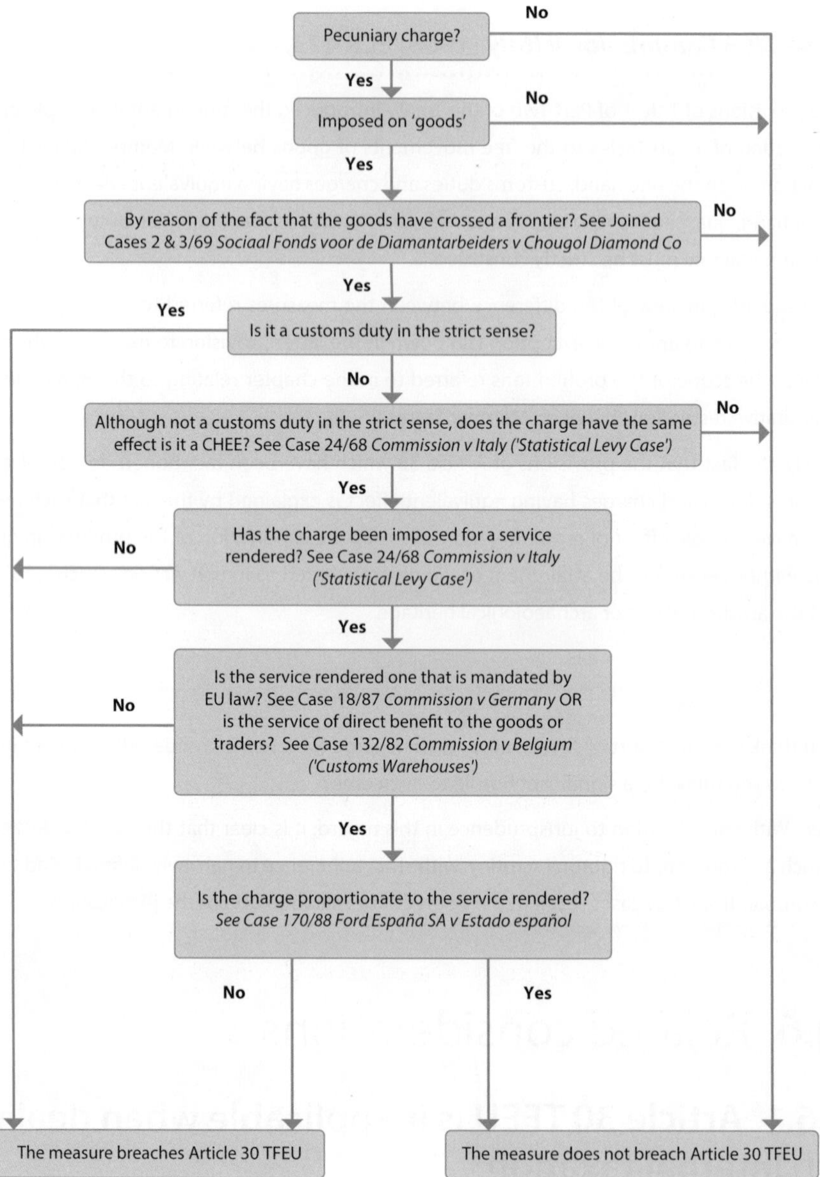

Figure 10.1 Article 30 TFEU

If a measure amounts to a customs duty or a CHEE, it must be abolished. Article 30 TFEU prohibits the imposition of such charges, reflecting the danger that such barriers pose to the existence of the customs union and the realization of the single market.

If the measure amounts to a matter of internal taxation, it is lawful subject to Article 110 TFEU. The Treaty does not prescribe an appropriate level of taxation, but is concerned with discriminatory or protective taxation measures.

10.6.3 The relevant Treaty Articles are mutually exclusive

It is important to appreciate from the outset that the relevant Treaty Articles are mutually exclusive. In Case 57/65 *Alfons Lütticke GmbH v Hauptzollamt Sarrelouis* [1966] ECR 293, a case concerning a German tax on imported powdered milk, the Court of Justice clarified the applicability of the two Articles to the same measure (although, on the facts, it was not required to do so).

Case 57/65 *Alfons Lütticke GmbH v Hauptzollamt Sarrelouis* [1966] ECR 293

2. It should however be made clear that Articles 12 [now Article 30 TFEU] and 13 [now repealed] on the one hand and Article 95 [now Article 110 TFEU] on the other cannot be applied jointly to one and the same case. Charges having an effect equivalent to customs duties on the one hand and internal taxation on the other hand are governed by different systems.

In most cases, determining the applicable Article is straightforward.

- Where the fiscal charge is imposed by reason of the fact that goods have entered a territory, it should be considered under Article 30 TFEU.
- Where the fiscal charge is part of a system of internal dues applied systematically and in accordance with the same criteria to domestic producers and imported products alike, it should be considered under Article 110 TFEU.

10.7 Article 110 TFEU: the prohibition of discriminatory taxation

Article 110 TFEU relates to national taxation systems operating internally. Case 132/78 *Denkavit v France* [1979] ECR 1923, at 1927, defined internal taxation as 'a general system of internal dues applied systematically and in accordance with the same criteria to domestic products and imported products alike'. Internal taxation is distinguished from customs duties and CHEEs. A charge is a tax if it is part of an internal system of taxation, as indicated by *Denkavit*. Customs duties and CHEEs are charges levied on goods by reason of importation.

Articles 110 and 30 TFEU are complementary, yet mutually exclusive (Case 10/65 *Deutschmann v Germany* [1965] ECR 469), so a charge on goods cannot be both a tax and a customs duty or CHEE. The distinction is important because if classed as a customs duty or

CHEE, it is unlawful under Article 30 TFEU. If classed as a tax, it is permissible, provided that it complies with Article 110 TFEU.

It is important to recognize that EU law does not prohibit national taxation, but it does prohibit taxation that discriminates between imported and domestically produced goods.

10.7.1 Article 110 TFEU prohibition

Article 110 TFEU draws a distinction between similar products and products in competition.

Article 110 TFEU

No Member State shall impose, directly or indirectly, on the products of other Member States any internal taxation of any kind in excess of that imposed directly or indirectly on similar domestic products.

Furthermore, no Member State shall impose on the products of other Member States any internal taxation of such nature as to afford indirect protection to other products.

Thus the first paragraph prohibits unequal taxation of similar products, whereas the second paragraph prohibits internal taxation that indirectly protects domestic products that, although not similar to the imported products, are nevertheless in competition with them.

The approach of the Court of Justice used to be to treat the concepts of similar and competing as interchangeable. Case 168/78 *Commission v France (Tax on Spirits)* [1980] ECR 347 is an example, with the Court of Justice considering differential tax rates for fruit-based and non-fruit-based spirits.

The Court of Justice considered first the differing functions of the two paragraphs of Article 110 TFEU.

Case 168/78 *Commission v France (Tax on Spirits)* [1980] ECR 347

5. The first paragraph of Article 95 [EC, now Article 110 TFEU], which is based on a comparison of the tax burdens imposed on domestic products and on imported products which may be classified as 'similar', is the basic rule in this respect. This provision, as the court has had occasion to emphasize in its judgment of 10 October 1978 in Case 148/77, *H. Hansen Jun. & O. C. Balle GMBH & Co. v Hauptzollamt Flensburg* (1978) ECR 1787, must be interpreted widely so as to cover all taxation procedures which conflict with the principle of the equality of treatment of domestic products and imported products; it is therefore necessary to interpret the concept of 'similar products' with sufficient flexibility. The court specified in the judgment of 17 February 1976 in the *Rewe* case (Case 45/75 (1976) ECR 181) that it is necessary to consider as similar products which 'have similar characteristics and meet the same needs from the point of view of consumers'. It is therefore necessary to determine the scope of the first

paragraph of Article 95 on the basis not of the criterion of the strictly identical nature of the products but on that of their similar and comparable use.

6. The function of the second paragraph of Article 95 is to cover, in addition, all forms of indirect tax protection in the case of products which, without being similar within the meaning of the first paragraph, are nevertheless in competition, even partial, indirect or potential, with certain products of the importing country. The court has already emphasized certain aspects of that provision in its judgment of 4 April 1978 in Case 27/77, *Firma Fink-Frucht GMBH v Hauptzollamt Munchen-Landsbergerstrasse* (1978) ECR 223, in which it stated that for the purposes of the application of the first paragraph of Article 95 it is sufficient for the imported product to be in competition with the protected domestic production by reason of one or several economic uses to which it may be put, even though the condition of similarity for the purposes of the first paragraph of Article 95 is not fulfilled.
7. Whilst the criterion indicated in the first paragraph of Article 95 consists in the comparison of tax burdens, whether in terms of the rate, the mode of assessment or other detailed rules for the application thereof, in view of the difficulty of making sufficiently precise comparisons between the products in question, the second paragraph of that Article is based upon a more general criterion, in other words the protective nature of the system of internal taxation.

In applying this to the subject matter of the case, the Court continued as follows.

Case 168/78 *Commission v France (Tax on Spirits)* [1980] ECR 347

13. It appears from the foregoing that Article 95 [EC, now Article 110 TFEU], taken as a whole, may apply without distinction to all the products concerned. It is sufficient therefore to examine whether the application of a given national tax system is discriminatory or, as the case may be, protective, in other words whether there is a difference in the rate or the detailed rules for levying the tax and whether that difference is likely to favour a given domestic production. It will be necessary to examine within this framework the economic relationships between the products concerned and the characteristics of the tax systems which form the subject-matter of the disputes in the case of each of the applications lodged by the Commission.

    [...]

39. After considering all these factors the court deems it unnecessary for the purposes of solving this dispute to give a ruling on the question whether or not the spirituous beverages concerned are wholly or partly similar products within the meaning of the first paragraph of Article 95 when it is impossible reasonably to contest that without exception they are in at least partial competition with the domestic products to which the application refers and that it is impossible to deny the protective nature of the French tax system within the second paragraph of Article 95.

Thus the Court of Justice rather glossed over the distinction between the two paragraphs and the effect of each, treating them as one. However, classifying correctly under Article 110 TFEU is important as the action needed to be taken by the relevant Member State is dependent upon this classification. If the first paragraph of Article 110 is breached, the Member State must equalize taxation. If the second paragraph is breached, the Member State has only to remove the competitive effect of the tax regulation. Later cases (see Case 170/78 *Commission v United Kingdom (Excise Duties on Wine)* [1980] ECR 417) show a greater focus by the Court of Justice on determining the relevant paragraph.

Before turning to the interpretation of these paragraphs in more detail, the concepts of direct and indirect discrimination are considered, since both kinds of discrimination can infringe Article 110 TFEU.

10.7.2 Direct and indirect discrimination

Article 110 TFEU provides a clear example of the importance of the general principle of non-discrimination (Article 18 TFEU) in ensuring the free movement of goods. Discrimination can, of course, be both direct and indirect in form, and being able to distinguish between them is important in dealing with arguments of potential justification.

?! THINKING POINT

As you read the following section, consider why one form of discrimination is capable of justification, whilst the other is not. Which form of discrimination seems more serious?

Measures that openly tax imported and domestic goods at different rates are directly discriminatory.

Direct discrimination is rarely seen in practice. It is easily identified and therefore usually avoided. However, it has occasionally occurred, for example in Case 57/65 *Alfons Lütticke GmbH v Hauptzollamt Sarrelouis* [1966] ECR 293, concerning a German tax on imported, but not domestically produced, powdered milk.

Case C-90/94 *Haahr Petroleum* [1997] ECR I-4085 provides a further example of directly discriminatory taxation. In *Haahr*, all goods unloaded at certain Danish ports were subject to a shipping tax. However, where imported goods were being unloaded, these imported goods were subject to an additional 40 per cent surcharge. The Court of Justice was very clear in its judgment that such directly discriminatory behaviour breached what is now Article 110 TFEU.

Case C-90/94 *Haahr Petroleum* [1997] ECR I-4085

27. Next, Article 95 of the [EC] Treaty [now Article 110 TFEU] provides that no Member State is to impose, directly or indirectly, on the products of other Member States internal taxation

> in excess of that imposed on similar domestic products or of such a nature as to afford indirect protection to other domestic products. It is therefore beyond question that application of a higher charge to imported products than to domestic products or application to imported products alone of a surcharge in addition to the duty payable on domestic and imported products is contrary to the prohibition of discrimination laid down in Article 95.

Indirectly discriminatory taxation is taxation that appears (in law) not to discriminate between imported and domestically produced goods, but which nevertheless has a discriminatory effect in reality. Such measures are usually more difficult to identify. Case 112/84 *Humblot v Directeur des Services Fiscaux* [1985] ECR 1367 provides a useful illustration of just such an indirectly discriminatory measure.

In *Humblot*, French annual tax on cars differentiated between cars below 16 horsepower (hp) and above 16 hp, with those in the higher power rating category being taxed at several times the rate of those below. French manufacturers did not produce cars above 16 hp. Humblot purchased a Mercedes in France and challenged the French taxation measure. The Court of Justice held that the French law was protectionist and discriminatory in respect of cars imported from other Member States, and therefore breached what is now Article 110 TFEU.

Case 112/84 *Humblot v Directeur des Services Fiscaux* [1985] ECR 1367

> 14. … Under that system there are two distinct taxes: a differential tax which increases progressively and is charged on cars not exceeding a given power rating for tax purposes and a fixed tax on cars exceeding that rating which is almost five times as high as the highest rate of the differential tax. Although the system embodies no formal distinction based on the origin of products it manifestly exhibits discriminatory or protective features contrary to Article [110 TFEU], since the power rating determining liability to the special tax has been fixed at a level such that only imported cars, in particular from other Member States, are subject to the special tax whereas all cars of domestic manufacture are liable to the distinctly more advantageous differential tax.

This passage is interesting, drawing attention as it does to the nature of the system in place—a progressive rate to which domestic products were also subject and a flat rate almost five times in excess of the next highest rate to which, coincidentally, domestic products were not subject.

Case 140/79 *Chemial Farmaceutici SpA v DAF SpA* [1981] ECR 1 provides a further example of indirectly discriminatory taxation relating this time to alcohol products, one derived from petroleum (synthetic ethyl alcohol) and the other produced by distilling products of the soil (fermented ethyl alcohol). The two products were found to not only be similar under what is now the first paragraph of Article 110 TFEU, but were found to be chemically identical and therefore fully interchangeable. Despite this, the Italians taxed synthetic ethyl alcohol at six times the rate at which it taxed fermented ethyl alcohol. Moreover, synthetic ethyl alcohol was

→ CROSS-REFERENCE
See Case C-132/88 *Commission v Greece* [1990] ECR I-1567, at 10.7.4.

not produced in Italy, meaning that the higher rate of tax in effect applied only to imported products.

10.7.3 Methods of tax collection and the basis of assessment

In some cases, the discrimination is not down to the rate of taxation levied, but the rules relating to collection or the basis of assessment.

In Case 55/79 *Commission v Ireland (Taxation of Alcohol)* [1980] ECR 481, the focus was upon the timing with which importers were required to pay the relevant tax.

Case 55/79 *Commission v Ireland (Taxation of Alcohol)* [1980] ECR 481

2. The facts which gave rise to the action are not contested by Ireland. It is in fact common ground that the legal provisions applicable in Ireland, in particular pursuant to the Imposition of Duties (No 221) (Excise Duties) Order 1975, provide in favour of producers of spirits, beer and made wine for deferment of payment of between four and six weeks according to the product whereas, in the case of the same products from other Member States, the duty is payable either at the date of importation or of delivery from the customs warehouse.
3. The Commission acknowledges that there is no discrimination as regards the rates of duty applicable. On the other hand, it considers that the fact that Irish products are granted deferment of payment beyond the date on which the products are put on the market amounts to conferring on national producers a financial benefit in comparison with importers who are obliged to pay the duty on the actual date on which the products are released to the market. This results, according to the Commission, in a disadvantage to imported products in competition with the corresponding Irish national production …
5. The government of Ireland claims in its defence that the detailed arrangements for levying the duty have to be adaptable to the different circumstances of home-produced products and imported products. It states that the decisive criterion is the rate of duty applied, whilst the wording of Article 95 merely prohibits the Member States from imposing on the products of other Member States taxation 'in excess' of that imposed on domestic products; to introduce factors which do not appear in its wording is to do violence to that provision.

In rejecting the argument of the Irish government, the Court of Justice held that Ireland was in breach of what is now Article 110 TFEU by bringing into force and applying tax measures that benefited domestic producers and were not available to importers of the same products from other Member States.

In Case C-213/96 *Outokumpu Oy* [1998] ECR I-1777, the question concerned how the rate of tax was calculated. The referring court usefully summarized the facts.

Case C-213/96 *Outokumpu Oy* [1998] ECR I-1777

17. [...]

'Under Finnish national legislation on the taxation of energy, excise duty on electricity is levied in Finland on electrical energy produced there, the amount of the duty depending on the method of production of the electricity. On electricity produced by nuclear power, the excise duty charged is a basic duty of 1.5 p/kWh and an additional duty of 0.9 p/kWh. On electricity produced by water power, the excise duty charged is only an additional duty of 0.4 p/kWh. On electricity produced by other methods, for example from coal, excise duty is charged on the basis of the amount of input materials used to produce the electricity. On electrical energy produced by some methods, for example in a generator with an output below two megavolt-amperes, no excise duty at all is charged. On imported electricity, the excise duty charged, regardless of the method of production of the electricity, is a basic duty of 1.3 p/kWh and an additional duty of 0.9 p/kWh. The excise duty on electricity is thus determined with respect to imported electricity on a different basis from that applied to electricity produced in Finland. The levying of excise duties determined on the basis of the method of production of the energy is founded on environmental grounds in the drafting history of the law. The amount of duty chargeable on imported electricity is not, however, determined on the basis of the method of production of the electricity. The excise duty chargeable on imported electricity is higher than the lowest excise duty chargeable on electricity produced in Finland, but lower than the highest excise duty chargeable on electricity produced in Finland. The excise duty on imported electricity is levied on the importer, whereas the excise duty relating to electricity produced in Finland is levied on the electricity producer. ...'

The Court of Justice was therefore required to consider whether such a basis for calculation amounted to a breach of what is now Article 110 TFEU.

Case C-213/96 *Outokumpu Oy* [1998] ECR I-1777

34. The Court has consistently held that that provision is infringed where the taxation on the imported product and that on the similar domestic product are calculated in a different manner on the basis of different criteria which lead, if only in certain cases, to higher taxation being imposed on the imported product (see, in particular, Case C-152/89 *Commission v Luxembourg* [1991] ECR I-3141, paragraph 20).
35. That is the case where, under a system of differential taxation of the kind at issue in the main proceedings, imported electricity distributed via the national network is subject, whatever its method of production, to a flat-rate duty which is higher than the lowest duty charged on electricity of domestic origin distributed via the national network.
36. The fact that electricity of domestic origin is in some cases taxed more heavily than imported electricity is immaterial in this connection since, in order to ascertain whether the system in question is compatible with Article 95 of the [EC] Treaty [now Article 110 TFEU], the tax burden imposed on imported electricity must be compared with the lowest tax burden imposed on electricity of domestic origin (see, to that effect, *Commission v Luxembourg*, paragraphs 21 and 22).
37. The Finnish Government raises the objection that in view of the characteristics of electricity, the origin and consequently the method of production of which cannot be determined

once it has entered the distribution network, the differential rates applicable to electricity of domestic origin cannot be applied to imported electricity. It submits that in those circumstances application of a flat rate, calculated so as to correspond to the average rate levied on electricity of domestic origin, is the only logical way of treating imported electricity in an equitable manner.

38. The Court has already had occasion to point out that practical difficulties cannot justify the application of internal taxation which discriminates against products from other Member States (see, inter alia, Case C-375/95 *Commission v Greece* [1997] ECR I-5981, paragraph 47).

39. While the characteristics of electricity may indeed make it extremely difficult to determine precisely the method of production of imported electricity and hence the primary energy sources used for that purpose, the Finnish legislation at issue does not even give the importer the opportunity of demonstrating that the electricity imported by him has been produced by a particular method in order to qualify for the rate applicable to electricity of domestic origin produced by the same method.

[…]

41. In the light of the foregoing considerations, the answer must be that the first paragraph of Article 95 of the EC Treaty precludes an excise duty which forms part of a national system of taxation on sources of energy from being levied on electricity of domestic origin at rates which vary according to its method of production while being levied on imported electricity, whatever its method of production, at a flat rate which, although lower than the highest rate applicable to electricity of domestic origin, leads, if only in certain cases, to higher taxation being imposed on imported electricity.

Thus the Court of Justice held that there is a breach of what is now Article 110 TFEU where a different method of calculation leads, if only in certain cases, to a higher tax on the imported product. It is interesting to note also the swift dismissal of the attempted justification relating to the practical difficulties in applying the same regime to both domestic and imported products. In so doing, the importance of the fundamental principle of non-discrimination was upheld.

10.7.4 Objective justification

The distinction between directly and indirectly discriminatory measures is all-important. In this regard, it is worth noting that there are no express defences to Article 110 TFEU in the Treaty. As such, directly discriminatory taxation can never be justified and always breaches Article 110 TFEU, underlining the importance of the principle of non-discrimination.

By contrast, indirectly discriminatory taxation may be objectively justified if there exists some objective policy reason that is acceptable to the EU. Such objective justifications have developed through the case law of the Court of Justice.

In Case 140/79 *Chemial Farmaceutici SpA v DAF SpA* [1981] ECR 1, the Italian government argued that its taxation of two interchangeable products at different rates according to the way in which they were produced was justified. The Italian government said that the higher taxation of synthetic alcohol constituted a legitimate choice of economic policy aimed to encourage production using a different raw material (agricultural products), leaving the existing raw material (petroleum ingredients) for more important uses.

Case 140/79 *Chemial Farmaceutici SpA v DAF SpA* [1981] ECR 1

14. As the court has stated on many occasions, particularly in the judgments cited by the Italian government, in its present stage of development Community law [now EU law] does not restrict the freedom of each Member State to lay down tax arrangements which differentiate between certain products on the basis of objective criteria, such as the nature of the raw materials used or the production processes employed. Such differentiation is compatible with Community law if it pursues economic policy objectives which are themselves compatible with the requirements of the Treaty and its secondary law and if the detailed rules are such as to avoid any form of discrimination, direct or indirect, in regard to imports from other Member States or any form of protection of competing domestic products.
15. Differential taxation such as that which exists in Italy for denatured synthetic alcohol on the one hand and denatured alcohol obtained by fermentation on the other satisfies these requirements. It appears in fact that that system of taxation pursues an objective of legitimate industrial policy in that it is such as to promote the distillation of agricultural products as against the manufacture of alcohol from petroleum derivatives. That choice does not conflict with the rules of Community law or the requirements of a policy decided within the framework of the Community [now the Union].

In Case C-132/88 *Commission v Greece* [1990] ECR I-1567, the Court of Justice considered an environmental justification for a car tax system providing for differential rates according to power rating. Greece imposed a tax on new and second-hand cars wherever they were produced and, once over a 1.8 litre engine, the tax rose steeply. Greece did not produce cars with engines above 1.6 litres.

→ CROSS-REFERENCE
See Case 112/84 *Humblot v Directeur des Services Fiscaux* [1985] ECR 1367, at 10.7.2.

Case C-132/88 *Commission v Greece* [1990] ECR I-1567

17. It must be emphasized in this regard that Article 95 of the [EC] Treaty [now Article 110 TFEU] does not provide a basis for censuring the excessiveness of the level of taxation which the Member States might adopt for particular products in the light of considerations of social policy. As the Court held in particular in *Humblot* [Case 112/84 *Humblot v Directeur des Services Fiscaux* [1985] ECR 1367] … as Community law [now EU law] stands at present, the Member States are at liberty to subject products such as cars to a system of tax which

increases progressively in amount according to an objective criterion, such as cylinder capacity, provided that the system of taxation is free from any discriminatory or protective effect.

18. It must be made clear that a system of taxation cannot be regarded as discriminatory solely because only imported products, in particular those from other Member States, come within the most heavily taxed category (see judgment of 14 January 1981 in Case 140/79 *Chemial Farmaceutici v DAF* [1981] ECR 1, paragraph 18).

19. In order to determine whether [relevant taxes] have a discriminatory or protective effect, it is necessary to consider whether they are capable of discouraging consumers from purchasing cars of a cylinder capacity in excess of 1,800 cc, which are all manufactured abroad, in such a way as to benefit domestically produced cars.

20. If it is assumed that the particular features of the system of taxation at issue actually discourage certain consumers from purchasing cars of a cylinder capacity greater than 1,800 cc, those consumers will choose either a model in the range of cars having cylinder capacities between 1,600 and 1,800 cc or a model in the range of cars having cylinder capacities below 1,600 cc. All the models in the first-mentioned range are of foreign manufacture. The second range includes cars of both foreign and Greek manufacture. Consequently, the Commission has not shown how the system of taxation at issue might have the effect of favouring the sale of cars of Greek manufacture.

Thus the Court of Justice held that the tax measure would escape Article 110 TFEU notwithstanding that all higher-taxed cars were imported because the taxation did not have the effect of discouraging Greeks from purchasing foreign cars. On the facts, the tax was motivated by other considerations and there was no discernible protective effect.

10.7.5 Article 110 TFEU, first paragraph: 'similar' products

?! THINKING POINT

Reflect on the decision in Case 112/84 *Humblot v Directeur des Services Fiscaux* [1985] ECR 1367 in the light of Case C-132/88 *Commission v Greece* [1990] ECR I-1567, paras 17–20. Can you distinguish the two cases?

Since the first paragraph of Article 110 TFEU prohibits the differential taxation of 'similar' products, the 'similarity' of the imported and domestic products is clearly important. In a number of cases concerning alcoholic drinks, the Court of Justice has interpreted 'similar' broadly, to mean similar characteristics and comparable use.

NOTE

Directly discriminatory measures can never be justified. Indirectly discriminatory measures may be objectively justified if there exists some objective policy reason that is acceptable to the EU.

In Case 168/78 *Commission v France (Tax on Spirits)* [1980] ECR 347, the Court of Justice considered the relative similarity of non-fruit-based spirits (such as whisky, gin, and vodka) and fruit-based spirits (such as brandy, armagnac, and calvados). Acknowledging the need to interpret 'similar' with 'sufficient flexibility', the Court stated, at para 5, that '[i]t is therefore necessary to determine the scope of the first paragraph of Article [110] on the basis not of the criterion of the strictly identical nature of the products but on that of their similar and comparable use.'

The Court of Justice in Case 243/84 *John Walker v Ministeriet for Skatter* [1986] ECR 875 considered the similarity of Scotch whisky and liqueur fruit wine and, with reference to the 'similar characteristics and comparable use' approach, decided as follows.

Case 243/84 *John Walker v Ministeriet for Skatter* [1986] ECR 875

11. … [I]n order to determine whether products are similar it is necessary first to consider certain objective characteristics of both categories of beverages, such as their origin, the method of manufacture and their organoleptic properties, in particular taste and alcohol content, and secondly to consider whether or not both categories of beverages are capable of meeting the same needs from the point of view of consumers.

In this regard, the Court considered the goods in question and applied the test in the following way, reaching the conclusion that the products were not similar within the meaning of Article 110 TFEU.

Case 243/84 *John Walker v Ministeriet for Skatter* [1986] ECR 875

12. It should be noted that the two categories of beverages exhibit manifestly different characteristics. Fruit wine of the liqueur type is a fruit-based product obtained by natural fermentation, whereas Scotch whisky is a cereal-based product obtained by distillation. The organoleptic properties of the two products are also different … [T]he fact that the same raw material, for example alcohol, is to be found in the two products is not sufficient reason to apply the prohibition contained in the first paragraph of Article 95 [EC, now Article 110 TFEU]. For the products to be regarded as similar that raw material must also be present in more or less equal proportions in both products. In that regard, it must be pointed out that the alcoholic strength of Scotch whisky is 40 per cent by volume, whereas the alcoholic strength of fruit wine of the liqueur type, to which the Danish tax legislation applies, does not exceed 20 per cent by volume.

13. The contention that Scotch whisky may be consumed in the same way as fruit wine of the liqueur type, as an aperitif diluted with water or with fruit juice, even if it were established, would not be sufficient to render Scotch whisky similar to fruit wine of the liqueur type, whose intrinsic characteristics are fundamentally different.

10.7.6 Article 110 TFEU, second paragraph: 'indirect protection to other products'

Under the second paragraph of Article 110 TFEU, where imported and domestic goods are not 'similar', but simply in competition with each other, national taxation must not give advantage to the domestic product.

Reaching such a determination of being in competition is a complex matter indeed and a number of factors are taken into account. One such approach is to look at the concept of cross-elasticity of demand, something which will be considered in some detail in relation to competition law (see Chapter 14). In essence, the question to be asked is whether demand in one product increases due to an increase in price or reduction in the availability of the other.

Manufacturing processes, product composition, and present and future consumer preferences are also considered in reaching a conclusion as to whether the measure in question affords indirect protection to the domestic product.

The case that best illustrates the complexity of this consideration is Case 170/78 *Commission v United Kingdom (Excise Duties on Wine)* [1980] ECR 417, in which the Court of Justice looked at differential taxation of beer and wine. The Commission argued that beer and wine could be substituted and met the same purposes as thirst-quenching and meal-accompanying beverages. As such, the argument was that the difference in tax amounted to discrimination against imported wine, which encouraged customers to buy beer (the domestic product). The UK argued that the products had entirely different manufacturing processes, differing alcoholic strengths, and entirely different pricing structures since wine was appreciably more expensive than beer. As regards consumer habits, the UK stated that, in accordance with long-established tradition, beer was a popular drink consumed preferably in public houses or in connection with work; domestic consumption and consumption with meals was negligible. In contrast, the consumption of wine was more unusual and special from the point of view of social custom.

Following years of information-gathering and detailed evidence on volume, price, and alcoholic strength, the Court of Justice reached the following conclusion.

Case 170/78 *Commission v United Kingdom (Excise Duties on Wine)* [1980] ECR 417

27. It is clear, therefore, following the detailed inquiry conducted by the court—whatever criterion for comparison is used, there being no need to express a preference for one or the

> other—that the United Kingdom's tax system has the effect of subjecting wine imported from other Member States to an additional tax burden so as to afford protection to domestic beer production ... Since such protection is most marked in the case of the most popular wines, the effect of the United Kingdom tax system is to stamp wine with the hallmarks of a luxury product which, in view of the tax burden which it bears, can scarcely constitute in the eyes of the consumer a genuine alternative to the typical domestically produced beverage.

The Court of Justice therefore held that the UK had imposed a higher duty on wine to give protection to beer. Beer was generally a domestic product, whilst wine was generally imported. As the tax favoured the domestic product, the second paragraph of Article 110 TFEU had been breached.

It should be noted that emphasis was placed upon competition existing between beer and the cheaper wines with lower alcoholic content. Importantly, the Court also stressed the need to assess not only the situation now, but also whether they would potentially be in competition in the future. The case is now almost 40 years old and has proven to be a shrewd judgment, as it can be argued that these products are more in competition now than ever.

For an overview of the operation of Article 110 TFEU, see Figure 10.2.

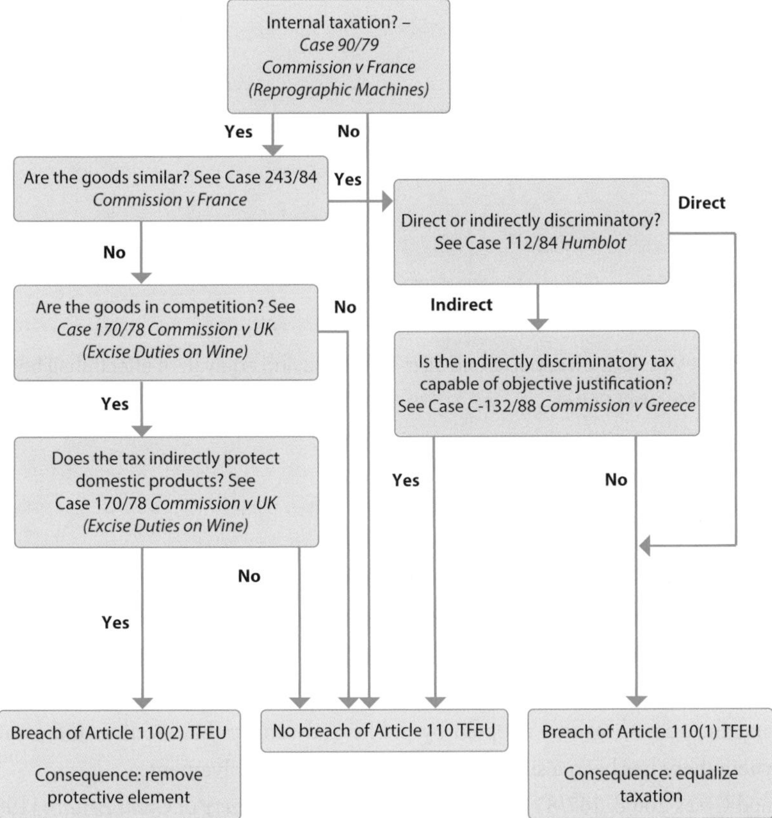

Figure 10.2 Article 110 TFEU

10.7.6.1 Harmonization of taxation

Harmonization of taxation within the EU could solve the problems arising from discriminatory taxation. However, whilst progress has been made on the approximation of value added tax (VAT), excise duty, and corporation tax, Member States remain resistant to further transfer of control to the EU in this area.

10.8 Articles 34 and 35 TFEU: the prohibition of quantitative restrictions and measures having equivalent effect

Merely removing customs duties and CHEEs and prohibiting discriminatory taxation is not enough to secure the free movement of goods within the EU.

As well as these pecuniary restrictions, there are other barriers of a non-pecuniary nature, such as administrative rules or procedures, which can prevent the free movement of goods. It is these that Articles 34 and 35 TFEU are concerned with.

Article 34 TFEU

Quantitative restrictions on imports, and all measures having equivalent effect, shall be prohibited between Member States.

Article 35 TFEU

Quantitative restrictions on exports, and all measures having equivalent effect, shall be prohibited between Member States.

10.8.1 Scope

Article 34 TFEU sets out the prohibition on quantitative restrictions and measures having equivalent effect to quantitative restrictions (MEQRs) on imports. Article 35 TFEU extends this to exports. The prohibition is addressed to Member States, but it has been interpreted widely, and includes measures adopted by public and semi-public bodies, and even private bodies where there has been a significant amount of State involvement.

In Joined Cases 266 & 267/87 *R v Royal Pharmaceutical Society of Great Britain* [1989] ECR 1295, it was held that Article 34 TFEU applied to the Royal Pharmaceutical Society, an organization that regulated the conduct of and set standards for chemists and pharmacists.

Article 34 TFEU applies also to measures applied to only part of a Member State's territory.

In Case C-67/97 *Ditlev Bluhme* [1998] ECR I-8033, a legislative measure prohibiting the keeping on the Danish island of Læsø of any species of bee other than the subspecies *Apis mellifera mellifera* (Læsø brown bee) constituted an MEQR despite the fact that the measure applied to only part of the national territory.

10.8.2 Quantitative restrictions

Quantitative restrictions are measures that limit the import or export of goods by reference to an amount or value. In Case 2/73 *Geddo v Ente Nazionale Risi* [1973] ECR 865, at 879, the Court of Justice defined them as 'measures which amount to a total or partial restraint of, according to the circumstances, imports, exports, or goods in transit'.

In Case 34/79 *R v Henn and Darby* [1979] ECR 3795, a ban on the import of pornographic material amounted to a quantitative restriction under Article 34 TFEU.

REVIEW QUESTION

Do you think the *Geddo* definition is a narrow or wide definition?

Answer: The definition from *Geddo* is clearly quite wide. It incorporates both partial restrictions in the form of quotas (such as a measure limiting the importation of wine to 10,000 litres) and total restrictions in the form of bans.

10.8.3 Measures having equivalent effect to quantitative restrictions

Measures having equivalent effect to quantitative restrictions are much more difficult to identify than quantitative restrictions. They take many different forms, including health and safety requirements, packaging requirements, and requirements relating to the composition or marketing of goods. The Court of Justice defined MEQRs in Case 8/74 *Procureur du Roi v Dassonville* [1974] ECR 837, at para 5, in what has become known as the '*Dassonville* formula': 'All trading rules enacted by Member States which are capable of hindering, directly or indirectly, actually or potentially, intra-Community [now Union] trade are to be considered as measures having an effect equivalent to quantitative restrictions.'

Although the test has undergone minor modifications in subsequent case law (the term 'trading rules' does not usually appear in more recent cases, for it is clear that the *Dassonville* formula is not merely limited to trading rules, but also includes, for example, technical regulations), this definition remains the decisive test for an MEQR.

REVIEW QUESTION

Do you think the *Dassonville* formula provides a narrow or a wide definition?

Answer: As with *Geddo* in the previous review question, it is important that you appreciate just how wide this definition is. It covers those measures that merely have the capability of hindering trade.

Indeed, virtually any measure that could hinder imports or exports in any way could be caught. Thus the crucial factor is the effect, with a discriminatory intent not needing to be identified.

The *Dassonville* formula emerged in a preliminary reference to the Court of Justice (see Chapter 6) arising from criminal proceedings in a Belgian court against traders who acquired a consignment of Scotch whisky in free circulation in France and imported it into Belgium without being in possession of a certificate of origin from the British customs authorities, thereby infringing Belgian rules. The national court asked whether a national provision prohibiting the import of goods bearing a designation of origin, where those goods are not accompanied by an official document issued by the government of the exporting country certifying their right to such designation, constitutes an MEQR within the meaning of what is now Article 34 TFEU. The Court of Justice articulated the decisive test for the existence of an MEQR and, applying this to the facts before it, concluded as follows.

Case 8/74 *Procureur du Roi v Dassonville* [1974] ECR 837

9. … [T]he requirement by a Member State of a certificate of authenticity which is less easily obtainable by importers of an authentic product which has been put into free circulation in a regular manner in another Member State than by importers of the same product coming directly from the country of origin constitutes a measure having an effect equivalent to a quantitative restriction as prohibited by the Treaty.

In essence, because it was very difficult for anyone but the original producers to obtain the certificate, to require it was, in effect, to restrict the importation of the goods to which it applied, contrary to the fundamental principle of the free movement of goods. Commission Directive 70/50/EEC of 22 December 1969 based on the provisions of Article 33(7), on the abolition of measures which have an effect equivalent to quantitative restrictions on imports and are not covered by other provisions are adopted in pursuance of the EEC Treaty, OJ 1970 L13/29, provides further guidance on the scope of MEQRs.

10.8.4 Directive 70/50

Directive 70/50 was a transitional measure introduced to provide guidance during a transitional period when the common market was becoming established. As such, it is no longer formally applicable, but it does indicate the Commission's view of MEQRs, and shows a clear intention to catch both those measures that provide different treatment for domestic and imported goods and those that are applied to them equally. As such, we can delineate between what are referred to as 'distinctly applicable' measures and 'indistinctly applicable' measures.

10.8.4.1 Distinctly applicable measures

Distinctly applicable measures are those other than those applicable equally to domestic or imported products. Thus they distinguish between imported goods and domestic products.

These measures are contained within Article 2 of the Directive, and a non-exhaustive list is set out in Article 2(3).

Commission Directive 70/50/EEC of 22 December 1969 based on the provisions of Article 33(7), on the abolition of measures which have an effect equivalent to quantitative restrictions on imports and are not covered by other provisions adopted in pursuance of the EEC Treaty, OJ 1970 L13/29

Article 2

1. This Directive covers measures, other than those applicable equally to domestic or imported products, which hinder imports which could otherwise take place, including measures which make importation more difficult or costly than the disposal of domestic production.
2. In particular, it covers measures which make imports or the disposal, at any marketing stage, of imported products subject to a condition—other than a formality—which is required in respect of imported products only, or a condition differing from that required for domestic products and more difficult to satisfy. Equally, it covers, in particular, measures which favour domestic products or grant them a preference, other than an aid, to which conditions may or may not be attached.
3. The measures referred to must be taken to include those measures which:
   (a) lay down, for imported products only, minimum or maximum prices below or above which imports are prohibited, reduced or made subject to conditions liable to hinder importation;
   (b) lay down less favourable prices for imported products than for domestic products;
   (c) fix profit margins or any other price components for imported products only or fix these differently for domestic products and for imported products, to the detriment of the latter;
   (d) preclude any increase in the price of the imported product corresponding to the supplementary costs and charges inherent in importation;
   (e) fix the prices of products solely on the basis of the cost price or the quality of domestic products at such a level as to create a hindrance to importation;
   (f) lower the value of an imported product, in particular by causing a reduction in its intrinsic value, or increase its costs;
   (g) make access of imported products to the domestic market conditional upon having an agent or representative in the territory of the importing Member State;
   (h) lay down conditions of payment in respect of imported products only, or subject imported products to conditions which are different from those laid down for domestic products and more difficult to satisfy;
   (i) require, for imports only, the giving of guarantees or making of payments on account;
   (j) subject imported products only to conditions, in respect, in particular of shape, size, weight, composition, presentation, identification or putting up, or subject imported

products to conditions which are different from those for domestic products and more difficult to satisfy;

(k) hinder the purchase by private individuals of imported products only, or encourage, require or give preference to the purchase of domestic products only;

(l) totally or partially preclude the use of national facilities or equipment in respect of imported products only, or totally or partially confine the use of such facilities or equipment to domestic products only;

(m) prohibit or limit publicity in respect of imported products only, or totally or partially confine publicity to domestic products only;

(n) prohibit, limit or require stocking in respect of imported products only; totally or partially confine the use of stocking facilities to domestic products only, or make the stocking of imported products subject to conditions which are different from those required for domestic products and more difficult to satisfy;

(o) make importation subject to the granting of reciprocity by one or more Member States;

(p) prescribe that imported products are to conform, totally or partially, to rules other than those of the importing country;

(q) specify time limits for imported products which are insufficient or excessive in relation to the normal course of the various transactions to which these time limits apply;

(r) subject imported products to controls or, other than those inherent in the customs clearance procedure, to which domestic products are not subject or which are stricter in respect of imported products than they are in respect of domestic products, without this being necessary in order to ensure equivalent protection;

(s) confine names which are not indicative of origin or source to domestic products only.

10.8.4.2 Indistinctly applicable measures

Indistinctly applicable measures are those that are equally applicable to domestic and imported products. Article 3 of the Directive again sets out a non-exhaustive list and draws attention to the importance of a test of proportionality.

Commission Directive 70/50/EEC of 22 December 1969 based on the provisions of Article 33(7), on the abolition of measures which have an effect equivalent to quantitative restrictions on imports and are not covered by other provisions adopted in pursuance of the EEC Treaty, OJ 1970 L13/29

Article 3

This Directive also covers measures governing the marketing of products which deal, in particular, with shape, size, weight, composition, presentation, identification, or putting up and which are equally applicable to domestic and imported products, where the restrictive effect of such measures on the free movement of goods exceeds the effects intrinsic to trade rules.

This is the case, in particular, where:

- the restrictive effects on the free movement of goods are out of proportion to their purpose;
- the same objective can be attained by other means which are less of a hindrance to trade.

?! THINKING POINT

Why do you think a distinction is drawn between these two types of measure? Reflect upon this when you have worked through the remainder of the chapter.

In Joined Cases 51–54/71 *International Fruit Company v Produktschap voor Groenten en Fruit (No 2)* [1971] ECR 1108, the Court of Justice made it clear that the mere requirement of an import or export licence would amount to an MEQR even if the granting of such a licence was a mere formality.

Applying *Dassonville* to this requirement, it can be seen that such a requirement hinders trade in three ways:

- goods are effectively banned pending processing of the application;
- there is, at least in theory, the potential for rejection; and
- any additional paperwork will result in additional costs, which will need to be accounted for in determining the price of the goods, and this may impact upon the eventual sales figures.

In Case 113/80 *Commission v Ireland ('Irish Souvenirs')* [1981] ECR 1625, Irish legislation required imported goods bearing or possessing characteristics suggesting that they were souvenirs of Ireland to bear an indication of the country of origin or the word 'Foreign'. The Court of Justice found as follows.

Case 113/80 *Commission v Ireland ('Irish Souvenirs')* [1981] ECR 1625

17. Thus by granting souvenirs imported from other Member States access to the domestic market solely on condition that they bear a statement of origin, whilst no such statement is required in the case of domestic products, the provisions contained in the sale order and the importation order indisputably constitute a discriminatory measure.
18. The conclusion to be drawn therefore is that by requiring all souvenirs and Articles of jewellery imported from other Member States which are covered by the sale order and the importation order to bear an indication of origin or the word 'foreign', the Irish rules constitute a measure having equivalent effect within the meaning of [Article 34 TFEU].

?! THINKING POINT

Think carefully about this case and others in this section, and consider the application of *Dassonville*. Identifying MEQRs can be quite difficult in practice and therefore reflecting upon decided cases, with a view to understanding how and why they fall within the *Dassonville* formula, is important.

10.8.4.3 Case law examples of indistinctly applicable measures

In Case 261/81 *Walter Rau Lebensmittelwerke v de Smedt PvbA* [1982] ECR 3961, a Belgian requirement that all margarine for sale should be in cube-shaped form or cube-shaped packaging was questioned as to its validity under what is now Article 34 TFEU. The imported product was supplied and packaged in plastic tubs having the shape of a truncated cone. It should be noted that the Belgian requirement applied to all margarine sold in Belgium, and therefore did not discriminate between the domestic and imported product. However, the Court of Justice held the measure to be an MEQR, with consideration of the effects of the measure.

Case 261/81 *Walter Rau Lebensmittelwerke v de Smedt PvbA* [1982] ECR 3961

13. Although the requirement that a particular form of packaging must also be used for imported products is not an absolute barrier to the importation into the Member State concerned of products originating in other Member States, nevertheless it is of such a nature as to render the marketing of those products more difficult or more expensive either by barring them from certain channels of distribution or owing to the additional costs brought about by the necessity to package the products in question in special packs which comply with the requirements in force on the market of their destination.
14. In this case the protective effect of the Belgian rules is moreover demonstrated by the fact, affirmed by the Commission and not disputed by the Belgian government, that despite prices appreciably higher than those in some other Member States there is practically no margarine of foreign origin to be found on the Belgian market.
15. Therefore it may not be claimed that the requirement of special packaging for the product is not an obstacle to marketing.

Attention should be drawn to the effects-based reasoning used by the Court of Justice. Applying *Dassonville*, the potential to hinder trade is clear from the reasoning given: the marketing of such products would be more difficult or more costly as a result of the additional costs of altering production processes to comply with the Belgian requirement.

In Case 207/83 *Commission v United Kingdom* [1985] ECR 1201, the Trade Descriptions (Origin Marking) (Miscellaneous Goods) Order 1981, SI 1981/121, required certain goods to be marked with the country of origin. Again, this was a measure that applied equally to domestic and imported goods. The Commission pointed out that the order imposed a not inconsiderable burden upon the retailer of any product listed in one of the four categories of goods covered by the Order. Under the scheme introduced by the Order, it remained for the retailer to prepare appropriate notices, display them near the goods, and ensure throughout the day that the notices were not detached, knocked over, obscured, or moved. None of those problems would arise if the product were already origin-marked at the time when it was delivered to the retailer, which would encourage the retailer to choose to sell only goods that were already origin-marked. The burden of the requirements laid down in the Order would inevitably be passed up the sales chain and come to rest on the manufacturer, who, anxious to retain its customers, would feel obliged to origin-mark its products. Such a requirement would necessarily increase the production costs of the imported article and make it more expensive. The Court of Justice, whilst acknowledging that the measure applied equally to domestic and imported goods, held as follows.

Case 207/83 *Commission v United Kingdom* [1985] ECR 1201

17. … [T]he origin-marking requirement not only makes the marketing in a Member State of goods produced in other Member States in the sectors in question more difficult; it also has the effect of slowing down economic interpenetration in the Community [now Union] by handicapping the sale of goods produced as the result of a division of labour between Member States.
18. It follows from those considerations that the United Kingdom provisions in question are liable to have the effect of increasing the production costs of imported goods and making it more difficult to sell them on the United Kingdom market.

[…]

22. Those considerations lead to the conclusion that Article 2 of the order constitutes a measure which makes the marketing of goods imported from other Member States more difficult than the marketing of domestically-produced goods and for which Community law [now EU law] does not recognize any ground of justification. That provision therefore falls within the prohibition laid down in Article 30 of the EEC Treaty [now Article 34 TFEU].

10.8.5 Obligation of Member States to ensure free movement of goods

Article 34 TFEU also applies where a Member State fails to adopt the necessary measures in order to ensure the free movement of goods, even where obstacles are not caused by the State.

This obligation to ensure the free movement of goods is an obligation arising from the Treaty itself. In Case C-265/95 *Commission v France* [1997] ECR I-6959, the Commission stated that, for more than a decade, it had regularly received complaints concerning the passivity of the

French authorities in the face of violent acts committed by private individuals and by protest movements of French farmers directed against agricultural products from other Member States. Those acts consisted of the interception of lorries transporting such products in France and the destruction of their loads, violence against lorry drivers, threats against French supermarkets selling agricultural products originating in other Member States, and the damaging of those goods when on display in shops in France.

Considering what is now Article 34 TFEU, the Court of Justice held as follows.

Case C-265/95 *Commission v France* [1997] ECR I-6959

29. That provision, taken in its context, must be understood as being intended to eliminate all barriers, whether direct or indirect, actual or potential, to flows of imports in intra-Community [now Union] trade.
30. As an indispensable instrument for the realization of a market without internal frontiers, Article 30 [EC, now Article 34 TFEU] therefore does not prohibit solely measures emanating from the State which, in themselves, create restrictions on trade between Member States. It also applies where a Member State abstains from adopting the measures required in order to deal with obstacles to the free movement of goods which are not caused by the State.
31. The fact that a Member State abstains from taking action or, as the case may be, fails to adopt adequate measures to prevent obstacles to the free movement of goods that are created, in particular, by actions by private individuals on its territory aimed at products originating in other Member States is just as likely to obstruct intra-Community trade as is a positive act.
32. Article 30 therefore requires the Member States not merely themselves to abstain from adopting measures or engaging in conduct liable to constitute an obstacle to trade but also, when read with Article 5 of the Treaty [replaced, in substance, by Article 9 TEU (renumbered 13)], to take all necessary and appropriate measures to ensure that that fundamental freedom is respected on their territory.

In Case C-112/00 *Schmidberger v Austria* [2003] ECR I-5659, the Austrian authorities had actually implicitly granted environmental protesters permission for a demonstration to take place, the effect of which was to close a motorway for almost 30 hours. The national court made a reference to the Court of Justice under Article 267 TFEU asking a number of questions, the most important of which related to what is now Article 34 TFEU.

Case C-112/00 *Schmidberger v Austria* [2003] ECR I-5659

1. (1) Are the principles of the free movement of goods under Article 30 et seq. of the EC Treaty (now Article 28 et seq. EC) [now Article 34 TFEU], or other provisions of Community law, to be interpreted as meaning that a Member State is obliged, either absolutely or at

least as far as reasonably possible, to keep major transit routes clear of all restrictions and impediments, inter alia, by requiring that a political demonstration to be held on a transit route, of which notice has been given, may not be authorised or must at least be later dispersed, if or as soon as it can also be held at a place away from the transit route with a comparable effect on public awareness?

[...]

The Court addressed this question by restating the importance of the free movement of goods and making reference to the judgment in Case C-265/95 *Commission v France* [1997] ECR I-6959.

Case C-265/95 *Commission v France* [1997] ECR I-6959

51. It should be stated at the outset that the free movement of goods is one of the fundamental principles of the Community [now Union].
52. Thus, Article 3 of the EC Treaty (now, after amendment, Article 3 EC [now Article 8 TFEU]), inserted in the first part thereof, entitled Principles, provides in subparagraph (c) that for the purposes set out in Article 2 of the Treaty [now repealed] the activities of the Community are to include an internal market characterised by the abolition, as between Member States, of obstacles to *inter alia* the free movement of goods.
53. The second paragraph of Article 7a of the EC Treaty (now, after amendment, Article 14 EC [now Article 26 TFEU/TEU]) provides that the internal market is to comprise an area without internal frontiers in which the free movement of goods is ensured in accordance with the provisions of the Treaty.
54. That fundamental principle is implemented primarily by Articles 30 and 34 of the Treaty [now Articles 36 and 40 TFEU/TEU].
55. In particular, Article 30 provides that quantitative restrictions on imports and all measures having equivalent effect are prohibited between Member States. Similarly, Article 34 prohibits, between Member States, quantitative restrictions on exports and all measures having equivalent effect.
56. It is settled case-law since the judgment in Case 8/74 *Dassonville* ([1974] ECR 837, paragraph 5) that those provisions, taken in their context, must be understood as being intended to eliminate all barriers, whether direct or indirect, actual or potential, to trade flows in intra-Community trade (see, to that effect, Case C-265/95 *Commission* v *France* [1997] ECR I-6959, paragraph 29).
57. In this way the Court held in particular that, as an indispensable instrument for the realisation of a market without internal frontiers, Article 30 does not prohibit only measures emanating from the State which, in themselves, create restrictions on trade between Member States. It also applies where a Member State abstains from adopting the measures

required in order to deal with obstacles to the free movement of goods which are not caused by the State (*Commission* v *France*, cited above, paragraph 30).

58. The fact that a Member State abstains from taking action or, as the case may be, fails to adopt adequate measures to prevent obstacles to the free movement of goods that are created, in particular, by actions by private individuals on its territory aimed at products originating in other Member States is just as likely to obstruct intra-Community trade as is a positive act (*Commission* v *France*, cited above, paragraph 31).

59. Consequently, Articles 30 and 34 of the Treaty require the Member States not merely themselves to refrain from adopting measures or engaging in conduct liable to constitute an obstacle to trade but also, when read with Article 5 of the Treaty [replaced, in substance, by Article 9 TEU (renumbered 13)], to take all necessary and appropriate measures to ensure that that fundamental freedom is respected on their territory (*Commission* v *France*, cited above, paragraph 32). Article 5 of the Treaty requires the Member States to take all appropriate measures, whether general or particular, to ensure fulfilment of the obligations arising out of the Treaty and to refrain from any measures which could jeopardise the attainment of the objectives of that Treaty.

60. Having regard to the fundamental role assigned to the free movement of goods in the Community system, in particular for the proper functioning of the internal market, that obligation upon each Member State to ensure the free movement of products in its territory by taking the measures necessary and appropriate for the purposes of preventing any restriction due to the acts of individuals applies without the need to distinguish between cases where such acts affect the flow of imports or exports and those affecting merely the transit of goods …

61. In the light of the foregoing, the fact that the competent authorities of a Member State did not ban a demonstration which resulted in the complete closure of a major transit route such as the Brenner motorway for almost 30 hours on end is capable of restricting intra-Community trade in goods and must, therefore, be regarded as constituting a measure of equivalent effect to a quantitative restriction which is, in principle, incompatible with the Community law [now EU law] obligations arising from Articles 30 and 34 of the Treaty, read together with Article 5 thereof, unless that failure to ban can be objectively justified.

Thus it is clear that Article 34 TFEU is concerned not only with measures that a Member State puts into place that could hinder the free movement of goods, but also failure by a Member State to adopt adequate measures to prevent obstacles.

10.8.6 *Cassis de Dijon*

As detailed earlier, measures that apply equally to domestic and imported products are called indistinctly applicable measures. Article 3 of Directive 70/50 stated that such measures would breach Article 34 TFEU only where the restrictive effect on the free movement of goods exceeds the effects necessary for the trade rules—that is, only in the case of those measures that are disproportionate and tend to protect domestic products at the expense of imported products.

?! THINKING POINT

Reflect upon the difference between distinctly and indistinctly applicable measures, and consider the following material in the context of the reason why such a distinction is made.

Although *Dassonville* does not make provision for indistinctly applicable measures to be justified on certain grounds, there are dicta acknowledging the possibility.

Case 8/74 *Procureur du Roi v Dassonville* [1974] ECR 837

6. In the absence of a Community [now Union] system guaranteeing for consumers the authenticity of a product's designation of origin, if a Member State takes measures to prevent unfair practices in this connexion, it is however subject to the condition that these measures should be reasonable and that the means of proof required should not act as a hindrance to trade between Member States and should, in consequence, be accessible to all Community nationals.

Thus, without focusing on whether such a measure is distinctly or indistinctly applicable, the possibility for justification was noted.

This was developed further in Case 120/78 *Rewe-Zentral AG v Bundesmonopolverwaltung für Branntwein ('Cassis de Dijon')* [1979] ECR 649, recognizing the difficulties that flow from indistinctly applicable measures introduced for arguably good reason. In this vitally important case, the Court of Justice developed a basis for the justification of such indistinctly applicable measures.

In *Cassis*, German legislation required fruit liqueurs to have a minimum alcohol content of 25 per cent if they are to be marketed lawfully in Germany. French Cassis had an alcohol content of only between 15–20 per cent and therefore could not be sold in the German market. It was argued that the condition was an MEQR. The Court of Justice established two important principles:

- the principle of mutual recognition; and
- the rule of reason.

10.8.6.1 The principle of mutual recognition

The principle of mutual recognition works as a presumption to be applied to differing Member State requirements. The presumption is that where goods have been lawfully produced and marketed in one Member State, there is no reason why they should not be introduced into another Member State. As stated in Case 120/78 *Rewe-Zentral AG v Bundesmonopolverwaltung für Branntwein ('Cassis de Dijon')* [1979] ECR 649, at para 14: 'There is therefore no valid reason why, provided that they have been lawfully produced and marketed in one of the Member States, alcoholic beverages should not be introduced into any other Member State; ...'

In Case 16/83 *Prantl* [1984] ECR 1299, Italian wine was imported in an Italian *bocksbeutel* bottle. This has a characteristic bulbous shape similar to a German (*Franconia bocksbeutel*) bottle used for a wine of particular quality. The Court of Justice noted that bulbous wine bottles had been manufactured in Italy for over 100 years and therefore found as follows.

Case 16/83 *Prantl* [1984] ECR 1299

30. The answer ... must therefore be that Article 30 of the EEC Treaty [now Article 34 TFEU] must be interpreted as meaning that the application by a Member State to imports of wine originating in another Member State of national legislation allowing only certain national producers to use a specific shape of bottle when the use of that shape or a similar shape of bottle accords with a fair and traditional practice in the state of origin constitutes a measure having an effect equivalent to a quantitative restriction.

However, although an important principle, it is merely a presumption and can therefore be rebutted with reference to the rule of reason.

10.8.6.2 The rule of reason

Case 120/78 *Rewe-Zentral AG v Bundesmonopolverwaltung für Branntwein ('Cassis de Dijon')* [1979] ECR 649

8. ... Obstacles to movement within the Community [now Union] resulting from disparities between the national laws relating to the marketing of the products in question must be accepted in so far as those provisions may be recognized as being necessary in order to satisfy mandatory requirements relating in particular to the effectiveness of fiscal supervision, the protection of public health, the fairness of commercial transactions and the defence of the consumer.

The Court of Justice therefore, appreciating that indistinctly applicable measures may be introduced for good reason, set out particular, but non-exhaustive, grounds whereby such measures could be justified—namely:

- the effectiveness of fiscal supervision;
- the protection of public health;
- the fairness of commercial transactions; and
- the defence of the consumer.

In *Cassis*, the German government argued on two main grounds. First, it argued that the measure was in place to protect public health on the basis that it avoids the proliferation of alcoholic beverages on the national market—in particular, alcoholic beverages with a low alcohol content, since, in its view, such products may more easily induce a tolerance towards alcohol than more highly alcoholic beverages. Secondly, the German government argued that the measure protected the fairness of commercial transactions as the lower alcohol provided a price advantage for the imported products that was unfair, and which would force down alcohol rates and quality of drinks. The Court was unconvinced by these arguments. The result was effectively an indirect ban. As such, the measure was held to be a breach of what is now Article 34 TFEU.

Scope of the rule of reason

It is important to note that the rule of reason applies to indistinctly applicable measures only.

In Case 113/80 *Commission v Ireland ('Irish Souvenirs')* [1981] ECR 1625, Irish legislation required Irish souvenirs not manufactured in Ireland to bear the label 'foreign'. The Commission argued that this breached what is now Article 34 TFEU on the basis that the measure had the effect of lowering the value of an imported product by causing a reduction in value or an increase in costs. The Irish government argued that it was justified on the basis of consumer protection. However, as the measure applied only to imported products, it was a distinctly applicable measure and therefore could not be covered by the rule of reason principle in *Cassis*.

?! THINKING POINT

Why does the *Cassis* rule of reason apply only to indistinctly applicable measures? What is it about these measures that differentiates them such that this basis of justification is reserved only to them?

It should be noted that a number of more recent cases, including Case C-320/03 *Commission v Austria ('Brenner')* [2005] ECR I-9871, have appeared to indicate that the Court has relaxed its approach of needing an indistinctly applicable measure for the *Cassis* rule of reason to apply, but it is important to state that it has never been repudiated and, until it has, it remains correct to draw this distinction between *Cassis* and Article 36 TFEU.

No harmonizing rules

The *Cassis* rule of reason applies only in the absence of EU rules governing the interest concerned. If there is EU harmonizing legislation in a particular area, Member States may not impose additional requirements, unless that legislation expressly permits them to do so.

10.8.6.3 Application of the principle of proportionality

In order to satisfy the rule of reason, the measures used must be no more than is necessary to achieve their aim. If the measure goes beyond what is necessary, it will fall outside *Cassis* and will therefore be classified as a breach of Article 34 TFEU.

In Case 120/78 *Rewe-Zentral AG v Bundesmonopolverwaltung für Branntwein ('Cassis de Dijon')* [1979] ECR 649, the German government's arguments were met by a consideration of proportionality, with the Court of Justice noting that the proposed aims could be met with clearer labelling. The measure in question therefore amounted to a breach of Article 34 TFEU.

In Case 261/81 *Walter Rau Lebensmittelwerke v de Smedt PvbA* [1982] ECR 3961, the Belgian requirement that all margarine for sale should be in cube-shaped form or cube-shaped packaging was argued to be in place for the defence or protection of the consumer, on the basis that the Belgian consumer was so used to purchasing margarine in this particular form that to sell margarine in other forms may cause confusion. The Court of Justice's response to this argument was both clear, yet subtle.

Case 261/81 *Walter Rau Lebensmittelwerke v de Smedt PvbA* [1982] ECR 3961

17. It cannot be reasonably denied that in principle legislation designed to prevent butter and margarine from being confused in the mind of the consumer is justified. However, the application by one Member State to margarine lawfully manufactured and marketed in another Member State of legislation which prescribes for that product a specific kind of packaging such as the cubic form to the exclusion of any other form of packaging considerably exceeds the requirements of the object in view. Consumers may in fact be protected just as effectively by other measures, for example by rules on labelling, which hinder the free movement of goods less.

Thus, if the aim of the measure was to prevent confusion amongst Belgian consumers, this could be achieved in a way that was more proportionate and therefore less of a hindrance to the free movement of goods—namely, effective labelling.

?! THINKING POINT

Do you understand the application of the principle of proportionality within *Walter Rau*? The case provides a useful and engaging example of the application of the principle in practice.

A more recent example of a potentially justifiable restriction falling foul of the principle of proportionality is Case C-15/15 *New Valmar BVBA v Global Pharmacies Partner Health Srl* EU:C:2016:464. In this 2016 preliminary reference, the Court of Justice considered the 'effectiveness of fiscal supervision' mandatory requirement in relation to Belgian legislation requiring every undertaking established within a federated entity (in this case, the Dutch-speaking region of the Kingdom of Belgium) to draw up invoices relating to cross-border transactions only in the official language of that entity. Indeed, the legislation in question provided that any invoices falling foul of the requirement were to be declared null and void by the national court.

Case C-15/15 *New Valmar BVBA v Global Pharmacies Partner Health Srl* EU:C:2016:464

55. Thus, as regards the objective of ensuring the effectiveness of fiscal supervision, the Belgian Government itself indicated, at the hearing, that, according to an administrative circular of 23 January 2013, the right of deduction of VAT cannot be refused by the tax authorities on the sole ground that the details that are required by law to be in an invoice were drawn up in a language other than Dutch, which tends to suggest that the use of another language is not liable to prevent the attainment of that objective.
56. In the light of all the foregoing, it must be held that legislation such as that at issue in the main proceedings goes beyond what is necessary to attain the objectives referred to in paragraphs 49 to 51 of this judgment [ie 'encouraging the use of the official language of the linguistic region concerned'] and cannot therefore be regarded as proportionate.

This case is an example of the extension of the mandatory requirements.

10.8.7 Extension of the mandatory requirements

The list of mandatory requirements set out in *Cassis* under the rule of reason was never articulated as an exhaustive list. As such, they have been developed further by the Court of Justice in subsequent case law and no doubt will continue to be developed still further in the future.

An example of a requirement developed post *Cassis* is found in Case 302/86 *Commission v Denmark* [1988] ECR 4607, in which Danish legislation required certain drinks sold in Denmark to be packaged in reusable containers and deposit-and-return schemes to be established. These measures were all designed to protect the environment. The Court of Justice recognized environmental protection as a mandatory requirement, but was clear that the measures were still required to satisfy the test of proportionality. Unfortunately for the Danish government, they did not.

In Case 155/80 *Oebel* [1981] ECR 1994, the Court of Justice found that German legislation prohibiting night working in bakeries and night deliveries of bakery products, which, it was claimed, restricted deliveries into neighbouring Member States in time for breakfast, was compatible with Article 34 TFEU because trade within the EU remained possible at all times. Whilst it was not necessary for the German government to justify the legislation, the Court recognized that legitimate interests of economic and social policy, designed to improve working conditions, could constitute a mandatory requirement.

In Case 145/88 *Torfaen Borough Council v B&Q plc* [1989] ECR 3851, consideration was given to the Shops Act 1950, which, with limited exceptions, prohibited Sunday trading in the UK. B&Q argued that this provision was an MEQR because its consequence was to reduce sales, and hence the volume of imports, from other Member States. The Court of Justice found that the Sunday trading rules were justified because they were in accord with national or regional socio-cultural characteristics. In including these, the mandatory requirements were again developed further.

As such, when considering an indistinctly applicable MEQR, if an objective justifiable reason for having such a measure in place can be identified, this reason can be argued under the non-exhaustive *Cassis* rule of reason.

10.8.8 Development of principles relating to indistinctly applicable measures

The expansive interpretation of MEQRs under *Dassonville* and the treatment of indistinctly applicable MEQRs was problematic in that the Court of Justice was inconsistent in dealing with 'equal burden rules'—that is, those rules that apply to all goods that may have an impact upon the overall volume of sales, but which do not have a protectionist effect.

In some cases, such equal burden rules were deemed by the Court to be within Article 34 TFEU subject to justification under the rule of reason or Article 36 TFEU (see 10.8.6). Thus, in Case 145/88 *Torfaen BC v B&Q plc* [1989] ECR 3851, the national court found that a ban on Sunday trading had the effect of reducing B&Q's total sales, that approximately 10 per cent of the goods sold by B&Q came from other Member States, and that a corresponding reduction of imports from other Member States would therefore ensue. Recognizing that national rules governing the hours of work, delivery, and sale constitute a legitimate part of economic and social policy, consistent with the objectives of public interest pursued by the Treaty, the Court of Justice stated as follows.

Case 145/88 *Torfaen BC v B&Q plc* [1989] ECR 3851

14. Such rules reflect certain political and economic choices in so far as their purpose is to ensure that working and non-working hours are so arranged as to accord with national or regional socio-cultural characteristics, and that, in the present state of Community law [now EU law], is a matter for the Member States. Furthermore, such rules are not designed to govern the patterns of trade between Member States.
15. Secondly, it is necessary to ascertain whether the effects of such national rules exceed what is necessary to achieve the aim in view. As is indicated in Article 3 of Commission Directive 70/50/EEC of 22 December 1969 (Official Journal, English Special Edition 1970 (I), p. 17), the prohibition laid down in Article 30 [now Article 34 TFEU] covers national measures governing the marketing of products where the restrictive effect of such measures on the free movement of goods exceeds the effects intrinsic to trade rules.
16. The question whether the effects of specific national rules do in fact remain within that limit is a question of fact to be determined by the national court.

Thus such a measure fell within Article 34 TFEU, but could be justified to the extent that it was proportionate (see 10.8.6.3). This was a matter for the national court to judge.

In other cases, equal burden rules were held to be outside Article 34 TFEU where the rule did not relate to the characteristics of the product, but only the conditions in which they were sold.

Thus, in Case 155/80 *Oebel* [1981] ECR 1994, when considering German rules on night work in bakeries whereby, subject to certain exceptions, no person would be permitted to work on the making of baker's wares between the hours of 10 pm and 4 am, the Court of Justice, when looking at whether such measures fell within Article 34 TFEU, held as follows.

Case 155/80 *Oebel* [1981] ECR 1994

15. … Article 34 concerns national measures which have as their specific object or effect the restriction of patterns of exports and thereby the establishment of a difference in treatment between the domestic trade of a Member State and its export trade, in such a way as to provide a particular advantage for national production or for the domestic market of the state in question.
16. This is clearly not the case with rules such as those in issue, which are part of economic and social policy and apply by virtue of objective criteria to all the undertakings in a particular industry which are established within the national territory, without leading to any difference in treatment whatsoever on the ground of the nationality of traders and without distinguishing between the domestic trade of the state in question and the export trade.

[…]

21. The reply to the second question must therefore be that Articles 30 and 34 of the EEC Treaty [now Articles 36 and 40 TFEU] do not apply to national rules which prohibit the production of ordinary and fine baker's wares and also their transport and delivery to individual consumers and retail outlets during the night up to a certain hour.

In the light of these inconsistent judgments, a general rule was needed for equal burden cases and, in *Keck*, the Court of Justice produced just such a rule.

10.8.9 The *Keck* judgment: selling arrangements

In Joined Cases C-267 & 268/91 *Keck and Mithouard* [1993] ECR I-6097, the issue of equal burden rules was raised in a preliminary reference concerning criminal proceedings brought by the French authorities against Keck and Mithouard. Keck and Mithouard were being prosecuted for reselling products in an unaltered state at prices lower than their actual purchase price, contrary to French law stating that goods could not be resold at a loss. The Court of Justice summed up the issue in relation to free movement of goods thus.

Joined Cases C-267 & 268/91 *Keck and Mithouard* [1993] ECR I-6097

11. By virtue of Article 30 [now Article 34 TFEU], quantitative restrictions on imports and all measures having equivalent effect are prohibited between Member States. The Court has

consistently held that any measure which is capable of directly or indirectly, actually or potentially, hindering intra-Community [now Union] trade constitutes a measure having equivalent effect to a quantitative restriction.

12. National legislation imposing a general prohibition on resale at a loss is not designed to regulate trade in goods between Member States.

13. Such legislation may, admittedly, restrict the volume of sales, and hence the volume of sales of products from other Member States, in so far as it deprives traders of a method of sales promotion. But the question remains whether such a possibility is sufficient to characterize the legislation in question as a measure having equivalent effect to a quantitative restriction on imports.

Thus the question ultimately became: do selling arrangements that may have an effect upon trade between Member States, but which are not designed to regulate it, fall within Article 34 TFEU? In re-examining and clarifying its case law on this matter, the Court of Justice concluded as follows.

Joined Cases C-267 & 268/91 *Keck and Mithouard* [1993] ECR I-6097

15. It is established by the case-law beginning with 'Cassis de Dijon' (Case 120/78 *Rewe-Zentral v Bundesmonopolverwaltung für Branntwein* [1979] ECR 649) that, in the absence of harmonization of legislation, obstacles to free movement of goods which are the consequence of applying, to goods coming from other Member States where they are lawfully manufactured and marketed, rules that lay down requirements to be met by such goods (such as those relating to designation, form, size, weight, composition, presentation, labelling, packaging) constitute measures of equivalent effect prohibited by Article 30 [now Article 34 TFEU]. This is so even if those rules apply without distinction to all products unless their application can be justified by a public-interest objective taking precedence over the free movement of goods.

16. By contrast, contrary to what has previously been decided, the application to products from other Member States of national provisions restricting or prohibiting certain selling arrangements is not such as to hinder directly or indirectly, actually or potentially, trade between Member States within the meaning of the *Dassonville* judgment (Case 8/74 [1974] ECR 837), so long as those provisions apply to all relevant traders operating within the national territory and so long as they affect in the same manner, in law and in fact, the marketing of domestic products and of those from other Member States.

17. Provided that those conditions are fulfilled, the application of such rules to the sale of products from another Member State meeting the requirements laid down by that State is not by nature such as to prevent their access to the market or to impede access any more than it impedes the access of domestic products. Such rules therefore fall outside the scope of Article 30.

REVIEW QUESTION

What are the key requirements to be met in determining whether a measure falls outside Dassonville as a legitimate selling arrangement?

Answer: Following *Keck*, it is clear that certain selling arrangements do not fall within the *Dassonville* formula, provided that those provisions apply to all affected traders operating within the national territory and provided that they affect in the same manner, in law and in fact, the marketing of domestic products and of those from other Member States.

10.8.9.1 'Selling arrangements'

Many references have been made to 'selling arrangements'. Selling arrangements can be defined as rules relating to the market circumstances in which the goods are sold, as opposed to rules relating to the composition of the product or its packaging. Selling arrangements have been held to include rules relating to:

- where or by whom goods may be sold (Case C-254/98 *Schutzverband gegen unlauteren Wettbewerb v TK-Heimdienst Sass GmbH* [2000] ECR I-151; Case C-391/92 *Commission of the European Communities v Hellenic Republic* [1995] ECR I-1621);
- when goods may be sold (Joined Cases C-418–21, 460–2, & 464/93 and C-9–11, 14, 15, 23, 24, & C-332/94 *Semeraro Casa Uno Srl v Sindaco del Comune di Erbusco* [1996] ECR I-2975);
- advertising restrictions (Cases C-34–6/95 *Konsumentombudsmannen (KO) v De Agostini (Svenska) Forlag AB* [1997] ECR I-3843); and
- price controls (Joined Cases C-267 & 268/91 *Keck and Mithouard* [1993] ECR I-6097).

In Joined Cases C-401 & 402/92 *Tankstation 't Heukske* [1994] I-2199, the Court of Justice held that Article 34 TFEU did not apply to rules concerning the opening times of shops at petrol stations that applied to all and affected all in the same manner. Such matters amounted to selling arrangements.

However, those discriminatory restrictions that do not satisfy the *Keck* test will remain within Article 34 TFEU and fall to be considered within Article 36 TFEU or *Cassis* (as appropriate).

Case C-254/98 *Schutzverband gegen unlauteren Wettbewerb v TK-Heimdienst Sass GmbH* [2000] ECR I-151 concerned Austrian legislation prohibiting door-to-door sales unless the sellers also carried on the trade from permanent premises in the same area. Although it applied to all traders, it had a discriminatory effect on traders from other Member States, as they would have the additional cost of setting up a permanent base. Therefore it impeded access to the Austrian market and thus breached Article 34 TFEU.

Joined Cases C-34–6/95 *Konsumentombudsmannen (KO) v De Agostini (Svenska) Forlag AB* [1997] ECR I-3843 concerned a ban on television advertising aimed at children under the age of 12. The Court of Justice found that where a producer is unable to advertise its product, it may be prevented from accessing a market. These same restrictions may have less impact on domestic products, as they will already be known and are less reliant upon television advertising as a means of penetrating the market. Thus the measure fell outside *Keck* due to the discriminatory effect and, as an MEQR, it fell to be considered under Article 36 TFEU or *Cassis*.

10.8.10 Further developments: a further category of MEQRs?

In a number of recent cases, the Court of Justice has been faced with circumstances involving tariff barriers to trade that affect market access, but which do not fall easily within either of the categories considered earlier. As such, a new category has started to develop. These barriers are characterized by the imposition of restrictions on the *use* of a product, rather than the characteristics or the market circumstances in which it is sold.

An example can be found in Case C-110/05 *Commission v Italy ('Italian Trailers')* [2009] ECR I-519, in which Italian legislation (set out in article 56 of the Highway Code) imposed a ban on the towing of trailers by two- and three-wheeled vehicles. The Court of Justice began its judgment by considering the types of measure that fall within what is now Article 34 TFEU as MEQRs and restating the *Dassonville* formula.

Case C-110/05 *Commission v Italy ('Italian Trailers')* [2009] ECR I-519

Preliminary observations

33. It should be recalled that, according to settled case-law, all trading rules enacted by Member States which are capable of hindering, directly or indirectly, actually or potentially, intra-Community [now Union] trade are to be considered as measures having an effect equivalent to quantitative restrictions and are, on that basis, prohibited by Article 28 EC [now Article 34 TFEU] (see, in particular, *Dassonville*, paragraph 5).
34. It is also apparent from settled case-law that Article 28 EC reflects the obligation to respect the principles of non-discrimination and of mutual recognition of products lawfully manufactured and marketed in other Member States, as well as the principle of ensuring free access of Community products to national markets (see, to that effect, Case 174/82 *Sandoz* [1983] ECR 2445, paragraph 26; Case 120/78 *Rewe-Zentral* (*'Cassis de Dijon'*) [1979] ECR 649, paragraphs 6, 14 and 15; and *Keck and Mithouard*, paragraphs 16 and 17).
35. Hence, in the absence of harmonisation of national legislation, obstacles to the free movement of goods which are the consequence of applying, to goods coming from other Member States where they are lawfully manufactured and marketed, rules that lay down requirements to be met by such goods constitute measures of equivalent effect to quantitative restrictions even if those rules apply to all products alike (see, to that effect, *'Cassis de Dijon'*, paragraphs 6, 14 and 15; Case C-368/95 *Familiapress* [1997] ECR I-3689, paragraph 8; and Case C-322/01 *Deutscher Apothekerverband* [2003] ECR I-14887, paragraph 67).

36. By contrast, the application to products from other Member States of national provisions restricting or prohibiting certain selling arrangements is not such as to hinder directly or indirectly, actually or potentially, trade between Member States for the purposes of the case-law flowing from *Dassonville*, on condition that those provisions apply to all relevant traders operating within the national territory and that they affect in the same manner, in law and in fact, the marketing of domestic products and of those from other Member States. Provided that those conditions are fulfilled, the application of such rules to the sale of products from another Member State meeting the requirements laid down by that State is not by nature such as to prevent their access to the market or to impede access any more than it impedes the access of domestic products (see *Keck and Mithouard*, paragraphs 16 and 17).

37. Consequently, measures adopted by a Member State the object or effect of which is to treat products coming from other Member States less favourably are to be regarded as measures having equivalent effect to quantitative restrictions on imports within the meaning of Article 28 EC, as are the measures referred to in paragraph 35 of the present judgment. Any other measure which hinders access of products originating in other Member States to the market of a Member State is also covered by that concept.

Paragraph 37 of *Italian Trailers* is a clear recognition of the breadth of the MEQR concept and, in finishing the paragraph in this way, the Court ensures flexibility in approach, recognizing that it is the object or effect of a measure that is paramount regardless of whether it neatly falls within existing categories.

The Court continued, explaining why the measure in question amounted to an MEQR.

Case C-110/05 *Commission v Italy ('Italian Trailers')* [2009] ECR I-519

56. It should be noted in that regard that a prohibition on the use of a product in the territory of a Member State has a considerable influence on the behaviour of consumers, which, in its turn, affects the access of that product to the market of that Member State.

57. Consumers, knowing that they are not permitted to use their motorcycle with a trailer specially designed for it, have practically no interest in buying such a trailer (see, by analogy, Case C-265/06 *Commission* v *Portugal* [2008] ECR I-0000, paragraph 33, concerning the affixing of tinted film to the windows of motor vehicles). Thus, Article 56 of the Highway Code prevents a demand from existing in the market at issue for such trailers and therefore hinders their importation.

58. It follows that the prohibition laid down in Article 56 of the Highway Code, to the extent that its effect is to hinder access to the Italian market for trailers which are specially designed for motorcycles and are lawfully produced and marketed in Member States other than the Italian Republic, constitutes a measure having equivalent effect to quantitative restrictions on imports within the meaning of Article 28 EC [now Article 34 TFEU], unless it can be justified objectively.

It is therefore clear that the restrictions on the use of the product amounted to an MEQR on the basis that market access was affected.

Case C-142/05 *Åklagaren v Percy Mickelsson and Joakim Roos ('Swedish Jet Skis')* [2009] ECR I-4273 provides a further example of an MEQR falling within the 'use of a product' category. In *Åklagaren*, Swedish legislation placed restrictions on the use of jet skis, limiting their use to generally navigable waterways, of which there were very few and which, in any event, were generally unsuitable for jet-ski use. Again, the Court of Justice considered whether restrictions on the use of a product could amount to an MEQR within what is now Article 34 TFEU.

Case C-142/05 *Åklagaren v Percy Mickelsson and Joakim Roos ('Swedish Jet Skis')* [2009] ECR I-4273

24. It must be borne in mind that measures taken by a Member State, the aim or effect of which is to treat goods coming from other Member States less favourably and, in the absence of harmonisation of national legislation, obstacles to the free movement of goods which are the consequence of applying, to goods coming from other Member States where they are lawfully manufactured and marketed, rules that lay down requirements to be met by such goods, even if those rules apply to all products alike, must be regarded as 'measures having equivalent effect to quantitative restrictions on imports' for the purposes of Article 28 EC [now Article 34 TFEU] (see to that effect, Case 120/78 *Rewe-Zentral (Cassis de Dijon)* [1979] ECR 649, paragraphs 6, 14 and 15; Case C-368/95 *Familiapress* [1997] ECR I-3689, paragraph 8; and Case C-322/01 *Deutscher Apothekerverband* [2003] ECR I-14887, paragraph 67). Any other measure which hinders access of products originating in other Member States to the market of a Member State is also covered by that concept (see Case C-110/05 *Commission* v *Italy* [2009] ECR I-0000, paragraph 37).
25. It is apparent from the file sent to the Court that, at the material time, no waters had been designated as open to navigation by personal watercraft, and thus the use of personal watercraft was permitted on only general navigable waterways. However, the accused in the main proceedings and the Commission of the European Communities [now EU] maintain that those waterways are intended for heavy traffic of a commercial nature making the use of personal watercraft dangerous and that, in any event, the majority of navigable Swedish waters lie outside those waterways. The actual possibilities for the use of personal watercraft in Sweden are, therefore, merely marginal.
26. Even if the national regulations at issue do not have the aim or effect of treating goods coming from other Member States less favourably, which is for the national court to ascertain, the restriction which they impose on the use of a product in the territory of a Member State may, depending on its scope, have a considerable influence on the behaviour of consumers, which may, in turn, affect the access of that product to the market of that Member State (see to that effect, *Commission* v *Italy*, paragraph 56).
27. Consumers, knowing that the use permitted by such regulations is very limited, have only a limited interest in buying that product (see to that effect, *Commission* v *Italy*, paragraph 57).

28. In that regard, where the national regulations for the designation of navigable waters and waterways have the effect of preventing users of personal watercraft from using them for the specific and inherent purposes for which they were intended or of greatly restricting their use, which is for the national court to ascertain, such regulations have the effect of hindering the access to the domestic market in question for those goods and therefore constitute, save where there is a justification pursuant to Article 30 EC or there are overriding public interest requirements, measures having equivalent effect to quantitative restrictions on imports prohibited by Article 28 EC.

Thus the Court concluded that the restrictive measure amounted to an MEQR on the basis that demand for jet skis would be limited as consumers would not be able to use them and therefore market access would be hindered. The Court further considered a potential justification on the basis of protection of health, life, and the environment, but found the measure to be disproportionate even in this regard, because the restrictions prevented use on some waterways where risks to health and the environment did not exist.

?! THINKING POINT

Can you identify the different categories that an MEQR can fall into?

10.8.11 Article 36 TFEU

Article 36 TFEU provides exceptions to the prohibition in Article 34 and 35 TFEU. It allows Member States to restrict the free movement of goods for certain specific reasons only. In contrast to the *Cassis* list of mandatory requirements (see 10.8.6), the Article 36 TFEU list of derogations is exhaustive.

Article 36 TFEU

The provisions of Articles 34 and 35 shall not preclude prohibitions or restrictions on imports ... justified on grounds of public morality, public policy or public security; the protection of health and life of humans, animals or plants ... protection of national treasures ... protection of industrial and commercial property. Such prohibitions or restrictions shall not, however, constitute a means of arbitrary discrimination or a disguised restriction on trade between Member States.

The following cases provide examples of obstacles to the free movement of goods that have been justified on Article 36 TFEU grounds.

10.8.11.1 Public morality

The 'public morality' ground was considered in two cases concerning restrictions on imports of pornography.

In Case 34/79 *R v Henn and Darby* [1979] ECR 3795 (see 6.4.1 and 9.2.2), a ban on the import of pornographic material amounted to a quantitative restriction under Article 34 TFEU. Such a ban was held to be justified on the ground of public morality, with the Court of Justice noting that it is for each Member State to determine standards. The legislation banning the material in question was found not to discriminate in favour of a domestic product and therefore was justified under Article 36 TFEU.

In Case 121/85 *Conegate Ltd v HM Customs and Excise* [1986] ECR 1007 (see 9.2.2), inflatable dolls that were clearly of a sexual nature and other erotic articles were seized by UK customs authorities. The UK government argued that the ban was justified on the basis of public morality under Article 36 TFEU. However, a distinction was drawn between this case and *R v Henn and Darby*.

Case 121/85 *Conegate Ltd v HM Customs and Excise* [1986] ECR 1007

15. However, although Community law [now EU law] leaves the Member States free to make their own assessments of the indecent or obscene character of certain articles, it must be pointed out that the fact that goods cause offence cannot be regarded as sufficiently serious to justify restrictions on the free movement of goods where the Member State concerned does not adopt, with respect to the same goods manufactured or marketed within its territory, penal measures or other serious and effective measures intended to prevent the distribution of such goods in its territory.
16. It follows that a Member State may not rely on grounds of public morality in order to prohibit the importation of goods from other Member States when its legislation contains no prohibition on the manufacture or marketing of the same goods on its territory.

?! THINKING POINT

Can you identify the distinction drawn by the Court of Justice?

10.8.11.2 Public policy

Although the ground is potentially wide in scope, 'public policy' has nevertheless been interpreted narrowly by the Court of Justice. This ground cannot be used as a general justification embracing more specific defences, such as consumer protection, but must be given its own independent meaning (Case 7/61 *Commission v Italy (Re Ban on Pork Imports)* [1961] ECR 317). The public policy ground has rarely been invoked.

In Case 7/78 *R v Thompson* [1978] ECR 2247, a ban on the unlawful importation into the UK of krugerrands (South African gold coins) and a ban on the export of coins was at issue. The Court of Justice held that the right to mint and thus control coinage was a fundamental interest of the State. Thus a State that prohibits the destruction of a coinage and imposes a ban to prevent their destruction abroad is justified in doing so on the basis of public policy under Article 36 TFEU.

10.8.11.3 Public security

In Case 72/83 *Campus Oil Ltd v Minister for Industry and Energy* [1984] ECR 2727, Irish legislation ensuring that a percentage of oil was bought from the State-owned refinery was argued to be in place to ensure that Ireland could continue with its refining capability, which ensured its public security. The Court of Justice held that as an interruption of supplies could seriously threaten public security, the maintenance of essential oil supplies was covered by the public security exception and therefore the measure was justified under Article 36 TFEU.

10.8.11.4 Protection of health and life of humans, animals, or plants

Two contrasting decisions elucidate the scope of this ground. In Case 4/75 *Rewe-Zentralfinanz v Landwirtschaftskammer Bonn ('San Jose Scale')* [1975] ECR 843, German inspections of imported (but not domestically produced) apples were held to be justified on health grounds as the imported fruit presented a genuine health risk not present in domestic apples. By contrast, the Court of Justice rejected health justifications (the aim of avoiding the spread of Newcastle disease) for the UK's prohibition on the import of poultry meat and the adoption of an import licensing system in Case 40/82 *Commission v UK (Imports of Poultry Meat)* [1984] ECR 283. Whilst it was acknowledged that Article 36 TFEU presented an appropriate ground for potential justification, the argument failed for a number of other reasons. The measures were not part of a seriously considered health policy and constituted a disguised restriction on trade.

The issue of health risk was assessed in Case C-322/01 *Deutsche Apothekerverband v 0800 DocMorris NV* [2003] ECR I-14887 concerning a German ban on the sale of medicines by mail order and over the Internet. The measure related to 'selling arrangements', but fell outside *Keck* because it had a greater impact on imports than on domestic products (see 10.8.9). Thus the ban infringed what is now Article 34 TFEU. The Court of Justice held that the measure could be justified on health grounds in relation to prescription medicines because consumers needed to receive individual advice and the authenticity of prescriptions must be checked. By contrast, non-prescription medicines did not present a risk because the 'virtual pharmacy' could provide an equal or better level of advice than traditional pharmacies. Here, the prohibition was not justified.

One difficult area is the use of additives in foodstuffs, since there may be scientific uncertainty as to the extent of any risk.

Case 174/82 *Officier van Justitie v Sandoz BV* [1983] ECR 2445 concerned a Dutch prohibition on the sale of muesli bars with added vitamins. The Dutch argued that the vitamins were harmful to health, although they were freely available in Germany and Belgium. The vitamins themselves presented no health risk and were in fact necessary to human health, but their overconsumption across a range of foodstuffs would constitute a risk. As scientific research had been unable to determine the critical amount or the precise effects, the Court of Justice declared that it was for Member States to decide the appropriate degree of public health protection, whilst observing the principle of proportionality. Member States must authorize marketing when the addition of vitamins to foodstuffs meets a technical or nutritional need.

In Case 178/84 *Commission v Germany (Re Beer Purity Laws)* [1987] ECR 1227, German rules stated that all beer in Germany under the designation 'Bier' could be made only from certain ingredients and that beers containing additives could not be marketed. One of the arguments advanced by the German government was that, due to the extent of German consumption of the products in question, the use of additives was more of a problem for German nationals than it was for nationals of other countries. Noting that Germany permitted additives in virtually all other drinks, the Court of Justice decided that high beer consumption did not justify banning all additives in this particular product.

In Case C-148/15 *Deutsche Parkinson Vereinigung eV v Zentrale zur Bekämpfung unlauteren Wettbewerbs eV* EU:C:2016:776, the Court held that a system of fixed prices of prescription-only medicines for sale in pharmacies amounted to an MEQR within Article 34 TFEU. In considering whether the measure could be justified under the Article 36 TFEU ground of public health, the Court began by setting out some key principles.

Case C-148/15 *Deutsche Parkinson Vereinigung eV v Zentrale zur Bekämpfung unlauteren Wettbewerbs eV* EU:C:2016:776

30. As regards a national measure coming within the field of public health, the Court has on numerous occasions held that the health and life of humans rank foremost among the assets and interests protected by the Treaty and that it is for the Member States to determine the level of protection which they wish to afford to public health and the way in which that level is to be achieved. Since that level may vary from one Member State to another, Member States should be allowed a measure of discretion (see judgment of 12 November 2015, *Visnapuu*, C-198/14, EU:C:2015:751, paragraph 118 and the case-law cited).
31. In particular, the need to ensure that the country has reliable supplies for essential medical purposes may, so far as Article 36 TFEU is concerned, justify a barrier to trade between Member States if that objective is one of protecting the health and life of humans (see judgment of 28 March 1995, *Evans Medical and Macfarlan Smith*, C-324/93, EU:C:1995:84, paragraph 37).

[...]

36. It follows that, where a national court examines national legislation in the light of the justification relating to protection of the health and life of humans under Article 36 TFEU, that court must examine objectively, through statistical or ad hoc data or by other means, whether it may reasonably be concluded from the evidence submitted by the Member State concerned that the means chosen are appropriate for the attainment of the objectives pursued and whether it is possible to attain those objectives by measures that are less restrictive of the free movement of goods (see, to that effect, judgment of 23 December 2015, *The Scotch Whisky Association and Others*, C-333/14, EU:C:2015:845, paragraph 59).

The Court then evaluated each of the arguments put forward to justify the measure.

Case C-148/15 *Deutsche Parkinson Vereinigung eV v Zentrale zur Bekämpfung unlauteren Wettbewerbs eV* EU:C:2016:776

37. As to whether the national legislation at issue in the main proceedings is appropriate for attaining the objectives invoked, it must be stated that there is no evidence to substantiate the contention that it is necessary to ensure a uniform supply of prescription-only medicinal products for essential medical purposes throughout Germany that satisfies the conditions set out in paragraph 35 above. In particular, by the general nature of the contentions made in the present case in that regard, it has not been demonstrated, as the Advocate General has, in essence, noted in point 51 of his Opinion, how setting fixed prices for such medicinal products allows for a better geographical allocation of traditional pharmacies in Germany.
38. Quite to the contrary, certain factors on which the Commission relies tend to suggest that increased price competition between pharmacies would be conducive to a uniform supply of medicinal products by encouraging the establishment of pharmacies in regions where the scarcity of dispensaries allows for higher prices to be charged.
39. As regards the argument based on a high-quality supply of prescription-only medicinal products, it must be found that, contrary to what the German Government claims, no factor has been laid before the Court that is capable of establishing that, in the absence of a system such as that at issue in the main proceedings, mail-order pharmacies would be able to compete in terms of price in such a way that essential services, such as emergency care, could no longer be ensured in Germany due to a consequential fall in the number of dispensing pharmacies. In that regard, it must be reiterated that competition factors other than price, such as those set out in paragraph 24 above, could potentially allow traditional pharmacies, faced with competition from mail-order sales, to remain competitive in the German market.
40. Similarly, the elements laid before the Court in the present case do not suffice to show that price competition for prescription-only medicinal products would adversely affect traditional pharmacies in performing certain activities in the general interest, such as producing prescription medicinal products or maintaining a given stock and selection of medicinal products. On the contrary, as the Advocate General stated, in essence, in point 47 in his Opinion, it may be that, faced with price competition from mail-order pharmacies, traditional pharmacies will be encouraged to improve such activities.
41. Nor has the alleged relationship between the fixed sales price in the case in the main proceedings and a consequential reduction of the risk that patients might attempt to pressurise doctors in order to obtain prescriptions of convenience been established in compliance with the conditions cited in paragraph 35 above.
42. As regards the argument put forward by the ZBUW and the German Government that a patient in poor health ought not to be required to carry out a market analysis in order

to determine which pharmacy offers the medicinal product sought at the most attractive price, it should be noted that the existence of a genuine risk to human health must be measured, not according to the yardstick of general conjecture, but on the basis of relevant scientific research (see, to that effect, judgment of EU:C:2016:776 7 JUDGMENT OF 19. 10. 2016—CASE C-148/15 DEUTSCHE PARKINSON VEREINIGUNG 14 July 1994, *van der Veldt*, C-17/93, EU:C:1994:299, paragraph 17). Such general conjecture made in that regard does not in any way suffice to prove that the possibility for the consumer to seek to acquire prescription-only medicinal products at lower prices poses an actual risk to public health.

43. Moreover, the Court notes, as did DPV and the Netherlands Government, that, in the present case, price competition could be capable of benefiting the patient in so far as it would allow, where relevant, for prescription-only medicinal products to be offered in Germany at more attractive prices than those currently imposed by that Member State. As the Court has previously held, the effective protection of health and life of humans demands, inter alia, that medicinal products be sold at reasonable prices (see judgment of 20 May 1976, *de Peijper*, 104/75, EU:C:1976:67, paragraph 25).
44. Finally, it should be added that the fact that there are other national measures, such as the rule excluding non-pharmacists from the right to own and operate pharmacies, which have the objective, according to the documents before the Court, of supplying safe and high-quality prescription-only medicinal products in Germany, does not affect the Court's assessment of the fixed-price system at issue in the case in the main proceedings.
45. Having regard to all of the foregoing considerations, it must be found that a restriction such as that resulting from the legislation at issue in the main proceedings has not been shown to be an appropriate means of attaining the objectives relied on and cannot therefore be regarded as justified by the attainment of those objectives.

The analysis given of the various arguments justifying the measure provides a useful insight into the restrictive approach of the Court of Justice when considering potential justifications. Clearly, in this case, the Court remained unconvinced.

10.8.11.5 Protection of national treasures possessing artistic, historic, or archaeological value

The scope of this justification remains uncertain. In Case 7/68 *Commission v Italy (Export Tax on Art Treasures, No 1)* [1968] ECR 423, the Court of Justice indicated that quantitative restrictions (but not charges) would be justified where the object of those restrictions was to prevent art treasures from being exported from a Member State.

10.8.11.6 Protection of industrial and commercial property

EU law protects the ownership of industrial and commercial property rights, such as patents, copyright, trade marks, and design rights. However, any improper use of these rights, constituting an obstacle to trade, will be condemned by the Court of Justice.

It is therefore clear that the interpretation and application of Article 36 TFEU by the Court of Justice, as with all the other potential means by which obstacles to the free movement of goods may be justified, is quite restrictive in practice, with a significant burden placed upon those seeking to justify such obstacles.

10.8.12 No arbitrary discrimination, disguised restriction on trade

Article 36 TFEU, emphasis added

The provisions of Articles 34 and 35 shall not preclude prohibitions or restrictions on imports, exports or goods in transit justified on grounds of public morality, public policy or public security; the protection of health and life of humans, animals or plants; the protection of national treasures possessing artistic, historic or archaeological value; or the protection of industrial and commercial property. *Such prohibitions or restrictions shall not, however, constitute a means of arbitrary discrimination or a disguised restriction on trade between Member States.*

In essence, the final element of Article 36 TFEU requires that any claims of justification under the Article must conform to the overall desire to ensure the free movement of goods. Thus they cannot be an attempt merely to discriminate between products or an attempt, albeit disguised, to restrict trade between Member States.

In Case 40/82 *Commission v UK (Imports of Poultry Meat)* [1982] ECR 2793, the UK's argument that prohibition of the importation of poultry products and the adoption of an import licensing system had the aim of avoiding the spread of Newcastle disease failed. Amongst the reasons identified was a failure to fully recognize measures taken elsewhere, the likelihood of spread of the disease, lobbying by farmers, and the timing of the measure.

→ CROSS-REFERENCE
See 10.8.6.3 on proportionality.

Case 40/82 *Commission v UK (Imports of Poultry Meat)* [1982] ECR 2793

37. Certain established facts suggest that the real aim of the 1981 measures was to block, for commercial and economic reasons, imports of poultry products from other Member States, in particular from France. The United Kingdom government had been subject to pressure from British poultry producers to block these imports. It hurriedly introduced its new policy with the result that French Christmas turkeys were excluded from the British market for the 1981 season. It did not inform the Commission and the Member States concerned in good time, as the letter in which the Commission was informed of the new measures—which took effect on 1 September 1981—was dated 27 August 1981. It did not find it necessary to discuss the effects of the new measures on imports with the Community [now Union] institutions, with the standing veterinary committee or with the Member States concerned.

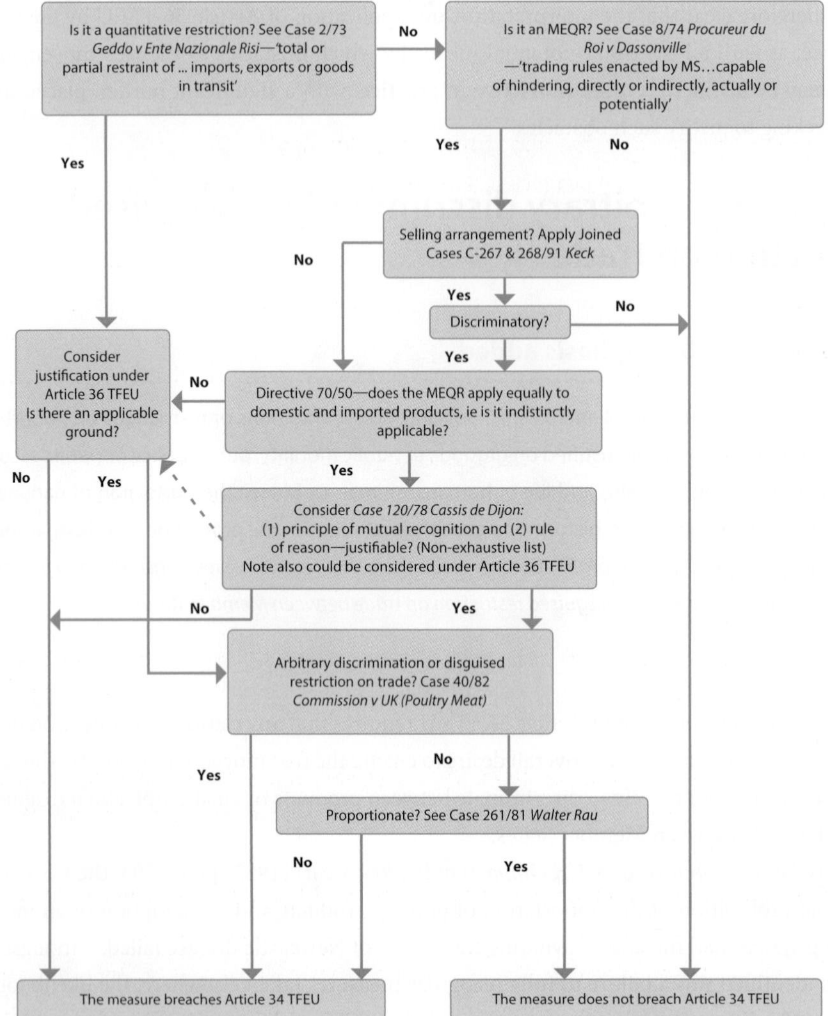

Figure 10.3 Article 34 TFEU

For an overview of Article 34 TFEU, see Figure 10.3.

10.8.13 Proportionality

As with *Cassis*, the measures must go no further than is necessary to achieve the desired aim. In Case 40/82 *Commission v UK (Imports of Poultry Meat)* [1982] ECR 2793, the UK government's argument for the restrictive measures in place also failed on the basis of their lack of proportionality to the risk identified.

10.8.13.1 No harmonizing rules

Article 36 TFEU applies only in the absence of EU rules governing the interest concerned. If there is harmonizing legislation in a particular area, Member States may not impose additional requirements unless the legislation expressly permits them to do so.

SUMMARY

- Article 30 TFEU prohibits customs duties and charges having an equivalent effect (CHEEs).
- The concept of a customs duty incorporates two elements—namely, (a) a pecuniary charge that is (b) imposed on goods by reason of crossing a frontier.
- The concept of a CHEE is wider and includes measures that are not customs duties in the strict sense, but which have the same effect even in the absence of a protective or discriminatory purpose. Thus the emphasis is upon the effect of the measure and not its purpose.
- There are exceptions: Article 30 TFEU is not breached if the charge is justified as a fee for a service rendered, in which case it must be of direct benefit to the goods or traders, or if it is mandated by EU law and proportionate to the service rendered.
- The first paragraph of Article 110 TFEU prohibits unequal taxation of similar products and the second prohibits internal taxation which indirectly protects domestic products that, although not similar to the imported products, are nevertheless in competition with them.
- A distinction can be drawn between direct and indirect discrimination.
  - Measures that openly tax imported and domestic goods at different rates are directly discriminatory.
  - Indirectly discriminatory taxation is taxation that appears (in law) not to discriminate between imported and domestically produced goods, but which nevertheless has a discriminatory effect in reality.
- Directly discriminatory measures can never be justified. Indirectly discriminatory measures may be objectively justified if there exists some objective policy reason that is acceptable to the European Union (EU).
- 'Similar products' within the first paragraph of Article 110 TFEU has been interpreted by the Court of Justice broadly to mean similar characteristics and comparable use.
- In determining the meaning of 'indirect protection to other products' within the second paragraph of Article 110 TFEU, the Court needs to establish whether the products are in competition. A number of factors are taken into account, including cross-elasticity of demand, manufacturing processes, product composition, and present and future consumer preferences.
- If the first paragraph of Article 110 TFEU is breached, the Member State must equalize taxation.
- If the second paragraph of Article 110 TFEU is breached, the Member State has to remove the competitive effect of the tax regulation.
- Article 34 TFEU prohibits quantitative restrictions and measures having equivalent effect to quantitative restrictions (MEQRs).
- Quantitative restrictions are measures that limit the import or export of goods by reference to an amount or value.
- The *Dassonville* formula defines MEQRs as 'all trading rules enacted by Member States which are capable of hindering, directly or indirectly, actually or potentially, intra-community trade'.
- A distinction can be drawn between distinctly and indistinctly applicable measures.
  - Distinctly applicable measures are those other than those applicable equally to domestic or imported products.

  - Indistinctly applicable measures are those that are equally applicable to domestic and imported products.
- *Cassis de Dijon* established two important principles: (a) the principle of mutual recognition; and (b) the rule of reason. These exceptions apply to indistinctly applicable MEQRs only.
- In order to satisfy the rule of reason, the measures used must be no more than is necessary to achieve their aim (proportionality).
- Certain selling arrangements do not fall within the *Dassonville* formula provided that they apply to all affected traders operating within the national territory and affect in the same manner, in law and in fact, the marketing of domestic and imported products.
- Article 36 TFEU allows Member States to restrict the free movement of goods for certain specific reasons only. Measures must not amount to arbitrary discrimination or a disguised restriction on trade and must be proportionate.
- Article 36 TFEU and *Cassis* mandatory requirements can be compared as follows.
  - Article 36 TFEU applies to distinctly and indistinctly applicable measures and is exhaustive.
  - *Cassis* applies only to indistinctly applicable MEQRs and is non-exhaustive.

FURTHER READING

Articles

R Barents, 'Charges of Equivalent Effect to Customs Duties' (1978) 15 CML Rev 415

Focuses on tariff barriers to trade.

T Connor, 'Accentuating the Positive: The "Selling Arrangement", the First Decade and Beyond' (2005) 54 ICLQ 127

Reflects upon the development of the *Keck* judgment.

P Oliver, 'Of Trailers and Jet Skis: Is the Case Law on Article 34 TFEU Hurtling in a New Direction?' (2011) 33(5) Fordham International LJ 1470

A useful chronology of case developments concerning Article 34 TFEU and interesting consideration of future developments.

A Tryfonidou, 'Was *Keck* a Half-Baked Solution After All?' (2007) 34 Legal Issues of Economic Integration 167

A critical consideration of *Keck*.

D Wilsher, 'Does *Keck* Discrimination Make Any Sense? An Assessment of the Non-Discrimination Principle within the European Single Market' (2008) 33 EL Rev 3

Focuses on the requirements for selling arrangements under *Keck*.

Books

P Oliver, *Oliver on Free Movement of Goods in the European Union*, 5th edn (Oxford: Hart, 2010)

A specialist text for academics and practitioners on all aspects of the free movement of goods.

L Woods, *Free Movement of Goods and Services within the European Community* (Farnham: Ashgate, 2004)

A specialist text focusing on two fundamental freedoms of the EU internal market.

QUESTION

SOUPS YOU SIR Ltd is an English company that manufactures a range of soups. Tom Ato, managing director, has been looking for opportunities to expand the business and has recently concluded that the time is right to export to the rest of Europe. However, things have not been straightforward.

The Latvian authorities have informed Tom that he will be unable to sell soup in Latvia unless changes are made to the way in which the products are packaged. SOUPS YOU SIR Ltd has always sold its products in cartons and has invested heavily in packaging processes, with the up-market cartons being a key element in the branding of the range. However, the Latvian authorities insist that if SOUPS YOU SIR Ltd products are to be sold in Latvia, they must be sold in jars.

Recent Belgian legislation aimed at tackling a rise in the obesity figures bans television advertising of all food products. Tom fears that the legislation may prevent SOUPS YOU SIR Ltd's products from breaking into the Belgian market.

The German authorities have informed Tom that all soup imported into Germany is subject to a €3 fee. When Tom queried this, he was informed that the fee is levied 'for the compilation of data deemed beneficial to importers'.

Finally, Polish taxation policy taxes soups in cartons at 15 per cent, whilst soups in tins are taxed at 1.5 per cent. Poland does not produce soups in cartons and Polish officials insist that the measure is justified, as tins are easier and cheaper to recycle than cartons.

Advise Tom as to the impact of relevant EU law in relation to the free movement of goods.

To view an outline answer to this question plus further resources to support your EU law studies, visit the Online Resources for this book at www.oup.com/uk/eulaw-complete4e

11 Free movement of persons

KEY POINTS

By the end of this chapter, you should be able to:

- define the scope of the right of free movement of persons in the European Union (EU);
- identify the relevant Treaty provisions and secondary legislation provisions regarding the free movement of persons in the EU;
- explain and apply the relevant legislation in order to determine and describe the specific rights granted to EU citizens and those holding the status of worker under their general right of free movement; and
- explain and apply the relevant legislation concerning measures restricting the free movement of persons in the EU.

INTRODUCTION

The free movement of persons is one of the four fundamental freedoms in EU law. The right for people to move freely between Member States is a distinguishing characteristic of an internal market. In particular, Article 26 TFEU provides that 'the internal market shall comprise an area without internal frontiers in which the free movement of goods, persons, services and capital is ensured'.

Initially, the free movement of persons did not entail a right of free movement for all persons; the emphasis was on the right of free movement for economically active persons, such as workers. Those people enjoyed, and continue to enjoy, a right to equal treatment compared to nationals of the host Member State in which they resided. Historically, the purpose or policy underlying the right of free movement for the economically active was primarily of an economic nature. It was thought that it would lead to an optimal allocation of resources, with workers viewed as factors of production.

However, there was also a social dimension to the free movement of the economically active: to form an ever-closer union of the peoples of Europe, it should be regarded as attractive and natural for people within the European Union (EU) to work in a Member State other than their own.

The free movement of persons is governed by Treaty provisions, as well as secondary legislation. Over the years, secondary legislation has demonstrated that the link between economic activity and free movement has become weaker, and that workers are no longer viewed as mere production factors; rather, they are now viewed as individual human beings who have certain rights in the host Member State, based on EU law.

→ CROSS-REFERENCE
See 1.13 on the TEU.

Furthermore, the category of non-economically active persons with free movement rights has expanded greatly over the years, culminating in a right of free movement for all EU citizens, a concept formally introduced by the Treaty on European Union (TEU).

11.1 EU citizenship

Whilst the rights of free movement of persons within the internal market began with the economically active, the Maastricht Treaty (TEU 1992) introduced the status of citizenship of the European Union. The significance of this status may not have been realized by some at this time, but, in a series of important cases, the Court of Justice interpreted the provisions on citizenship status as a basis for rights, declaring in Case C-184/99 *Grzelczyk v Centre public d'aide sociale d'Ottignies-Louvain-la-Neuve* [2001] ECR I-6193, at para 31, that 'Union citizenship is destined to be the fundamental status of nationals of the Member States, enabling those who find themselves in the same situation to enjoy the same treatment in law irrespective of their nationality, subject to such exceptions as are expressly provided for.'

As such, it seems fitting to begin by discussing the relevant provisions that apply to EU citizens before considering in detail the rights provided to workers.

Article 20 TFEU

1. Citizenship of the Union is hereby established. Every person holding the nationality of a Member State shall be a citizen of the Union. Citizenship of the Union shall be additional to and not replace national citizenship.
2. Citizens of the Union shall enjoy the rights and be subject to the duties provided for in the Treaties. They shall have, inter alia:
   (a) the right to move and reside freely within the territory of the Member States;
   (b) the right to vote and to stand as candidates in elections to the European Parliament and in municipal elections in their Member State of residence, under the same conditions as nationals of that State;
   (c) the right to enjoy, in the territory of a third country in which the Member State of which they are nationals is not represented, the protection of the diplomatic and consular authorities of any Member State on the same conditions as the nationals of that State;
   (d) the right to petition the European Parliament, to apply to the European Ombudsman, and to address the institutions and advisory bodies of the Union in any of the Treaty languages and to obtain a reply in the same language.

   These rights shall be exercised in accordance with the conditions and limits defined by the Treaties and by the measures adopted thereunder.

Article 21 TFEU

1. Every citizen of the Union shall have the right to move and reside freely within the territory of the Member States, subject to the limitations and conditions laid down in the Treaties and by the measures adopted to give them effect.

2. If action by the Union should prove necessary to attain this objective and the Treaties have not provided the necessary powers, the European Parliament and the Council, acting in accordance with the ordinary legislative procedure, may adopt provisions with a view to facilitating the exercise of the rights referred to in paragraph 1.
3. For the same purposes as those referred to in paragraph 1 and if the Treaties have not provided the necessary powers, the Council, acting in accordance with a special legislative procedure, may adopt measures concerning social security or social protection. The Council shall act unanimously after consulting the European Parliament.

11.1.1 EU citizens

It follows from Article 20(1) TFEU that an EU citizen is anyone who has the nationality of one of the Member States of the EU.

REVIEW QUESTION

Does the EU decide who is an EU citizen or do the Member States set out the criteria?

Answer: It is under the Member States' exclusive competence to decide who can obtain that State's nationality and under what conditions. Therefore the Member States decide who is an EU citizen, and the EU has no power to grant or remove nationality and, consequently, citizenship of the EU. Similarly, other Member States cannot interfere with a Member State's decision to grant nationality or the conditions for acquiring that nationality.

?! THINKING POINT

Why do you think this approach is taken?

In Case C-369/90 *Micheletti* [1992] ECR I-4239, a person with both Argentine and Italian nationalities wanted to set up as a dentist in Spain. The Spanish authorities denied him the right of permanent residence in Spain based on the Spanish Civil Code, according to which, in cases of dual nationality in which neither nationality is Spanish, the nationality corresponding to the habitual residence of the person concerned before his arrival in Spain is to take precedence. In the case of Mr Micheletti, that was Argentine nationality and therefore, under Spanish law, he was viewed as a third-country national. The Court of Justice ruled that, under international law, it was for each Member State, having due regard to EU law, to lay down the conditions for the acquisition and loss of nationality. It was not permissible for the legislation of a Member State to restrict the effects of the grant of nationality of another Member State by imposing an additional condition for recognition of that nationality with a view to restricting the exercise of the fundamental freedoms provided for in the Treaty.

The Member States also have the power to grant different rights to different categories of nationals. In Case C-192/99 *Kaur* [2001] ECR I-1237, a British citizen born in Kenya was denied the right to reside in the UK. Upon its accession to the EU, the UK had made a declaration in which it specified which UK nationals would benefit from the provisions regarding free movement of persons. Ms Kaur was not one of them. The Court of Justice held that this declaration did not deprive her of rights under EU law because such rights never arose for her in the first place. The UK had the competence to decide which nationals gain the right to reside in its territory and which nationals were considered EU citizens.

However, the Court of Justice has emphasized that the Member States, when laying down the conditions for the acquisition and loss of nationality, must have due regard to EU law. A case in which this was at issue was Case C-135/08 *Rottmann* [2010] ECR I-1449. Mr Rottmann was Austrian by birth and moved to Germany, where he successfully applied for German nationality. Austrian law provided that, as a result, he lost his Austrian nationality. During the application procedure, however, he failed to mention that he was under investigation for fraud in Austria, where a warrant for his arrest had been issued. His German naturalization was withdrawn for deception, rendering him stateless. The Court of Justice held that although a decision to withdraw naturalization fell within the competence of the Member States, the situation of an EU citizen who lost his status and the rights attached to it because of a Member State decision fell within the scope of EU law. A decision withdrawing naturalization because of deception was in itself compatible with EU law even if it meant that the person lost not only nationality of the Member State, but also citizenship of the EU. In such a case, however, the national court must ascertain whether the withdrawal decision was proportionate, given the consequences. In particular, the national court must establish whether the loss of the rights the person had as an EU citizen was justified in relation to the gravity of the offence committed, to the lapse of time between the naturalization decision and the withdrawal decision, and to whether it was possible for that person to recover their original nationality.

11.1.2 Dual EU–UK citizens

In Case C-165/16 *Toufik Lounes v Secretary of State for the Home Department* EU:C:2017:862, the Court of Justice considered the circumstances of a Spanish national who exercised free movement rights as an EU citizen, and subsequently acquired permanent residency rights and was naturalized as British. She later married an Algerian national, who applied for residence on the basis of being a family member of an EU citizen. The question arose as to whether the third-country national acquired residency rights on the basis of being a family member of an EU citizen.

Case C-165/16 *Toufik Lounes v Secretary of State for the Home Department* EU:C:2017:862

58. … [I]t would be contrary to the underlying logic of gradual integration that informs Article 21(1) TFEU to hold that such citizens, who have acquired rights under that provision as a result of having exercised their freedom of movement, must forego those rights—in particular the right to family life in the host Member State—because they have sought,

by becoming naturalised in that Member State, to become more deeply integrated in the society of that State.

59. It would also follow that Union citizens who have exercised their freedom of movement and acquired the nationality of the host Member State in addition to their nationality of origin would, so far as their family life is concerned, be treated less favourably than Union citizens who have also exercised that freedom but who hold only their nationality of origin. The rights conferred on Union citizens in the host Member State, particularly the right to a family life with a third-country national, would thus be reduced in line with their increasing degree of integration in the society of that Member State and according to the number of nationalities that they hold.

60. It follows from the foregoing that, if the rights conferred on Union citizens by Article 21(1) TFEU are to be effective, citizens in a situation such as Ms Ormazabal's must be able to continue to enjoy, in the host Member State, the rights arising under that provision, after they have acquired the nationality of that Member State in addition to their nationality of origin and, in particular, must be able to build a family life with their third-country-national spouse, by means of the grant of a derived right of residence to that spouse.

61. The conditions for granting that derived right of residence must not be stricter than those provided for by Directive 2004/38 for the grant of a derived right of residence to a third-country national who is a family member of a Union citizen who has exercised his right of freedom of movement by settling in a Member State other than that of which he is a national. Even though Directive 2004/38 does not cover a situation such as that mentioned in the preceding paragraph of this judgment, it must be applied, by analogy, to that situation (see, by analogy, judgments of 12 March 2014, O. and B., C-456/12, EU:C:2014:135, paragraphs 50 and 61, and of 10 May 2017, Chavez-Vilchez and Others, C-133/15, EU:C:2017:354, paragraphs 54 and 55).

62. In view of all the foregoing, the answer to the question is that Directive 2004/38 must be interpreted as meaning that, in a situation in which a Union citizen (i) has exercised his freedom of movement by moving to and residing in a Member State other than that of which he is a national, under Article 7(1) or Article 16(1) of that directive, (ii) has then acquired the nationality of that Member State, while also retaining his nationality of origin, and (iii) several years later, has married a third-country national with whom he continues to reside in that Member State, that third-country national does not have a derived right of residence in the Member State in question on the basis of Directive 2004/38. The third-country national is however eligible for a derived right of residence under Article 21(1) TFEU, on conditions which must not be stricter than those provided for by Directive 2004/38 for the grant of such a right to a third-country national who is a family member of a Union citizen who has exercised his right of freedom of movement by settling in a Member State other than the Member State of which he is a national.

The Court therefore decided that such a right derived from the EU citizen's Article 21(1) TFEU rights.

11.1.3 Article 21(1) TFEU: direct effect

Like the other free movement provisions, the Court of Justice has affirmed that Article 21(1) TFEU has direct effect.

→ CROSS-REFERENCE
See 4.1 on direct effect.

The question first arose in Case C-413/99 *Baumbast* [2002] ECR I-7091, a case in which Mr Baumbast was a German national married to a Colombian, with two children. He lived in the UK with his family for three years while working there, after which he was employed by German companies in China and Lesotho. Mrs Baumbast applied for indefinite leave to remain in the UK for herself, her husband, and their children. When this was refused, the case was sent to the Court of Justice for a preliminary ruling. The question arose whether Mr Baumbast had an independent right of residence in the UK as an EU citizen since he was no longer a worker and therefore no longer had that right as a worker.

The Court held that, although before the TEU entered into force the right of residence was subject to the condition that the person concerned was carrying out an economic activity, since then EU citizenship had been introduced into what is now the TFEU.

→ CROSS-REFERENCE
See 1.13 on the TEU.

Article 21(1) TFEU confers a right for every citizen to move and reside freely within the territory of the Member States and EU citizenship is destined to be the fundamental status of nationals of the Member States. The Treaty did not require that EU citizens pursued a professional or trade activity in order to enjoy the rights provided for them. Furthermore, there was nothing in the text of the Treaty that suggested that citizens who had established themselves in another Member State in order to carry out an activity as an employed person there were deprived, when that activity came to an end, of the rights that they had by virtue of their citizenship. As regards, in particular, the right to reside within the territory of the Member States under Article 21(1) TFEU, that right was conferred directly on every citizen of the EU by a clear and precise provision of the Treaty. Purely as a national of a Member State and consequently a citizen of the EU, Mr Baumbast therefore had the right to rely on Article 21(1) TFEU.

The direct effect of Article 21(1) TFEU was confirmed in Case C-200/02 *Chen* [2004] ECR I-9925, which concerned a child with parents who were third-country nationals. Mrs Chen and her husband both held Chinese nationality. Mrs Chen went to the UK when she was about six months pregnant. When about eight months pregnant, Mrs Chen went to Ireland and gave birth to her daughter, Catherine, who obtained Irish nationality, since Irish law allowed any person born on the island of Ireland to acquire its nationality. Afterwards, mother and daughter went to live in the UK. It was clear that Mrs Chen had gone to give birth in Ireland for the purpose of her child obtaining Irish nationality and to enable her, as a consequence, to acquire the right to reside with her child in the UK. Both mother and child were refused a long-term residence permit in the UK on the grounds that the child was not exercising any EU law rights and her mother was not entitled to reside in the UK under EU law.

The Court reiterated that the right to reside in the territory of the Member States provided for in Article 21(1) TFEU was granted directly to every citizen of the EU by a clear and precise provision of the Treaty. Purely as a national of a Member State and therefore as a citizen of the EU, the child was entitled to rely on Article 21(1) TFEU. Her age meant that she was dependent on her mother, both emotionally and financially, and the Court therefore had to address whether her mother had a right to reside as the child's primary carer. It decided that a refusal to allow the parent-carer of a child with a citizen's right of residence to reside with the child in the host Member State, regardless of whether the parent-carer was a national of a Member State, would deprive the child's right of residence of any useful effect. Enjoyment by a young child of a right of residence necessarily implied that the child was entitled to be accompanied by the person who was their primary carer and, accordingly, that carer must be in a position to reside with the child in the host Member State for the duration of such residence.

11.1.4 The rights of EU citizens and their families

Articles 20–24 TFEU are the primary legislation regarding EU citizenship. The secondary legislation is now consolidated in the Citizenship Directive (Directive 2004/38/EC of the European Parliament and of the Council of 29 April 2004 on the right of citizens of the Union and their family members to move and reside freely within the territory of the Member States . . . , OJ 2004 L158/77), which replaced a range of legislation with one instrument. An overview of the key provisions is provided in Figure 11.1.

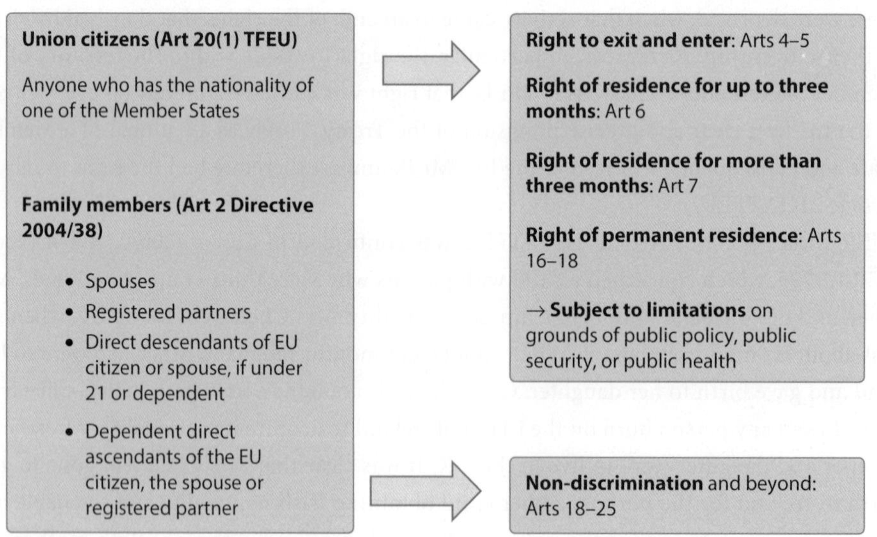

Figure 11.1 Overview of the rights of EU citizens and their families

Interestingly, the Preamble to the Citizenship Directive clearly echoes the sentiment of the Court of Justice in *Grzelczyk*.

Directive 2004/38/EC of the European Parliament and of the Council of 29 April 2004 on the right of citizens of the Union and their family members to move and reside freely within the territory of the Member States ... , OJ 2004 L158/77

Preamble

(1) Citizenship of the Union confers on every citizen of the Union a primary and individual right to move and reside freely within the territory of the Member States, subject to the limitations and conditions laid down in the Treaty and to the measures adopted to give it effect.

(2) The free movement of persons constitutes one of the fundamental freedoms of the internal market, which comprises an area without internal frontiers, in which freedom is ensured in accordance with the provisions of the Treaty.

(3) Union citizenship should be the fundamental status of nationals of the Member States when they exercise their right of free movement and residence. It is therefore necessary to codify and review the existing Community instruments dealing separately with workers, self-employed persons, as well as students and other inactive persons in order to simplify and strengthen the right of free movement and residence of all Union citizens.

11.1.4.1 The right to exit and enter

Chapter II of the Citizenship Directive is entitled 'Right of exit and entry' and contains two Articles.

Directive 2004/38/EC of the European Parliament and of the Council of 29 April 2004 on the right of citizens of the Union and their family members to move and reside freely within the territory of the Member States ... , OJ 2004 L158/77

Article 4

Right of exit

1. Without prejudice to the provisions on travel documents applicable to national border controls, all Union citizens with a valid identity card or passport and their family members who are not nationals of a Member State and who hold a valid passport shall have the right to leave the territory of a Member State to travel to another Member State.
2. No exit visa or equivalent formality may be imposed on the persons to whom paragraph 1 applies.
3. Member States shall, acting in accordance with their laws, issue to their own nationals, and renew, an identity card or passport stating their nationality.

4. The passport shall be valid at least for all Member States and for countries through which the holder must pass when travelling between Member States. Where the law of a Member State does not provide for identity cards to be issued, the period of validity of any passport on being issued or renewed shall be not less than five years.

Article 5

Right of entry

1. Without prejudice to the provisions on travel documents applicable to national border controls, Member States shall grant Union citizens leave to enter their territory with a valid identity card or passport and shall grant family members who are not nationals of a Member State leave to enter their territory with a valid passport. No entry visa or equivalent formality may be imposed on Union citizens.
2. Family members who are not nationals of a Member State shall only be required to have an entry visa in accordance with Regulation (EC) No 539/2001 or, where appropriate, with national law. For the purposes of this Directive, possession of the valid residence card referred to in Article 10 shall exempt such family members from the visa requirement. Member States shall grant such persons every facility to obtain the necessary visas. Such visas shall be issued free of charge as soon as possible and on the basis of an accelerated procedure.
3. The host Member State shall not place an entry or exit stamp in the passport of family members who are not nationals of a Member State provided that they present the residence card provided for in Article 10.
4. Where a Union citizen, or a family member who is not a national of a Member State, does not have the necessary travel documents or, if required, the necessary visas, the Member State concerned shall, before turning them back, give such persons every reasonable opportunity to obtain the necessary documents or have them brought to them within a reasonable period of time or to corroborate or prove by other means that they are covered by the right of free movement and residence.
5. The Member State may require the person concerned to report his/her presence within its territory within a reasonable and non-discriminatory period of time. Failure to comply with this requirement may make the person concerned liable to proportionate and non-discriminatory sanctions.

Article 4 of the Directive provides that EU citizens have the right to depart their home state by producing a valid identity card or passport, which must be issued and renewed by their Member State. Their non-EU citizen family members must produce a valid passport. There are no additional formalities. Similarly, Article 5 of the Directive provides that EU citizens are allowed to enter the host State with a valid identity card or passport. Family members who are not EU citizens may be required to obtain an entry visa, in accordance with EU or national law, although a visa is not required if the family member has a valid residence card, which is a document giving them the right to establish themselves in a Member State with an EU citizen as their family member or partner. If an EU citizen or their family member lacks the necessary travel documents or visas, the host Member State has to give them ample opportunity to obtain the documents or to prove their right of free movement and residence before turning them back. EU citizens and their family members may be required to report their presence in the territory of the host Member State within a reasonable and non-discriminatory period. Failure to comply may result in a sanction, which must be proportionate and non-discriminatory.

11.1.4.2 The right of residence for up to three months

Directive 2004/38/EC of the European Parliament and of the Council of 29 April 2004 on the right of citizens of the Union and their family members to move and reside freely within the territory of the Member States ..., OJ 2004 L158/77

Article 6

1. Union citizens shall have the right of residence on the territory of another Member State for a period of up to three months without any conditions or any formalities other than the requirement to hold a valid identity card or passport.
2. The provisions of paragraph 1 shall also apply to family members in possession of a valid passport who are not nationals of a Member State, accompanying or joining the Union citizen.

Based on this provision, all EU citizens, whether economically active or not, whether jobseeking or not, and whether having sufficient resources or health insurance or not, have a right of residence for up to three months in another Member State. Their non-EU citizen family members have the same right derived from that of the citizen. It must be noted, however, that Article 14(2) of the Directive provides that the host Member State is not obliged to confer entitlement to social assistance during the first three months of residence. Furthermore, following Article 6, EU citizens and their family members no longer have the right of residence in another Member State for up to three months if they become an unreasonable burden on the social assistance system of the host Member State.

11.1.4.3 The right of residence for more than three months

Directive 2004/38/EC of the European Parliament and of the Council of 29 April 2004 on the right of citizens of the Union and their family members to move and reside freely within the territory of the Member States ..., OJ 2004 L158/77

Article 7

1. All Union citizens shall have the right of residence on the territory of another Member State for a period of longer than three months if they:
   (a) are workers or self-employed persons in the host Member State; or

(b) have sufficient resources for themselves and their family members not to become a burden on the social assistance system of the host Member State during their period of residence and have comprehensive sickness insurance cover in the host Member State; or

(c)

- are enrolled at a private or public establishment, accredited or financed by the host Member State on the basis of its legislation or administrative practice, for the principal purpose of following a course of study, including vocational training; and
- have comprehensive sickness insurance cover in the host Member State and assure the relevant national authority, by means of a declaration or by such equivalent means as they may choose, that they have sufficient resources for themselves and their family members not to become a burden on the social assistance system of the host Member State during their period of residence; or

(d) are family members accompanying or joining a Union citizen who satisfies the conditions referred to in points (a), (b) or (c).

2. The right of residence provided for in paragraph 1 shall extend to family members who are not nationals of a Member State, accompanying or joining the Union citizen in the host Member State, provided that such Union citizen satisfies the conditions referred to in paragraph 1(a), (b) or (c).

Article 7 gives persons the right to reside in another Member State for more than three months and up to five years if they are workers or self-employed, if they have sufficient resources and comprehensive medical insurance, or if they are students with sufficient resources and comprehensive medical insurance. Family members accompanying such persons have the same right of residence, regardless of whether they are Member State nationals. Article 14(2) of the Directive provides that Member States may verify whether the conditions in Article 7 are fulfilled in specific cases in which there is a reasonable doubt as to whether an EU citizen or their family members satisfy the conditions. Such verification may not, however, be carried out systematically.

→ CROSS-REFERENCE
See 11.2.3 on the rights of workers.

These four categories of persons having the right to reside for more than three months in the territory of another Member State will now be looked at more closely.

Economically active citizens

Economically active citizens are workers and self-employed persons. Workers have extensive rights under EU law in terms of equal treatment and these are discussed more fully at 11.2.

They also have a right to reside in another Member State for a period longer than three months. Regarding their right to reside, EU citizens who are no longer a worker or self-employed retain their status under certain circumstances. These are set out in Article 7(3) of the Citizenship Directive.

Directive 2004/38/EC of the European Parliament and of the Council of 29 April 2004 on the right of citizens of the Union and their family members to move and reside freely within the territory of the Member States ..., OJ 2004 L158/77

Article 7(3)

For the purposes of paragraph 1(a), a Union citizen who is no longer a worker or self-employed person shall retain the status of worker or self-employed person in the following circumstances:

(a) he/she is temporarily unable to work as the result of an illness or accident;

(b) he/she is in duly recorded involuntary unemployment after having been employed for more than one year and has registered as a job-seeker with the relevant employment office;

(c) he/she is in duly recorded involuntary unemployment after completing a fixed-term employment contract of less than a year or after having become involuntarily unemployed during the first twelve months and has registered as a job-seeker with the relevant employment office. In this case, the status of worker shall be retained for no less than six months;

(d) he/she embarks on vocational training. Unless he/she is involuntarily unemployed, the retention of the status of worker shall require the training to be related to the previous employment.

This provision is important because it means that a person no longer working or self-employed, under the conditions set out in the previous extract, retains the right to reside in the host Member State without any additional requirements such as sufficient resources or health insurance. Furthermore, Article 14(4) of the Directive provides that an expulsion measure may in no case be adopted against EU citizens or their family members if they are workers or self-employed persons or if they entered the territory of the host Member State in order to seek employment. In the latter case, the EU citizens and their family members may not be expelled for as long as the EU citizens can prove that they are continuing to seek employment and that they have a genuine chance of being employed.

The recent case of Case C-442/16 *Florea Gusa v Minister for Social Protection, Ireland and Attorney General* EU:C:2017:1004 involved a Romanian national working in Ireland as a self-employed plasterer. When work dried up due to an economic downturn, Mr Gusa applied for a jobseekers' allowance, but it was refused on the grounds that he no longer satisfied the requirements for a right of residence. Mr Gusa argued that he retained self-employed status within Article 7. In drawing an analogy with a worker who has involuntarily lost their job, the Court decided that such status was retained.

Case C-442/16 *Florea Gusa v Minister for Social Protection, Ireland and Attorney General* EU:C:2017:1004

45. It follows from all of the foregoing that a person who has ceased to work in a self-employed capacity, because of an absence of work owing to reasons beyond his control, after having car-

> ried on that activity for more than one year, is, like a person who has involuntarily lost his job after being employed for that period, eligible for the protection afforded by Article 7(3)(b) of Directive 2004/38. As set out in that provision, that cessation of activity must be duly recorded.
>
> 46. Accordingly, the answer to the first question is that Article 7(3)(b) of Directive 2004/38 must be interpreted as meaning that a national of a Member State retains the status of self-employed person for the purposes of Article 7(1)(a) of that directive where, after having lawfully resided in and worked as a self-employed person in another Member State for approximately four years, that national has ceased that activity, because of a duly recorded absence of work owing to reasons beyond his control, and has registered as a jobseeker with the relevant employment office of the latter Member State.

It is important to note here that, according to Article 24(2) of the Citizenship Directive, the Member States are not obliged to confer entitlement to a jobseekers' allowance. Case C-138/02 *Collins* [2004] ECR I-2703, however, made it clear that Member States cannot always deny a jobseeker's claim for social assistance. While it is legitimate to require a genuine link between the jobseeker and the employment market of the State in question, and while the existence of such a link may be established by a residence requirement, the period of residence required must not exceed that necessary in order to assess whether the jobseeker is genuinely seeking work in the employment market of the host Member State. Furthermore, Joined Cases C-22 & 23/08 *Vatsouras and another v Arbeitsgemeinschaft (ARGE) Nurnberg 900* [2009] ECR I-4585, which was decided after the entry into force of the Citizenship Directive, established that a jobseekers' allowance is not 'social assistance' within the meaning of Article 24(2) of the Directive.

→ CROSS-REFERENCE
For a more in-depth discussion of *Collins*, see 11.2.2. On *Vatsouras*, see 11.2.3.2.

Economically independent citizens

The second category of EU citizens having a right of residence in the territory of another Member State for a period longer than three months are persons who have sufficient resources for themselves and their family members not to become a burden on the social assistance system of the host Member State during their period of residence and who have comprehensive sickness insurance cover in the host Member State.

Article 8(4) of the Citizenship Directive provides that Member States may not lay down a fixed amount that they regard as 'sufficient resources', but they must take into account the personal situation of the person concerned. In all cases, the amount shall not be higher than the threshold below which nationals of the host Member State become eligible for social assistance or, where this criterion is not applicable, higher than the minimum social security pension paid by the host Member State.

In Case C-200/02 *Chen* [2004] ECR I-9925, which concerned a newborn EU citizen, the Court of Justice made it clear that the resources required need not be the citizen's own; they may be provided by a family member—in this case, the baby's mother.

→ CROSS-REFERENCE
On *Chen*, see 11.1.3.

In Case C-408/03 *Commission v Belgium* [2006] ECR I-2647, it was pointed out that it is sufficient for the nationals of Member States to 'have' the necessary resources and that there are no requirements whatsoever as to the origin of the resources. There does not have to be a legal link between the provider and the recipient of the resources.

Regarding required medical insurance, Case C-413/99 *Baumbast* [2002] ECR I-7091 established that the fact that an EU citizen is covered only partially by insurance does not justify a Member State's refusal to renew his residence permit. Again, regard must be had to the individual circumstances and the principle of proportionality.

→ CROSS-REFERENCE
Baumbast is discussed at 11.1.3.

Finally, Article 14(3) of the Citizenship Directive provides that an expulsion measure shall not be the automatic consequence of an EU citizen's or their family member's recourse to the social assistance system of the host Member State. Prior to the acquisition of the right of permanent residence, though, the host Member State is not obliged to grant maintenance aid for studies, including vocational training, consisting in student grants or student loans to persons other than workers, self-employed persons, persons who retain such status, and members of their family (Article 24(2) of the Directive). Moreover, if an economically inactive citizen becomes a burden on the social assistance system of the host Member State, they may lose their right of residence.

In regards to the entitlement of non-active EU citizens to social advantages, the decision in C-333/13 *Dano v Jobcentre Leipzig* EU:C:2014:2358 clarified the position under EU law. Ms Dano and her son Florin, both Romanian nationals, resided in Germany with Ms Dano's sister. Ms Dano never worked in Germany and there was nothing to indicate that she had looked for a job. She received a child benefit for her son, but when she applied for social benefits by way of basic provision, this was refused. Ms Dano objected to this refusal, relying on EU law—specifically, the prohibition of discrimination based on nationality in Article 18 TFEU and Article 24 of the Citizenship Directive.

The Court of Justice pointed out that, pursuant to Article 24(1) of the Directive, EU citizens can indeed claim equal treatment with nationals of the host Member State, but only if their residence has complied with the conditions of the Directive. For residence between three months and five years, such as that of Ms Dano and her son, the relevant provision is Article 7(1) of the Directive. According to this provision, persons who are economically inactive must meet the condition that they have sufficient resources of their own in order to have a right of residence. When assessing whether such persons have sufficient resources, the social assistance applied for cannot be taken into account, as the person does not have sufficient resources without such social assistance. Since Ms Dano and her son did not have sufficient resources, they could not claim a right of residence in Germany and therefore they could not invoke the principle of non-discrimination applicable to EU citizens residing in another Member State.

→ CROSS-REFERENCE
Article 16(2) of the Citizenship Directive on family members is discussed later at 11.1.4.4.

Students

Persons enrolled at a private or public establishment accredited or financed by the host Member State have a right to reside in another Member State for more than three months if they have sufficient resources and comprehensive health insurance. The fact that they have sufficient funds for themselves and their family members not to become a burden on the social assistance system of the host Member State may be proven by means of a simple declaration. Like the category of economically independent citizens, this means they may lose their residence right if they become an unreasonable burden on the host Member State's social system.

Since students are economically inactive, according to Article 24(2) of the Citizenship Directive the host Member State has no obligation to provide them with maintenance grants or student loans before the right of permanent residence has been acquired. The Court of Justice decided in Case C-209/03 *R v London Borough of Ealing and Secretary of State for Education, ex p Bidar* [2005] ECR I-2119, however, that encouragement and support for cooperation in education matters had been incorporated into EU law. Therefore, there must be equality between EU students in relation to loans and grants. A condition requiring a certain degree of integration into the host Member State's society, however, is justified.

The existence of a certain degree of integration may be evaluated through a residence requirement. This was established in Case C-158/07 *Forster v Hoofddirectie van de Informatie Beheer Groep* [2008] ECR I-8507, in which a requirement of at least five years' uninterrupted lawful residence before claiming a maintenance grant was held to be compatible with EU law.

Family members

Family members of EU citizens have a right of residence dependent on the citizen's right of residence. Article 2(2) of the Citizenship Directive defines 'family member'.

Directive 2004/38/EC of the European Parliament and of the Council of 29 April 2004 on the right of citizens of the Union and their family members to move and reside freely within the territory of the Member States ..., OJ 2004 L158/77

Article 2

For the purposes of this Directive:

[...]

2. "Family member" means:

(a) the spouse;

(b) the partner with whom the Union citizen has contracted a registered partnership, on the basis of the legislation of a Member State, if the legislation of the host Member State treats registered partnerships as equivalent to marriage and in accordance with the conditions laid down in the relevant legislation of the host Member State;

(c) the direct descendants who are under the age of 21 or are dependants and those of the spouse or partner as defined in point (b);

(d) the dependent direct relatives in the ascending line and those of the spouse or partner as defined in point (b);

[...]

11.1.4.4 The right of permanent residence

General rule for all EU citizens

Directive 2004/38/EC of the European Parliament and of the Council of 29 April 2004 on the right of citizens of the Union and their family members to move and reside freely within the territory of the Member States ..., OJ 2004 L158/77

Article 16

1. Union citizens who have resided legally for a continuous period of five years in the host Member State shall have the right of permanent residence there. This right shall not be subject to the conditions provided for in Chapter III.

 [...]

3. Continuity of residence shall not be affected by temporary absences not exceeding a total of six months a year, or by absences of a longer duration for compulsory military service, or by one absence of a maximum of twelve consecutive months for important reasons such as pregnancy and childbirth, serious illness, study or vocational training, or a posting in another Member State or a third country.
4. Once acquired, the right of permanent residence shall be lost only through absence from the host Member State for a period exceeding two consecutive years.

?! THINKING POINT

Why do you think an EU citizen acquires the right of permanent residence after five years in the host Member State? How is a right of permanent residence different from a right of residence for up to five years?

After an EU citizen has legally resided in the host Member State for a continuous period of five years, it is deemed that there is a very strong link between that person and the host Member State that makes the person comparable to a national of that Member State. The right of permanent residence is seen as a vehicle for integration into the society of the host Member State. Therefore this right, once acquired, is not subject to the conditions set out for a right of residence for up to five years. In particular, after five years of continuous legal residence, the citizen does not have to be economically active or economically independent with comprehensive health insurance.

Article 16 of the Citizenship Directive specifies that the acquisition of five years' continuity of residence in the host Member State is not affected by temporary absences. Furthermore, after those five years, when the right of permanent residence is acquired, it can be lost only through absence from the host Member State for more than two consecutive years.

→ CROSS-REFERENCE
On the right of residence for more than three months and the conditions that have to be met to acquire this right, see 11.1.4.3.

More favourable rule for the formerly economically active

Directive 2004/38/EC of the European Parliament and of the Council of 29 April 2004 on the right of citizens of the Union and their family members to move and reside freely within the territory of the Member States ..., OJ 2004 L158/77

Article 17

1. By way of derogation from Article 16, the right of permanent residence in the host Member State shall be enjoyed before completion of a continuous period of five years of residence by:

   (a) workers or self-employed persons who, at the time they stop working, have reached the age laid down by the law of that Member State for entitlement to an old age pension or workers who cease paid employment to take early retirement, provided that they have been working in that Member State for at least the preceding twelve months and have resided there continuously for more than three years.

   If the law of the host Member State does not grant the right to an old age pension to certain categories of self-employed persons, the age condition shall be deemed to have been met once the person concerned has reached the age of 60;

   (b) workers or self-employed persons who have resided continuously in the host Member State for more than two years and stop working there as a result of permanent incapacity to work.

   If such incapacity is the result of an accident at work or an occupational disease entitling the person concerned to a benefit payable in full or in part by an institution in the host Member State, no condition shall be imposed as to length of residence;

   (c) workers or self-employed persons who, after three years of continuous employment and residence in the host Member State, work in an employed or self-employed capacity in another Member State, while retaining their place of residence in the host Member State, to which they return, as a rule, each day or at least once a week.

   For the purposes of entitlement to the rights referred to in points (a) and (b), periods of employment spent in the Member State in which the person concerned is working shall be regarded as having been spent in the host Member State.

   Periods of involuntary unemployment duly recorded by the relevant employment office, periods not worked for reasons not of the person's own making and absences from work or cessation of work due to illness or accident shall be regarded as periods of employment.

2. The conditions as to length of residence and employment laid down in point (a) of paragraph 1 and the condition as to length of residence laid down in point (b) of paragraph 1 shall not apply if the worker's or the self-employed person's spouse or partner as referred to in point 2(b) of Article 2 is a national of the host Member State or has lost the nationality of that Member State by marriage to that worker or self-employed person.

[...]

Citizens who were economically active in the host Member State acquire the right of permanent residence more easily than citizens who were not economically active. This means that, in order to have a right of permanent residence, a shorter period of residence in the host Member State is required for people who have reached pensionable age, for people who can no longer work because of permanent incapacity, and for so-called frontier workers.

People who are no longer working because they have reached pensionable age have the right of permanent residence if they worked in the host Member State for at least one year preceding that birthday and provided that they resided there continuously for more than three years.

People who are no longer working because they are permanently incapacitated have the right of permanent residence if they have continuously resided in the host Member State for more than two years. Furthermore, if the incapacity is a result of an accident at work or an occupational illness, they have the right of permanent residence without any condition as to length of residence.

Frontier workers—that is, those who reside in one Member State and work in another—have the right of permanent residence even if they worked in the host Member State for less than five years, as long as they worked there for at least three years before starting to work in another Member State and still reside in the host Member State and return there at least once a week.

A worker or self-employed person who is married to someone who has the nationality of the host Member State, or to someone who has lost this nationality as a consequence of marriage, does not have to satisfy any condition as to length of residence or employment in order to have a right of permanent residence. This rule brings us to the rights of permanent residence for family members of EU citizens, which is discussed in the next section.

Directive 2004/38/EC of the European Parliament and of the Council of 29 April 2004 on the right of citizens of the Union and their family members to move and reside freely within the territory of the Member States ..., OJ 2004 L158/77

Article 16

[...]

2. Paragraph 1 shall apply also to family members who are not nationals of a Member State and have legally resided with the Union citizen in the host Member State for a continuous period of five years.

Article 17

[...]

3. Irrespective of nationality, the family members of a worker or a self-employed person who are residing with him in the territory of the host Member State shall have the right of permanent residence in that Member State, if the worker or self-employed person has acquired himself the right of permanent residence in that Member State on the basis of paragraph 1.

4. If, however, the worker or self-employed person dies while still working but before acquiring permanent residence status in the host Member State on the basis of paragraph 1, his family members who are residing with him in the host Member State shall acquire the right of permanent residence there, on condition that:
   (a) the worker or self-employed person had, at the time of death, resided continuously on the territory of that Member State for two years; or
   (b) the death resulted from an accident at work or an occupational disease; or
   (c) the surviving spouse lost the nationality of that Member State following marriage to the worker or self-employed person.

Article 18

Without prejudice to Article 17, the family members of a Union citizen to whom Articles 12(2) and 13(2) apply, who satisfy the conditions laid down therein, shall acquire the right of permanent residence after residing legally for a period of five consecutive years in the host Member State.

Family members

→ CROSS-REFERENCE
For the definition of 'family member', see Article 2(2) of the Citizenship Directive, set out at 11.1.4.3.

Family members of an EU citizen will also have a right of permanent residence, derived from that of the citizen, regardless of whether they are citizens or third-country nationals.

If the worker or self-employed person acquires a right of permanent residence after two or three years of residence or even without satisfying any residence requirement at all, as set out earlier in this section, their family members also acquire this right and they acquire it at the same time as does the worker or self-employed person. Equally, if the citizen acquires their right of permanent residence after five years of residence in the host Member State based on Article 16(1) of the Citizenship Directive, their family members will also acquire this right after five years.

Furthermore, if the worker or self-employed person dies while still working, but before they acquired the right of permanent residence, their family members will still acquire the right of permanent residence in the host Member State provided that one of three conditions are met:

(1) at the time of death, the worker or self-employed person had resided continuously for more than two years in the host Member State; or

(2) the worker or self-employed person died as a result of an accident at work or an occupational illness; or

(3) the surviving spouse lost the nationality of the host Member State as a consequence of marriage to the worker or self-employed person.

From case law, it appears that these conditions are interpreted in a strict manner. In Case C-257/00 *Givane* [2003] ECR I-345, an Indian widow and three children were denied the right of permanent residence in the UK. The deceased husband was a Portuguese national who had worked in the UK for three years as a chef, after which he went to India for ten months. He died less than two years after returning to the UK. Because he had resided for less than two years in the UK immediately preceding his death, the Court of Justice upheld the UK's refusal to grant his family members a permanent right of residence.

Finally, in the case of divorce or annulment of marriage, or in the case of death or departure of the EU citizen, family members who legally remain in the host Member State for a period of five consecutive years will acquire a right of permanent residence.

11.1.4.5 The right to equal treatment and beyond

Part Two of the TFEU (Articles 18–25) is entitled 'Non-discrimination and citizenship of the Union'. Non-discrimination and the corresponding right to equal treatment is one of the cornerstones of the EU and entails non-discrimination on a variety of grounds. In the context of the free movement of persons, however, equal treatment and the prohibition of discrimination based on nationality are of particular importance. The right to equal treatment regarding social assistance has already been discussed under the different relevant headings in this chapter. It will therefore not be expanded upon here.

Article 18 TFEU

Within the scope of application of the Treaties, and without prejudice to any special provisions contained therein, any discrimination on grounds of nationality shall be prohibited.

The European Parliament and the Council, acting in accordance with the ordinary legislative procedure, may adopt rules designed to prohibit such discrimination.

Directive 2004/38/EC of the European Parliament and of the Council of 29 April 2004 on the right of citizens of the Union and their family members to move and reside freely within the territory of the Member States ..., OJ 2004 L158/77

Article 24

1. Subject to such specific provisions as are expressly provided for in the Treaty and secondary law, all Union citizens residing on the basis of this Directive in the territory of the host Member State shall enjoy equal treatment with the nationals of that Member State within the scope of the Treaty. The benefit of this right shall be extended to family members who are not nationals of a Member State and who have the right of residence or permanent residence.
2. By way of derogation from paragraph 1, the host Member State shall not be obliged to confer entitlement to social assistance during the first three months of residence or, where appropriate, the longer period provided for in Article 14(4)(b), nor shall it be obliged, prior to acquisition of the right of permanent residence, to grant maintenance aid for studies, including vocational training, consisting in student grants or student loans to persons other than workers, self-employed persons, persons who retain such status and members of their families.

?! THINKING POINT

Read Article 24(2) of the Citizenship Directive carefully. Can you identify the relevant derogations to the general principle of equal treatment in Article 24(1)? Note the reference to permanent residence and its significance in this regard.

EU citizens have a right to equal treatment in all matters having a connection with free movement rights, even if this connection is only very remote. This became clear after Case C-148/02 *Garcia Avello* [2003] ECR I-11613—a case that did not concern different treatment of similar situations, but rather similar treatment of different situations. Mr Garcia Avello, a Spanish national, was married to Ms Weber, a Belgian national. They were resident in Belgium, where their two children were born. The children had dual Spanish and Belgian nationality. In accordance with Belgian law, the children received their father's surname upon registration—that is, Garcia Avello. Their parents requested the children's surname to be changed to Garcia Weber in accordance with Spanish custom, which was that the surname of children of a married couple consisted of the first surname of the father followed by that of the mother. They had already registered the children under that name at the Spanish embassy. Their request was denied and the authorities merely changed the children's name to Garcia. A case was brought against the Belgian authorities and the Belgian court made a preliminary reference to the Court of Justice, asking whether EU law prevented the Belgian authorities from rejecting the requested change of surname.

→ CROSS-REFERENCE
On preliminary references, see Chapter 6.

Case C-148/02 *Garcia Avello* [2003] ECR I-11613

26. Citizenship of the Union, established by Article 17 EC [now Article 20 TFEU], is not … intended to extend the scope *ratione materiae* of the Treaty … to internal situations which have no link with Community law [now EU law].
27. Such a link with Community law does, however, exist in regard to persons in a situation such as that of the children of Mr Garcia Avello, who are nationals of one Member State lawfully resident in the territory of another Member State.
28. That conclusion cannot be invalidated by the fact that the children involved in the main proceedings also have the nationality of the Member State in which they have been resident since their birth and which, according to the authorities of that State, is by virtue of that fact the only nationality recognised by the latter. It is not permissible for a Member State to restrict the effects of the grant of the nationality of another Member State by imposing an additional condition for recognition of that nationality with a view to the exercise of the fundamental freedoms provided for in the Treaty. Furthermore, Article 3 of the Hague Convention, on which the Kingdom of Belgium relies in recognising only the nationality of the forum where there are several nationalities, one of which is Belgian, does not impose an obligation but simply provides an option for the contracting parties to give priority to that nationality over any other.

29. That being so, the children of the applicant in the main proceedings may rely on the right set out in Article 12 EC [now Article 18 TFEU] not to suffer discrimination on grounds of nationality in regard to the rules governing their surname.

[...]

35. In contrast to persons having only Belgian nationality, Belgian nationals who also hold Spanish nationality have different surnames under the two legal systems concerned. More specifically, in a situation such as that in issue in the main proceedings, the children concerned are refused the right to bear the surname which results from application of the legislation of the Member State which determined the surname of their father.

36. As the Advocate General has pointed out in paragraph 56 of his Opinion, it is common ground that such a discrepancy in surnames is liable to cause serious inconvenience for those concerned at both professional and private levels resulting from, inter alia, difficulties in benefiting, in one Member State of which they are nationals, from the legal effects of diplomas or documents drawn up in the surname recognised in another Member State of which they are also nationals. As has been established in paragraph 33 of the present judgment, the solution proposed by the administrative authorities of allowing children to take only the first surname of their father does not resolve the situation of divergent surnames which those here involved are seeking to avoid.

37. In those circumstances, Belgian nationals who have divergent surnames by reason of the different laws to which they are attached by nationality may plead difficulties specific to their situation which distinguish them from persons holding only Belgian nationality, who are identified by one surname alone.

In this case, the sole fact of dual nationality was enough to trigger the operation of the Treaty provisions on equal treatment, regardless of the fact that there was no actual movement. The Court looked at the fact that the children might want to exercise their free movement rights in the future, in which case the discrepancy between their surnames (Garcia on Belgian documents and Garcia Weber on Spanish documents) could cause them serious inconvenience.

The Court's willingness to apply the Treaty to cases that have a very remote, if not merely potential, link with free movement was confirmed in Case C-34/09 *Ruiz Zambrano* [2011] ECR I-1177. Mr Zambrano, a Colombian national, applied for asylum in Belgium in 1999. His wife, also a Colombian national, applied for refugee status in Belgium in 2000. Their applications were refused, but they were not ordered to be sent back to Colombia in view of the civil war in that country. Mr Zambrano unsuccessfully tried to have his situation regularized, but managed to find a permanent full-time job despite the fact that he did not hold a work permit. The couple remained in Belgium, where their second and third children were born, and these children obtained Belgian nationality. Mr and Mrs Zambrano claimed that they had a right of residence directly by virtue of the Treaty and the Citizenship Directive or, at the very least, a derived right of residence, as recognized in Case C-200/02 *Chen* [2004] ECR I-9925, because they were the ascendants of minor children who were Member State nationals.

→ CROSS-REFERENCE
On *Chen*, see 11.1.3.

The Court of Justice decided that Article 20 TFEU precluded national measures that have the effect of depriving EU citizens of the genuine enjoyment of the substance of the rights conferred by virtue of their status as citizens. The refusal to grant a right of residence and a work permit to the children's parents had such an effect because it could lead to a situation in which those children would have to leave the territory of the EU in order to accompany their parents.

11.1.4.6 Other EU citizens' rights

Following Article 22 TFEU, every citizen of the EU has a right to vote and to stand as a candidate at municipal elections and in elections to the European Parliament in the Member State in which they reside and of which they are not a national under the same conditions as nationals of that State. The Article, however, allows for derogations, provided that they are warranted by problems specific to a Member State.

It must be noted that although the Member States decide on the conditions for the exercise of the right to vote in elections to the European Parliament (for example age), this right is not unlimited, since the principle of equal treatment does not allow for unjustified differences in treatment of nationals in comparable situations. In Case C-300/04 *Eman and Servinger* [2006] ECR I-8055, two Dutch citizens residing in Aruba complained because they did not have the right to vote in elections to the European Parliament. Dutch law specified that persons resident in the overseas territories could not vote for elections on the mainland and, as a consequence, they could not vote in elections to the European Parliament either. Although the Netherlands could define the conditions for voting and standing in elections to the European Parliament, this was subject to the principle of equality. Since Dutch citizens residing elsewhere in the world were allowed to vote and the exclusion applied only to those residing in the overseas territories, the Dutch legislation breached the principle of equality.

Article 23 TFEU provides that every EU citizen is entitled to protection by the diplomatic or consular authorities of another Member State on the same conditions as the nationals of that State in the territory of third countries.

THINKING POINT

What do you think such diplomatic or consular protection includes?

Decision 95/553EC of the Representatives of the Governments of the Member States meeting within the Council of 19 December 1995 regarding protection for citizens of the European Union by diplomatic and consular representations, OJ 1995 L314/73, specifies what protection the Member States will offer EU citizens. The protection concerns assistance in cases of death, serious accident or serious illness, and arrest or detention. Assistance is also available for victims of violent crime, and relief and repatriation will be provided for distressed citizens. The Member States' diplomatic representations or consular agents in third countries may also come to the assistance of any EU citizen who requests it in any other circumstance insofar as it is within their powers to do so.

Article 24 TFEU grants EU citizens the right of initiative and the right to petition the European Parliament, in accordance with Article 227 TFEU. The right of initiative, according to Article 11(4) TEU, is the right to invite the Commission to submit a proposal on matters where EU citizens consider a legal act of the EU to be required for the purpose of implementing the Treaties. Such an initiative must be supported by at least 1 million EU citizens who are nationals of a significant number of Member States. Furthermore, every citizen has a right to apply to the European Ombudsman, in accordance with Article 228 TFEU. Lastly, Article 24 TFEU provides that every citizen has the right to write to the EU institutions or the Ombudsman in any of the EU's languages and to receive an answer in the same language.

11.2 Free movement of workers: substantive rights

11.2.1 Article 45 TFEU

Article 45 TFEU sets out the principles regarding the free movement of workers.

Article 45 TFEU

1. Freedom of movement for workers shall be secured within the Union.
2. Such freedom of movement shall entail the abolition of any discrimination based on nationality between workers of the Member States as regards employment, remuneration and other conditions of work and employment.
3. It shall entail the right, subject to limitations justified on grounds of public policy, public security or public health:
   (a) to accept offers of employment actually made;
   (b) to move freely within the territory of Member States for this purpose;
   (c) to stay in a Member State for the purpose of employment in accordance with the provisions governing the employment of nationals of that State laid down by law, regulation or administrative action;
   (d) to remain in the territory of a Member State after having been employed in that State, subject to conditions which shall be embodied in regulations to be drawn up by the Commission.
4. The provisions of this Article shall not apply to employment in public service.

It was established in Case 41/74 *Van Duyn v Home Office* [1974] ECR 1337 that Article 45 TFEU has vertical direct effect, which means that it can be relied upon by an individual against public authorities.

→ CROSS-REFERENCE See 4.1.4 for an explanation of vertical and horizontal direct effect.

In Case 36/74 *Walrave and Koch* [1974] ECR 1405, at 1406, it was held that Article 45 TFEU 'applies to all legal relationships which can be located within the territory of the Community [now Union] by reason either of the place where they are entered into or of the place where they take effect'. This means that the rule on non-discrimination can be relied upon when the legal relationship is entered into in the EU even if the work is performed outside the EU.

→ CROSS-REFERENCE For a full explanation and discussion of direct effect, see 4.1.

Furthermore, it was ruled in *Walrave and Koch* and in Case C-415/93 *Bosman* [1995] ECR I-1921 that Article 45 TFEU had not only vertical direct effect, but also horizontal direct effect.

Both cases concerned rules made by sporting associations: cycling, in *Walrave and Koch*, and football, in *Bosman*. These associations were not public authorities, but the Court of Justice decided that the prohibition of discrimination also applied to rules aimed at regulating gainful employment in a collective manner, but not emanating from a public authority. The reason for this decision is that, in several Member States, working conditions and relations are regulated not only by law, but also by collective agreements, which are agreements concluded between an employer or an employers' association, on the one hand, and one or more trade unions, on the other hand. Thus limiting the prohibitions in Article 45 TFEU to acts of public authorities would greatly reduce their effect and could create inequality in their application.

In Case C-281/98 *Angonese* [2000] ECR I-4139, the Court of Justice went even further. A private bank in Italy required a certificate of bilingualism from anyone wishing to apply for a job with it. The certificate was to be issued by the local authority after an examination held only in the province of Bolzano. Since this certificate used to be required for a career in the local public service, it was very usual for residents of the province to obtain it. Since the majority of residents in the province of Bolzano were Italian nationals, in effect the required certificate put nationals of other Member States at a disadvantage. It was therefore held by the Court that the prohibition of discrimination based on nationality also applied to private employers.

→ CROSS-REFERENCE For more on *Angonese*, see 11.2.3.

Finally, it must be noted that Article 45 TFEU can be relied upon not only by the worker, but also by the employer. Case C-350/96 *Clean Car Autoservice* [1998] ECR I-2521 concerned Austrian legislation that prohibited businesses in Austria from employing as managers persons not resident in the country. The Court of Justice decided that 'while [the rights in Article 45 TFEU] are undoubtedly enjoyed by those directly referred to—namely, workers—there is nothing in the wording of [Article 45 TFEU] to indicate that they may not be relied upon by others, in particular employers' (*Clean Car Autoservice*, at para 19).

11.2.2 The definition of 'worker'

11.2.2.1 An autonomous EU concept

The concept of 'worker' is not defined in the TFEU or any secondary legislation, but has been developed through the Court of Justice's case law. An overview of the relevant case law is provided in Figure 11.2. It is an autonomous EU concept, which means that its meaning is determined solely by EU law, without reference to the national laws of the Member States. In Case 75/63 *Hoekstra* [1964] ECR 177, the Court held that the relevant Treaty Articles would be deprived of all effect if the meaning of the concept of 'worker' could be fixed or modified by national law.

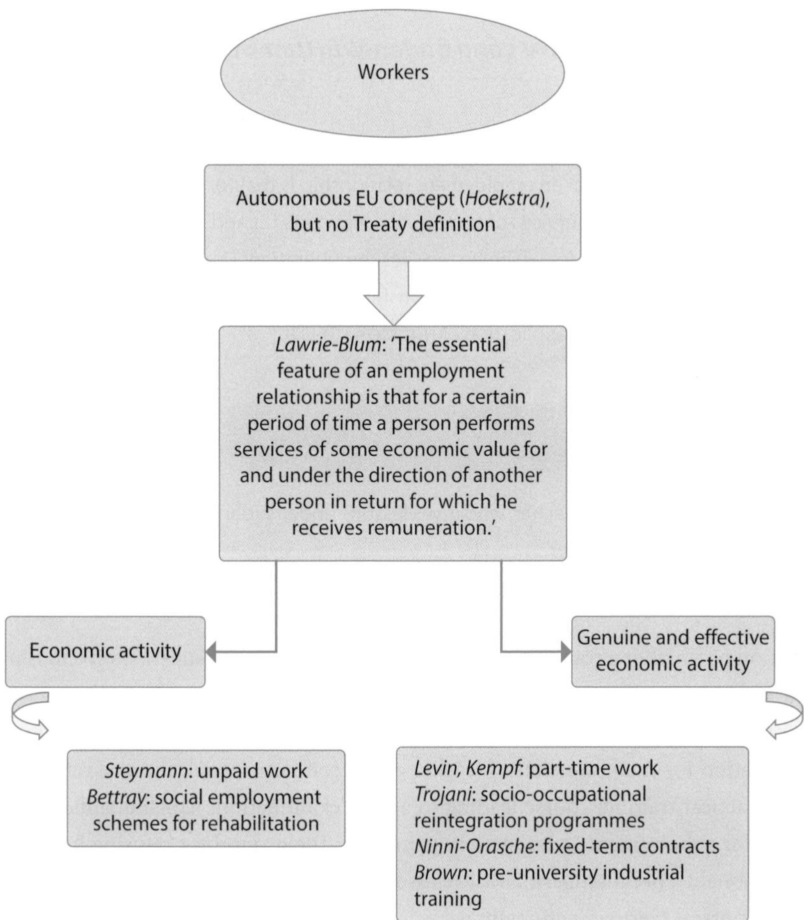

Figure 11.2 Overview: The concept of 'worker'

?! THINKING POINT

Why do you think the Court of Justice decided this? What would be the consequences if the Member States could determine or modify the meaning of the concept of 'worker'?

After all, if the definition of the concept of worker were a matter of national law, each Member State could decide or modify, through its national law, which persons or categories of persons would be protected under the Treaty. This could severely undermine the effect and the objectives of the Treaty, since national laws would be able to exclude certain categories of persons from the benefit of the Treaty without any control by the EU institutions.

11.2.2.2 The essential feature of an employment relationship

The Court of Justice has pointed out the essential feature of an employment relationship in Case 66/85 *Lawrie-Blum v Land Baden-Württemberg* [1986] ECR 2121.

Case 66/85 *Lawrie-Blum v Land Baden-Württemberg* [1986] ECR 2121

Summary

1. ... The essential feature of an employment relationship is that for a certain period of time a person performs services of some economic value for and under the direction of another person in return for which he receives remuneration. The sphere in which they are provided and the nature of the legal relationship between employee and employer are immaterial as regards the application of [Article 45 TFEU].

?! THINKING POINT

Do you think that a trainee teacher, who gives lessons under supervision and is paid for this, is a 'worker' according to EU law?

The question of whether a trainee teacher, who gives lessons under supervision and is paid for this, is a 'worker' arose in *Lawrie-Blum*.

Deborah Lawrie-Blum was a British national living and working in Germany. After passing the examination for the profession of teacher at a secondary school, she was refused admission to a practical training course leading to a state examination, which qualified successful candidates for appointment as teachers in gymnasia. The ground for refusing her admission was her nationality, because German law classed trainee teachers as temporary civil servants, who had to possess German nationality.

The German court asked for a preliminary ruling on the question of whether trainee teachers were 'workers' under EU law.

Case 66/85 *Lawrie-Blum v Land Baden-Württemberg* [1986] ECR 2121

18. In the present case, it is clear that during the entire period of preparatory service the trainee teacher is under the direction and supervision of the school to which he is assigned. It is the school that determines the services to be performed by him and his working hours and it is the school's instructions that he must carry out and its rules that he must observe. During a substantial part of the preparatory service he is required to give lessons to the school's pupils and thus provides a service of some economic value to the school. The amounts which he receives may be regarded as remuneration for the services provided and for the duties involved in completing the period of preparatory service. Consequently, the three criteria for the existence of an employment relationship are fulfilled in this case.
19. The fact that teachers' preparatory service, like apprenticeships in other occupations, may be regarded as practical preparation directly related to the actual pursuit of the occupa-

tion in point is not a bar to the application of [Article 45 TFEU] if the service is performed under the conditions of an activity as an employed person.

20. Nor may it be objected that services performed in education do not fall within the scope of the … Treaty because they are not of an economic nature. All that is required for the application of [Article 45 TFEU] is that the activity should be in the nature of work performed for remuneration, irrespective of the sphere in which it is carried out … Nor may the economic nature of those activities be denied on the ground that they are performed by persons whose status is governed by public law since … the nature of the legal relationship between employee and employer, whether involving public law status or a private law contract, is immaterial as regards the application of [Article 45 TFEU].

The work performed must be an economic activity. In Case 196/87 *Steymann v Staatssecretaris van Justitie* [1988] ECR 6159, Mr Steymann carried out plumbing for a religious community and also took part in their commercial activities. He did not receive a salary, but the community took care of his material needs. According to the Court of Justice, he performed economic activities because the services the community provided to its members could be regarded as the indirect quid pro quo for the work they carried out.

A person taking part in a social employment scheme for the rehabilitation of drug addiction, however, is not a worker. The purpose of such a scheme is social and the activities carried out are not economic, but merely a means of rehabilitation or reintegration (Case 344/87 *Bettray v Staatssecretaris van Justitie* [1989] ECR 1621).

11.2.2.3 Part-time workers

The question can be asked whether someone working part-time or for a salary less than the minimum wage in the country concerned could be classed as a 'worker', since they would not earn sufficient money to support themselves and certainly not enough to support a family. This question was answered in Case 53/81 *Levin v Staatssecretaris van Justitie* [1982] ECR 1035.

Mrs Levin was a British citizen and married to a non-EU national husband. She worked part-time as a chambermaid and, because she worked only part-time, she earned less than what was considered the minimum for subsistence in the Netherlands. She applied for a permit to reside in the Netherlands, but this was refused. The reason for the refusal was that, according to Dutch legislation, Mrs Levin was not engaged in gainful employment in the Netherlands and therefore could not benefit from the EU legislation favourable to workers.

The Court of Justice emphasized that the terms 'worker' and 'activity as an employed person' are not to be defined by reference to the national laws of the Member States, but have an EU meaning. As these concepts define the field of application of one of the fundamental freedoms guaranteed by the Treaty, they must not be interpreted restrictively.

According to the Court of Justice, one of the objectives of the Treaty is the abolition, as between Member States, of obstacles to freedom of movement of persons, with the purpose of promoting throughout the EU the harmonious development of economic activities and raising the standard of living. Although part-time employment may provide an income lower than that considered to be the minimum required for subsistence, it constitutes, for a large number of persons, an effective means of improving their living conditions. The effectiveness of EU law would be impaired and the achievement of the Treaty objectives would be jeopardized if the enjoyment of the rights for workers were to be reserved solely to persons engaged in full-time employment and earning, as a result, a salary at least equivalent to the guaranteed minimum wage.

11.2.2.4 Genuine and effective economic activity

Although *Levin* established that part-time employment is not excluded from the field of application of the rules on freedom of movement for workers, the work performed must be effective and genuine, and not purely marginal and ancillary. The question as to which activities are considered effective and genuine was raised in Case 139/85 *Kempf v Staatssecretaris van Justitie* [1986] ECR 1741.

Mr Kempf was a German citizen who worked in the Netherlands as a part-time music teacher. Since he worked only 12 hours per week, he applied for and received supplementary benefits, which came out of public funds and were payable to persons having the status of workers. When he applied for a residence permit in the Netherlands in order to pursue an activity as an employed person, he was refused a permit. It was decided by the Dutch authorities that he was not a worker because he had received public funds and was therefore clearly unable to support himself out of the income received from his employment.

The Dutch government argued that work providing an income below the minimum means of subsistence cannot be regarded as effective and genuine work if the person who carries out the work claims social assistance from public funds.

The Court of Justice disagreed. It held that a person in effective and genuine employment who sought to supplement their income, which was below the level of minimum means of subsistence, was still a worker under EU law. It was irrelevant whether those supplementary means were derived from property or from the employment of a family member—as was the case in *Levin*—or whether they were obtained through financial assistance drawn from public funds of the Member State in which the worker resides.

However, work cannot be regarded as an effective and genuine economic activity if it constitutes merely a means of rehabilitation or reintegration for the persons concerned and if the purpose of the paid employment, which is adapted to the specific possibilities of each person, is to enable those persons to recover their capacity to take up ordinary employment or to lead a normal life (Case 344/87 *Bettray v Staatssecretaris van Justitie* [1989] ECR 1621).

In an apparently similar case, the Court of Justice left it to the national court to decide whether there was a real and genuine economic activity. In Case C-456/02 *Trojani* [2004] ECR I-7573, a French national, Mr Trojani, worked for approximately 30 hours per week as part of a personal socio-occupational reintegration programme in a Salvation Army hostel in return for board and lodging and some pocket money. The Court of Justice ruled that, in deciding whether Mr Trojani was a worker, the national court had to establish, by assessing the facts, whether the paid activity was real and genuine. In particular, the national court had to ascertain whether the services performed were capable of being regarded as forming part of the normal labour market. For that purpose, account could be taken of the status and practices of the hostel, the content of the social reintegration programme, and the nature and details of performance of the services.

Another scenario in which the question as to effective and genuine activities has arisen is that of employment of short duration. In Case C-413/01 *Ninni-Orasche* [2003] ECR I-13187, an Italian national worked as a waitress in Austria for a fixed term of two-and-a-half months. After unsuccessful attempts to find new employment, she decided to study romance languages in Austria. The question raised in this case was whether the short-term employment taken up by Mrs Ninni-Orasche could be regarded as an effective and genuine activity, therefore classing her as a worker. The Court held that the fact that a person has worked for a temporary period of two-and-a-half months can confer on them the status of worker within the meaning of the Treaty, provided that the activity performed as an employed person is not purely marginal and ancillary. The national court must assess the facts in order to determine whether this is the case. The Court of Justice emphasized that the national court, in examining whether a person is a worker, must look at objective criteria relating to the nature of the activities concerned and the employment relationship. Subjective factors, such as motive or the fact that the person abusively created a situation enabling them to claim the status of worker within the meaning of the Treaty, are irrelevant.

In Case 197/86 *Brown* [1988] ECR 3205, the claimant similarly worked before moving on to further education, although the Court reached a different conclusion from that in *Ninni-Orasche*. Mr Brown had both British and French nationalities. He worked for nine months for a company in Scotland in employment that was described as 'pre-university industrial training'. After this employment, he commenced studies leading to a degree in electrical engineering at Cambridge University. He applied for a maintenance grant to which he was not entitled under national regulations. He relied on his French nationality, however, claiming that he was a worker and therefore entitled to the grant under EU law. The Court of Justice decided that Mr Brown was a worker, but that this did not mean he was entitled to the maintenance grant. He had acquired his status of worker exclusively as a result of being accepted at university to undertake studies and, in such circumstances, the employment relationship was merely ancillary to the studies.

11.2.2.5 Jobseekers

The Court of Justice has decided in its case law that Article 45 TFEU applies not only to workers, but also to those seeking work.

It could be difficult to find work in one Member State while living in another. Therefore, if only persons already employed were allowed to move to another Member State, Article 45 TFEU would lose a considerable amount of its effect, since this would cover only a small group of people. For this reason, the Court of Justice has ruled that jobseekers are also covered by Article 45 TFEU, which means that they have the right to move to another Member State to seek employment. This does not mean, however, that jobseekers have exactly the same status and rights as workers, which is evidenced by the relevant case law.

?! THINKING POINT

Why do you think persons seeking work can also benefit from Article 45 TFEU, even though they have no employment of any kind in the Member State in which they want to live?

In Case C-292/89 *Antonissen* [1991] ECR I-745, a Belgian national had unsuccessfully sought work in the UK when he was sentenced to imprisonment for unlawful possession of cocaine with intent to supply. After his release from prison, the Secretary of State ordered his deportation. The question to be answered was whether Mr Antonissen was a worker within the meaning of the Treaty because, if he was, this would make him virtually immune from deportation. The Court of Justice acknowledged that, according to the strict wording of Article 45 TFEU, EU nationals are given the right to move freely within the territory of the Member States only to accept offers of employment actually made and the right to stay in the territory of a Member State is stated to be for the purpose of employment. However, such a strict interpretation would exclude the right of a national of a Member State to move freely and to stay in another Member State to seek employment. The Court decided that such an interpretation could not be upheld because it would jeopardize the actual chances of a jobseeker finding employment in another Member State and would therefore render Article 45 TFEU ineffective. As a consequence, the Court decided as follows.

Case C-292/89 *Antonissen* [1991] ECR I-745

13. It follows that Article 45 TFEU must be interpreted as enumerating, in a non-exhaustive way, certain rights benefiting nationals of Member States in the context of the free movement of workers and that that freedom also entails their right to move freely within the territory of the other Member States and to stay there for the purposes of seeking employment.

→ CROSS-REFERENCE See 11.1.4 and also the section therein on economically active citizens' right of residence for more than three months.

As mentioned at the beginning of this section, the status of a person seeking employment is not entirely the same as that of a worker. In that respect, it must be noted that the right to stay in a Member State to seek employment may be subject to a reasonable time limitation, unless the jobseeker can prove that they are continuing to seek employment and that they have genuine chances of being employed. This is provided for in Article 14(4)(b) of the Citizenship Directive.

Another difference between workers and jobseekers lies in their rights to certain social advantages, which was at issue in Case C-278/94 *Commission v Belgium* [1996] ECR I-4307. In this case, the Court of Justice said that national rules concerning unemployment insurance do not infringe EU law if they require a person to have participated in the employment market by exercising an effective and genuine occupational activity before they can use such insurance.

The right of jobseekers to social advantages was further discussed in Case C-138/02 *Collins* [2004] ECR I-2703, which concerned Mr Collins, an Irish national, who moved to the

UK. A little over a week after arriving in the UK, he applied for a jobseekers' allowance whilst seeking work. He was refused unemployment benefits because he was not habitually resident in the UK. The Court of Justice pointed out that Member State nationals who move to seek work benefit from the principle of equal treatment only as regards access to employment. This means that those who have already entered the employment market may claim the same social and tax advantages as national workers, but those who have not yet entered the employment market may not. It is legitimate for a Member State to grant a jobseekers' allowance only after it has become possible to establish that a genuine link exists between the person seeking work and the employment market of that State. The existence of such a link may be determined by establishing that the jobseeker has, for a reasonable period, genuinely sought work in the Member State. A residence requirement is, in principle, appropriate to ensure such a connection, but is has to be proportionate. That means it cannot go beyond what is necessary in order to achieve the objective. Therefore the period of residence required must not exceed that necessary to be able to assess whether the jobseeker is genuinely seeking work in the employment market of the host Member State.

→ CROSS-REFERENCE
For a further discussion of a jobseeker's right to social advantages, see 11.2.3.

NOTE

In 2004, when ten new Member States joined the EU, they were not given the immediate right to benefit from the free movement of workers because the other Member States feared that their labour markets would be flooded by workers from the new Member States. The 2003 Accession Treaty therefore provided for an optional transitional regime, which allowed for the deferral of the free movement of workers for a period up to seven years. The UK, Sweden, and Ireland did not opt into the regime, so that workers from the ten new Member States could, and did, move to work in those Member States from 2004 onwards. Other Member States implemented certain restrictions regarding the rights for workers from the new Member States, which were later abolished. The 2003 transitional regime expired altogether on 30 April 2011. Similar arrangements were made in the 2007 Accession Treaty of Bulgaria and Romania. This transitional regime, which was opted into by the UK and other Member States, expired on 31 December 2013.

→ CROSS-REFERENCE
On the enlargement of the EU, see 1.6.

11.2.3 The rights of workers under EU law

Article 45 TFEU is the primary legislation conferring rights on workers. In addition, there is secondary legislation governing workers' rights under EU law. For many years, this included one Directive and two Regulations:

- Council Directive 68/360/EEC of 15 October 1968 on the abolition of restrictions on movement and residence within the Community for workers of Member States and their families, OJ 1968 L257/13;
- Regulation (EEC) No 1612/68 of the Council of 15 October 1968 on freedom of movement for workers within the Community, OJ 1968 L257/2; and
- Regulation (EEC) No 1251/70 of the Commission of 29 June 1970 on the right of workers to remain in the territory of a Member State after having been employed in that State, OJ 1970 L142/24.

More recently, the Citizenship Directive replaced Directive 68/360 and Regulation 1251/70, as well as Articles 10 and 11 of Regulation 1612/68. Regulation (EU) No 492/2011 of the European Parliament and of the Council of 5 April 2011 on freedom of movement for workers within the Union, OJ 2011 L141/1, replaced the remainder of Regulation 1612/68. Since Regulation 492/2011 is a consolidation Regulation, it does not change the rights formerly contained in Regulation 1612/68. It must also be remembered that if there is a conflict between the Treaty provisions and any secondary legislation, the Treaty provisions prevail. An overview of the current relevant legislation is provided in Figure 11.3.

→ CROSS-REFERENCE
On the sources of EU law, see 3.4.

11.2.3.1 The right to move and reside freely

Article 45 TFEU gives workers the right to move freely within the territory of the Member States and to reside there. These rights can be restricted only on grounds of public policy, public security, or public health. Workers are not the only persons having these rights in the EU: the Citizenship Directive gives all EU citizens the right to move and reside freely within the territory of the EU. This is therefore discussed in detail in this chapter under EU citizenship rights.

→ CROSS-REFERENCE
See 11.1.4 on the rights of EU citizens and their families.

There are differences, however, between rights applicable to all EU citizens and those applicable only to workers specifically. Workers' specific rights will be the subject of the next sections.

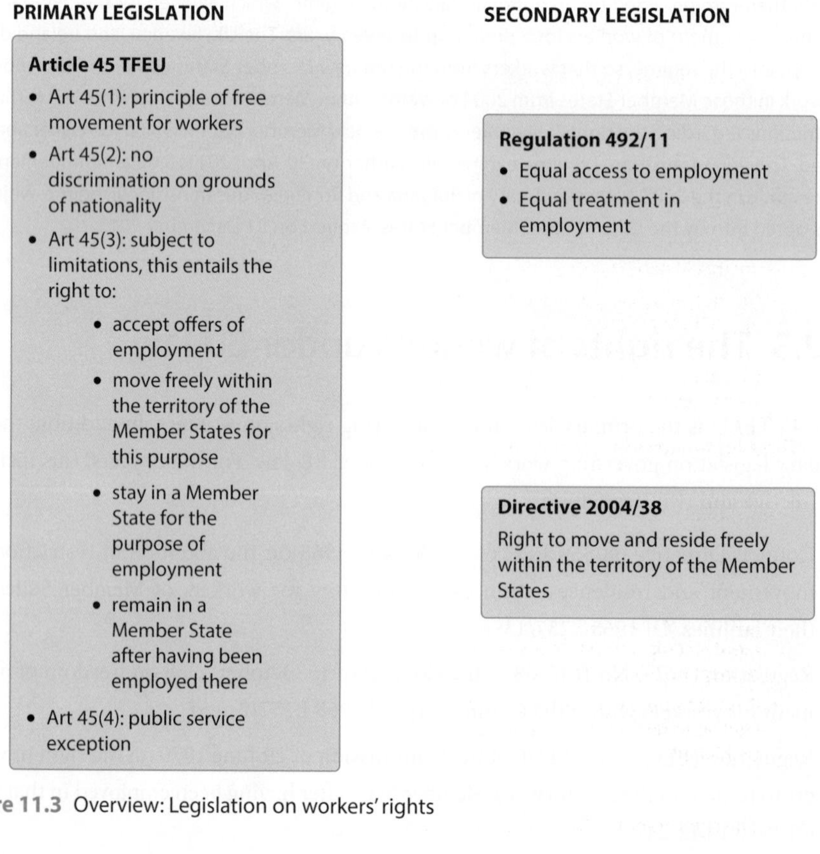

PRIMARY LEGISLATION

Article 45 TFEU
- Art 45(1): principle of free movement for workers
- Art 45(2): no discrimination on grounds of nationality
- Art 45(3): subject to limitations, this entails the right to:
  - accept offers of employment
  - move freely within the territory of the Member States for this purpose
  - stay in a Member State for the purpose of employment
  - remain in a Member State after having been employed there
- Art 45(4): public service exception

SECONDARY LEGISLATION

Regulation 492/11
- Equal access to employment
- Equal treatment in employment

Directive 2004/38
Right to move and reside freely within the territory of the Member States

Figure 11.3 Overview: Legislation on workers' rights

11.2.3.2 The right to equal treatment for workers

Article 45 TFEU states that the freedom of movement of workers shall entail the abolition of any discrimination based on nationality between workers of the Member States as regards employment, remuneration, and other conditions of work and employment. Regulation (EU) No 492/2011 of the European Parliament and of the Council of 5 April 2011 on freedom of movement for workers within the Union, OJ 2011 L141/1, implements this provision regarding the prohibition of discrimination and the corresponding right to equal treatment. It provides for equal treatment in terms of eligibility for employment—that is, equal access to employment—as well equal treatment in employment—that is, equal treatment while working. Article 24 of the Citizenship Directive also formulates a general right to equal treatment for all EU citizens, but this chapter concerns equal treatment in the specific context of workers.

Key case law on the right to equal treatment for workers is summarized in Figure 11.4.

WORKERS: EQUAL TREATMENT

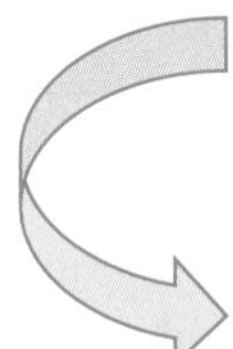

ELIGIBILITY FOR EMPLOYMENT

No direct discrimination

- *Bosman*: 3 + 2 rule regarding fielding of players
- *Commission v France*: nationality requirements and ratios on merchant ships
- *Commission v Italy*: nationality requirement for private security guards

No indirect discrimination

- *Scholz*: refusal to consider experience in another Member State
- *Groener*: language requirements can be justified under Art 3 Regulation 492/11
- *Angonese*: linguistic knowledge/certificate cannot be required to be acquired in a specific Member State

Obstacles to access the employment market

- *Bosman*: are in principle prohibited, but may be justified by reasons of public interest if they are proportionate
- *Terhoeve*: greater social contributions because of work in another Member State
- *Commission v Denmark*: requirement to register company cars for employees resident in Denmark
- *Graf*: obstacles must affect access of workers to the labour market to be prohibited

WORKING CONDITIONS

No direct discrimination

- *Marsmann*: protection against dismissal for German nationals resident in another Member State, but not for non-nationals resident there

No indirect discrimination

- *Ugliola*: refusal to take into account service in the military of another Member State for the calculation of seniority
- *Sotgiu*: different allowances for those not resident in the Member State at the time of recruitment

Figure 11.4 The right to equal treatment for workers

Eligibility for employment

The prohibition of discrimination based on nationality regarding access to employment is detailed in Article 1 of Regulation 492/2011.

Regulation (EU) No 492/2011 of the European Parliament and of the Council of 5 April 2011 on freedom of movement for workers within the Union, OJ 2011 L141/1

Article 1

1. Any national of a Member State shall, irrespective of his place of residence, have the right to take up an activity as an employed person, and to pursue such activity, within the territory of another Member State in accordance with the provisions laid down by law, regulation or administrative action governing the employment of nationals of that State.
2. He shall, in particular, have the right to take up available employment in the territory of another Member State with the same priority as nationals of that State.

Article 45 TFEU and Regulation 492/2011 envisage the prohibition of not only direct discrimination, but also indirect discrimination and even certain non-discriminatory measures, as can be seen from the Court of Justice's case law, which will be discussed in the following sections.

THINKING POINT

Do you think it is allowed, under EU law, to restrict the employment of foreign nationals in a business?

Direct discrimination

Direct discrimination entails that a national of a Member State is treated differently (usually more favourably) than a non-national of that Member State. In the context of the free movement of workers, it means that the non-national worker is treated less favourably than the national worker. As a rule, this is prohibited under EU law.

EU law does not prohibit the restriction of employment of foreign nationals provided that they are non-EU nationals. Article 45 TFEU provides that the freedom of movement of workers entails the abolition of any discrimination based on nationality between workers of the Member States. Furthermore, Article 4 of Regulation 492/2011, which implements Article 45 TFEU, provides that provisions that restrict by number or percentage the employment of foreign nationals shall not apply to nationals of the other Member States.

These provisions have been applied on a few occasions by the Court of Justice. In Case C-415/93 *Bosman* [1995] ECR I-1921, a preliminary ruling was requested on whether a rule made by UEFA infringed EU law. The rule concerned was the so-called 3 + 2 rule, which permitted each national football association to limit to three the number of foreign players that a club may field in any first division match in their national championships *plus* two players who have played in the country of the relevant national association for five years, including three years as a junior. The same limitation applied to UEFA matches in competitions for club teams. The Court of Justice held that such limitations on the employment of foreign nationals could not apply to Member State nationals because they would directly discriminate against them based on their nationality. The fact that the rule did not concern the employment of foreign Member State players, but only the extent to which they could be fielded by their clubs, was held to be irrelevant, since participation in matches was the essential purpose of a football player's activity. A rule that restricted that participation therefore also restricted the chances of employment of the player concerned.

In Case 167/73 *Commission v France* [1974] ECR 359, the rule in question was one of French law, which provided that certain crew members on merchant ships had to be of French nationality and employment on merchant ships generally had to be in the ratio of three French crew members to one non-French crew member. The Court of Justice decided that this rule infringed Article 45 TFEU and Article 4 of Regulation 492/2011.

Finally, Case C-283/99 *Commission v Italy* [2001] ECR I-4363 provides another example of a rule directly discriminating based on nationality. In particular, Italian law required that private security activities could be carried out only by private security firms holding Italian nationality and hiring only Italian nationals. The Court held that such a rule was prohibited under Article 45 TFEU because it prevented workers from other Member States from working in Italy as private security guards.

Indirect discrimination

It is not only direct discrimination based on nationality that is prohibited under the Treaty and the implementing Regulation. Indirect discrimination also constitutes an infringement of EU law.

Indirect discrimination exists when a rule, although neutral in terms of nationality, affects non-nationals of a Member State more severely than nationals of the Member State. In the context of eligibility for employment or access to work, this means that a rule will set a condition that is more easily satisfied by nationals than by non-nationals. Article 3(1) of Regulation 493/2011 provides that 'provisions laid down by law, regulation or administrative practices of a Member State shall not apply … where, though applicable irrespective of nationality, their exclusive or principal aim or effect is to keep nationals of other Member States away from the employment offered'.

THINKING POINT

Can you define 'indirect discrimination'? What do you think it means?

Several examples of case law involving indirect discrimination will be discussed here to illustrate the types of rule that are prohibited. In Case C-419/92 *Scholz* [1994] ECR I-505, the claimant was of German origin, but had acquired Italian nationality by marriage. She applied for a post as a member of the canteen staff at the University of Cagliari in Italy. Candidates entered an open competition based on tests and qualifications. The rules of the competition took account of previous employment in public service when drawing up the list of successful candidates. Mrs Scholz, the claimant, challenged her place on the list, saying it was unlawful for the selection board to refuse to take into account her previous employment with the German post office. The Court of Justice agreed and said that the board's refusal to take into consideration the claimant's employment in the public service of another Member State constituted unjustified indirect discrimination.

It was clear that there was no direct discrimination in this case since there were no nationality requirements for entering the open competition or restrictions on the employment of foreign Member State nationals and, in any event, Mrs Scholz had acquired Italian nationality by marriage. However, this did not mean that the principle of non-discrimination did not apply, since Mrs Scholz had exercised her right to freedom of movement for workers and could therefore rely on the relevant provisions irrespective of her place of residence or her nationality. The fact that the board would take account of experience in the public service of only its own State constituted indirect discrimination because it would be far easier for their own nationals to gain that experience than it would be for a foreign national, such as Mrs Scholz, who was a German national at the time she gained her experience with the German post office.

As well as requirements for a certain period of experience gained in the host Member State, residence requirements could also constitute indirect discrimination, since these requirements will similarly be met more easily by nationals of the Member State in question than by non-nationals. Case C-138/02 *Collins* [2004] ECR I-2703 is an illustration of this. English law required a person to be habitually resident in the UK in order to be able to claim a jobseekers' allowance. The Court of Justice held that this requirement was more easily met by the State's own nationals and could therefore be indirectly discriminatory as it placed at a disadvantage Member State nationals who had exercised their right of free movement in order to seek employment in another Member State. In *Collins*, however, the English rule could be justified.

→ CROSS-REFERENCE
See 11.2.2 for a full discussion of *Collins*.

Other examples of measures that could be indirectly discriminatory to non-nationals of a Member State in terms of eligibility for employment are language requirements. Non-nationals of a Member State will obviously be affected by such requirements more onerously since they are less likely to speak the languages required for employment in that Member State. Article 3(1) of Regulation 492/2011, however, expressly provides that such requirements are allowed for eligibility for employment. In particular, it provides that the principle of non-discrimination does not apply to 'conditions relating to the linguistic knowledge required by reason of the nature of the post to be filled'.

This provision was applied in Case 379/87 *Groener* [1989] ECR 3967. Mrs Groener, a Dutch national, was engaged on a temporary basis as a part-time art teacher at the College of Marketing and Design in Dublin. She applied for a permanent full-time position as a lecturer in art in that college, a position for which she was required to obtain a certificate of proficiency in the Irish language. After her unsuccessful application for an exemption, she completed a four-week beginner's course, following which she took an examination to assess her knowledge of the Irish language, which she failed. Since this prohibited her from taking up the full-time employment as an art lecturer, she started proceedings alleging that the language requirements for the job infringed the principle of non-discrimination in Article 45 TFEU and Regulation 492/2011.

The Court of Justice observed that the teaching of art at the College was conducted essentially or almost exclusively in English. Knowledge of the Irish language was therefore not required for the performance of those teaching duties. The imposition of the language requirement could, however, be justified under Article 45 TFEU and Article 3(1) of Regulation 492/2011 in the context of the policy followed by the Irish government for many years of aiming to maintain and promote the use of Irish as a means of expressing national identity and culture. Since education was crucial for the implementation of such a policy, it was not unreasonable to require teachers to have knowledge of the Irish language, provided that the level of knowledge required was not disproportionate in relation to the objective pursued. The Court emphasized, however, that the principle of non-discrimination prevented the imposition of any requirement that the linguistic knowledge must have been acquired within the national territory.

This last point was also addressed in Case C-281/98 *Angonese* [2000] ECR I-4139, a case that concerned a requirement for a certificate of bilingualism that could be obtained only in the province of Bolzano, Italy. The Court held that, even though the requirement to have a certain level of linguistic ability could be legitimate and the possession of a certificate could constitute a criterion to assess such ability, the fact that it was impossible to prove the required linguistic knowledge by any other means—in particular, by equivalent qualifications obtained in other Member States—was disproportionate in relation to the aim pursued.

Obstacles to access the employment market

Some national measures impede the freedom of movement of workers without being either directly or indirectly discriminatory based on nationality. It is apparent from the Court of Justice's case law that such measures can also breach Article 45 TFEU and Regulation 492/2011. In particular, they will be prohibited when they substantially obstruct access to the market. The issue first arose in Case C-415/93 *Bosman* [1995] ECR I-1921, in which the transfer system applied in professional football was in question.

Mr Bosman was a professional footballer of Belgian nationality who was employed by a Belgian first-division club. A few months before his contract was due to expire, his club offered him a new contract for one season, which drastically reduced his salary. Mr Bosman refused to sign and was put on the transfer list. Since no club showed any interest in a transfer, Mr Bosman contacted a French club in the second division, which led to him being hired. A contract was also made between the Belgian club and the French club for the temporary transfer of Mr Bosman for one year, against payment by the French club of a compensation fee. Both the contract between Mr Bosman and the French club and the contract between the Belgian club and the French club were subject to the condition that a transfer certificate must be sent in time for the first match of the season. The compensation fee was also payable at the time that the transfer certificate was received by the proper authorities. The Belgian club had doubts as to the French club's solvency and never requested the transfer certificate to be sent. Consequently, neither contract took effect. The Belgian club also suspended Mr Bosman and hence prevented him from playing for the entire season.

→ CROSS-REFERENCE
The *Bosman* case has been discussed already in relation to the direct effect of Article 45 TFEU (see 11.1.1) and direct discrimination regarding eligibility for employment earlier in this section.

The real question here was whether the transfer system developed by football associations breached Article 45 TFEU, since it required football clubs wanting to hire players to pay substantial amounts of money, in the form of compensation fees, to the clubs with which these players' contracts were about to expire. The Court of Justice therefore considered whether these transfer rules formed an obstacle to the freedom of movement for workers prohibited by Article 45 TFEU.

Case C-415/93 *Bosman* [1995] ECR I-1921

96. Provisions which preclude or deter a national of a Member State from leaving his country of origin in order to exercise his right to freedom of movement therefore constitute an obstacle to that freedom even if they apply without regard to the nationality of the workers concerned.

[...]

98. It is true that the transfer rules in issue in the main proceedings apply also to transfers of players between clubs belonging to different national associations within the same Member State and that similar rules govern transfers between clubs belonging to the same national association.

99. However, as has been pointed out by Mr Bosman, by the Danish Government and by the Advocate General in points 209 and 210 of his Opinion, those rules are likely to restrict the freedom of movement of players who wish to pursue their activity in another Member State by preventing or deterring them from leaving the clubs to which they belong even after the expiry of their contracts of employment with those clubs.

100. Since they provide that a professional footballer may not pursue his activity with a new club established in another Member State unless it has paid his former club a transfer fee agreed upon between the two clubs or determined in accordance with the regulations of the sporting associations, the said rules constitute an obstacle to freedom of movement for workers.

101. As the national court has rightly pointed out, that finding is not affected by the fact that the transfer rules adopted by UEFA in 1990 stipulate that the business relationship between the two clubs is to exert no influence on the activity of the player, who is to be free to play for his new club. The new club must still pay the fee in issue, under pain of penalties which may include its being struck off for debt, which prevents it just as effectively from signing up a player from a club in another Member State without paying that fee.

[...]

103. It is sufficient to note that, although the rules in issue in the main proceedings apply also to transfers between clubs belonging to different national associations within the same Member State and are similar to those governing transfers between clubs belonging to the same national association, they still directly affect players' access to the employment market in other Member States and are thus capable of impeding freedom of movement for workers.

> 104. Consequently, the transfer rules constitute an obstacle to freedom of movement for workers prohibited in principle by Article 48 of the [EC] Treaty [now Article 45 TFEU]. It could only be otherwise if those rules pursued a legitimate aim compatible with the Treaty and were justified by pressing reasons of public interest. But even if that were so, application of those rules would still have to be such as to ensure achievement of the aim in question and not go beyond what is necessary for that purpose.

Bosman principle Provisions that impede access to the employment market for workers are prohibited under Article 45 TFEU, even if they do not either directly or indirectly discriminate based on nationality. They may, however, be justified by reasons of public interest provided that they are proportionate.

The **_Bosman_ principle** has been applied in several subsequent cases. In Case C-18/95 *Terhoeve* [1999] ECR I-345, a Dutch national lived and worked in the UK for a time after being sent there by his Dutch employer. Because of this, he was required by Dutch law to pay more social contributions than if he had not worked in the UK. Dutch law could not be said to discriminate either directly or indirectly based on nationality since Mr Terhoeve was Dutch. The Court held, however, that provisions that precluded or deterred a national of a Member State from leaving their country of origin in order to exercise their right to freedom of movement constituted an obstacle to that freedom even if they applied without regard to the nationality of the worker concerned. This was because a national of a Member State could be deterred from leaving the Member State in which they resided to work in another Member State if they were required to pay greater social contributions than if they had continued to reside in that same Member State throughout the year. Legislation to that effect was therefore prohibited under Article 45 TFEU.

In Case C-464/02 *Commission v Denmark* [2005] ECR I-7929, Danish law required that a company car made available to an employee resident in Denmark by an employer established in another Member State be registered in Denmark. It was held that such a rule could impede access for employees resident in Denmark to employers in other Member States because the cost of registration of the vehicle, borne by the employer, made an employee resident in Denmark more expensive than an employee not resident there. The rule therefore infringed Article 45 TFEU.

In the light of this case law in which the so-called *Bosman* principle was applied, it can be questioned whether there are any boundaries to Article 45 TFEU, but in Case C-190/98 *Graf* [2000] ECR I-493 it was established that there are. Mr Graf was a German national who worked for an Austrian company but terminated his contract of employment in order to go and work in Germany. He was denied entitlement to compensation on termination of employment under Austrian law and claimed that such denial was precluded by Article 45 TFEU. The Court of Justice disagreed. The legislation in question granted entitlement to compensation on termination of employment to a worker whose contract ended without the termination being at their own initiative or attributable to themselves, but denied it to a worker who terminated their contract of employment themselves in order to take up employment with a new employer (whether in that Member State or in another Member State). Such legislation thus applied irrespective of the nationality of the worker. The Court then reiterated the *Bosman* principle, stating that provisions that, even if they applied without distinction, precluded or deterred a national of a Member State from leaving their country of origin in order to exercise their right to freedom of movement constitute an obstacle to that freedom. However, in order to be capable of constituting such an obstacle, such provisions must affect the access of workers to the labour market. The national provisions in *Graf* made entitlement to compensation dependent not on the choice of the worker whether or not to stay with their current employer, but on a future and hypothetical event—namely, the subsequent termination of the worker's contract without such termination being at their own initiative or attributable to themselves. Such an event was too uncertain and indirect a possibility for legislation to be capable of being regarded as liable to hinder the freedom of movement for workers.

The public service exception

Article 45(4) TFEU reads: 'The provisions of this Article shall not apply to employment in the public service.' This provision is inspired by the fact that the public service is part of the exercise of a State's sovereignty and so States wish to retain the ability to discriminate in favour of their own nationals in selecting the people who work in the public service. The extent to which this is allowed and the way in which Article 45(4) TFEU is applied becomes clear from the case law of the Court of Justice.

In Case 152/73 *Sotgiu* [1974] ECR 153, it was made clear that it was for the Court of Justice and not the Member States to define the scope of the exception. The Court emphasized that because of the fundamental nature of the principles of freedom of movement and equality of treatment of workers within the EU, the exceptions made by Article 45(4) TFEU must be read bearing in mind the aim in view of which this derogation was included. Although the derogation allows Member States to protect certain interests by allowing them to restrict the admission of foreign nationals to certain activities in the public service, it could not justify discriminatory measures against workers once they had been admitted to the public service. Furthermore, the exception concerns access to all posts forming part of the public services, and the nature of the legal relationship between the employee and the employing administration was of no consequence. It was therefore irrelevant to the application of Article 45(4) whether a worker was engaged as a workman, a clerk or an official, or even whether the terms on which they were employed came under public or private law.

?! THINKING POINT

Why do you think the legal relationship between the employee and the employing administration is irrelevant? Does it not seem relevant whether the person concerned was hired as a workman, a clerk or an official and whether the terms of their employment were governed by public or private law when determining whether their post forms part of the public services?

The question of whether an employee is hired as a workman, a clerk or an official and whether the terms of their employment are governed by public or private law when determining whether their post forms part of the public services may be relevant. However, it is for the Court of Justice to define the scope of Article 45(4) TFEU. The legal designations mentioned can be varied at the whim of national legislatures and, as such, the Member States would be able to determine the scope of the public service exception effectively. Therefore the legal relationship between the employee and the employing administration cannot provide an appropriate criterion for interpreting what constitutes 'public service'.

As already mentioned, not all posts in the public service fall within the scope of Article 45(4) TFEU. In Case 149/79 *Commission v Belgium No 1* [1980] ECR 3881, the Commission brought an action under Article 258 TFEU alleging that the requirement of Belgian nationality as a condition of recruitment for certain posts constituted an infringement of Article 45(4) TFEU. In particular, the Commission referred to vacancies among Belgian public undertakings and local authorities looking to fill posts for trainee train drivers, loaders, plate-layers, shunters, and signallers with the national railways, unskilled workers with the local railways, posts for hospital nurses, children's nurses, night-watchmen, plumbers, carpenters, electricians, garden hands, architects, and supervisors.

The Court noted that Article 45(4) TFEU removed from the range of Article 45(1)–(3) TFEU a series of posts that involve, first, direct or indirect participation in the exercise of powers conferred by public law and, secondly, duties designed to safeguard the general interests of the State or of other public authorities. Such posts in fact presumed, on the part of those occupying them, the existence of a special relationship of allegiance to the State and the reciprocity of rights and duties that form the foundation of the bond of nationality.

The Court did not consider itself in a position to rule on whether Belgium had infringed Article 45(4) TFEU, so it asked the Commission and Belgium to re-examine the issue in the light of its considerations and to report to the Court. In doing so, the Commission and Belgium reached a solution as to the posts of technical office supervisor, principal supervisor, works supervisor, stock controller, night-watchman, and architect with the municipality of Brussels. They agreed that these fell within the scope of Article 45(4) TFEU. The Court therefore had to make a decision regarding the other posts in question on which the Commission and Belgium had failed to reach an agreement. It did so two years later, in Case 149/79 *Commission v Belgium No 2* [1982] ECR 1845, holding that none of the other posts in question constituted employment in the public service.

This decision seems to suggest that only a limited number of positions will fall within the scope of Article 45(4) TFEU and that these will be mainly supervisory or managerial positions. Indeed, it is not easy to satisfy both conditions laid out by the Court for the public service exception to apply, which are that the position involves participation in the exercise of power conferred by public law *and* the safeguarding of the general interests of the State. This was also apparent in Case 225/85 *Commission v Italy* [1985] ECR 2625, in which it was held by the Court of Justice that research posts at the national research centre of a Member State do not constitute employment in the public service within the meaning of Article 45(4) TFEU. It was held that simply referring to the general tasks of the national research centre and listing the duties of all of its researchers is not sufficient to establish that the researchers are responsible for exercising powers conferred by public law or for safeguarding the general interests of the State. Only the duties of management or of advising the State on scientific and technical questions could be described as employment in the public service within the meaning of Article 45(4) TFEU.

In the absence of secondary legislation on Article 45(4) TFEU, the Court of Justice's case law clarifies the scope of the derogation from the general prohibition of discrimination based on nationality. As is clear from the case law discussed, the Court adheres to a functional approach, making an assessment case by case with regard to the nature of the tasks and responsibilities covered by the post in question. As such, it must be noted that an individual's position may change over time; it is possible for a worker to have equal access to a certain position as a non-national because it is not covered under Article 45(4) TFEU, but that later, when they are aiming for promotion, the new position may fall under the public service exception, so that they may not have equal access to that position.

REVIEW QUESTION

Bearing in mind the criteria developed by the Court of Justice to determine whether a position is covered by the public service employment exception, do you think the position of trainee teacher qualifies as employment in the public service? And what about the position of a nurse in a public hospital? Or of a foreign-language assistant at a university?

Answer: In Case 66/85 *Lawrie-Blum* [1986] ECR 2121, it was decided that the position of trainee teacher is not covered by Article 45(4) TFEU. In Case 307/84 *Commission v France* [1986] ECR 1725, it was decided that working as a nurse in a public hospital does not constitute employment in public service. And neither does working as a foreign-language assistant at a university, as was decided in Case 225/85 *Allué and Coonan* [1987] ECR 2625.

Working conditions

Under Article 45 TFEU, equal treatment must be provided not only regarding access to employment, but also during the exercise of the employment. This means that discrimination based on nationality is prohibited as regards eligibility for employment, as well as the terms and conditions of employment. The former prohibition was discussed earlier in this section. The latter prohibition will be discussed here.

Article 7(1) of Regulation 492/2011, which reiterates Article 45 TFEU, states as follows.

Regulation (EU) No 492/2011 of the European Parliament and of the Council of 5 April 2011 on freedom of movement for workers within the Union, OJ 2011 L141/1

Article 7(1)

[A] worker who is a national of a Member State may not, in the territory of another Member State, be treated differently from national workers by reason of his nationality in respect of any conditions of employment and work, in particular as regards remuneration, dismissal, and, should he become unemployed, reinstatement or re-employment.

There are few examples of case law regarding legislation that directly discriminates based on nationality. One can be found, however, in Case 44/72 *Marsmann* [1972] ECR 1243. Mr Marsmann was a Dutch national, resident in the Netherlands and employed in Germany. He suffered an industrial accident in Germany, resulting in a loss of earning capacity of more than 50 per cent. Under German law, workers enjoyed special protection against dismissal under such circumstances. Although this protection applied to Germans resident outside Germany, it did not apply to non-nationals resident in another Member State. It was held by the Court of Justice that this rule was discriminatory, and therefore prohibited, because the requirement of residence in Germany in order to enjoy the special protection against dismissal in the case of severe work-related injury applied only to non-nationals and not to nationals.

A substantial percentage of the cases regarding discrimination as to terms and conditions of employment involve indirectly discriminatory measures. A prime example can be found in Case 15/69 *Ugliola* [1969] ECR 363, which concerned the period of service in a Member State taken into account when calculating pay or other advantages. An Italian national employed in Germany asked for his period of military service in Italy to be taken into account in calculating his seniority with his German employer. German law provided that service in the German army was to be taken into account for such calculation, but was silent on whether service in the army of another Member State could also be taken into account. There was no direct discrimination here, since service in the German army by a non-national was to be taken into account and service of a German national in the army of another Member State was not to be taken into account. However, the Court held that this rule constituted prohibited indirect discrimination since it contained a criterion that, although theoretically applicable to both nationals and non-nationals, would in practice be fulfilled only by nationals.

Another example of measures that could lead to indirect discrimination is those containing residence requirements. As already explained, while discrimination based on nationality is, under certain conditions, allowed in terms of access to employment, it is not permissible once a non-national has been admitted to the public service. In Case 152/73 *Sotgiu* [1974] ECR 153, the question of discrimination arose regarding the payment of a so-called separation allowance, which was granted to workers allocated to posts away from their place of residence. Mr Sotgiu was an Italian national who worked for the German post office and was thus entitled to a separation allowance. German workers working away from home received the same allowance. At a certain point in time, however, the separation allowance was increased for those workers living in Germany at the time of recruitment, but not for those living in another Member State at the time of recruitment. Although this rule applied to Germans and non-Germans alike, it clearly affected non-Germans more, since they were less likely to have been resident in Germany at the time of recruitment.

Social and tax advantages

Following Article 7(2) of Regulation 492/2011, a worker who is a national of a Member State shall enjoy, in the territory of another Member State, the same social and tax advantages as national workers.

Social advantages

A definition of 'social advantages' in the context of Regulation 492/2011 can be found in the case law of the Court of Justice, which has defined the concept broadly. In particular, social advantages are not only those that national law confers on workers as such. The case of

Case 32/75 *Cristini v SNCF* [1975] ECR 1085 concerned an Italian widow with four children, whose husband, also an Italian, had worked in France and died there in an industrial accident. Mrs Cristini requested a discount card that the French railways, SNCF, offered to large families. This was refused, based on her nationality, since French law provided that the discount card was reserved for French nationals and foreigners whose country of origin had entered into a reciprocal treaty with France. This was not the case for Italy. The question then arose whether such a discount card was a social advantage, in the sense of Article 7(2) of Regulation 492/2011, since it was not connected with the contract of employment itself. The Court of Justice observed that, although certain provisions in the Article refer to relationships deriving from the contract of employment, there are others, such as those concerning reinstatement and re-employment should a worker become unemployed, which have nothing to do with such relationships and which even imply the termination of a previous employment. In these circumstances, the concept of 'social advantages' cannot be interpreted restrictively. In the view of equality of treatment, which Article 7(2) seeks to achieve, the substantive area must be delineated so as to include all social and tax advantages, whether or not attached to the contract of employment, such as reduction in fares for large families.

In Case 207/78 *Even* [1979] ECR 2019, the Court defined social advantages as follows.

Case 207/78 *Even* [1979] ECR 2019, 2020

… all those which, whether or not linked to a contract of employment, are generally granted to national workers primarily because of their objective status as workers or by virtue of the mere fact of their residence on the national territory and the extension of which to workers who are nationals of other Member States therefore seems suitable to facilitate their mobility within the Community [now Union].

The concept of 'social advantage' encompasses benefits granted by virtue of a right, but also benefits granted on a discretionary basis. In Case 65/81 *Reina v Landeskreditbank Baden-Württemberg* [1982] ECR 33, an Italian couple working in Germany applied for the grant of an interest-free childbirth loan on the birth of twins. Their application was rejected because the law required at least one of the spouses to be a German national. The Landeskreditbank, a credit institution incorporated under public law, argued that a childbirth loan was not a social advantage because it was granted mainly for reasons of demographic policy, assisting low-income families to stimulate the birth rate of the German population. As such, it was a measure adopted in the area of political rights, linked to nationality. Furthermore, it argued that the refusal to grant the loan in no way hindered the mobility of workers, and that the loan constituted a voluntary benefit and not one to which persons were entitled by virtue of a right. The Court of Justice acknowledged that the loans may be granted for reasons of demographic policy, but held that that did not mean that they could not be classed as social advantages. In particular, the Court viewed the interest-free childbirth loans as measures to alleviate the financial burden resulting from the birth of a child for low-income families and so the concept of 'social advantage' encompasses not only the benefits accorded by virtue of a right, but also those granted on a discretionary basis.

In Case C-237/94 *O'Flynn v Adjudication Officer* [1996] ECR I-2617, it was decided that social benefits to cover the costs of funeral expenses of family members were a social advantage within the meaning of Article 7(2) of Regulation 492/2011. In Case 59/85 *Reed* [1986] ECR 1283, it was held that the ability of a migrant worker to obtain permission for his unmarried companion to reside with him could assist his integration in the host Member State and thus contribute to the achievement of freedom of movement for workers. As a consequence, that possibility was a social advantage for the purposes of Article 7(2) of Regulation 492/2011. It must also be noted that this possibility has now been codified in the Citizenship Directive (Directive 2004/38/EC of the European Parliament and of the Council of 29 April 2004 on the right of citizens of the Union and their family members to move and reside freely within the territory of the Member States . . . , OJ 2004 L158/77).

→ CROSS-REFERENCE
For an in-depth discussion of the Citizenship Directive, see 11.1 on EU citizenship.

By contrast, in Case C-566/15 *Konrad Erzberger v TUI AG* EU:C:2017:562, German legislation preventing workers employed by a subsidiary of the TUI group located in a Member State other than Germany from participating in the composition of the TUI supervisory board was considered under the equal treatment provisions of Article 45 TFEU. Further, consideration was given to the fact that if a worker were a member of the TUI supervisory board and were to wish to exercise free movement rights by moving to a Member State other than Germany, that worker would lose membership of the supervisory board. Mr Erzberger argued that such legislation would prevent workers from exercising their free movement rights. However, the Court disagreed and held that Article 45 TFEU did not preclude such legislation.

Case C-566/15 *Konrad Erzberger v TUI AG* EU:C:2017:562

33. According to the Court's settled case-law, all the provisions of the Treaty on freedom of movement for persons are intended to facilitate the pursuit by Union nationals of occupational activities of all kinds throughout the EU, and preclude measures which might place Union nationals at a disadvantage when they wish to pursue an activity in the territory of a Member State other than their Member State of origin. In that context, nationals of the Member States have in particular the right, which they derive directly from the Treaty, to leave their Member State of origin to enter the territory of another Member State and reside there in order to pursue an activity there. As a result, Article 45 TFEU precludes any national measure which is capable of hindering or rendering less attractive the exercise by Union nationals of the fundamental freedoms guaranteed by that article (see, to that effect, judgments of 1 April 2008, *Government of the French Community and Walloon Government*, C-212/06, EU:C:2008:178, paragraphs 44 and 45, and of 10 March 2011, *Casteels*, C-379/09, EU:C:2011:131, paragraphs 21 and 22).
34. However, primary EU law cannot guarantee to a worker that moving to a Member State other than his Member State of origin will be neutral in terms of social security, since, given the disparities between the Member States' social security schemes and legislation, such a move may be more or less advantageous for the person concerned in that regard (see, by analogy, judgments of 26 April 2007, *Alevizos*, C-392/05, EU:C:2007:251, paragraph 76 and the case-law cited, and of 13 July 2016, *Pöpperl*, C-187/15, EU:C:2016:550, paragraph 24).

From the case law discussed, it is clear that the CJEU has defined the concept of 'social advantages' broadly. Where it has linked social advantages to the facilitation of mobility in *Even*, it has classed certain measures as social advantages even though it is difficult to see how or whether they in fact facilitate mobility of workers. Often, it is easier to see how they facilitate the integration of the worker in the host State, which was the criterion put forward in *Reed*.

Furthermore, the Court of Justice has decided that certain financial advantages, such as a jobseekers' allowance, are also social advantages. The issue has already been touched upon in relation to the definition of a 'worker'. In its earlier case law, the Court had decided that jobseekers did not enjoy the right to equal treatment in respect of social and tax advantages; their right to equal treatment was limited to eligibility for employment or access to the labour market. The case of Case C-138/02 *Collins* [2004] ECR I-2703, however, changed this position. An Irish national moved to the UK and applied for a jobseekers' allowance one week after arriving. It was held by the Court that, in view of the establishment of EU citizenship and the right to equal treatment enjoyed by citizens, it was no longer possible to exclude from the scope of Article 45(2) TFEU a benefit of a financial nature intended to facilitate access to employment in the labour market of a Member State.

This decision seemed peculiar. The Court said that the right to equal treatment is limited to access to the labour market and does not include equal treatment in respect of social advantages. Following this, and in the light of the introduction of the notion of EU citizenship, there must also be equal treatment regarding benefits of a financial nature facilitating access to employment. This decision seems to allow for so-called welfare tourism, which means that citizens could use their free movement rights to move to whichever Member State has the most advantageous welfare system. In order to try to remedy this, the Court emphasized that it is legitimate for the Member States to seek to ensure that there is a genuine link between an applicant for an allowance in the nature of a social advantage, within the meaning of Article 7(2) of Regulation 492/2011, and the geographic employment market in question. Such a link may be determined when a jobseeker has in fact genuinely sought work in the Member State in question. A residence requirement, which is usually indirectly discriminatory, can be appropriate to ensure this.

Although not all jobseekers will be entitled to benefits facilitating their access to employment, because there is a requirement of a link between the jobseeker and the employment market of the host State, it was still difficult to reconcile this case law with the Citizenship Directive, which provides in its Article 24(2) that the host Member State is not obliged to confer entitlement to social assistance during the first three months of residence or during a longer period for jobseekers.

The Court of Justice addressed these apparent inconsistencies in Joined Cases C-22 & 23/08 *Vatsouras and another v Arbeitsgemeinschaft (ARGE) Nurnberg 900* [2009] ECR I-4585. The Court decided that '[b]enefits of a financial nature which, independently of their status under national law, are intended to facilitate access to the labour market cannot be regarded as constituting "social assistance" within the meaning of Article 24(2) of Directive 2004/38' (*Vatsouras*, at para 45).

It is clear that the Court of Justice has stretched the application of Article 7(2) of Regulation 492/2011 to secure the free movement of workers. That does not mean, however, that there are no limits to the scope of this provision and the rights that can be claimed under it. In Case 207/78 *Even* [1979] ECR 2019, a French national receiving an early retirement pension in Belgium complained that he did not receive the increased rate given to Belgian nationals who served in the allied forces during the Second World War and suffered injury in service. The Court observed that the main reason for a benefit such as the increased early retirement pension rate was the service that those in receipt of the benefit had rendered in wartime to their own country and that its essential objective was to give those nationals an advantage by reason of the hardships suffered for their country. Such a benefit, which is based on a scheme of national recognition, cannot therefore be considered an advantage granted to a national worker by reason primarily of their status of worker or resident on the national territory and, for that reason, does not fulfil the essential characteristics of the 'social advantages' referred to in Article 7(2) of Regulation 492/2011.

In Case C-43/99 *Leclere* [2001] ECR I-4265, a Belgian couple were denied maternity, childbirth, and child-raising allowances in Luxembourg because they did not reside there. Mr Leclere had worked in Luxembourg and received an invalidity pension paid by the Luxembourg social security scheme. The question therefore arose whether he was entitled to these allowances as social advantages under Article 7(2) of Regulation 492/2011. The Court held that, once the employment relationship had ended, the person concerned lost his status as a worker. This status could, however, produce certain effects after the relationship had ended. Mr Leclere was therefore entitled to the advantages linked to his former employment, such as his invalidity pension, without discrimination and so without any residence requirement. However, since he was no longer a worker, he was not entitled to any new rights that did not derive from his previous professional activity, such as the childbirth allowances.

Tax advantages

Article 7(2) of Regulation 492/2011 states that a worker who is a national of a Member State shall enjoy, in the territory of another Member State, not only the same social advantages, but also the same tax advantages as national workers. Taxes, and therefore also tax advantages, are inherently territorial and fall within the competence of the Member States. This competence, however, must be exercised consistently with EU law. Because taxes are inherently territorial, most of the case law in this area concerns situations in which residents are treated differently from non-residents. A residence requirement will usually be indirectly discriminatory and therefore prohibited. Concerning taxation, however, this is not necessarily the case because residents and non-residents may be in non-comparable situations.

In Case C-279/93 *Schumacker* [1995] ECR I-225, a Belgian national, who worked in Germany and was taxed there as an employee, wanted to enjoy a tax advantage available for married persons. He was denied the advantage because he and his wife and children lived in Belgium. The Court of Justice noted that although tax benefits granted only to residents of a Member State could constitute indirect discrimination by reason of nationality, discrimination could arise only through the application of different rules to comparable situations or the application of the same rule to different situations. However, in relation to direct taxes, the situations of residents and non-residents were not, as a rule, comparable. Income received in the territory of a Member State by a non-resident was, in most cases, only part of that individual's total income, which was concentrated at their place of residence. Moreover, a non-resident's personal ability to pay tax, determined by reference to their aggregate income and their personal and family circumstances, was easier to assess at the place where their personal and financial interests were centred. In general, that was the place where the person resided. The situation of a resident was different insofar as the major part of their income was normally concentrated in the State of residence. Moreover, that State generally had available all of the information needed to assess the taxpayer's overall ability to pay tax, taking account of their personal and family circumstances. Consequently, the fact that a Member State did not grant to a non-resident certain tax benefits that it granted to a resident was not, as a rule, discriminatory, since those two categories of taxpayer were not in a comparable situation.

In the case of Mr Schumacker, however, the position was different because he did not receive significant income in the State of his residence—indeed, he had obtained the major part of his taxable income from an activity performed in the State of employment—with the result that the State of his residence was not in a position to grant him the benefits resulting from taking into account his personal and family circumstances. There was no objective difference between the situations of such a non-resident and a resident engaged in comparable employment such as to justify different treatment.

Another example of a tax advantage is the possibility of deducting from income tax the negative income relating to a house used as a dwelling. In Case C-527/06 *Renneberg v Staatssecretaris van Financiën* [2008] ECR I-7735, a Dutch national applied for such a deduction, but was unsuccessful because his house was located in Belgium. The Court observed that the relevant Dutch legislation treated non-resident taxpayers less advantageously than resident taxpayers. Because Mr Renneberg derived most of his taxable income from salaried employment in another Member State and he had no significant income in his Member State of residence, he was, for the purposes of taking into account his ability to pay tax, in a situation objectively comparable, with regard to his Member State of employment, to that of a resident of that Member State who was also in salaried employment there. Since there was no objective difference between the situation of a resident and a non-resident, the Dutch legislation was held to be discriminatory.

A discriminatory tax rule can be justified, for example, by reasons of effectiveness of fiscal supervision, as follows from *Schumacker*. There is little case law, however, where Member States have successfully relied on this justification. Another example of a justification for a discriminatory tax rule is the need to preserve the cohesion of the tax system. Again, however, this defence has often failed, mostly because there was no direct link between the discriminatory tax rule and the compensating tax advantage. An example of a situation in which a link did exist can be found in Case C-204/90 *Bachmann* [1992] ECR I-249. Belgian law gave individuals a choice regarding the cost of invalidity insurance and pension and life assurance premiums. They could choose to deduct the contributions from their taxable income and pay tax on the future benefits, or not to deduct them from their income and not pay tax on the future benefits. The contributions could not be deducted from taxable income earned in Belgium if they were paid in other Member States. The Court of Justice held that the Belgian rules were justified, even though they were discriminatory, because there was a connection between the deductibility of contributions and the liability to tax of sums payable under the insurance and assurance contracts.

11.3 Derogations to the free movement of persons

Article 45(3) TFEU expressly makes the rights following from the freedom of movement for workers subject to limitations justified on grounds of public policy, public security, or public health. Article 21 TFEU on the right of EU citizens to reside and move freely does not contain such an express derogation, although it states that this right is subject to the limitations and conditions laid down in the Treaties and by the measures adopted to give them effect. Read in conjunction with Chapter VI of the Citizenship Directive (Directive 2004/38/EC of the European Parliament and of the Council of 29 April 2004 on the right of citizens of the Union and their family members to move and reside freely within the territory of the Member States … , OJ 2004 L158/77), which is headed 'Restrictions on the right of entry and the right of residence on grounds of public policy, public security or public health', it becomes clear that these derogations or limitations apply to the rights of all EU citizens and their family members, economically active or not.

?! **THINKING POINT**

With consideration to all of the issues covered so far in this chapter, can you think of further circumstances that in essence amount to derogations to the free movement of persons? In particular, reflect upon the provisions concerning linguistic requirements in Regulation (EU) No 492/2011 of the European Parliament and of the Council of 5 April 2011 on freedom of movement for workers within the Union, OJ 2011 L141/1, and public service posts in Article 45(4) TFEU.

11.3.1 Public policy and public security

Directive 2004/38/EC of the European Parliament and of the Council of 29 April 2004 on the right of citizens of the Union and their family members to move and reside freely within the territory of the Member States … , OJ 2004 L158/77

Article 27

1. Subject to the provisions of this Chapter, Member States may restrict the freedom of movement and residence of Union citizens and their family members, irrespective of nationality, on grounds of public policy, public security or public health. These grounds shall not be invoked to serve economic ends.
2. Measures taken on grounds of public policy or public security shall comply with the principle of proportionality and shall be based exclusively on the personal conduct of the individual concerned.

> Previous criminal convictions shall not in themselves constitute grounds for taking such measures.
>
> The personal conduct of the individual concerned must represent a genuine, present and sufficiently serious threat affecting one of the fundamental interests of society. Justifications that are isolated from the particulars of the case or that rely on considerations of general prevention shall not be accepted.

Article 27 of the Citizenship Directive allows Member States to restrict the free movement rights of EU citizens and their families based on reasons of public policy, public security, and public health. Measures taken on grounds of public health are the subject of the next section (see 11.3.2). It is important to note here, in regards to measures taken on any of these grounds, however, that they will be scrutinized by the Court of Justice. Because the freedom of movement of persons is such a key freedom in the internal market, the Court of Justice has interpreted the limitations strictly. Any measure by a Member State limiting free movement rights without strict compliance with the requirements laid down in the Citizenship Directive will be contrary to EU law. It is also important to note here that such measures may not be taken for economic reasons (Article 27(1) *in fine*).

Measures taken on grounds of public policy or public security must be based exclusively on the personal conduct of the individual concerned, and this conduct must represent a genuine, present, and sufficiently serious threat affecting one of the fundamental interests of society.

11.3.1.1 Personal conduct of the individual concerned

EU law does not impose a uniform scale of values as regards the assessment of conduct that may be considered as contrary to public policy. Therefore case law illustrates how this provision is to be applied. A clear requirement is that the conduct concerned must be the personal conduct of the individual. In Case 41/74 *Van Duyn* [1974] ECR 1337, a Dutch national who wanted to work as a secretary for the Church of Scientology was refused entry into the UK because the authorities considered that organization's activities to be socially harmful. She argued that the public policy ground could not be invoked by the UK because her membership of the Church of Scientology did not constitute personal conduct. Although membership of the organization was not prohibited in the UK, the Court of Justice pointed out that the personal conduct concerned did not need to be unlawful before a Member State could rely on the public policy exception. The Court also held that a person's present association with an organization could constitute personal conduct because it reflects participation in the activities of the organization, as well as identification with its aims and design. In general, however, a person's past association with an organization cannot justify a decision refusing them the right to move freely within the EU.

→ CROSS-REFERENCE On *Van Duyn*, see also 4.2.1.

→ CROSS-REFERENCE See 11.3.3 regarding procedural safeguards in the case of expulsion.

Case law has also made it clear that legislation requiring automatic expulsion cannot be justified on grounds of public policy and public security. This principle is now protected by Article 33 of the Citizenship Directive.

This issue arose in Case C-348/96 *Calfa* [1999] ECR I-11. Ms Calfa, an Italian national, was charged with possession and use of prohibited drugs while on holiday in Greece. She was sentenced by the Greek court to three months' imprisonment and ordered to be expelled for life from Greek territory—an automatic expulsion prescribed by Greek law. The Court of Justice explained that Member States can, on public policy grounds, adopt measures against nationals of other Member States that they cannot adopt against their own nationals. It decided, however, that an automatic expulsion for life following a criminal conviction, as provided for by Greek legislation, was not permitted under EU law owing to its failure to take into account the personal conduct of the person concerned. Therefore the personal conduct of the convicted person had to be taken into account—in particular, whether that conduct created a genuine and sufficiently serious threat affecting one of the fundamental interests of society.

Similar issues arose in Joined Cases C-482 & 493/01 *Orfanopoulos and Oliveri* [2004] ECR I-5257. Orfanopoulos, a Greek national, and Oliveri, an Italian national, both suffered from drug addiction and were convicted of several offences in Germany, where they lived. Eventually they were both expelled, as provided under German law for aliens convicted of certain offences and/or sentenced to certain sentences. The Court of Justice held that such automatic expulsion was contrary to EU law, as regard must be had to the personal conduct of the offender and the danger that the person represents for the requirements of public policy.

11.3.1.2 A genuine, present, and sufficiently serious threat

Orfanopoulos and Oliveri also made it clear that the personal conduct of the person concerned must represent a *present* threat to the requirements of public policy. Mr Oliveri had argued that he had become more mature because of the difficult life he had led in prison and that he no longer posed a risk of reoffending. German law did not allow this argument to be taken into account by the authorities reviewing the original expulsion decision. The Court of Justice held that, in general, the threat to public policy and security must exist at the time of the expulsion order. However, a national practice whereby the authorities reviewing the lawfulness of the original expulsion order are prevented from taking into account factors that have arisen after the order and which indicate a diminution of the present threat to public policy and security of the person involved is contrary to EU law because the limitations to free movement rights must be interpreted and applied strictly. Such practice is all the more problematic if a long time has elapsed between the original expulsion order and the review of that original decision.

It has also been held by the Court of Justice that personal conduct may not be considered *sufficiently serious* where the host Member State does not adopt repressive measures or other genuine and effective measures intended to combat such conduct on the part of its own nationals. Joined Cases 115 & 116/81 *Adoui and Cornuaille* [1982] ECR 1665 concerned two French prostitutes who were refused a Belgian residence permit on the ground that their conduct was contrary to public policy. Although Belgian law prohibited certain activities incidental to prostitution, such as the exploitation of prostitution by third parties and incitement to debauchery, prostitution as such was not prohibited. Therefore the prostitutes' conduct was not sufficiently serious to refuse them a right of residence on grounds of public policy.

11.3.1.3 General preventative measures

Article 27(2) of the Citizenship Directive specifies that 'justifications that are isolated from the particulars of the case or that rely on considerations of general prevention shall not be accepted'. In other words, restrictions on the freedom of movement and residence of EU citizens, imposed by Member States, cannot be justified by considerations of general prevention. In Case 67/74 *Bonsignore* [1975] ECR 297, an Italian worker who lived in Germany was convicted for unlawful possession of a firearm and found guilty of accidentally causing his brother's death by his careless handling of the firearm. He was fined for unlawful possession of the firearm and an order for his deportation was subsequently issued. The German court considered that the only possible justification for the deportation would be reasons of a general preventive nature, based on the deterrent effect that the deportation of an alien, found in illegal possession of a firearm, would have in immigrant circles, having regard to the resurgence of violence in large urban areas. The Court of Justice emphasized that derogations from the rules concerning the free movement of persons constitute exceptions that must be strictly construed. The concept of 'personal conduct' required that a deportation order may be made only for breaches of the peace and public security that might be committed by the individual affected and not for general preventative reasons.

11.3.1.4 Previous criminal convictions

Article 27(2) of the Citizenship Directive specifies that previous criminal convictions do not in themselves constitute grounds for taking measures on grounds of public policy or security. In Case 34/77 *Bouchereau* [1977] ECR 1999, a French worker in the UK was convicted of illegal possession of drugs. Before ordering his deportation, the national court asked a preliminary ruling of the Court of Justice to ensure that such deportation would not constitute an infringement of EU law. It was held by the Court that a previous criminal conviction can be taken into account only insofar as the circumstances that give rise to that conviction are evidence of personal conduct constituting a present threat to the requirements of public policy. In general, a finding that such a threat exists implies a propensity of the individual concerned to act in the same way in the future. However, it is possible that past conduct alone may constitute such a threat to the requirements of public policy. The Court also emphasized that recourse by a national authority to the concept of public policy presupposes, in any event and in addition to the perturbation of the social order that any infringement of the law involves, the existence of a genuine and sufficiently serious threat to the requirements of public policy affecting one of the fundamental interests of society.

11.3.1.5 Proportionality

As with any limitation on an EU citizen's rights, the requirement of proportionality also applies here. This means that Member State measures restricting free movement rights must be proportionate to their aim. Therefore national authorities are not entitled to impose measures that are so disproportionate to the offence that they in effect constitute obstacles to the free movement of persons. An example of such disproportionality can be found in Case C-157/79

R v Pieck [1980] ECR-2171, in which expulsion was held to be a disproportionate penalty for non-compliance with administrative formalities.

Even for more serious crimes, it must be carefully monitored whether the measure imposed by the Member State is proportionate to the aim it is pursuing (ie the protection of public policy and public security). As such, in Joined Cases C-482/01 and C-493/01 *Orfanopoulos and Oliveri* [2004] ECR I-5257, in which the men had been convicted of drug-related offences and sentenced to imprisonment on a number of occasions, regard must still be had to the proportionality of expulsion as a penalty. In particular, the national authorities must take into account the seriousness of the offence(s), the length of residence in the host Member State, the time that has elapsed since the offences were committed, and the offender's family circumstances.

The requirement of proportionality is now laid down in Article 28 of the Citizenship Directive.

Directive 2004/38/EC of the European Parliament and of the Council of 29 April 2004 on the right of citizens of the Union and their family members to move and reside freely within the territory of the Member States ..., OJ 2004 L158/77

Article 28

1. Before taking an expulsion decision on grounds of public policy or public security, the host Member State shall take account of considerations such as how long the individual concerned has resided on its territory, his/her age, state of health, family and economic situation, social and cultural integration into the host Member State and the extent of his/her links with the country of origin.
2. The host Member State may not take an expulsion decision against Union citizens or their family members, irrespective of nationality, who have the right of permanent residence on its territory, except on serious grounds of public policy or public security.
3. An expulsion decision may not be taken against Union citizens, except if the decision is based on imperative grounds of public security, as defined by Member States, if they:
   (a) have resided in the host Member State for the previous ten years; or
   (b) are a minor, except if the expulsion is necessary for the best interests of the child, as provided for in the United Nations Convention on the Rights of the Child of 20 November 1989.

The host Member State thus has to take the personal circumstances of the EU citizen concerned into account before it can issue an expulsion order. Furthermore, once the EU citizen and their family members have acquired a right of permanent residence, an expulsion decision may be made only on *serious* grounds of public policy or public security. If the citizen concerned has resided in the host Member State for ten years or more, a decision of expulsion can be justified only on *imperative* grounds of public policy or public security.

Since the public policy and public security derogations are very strictly defined, these even stricter thresholds have made expulsion of an EU citizen after they have resided in the host Member State for more than five years extremely difficult.

?! THINKING POINT

Can you think of an example that would be so serious as to constitute a justification on either serious or imperative grounds of public policy or public security?

An example of a situation in which such a ground could be used to justify expulsion can be found in Case C-145/09 *Tsakouridis* [2010] ECR I-11979. In this case, it was held that the fight against crime in connection with dealing in narcotics as part of an organized group was capable of being covered by the concept of 'imperative grounds of public security', which may justify a measure expelling an EU citizen who has resided in the host Member State for the preceding ten years.

11.3.1.6 Partial restrictions

Article 22 of the Citizenship Directive now clearly provides as follows.

Directive 2004/38/EC of the European Parliament and of the Council of 29 April 2004 on the right of citizens of the Union and their family members to move and reside freely within the territory of the Member States ..., OJ 2004 L158/77

Article 22

The right of residence and the right of permanent residence shall cover the whole territory of the host Member State. Member States may impose territorial restrictions on the right of residence and the right of permanent residence only where the same restrictions apply to their own nationals.

This provision thus answers the question 'may measures restricting free movement rights prohibit residence in certain regions of a Member State only?' It appears they may not, unless such restrictions apply to their own nationals as well. The relevant case law, which preceded the Directive, provides clarity as to the relevance of the question.

In Case 36/75 *Rutili v Ministre de l'Intérieur* [1975] ECR 1219, Mr Rutili, an Italian national, was an enthusiastic trade union activist, living in France. The French authorities prevented him from living in certain regions in France, on the basis that 'he was likely to disturb public policy' there. The Court of Justice held that prohibitions on residence for reasons of public policy may be imposed only in respect of the whole of the national territory. Prohibitions on residence that were territorially limited—such as here, where the limitation was for certain regions only—were allowed only where they may be imposed on the Member State's own nationals as well.

This position is in line with the rule in Article 22 of the Citizenship Directive. It is therefore interesting to read what the Court of Justice decided in Case C-100/01 *Ministre de l'Intérieur v Olazabal* [2002] ECR I-10981. Mr Olazabal was a Spanish national of Basque origin who was sentenced to 18 months' imprisonment—of which eight were suspended—for conspiracy to disturb public order by intimidation or terror. Later, the French authorities prevented him from living near the Spanish frontier in the light of police reports that he still maintained relations with ETA. The Court of Justice, emphasizing that the requirement of proportionality must be borne in mind, made the following statement.

Case C-100/01 *Ministre de l'Intérieur v Olazabal* [2002] ECR I-10981

41. In situations where nationals of other Member States are liable to banishment or prohibition of residence, they are also capable of being subject to less severe measures consisting of partial restrictions on their right of residence, justified on grounds of public policy, without it being necessary that identical measures be capable of being applied by the Member State in question to its own nationals.

This decision seems contrary to the current rule in Article 22 of the Citizenship Directive. The rule in the Directive should, of course, be considered the current position at law, but it will be interesting to see how the Court of Justice responds to its prior case law, read together with the Directive.

11.3.2 Public health

Directive 2004/38/EC of the European Parliament and of the Council of 29 April 2004 on the right of citizens of the Union and their family members to move and reside freely within the territory of the Member States ..., OJ 2004 L158/77

Article 29

1. The only diseases justifying measures restricting freedom of movement shall be the diseases with epidemic potential as defined by the relevant instruments of the World Health Organisation [*sic*] and other infectious diseases or contagious parasitic diseases if they are the subject of protection provisions applying to nationals of the host Member State.
2. Diseases occurring after a three-month period from the date of arrival shall not constitute grounds for expulsion from the territory.
3. Where there are serious indications that it is necessary, Member States may, within three months of the date of arrival, require persons entitled to the right of residence to undergo, free of charge, a medical examination to certify that they are not suffering from any of the conditions referred to in paragraph 1. Such medical examinations may not be required as a matter of routine.

The restriction of freedom of movement of persons can be justified only in relation to diseases with epidemic potential. Furthermore, these diseases must be the subject of protection provisions applying to nationals of the host Member State. The derogation also applies only on first entry to a Member State or within three months of arrival. After that period, the public health derogation can no longer be relied upon to order expulsion. In that respect, this derogation is more limited than the public policy and public security derogation, which can be relied upon up to five years after the person's arrival in the host Member State. It is also exclusively within those first three months after arrival that the host Member State may require the person to undergo a (free) medical examination to ensure that they are not suffering from a disease with epidemic potential. Such a medical examination may be required only if there are serious indications that it is necessary and certainly not as a matter of routine.

11.3.3 Procedural safeguards in the case of expulsion

The Citizenship Directive provides a number of procedural safeguards for people who are refused rights of entry and residence.

Article 30 of the Directive provides that they must be notified of such refusal in writing, in such a way that they are able to comprehend the content of the decision and the implications of the decision for them. In particular, they must be informed of the public policy, public security, or public health grounds on which the decision was based, unless this is contrary to the interests of State security. The notification must also contain details of the possibilities to appeal the decision and the time allowed for the person to leave the territory of the Member State in question. Unless there are exceptional circumstances of urgency, the time allowed to leave must be at least one month.

In Case C-184/16 *Ovidiu-Mihăiță Petrea v Ypourgos Esoterikon kai Dioikitikis Anasygrotisis* EU:C:2017:684, a Romanian national was ordered to return to Romania from Greece on the grounds that he constituted a threat to public policy and security following a conviction for robbery. Mr Petrea claimed that he had not been notified of the relevant exclusion order in a language he understood. The Court considered this aspect, amongst others, clarifying the scope of the requirement that the person be notified of such refusal in writing, in such a way that they are able to comprehend the content of the decision and the implications of the decision for them.

Case C-184/16 *Ovidiu-Mihăiță Petrea v Ypourgos Esoterikon kai Dioikitikis Anasygrotisis* EU:C:2017:684

68. Consequently, it must be considered that, by its fifth question, the referring court asks, in essence, whether Article 30 of Directive 2004/38 requires a decision adopted under Article 27(1) of that directive to be notified to the person concerned in a language he understands, although he did not bring an application to that effect.
69. It should, first of all, be noted that such a requirement does not derive from the wording of Article 30(1) of that directive, which provides, more generally, that the persons concerned

are to be notified in writing of any decision taken under Article 27(1) 'in such a way that they are able to comprehend its content and the implications'.

70. Next, it follows from the preparatory works to Directive 2004/38, in particular from the proposal for a directive of the European Parliament and of the Council on the right of citizens of the Union and their family members to move and reside freely within the territory of the Member States [COM(2001) 257 final], that Article 30(1) of Directive 2004/38 does not mean that the removal order is to be translated into the language of the person concerned, but requires by contrast that the Member States take the necessary measures to ensure that the latter understands the content and implications of that decision, in accordance with the Court's findings in the judgment of 18 May 1982, *Adoui and Cornuaille* (115/81 and 116/81, EU:C:1982:183, paragraph 13).
71. Finally, it should be noted, concerning return decisions adopted against third-country nationals, that Article 12(2) of Directive 2008/115 provides that the Member States are to provide, upon request, a written or oral translation of the main elements of decisions related to return, including information on the available legal remedies in a language the third-country national understands or may reasonably be presumed to understand.
72. In the light of above, the answer to the fifth question is that Article 30 of Directive 2004/38 requires the Member States to take every appropriate measure with a view to ensuring that the person concerned understands the content and implications of a decision adopted under Article 27(1) of that directive, but that it does not require that decision to be notified to him in a language he understands or which it is reasonable to presume he understands, although he did not bring an application to that effect.

According to Article 31 of the Citizenship Directive, the persons concerned must have access to judicial and, where appropriate, administrative procedures in the host Member State to appeal against or seek review of a decision taken against them. When the person concerned appeals the expulsion decision and, at the same time, applies for an interim order to suspend their expulsion, they cannot be removed from the territory of the Member State until the decision on the interim order has been made, except under limited circumstances. The appeal procedures must allow for an examination of the legality of the expulsion decision and the facts of the case. They must also ensure that the decision is not disproportionate. Pending the appeal, the person concerned can be excluded from the territory of the host Member State, but this may not prevent them from submitting their defence in person, except if this would cause serious problems for public policy or public security, or when the appeal concerns a denial of entry to the host Member State.

Article 32 of the Directive provides for persons excluded on grounds of public policy or public security to submit an application for lifting the exclusion order after a reasonable period, depending on the circumstances, and in any event after three years from enforcement of the final exclusion order. The Member State concerned must reach a decision on this application within six months of the submission of the application.

It is important to note that a Member State cannot automatically expel an EU citizen from its territory for life. This issue arose in Case C-348/96 *Calfa* [1999] ECR I-11, in which Ms

CROSS-REFERENCE
On *Calfa*, see 11.3.1.

Calfa, an Italian national, was ordered by a Greek court to be expelled for life from Greek territory. The Court of Justice decided that an automatic expulsion for life following a criminal conviction, as provided for by Greek legislation, was not permitted under EU law. The personal conduct of the convicted person had to be taken into account—in particular, whether that conduct created a genuine and sufficiently serious threat affecting one of the fundamental interests of society.

11.4 Free movement of persons and Brexit

Since the outcome of the UK's referendum of 23 June 2016 on EU membership, there has been much speculation as to the extent to which rights of free movement will continue once the UK formally leaves the EU. Much will depend upon the nature of the relationship that the UK has with the internal market, as set out in Chapter 10. There are some in the 'Leave' camp who believe that it will be possible to negotiate a position whereby the UK enjoys the trade benefits of the internal market without being subject to provisions on the free movement of persons. However, Donald Tusk, President of the European Council, has, on many occasions, been clear in his view that that there can be 'no compromises' on retaining benefits such as access to the single market and customs union at the same time as rejecting the free movement of people.

European Council, Speech by President Donald Tusk at the European Policy Centre Conference, 13 October 2016

Our task will be to protect the interests of the EU as a whole and the interests of each of the 27 member states. And also to stick unconditionally to the Treaty rules and fundamental values. By this I mean, inter alia, the conditions for access to the single market with all four freedoms. There will be no compromises in this regard.

SUMMARY

- Free movement of workers (Article 45 TFEU):
  - A 'worker', for the purposes of European Union law is not defined within the Treaty or secondary legislation, but has been defined by case law to include performance of genuine and effective economic activity for remuneration and can include part-time working.
  - The Citizenship Directive, Directive 2004/38, provides more favourable rights to move and reside freely for workers than for the non-economically active.
  - A fundamental right to equal treatment exists, which includes the prohibition of direct and indirect discrimination and the prohibition of national measures that impede the free movement of workers (subject to justification).

- An exception to the right to equal treatment of workers can be found within the public service exception of Article 45 TFEU.
- EU citizenship (Article 20 TFEU):
  - All EU citizens have the right to exit and enter a Member State and reside for a period up to three months unless they are an unreasonable burden on the social assistance system of the host Member State.
  - EU citizens have a right of residence for more than three months (subject to conditions) if they are economically active/independent citizens or students.
  - EU citizens acquire a right of permanent residence after five years' residence, with a more favourable regime existing for formerly economically active citizens.
  - EU citizens have a fundamental right to equal treatment (subject to exceptions regarding social advantages).
  - EU citizens enjoy a number of other rights, which include diplomatic protection and the right of citizens' initiative.
- Derogations:
  - Derogations to free movement rights exist on the grounds of public policy, public security, and public health, with procedural safeguards in place.

FURTHER READING

Articles

J Lonbay, 'The Free Movement of Persons' (2004) 53(2) ICLQ 479

Critical discussion of developments in case law and legislation.

RCA White, 'Free Movement, Equal Treatment, and Citizenship of the Union' (2005) 54(4) ICLQ 885

Detailed discussion of EU citizens' right to free movement, with particular emphasis on the prohibition of discrimination.

Books

C Barnard, *The Substantive Law of the EU: The Four Freedoms*, 4th edn (Oxford: Oxford University Press, 2010), esp chs 11, 12, 15, and 16

Thorough analysis of relevant legislation and case law, with critical commentary, background, historical developments, and visual aids.

P Craig and G de Búrca, *EU Law: Text, Cases, and Materials*, 6th edn (Oxford: Oxford University Press, 2015), esp chs 21 and 23

Focused and accessible account of relevant cases and materials.

F Goudappel, *The Effects of EU Citizenship: Economic, Social and Political Rights in a Time of Constitutional Change* (The Hague: Asser Press, 2010)

Overview of developments and current situation regarding EU citizenship.

E Guild, S Peers, and J Tomkin, *The Citizens' Rights Directive* (Oxford: Oxford University Press, 2014)

Excellent, yet accessible, commentary on the Directive, with relevant case law.

A Kaczorowska, *European Union Law*, 4th edn (Abingdon: Routledge-Cavendish, 2016)

Comprehensive, but accessible, source of EU law.

QUESTION

Patrick, a UK national, is a librarian at his local library. He has recently been told that, due to the economic climate, a decision has been made to close a number of libraries and that, unfortunately, the library in which he works is one of those that will close. Patrick has looked for employment opportunities elsewhere in the UK, but, unsurprisingly, librarian posts are few and far between. Becoming increasingly concerned about his ability to support his family financially, Patrick has decided to go abroad to seek work and has identified France, where he has supportive friends, as a suitable destination.

Whilst he is looking for work, Patrick, his wife Shannon (a Canadian national), and his son James (a UK national) plan to live with Patrick's friends in France. Shannon hopes to find casual work and James plans to attend the local school. Patrick is confident that he will be able to find work within a year and he then plans to purchase a property. He has spotted a couple of part-time posts in French libraries, but it has been suggested that part-time employment would not provide him with a right to stay in France. He has also become concerned by a recent newspaper article suggesting that some French provinces reserve librarian posts for French nationals because of the 'public service' nature of such posts. Furthermore, the article went on to say that, at times, non-nationals were paid less and had less employment protection than French nationals.

As the day of departure approached, Patrick went out with friends for a farewell party. Unfortunately, Patrick drank heavily and, whilst in an intoxicated state, became involved in an altercation with another man. Patrick has since been charged with assault. Patrick fears that this charge will give the French authorities cause to deny him and his family entry.

Advise Patrick, Shannon, and James as to all of the issues raised in connection with the free movement of persons within the EU.

To view an outline answer to this question plus further resources to support your EU law studies, visit the Online Resources for this book at www.oup.com/uk/eulaw-complete4e

Freedom of establishment and freedom to provide and receive services

12

KEY POINTS

By the end of this chapter, you should be able to:

- define the scope of the freedom of establishment and the freedom to provide and receive services in the European Union (EU);
- identify the relevant Treaty provisions and secondary legislation regarding the freedom of establishment and freedom to provide and receive services in the EU;
- apply the relevant legislation in order to describe the specific rights granted under the freedom of establishment and freedom to provide and receive services; and
- explain the possibilities for Member States to implement measures derogating from the freedom of establishment and freedom to provide and receive services.

INTRODUCTION

The freedom of establishment and the freedom to provide and receive services form part of the fundamental freedoms of EU law, characteristic of the internal market. Chapter 11 discussed the free movement of workers and EU citizens and their families. Self-employed persons have rights similar to workers. The freedom of establishment and the freedom to provide services, however, also entail rights for companies.

The fundamental freedoms are guaranteed by the Treaty on the Functioning of the European Union (TFEU) and implemented in secondary legislation. For the self-employed, reference must be made to the Citizenship Directive (Directive 2004/38/EC of the European Parliament and of the Council of 29 April 2004 on the right of citizens of the Union and their family members to move and reside freely within the territory of the Member States . . . , OJ 2004 L158/77), which was discussed in Chapter 11. For companies, the Services Directive (Directive 2006/123/EC of the European Parliament and of the Council of 12 December 2006 on services in the internal market, OJ 2006 L376/36) was adopted. Furthermore, the Court of Justice's case law is an important source in this area.

There are many parallels between the freedom of establishment and the freedom to provide and receive services, on the one hand, and the other fundamental freedoms, on the other hand. These will be highlighted throughout the chapter.

The freedom of establishment is discussed first, making a distinction between the freedom of establishment for natural persons and the freedom of establishment for legal persons where relevant. The freedom to provide and receive services is discussed thereafter. Finally, the possible derogations to both freedoms are explained.

12.1 Freedom of establishment

12.1.1 Article 49 TFEU

Article 49 TFEU sets out the principle of freedom of establishment. This freedom comprises the right of EU citizens and companies to establish themselves in any Member State for a commercial purpose and, when they are already established in a Member State, to set up secondary establishments in another Member State.

Article 49 TFEU

Within the framework of the provisions set out below, restrictions on the freedom of establishment of nationals of a Member State in the territory of another Member State shall be prohibited. Such prohibition shall also apply to restrictions on the setting-up of agencies, branches or subsidiaries by nationals of any Member State established in the territory of any Member State.

Freedom of establishment shall include the right to take up and pursue activities as self-employed persons and to set up and manage undertakings, in particular companies or firms within the meaning of the second paragraph of Article 54, under the conditions laid down for its own nationals by the law of the country where such establishment is effected, subject to the provisions of the Chapter relating to capital.

The phrase 'within the framework of the provisions set out below' in Article 49 TFEU refers to the fact that the subsequent Treaty Articles provide that the prohibition of discrimination set out in Article 49 TFEU will be implemented in secondary legislation—specifically, Directives. This could suggest that, in the absence of such secondary legislation, Article 49 would be ineffective. The Court of Justice has made it clear, however, that this is not the case.

In Case 2/74 *Reyners* [1974] ECR 631, a Dutch national who had undertaken his legal education in Belgium was refused admission to the Belgian Bar based solely on his lack of Belgian nationality. He brought a claim and the Belgian court requested a preliminary ruling from the Court of Justice. Mr Reyners claimed that Article 49 TFEU was capable of producing direct effect and the Court agreed.

Case 2/74 *Reyners* [1974] ECR 631

26. In laying down that freedom of establishment shall be attained at the end of the transitional period, Article 52 [now Article 49 TFEU] thus imposes an obligation to attain a precise result, the fulfilment of which had to be made easier by, but not made dependent on, the implementation of a programme of progressive measures.

27. The fact that this progression has not been adhered to leaves the obligation itself intact beyond the end of the period provided for its fulfilment.
28. This interpretation is in accordance with Article 8(7) of the treaty [now Article 20 TFEU], according to which the expiry of the transitional period shall constitute the latest date by which all the rules laid down must enter into force and all the measures required for establishing the common market must be implemented.
29. It is not possible to invoke against such an effect the fact that the council has failed to issue the directives provided for by Articles 54 and 57 [now Articles 50 and 53 TFEU] or the fact that certain of the directives actually issued have not fully attained the objective of non-discrimination required by Article 52.
30. After the expiry of the transitional period the directives provided for by the chapter on the right of establishment have become superfluous with regard to implementing the rule on nationality, since this is henceforth sanctioned by the treaty itself with direct effect.

Article 49 TFEU, as then worded, required the freedom of establishment to be attained by the end of a transitional period and therefore imposed an obligation to attain a precise result: the abolition of discrimination on grounds of nationality. The fulfilment of this result had to be made easier by the implementation of a programme of progressive measures—Directives—but was not dependent on this. It was therefore possible for Mr Reyners to rely on Article 49 TFEU directly. The fact that Article 49 refers to the prohibition of discrimination 'within the framework of the provisions set out below' and that no Directives had been made in accordance with these provisions was relevant only during the transitional period. After that, the freedom of establishment was fully attained, allowing Mr Reyners to rely on it despite a lack of secondary legislation implementing it. The Court of Justice emphasized, however, that these Directives had not lost all relevance since they preserved an important role in the field of measures intended to make the effective exercise of the right of freedom of establishment easier (*Reyners*, at para 31).

The Court in *Reyners* also made it clear that Article 49 TFEU had vertical direct effect. The question could still be asked, though, whether it also had horizontal direct effect—in other words, whether it could be relied upon against private parties as well as against the Member States.

→ CROSS-REFERENCE
For an in-depth explanation and discussion of direct effect, see 4.1.

Case C-438/05 *International Transport Workers' Federation and Finnish Seamen's Union v Viking Line ABP and OÜ Viking Line Eesti* [2007] ECR I-779 only partially answered that question. Viking, a large Finnish ferry operator, operated a route between Finland and Estonia. Viking wanted to change its place of establishment to Estonia to provide its services from there, benefiting from the lower Estonian wage levels. Finnish trade union FSU, supported by the International Transport Workers' Federation, opposed these plans, and threatened strike action and other boycotts if the company failed to maintain the higher Finnish wage levels if and when moving to Estonia.

Case C-438/05 *International Transport Workers' Federation and Finnish Seamen's Union v Viking Line ABP and OÜ Viking Line Eesti* [2007] ECR I-779

34. Since working conditions in the different Member States are governed sometimes by provisions laid down by law or regulation and sometimes by collective agreements and other acts concluded or adopted by private persons, limiting application of the prohibitions laid down by these articles to acts of a public authority would risk creating inequality in its application (see, by analogy, *Walrave and Koch* [Case 36/74 *Walrave and Koch* [1974] ECR 1405], paragraph 19; *Bosman* [Case C-415/93 *Bosman* [1995] ECR I-1921], paragraph 84; and *Angonese* [Case C-281/98 *Angonese* [2000] ECR I-4139], paragraph 33).

[...]

57. The Court would point out that it is clear from its case-law that the abolition, as between Member States, of obstacles to freedom of movement for persons and freedom to provide services would be compromised if the abolition of State barriers could be neutralised by obstacles resulting from the exercise, by associations or organisations not governed by public law, of their legal autonomy (*Walrave and Koch*, paragraph 18; *Bosman*, paragraph 83; *Deliège* [Joined Cases C-51/96 & 191/97 *Deliège* [2000] ECR I-2549], paragraph 47; *Angonese*, paragraph 32; and *Wouters and Others* [Case C-309/99 *Wouters and others v Netherlands Bar* [2002] ECR I-1577], paragraph 120).

[...]

61. It follows that [Article 49 TFEU] must be interpreted as meaning that, in circumstances such as those in the main proceedings, it may be relied on by a private undertaking against a trade union or an association of trade unions.

[...]

65. There is no indication in ... case-law that could validly support the view that it applies only to associations or to organisations exercising a regulatory task or having quasi-legislative powers. Furthermore, it must be pointed out that, in exercising their autonomous power, pursuant to their trade union rights, to negotiate with employers or professional organisations the conditions of employment and pay of workers, trade unions participate in the drawing up of agreements seeking to regulate paid work collectively.

From this ruling, it is not entirely clear how far Article 49 TFEU can be relied upon against any private party. It could be argued that the fact that the Court of Justice recognized its horizontal direct effect implies that it can be relied upon against any person. However, the Court emphasized that trade unions have particular powers regarding the negotiation of collective regulation, which could suggest that a certain collective dimension is required. It is to be hoped that future case law resolves this uncertainty.

12.1.2 Meaning of 'establishment'

The concept of establishment implies the permanent or semi-permanent settlement of a person or a company for economic reasons. The right of establishment, therefore, is the right to set up in another Member State for the purpose of pursuing an economic activity there. The Court of Justice has confirmed, in Case C-55/94 *Gebhard* [1995] ECR I-4165, at para 25, that the concept of establishment is a broad one, 'allowing an EU national to participate, on a stable and continuous basis, in the economic life of a Member State other than his state of origin and to profit therefrom, so contributing to economic and social interpenetration within the Union, in the sphere of activities of self-employed persons'.

As such, it has been decided as follows.

Case 205/84 *Commission v Germany* [1986] ECR 3755

Summary

[...]

2. An insurance undertaking of another Member State which maintains a permanent residence in the Member State in question comes within the scope of the provisions of the Treaty on the right of establishment, even if that presence does not take the form of a branch or agency, but consists merely of an office managed by the undertaking's own staff or by a person who is independent but authorized to act on a permanent basis for the undertaking, as would be the case with an agency. . . .

In Case C-243/01 *Gambelli* [2003] ECR I-13031, the Court of Justice decided that a bookmaker established in the UK was also established in Italy, where it had a presence in the form of commercial agreements with Italian operators or intermediaries relating to the creation of data transmission centres. Those centres made electronic means of communication available to users, collected and registered the intentions to bet, and forwarded them to the bookmaker in the UK.

→ CROSS-REFERENCE
The distinction between establishment and the provision of services is discussed at 12.2.3.

The Court of Justice clarified the requirement of presence in the host Member State in Case C-386/04 *Stauffer* [2006] ECR I-8203. It held that, in order for the provisions on freedom of establishment to apply, it was generally necessary to have secured a permanent presence in the host Member State. Where immoveable property was purchased and held, that property should be actively managed. The Italian charitable organization in that case did not have any premises in Germany for the purposes of pursuing its activities and the services ancillary to the letting of its German property were provided by a German property agent. As a consequence, the Italian foundation was held not to be established in Germany.

→ CROSS-REFERENCE
On the definition of workers, see 11.2.2.

12.1.3 Beneficiaries

12.1.3.1 *Natural persons*

The TFEU does not define the concept of 'self-employed person', but like the concept of 'worker', it has been defined in the Court of Justice's case law.

Case C-268/99 *Jany* [2001] ECR I-8615 concerned Czech and Polish women working as prostitutes in the Netherlands. They paid rent to the owner of the premises where they conducted their activity and received a monthly income, which they declared to the tax authorities. The Dutch government argued that, because of the subordinate relationship of the prostitutes to their pimps, they were in fact in an employment relationship. The Court considered whether a prostitute could be considered to be a self-employed person and, in so doing, contrasted this concept with the concept of 'worker', providing a definition of the former.

Case C-268/99 *Jany* [2001] ECR I-8615

51. By its third question, the national court is asking in substance whether Article 44 of the Association Agreement between the Communities and Poland and Article 45 of the Association Agreement between the Communities and the Czech Republic must be construed as meaning that prostitution does not come under those provisions on the ground that it cannot be regarded as an economic activity pursued in a self-employed capacity, as defined in those provisions:
    - in view of its illegal nature;
    - for reasons of public morality;
    - on the ground that it would be difficult to control whether persons pursuing that activity are able to act freely and are therefore not, in reality, parties to disguised employment relationships.

[...]

71. ... [P]rostitution is an economic activity pursued by a self-employed person ... where it is established that it is being carried on by the person providing the service:
    - outside any relationship of subordination concerning the choice of that activity, working conditions and conditions of remuneration;
    - under that person's own responsibility; and
    - in return for remuneration paid to that person directly and in full.

It is for the national court to determine in each case, in the light of the evidence adduced before it, whether those conditions are satisfied.

NOTE

According to *Jany*, a self-employed person (a) provides a service (b) outside any relationship of subordination concerning the choice of that activity, working conditions, and conditions of remuneration (c) under that person's own responsibility (d) in return for remuneration paid to that person directly and in full.

?! **THINKING POINT**

Applying this definition, do you think that a prostitute could be considered a self-employed person?

In *Jany*, the Court of Justice held that prostitutes could be considered to be self-employed. The Court of Justice disagreed with the Dutch government's view, refusing to accept that a relationship of dependency could be equated to an employment relationship. The potentially immoral character of the activity did not change the Court's opinion. Prostitution was not illegal in the Netherlands and the Court considered that it was not its task to substitute its own assessment for that of the national legislature simply because a legal activity was allegedly immoral.

It is thus apparent that a self-employed person can engage in a wide range of activities. In particular, the Court has explained that a self-employed person may pursue activities of an industrial or commercial character, activities of craftsmen, or activities of the professions of a Member State (Case C-257/99 *Barkoci and Malik* [2001] ECR I-6557).

12.1.3.2 Legal persons

According to Article 54 TFEU, 'companies or firms' means 'companies or firms constituted under civil or commercial law, including cooperative societies, and other legal persons governed by public or private law, save for those which are non-profit-making'.

This definition is very wide and so it can cover many organizations. However, non-profit-making organizations are excluded. This means that, similarly to a self-employed person who pursues activities for remuneration, a company or a self-employed person must pursue economic activities. Charities are therefore excluded. That does not mean that a company must make a profit to be included in the definition. An organization making a loss or breaking even falls within the definition provided that it pursues economic activities—that is, activities intended to make a profit.

For natural persons, it is fairly easy to determine whether they are Member State nationals and consequently EU citizens.

→ CROSS-REFERENCE
See 11.1.1 on EU citizens.

For companies, nationality is determined by reference to the Member State in which they have their seat according to their statutes. It has been clarified by the Court of Justice that, for the application of the provisions on the right of establishment, it is required only that the company is formed in accordance with the law of a Member State and that it has its registered office, central administration, or principal place of business within the EU. In Case 79/85 *Segers* [1986] ECR 2375, the Court added that the fact that the company conducted its business through an agency, branch, or subsidiary solely in another Member State is immaterial. In other words, when a company is formed in accordance with the law of a Member State and has its registered office, central administration, or principal place of business somewhere in the EU, it is established in the Member State according to which law it is formed, even if it conducts no business whatsoever in that Member State. This position was confirmed in Case C-212/97 *Centros* [1999] ECR 1459, in which the Court of Justice held that it was immaterial that the company was formed in the first Member State only for the purpose of establishing itself in the second, where its main—or even its entire—business was to be conducted.

The situation is somewhat different if the company is formed in accordance with the law of a Member State, but has its registered office, central administration, or principal place of business outside the EU and only its seat prescribed by its statutes in the EU. The Council's General Programme for the Abolition of Restrictions on Freedom to Provide Services, OJ 1962 32/3, stipulates that, under these circumstances, for the company to be established in a Member State, the company's activities must have an effective and continuous link with the economy of a Member State, excluding the possibility that this link might depend on nationality—particularly, the nationality of the partners or the members of the managing or supervisory bodies, or of the persons holding the capital stock. Once established in a Member State, the company can set up branches and agencies in other Member States, even though it does not have its principal office in the EU.

REVIEW QUESTION

Which requirements must be met before organizations can benefit from the provisions on the freedom of establishment?

Answer: The company must have been formed in accordance with the law of a Member State. The company must also have its registered office, central administration, or principal place of business within the EU—that is, it must be located in a Member State. When only the seat prescribed by its statutes is in the EU, but not its registered office, central administration, or principal place of business, the company's activity must show a real and continuous link with the economy of a Member State. This link is not one of nationality, whether of the members of the company or firm, or of the persons holding managerial or supervisory posts therein, or of the holders of the capital.

12.1.4 Rights pertaining to the freedom of establishment

→ CROSS-REFERENCE
See 12.1.1 on Article 49 TFEU.

As mentioned earlier, Article 49 TFEU prohibits restrictions on the freedom of establishment. Since this provision has direct effect, a person has rights directly derived from the Treaty. Furthermore, there is secondary legislation that implements the prohibition.

The freedom of establishment entails several rights. Both self-employed persons and organizations can benefit from these rights, but not necessarily in the same way, given the differences between natural persons and legal persons. Where relevant, a distinction will therefore be made between those two categories for the discussion of the rights pertaining to the freedom of establishment.

12.1.4.1 Right of exit, entry, and residence

Natural persons

Council Directive 73/148/EEC of 21 May 1973 on the abolition of restrictions on movement and residence within the Community for nationals of Member States with regard to establishment and the provision of services, OJ 1973 L172/14, provided that Member States had to abolish restrictions on the movement and residence of nationals wishing to establish themselves in another Member State as self-employed persons or to provide services in another Member State or to enter another Member State to receive services. They also had to abolish restrictions on the movement and residence of the self-employed person's family members. This Directive has been replaced by the Citizenship Directive (Directive 2004/38/EC of the European Parliament and of the Council of 29 April 2004 on the right of citizens of the Union and their family members to move and reside freely within the territory of the Member States … , OJ 2004 L158/77), which was discussed at 11.1.4 on the rights of EU citizens and their families.

→ CROSS-REFERENCE
See 11.1.4 on the rights of EU citizens and their families.

Since all EU citizens have the right of free movement within the EU, EU citizens who are self-employed also enjoy this right. This chapter will not repeat what has been discussed earlier regarding the right of departure, entry, and residence. It will, however, be illustrated within the framework of the freedom of establishment specifically.

EU citizens have the right to leave their home Member State, with their family, to establish themselves in another Member State. This freedom of establishment should not be restricted. A case in which the Court of Justice held that it was restricted was Case C-9/02 *Hughes de Lasteyrie du Saillant v Ministère de l'Économie, des Finances et de l'Industrie* [2004] ECR I-2409.

Mr de Lasteyrie left France to go and live in Belgium. The French authorities charged him with an 'exit tax' on an unrealized increase in the value of securities that was payable when taxpayers transferred their residence outside France for tax purposes. The Court of Justice held that, even though the provisions concerning freedom of establishment were aimed particularly at ensuring that foreign nationals were treated in the host Member State in the same way as nationals of that State, Article 49 TFEU also prohibited the Member State of origin (France) from hindering the establishment in another Member State (Belgium) of one of its own nationals. The prohibition on Member States imposing restrictions on the freedom of establishment also applied to tax provisions. Although direct taxation did not, as such, fall within the scope of the EU's jurisdiction, Member States must exercise their powers in this area in compliance with EU law. Even if French tax legislation did not prevent a French taxpayer from exercising their right of establishment, it was nevertheless of such a nature as to restrict the exercise of that right, having at the very least a dissuasive effect on taxpayers wishing to establish themselves in another Member State. A taxpayer wishing to transfer their tax residence outside France, in exercise of the right guaranteed to them by Article 49 TFEU, was subjected to disadvantageous treatment in comparison with a person who maintained their residence in France. Mr de Lasteyrie had become liable, simply because of the transfer, to tax on income that had not yet been realized and which he therefore did not have, whereas had he remained in France, he would have become liable to pay tax on the income only when and to the extent that it was actually realized.

The French court had also inquired in its preliminary question whether there could be any justification on the ground of preventing tax avoidance. The Court of Justice considered that the French legislation in question was not specifically designed to exclude from a tax advantage purely artificial arrangements aimed at circumventing French tax law. It was aimed, more generally, at any situation in which a taxpayer with substantial holdings in a company subject to corporation tax transferred their tax residence outside France for whatever reason. The transfer of a physical person's tax residence outside the territory of a Member State did not, in itself, imply tax avoidance and could not justify a national fiscal measure that compromised the exercise of a fundamental freedom guaranteed by the Treaty.

Legal persons

→ CROSS-REFERENCE
On Case C-446/03 *Marks & Spencer plc v David Halsey* [2005] ECR I-2647, see 12.1.4.2.

Although the Citizenship Directive, which sets out the rights of EU citizens and their families (ie natural persons) to move and reside freely within the territory of the Member States, does not apply to organizations, that does not mean that companies do not have these rights. They can rely on Article 49 TFEU directly. As the Court held in Case C-446/03 *Marks & Spencer plc v David Halsey* [2005] ECR I-2647, similarly to self-employed persons, a company's right of establishment can be hindered in practice not only by the law of the host Member State, but also by the law of the home Member State. As a rule, this is not allowed under EU law.

This does not mean, however, that companies have an unfettered right under the freedom of establishment to move their registered office, central administration, or principal place of business to another Member State while retaining an establishment in the home Member State. This was made clear in Case 81/87 *The Queen v HM Treasury and Commissioners of Inland Revenue, ex p Daily Mail and General Trust plc* [1988] ECR 5483.

Daily Mail, an investment holding company incorporated under UK legislation and with its registered office in the UK, wanted to transfer its central management and control to the Netherlands. Dutch legislation did not prevent foreign companies from establishing their central management there. UK tax law provided that companies resident in the UK for tax purposes could not cease to be resident there without the consent of HM Treasury. Daily Mail applied for consent, but, without waiting for it, decided to open an investment management office in the Netherlands with a view to providing services to third parties. The main reason for the proposed transfer of central management and control was to enable Daily Mail, after establishing its residence for tax purposes in the Netherlands, to sell a significant part of its non-permanent assets and to use the proceeds of that sale to buy its own shares without having to pay the tax to which such transactions would make it liable under UK tax law. Daily Mail argued that the requirement to obtain consent from HM Treasury breached EU law and the English court asked the Court of Justice for a preliminary ruling.

Case 81/87 *The Queen v HM Treasury and Commissioners of Inland Revenue, ex p Daily Mail and General Trust plc* [1988] ECR 5483

11. The first question seeks in essence to determine whether Articles 52 and 58 of the Treaty [now Articles 49 and 54 TFEU] give a company incorporated under the legislation of a Member State and having its registered office there the right to transfer its central management and control to another Member State. If that is so, the national court goes on to ask whether the Member State of origin can make that right subject to the consent of national authorities, the grant of which is linked to the company's tax position.
12. With regard to the first part of the question, the applicant claims essentially that Article 58 of the Treaty expressly confers on the companies to which it applies the same right of pri-

mary establishment in another Member State as is conferred on natural persons by Article 52. The transfer of the central management and control of a company to another Member State amounts to the establishment of the company in that Member State because the company is locating its centre of decision-making there, which constitutes genuine and effective economic activity.

[...]

15. The Court must first point out, as it has done on numerous occasions, that freedom of establishment constitutes one of the fundamental principles of the Community and that the provisions of the Treaty guaranteeing that freedom have been directly applicable ... Those provisions secure the right of establishment in another Member State not merely for Community nationals but also for ... companies ...
16. Even though those provisions are directed mainly to ensuring that foreign nationals and companies are treated in the host Member State in the same way as nationals of that State, they also prohibit the Member State of origin from hindering the establishment in another Member State of one of its nationals or of a company incorporated under its legislation which comes within the definition contained in [Article 54].
17. In the case of a company, the right of establishment is generally exercised by the setting-up of agencies, branches or subsidiaries, as is expressly provided for in the second sentence of the first paragraph of Article 52. Indeed, that is the form of establishment in which the applicant engaged in this case by opening an investment management office in the Netherlands. A company may also exercise its right of establishment by taking part in the incorporation of a company in another Member State, and in that regard Article 221 of the Treaty ensures that it will receive the same treatment as nationals of that Member State as regards participation in the capital of the new company.
18. The provision of United Kingdom law at issue in the main proceedings imposes no restriction on transactions such as those described above. Nor does it stand in the way of a partial or total transfer of the activities of a company incorporated in the United Kingdom to a company newly incorporated in another Member State, if necessary after winding-up and, consequently, the settlement of the tax position of the United Kingdom company. It requires Treasury consent only where such a company seeks to transfer its central management and control out of the United Kingdom while maintaining its legal personality and its status as a United Kingdom company.
19. In that regard it should be borne in mind that, unlike natural persons, companies are creatures of the law and, in the present state of Community law, creatures of national law. They exist only by virtue of the varying national legislation which determines their incorporation and functioning.
20. As the Commission has emphasized, the legislation of the Member States varies widely in regard to both the factor providing a connection to the national territory required for the incorporation of a company and the question whether a company incorporated under the legislation of a Member State may subsequently modify that connecting factor ...

21. The Treaty has taken account of that variety in national legislation ...

[...]

24. Articles 52 and 58 of the Treaty [now Articles 49 and 54 TFEU] cannot be interpreted as conferring on companies incorporated under the law of a Member State a right to transfer their central management and control and their central administration to another Member State while retaining their status as companies incorporated under the legislation of the first Member State.

The *Daily Mail* case established that the Member State from which a company wants to move its registered office, central administration, or principal place of business can subject the company to certain conditions. In this case, the UK could require the Daily Mail to settle its taxes and even to wind up the UK company. Because Member State corporate laws have not been harmonized, different Member States define the place of incorporation of a company differently. The question of how far companies can rely on Article 49 TFEU to use these differences in national legislation in order to set up different forms of establishment in different Member States also arose in Case C-212/97 *Centros* [1999] ECR I-1459.

In *Centros,* Mrs Bryde was a Danish national who registered her company, Centros, in the UK because UK law did not impose any requirements on limited liability companies for the provision for, or paying up of, minimum share capital. The company never traded in the UK and Mrs Bryde's main purpose was to conduct business in Denmark through a branch office. Danish conditions for minimum capital requirements were far stricter than those in the UK, and Mrs Bryde wanted to avoid these by registering the company in the UK and establishing a secondary establishment in Denmark. The Danish authorities refused to register the branch in Denmark on the grounds that Mrs Bryde was, in fact, not seeking to establish a branch, but a principal establishment, while circumventing Danish national rules.

The Court of Justice ruled that it was contrary to Articles 49 and 54 TFEU for a Member State to refuse on those grounds to register a branch of a company formed in accordance with the law of a Member State in which it has its registered office. National rules aimed at preventing fraud could not justify restrictions on the freedom of establishment of companies. The fact that Mrs Bryde chose to form her company in that Member State in which the rules of company law seemed the least restrictive to her and to set up branches in other Member States did not, in itself, constitute an abuse of the right of establishment.

It could be argued that the decision in *Centros* contradicted the decision in *Daily Mail.* In *Daily Mail,* the Court of Justice held that a Member State could impose certain conditions on a company wanting to move its centre of administration. Such conditions are in effect a restriction on the freedom of establishment as they make it more difficult for the company to establish itself in another Member State. *Centros* had a fact pattern similar to that in *Daily Mail* in the sense that, in both cases, the companies used their freedom of establishment to benefit from a more favourable legal regime. In *Centros,* however, the Court of Justice held that the restrictions on the freedom of establishment imposed by the Member State could not be justified. Case C-208/00 *Überseering* [2002] ECR I-9919 clarified the Court of Justice's approach.

Überseering was a company incorporated under Dutch law, with its registered office in the Netherlands. It wanted to transfer its centre of administration to Germany and sold its entire share capital to German shareholders. Dutch law did not prevent Überseering from keeping its establishment there through its continued incorporation, despite transferring its central administration to another Member State. German law, however, did not recognize the legal capacity of a company incorporated in another Member State. Therefore Überseering had to reincorporate in Germany if it wanted to appear before the German courts. The Court of Justice distinguished *Daily Mail* from the facts of *Überseering. Daily Mail* concerned a company emigrating and the restrictions were imposed by the Member State of incorporation; *Überseering* concerned a company immigrating and the restrictions were imposed by the hosting Member State, which refused to recognize a company incorporated under the law of another Member State.

The Court held that overriding requirements relating to the general interest could justify restrictions on the freedom of establishment. They could not, however, justify an outright negation of the freedom of establishment. The requirement of reincorporation of the same company in Germany in *Überseering* was tantamount to such negation and therefore prohibited.

12.1.4.2 Equal treatment

Prohibition of discrimination

The second paragraph of Article 49 TFEU states as follows.

Article 49 TFEU

[…]

Freedom of establishment shall include the right to take up and pursue activities as self-employed persons and to set up and manage undertakings, in particular companies or firms within the meaning of the second paragraph of Article 54, under the conditions laid down for its own nationals by the law of the country where such establishment is effected …

From the wording of Article 49 TFEU, it is clear that direct or indirect discrimination based on nationality is prohibited. In this respect, there are clear parallels between the prohibition of discrimination regarding workers, EU citizens, and the self-employed and companies.

Measures interfering with the free movement of establishment, however, will not necessarily be discriminatory. In line with its case law on the free movement of goods, services, and workers, the Court of Justice has also applied a broader approach in the area of freedom of establishment, focusing not necessarily on the prohibition of discrimination, but also on non-discriminatory restrictions. These will be the subject of the discussion under the next subheading.

→ CROSS-REFERENCE
On equal treatment of workers, see 11.2.3; on equal treatment of EU citizens, see 11.1.4.

→ CROSS-REFERENCE
See 10.8.3 on goods, 12.2.3 on services, 12.1.4 on establishment, and 11.2.3 on workers.

Natural persons

An illustration of the prohibition of discrimination regarding the freedom of establishment can be found in Case 2/74 *Reyners* [1974] ECR 631, which involved direct discrimination

→ CROSS-REFERENCE
For a full discussion of *Reyners*, see 12.1.1.

based on nationality. Mr Reyners was refused admission to the Bar in Belgium based solely on his lack of Belgian nationality.

In Case C-162/99 *Commission v Italy (Dentists)* [2001] ECR I-541, the national measure in question was an Italian law stating that dentists moving their residence to another Member State lost their registration with the Italian dental association unless they had Italian nationality. Because this law was directly discriminatory, it breached Article 49 TFEU. Similarly, a Belgian rule requiring non-Belgian nationals to have been resident or established in Belgium for at least one year in order to be able to register an aircraft there was prohibited under Article 49 TFEU, because it clearly constituted discrimination on grounds of nationality (Case C-203/98 *Commission v Belgium* [1999] ECR I-4899).

An example of indirect discrimination can be found in Case C-145/99 *Italy v Commission (Lawyers)* [2002] ECR I-2235. Italian law required members of the Bar to reside in the judicial district of the court to which their Bar was attached. As such, members of the Bar established in another Member State could not maintain an establishment in Italy. The Italian rule therefore breached Article 49 TFEU.

Legal persons

The question of discrimination in respect of legal persons often arises in cases concerning taxation. It must be pointed out that Member States are allowed to treat, for tax purposes, resident and non-resident companies differently. This is in accordance with the fiscal principle of territoriality, which was applied in Case C-250/95 *Futura Participations* [1997] ECR I-2471. Luxembourg law provided that all income earned by resident taxpayers was taxable, regardless of where it was earned; for non-resident taxpayers, only income earned in Luxembourg was taxable. The Court of Justice held that the law in question was not discriminatory and did not breach Article 49 TFEU because it was in conformity with the fiscal principle of territoriality.

→ CROSS-REFERENCE
See 12.1.3 for more detail on the nationality of companies.

An example of direct discrimination can be found in Case C-311/97 *Royal Bank of Scotland* [1999] ECR I-2651. As explained earlier, the nationality of a company is determined by where it has its seat.

Direct discrimination on grounds of a company's nationality therefore exists when there is a difference in treatment based on where the company has its seat. In *Royal Bank of Scotland*, this difference in treatment consisted of Greek taxation of company profits at a higher rate for companies with their seat in another Member State. In other words, Greek law provided that the profits of companies with their seat in Greece were taxed at a lower rate than those of companies with their seat in another Member State. Greek law therefore breached Article 49 TFEU.

The Court of Justice found that there was indirect discrimination in Case C-270/83 *Commission v France* [1986] ECR 273. The Court drew an analogy between the place of residence of a natural person and the location of the registered office of a company. The case concerned French law, which granted tax credits to companies with their registered office in France. Companies with only a branch or agency in France and their registered office in another Member State did not benefit from these tax credits. The Court held that Article 49 TFEU expressly left traders free to choose the appropriate legal form in which to pursue their activities in another Member State and that this freedom of choice could not be limited by discriminatory tax provisions.

In Case C-250/95 *Futura Participations* [1997] ECR I-2471, the Court of Justice stated that it was permissible for Member States to impose certain restrictions on the freedom of establishment if they could be justified on the ground of ensuring the effectiveness of fiscal supervision. As such, conditions regarding the keeping of accounts and the location where losses were incurred for non-resident companies could be justified. However, the Court applied a strict proportionality test, which meant that the rule in question in this case was held to be too restrictive and therefore not allowed under Article 49 TFEU.

Non-discriminatory restrictions

Some national measures could create barriers to the freedom of establishment even though they apply without distinction to all persons established in a Member State—that is, to nationals, as well as non-nationals—and are therefore not discriminatory. It could be thought that they are not prohibited under Article 49 TFEU—but the case law of the Court of Justice has proven otherwise.

Natural persons

The ruling in Case C-55/94 *Gebhard* [1995] ECR I-4165 made it clear that the Court of Justice interpreted Article 49 TFEU broadly, applying the same principles and interpretation to the provisions on free movement of goods, services, workers, and establishment. Mr Gebhard was a German national residing in Italy, with his Italian wife and three children. He found himself the subject of disciplinary proceedings, opened by the Milan Bar Council, for pursuing a professional activity in Italy on a permanent basis in chambers set up by him whilst using the title *avvocato*. Mr Gebhard was a member of the Bar of Stuttgart, Germany, and had applied to the Milan Bar Council to be entered on its roll of members. The Milan Bar Council, however, had not taken any formal decision on the application.

The Court held that whether it is possible for a national of a Member State to exercise their right of establishment and the conditions for exercise of that right must be determined in the light of the activities that the individual intended to pursue on the territory of the host Member State. The freedom of establishment was to be exercised under the conditions laid down for its own nationals by the law of the country where establishment was effected. If the specific activities in question were not subject to any rules in the host Member State, so that a national of that Member State did not have to have any specific qualification in order to pursue them, a national of another Member State was entitled to establish themselves on the territory of the first State and to pursue those activities there. However, the taking up and pursuit of certain self-employed activities could be conditional on complying with certain provisions justified by the general good, such as rules relating to organization, qualifications, professional ethics, supervision, and liability. Where this was the case, a national of another Member State intending to pursue those activities must, in principle, comply with those conditions.

The Court added the following.

Case C-55/94 *Gebhard* [1995] ECR I-4165

37. It follows, however, from the Court's case-law that national measures liable to hinder or make less attractive the exercise of fundamental freedoms guaranteed by the Treaty must fulfil four conditions: they must be applied in a non-discriminatory manner; they must be justified by imperative requirements in the general interest; they must be suitable for securing the attainment of the objective which they pursue; and they must not go beyond what is necessary in order to attain it …

From the *Gebhard* ruling, it follows that not only could (directly or indirectly) discriminatory rules be in breach of the TFEU, but also any national rule that hinders or makes less attractive the exercise of the fundamental freedom of establishment could violate the TFEU unless it is justified. As such, the Court of Justice adopts an obstacle-based approach rather than a discrimination-based approach. This position was confirmed in its later case law, such as Case C-400/08 *Commission v Spain* [2011] ECR I-1915. This case concerned Spanish legislation imposing certain restrictions on the establishment of large retail outlets. The Commission was of the opinion that the rules in question were indirectly discriminatory because those wishing to set up large retail establishments were often from other Member States, while smaller retail establishments were usually Spanish, so that the rules favoured these Spanish businesses. The Court of Justice held that the Commission had not been successful in establishing that the rules were indirectly discriminatory. It reiterated, however, that Article 49 TFEU precludes any national measure that, even though it is applicable without distinction on grounds of nationality, is liable to hinder or to render less attractive the exercise by EU citizens of the freedom of establishment that is guaranteed by the Treaty. In that context, the concept of 'restriction' for the purposes of Article 49 TFEU covers measures taken by Member States that, although applicable without distinction, affect access to the market for undertakings from other Member States and thereby hinder intra-EU trade.

Whether a restriction on the freedom of establishment is discriminatory is still relevant for two reasons. First and on the one hand, if a rule is directly discriminatory, it automatically falls within the scope of the prohibition in Article 49 TFEU. A non-discriminatory restriction, on the other hand, must still constitute a sufficient hindrance to the freedom of establishment. This requirement that there be sufficient hindrance, or sufficient effect on inter-State trade, due to a national rule for there to be a breach of EU law on the fundamental freedoms has been established in the Court of Justice's case law regarding the free movement of goods and workers.

Secondly, a directly discriminatory restriction can be justified only on the grounds provided for in Article 52 TFEU (ie public policy, public security, or public health). A non-discriminatory restriction could be justified on the grounds in Article 52, but could also be based on broader objective justifications.

?! THINKING POINT

Since the Court of Justice applies this obstacle-based approach, rather than a discrimination-based approach, is there any relevance left to the discriminatory nature of a restriction?

A case in which the question arose as to whether there were objective justifications for a restriction was Case C-171/07 *Commission v Italy* [2009] ECR I-4171, which concerned national legislation preventing persons who did not have the status of pharmacists from owning and operating pharmacies. The Court held that such a rule constituted a restriction within the meaning of Article 49 TFEU because it allowed only pharmacists to operate pharmacies, denying other economic operators access to this self-employed activity in the Member State concerned. However, this restriction could be justified by the protection of public health—more specifically, by the objective of ensuring that the provision of medicinal products to the public is reliable and of good quality.

→ CROSS-REFERENCE
See 10.8.3 on goods and 11.2.3 on workers.

In Joined Cases C-570 & 571/07 *José Manuel Blanco Pérez and María del Pilar Chao Gómez v Consejería de Salud y Servicios Sanitarios and Principado de Asturias* [2010] ECR I-4629, Spanish legislation provided that administrative authorization was required prior to setting up a new pharmacy. The authorities in the region of Asturias, Spain, launched a call for applications with a view to issuing new pharmacy licences according to a system that limited the number of pharmacies per area depending on the population and the nearest other pharmacy. Furthermore, there were criteria for the selection of pharmacists based on professional and teaching experience. Mr Pérez and Mrs Gómez wanted to open a new pharmacy in Asturias without having to comply with this territorial planning system, and brought an action against the rules in question. The Spanish court referred the matter to the Court of Justice for a preliminary ruling.

The Court held that the conditions, linked to population density and minimum distance between pharmacies, constituted a restriction on the freedom of establishment. Applying the conditions set out in *Gebhard*, however, the Court assessed whether this restriction could be justified.

?! THINKING POINT

What were the four conditions in *Gebhard* and how might they be applied here?

The first condition was met, since the conditions linked to population density and minimum distance between pharmacies applied without discrimination on grounds of nationality. The second condition was also met, since the objective of the restrictions was to ensure that the provision of medicinal products to the public was reliable and of good quality. As a consequence, the objective constituted an overriding reason relating to the general interest. As to the third condition, the Court considered whether the restriction was appropriate for attaining the objective pursued and held that it was, because it was conceivable that there would not be enough pharmacies in certain areas to ensure a reliable and qualitative service if there were no regulations. The fourth condition was also met, since the Court held that the rules in question did not go beyond those necessary to attain the objective pursued. Since all four conditions were met, the restrictions were not in breach of the freedom of establishment.

From these cases, it is clear that the Court of Justice has adopted the same approach as with other freedoms in assessing whether national legislation breaches EU law regarding the freedom of establishment. Often, the Court will find that there is a potential breach of Article 49 TFEU because the legislation in question is liable to hinder or to render less attractive the exercise by EU citizens of the freedom of establishment that is guaranteed by the Treaty. The Court then assesses, however, whether the national rule could be justified, which will often be the case, although not always.

NOTE

The *Gebhard* test

National rules that hinder or make less attractive the exercise of the fundamental freedom of establishment violate the TFEU unless they are justified. They are justified when they fulfil four conditions, as follows.

(1) They must be applied in a non-discriminatory manner.

(2) They must be justified by imperative requirements in the general interest.

(3) They must be suitable for securing the attainment of the objective that they pursue.

(4) They must not go beyond what is necessary in order to attain it.

An example of a case in which the Court of Justice concluded that there was no objective justification is Case C-140/03 *Commission v Greece* [2005] ECR I-3177. According to Greek law, an optician could manage only one optician's shop. The Greek government claimed that the prohibition on operating more than one shop was enacted for overriding reasons of general interest in relation to the protection of public health. The government explained that the measure in question aimed to safeguard the personal relationship of trust within the optician's shop, as well as, in the event of fault, the absolute and unlimited liability of the optician who operated or owned the shop. Only an optician who participated directly in the running of their shop without expending physical or mental energy on running other shops could guarantee this result. The Court of Justice disagreed. It ruled that the national measure, even though it applied without discrimination on grounds of nationality, could hinder or render less attractive the exercise of fundamental freedoms guaranteed under EU law. Such a measure could be justified by overriding reasons of general interest, provided that the measure in question was appropriate for ensuring attainment of the objective pursued and did not go beyond that necessary for the purpose. In this case, the Court held that the objective of protecting public health could be achieved by measures that were less restrictive of the freedom of establishment, for example by requiring the presence of qualified, salaried opticians or associates in each optician's shop, rules concerning civil liability for the actions of others, and rules requiring professional indemnity insurance. Because the restrictions went beyond those required to achieve the objective pursued, there was no justification for them.

Commission v Greece established that the Court of Justice, although it recognizes a diverse range of justifications for national measures hindering the fundamental freedoms, applies a strict proportionality test. The measure in question cannot be justified if the objective pursued could be achieved by a less restrictive measure.

Legal persons

The position of the Court of Justice regarding non-discriminatory restrictions on the freedom of establishment for companies can be illustrated by Case C-446/03 *Marks & Spencer plc v David Halsey* [2005] ECR I-2647. Marks & Spencer, a company established in the UK, had subsidiaries in the UK and in a number of other Member States, including Belgium, France, and Germany. According to UK tax law, a parent company established in the UK was liable for corporation tax only in respect of the profits attributable to its branches or agencies established in the UK. Correspondingly, the parent company could deduct from its taxable profits only losses made by its subsidiaries established in the UK and not losses made by its subsidiaries in other Member States. Marks & Spencer wanted to deduct losses incurred by its subsidiaries in Belgium, France, and Germany, but the UK tax authorities rejected its claim.

The Court of Justice reiterated that, although direct taxation falls within the competence of the Member States, this competence must be exercised in compliance with EU law. UK tax law constituted a restriction on the freedom of establishment because it treated differently for tax purposes the losses incurred by a resident subsidiary and those incurred by a non-resident subsidiary. This could deter a parent company from setting up subsidiaries in other Member States. The Court acknowledged, however, that such a restriction could be permitted if it were in pursuit of a legitimate objective compatible with EU law and justified by imperative reasons in the public interest—in other words, if the restriction could be objectively justified. The Court set out the relevant objective criteria as being:

- the protection of a balanced allocation of the power to impose taxation between the different Member States concerned;
- the avoidance of the double deduction of losses (once in the Member State in which the parent company was established and once in the Member State in which the subsidiaries were established); and
- the prevention of tax avoidance.

The Court held that the UK tax law at issue pursued legitimate objectives that were compatible with EU law and constituted overriding reasons in the public interest. However, it held that UK tax law would not comply with the principle of proportionality and went beyond that necessary to attain the objectives pursued if the non-resident subsidiary had exhausted the possibilities available in its State of residence of having the losses taken into account for the accounting period concerned by the claim for relief and also for previous accounting periods, if necessary by transferring those losses to a third party or by off-setting the losses against the profits made by the subsidiary in previous periods, and there was no possibility for the foreign subsidiary's losses to be taken into account in its State of residence for future periods, either by the subsidiary itself or by a third party, in particular where the subsidiary has been sold to that third party.

As a consequence, where, in one Member State, the resident parent company had demonstrated to the tax authorities that those conditions were fulfilled, it was contrary to the freedom of establishment to preclude the possibility for the parent company to deduct from its taxable profits in that Member State the losses incurred by its non-resident subsidiary.

controlled foreign company
A CFC is a foreign company in which a UK resident company owns a holding of more than 50 per cent.

In Case C-196/04 *Cadbury Schweppes* [2006] ECR I-7995, the national rule at issue was a UK rule according to which the profits of a **controlled foreign company (CFC)** were attributed to the resident company and subjected to tax in the UK when the corporation tax in the foreign country was less than three-quarters of the tax that would have been payable in the UK.

The resident company was given a tax credit for the tax paid by the CFC. The aim of this rule was to make the resident company pay the difference between the tax paid in the foreign country and the tax it would have paid had the company been resident in the UK. Cadbury Schweppes established a subsidiary in Ireland and was charged approximately £9 million in corporation tax in the UK.

The Court of Justice held that the fact that a company was established in a Member State for the purpose of benefiting from more favourable legislation did not in itself suffice to constitute abuse of the freedom of establishment.

The Court further held that the separate tax treatment under the legislation on CFCs and the resulting disadvantage for resident companies that have a subsidiary subject in another Member State to a lower level of taxation hindered the exercise of the freedom of establishment by such companies and therefore constituted a restriction on this freedom within the meaning of EU law. The Court added, however, that a national measure restricting freedom of establishment could be justified where it specifically related to wholly artificial arrangements aimed at circumventing the application of the legislation of the Member State concerned. In other words, legislation restricting the freedom of establishment could be justified when it was aimed at preventing the avoidance of national taxes by setting up 'letterbox subsidiaries' in another country.

REVIEW QUESTION

In which case did the Court of Justice establish this principle?

Answer: This principle was established in Case C-212/97 *Centros* [1999] ECR 1459.

Professional qualifications

Certain trades and professions are subject to national professional qualification requirements. Since they are more easily met by nationals than by non-nationals, they may hinder free movement. An example of this can be found in Case 71/76 *Thieffry v Conseil de l'Ordre des Avocats à la Cour de Paris* [1977] ECR 765. Mr Thieffry, who held a doctorate in Belgian law, established himself in Paris, where he wanted to join the Paris Bar. He was refused admission to that Bar because he did not have the required qualifications, despite the fact that he had obtained recognition of the diploma for his doctorate in Belgian law as a qualification equivalent to a licentiate's degree in French law. The Court of Justice held that this was an unjustified restriction on the freedom of establishment since the only reason why Mr Thieffry was refused admission to the Paris Bar was that he did not have a French diploma, while French law recognized his Belgian diploma as equivalent.

Where qualifications are not recognized as equivalent, they must be compared with the relevant national requirements and they must be accepted, if equivalent. If they are not found to be equivalent based upon this comparison, evidence of relevant knowledge, or aptitude, and experience may be required, as in Case 340/89 *Vlassopoulou v Ministerium für Justiz* [1991] ECR I-2357, a case involving a lawyer who wanted to practise in Greece, as well as Germany.

It must be noted also that harmonization efforts have been made in the area of mutual recognition of qualifications. To that effect, a range of sectoral Directives was adopted, regulating the requirements for specific trades and professions. In addition, Council Directive 89/48/EEC of 21 December 1988 on a general system for the recognition of higher-education diplomas awarded on completion of professional education and training of at least three years' duration, OJ 1989 L19/16, Directive 92/51/EEC of 18 June 1992 on a second general system for the recognition of professional education and training to supplement Directive 89/48/EEC, OJ 1992 L209/25, and Directive 1999/42/EC of the European Parliament and of the Council of 7 June 1999 establishing a mechanism for the recognition of qualifications in respect of the professional activities covered by the Directives on liberalisation and transitional measures and supplementing the general systems for the recognition of qualifications, OJ 1999 L201/77, provided for the mutual recognition of qualifications involving three years' professional education, one-year post-secondary courses, and a range of industrial and professional areas, respectively.

Finally, Directive 2005/36/EC of the European Parliament and of the Council of 7 September 2005 on the recognition of professional qualifications, OJ 2005 L255/22, replaced and consolidated most existing Directives, aiming to liberalize the provision of services and to retain the system of mutual recognition of qualifications.

12.2 Freedom to provide services

12.2.1 Articles 56 and 57 TFEU: direct effect

Article 56 TFEU

Within the framework of the provisions set out below, restrictions on freedom to provide services within the Union shall be prohibited in respect of nationals of Member States who are established in a Member State other than that of the person for whom the services are intended …

Article 57 TFEU

… Without prejudice to the provisions of the Chapter relating to the right of establishment, the person providing a service may, in order to do so, temporarily pursue his activity in the Member State where the service is provided, under the same conditions as are imposed by that State on its own nationals.

Similarly to Article 49 TFEU, Article 56 states that restrictions on freedom to provide services are prohibited 'within the framework of the provisions set out below'. In particular, this refers to secondary legislation, in the form of Directives, which is meant to implement the Treaty provisions. Regarding the freedom of establishment, the ruling in Case 2/74 *Reyners* [1974] ECR 631 made it clear that Article 49 TFEU had direct effect, even absent secondary legislation.

→ CROSS-REFERENCE On *Reyners* and the direct effect of Article 49 TFEU, see 12.1.1.

Shortly after *Reyners*, the question on the direct effect of Article 56 TFEU was raised before the Court of Justice. In Case 33/74 *van Binsbergen v Bestuur van de Bedrijfsvereniging voor de Metaalnijverheid* [1974] ECR 1299 a Dutch national, Mr Kortmann, acted as a legal adviser and representative of Mr van Binsbergen in social security proceedings before a Dutch court. During the course of the proceedings, Mr Kortmann transferred his residence from the Netherlands to Belgium. He was told that he could no longer represent Mr van Binsbergen because Dutch law stated that legal representation in social security matters could be provided only by persons established in the Netherlands. The Court of Justice was asked for a preliminary ruling on the direct effect of Article 56 TFEU and the permissibility of a residence requirement as a condition to the provision of services in a Member State.

The case clearly did not concern direct discrimination based on grounds of nationality as Mr Kortmann (the legal adviser), Mr van Binsbergen (the client), the court, and the law in question were all Dutch. The Court of Justice held, however, that the restrictions to be abolished pursuant to Articles 56 and 57 TFEU included all requirements imposed on the person providing the service by reason in particular of their nationality or of the fact that they do not habitually reside in the State where the service is provided, which do not apply to persons established within the national territory or which may prevent or otherwise obstruct the activities of the person providing the service. In particular, a requirement that the person providing the service must be habitually resident within the territory of the State where the service is to be provided could have the result of depriving Article 56 TFEU of all useful effect.

The Court then ruled on the direct effect of Article 56 TFEU. It held that the issuing of Directives, provided for in the Treaty, was intended to accomplish different functions. The first function was to abolish restrictions on the freedom to provide services during the transitional period. The second function was to introduce into the law of the Member States a set of provisions intended to facilitate the exercise of this freedom. These Directives also had the task of resolving the specific problems resulting from the fact that, where the person providing the service is not established, on a habitual basis, in the State where the service is performed, that person may not be fully subject to the professional rules of conduct in force in that State.

The provisions of Article 56 TFEU, the application of which was to be prepared by Directives issued during the transitional period, therefore became unconditional on the expiry of that period. As a consequence, at least regarding the specific requirement of nationality or residence, Article 56 TFEU imposes a well-defined obligation, the fulfilment of which by the Member State cannot be delayed or jeopardized by the absence of provisions that were to be adopted.

In summary, the first paragraph of Article 56 TFEU has direct effect and can be relied on before national courts, at least insofar as it seeks to abolish any discrimination against a person providing a service by reason of their nationality or of the fact that they reside in a Member State other than that in which the service is to be provided.

12.2.2 The scope of Article 56 TFEU

12.2.2.1 *Requirement of a cross-border element*

As with the other EU freedoms, Article 56 TFEU does not apply to purely internal situations. An example of this can be found in Case C-97/98 *Jägerskiöld* [1999] ECR I-7319. Mr Gustafsson paid a fishing licence fee, which, according to Finnish law, gave him the right to fish even in private waters. When Mr Gustafsson fished in Mr Jägerskiöld's waters, the latter complained, arguing that Finnish law breached EU law on the free movement of goods and services. The Court of Justice held that the provisions on the free movement of goods did not apply. Those on the freedom to provide services could apply in theory, but they did not apply to activities that were confined in all respects within a single Member State. The proceedings concerned were between two Finnish nationals, both established in Finland, concerning the right of Mr Gustafsson to fish in waters belonging to Mr Jägerskiöld and situated in Finland. Such a situation did not present any link to any of the situations envisaged by EU law in the field of the free provision of services.

?! THINKING POINT

Do you think the Court of Justice takes a narrow or a wide interpretation of the requirement for a cross-border element?

In Case 15/78 *Koestler* [1978] ECR 1971, a French bank provided services, in the form of stock exchange orders and current account transactions, to a customer established in France. The Court of Justice held that there was a provision of services within the meaning of the Treaty, however, since the person in receipt of the services had taken up residence in another Member State (Germany) before the termination of the contractual relations between the parties.

Case C-17/00 *De Coster* [2001] ECR I-9445 concerned a municipal tax on satellite dishes. The cross-border element found by the Court of Justice was the receipt, through these dishes, of foreign satellite television, which could come from another Member State.

Joined Cases C-51/96 & 191/97 *Deliège* [2000] ECR I-2549 was a case in which a Belgian athlete challenged the selection rules of the Belgian Judo Federation. It was argued that the proceedings concerned a purely internal situation. The Court of Justice held that it was true that the Treaty provisions on the freedom of services did not apply to activities that were confined in all respects within a single Member State. It held, however, that a degree of extraneity could derive from the fact that an athlete participates in a competition in a Member State other than that in which they are established.

It becomes clear from this case law that the requirement of a cross-border element is often easily satisfied.

12.2.2.2 Remuneration

Article 57 TFEU

Services shall be considered to be 'services' within the meaning of the Treaties where they are normally provided for remuneration, in so far as they are not governed by the provisions relating to freedom of movement for goods, capital and persons ...

The services must be commercial in nature or, in the wording of Article 57 TFEU, they must be normally provided for remuneration. Case C-70/95 *Sodemare* [1997] ECR I-3395 established that services do not lose their commercial nature because they are provided by a non-profit organization nor do they lose their economic nature because there is an element of chance involved, such as in Case C-275/92 *Schindler* [1994] ECR I-1039.

The essential characteristics of remuneration were clarified in Case 263/86 *Belgium v Humbel* [1988] ECR 5365. The Court of Justice held that 'the essential characteristic of remuneration ... lies in the fact that it constitutes consideration for the service in question, and is normally agreed upon between the provider and the recipient of the service' (*Belgium v Humbel*, at para 17). The Court added as follows.

Case 263/86 *Belgium v Humbel* [1988] ECR 5365

18. That characteristic is, however, absent in the case of courses provided under the national education system. First of all, the State, in establishing and maintaining such a system, is not seeking to engage in gainful activity but is fulfilling its duties towards its own population in the social, cultural and educational fields. Secondly, the system in question is, as a general rule, funded from the public purse and not by pupils or their parents.
19. The nature of the activity is not affected by the fact that pupils or their parents pay teaching or enrolment fees in order to make a certain contribution to the operating expenses of the system ...

Education could constitute a service, however, if it is provided by an institution that seeks to make profit and if it is paid for mainly from private funds (Case C-109/92 *Wirth* [1993] ECR I-6447).

The Court of Justice's approach must be nuanced against the background of its case law regarding cross-border health care. Case C-157/99 *Geraets-Smits/Peerbooms* [2001] ECR I-5473 concerned two people who were insured for medical costs under a Dutch social insurance scheme for people with low incomes. In order to be eligible for reimbursement of medical costs incurred abroad, the insured had to obtain authorization before receiving the treatment. The applicants in this case received treatment in Germany and Austria without prior authorization, and the question arose whether such authorization was prohibited under EU law. It was argued by several governments, applying the principles established in *Belgium v Humbel*, that hospital services did not constitute an economic activity.

REVIEW QUESTION

Applying *Belgium v Humbel*, what do you think the argument was for saying that hospital services did not constitute an economic activity?

Answer: A number of governments argued that hospital services could not constitute an economic activity, particularly when they were provided in kind and free of charge under the relevant sickness insurance scheme. Relying on *Belgium v Humbel*, they argued that there was no remuneration where the patient received care in a hospital infrastructure without having to pay for it themselves or where all or part of the amount they paid was reimbursed.

Some of the governments added to that, relying on *Wirth*, that a further condition to be satisfied before a service can constitute an economic activity was that the person providing the service must do so with a view to making a profit.

The Court of Justice held as follows.

Case C-157/99 *Geraets-Smits v Stichting Ziekenfonds; Peerbooms v Stichting CZ Groep Zorgverzekeringen* [2001] ECR I-5473

55. With regard more particularly to the argument that hospital services provided in the context of a sickness insurance scheme providing benefits in kind, such as that governed by the ZFW, should not be classified as services within the meaning of Article 60 of the Treaty, it should be noted that, far from falling under such a scheme, the medical treatment at issue in the main proceedings, which was provided in Member States other than those in which the persons concerned were insured, did lead to the establishments providing the treatment being paid directly by the patients. It must be accepted that a medical service provided in one Member State and paid for by the patient should not cease to fall within the scope of the freedom to provide services guaranteed by the Treaty merely because reimbursement of the costs of the treatment involved is applied for under another Member State's sickness insurance legislation which is essentially of the type which provides for benefits in kind.

The fact that hospital medical treatment was financed directly by sickness insurance funds on the basis of agreements and a pre-set scale of fees was not, in any event, such as to remove treatment from the sphere of services within the meaning of Article 57 TFEU.

12.2.2.3 The meaning of 'services'

Article 57 TFEU

... 'Services' shall in particular include:

(a) activities of an industrial character;

(b) activities of a commercial character;

(c) activities of craftsmen;

(d) activities of the professions.

Even though Article 57 TFEU contains a list of activities that constitute services, this list is not exhaustive. As may become clear from the examples of case law discussed throughout this chapter, the Court of Justice has accepted a diverse list of activities as services under EU law.

REVIEW QUESTION

Can you think of some examples of activities that constitute services according to the Court of Justice's case law?

Answer: Examples include prostitution (Case C-268/99 *Jany* [2001] ECR I-8615), education services (Case C-109/92 *Wirth* [1993] ECR I-6447), television signals (Case C-17/00 *De Coster* [2001] ECR I-9445), medical treatment (Case C-157/99 *Geraets-Smits/Peerbooms* [2001] ECR I-5473), and legal advice (Case 33/74 *van Binsbergen v Bestuur van de Bedrijfsvereniging voor de Metaalnijverheid* [1974] ECR 1299).

12.2.2.4 Illegal activities

Some activities are legal in one Member State and illegal in another Member State. The fact that they are illegal does not necessarily mean, however, that they will escape the application of Article 56 TFEU. This can be illustrated through a range of relatively recent cases.

In Case C-159/90 *SPUC v Grogan* [1991] ECR I-4685, a students' union in Dublin provided information about lawful abortion in London. Abortion was illegal in Ireland at the time (and it remains so after the first 12 weeks of pregnancy), subject only to limited exceptions such as situations in which the life of the expecting mother is at risk, and Irish law contained restrictions on the publication of information regarding abortion services in other Member States. The Society for the Protection of Unborn Children (SPUC) took the students' union to court and the Court of Justice was asked for a preliminary ruling. The Court held that the provision of abortion could constitute a service—but, because the students' union was not providing the information on behalf of the economic operators (the abortion clinics), the Irish restrictions were allowed.

Case C-275/92 *Schindler* [1994] ECR I-1039 concerned agents of a German public lottery seeking to promote the lottery in the UK. Since they were in breach of UK lotteries legislation, they were charged with an offence. Several Member States intervening in the case argued that lotteries were not economic activities because they are usually subject to very strict control and often operated by public authorities. The Court of Justice disagreed. It held that lotteries were services provided for remuneration. The Court considered UK legislation prohibiting lotteries to be a non-discriminatory obstacle to the freedom to provide services. As such, however, it could be justified on social and cultural grounds, the concern to prevent fraud, the protection of players, or the maintenance of order in society.

In Case C-268/99 *Jany* [2001] ECR I-8615, the Court of Justice held that a prostitute's services were services provided for remuneration under EU law. The Court reiterated what it had also pointed out previously in *SPUC v Grogan* and *Schindler*, and said that, far from being prohibited in all Member States, prostitution is tolerated or even regulated by most Member States.

→ CROSS-REFERENCE
On *Jany*, see 12.1.3.

In Case C-137/09 *Josemans* [2010] ECR I-13019, the Court of Justice looked into the prohibition of access for non-residents to coffee shops (shops selling cannabis) in the Netherlands. Marketing of cannabis was tolerated, but not legal, in the Netherlands. Therefore the owner of a coffee shop could not rely on the provisions regarding freedom of services for the marketing of cannabis. In relation to the food and drinks he sold in his establishment, however, he could rely on the freedom to provide services and Article 56 TFEU. As such, the national rules, precluding non-residents from entering coffee shops, were indirectly discriminatory because non-residents were more likely to be non-Dutch nationals. However, the rule could be justified by the legitimate aim of combating drug tourism.

This decision seems to contradict prior decisions because illegal, yet tolerated, activities escape the application of the provisions on freedom of services, where they had not previously done so. This can be explained by differences in circumstances, as the Court of Justice distinguished *Josemans* from its previous case law. In *Josemans*, the activity concerned was the marketing of narcotics, which was illegal in all Member States, while the activities concerned in the other cases were not illegal in all Member States, but only in some.

From this case law, it seems that a remunerated activity constitutes a service for the purposes of EU law provided that it is legal in some Member States. Restrictions on the freedom to provide such services, however, may be justified.

12.2.2.5 Freedom to receive services

Article 56 TFEU expressly refers to providers of services, but is silent on the recipients of services. Secondary legislation, however, also gives certain rights to the recipients.

→ CROSS-REFERENCE
See 11.1.4 on the rights of EU citizens.

Furthermore, the Court of Justice has confirmed in its case law that Article 56 TFEU applies not only to providers of services, but also to recipients of services.

Joined Cases 286/82 & 26/83 *Luisi and Carbone* [1984] ECR 377 concerned two Italian nationals who were prosecuted for attempting to export more Italian currency than the legal maximum. They argued that they needed it to pay for services as tourists and medical treatment, and that the restrictions as to how much currency they could export infringed EU law. The Court of Justice held that, in order to enable services to be provided, the person providing the services could go to the Member State where the person for whom it is to be provided is established or the person for whom it is to be provided may go to the Member State in which the service provider is established. While the former possibility is expressly mentioned in Article 57 TFEU, the latter possibility is the necessary corollary thereof, which fulfils the objective of liberalizing all gainful activity not covered by the free movement of goods, persons, and capital.

→ CROSS-REFERENCE
On the freedom to move, see 12.2.3.

The Court explained as follows.

Joined Cases 286/82 & 26/83 *Luisi and Carbone* [1984] ECR 377, 377

The freedom to provide services includes the freedom to, for the recipient of services, go to another Member State in order to receive a service there, without being obstructed by restrictions, even in relation to payments, and that tourists, persons receiving medical treatment and persons travelling for the purposes of education or business are to be regarded as recipients of services.

Another case regarding recipients of services was Case 186/87 *Cowan v Le Trésor Public* [1989] ECR 195. A British tourist was violently assaulted when exiting a metro station during a brief visit to Paris. Since the assailants could not be identified, Mr Cowan applied for compensation from the French State. He was denied such compensation since, under French law, this was available to French nationals only. Mr Cohan, relying on the prohibition of discrimination in Article 18 TEU, challenged this denial. The Court observed that tourists must be regarded as recipients of services and, as such, they must not be discriminated against as compared to nationals of the Member State in question. They are entitled to equal treatment, including the protection from harm in the Member State in question and the right to obtain financial compensation provided for by national law when the risk of harm materializes.

12.2.3 Rights pertaining to the freedom to provide services

12.2.3.1 The right to move and reside

→ CROSS-REFERENCE
See 11.1.4 on the rights of EU citizens and their families.

The right to move and reside has been discussed in detail in Chapter 11. Council Directive 73/148/EEC of 21 May 1973 on the abolition of restrictions on movement and residence within the Community for nationals of Member States with regard to establishment and the provision of services, OJ 1973 L172/14, was the original secondary legislation implementing the rights of entry and residence for service providers and recipients. This Directive has, however, been repealed by the Citizenship Directive (Directive 2004/38/EC of the European Parliament and of the Council of 29 April 2004 on the right of citizens of the Union and their family members to move and reside freely within the territory of the Member States . . . , OJ 2004 L158/77).

→ CROSS-REFERENCE
See 12.1.2 on the meaning of 'establishment'.

It is relevant to note here that although the right of establishment and the freedom to provide services share common features and provisions, they constitute two separate branches of EU law. The meaning of establishment has been explained earlier.

Where establishment means integration into a national economy, the freedom to provide services does not. This freedom to provide services merely enables a self-employed person established in a Member State in which that person is integrated to exercise their activity in another Member State (Case C-55/94 *Gebhard* [1995] ECR I-4165). The provision of services often involves temporary and/or occasional pursuit of economic activities in another Member State, and it does not require the provider, as a matter of principle, to reside in that Member State. It was held in *Gebhard* that establishment and the provision of services are mutually exclusive, therefore distinguishing the rules governing the two types of activity. The key distinguishing feature is duration, and the temporary nature of services must be determined in the light not only of the duration of the provision of the service, but also of its regularity, periodicity, or continuity.

12.2.3.2 Equal treatment

Prohibition of discrimination

Article 56 TFEU

Within the framework of the provisions set out below, restrictions on freedom to provide services within the Union shall be prohibited in respect of nationals of Member States who are established in a Member State other than that of the person for whom the services are intended . . .

Article 57 TFEU

... Without prejudice to the provisions of the Chapter relating to the right of establishment, the person providing a service may, in order to do so, temporarily pursue his activity in the Member State where the service is provided, under the same conditions as are imposed by that State on its own nationals.

Both direct and indirect discrimination are prohibited under Article 57 TFEU. In Case C-288/89 *Gouda* [1991] ECR I-4007, the Court of Justice explained the meaning of direct discrimination in the context of the freedom to provide services.

Case C-288/89 *Gouda* [1991] ECR I-4007

Summary

1. ... Article 59 of the Treaty [now Article 56 TFEU] entails, in the first place, the abolition of any discrimination against a person providing services on the grounds of his nationality or the fact that he is established in a Member State other than the one in which the service is provided.

   National rules which are not applicable to services without discrimination as regards their origin are compatible with Community law [now EU law] only if they can be brought within an express derogation, such as that contained in Article 56 of the Treaty [now Article 52 TFEU] ...

A case in which there was such direct discrimination was Case C-17/92 *FDC* [1993] ECR I-2239. Spanish law provided that film distributors were granted a licence to dub foreign language films on condition that they distributed a Spanish-language film at the same time. According to the Court of Justice, this rule breached Article 56 TFEU because it gave preferential treatment to the producers of national films in comparison with producers established in other Member States, since the former had a guarantee that their films would be distributed, whereas the latter were dependent solely on the choice of the Spanish distributors. The obligation to distribute a Spanish film therefore had the effect of protecting undertakings producing Spanish films and, by the same token, it placed undertakings of the same type established in other Member States at a disadvantage. Since the producers of films from other Member States were thus deprived of the advantage granted to the producers of Spanish films, that restriction was discriminatory.

An example of indirect discrimination can be found in Case 33/74 *van Binsbergen v Bestuur van de Bedrijfsvereniging voor de Metaalnijverheid* [1974] ECR 1299, in which a Dutch rule requiring legal representatives to be resident in the Netherlands was found to breach EU law because, although it could be objectively justified on the ground of professional rules of conduct connected with the administration of justice, it was disproportionate.

→ CROSS-REFERENCE
See 12.2.1 for a more detailed discussion of *van Binsbergen*.

Non-discriminatory restrictions

As with the other freedoms, the case law of the Court of Justice has evolved to a point at which not only discriminatory rules are prohibited under EU law, but also measures that are liable to prohibit or otherwise impede the activities of a provider of services. The milestone case in this respect is Case C-76/90 *Säger v Dennemeyer* [1991] ECR I-4221. Dennemeyer was a specialist in patent renewal services, based in the UK. It had clients in Germany for whom it monitored patents and it informed them when renewal fees were due. German law required persons attending to the legal affairs of others, such as the monitoring of patents, to have a licence. Dennemeyer did not have such a licence and a German patent agent, Säger, complained. Dennemeyer argued that German law breached Article 56 TFEU.

The Court of Justice ruled that Article 56 TFEU requires not only the elimination of all discrimination against a person providing services on the ground of their nationality, but also the abolition of any restriction, even if it applies without distinction to national providers of services and to those of other Member States, when it is liable to prohibit or otherwise impede the activities of a provider of services established in another Member State where that person lawfully provides similar services. It continued that the freedom to provide services can be limited only by rules that are justified by imperative reasons relating to the public interest and which apply to all persons or undertakings pursuing an activity in the State of destination, insofar as that interest is not protected by the rules to which the person providing the services is subject in the Member State in which they are established. In particular, those objectives must be objectively necessary in order to ensure compliance with professional rules and to guarantee the protection of the recipient of services, and they must not exceed what is necessary to attain those objectives.

This ruling confirms that the same principles apply to all EU freedoms. Discrimination is not required for a national measure to constitute an impediment to freedom of movement; Article 56 TFEU captures all national measures that are liable to prohibit, impede, or render less advantageous the activities of a provider of services established in another Member State where that person lawfully provides similar services (Joined Cases C-369 & 376/96 *Arblade* [1999] ECR I-8453).

NOTE

The *Säger* test

A national measure restricting the freedom to provide services can be justified if:

- it is non-discriminatory;
- it is justified by imperative requirements in the general interest;
- it is suitable to attain the objective it pursues; and
- it does not go beyond what is necessary in order to attain its objective.

?! THINKING POINT

Bearing in mind the case law regarding the free movement of goods, do you think that advertising restrictions could breach Article 56 TFEU? And how could they be justified?

Case C-405/98 *Gourmet* [2001] ECR I-1795 confirmed that a prohibition on advertising, even if it is non-discriminatory, had a particular effect on the cross-border supply of advertising space and thereby constituted a restriction on the freedom to provide services within the meaning of Article 56 TFEU. Such a restriction could be justified, however, by the protection of public health.

A wide range of national measures could constitute a restriction on the freedom to provide services prohibited under Article 56 TFEU. Correspondingly, however, there is a wide range of public interest grounds that could justify such restrictions, rendering them permissible under EU law.

In Case C-384/93 *Alpine Investments* [1995] ECR 1141, the restriction in question was the Dutch prohibition on cold calling—that is, the making of phone calls without prior consent in order to offer services. The Court of Justice held that such a prohibition, although it was general and non-discriminatory, could constitute a restriction on the freedom to provide cross-border services. Maintaining the good reputation of the national financial sector, however, could constitute an imperative reason of public interest capable of justifying restrictions on the freedom to provide financial services.

12.2.4 The Services Directive

The Services Directive (Directive 2006/123/EC of the European Parliament and of the Council of 12 December 2006 on services in the internal market, OJ 2006 L376/36) implements the TFEU provisions on the freedom of establishment and the free movement of services. In its Article 1, the Directive articulates that it establishes general provisions facilitating the exercise of the freedom of establishment for service providers and the free movement of services, while maintaining a high quality of services.

The Directive aims to facilitate these freedoms by removing legal and administrative barriers. It pursues four main objectives:

(1) to ease freedom of establishment and the freedom to provide services;

(2) to strengthen the rights of recipients of services;

(3) to promote the quality of services; and

(4) to establish administrative cooperation between the Member States.

To ease the freedom of establishment, the Directive provides that Member States cannot make access to a service activity or the exercise thereof subject to an authorization scheme unless it does not discriminate and it is justified by an overriding reason relating to the public interest (Article 9). It also contains certain principles regarding the conditions and procedures of authorization. Furthermore, the Directive lists certain requirements that are prohibited under EU law, as well as requirements that need to be evaluated.

To ease the freedom to provide services, the Directive puts in place points of single contact for service providers to complete all formalities (Article 6) and provides that this should be made possible online (Article 8).

Article 16 of the Directive provides that the Member States must ensure free access to and free exercise of a service activity within their territory. They cannot make access to or exercise of a service activity subject to compliance with any requirements, unless these requirements are non-discriminatory, necessary, and proportionate.

The Directive protects the rights of service recipients by guaranteeing their right to use services from another Member State (Article 19), and by providing them with certain information on the service and the service provider (Article 22).

To promote the quality of services, the Directive encourages certain voluntary action, such as certification by independent bodies, the drawing up of quality charters, and the drawing up of European standards (Article 26).

Regarding administrative cooperation, the Directive contains the obligation of mutual assistance between the Member States (Articles 28–29). Essential to achieving this is the development of an electronic system to exchange information, which is provided for in Article 34.

12.3 Derogations to the freedom of establishment and the freedom to provide and receive services

12.3.1 The official authority exception

Article 51 TFEU

The provisions of this Chapter shall not apply, so far as any given Member State is concerned, to activities which in that State are connected, even occasionally, with the exercise of official authority.

→ CROSS-REFERENCE
See 11.2.3 on the rights of workers under EU law.

Article 62 TFEU

The provisions of Articles 51 to 54 shall apply to the matters covered by this Chapter.

The Chapter to which Article 51 TFEU refers is Chapter 2, headed 'Right of establishment'. The Chapter referred to in Article 62 TFEU is Chapter 3, headed 'Services'.

→ CROSS-REFERENCE
On *Reyners*, see 12.1.1.

In Case 2/74 *Reyners* [1974] ECR 631, the Court of Justice clarified the scope of the official authority exception.

The question at issue here was whether, within a profession such as that of *avocat* (lawyer), only those activities inherent in this profession that were connected with the exercise of official authority were excepted from the application of the Chapter on the right of establishment, or whether the whole profession was excepted because it comprised activities connected with the exercise of this authority. The Luxembourg government and the Belgian Bar argued that the whole profession was exonerated from the rules on the right of establishment because it was connected organically with the functioning of the public service of the administration of justice.

The Court of Justice held that the first paragraph of Article 51 TFEU enables Member States to exclude non-nationals from taking up functions involving the exercise of official authority that were connected with an activity as a self-employed person. This need was fully satisfied when the exclusion was limited to those activities that, taken on their own, constituted a direct and specific connection with the exercise of official authority. An extension of the exception allowed by Article 51 TFEU to a whole profession would be possible only in cases in which such activities were linked with that profession in such a way that the freedom of establishment would result in imposing on the Member State concerned the obligation to allow the exercise, even occasionally, by non-nationals of functions appertaining to official authority. This extension was, however, not possible when, within the framework of an independent profession, the activities connected with the exercise of official authority were separable from the professional activity in question taken as a whole.

The Court of Justice has construed the official authority exception narrowly. In Case C-306/89 *Commission v Greece* [1991] ECR I-5863, it held that road traffic experts did not come under the exception in Article 51 TFEU. In Case C-272/91 *Commission v Italy* [1994] ECR I-1409, it was decided that the concession of computer services for the state lottery did not come within the scope of the exception either. Finally, in Case C-47/08 *Commission v Belgium* [2011] ECR I-4105, the Court of Justice ruled that the activities of notaries were not connected with the exercise of official authority within the meaning of Article 51 TFEU.

?! THINKING POINT

These provisions have a role similar to which exception relating to free movement of workers considered in Chapter 11?

12.3.2 Public policy, public security, and public health

Article 52 TFEU

The provisions of this Chapter and measures taken in pursuance thereof shall not prejudice the applicability of provisions laid down by law, regulation or administrative action providing for special treatment for foreign nationals on grounds of public policy, public security or public health . . .

Article 62 TFEU

The provisions of Articles 51 to 54 shall apply to the matters covered by this Chapter.

→ CROSS-REFERENCE
See 11.3.1 and 11.3.2 on derogations to the free movement of persons for reasons of public policy and public security, and public health, respectively.

→ CROSS-REFERENCE
See 12.2.4 on the Services Directive.

→ CROSS-REFERENCE
For further discussion on the derogations, see 11.3.1 and 11.3.2, and on goods, see 10.8.12.

Similar to the provisions on the official authority exception, Article 52 TFEU refers to Chapter 2 on 'Right of establishment' and Article 62 refers to Chapter 3 on 'Services'. These derogations are regulated in secondary legislation. For natural persons, that is the Citizenship Directive (Directive 2004/38/EC of the European Parliament and of the Council of 29 April 2004 on the right of citizens of the Union and their family members to move and reside freely within the territory of the Member States ..., OJ 2004 L158/77), which applies not only to the self-employed, but also to all EU citizens and their families.

For companies, the Services Directive (Directive 2006/123/EC of the European Parliament and of the Council of 12 December 2006 on services in the internal market, OJ 2006 L376/36) applies. The Services Directive reflects the Court of Justice's case law, including the principle of proportionality.

The derogations and their application in the area of freedom of establishment and free movement of services will be illustrated by the relevant case law.

In Case 79/85 *Segers* [1986] ECR 2375, the Court of Justice held that, as regards the freedom of establishment, Article 52 TFEU allowed different treatment for companies formed in accordance with the law of another Member State, provided that the different treatment was justified on grounds of public policy, public security, or public health. The need to combat fraud could constitute such a ground justifying different treatment. The mere risk of tax avoidance, however, could not justify discriminatory treatment.

Case C-36/02 *Omega* [2004] ECR I-9609 concerned the prohibition of certain laser games involving the simulation of acts of violence against people—in particular, the representation of acts of homicide. The Court of Justice accepted that the protection of human dignity constituted a ground of public policy that could justify the restriction on the freedom to provide services, provided that the measure was proportionate. It was held that, by prohibiting only the commercial exploitation of that variant of the game which involved playing at killing people, the prohibition did not go beyond that necessary to attain the objective pursued—that is, the respect for human dignity—and was therefore justified under EU law.

Case C-158/96 *Kohll* [1998] ECR I-1931 concerned national legislation under which reimbursement of the cost of dental treatment provided by an orthodontist, established in another Member State, was subject to authorization by the person's social security institution. The Court of Justice held that although the freedom to provide services could be limited on grounds of public health, that did not permit the Member States from excluding the public health sector, as a sector of economic activity and from the point of view of freedom to provide services, from the application of the fundamental principle of freedom of movement. The Member States were allowed to restrict the freedom to provide medical and hospital services insofar as the maintenance of a treatment facility or medical service on national territory was essential for the public health and even the survival of the population.

In Case C-429/02 *Bacardi France* [2004] ECR I-6613, the question that arose was whether Article 56 TFEU precluded the prohibition of television advertising for alcoholic beverages marketed in a Member State in the case of indirect television advertising resulting from the appearance on screen of hoardings visible during the retransmission of binational sporting events taking place in other Member States. The Court of Justice ruled that such rules on television advertising constituted a restriction on freedom to provide services because the owners of the advertising hoardings had to refuse advertising for alcoholic drinks if the sporting event was likely to be transmitted in another Member State. Such rules also impeded the provision of broadcasting services since broadcasters from the Member State concerned had to refuse all retransmission of sporting events in which hoardings bearing advertising for alcoholic drinks may be visible. The restriction was justified, however, according to the Court, because it pursued an objective relating to the protection of public health—in particular, the objective of combating alcohol abuse.

Finally, it is important to bear in mind that economic aims do not constitute grounds of public policy within the meaning of Article 52 TFEU (Case C-288/89 *Gouda* [1991] ECR I-4007).

→ CROSS-REFERENCE
For a discussion of *Gouda*, see 12.2.3.

Furthermore, in line with the Court's judgment in Case C-158/96 *Kohll* [1998] ECR I-1931, it was held that Article 52 TFEU did not permit a Member State to exclude an entire economic sector from the application of the provisions on freedom of establishment and services (Case C-496/01 *Commission v France* [2004] ECR I-2351).

REVIEW QUESTION

How is this decision in line with the judgment in *Kohll*?

Answer: In *Kohll*, the Court of Justice had ruled to that effect regarding the public health sector, which could not, as a sector of economic activity, be excluded in its entirety from the application of the fundamental principle of freedom of movement.

SUMMARY

- The freedom of establishment (Article 49 TFEU):
  - 'Establishment', for the purposes of European Union law implies the permanent or semi-permanent settlement for economic reasons and can be enjoyed by both self-employed persons (defined widely) and companies.
  - Rights include the right of exit, entry, and residence, provided by Directive 2004/38 for the self-employed and by Article 49 TFEU and case law for companies.
  - A fundamental right of equal treatment exists, which includes the prohibition of direct or indirect discrimination, and the prohibition of measures which hinder or make less attractive the exercise of the freedom of establishment, unless justified.
- The freedom to provide services (Articles 56–57 TFEU):
  - A cross-border element is required (a wholly internal situation is not covered by the rules).
  - Services should normally be provided for remuneration and may include illegal activities where such activity is legal in some Member States.

- Whilst Article 56 is silent on the freedom to receive services, case law has confirmed that it includes this corresponding right.
- The right to move and reside is provided by Directive 2004/38.
- A fundamental right of equal treatment exists, which includes the prohibition of direct or indirect discrimination, and the prohibition of measures which prohibit, impede, or render less advantageous the freedom to provide services, unless justified.
- Directive 2006/123 provides general provisions facilitating the exercise of the freedom of establishment and the free movement of services.

- Derogations to the freedom of establishment and freedom to provide and receive services can be found in the official authority exception (Articles 51 and 62 TFEU) and on the grounds of public policy, public security, and public health (Articles 52 and 62 TFEU).

FURTHER READING

Articles

WH Roth, 'From *Centros* to *Überseering*: Free Movement of Companies, Private International Law, and Community Law' (2003) 52(1) ICLQ 177

In-depth analysis of the issues underlying *Centros*, as well as further developments.

Books

M Andenas and WH Roth, *Services and Free Movement in EU Law* (Oxford: Oxford University Press, 2003)

Critical analysis of the recent state of EU services law as well as contribution to the development of the right to provide services.

C Barnard, *The Substantive Law of the EU: The Four Freedoms*, 5th edn (Oxford: Oxford University Press, 2016)

Thorough analysis of relevant legislation and case law, with critical commentary, background, historical developments, and visual aids.

P Craig and G de Búrca, *EU Law: Text, Cases, and Materials*, 6th edn (Oxford: Oxford University Press, 2015), esp ch 22

Focused and accessible account of relevant cases and materials.

A Kaczorowska, *European Union Law*, 4th edn (Abingdon: Routledge-Cavendish, 2016), esp ch 24

Comprehensive, but accessible, source of EU law.

QUESTION

James owns a successful patisserie in Paris, France renowned for authentic French pastries. The business has been successful over a number of years and he is keen to capitalize on the recent baking trend in the UK. James has identified suitable premises in Oxford, England where he can expand and establish a new patisserie, recruiting skilled local staff to work as pastry chefs. However, James is unfamiliar with UK leasehold arrangements and contacts the (fictitious) UK Food Manufacturers Association who advertise free advice on such matters. When James receives a letter from the Association informing him he is ineligible for free advice as he is not a UK national, he begins to wonder about his rights.

Advise James on his rights under EU law in relation to all aspects of this scenario.

To view an outline answer to this question plus further resources to support your EU law studies, visit the Online Resources for this book at www.oup.com/uk/eulaw-complete4e

13 Competition law: Article 101 TFEU

KEY POINTS

By the end of this chapter, you should be able to:

- understand and appreciate the general aims of EU competition law;
- explain and analyse the scope of the Article 101(1) TFEU prohibition;
- explain and analyse the key elements of Article 101 TFEU; and
- understand the applicability and scope of the exceptions under Article 101(3) TFEU, both individual and block.

INTRODUCTION

Competition law

As was discussed as early as Chapter 1, the creation of an internal market has been a fundamental aim of the European Union (EU) since 1957. In this regard, there are a number of Articles contained in the Treaties that prohibit tariff and non-tariff barriers to trade, with a view to ensuring the free movement of goods—one of the four fundamental freedoms. These rules have been, and indeed continue to be, vital to the effective operation of the internal market. Such measures target restrictions implemented by Member States, usually in the form of national legislation. It must be recognized, however, that Member State action is not the only threat to effective operation of the internal market; restrictive business practices can also have harmful consequences. Indeed, not only do such practices prejudice the operation of the internal market, but also they can have a detrimental effect on business efficiency, can harm consumers, and, if engaged in by large and powerful companies, are likely to disadvantage small and medium-sized enterprises (SMEs).

The two key Articles concerning the prohibition of anti-competitive behaviour are Articles 101 and 102 TFEU. This chapter focuses on Article 101 TFEU (agreements between businesses that may affect competition and interstate trade), whilst Chapter 14 focuses on Article 102 TFEU (abuse of a dominant position). Finally, Chapter 15 focuses on the enforcement of EU competition law.

Article 101 TFEU

The focus of Article 101 TFEU is upon trade agreements or less formal trade arrangements that are intended to or have the possibility of preventing, restricting, or distorting competition within the internal market to the extent that such agreements/arrangements affect trade between Member States.

For example, suppose that Pear Ltd and Melon Ltd, two UK-based technology companies that, together, supply 85 per cent of all laptops sold in the EU, decide that it is not in their interests to constantly compete against each other. Doing so has resulted in each company making only a very small profit margin and has resulted in huge marketing costs. They agree that if they each concentrate on the markets in separate countries and agree set prices, then their advertising budgets could be reduced and their profit margins restored to healthy rates. They suspect that this may not be totally legitimate and so are careful not to create a formal contract between them. Nevertheless, they reach an agreement whereby the EU market is divided up between them along national boundaries and a set pricing scheme is introduced.

It is this type of agreement that Article 101 TFEU is designed to prevent. Such an agreement ensures that Pear Ltd and Melon Ltd are, to a large extent, free from competitive pressures in their respective markets—but consumer choice is reduced and the expectation is that prices would be set at artificially high levels. Furthermore, it would be difficult for potential new competitors to access the market as Pear Ltd and Melon Ltd would each have a virtual monopoly in each Member State due to the market portioning resulting from the agreement. Thus the agreement has adverse effects on both consumers and potential competitors, and hence, as the agreement has the object of distorting competition within the internal market and will affect trade between Member States, it is likely to be within the scope of Article 101 TFEU.

13.1 Outline of Article 101 TFEU

Article 101 TFEU

1. The following shall be prohibited as incompatible with the internal market: all agreements between undertakings, decisions by associations of undertakings and concerted practices which may affect trade between Member States and which have as their object or effect the prevention, restriction or distortion of competition within the internal market, and in particular those which:
   (a) directly or indirectly fix purchase or selling prices or any other trading conditions;
   (b) limit or control production, markets, technical development, or investment;
   (c) share markets or sources of supply;
   (d) apply dissimilar conditions to equivalent transactions with other trading parties, thereby placing them at a competitive disadvantage;
   (e) make the conclusion of contracts subject to acceptance by the other parties of supplementary obligations which, by their nature or according to commercial usage, have no connection with the subject of such contracts.
2. Any agreements or decisions prohibited pursuant to this Article shall be automatically void.
3. The provisions of paragraph 1 may, however, be declared inapplicable in the case of:
   - any agreement or category of agreements between undertakings,
   - any decision or category of decisions by associations of undertakings,
   - any concerted practice or category of concerted practices,

   which contributes to improving the production or distribution of goods or to promoting technical or economic progress, while allowing consumers a fair share of the resulting benefit, and which does not:
   (a) impose on the undertakings concerned restrictions which are not indispensable to the attainment of these objectives;
   (b) afford such undertakings the possibility of eliminating competition in respect of a substantial part of the products in question.

Article 101 TFEU is broad, covering formal agreements and also informal arrangements.

Under Article 101(2) TFEU, agreements or decisions within Article 101(1) are automatically void, although if it is possible to sever (that is, remove) restrictive clauses from an agreement, only those clauses will be void (Joined Cases 56 & 58/64 *Établissements Consten SaRL and Grundig-Verkaufs-GmbH v Commission* [1966] ECR 299).

Article 101(3) TFEU provides for exemption, so that Article 101(1) may be declared inapplicable to an agreement, decision, or concerted practice if certain conditions are satisfied.

13.2 Article 101(1) TFEU: the prohibition

It is therefore important, in applying Article 101(1) TFEU, to take a structured approach.

REVIEW QUESTION

Article 101(1) TFEU can be broken into three distinct elements. Can you identify them?

Answer: Article 101(1) covers (a) agreements between undertakings, decisions by associations of undertakings, and concerted practices that (b) may affect trade between Member States and (c) have as their object or effect the prevention, restriction, or distortion of competition within the internal market.

13.2.1 Agreements between undertakings, decisions by associations of undertakings, and concerted practices

Before considering the nature of the agreements, etc that fall within Article 101(1) TFEU, it is first important to ensure that we are dealing with 'undertakings'.

The term itself is not defined within the Treaty. As such, we need to consider its interpretation within case law.

13.2.1.1 Undertakings

In Case C-41/90 *Höfner and Elser* [1991] ECR I-1979, the Court of Justice considered the capacity of an employment agency. The Commission took the view that such an agency fell within the meaning of an undertaking within what is now Article 101(1) TFEU. The German government did not feel that this was the case with a public employment agency insofar as the employment procurement services were provided free of charge, as was the case here. The Court of Justice, in applying a wide definition of the term 'undertaking', held as follows.

Case C-41/90 *Höfner and Elser* [1991] ECR I-1979

21. It must be observed, in the context of competition law, first that the concept of an undertaking encompasses every entity engaged in an economic activity, regardless of the legal status of the entity and the way in which it is financed and, secondly, that employment procurement is an economic activity.
22. The fact that employment procurement activities are normally entrusted to public agencies cannot affect the economic nature of such activities. Employment procurement has not always been, and is not necessarily, carried out by public entities. That finding applies in particular to executive recruitment.
23. It follows that an entity such as a public employment agency engaged in the business of employment procurement may be classified as an undertaking for the purpose of applying the Community [now Union] competition rules.

Thus the term 'undertaking' has been interpreted widely and includes any legal or natural person engaged in some form of economic or commercial activity.

13.2.1.2 Agreements

'Agreement' clearly covers formal binding contracts, but it is not, on the face of it, clear whether it extends to less formal agreements. This matter was considered by the Court of Justice in Case 41/69 *ACF Chemiefarma NV v Commission ('Quinine Cartel')* [1970] ECR 661.

?! THINKING POINT

Why do you think the term 'agreement' does not have a Treaty definition?

In the *Quinine Cartel* case, the companies concerned agreed to retain their respective domestic markets and provided for the fixing of prices, rebates, and the allocation of export quotas for the export of quinine and quinidine to other countries. This was extended to all sales within the internal market by way of a 'gentlemen's agreement'. The companies argued that such an agreement did not constitute an 'agreement' within the meaning of what is now Article 101(1) TFEU. The Court of Justice held that '[a] gentlemen' s agreement constitutes a measure which may fall under the prohibition contained in Article 85(1) [EC, now Article 101(1) TFEU] if it contains clauses restricting competition in the common market within the meaning of that Article and its clauses amount to a faithful expression of the joint intention of the parties' (*Quinine Cartel*, at para 9).

It is therefore clear that the term 'agreement' is interpreted widely to include both formally and non-formally constituted agreements. In this regard, it would seem that the emphasis is on substance above form.

?! **THINKING POINT**

Why do you think that identifying the precise boundaries of an 'agreement' is less important than it otherwise might be? Reflect upon this as you familiarize yourself with all elements of Article 101(1) TFEU.

13.2.1.3 Decisions by associations of undertakings

The focus of 'decisions by undertakings' is trade associations. A trade association is simply an organization made up of members involved in a particular trade or business to promote a common interest. Such associations usually lay down membership rules that have the effect of regulating standards and behaviour. The decisions of such are therefore subject to Article 101(1) TFEU insofar as they are intended or have the possibility of preventing, restricting, or distorting competition within the internal market and to the extent that they are capable of affecting trade between Member States. An example of a decision by an association of undertakings therefore would be where a trade association for mobile phone manufacturers lays down rules stating that all manufacturers are to impose restrictive clauses in sales contracts.

In Joined Cases 96–102, 104, 105, 108, & 110/82 *IAZ International Belgium NV v Commission* [1983] ECR 3369, even a non-binding recommendation of a trade association concerning the connection of washing machines and dishwashers to the water supply was held to fall within Article 101(1) TFEU. Attention was drawn to the fact that such a recommendation, even if it had no binding effect, could not escape what is now Article 101(1) where compliance with the recommendation by the undertakings to which it was addressed would have an appreciable influence on competition in the market in question.

The focus of 'decisions of undertakings' is arguably upon trade associations, but, as with other elements of Article 101(1) TFEU, this has been interpreted widely to include professional associations. Thus, in Case C-309/99 *Wouters and others v Netherlands Bar* [2002] ECR I-1577, consideration was given to a regulation of the Dutch Bar Association prohibiting multidisciplinary partnerships and whether this was a decision of an association of undertakings, since it expressed the intention of members to carry out their economic activity in a particular way. It was held by the Court of Justice that, in such situations, the Dutch Bar Association acts as the regulatory body of a profession, the practice of which constitutes an economic activity.

Case C-309/99 *Wouters and others v Netherlands Bar* [2002] ECR I-1577

66. ... The legal framework within which such agreements are concluded and such decisions taken, and the classification given to that framework by the various national legal systems, are irrelevant as far as the applicability of the Community [now Union] rules on competition, and in particular Article 85 of the Treaty [now Article 101 TFEU], are concerned ...

[...]

71. … [A] regulation concerning partnerships between members of the Bar and members of other liberal professions … adopted by a body such as the Bar of the Netherlands, must be regarded as a decision adopted by an association of undertakings within the meaning of Article 85(1) of the Treaty [now Article 101(1) TFEU].

13.2.1.4 Concerted practices

A concerted practice is less easy to define than an agreement or a decision and a finding of such often requires a careful analysis over time of the interaction between undertakings in the absence of a formally or informally constituted agreement.

The first case to consider the meaning of 'concerted practice' was the leading case of Case 48/69 *Imperial Chemical Industries Ltd v Commission ('Dyestuffs')* [1972] ECR 619, which followed three general and uniform increases in the prices of dyestuffs between January 1964 and October 1967. A Commission Decision found that such uniform increases in prices were a result of coordinated behaviour between the undertakings concerned amounting to a concerted practice within Article 101(1) TFEU. Attention was drawn to the fact that the prices introduced for each increase by the different producers in each country were the same, that, with very rare exceptions, the same dyestuffs were involved, and that the increases were put into effect over only a very short period, if not actually on the same date. However, this was challenged by ICI, which argued that the simultaneous increases in price could be explained by, amongst other things, the nature of the **oligopolistic market** within which the undertakings were operating.

oligopolistic market
An oligopolistic market is a market within which only a few undertakings operate.

?! THINKING POINT

Why do you think that the behaviour of undertakings in an oligopolistic market is more likely to raise questions pertaining to a concerted practice than a market in which many undertakings operate?

The Court of Justice considered the content of what is now Article 101(1) TFEU and, in so doing, provided a definition that drew a distinction between market forces and evidence of collusion.

Case 48/69 *Imperial Chemical Industries Ltd v Commission ('Dyestuffs')* [1972] ECR 619

64. Article 85 [EC, now Article 101 TFEU] draws a distinction between the concept of 'concerted practices' and that of 'agreements between undertakings' or of 'decisions by associations of undertakings'; the object is to bring within the prohibition of that Article a form

of coordination between undertakings which, without having reached the stage where an agreement properly so-called has been concluded, knowingly substitutes practical cooperation between them for the risks of competition.

65. By its very nature, then, a concerted practice does not have all the elements of a contract but may inter alia arise out of coordination which becomes apparent from the behaviour of the participants.

66. Although parallel behaviour may not by itself be identified with a concerted practice, it may however amount to strong evidence of such a practice if it leads to conditions of competition which do not correspond to the normal conditions of the market, having regard to the nature of the products, the size and number of the undertakings, and the volume of the said market.

67. This is especially the case if the parallel conduct is such as to enable those concerned to attempt to stabilize prices at a level different from that to which competition would have led, and to consolidate established positions to the detriment of effective freedom of movement of the products in the common market and of the freedom of consumers to choose their suppliers.

The Court held that the companies had not reacted spontaneously to each other's pricing strategies. There were sufficient producers to allow natural competition to take place and the firms could realistically be expected to adopt their own pricing strategies, especially since the market was broken down into five separate national markets. Advance announcements of price increases had eliminated all uncertainty between them as to their future conduct and their actions demonstrated a 'common intention' to fix prices. The Court therefore held that the behaviour was not the result of an oligopolistic market, but the result of a concerted practice.

The case can be usefully compared to Joined Cases C-89, 104, 114, 116, 117, & 125–9/85 *Ahlström and others v Commission ('Woodpulp')* [1988] ECR 5193. *Woodpulp* concerned bleached sulphate pulp, which is used in the production of high-quality paper. The practice of quarterly announcements was well established on the European pulp market, whereby some weeks—even, at times, some days—before the beginning of each quarter, producers communicated to their customers and agents the prices that they wished to obtain.

After carrying out investigations, the Commission stated that it had discovered the existence in the pulp industry of a number of restrictive practices and agreements, and had decided to commence a proceeding against 57 pulp producers that were alleged to have participated in price-fixing by way of concerted practices and in decisions by associations.

The Court of Justice accepted that the market consisted of a series of oligopolies and that the quarterly price announcements were at the request of customers. It considered the market to be highly transparent and this explained the near-simultaneous price announcements. There was no evidence of communication between the parties and the parallel conduct could therefore be explained by the nature of the market.

?! THINKING POINT

Refer back to the definition of 'concerted practice' in *Dyestuffs*, and in particular the following extract. Do you think a clear distinction between a concerted practice and the usual behaviour of an oligopolistic market can ever be made?

Case 48/69 *Imperial Chemical Industries Ltd v Commission ('Dyestuffs')* [1972] ECR 619

66. Although parallel behaviour may not by itself be identified with a concerted practice, it may however amount to strong evidence of such a practice if it leads to conditions of competition which do not correspond to the normal conditions of the market, having regard to the nature of the products, the size and number of the undertakings, and the volume of the said market.

It is clear that, with such a wide definition of concerted practice under Article 101(1) TFEU, the precise boundaries of an agreement are not a key consideration in a finding of a breach.

13.2.1.5 Cartels

A cartel is a group of independent, but similar, undertakings that work together to reach agreements that have anti-competitive effects. Such cartels reveal information between the companies involved about the course of action each plans to take and agreements may be made regarding pricing, marketing, and market-sharing. Whilst it is clear that such activity is anti-competitive and damaging to customers and potential competitors, cartels are difficult to find for the authorities. They are secretive in nature and have often developed quite sophisticated strategies to ensure that their operations remain undetected.

In view of this, the Commission has provided incentives to cartel members willing to reveal details about the cartel. The Commission's reasoning is clear.

Commission Notice on immunity from fines and reduction of fines in cartel cases, OJ 2006 C298/17

I. Introduction

(1) This notice sets out the framework for rewarding cooperation in the Commission investigation by undertakings which are or have been party to secret cartels affecting the Community [now Union]. Cartels are agreements and/or concerted practices between two or more competitors aimed at coordinating their competitive behaviour on the market and/or influencing the relevant parameters of competition through practices such as the fixing of purchase or selling prices or other trading conditions, the allocation of production

or sales quotas, the sharing of markets including bid-rigging, restrictions of imports or exports and/or anti-competitive actions against other competitors. Such practices are among the most serious violations of Article 81 EC [now Article 101 TFEU].

(2) By artificially limiting the competition that would normally prevail between them, undertakings avoid exactly those pressures that lead them to innovate, both in terms of product development and the introduction of more efficient production methods. Such practices also lead to more expensive raw materials and components for the Community companies that purchase from such producers. They ultimately result in artificial prices and reduced choice for the consumer. In the long term, they lead to a loss of competitiveness and reduced employment opportunities.

(3) By their very nature, secret cartels are often difficult to detect and investigate without the cooperation of undertakings or individuals implicated in them. Therefore, the Commission considers that it is in the Community interest to reward undertakings involved in this type of illegal practices which are willing to put an end to their participation and co-operate in the Commission's investigation, independently of the rest of the undertakings involved in the cartel. The interests of consumers and citizens in ensuring that secret cartels are detected and punished outweigh the interest in fining those undertakings that enable the Commission to detect and prohibit such practices.

(4) The Commission considers that the collaboration of an undertaking in the detection of the existence of a cartel has an intrinsic value. A decisive contribution to the opening of an investigation or to the finding of an infringement may justify the granting of immunity from any fine to the undertaking in question, on condition that certain additional requirements are fulfilled.

(5) Moreover, co-operation by one or more undertakings may justify a reduction of a fine by the Commission. Any reduction of a fine must reflect an undertaking's actual contribution, in terms of quality and timing, to the Commission's establishment of the infringement. Reductions are to be limited to those undertakings that provide the Commission with evidence that adds significant value to that already in the Commission's possession.

(6) In addition to submitting pre-existing documents, undertakings may provide the Commission with voluntary presentations of their knowledge of a cartel and their role therein prepared specially to be submitted under this leniency programme. These initiatives have proved to be useful for the effective investigation and termination of cartel infringements and they should not be discouraged by discovery orders issued in civil litigation. Potential leniency applicants might be dissuaded from cooperating with the Commission under this Notice if this could impair their position in civil proceedings, as compared to companies who do not cooperate. Such undesirable effect would significantly harm the public interest in ensuring effective public enforcement of Article 81 EC in cartel cases and thus its subsequent or parallel effective private enforcement.

(7) The supervisory task conferred on the Commission by the Treaty in competition matters does not only include the duty to investigate and punish individual infringements, but also

encompasses the duty to pursue a general policy. The protection of corporate statements in the public interest is not a bar to their disclosure to other addressees of the statement of objections in order to safeguard their rights of defence in the procedure before the Commission, to the extent that it is technically possible to combine both interests by rendering corporate statements accessible only at the Commission premises and normally on a single occasion following the formal notification of the objections. Moreover, the Commission will process personal data in the context of this notice in conformity with its obligations under Regulation (EC) No 45/2001.

Thus those members of a cartel who are willing to cooperate with the Commission and thereby enable it to detect and investigate the cartel may be entitled to substantial benefits in terms of reductions in, and sometimes even total immunity from, fines.

→ CROSS-REFERENCE
See Chapter 15 on enforcement of EU competition law.

13.2.1.6 *Vertical and horizontal agreements*

In its wording, Article 101(1) TFEU does not distinguish between **horizontal agreements** and **vertical agreements**.

In Joined Cases 56 & 58/64 *Établissements Consten SaRL and Grundig-Verkaufs-GmbH v Commission* [1966] ECR 299, Grundig, under a dealership agreement, supplied its electronic products to Consten, as its only French distributor, for resale in France. Under the agreement, Consten had to take a minimum order, had to provide publicity and an after-sales service, and could not sell the Grundig products directly or indirectly outside France or sell the products of competing manufacturers. Grundig assigned its trade mark to Consten, which could use it against unauthorized sales in France. Grundig distributors in other countries could not sell Grundig products in France. This ensured that Consten had absolute territorial protection in France, as did other distributors in other countries.

When a company purchased Grundig goods and then sold them in France at a price below that of Consten, Consten took action for infringement of its trade mark. The question arose as to whether the agreement breached what is now Article 101(1) TFEU.

horizontal agreements
Horizontal agreements are agreements between parties operating at the same level of the production/distribution chain, for instance an agreement between manufacturers or between retailers.

vertical agreementS
Vertical agreements are agreements between parties operating at different levels of the production/distribution chain, for instance a distribution agreement between a manufacturer and a distributor.

?! THINKING POINT

Was the agreement between Consten and Grundig a vertical or horizontal agreement? Look back at the definitions given.

This agreement was between a manufacturer and a distributor; thus it was a vertical agreement. Consten submitted that the prohibition in what is now Article 101 TFEU applied only to horizontal agreements. However, the Court of Justice disagreed.

Joined Cases 56 & 58/64 *Établissements Consten SaRL and Grundig-Verkaufs-GmbH v Commission* [1966] ECR 299, 339

Neither the wording of Article 85 [EC, now Article 101 TFEU] nor that of Article 86 [EC, now Article 102 TFEU] gives any ground for holding that distinct areas of application are to be assigned to each of the two Articles according to the level in the economy at which the contracting parties operate. Article 85 refers in a general way to all agreements which distort competition within the common market and does not lay down any distinction between those agreements based on whether they are made between competitors operating at the same level in the economic process or between non-competing persons operating at different levels. In principle, no distinction can be made where the Treaty does not make any distinction.

Therefore it is clear that, given that the Treaty makes no such distinction, Article 101 TFEU applies to both horizontal and vertical agreements.

13.2.2 Which may affect trade between Member States

Remember that, for the purposes of the structure of arguments in this area, the three elements of the prohibition under Article 101(1) TFEU are (a) agreements between undertakings, decisions by associations of undertakings, and concerted practices that (b) may affect trade between Member States and which (c) have as their object or effect the prevention, restriction, or distortion of competition within the internal market. We shall now turn to the second of these.

Article 101(1) TFEU is breached only if the agreement, decision, or concerted practice is one that may affect trade between Member States. The function of the notion 'may affect' is to define the nature of the required impact on trade between EU countries.

In line with the Court of Justice's approach to most provisions for the protection of effective competition, the interpretation of this second requirement has been (unsurprisingly) wide.

In Case 56/65 *Société Technique Minière v Maschinenbau Ulm GmbH* [1966] ECR 235, Maschinenbau (MU) was a German manufacturer of grading equipment, and an agreement between MU and Société Technique Minière (STM) provided that STM would sell this equipment in France. The terms of the agreement provided that STM had an exclusive right to sell the equipment in France. However, and in contrast with *Consten*, STM could also sell the equipment outside France and French buyers were able to source the equipment from other suppliers outside France. The relationship between the parties deteriorated and STM argued that the agreement breached Article 101 TFEU. The Court of Justice stated as follows, in considering the second element of the Article 101(1) prohibition and ultimately concluding that the agreement did not breach the Article.

Case 56/65 *Société Technique Minière v Maschinenbau Ulm GmbH* [1966] ECR 235, 249

... It is in fact to the extent that the agreement may affect trade between Member States that the interference with competition caused by that agreement is caught by the prohibitions in Community law [now EU law] found in Article 85 [EC, now Article 101 TFEU], whilst in the converse case it escapes those prohibitions. For this requirement to be fulfilled it must be possible to foresee with a sufficient degree of probability on the basis of a set of objective factors of law or of fact that the agreement in question may have an influence, direct or indirect, actual or potential, on the pattern of trade between Member States. Therefore, in order to determine whether an agreement which contains a clause 'granting an exclusive right of sale' comes within the field of application of Article 85, it is necessary to consider in particular whether it is capable of bringing about a partitioning of the market in certain products between Member States and thus rendering more difficult the interpenetration of trade which the Treaty is intended to create.

Thus there would be an effect on trade wherever it was 'possible to foresee with a sufficient degree of probability on the basis of a set of objective factors of law or of fact that the agreement in question may have an influence, direct or indirect, actual or potential, on the pattern of trade between Member States'. This broad test is easily satisfied.

In Commission Decision 77/160/EEC of 20 January 1977 relating to a proceeding under Article 85 of the EEC Treaty (IV/27.442 – *Vacuum Interrupters Ltd*), OJ 1977 L48/32, Associated Electrical Industries Ltd and Reyrolle Parsons Ltd, two UK companies, were major manufacturers of switchgear apparatus used for switching on and off the power flowing from generating stations and acting as a safety device in the event of faults. They were both working on a new product, a vacuum interrupter. However, the cost of development was significant, and the two companies decided to collaborate and pool resources, establishing a joint facility for research and development by way of a joint venture agreement. When applying the provisions of what is now Article 101(1) TFEU, the Commission gave consideration as to whether the joint venture agreement may affect trade between Member States. Giving consideration to the future possibility of impact, the Commission found as follows.

Commission Decision 77/160/EEC of 20 January 1977 relating to a proceeding under Article 85 of the EEC Treaty (IV/27.442 – *Vacuum Interrupters Ltd*), OJ 1977 L48/32

17. ... It is reasonable to assume that if a market were to develop in the other Member States of the EEC [now EU] for the vacuum interrupter and if both Associated Electrical Industries Ltd and/or their associated companies and Reyrolle Parsons Ltd had developed and manufactured the vacuum type interrupter independently of each other, each should

> have been able to obtain a market for it in the other Member States, where they would have been in direct competition not only with each other but also with such other undertakings as might manufacture this type of interrupter. There could have developed an export trade between each of these undertakings in the United Kingdom and customers in other Member States in which each would have been in competition with the other and with local manufactures. Exports from the UK to other Member States are now likely to start earlier and form a different pattern, thus affecting the flow of trade from the United Kingdom to other Member States. Further, both Associated Electrical Industries Ltd and Reyrolle Parsons Ltd have as customers in the United Kingdom the Central Electricity Generating Board and other area boards and most of the large industrial undertakings which take electricity from high voltage lines. The fact that two companies, each with an important market position in heavy electrical equipment in the United Kingdom, have combined their activity in the field of vacuum interrupters in a joint subsidiary must reduce the possibility that another manufacturer or other manufacturers of electrical equipment from other Member States of the EEC would be able to enter the United Kingdom for the purpose of manufacturing and selling or selling only the vacuum interrupter in competition with Vacuum Interrupters Ltd. It might well have been easier for such manufacturers to build up a market for the vacuum interrupter in the United Kingdom if they were not to be in competition with one economically and technically strong competitor but with two competitors, each separately economically and technically weaker. The market position of Vacuum Interrupters Ltd, having regard to that of the parent undertakings and of other manufacturers of switchgear equipment in the UK who are also in a position to sell switchgear equipment utilizing the interrupters designed and made by Vacuum Interrupters Ltd, would make it more difficult for new market entrants to capture a share of the market. The result therefore of the establishment of Vacuum Interrupters Ltd is that the economic penetration of the United Kingdom by manufacturers of electrical apparatus from the other Member States of the EEC will be rendered more difficult. Thus the effect of the restriction on competition arising from the creation of the joint subsidiary with which this decision is concerned is that the potential competition between the parent companies to be offered from the United Kingdom to other Member States will be reduced, as will the potential for competition by companies from other Member States within the United Kingdom. Further, because there are no other manufacturers of vacuum interrupters in the common market at present and there are relatively few potential manufacturers therein, a joint venture between two potential manufacturers affects the structure of competition in the common market. Trade between Member States may thus be affected by the agreement of 25 March 1970.

Thus the Commission concluded that although the two companies concerned were both based in the UK, the possibility of a rival company emerging was reduced due to the combined strength the joint venture had afforded them. Furthermore, the pattern of trade between Member States was likely to be different from that which may have arisen if each independent company had developed a product separately and become export competitors. As such, the agreement was found to have been capable of affecting trade between Member States.

The 'legal and economic context' of an agreement, concerted practice, or decision will also be a factor to take into account. In considering this, it is clear that the existence of similar contracts should be analysed when, if such similar contracts are considered together, they may result in an effect on Member State trade. In Case 23/67 *Brasserie de Haecht SA v Wilkin (No 1)* [1967] ECR 407, Mr and Mrs Wilkin had undertaken to obtain all of their supplies of beer and soft drinks exclusively from the brewery under which they had made loan agreements. When Mr and Mrs Wilkin breached the obligation by purchasing beverages elsewhere, the brewery sought repayment of the loan. In legal proceedings relating to this breach of contract, the argument was advanced that the agreement in question breached what is now Article 101(1) TFEU. A key consideration for the Court of Justice in assessing the validity or otherwise of the agreement alongside EU competition law was whether the agreement and its effect on Member State trade should be assessed solely on the basis of the single agreement in question or whether the context of a network of similar agreements was a factor.

Case 23/67 *Brasserie de Haecht SA v Wilkin (No 1)* [1967] ECR 407, 415

The prohibition in Article 85(1) of the Treaty [now Article 101(1) TFEU] rests on three factors essential for a reply to the question referred. After stating the limits within which the prohibition is to apply, Article 85(1) mentions agreements, decisions and practices. By referring in the same sentence to agreements between undertakings, decisions by associations of undertakings and concerted practices, which may involve many parties, Article 85(1) implies that the constituent elements of those agreements, decisions and practices may be considered together as a whole.

Furthermore, by basing its application to agreements, decisions or practices not only on their subject-matter but also on their effects in relation to competition, Article 85(1) implies that regard must be had to such effects in the context in which they occur, that is to say, in the economic and legal context of such agreements, decisions or practices and where they might combine with others to have a cumulative effect on competition. In fact, it would be pointless to consider an agreement, decision or practice by reason of its effects if those effects were to be taken distinct from the market in which they are seen to operate and could only be examined apart from the body of effects, whether convergent or not, surrounding their implementation. Thus in order to examine whether it is caught by Article 85(1) an agreement cannot be examined in isolation from the above context, that is, from the factual or legal circumstances causing it to prevent, restrict or distort competition. The existence of similar contracts may be taken into consideration for this objective to the extent to which the general body of contracts of this type is capable of restricting the freedom of trade.

Lastly, it is only to the extent to which agreements, decisions or practices are capable of affecting trade between Member States that the alteration of competition comes under Community [now Union] prohibitions. In order to satisfy this condition, it must be possible for the agreement, decision or practice, when viewed in the light of a combination of the objective, factual or legal circumstances, to appear to be capable of having some influence, direct or indirect, on trade between Member States, of being conducive to a partitioning of the market and of hampering the economic interpenetration sought by the Treaty. When this point is considered the agreement, decision or practice cannot therefore be isolated from all the others of which it is one.

The existence of similar contracts is a circumstance which, together with others, is capable of being a factor in the economic and legal context within which the contract must be judged. Accordingly, whilst such a situation must be taken into account it should not be considered as decisive by itself, but merely as one among others in judging whether trade between Member States is capable of being affected through any alteration in competition. …

The existence of similar contracts is therefore a key factor to be taken into account.

Guidance is provided by the Commission Notice, *Guidelines on the effect on trade concept contained in Articles 81 and 82 of the Treaty* [now Articles 101 and 102 TFEU], OJ 2004 C101/81.

Commission Notice: Guidelines on the effect on trade concept contained in Articles 81 and 82 of the Treaty [now Articles 101 and 102 TFEU], OJ 2004 C101/81

52. The Commission holds the view that in principle agreements are not capable of appreciably affecting trade between Member States when the following cumulative conditions are met:

(a) The aggregate market share of the parties on any relevant market within the Community [now Union] affected by the agreement does not exceed 5 per cent, and

(b) In the case of horizontal agreements, the aggregate annual Community turnover of the undertakings concerned in the products covered by the agreement does not exceed 40 million euro …

In the case of vertical agreements, the aggregate annual Community turnover of the supplier in the products covered by the agreement does not exceed 40 million euro …

Thus, unless the parties' aggregate market share on any relevant EU market affected by the agreement exceeds 5 per cent and (for horizontal agreements) their aggregate turnover does not exceed €40 million or (for vertical agreements) the aggregate EU turnover of the supplier does not exceed €40 million, the agreement in question is not capable of affecting trade between Member States.

Of course, market shares can be determined only with reference to a 'relevant market'. This concept is discussed in detail in Chapter 14 in relation to Article 102 TFEU, but is equally applicable to Article 101 TFEU.

13.2.3 Object or effect: prevention, restriction, or distortion of competition

Returning to the three elements of the prohibition under Article 101(1) TFEU—that is, (a) agreements between undertakings, decisions by associations of undertakings, and concerted practices that (b) may affect trade between Member States and which (c) have as their object or effect the prevention, restriction, or distortion of competition within the internal market—we shall now consider the third element.

Article 101(1) TFEU is breached only if the agreement, decision, or concerted practice is one that not only may affect trade between Member States, but also has as its 'object or effect' the prevention, restriction, or distortion of competition.

In Case 56/65 *Société Technique Minière v Maschinenbau Ulm GmbH* [1966] ECR 235, the Court of Justice also considered the third element of the Article 101(1) prohibition.

Case 56/65 *Société Technique Minière v Maschinenbau Ulm GmbH* [1966] ECR 235, 249

The fact that these are not cumulative but alternative requirements, indicated by the conjunction 'or', leads first to the need to consider the precise purpose of the agreement, in the economic context in which it is to be applied. This interference with competition referred to in Article 85(1) [EC, now Article 101(1) TFEU] must result from all or some of the clauses of the agreement itself. Where, however, an analysis of the said clauses does not reveal the effect on competition to be sufficiently deleterious, the consequences of the agreement should then be considered and for it to be caught by the prohibition it is then necessary to find that those factors are present which show that competition has in fact been prevented or restricted or distorted to an appreciable extent.

Thus, as there clearly was no object of preventing, restricting, or distorting competition, it was necessary to see whether this was the effect of the agreement.

The Commission has stated that, with regard to particularly objectionable restrictions, such as horizontal price-fixing or market-sharing, it will be unnecessary to establish any actual effect on the market. The mere existence of such a restriction is sufficient.

Commission Notice, Guidelines on the application of Article 81(3) of the Treaty [now Article 101(3) TFEU], OJ 2004 C101/97

20. The distinction between restrictions by object and restrictions by effect is important. Once it has been established that an agreement has as its object the restriction of competition, there is no need to take account of its concrete effects. In other words, for the purpose of applying Article 81(1) [EC, now Article 101(1) TFEU] no actual anti-competitive effects need to be demonstrated where the agreement has a restriction of competition as its object. Ar-

ticle 81(3) [EC, now Article 101(3) TFEU], on the other hand, does not distinguish between agreements that restrict competition by object and agreements that restrict competition by effect. Article 81(3) applies to all agreements that fulfil the four conditions contained therein.

21. Restrictions of competition by object are those that by their very nature have the potential of restricting competition. These are restrictions which in light of the objectives pursued by the Community [now Union] competition rules have such a high potential of negative effects on competition that it is unnecessary for the purposes of applying Article 81(1) to demonstrate any actual effects on the market. This presumption is based on the serious nature of the restriction and on experience showing that restrictions of competition by object are likely to produce negative effects on the market and to jeopardise the objectives pursued by the Community competition rules. Restrictions by object such as price fixing and market sharing reduce output and raise prices, leading to a misallocation of resources, because goods and services demanded by customers are not produced. They also lead to a reduction in consumer welfare, because consumers have to pay higher prices for the goods and services in question.

22. The assessment of whether or not an agreement has as its object the restriction of competition is based on a number of factors. These factors include, in particular, the content of the agreement and the objective aims pursued by it. It may also be necessary to consider the context in which it is (to be) applied and the actual conduct and behaviour of the parties on the market. In other words, an examination of the facts underlying the agreement and the specific circumstances in which it operates may be required before it can be concluded whether a particular restriction constitutes a restriction of competition by object. The way in which an agreement is actually implemented may reveal a restriction by object even where the formal agreement does not contain an express provision to that effect. Evidence of subjective intent on the part of the parties to restrict competition is a relevant factor but not a necessary condition.

23. Non-exhaustive guidance on what constitutes restrictions by object can be found in Commission block exemption regulations, guidelines and notices. Restrictions that are blacklisted in block exemptions or identified as hardcore restrictions in guidelines and notices are generally considered by the Commission to constitute restrictions by object. In the case of horizontal agreements restrictions of competition by object include price fixing, output limitation and sharing of markets and customers. As regards vertical agreements the category of restrictions by object includes, in particular, fixed and minimum resale price maintenance and restrictions providing absolute territorial protection, including restrictions on passive sales.

The determination of whether or not an agreement has as its object or effect the prevention, restriction, or distortion of competition within the internal market is increasingly important in view of the Commission Notice on agreements of minor importance which do not appreciably restrict competition under Article 101(1) of the Treaty on the Functioning of the European Union ('*De Minimis* Notice'), OJ 2014 C291/1, considered next.

13.2.3.1 Agreements of minor importance

The Court of Justice, in Case 5/69 *Volk v Établissements Vervaecke Sprl* [1969] ECR 295, considered the conditions of Article 101(1) TFEU alongside the potential effect on the market. Clearly, the extent to which an agreement may have an effect on a market can vary greatly due to the market strength of the undertakings concerned.

Case 5/69 *Volk v Établissements Vervaecke Sprl* [1969] ECR 295, 302

If an agreement is to be capable of affecting trade between Member States it must be possible to foresee with a sufficient degree of probability on the basis of a set of objective factors of law or of fact that the agreement in question may have an influence, direct or indirect, actual or potential, on the pattern of trade between Member States in such a way that it might hinder the attainment of the objectives of a single market between states. Moreover the prohibition in Article 81(1) [EC, now Article 101(1) TFEU] is applicable only if the agreement in question also has as its object or effect the prevention, restriction or distortion of competition within the common market. Those conditions must be understood by reference to the actual circumstances of the agreement. Consequently an agreement falls outside the prohibition in Article 81 when it has only an insignificant effect on the markets, taking into account the weak position which the persons concerned have on the market of the product in question. …

This passage of the judgment draws attention to the fact that where an agreement's effect on the market does not meet a particular level (or has only an insignificant effect upon it), the agreement will fall outside Article 101(1) TFEU. Thus it recognizes a 'safe harbour' or a *de minimis* standard. However, the Court failed in *Volk* to quantify the relevant level against which that agreement's effect is to be assessed.

de minimis
From the Latin, meaning 'of minor importance'.

THINKING POINT

Why should an appreciable effect on the market be required? Does this mean that smaller undertakings can effectively behave as they would like?

The Commission Notice on agreements of minor importance which do not appreciably restrict competition under Article 101(1) of the Treaty on the Functioning of the European Union ('*De Minimis* Notice'), OJ 2014 C291/1, sets out the Commission's view of *de minimis* agreements.

Commission Notice on agreements of minor importance which do not appreciably restrict competition under Article 101(1) of the Treaty on the Functioning of the European Union ('*De Minimis* Notice'), OJ 2014 C291/1

1. Article 101(1) of the Treaty on the Functioning of the European Union prohibits agreements between undertakings which may affect trade between Member States and which have as their object or effect the prevention, restriction or distortion of competition within the

internal market. The Court of Justice of the European Union has clarified that that provision is not applicable where the impact of the agreement on trade between Member States or on competition is not appreciable.

2. The Court of Justice has also clarified that an agreement which may affect trade between Member States and which has as its object the prevention, restriction or distortion of competition within the internal market constitutes, by its nature and independently of any concrete effects that it may have, an appreciable restriction of competition. This Notice therefore does not cover agreements which have as their object the prevention, restriction or distortion of competition within the internal market.

Paragraph 2 sees a departure from the approach taken in the 2001 *De Minimis* Notice (Commission Notice on agreements of minor importance which do not appreciably restrict competition under Article 81(1) of the Treaty establishing the European Community, OJ 2001 C 368/13) in that it is made clear that agreements which have as their *object* the prevention, restriction, or distortion of competition cannot benefit from the Notice. This builds upon the decision in Case 226/11 *Expedia Inc v Autorité de la concurrence and others* EU:C:2012:795 concerning a number of agreements between SNCF and Expedia in relation to the sale of train tickets and travel over the Internet. It was clear that the agreements in question breached Article 101(1) TFEU, but the market shares fell below those provided in the *De Minimis* Notice. The national court made a reference to the Court of Justice under Article 267 TFEU regarding the applicability of the Notice. The Court of Justice, in considering the question before it, drew attention to the difference between 'infringements by object' and 'infringements by effect'.

Case 226/11 *Expedia Inc v Autorité de la concurrence and others* EU:C:2012:795

36. In that regard, the Court has emphasised that the distinction between 'infringements by object' and 'infringements by effect' arises from the fact that certain forms of collusion between undertakings can be regarded, by their very nature, as being injurious to the proper functioning of normal competition (Case C-209/07 Beef Industry Development Society and Barry Brothers ('BIDS') [2008] ECR I-8637, paragraph 17, and Case C-8/08 T-Mobile Netherlands and Others [2009] ECR I-4529, paragraph 29).

37. It must therefore be held that an agreement that may affect trade between Member States and that has an anti-competitive object constitutes, by its nature and independently of any concrete effect that it may have, an appreciable restriction on competition.

38. In light of the above, the answer to the question referred is that Article 101(1) TFEU and Article 3(2) of Regulation No 1/2003 must be interpreted as not precluding a national competition authority from applying Article 101(1) TFEU to an agreement between

undertakings that may affect trade between Member States, but that does not reach the thresholds specified by the Commission in its de minimis notice, provided that that agreement constitutes an appreciable restriction of competition within the meaning of that provision.

The Court of Justice therefore concluded that an 'infringement by object' in itself has an appreciable effect on competition, even though the relevant market share may fall below the thresholds set out.

However, the thresholds remain important when considering agreements that have as their *effect* the prevention, restriction, or distortion of competition. The 2014 *De Minimis* Notice retains the thresholds set out in the 2001 *De Minimis* Notice. Remember, though, that market shares can be determined only with reference to a 'relevant market'. This concept is discussed in detail in Chapter 14 in relation to Article 102 TFEU, but is equally applicable to Article 101 TFEU.

Commission Notice on agreements of minor importance which do not appreciably restrict competition under Article 101(1) of the Treaty on the Functioning of the European Union ('*De Minimis* Notice'), OJ 2014 C291/1

8. The Commission holds the view that agreements between undertakings which may affect trade between Member States and which may have as their effect the prevention, restriction or distortion of competition within the internal market, do not appreciably restrict competition within the meaning of Article 101(1) of the Treaty:
   - if the aggregate market share held by the parties to the agreement does not exceed 10 per cent on any of the relevant markets affected by the agreement, where the agreement is made between undertakings which are actual or potential competitors on any of those markets (agreements between competitors); or
   - if the market share held by each of the parties to the agreement does not exceed 15 per cent on any of the relevant markets affected by the agreement, where the agreement is made between undertakings which are not actual or potential competitors on any of those markets (agreements between non-competitors).

   In cases where it is difficult to classify the agreement as either an agreement between competitors or an agreement between non-competitors the 10 per cent threshold is applicable.

However, the safe harbour provided by the *De Minimis* Notice does not apply to all types of agreement. Point 13 of the Notice reiterates the approach in relation to agreements that have as their object the prevention, restriction, or distortion of competition, as set out in points 1 and 2. Furthermore, agreements containing 'hardcore restrictions' that are listed in block exemption Regulations are also unable to benefit from the Notice.

Commission Notice on agreements of minor importance which do not appreciably restrict competition under Article 101(1) of the Treaty on the Functioning of the European Union ('*De Minimis* Notice'), OJ 2014 C291/1

13. In view of the clarification of the Court of Justice referred to in point 2, this Notice does not cover agreements which have as their object the prevention, restriction or distortion of competition within the internal market. The Commission will thus not apply the safe harbour created by the market share thresholds set out in points 8, 9, 10 and 11 to such agreements. For instance, as regards agreements between competitors, the Commission will not apply the principles set out in this Notice to, in particular, agreements containing restrictions which, directly or indirectly, have as their object: a) the fixing of prices when selling products to third parties; b) the limitation of output or sales; or c) the allocation of markets or customers. Likewise, the Commission will not apply the safe harbour created by those market share thresholds to agreements containing any of the restrictions that are listed as hardcore restrictions in any current or future Commission block exemption regulation, which are considered by the Commission to generally constitute restrictions by object.

These 'hardcore' restrictions, such as price-fixing and market-sharing, will therefore not enjoy the protection that the *De Minimis* Notice affords.

13.2.3.2 Prevention, restriction, and distortion of competition

Article 101(1) TFEU lists examples of anti-competitive behaviour.

Article 101(1) TFEU

[...]

(a) directly or indirectly fix purchase or selling prices or any other trading conditions;

(b) limit or control production, markets, technical development, or investment;

(c) share markets or sources of supply;

(d) apply dissimilar conditions to equivalent transactions with other trading parties, thereby placing them at a competitive disadvantage;

(e) make the conclusion of contracts subject to acceptance by the other parties of supplementary obligations which, by their nature or according to commercial usage, have no connection with the subject of such contracts.

It is a non-exhaustive list, but it includes agreements or individual restrictions that would amount to a 'prevention, restriction or distortion of competition'. It should be noted that there is no obvious distinction drawn between these terms.

13.3 Article 101(2) TFEU

Article 101(2) TFEU provides as follows.

Article 101(2) TFEU

Any agreements or decisions prohibited pursuant to this Article shall be automatically void.

However, if it is possible to sever (remove) restrictive clauses from an agreement, only those clauses will be void. Joined Cases 56 & 58/64 *Établissements Consten SaRL and Grundig-Verkaufs-GmbH v Commission* [1966] ECR 299 provides an illustration of such.

Joined Cases 56 & 58/64 *Établissements Consten SaRL and Grundig-Verkaufs-GmbH v Commission* [1966] ECR 299, 344

The provision in Article 85(2) [EC, now Article 101(2) TFEU] that agreements prohibited pursuant to Article 85 shall be automatically void applies only to those parts of the agreement which are subject to the prohibition, or to the agreement as a whole if those parts do not appear to be severable from the agreement itself. The Commission should, therefore, either have confined itself in the operative part of the contested Decision to declaring that an infringement lay in those parts only of the agreement which came within the prohibition, or else it should have set out in the preamble to the Decision the reasons why those parts did not appear to it to be severable from the whole agreement.

13.4 Article 101(3) TFEU: exemption from Article 101(1)

Article 101(3) TFEU provides that Article 101(1) may be declared inapplicable to any agreement or category of agreements between undertakings, any decision or category of decisions by associations of undertakings, or any concerted practice or category of concerted practices that contributes to improving the production or distribution of goods, or to promoting technical or economic progress, while allowing consumers a fair share of the resulting benefit, and which does not impose on the undertakings concerned restrictions that are not indispensable to the attainment of these objectives or afford such undertakings the possibility of eliminating competition in respect of a substantial part of the products in question.

REVIEW QUESTION

Can you identify the four elements to Article 101(3) TFEU?

Answer: The first two are expressed as positive requirements, whilst the latter two are expressed in the negative. In short, they are (a) that the agreements, etc must contribute to improving production, distribution, promoting technical or economic progress and (b) consumers must benefit *and* there should be (c) no unnecessary restrictions (ie proportionality) and (d) no substantial elimination of competition.

The wording used is clear that the exemption in Article 101(3) TFEU can apply both to individual agreements that are not covered by any of the block exemptions (regulations exempting certain groups of agreements) and to particular types of agreement that have been covered by a block exemption.

?! THINKING POINT

Why do you think Article 101(3) TFEU makes reference both to agreements, decisions, or concerted practices *and* categories of agreements, decisions, or concerted practices?

13.4.1 Individual exemption

Under Council Regulation (EC) No 1/2003 of 16 December 2002 on the implementation of the rules on competition laid down in Articles 81 and 82 of the Treaty [now Articles 101 and 102 TFEU], OJ 2003 L1/1, the main circumstance in which the question of whether an agreement is individually exempted will arise will be in relation to it being raised as a defence to enforcement proceedings by the Commission or national competition authorities (NCAs) or, indeed, in private actions against an undertaking. This is in stark contrast to the position before Regulation 1/2003, whereby it was, in principle, the Commission alone that had the power to pronounce whether Article 101(3) TFEU applied. Guidance on individual exemption is provided by Commission Notice: Guidelines on the application of Article 81(3) of the Treaty [now Article 101(3) TFEU], OJ 2004 C101/97.

13.4.1.1 Improving production or distribution of goods or promoting technical or economic progress

The Commission's 2004 guidelines concerning the first condition refer to 'efficiency gains'.

Commission Notice, Guidelines on the application of Article 81(3) of the Treaty [now Article 101(3) TFEU], OJ 2004 C101/97

50. The purpose of the first condition of Article 81(3) [EC, now Article 101(3) TFEU] is to define the types of efficiency gains that can be taken into account and be subject to the further tests of the second and third conditions of Article 81(3). The aim of the analysis is to ascertain what are the objective benefits created by the agreement and what is the economic importance of such efficiencies. Given that for Article 81(3) to apply the pro-competitive effects flowing from the agreement must outweigh its anti-competitive effects, it is necessary to verify what is the link between the agreement and the claimed efficiencies and what is the value of these efficiencies.

These efficiency gains are categorized in the following way by the Commission.

Commission Notice, Guidelines on the application of Article 81(3) of the Treaty [now Article 101(3) TFEU], OJ 2004 C101/97

56. In the case of claimed cost efficiencies the undertakings invoking the benefit of Article 81(3) [EC, Article 101(3) TFEU] must as accurately as reasonably possible calculate or estimate the value of the efficiencies and describe in detail how the amount has been computed. They must also describe the method(s) by which the efficiencies have been or will be achieved. The data submitted must be verifiable so that there can be a sufficient degree of certainty that the efficiencies have materialized or are likely to materialize.
57. In the case of claimed efficiencies in the form of new or improved products and other non-cost based efficiencies, the undertakings claiming the benefit of Article 81(3) must describe and explain in detail what is the nature of the efficiencies and how and why they constitute an objective economic benefit.

Thus it would seem that benefits can be both cost-based improvements (para 56) and quality-based improvements (para 57). It is clear from the Notice that there must be a sufficient and direct causal link between the restrictive agreement and the claimed efficiencies.

In Commission Decision 94/986/EEC of 21 December 1994 relating to a proceeding pursuant to Article 85 of the EC Treaty and Article 53 of the EEA Agreement (IV/34.252 – *Philips-Osram*) OJ 1994 L378/37, the two parties entered into a joint venture agreement regarding the manufacture and sale of certain lead glass tubing for incandescent and fluorescent lamps. The joint venture company was to be based in Belgium, where the relevant factory had the necessary equipment, including complex and expensive hazardous gas conversion equipment to reduce the problems inherent in the production of lead glass—namely, dangerous emissions.

In considering the relevant efficiency gains, the Commission Decision stated as follows.

Commission Decision 94/986/EEC of 21 December 1994 relating to a proceeding pursuant to Article 85 of the EC Treaty and Article 53 of the EEA Agreement (IV/34.252 – *Philips-Osram*) OJ 1994 L378/37

(25) The joint venture achieves rationalization of production by allowing Osram to eliminate its obsolete facilities in Berlin and allowing Philips to relocate certain non-lead glass production from Lommel to other glass factories in the Philips group. The joint venture will offer greater flexibility in quantities and types of product and a lower risk of breakdown, and will have a production capacity substantially higher than that resulting from the combination of the production capacity of the facilities of the parent companies in the EEA [European Economic Area] for the production of lead glass prior to the creation of the present joint venture. The joint venture will result in lower total energy usage and a better prospect of realizing energy reduction and waste emission programmes.

In addition, the parties will concentrate their R&D [research and development] activities in Philips' laboratories, achieving savings and economies of scale and a concentration of effort to tackle properly the common challenge of developing lead-free materials.

Thus the efficiencies in this case were both cost-based and quality-based.

13.4.1.2 Allowing consumers a fair share of the resulting benefit

Commission Notice, Guidelines on the application of Article 81(3) of the Treaty [now Article 101(3) TFEU], OJ 2004 C101/97

85. The concept of 'fair share' implies that the pass-on of benefits must at least compensate consumers for any actual or likely negative impact caused to them by the restriction of competition found under Article 81(1) [EC, now Article 101(1) TFEU]. In line with the overall objective of Article 81 to prevent anti-competitive agreements, the net effect of the agreement must at least be neutral from the point of view of those consumers directly or likely to be affected by the agreement. If such consumers are worse off following the agreement, the second condition of Article 81(3) is not fulfilled. The positive effects of an agreement must be balanced against and compensate for its negative effects on consumers. When that is the case consumers are not harmed by the agreement. Moreover, society as a whole benefits where the efficiencies lead either to fewer resources being used to produce the output consumed or to the production of more valuable products and thus to a more efficient allocation of resources.
86. It is not required that consumers receive a share of each and every efficiency gain identified under the first condition. It suffices that sufficient benefits are passed on to compensate for the negative effects of the restrictive agreement. In that case consumers obtain a fair share of the overall benefits. If a restrictive agreement is likely to lead to higher prices, consumers must be fully compensated through increased quality or other benefits. If not, the second condition of Article 81(3) is not fulfilled.

13.4.1.3 No restrictions that are not indispensable

The third condition for individual exemption under Article 101(3) TFEU amounts to the application of the principle of proportionality. Thus it is not simply enough that benefits are gained and that the consumer enjoys these benefits. Recognizing the restrictions placed upon free competition, it is essential that those restrictions have been achieved in a way that goes no further than is necessary.

Commission Decision 94/986/EEC of 21 December 1994 relating to a proceeding pursuant to Article 85 of the EC Treaty and Article 53 of the EEA Agreement (IV/34.252 – *Philips-Osram*) OJ 1994 L378/37

(28) The joint venture is indispensable for achieving the improvements in terms of rationalization, flexibility, energy and cost savings, pooling of R&D efforts and lower emissions resulting from the declaration of intent.

> An alternative to the joint venture would have been for Osram to set up a new facility. However this would have resulted in a disproportionately high and risky investment, in terms of the time required for the new facility to be operational and in terms of the money required not only to set up the factory but also to install the necessary equipment to comply with environmental protection requirements. In this respect, Philips' current facility can be adapted much more quickly and has the environmental protection equipment already installed.
>
> Another alternative would have been for Osram to enter into a long-term supply agreement with Philips (and possibly other suppliers). Osram has, however, explicitly stated that it was not interested in such an arrangement because it would have made Osram very dependent. As to Philips, such an agreement might not have provided sufficient certainty to make on its own the investments now made. This is the more so because of the limited size and the mature character of the market. The improvements resulting from the joint venture might therefore not have been achieved. Such an alternative would, therefore, most likely have resulted in a smaller quantity of lead glass being available for third parties than will be available due to the joint venture, the capacity of which will indeed be bigger than the combined previous capacity of the parent companies in the EEA.
>
> As to the possibility of Osram obtaining supplies from its Sylvania facilities in the USA, it is sufficient to indicate that Osram Sylvania's spare capacity in the United States is not big enough to cover all of Osram's European lead glass needs.

It is therefore clear that some analysis is required by the Court of the alternative ways in which the benefits claimed by the undertakings could be achieved. In *Philips/Osram*, the Court of Justice held that the competitive restrictions were proportionate to the benefits by analysing the alternative ways in which such benefits may be realized.

13.4.1.4 No elimination of competition

Commission Notice, Guidelines on the application of Article 81(3) of the Treaty [now Article 101(3) TFEU], OJ 2004 C101/97

> 105. According to the fourth condition of Article 81(3) [EC, now Article 101(3) TFEU] the agreement must not afford the undertakings concerned the possibility of eliminating competition in respect of a substantial part of the products concerned. Ultimately the protection of rivalry and the competitive process is given priority over potentially pro-competitive efficiency gains which could result from restrictive agreements. The last condition of Article 81(3) recognises the fact that rivalry between undertakings is an essential driver of economic efficiency, including dynamic efficiencies in the shape of innovation. In other words, the ultimate aim of Article 81 is to protect the competitive process. When competition is eliminated the competitive process is brought to an end and short-term efficiency gains are outweighed by longer-term losses stemming inter alia from expenditures incurred by the incumbent to maintain its position (rent seeking), misallocation of resources, reduced innovation and higher prices.

?! **THINKING POINT**

Which fundamental principle of EU law can you identify here?

13.4.2 Block exemption

As has been explained in 13.4.1, Article 101(3) TFEU allows Article 101(1) to be declared inapplicable to categories of agreements in addition to individual agreements.

Block exemption Regulations remove certain categories of agreement from the Article 101(1) TFEU prohibition. They arise in a number of different areas and include specific industries or sectors, specialization agreements, technology transfer agreements, and research and development agreements (amongst others). One particularly wide block exemption will be considered in detail by way of example.

13.4.2.1 Regulation 330/2010

Commission Regulation (EU) No 330/2010 of 20 April 2010 on the application of Article 101(3) of the Treaty on the Functioning of the European Union to categories of vertical agreements and concerted practices, OJ 2010 L102/1, concerns a block exemption for vertical supply and distribution agreements. It provides an excellent example of the Commission's effect-based approach. Indeed, the words of Joaquin Almunia, Vice-President of the Commission and Competition Commissioner, when announcing the block exemption (which replaced Commission Regulation (EC) No 2790/1999 of 22 December 1999 on the application of Article 81(3) of the Treaty to categories of vertical agreements and concerted practices, OJ 1999 L336/21), are notable in this regard.

European Commission, 'Antitrust: Commission adopts revised competition rules for distribution of goods and services', Press release IP/10/445, 20 April 2010

'A clear and predictable application of the competition rules to supply and distribution agreements is essential for the competitiveness of the EU economy and for consumer welfare. Distributors should be free to satisfy consumer demand, whether in brick and mortar shops or on the Internet. The rules adopted today will ensure that consumers can buy goods and services at the best available prices wherever they are located in the EU while leaving companies without market power essentially free to organise their sales network as they see best,' said Vice-President of the Commission and Competition Commissioner Joaquin Almunia.

?! THINKING POINT

Think back to the concepts of horizontal and vertical agreements. Can you remember the difference between them? Why do you think a block exemption for vertical agreements exists, whilst there is no comparable block exemption for horizontal agreements?

Commission Regulation (EU) No 330/2010 of 20 April 2010 on the application of Article 101(3) of the Treaty on the Functioning of the European Union to categories of vertical agreements and concerted practices, OJ 2010 L102/1

Article 2

Exemption

1. Pursuant to Article 101(3) of the Treaty and subject to the provisions of this Regulation, it is hereby declared that Article 101(1) of the Treaty shall not apply to vertical agreements.

   This exemption shall apply to the extent that such agreements contain vertical restraints.

In broad terms, Article 2 of Regulation 330/2010 exempts from Article 101(1) TFEU vertical agreements relating to the conditions under which the parties may purchase, sell, or resell certain goods or services, to the extent that these agreements contain otherwise prohibited restrictions. These include, for instance, exclusive distribution, distribution franchise, and selective distribution agreements.

Commission Regulation (EU) No 330/2010 of 20 April 2010 on the application of Article 101(3) of the Treaty on the Functioning of the European Union to categories of vertical agreements and concerted practices, OJ 2010 L102/1

Article 3

Market share threshold

1. The exemption provided for in Article 2 shall apply on condition that the market share held by the supplier does not exceed 30 per cent of the relevant market on which it sells the contract goods or services and the market share held by the buyer does not exceed 30 per cent of the relevant market on which it purchases the contract goods or services.

The exemption is therefore subject to market-share thresholds. It applies only where both the supplier's market share does not exceed 30 per cent of the relevant market on which it sells the contract goods or services and the buyer's market share does not exceed 30 per cent of the relevant market on which it purchases the contract goods or services.

Commission Regulation (EU) No 330/2010 of 20 April 2010 on the application of Article 101(3) of the Treaty on the Functioning of the European Union to categories of vertical agreements and concerted practices, OJ 2010 L102/1

Article 4

Restrictions that remove the benefit of the block exemption—hardcore restrictions

The exemption provided for in Article 2 shall not apply to vertical agreements which, directly or indirectly, in isolation or in combination with other factors under the control of the parties, have as their object:

(a) the restriction of the buyer's ability to determine its sale price, without prejudice to the possibility of the supplier to impose a maximum sale price or recommend a sale price, provided that they do not amount to a fixed or minimum sale price as a result of pressure from, or incentives offered by, any of the parties;

(b) the restriction of the territory into which, or of the customers to whom, a buyer party to the agreement, without prejudice to a restriction on its place of establishment, may sell the contract goods or services, except:

(i) the restriction of active sales into the exclusive territory or to an exclusive customer group reserved to the supplier or allocated by the supplier to another buyer, where such a restriction does not limit sales by the customers of the buyer,

(ii) the restriction of sales to end users by a buyer operating at the wholesale level of trade,

(iii) the restriction of sales by the members of a selective distribution system to unauthorised distributors within the territory reserved by the supplier to operate that system, and

(iv) the restriction of the buyer's ability to sell components, supplied for the purposes of incorporation, to customers who would use them to manufacture the same type of goods as those produced by the supplier;

(c) the restriction of active or passive sales to end users by members of a selective distribution system operating at the retail level of trade, without prejudice to the possibility of prohibiting a member of the system from operating out of an unauthorised place of establishment;

(d) the restriction of cross-supplies between distributors within a selective distribution system, including between distributors operating at different level of trade;

(e) the restriction, agreed between a supplier of components and a buyer who incorporates those components, of the supplier's ability to sell the components as spare parts to end-users or to repairers or other service providers not entrusted by the buyer with the repair or servicing of its goods.

The benefit of the block exemption does not apply to vertical agreements containing certain hardcore restrictions, listed in Article 4 of the Regulation.

The impact of this is that an agreement containing hardcore restrictions is, in its entirety, outside the scope of the block exemption. The offending clauses cannot be removed.

Commission Regulation (EU) No 330/2010 of 20 April 2010 on the application of Article 101(3) of the Treaty on the Functioning of the European Union to categories of vertical agreements and concerted practices, OJ 2010 L102/1

Article 5

Excluded restrictions

1. The exemption provided for in Article 2 shall not apply to the following obligations contained in vertical agreements:

   (a) any direct or indirect non-compete obligation, the duration of which is indefinite or exceeds five years;

   (b) any direct or indirect obligation causing the buyer, after termination of the agreement, not to manufacture, purchase, sell or resell goods or services;

   (c) any direct or indirect obligation causing the members of a selective distribution system not to sell the brands of particular competing suppliers.

   For the purposes of point (a) of the first subparagraph, a non-compete obligation which is tacitly renewable beyond a period of five years shall be deemed to have been concluded for an indefinite duration.

Article 5 of the Regulation also provides that the block exemption does not apply to certain obligations contained in agreements. In contrast to Article 4, although the Article 5 restrictions themselves fall outside the block exemption, they may be severed, allowing the remainder of the agreement to be block-exempted. Severable restrictions comprise certain non-compete obligations (obligations on the buyer not to sell competing goods), including non-compete clauses (obligations causing the buyer not to manufacture, purchase, sell, or resell goods or services that compete with the contract goods or services) exceeding five years.

Any restriction not referred to in Articles 4 and 5 is permitted.

SUMMARY

- Article 101(1) TFEU prohibits agreements between undertakings, decisions by associations of undertakings, and concerted practices that may affect trade between Member States and which have as their object or effect the prevention, restriction, or distortion of competition within the internal market.
- All three elements must be satisfied to establish a breach of Article 101(1) TFEU.
- The term 'undertaking' has been interpreted widely and includes any legal or natural person engaged in some form of economic or commercial activity.

- The term 'agreement' is interpreted widely and includes both formally and non-formally constituted agreements. In this regard, it would seem that the emphasis is on substance above form.
- In relation to decisions by associations of undertakings, the focus is upon trade associations, but, as with other elements of Article 101(1) TFEU, this has been interpreted widely to include professional associations.
- A 'concerted practice' is a form of coordination between undertakings that, without having reached the stage at which an agreement properly so-called has been concluded, knowingly substitutes practical cooperation between them for the risks of competition (*Dyestuffs*). This should be compared with the behaviour of a true oligopolistic market (*Woodpulp*).
- Article 101(1) TFEU applies to both horizontal and vertical agreements.
- The effect on trade between Member States will emerge wherever it is 'possible to foresee with a sufficient degree of probability on the basis of a set of objective factors of law or of fact that the agreement in question may have an influence, direct or indirect, actual or potential, on the pattern of trade between Member States' (*STM*).
- The 'legal and economic context' of an arrangement will also be taken into account (*Wilkin*).
- *Object or effect: prevention, restriction, or distortion of competition*: these are all alternative requirements. Note the important determination under the new (2014) *De Minimis* Notice.
- In relation to agreements of minor importance, an agreement is caught by Article 101(1) TFEU only if it has an 'appreciable' effect on the market (*Volk*).
- The prevention, restriction, and distortion of competition cover all forms of anti-competitive behaviour. Article 101(1)(a)–(e) TFEU provides examples.
- Any agreements or decisions prohibited pursuant to Article 101(2) TFEU shall be automatically void. However, if it is possible to sever (remove) restrictive clauses from an agreement, only those clauses will be void.
- Article 101(3) TFEU applies to both 'individual exemptions' and 'block exemptions'.
- To qualify for individual exemption, agreements must contribute to improving production, distribution, promoting technical or economic progress *and* must benefit the consumer *and* there must be no unnecessary restrictions *and* no substantial elimination of competition.
- Block exemptions apply to categories of agreement.
- Regulation 330/2010 comprises a block exemption for vertical agreements.

FURTHER READING

Articles

A Jones, '*Woodpulp*: Concerted Practice and/or Conscious Parallelism?' (1993) 14 ECL Rev 273

A detailed look at the concerted practice/oligopolistic market issue.

L Kjølbye, 'The New Commission Guidelines on the Application of Article 81(3): An Economic Approach to Article 81' (2004) 25(9) ECL Rev 566

Consideration of application and policy surrounding what is now Article 101(3) TFEU.

B Meyring, '*T-Mobile*: Further Confusion on Information Exchanges between Competitors—C-8/08 *T-Mobile Netherlands and Others* [2009] ECR I-4529' (2009) 1(1) Journal of European Competition Law & Practice Advance 30

Detailed focus on a contemporary case within Article 101 TFEU.

D Roitman, 'Legal Uncertainty for Vertical Distribution Agreements: The Block Exemption Regulation 2790/99 (BER) and Related Aspects of the New Regulation 1/2003' (2006) 27(5) ECL Rev 261

Historically interesting for consideration of change in approach to vertical agreements.

Books

C Graham, *EU and UK Competition Law* (London: Pearson, 2013)

A specialized competition law text, with substantive coverage of Article 101 TFEU and the EU/UK approach.

O Odudu, *The Boundaries of EC Competition Law: The Scope of Article 81* (Oxford: Oxford University Press, 2006)

A comprehensive account of Article 101 TFEU.

QUESTION

Kettles r us Ltd (Kettles), a UK-based kettle manufacturer with a 28 per cent share of the relevant market, is in supply negotiations with PotsnPans Ltd, an Irish wholesaler with an 18 per cent share of the relevant market. PotsnPans is very keen to make an agreement with Kettles for its unique products, especially given Kettles' willingness to grant PotsnPans sole wholesaler status in Ireland. In return, PotsnPans is considering agreeing not to sell any other kettles for an indefinite period and to accept the resale prices stipulated by Kettles.

Advise the parties as to the validity of the proposed agreement under Article 101 TFEU and consider whether Regulation 330/2010 applies as it stands, as well as what amendments could or should be made.

To view an outline answer to this question plus further resources to support your EU law studies, visit the Online Resources for this book at **www.oup.com/uk/eulaw-complete4e**

14 Competition law: Article 102 TFEU

KEY POINTS

By the end of this chapter, you should be able to:

- explain the key elements of an abuse of a dominant position contained in Article 102 TFEU;
- explain and analyse the concept of dominance;
- explain, analyse, and apply the concept of relevant markets, including economic indicators; and
- identify and apply abusive behaviour.

INTRODUCTION

Whereas Article 101 TFEU applies to restrictive arrangements and concerted practices between businesses, the focus of Article 102 TFEU is the abuse of market power, or 'dominance', within the internal market. It is important to note that dominance itself is not prohibited; the emphasis is upon an abuse of such a position to the extent that it is capable of affecting trade. Like Article 101 TFEU, Article 102 is enforced by the European Commission, national competition authorities (NCAs), and national courts under powers conferred by Council Regulation (EC) No 1/2003 of 16 December 2002 on the implementation of the rules on competition laid down in Articles 81 and 82 of the Treaty [now Articles 101 and 102 TFEU], OJ 2003 L1/1.

For example, suppose that Bagsaflavour, a UK teabag manufacturer with a 70 per cent share of the relevant market supplying teabags across the European Union (EU), becomes alarmed to hear of a potential competitor emerging in Western Europe. It therefore contacts each of its customers in the UK, offering loyalty discounts for those willing to commit to only buying teabags from Bagsaflavour. However, such discounts are not available in Romania, where demand for UK tea is exceptionally high. As a result, Bagsaflavour has been charging wholesalers in Romania prices three times as high as those in the UK.

Bagsaflavour appears to have an erratic pricing structure aimed at removing competition and exploiting customers in countries in which competition does not exist or is reduced. Such behaviour is likely to be a breach of Article 102 TFEU.

14.1 Outline of Article 102 TFEU

Article 102 TFEU

Any abuse by one or more undertakings of a dominant position within the internal market or in a substantial part of it shall be prohibited as incompatible with the internal market in so far as it may affect trade between Member States.

Such abuse may, in particular, consist in:

(a) directly or indirectly imposing unfair purchase or selling prices or other unfair trading conditions;

(b) limiting production, markets or technical development to the prejudice of consumers;

(c) applying dissimilar conditions to equivalent transactions with other trading parties, thereby placing them at a competitive disadvantage;

(d) making the conclusion of contracts subject to acceptance by the other parties of supplementary obligations which, by their nature or according to commercial usage, have no connection with the subject of such contracts.

Article 102 TFEU is similar in approach to Article 101 in that a clear prohibition is set out, followed by examples of behaviour that would amount to a breach. It prohibits, as incompatible with the internal market, '[a]ny abuse by one or more undertakings of a dominant position within the internal market or in a substantial part of it ... in so far as it may affect trade between Member States'.

14.2 Article 102 TFEU: the prohibition

The undertaking (a) must have a dominant position within the internal market or in a substantial part of it, which (b) it must have abused, and (c) the abuse must be capable of affecting trade between Member States.

?! THINKING POINT

Article 102 TFEU can be broken into three distinct elements. Can you identify them?

If all three elements are satisfied, a breach of Article 102 TFEU is established. If any one of the three elements is not satisfied, the behaviour does not fall within the prohibition within Article 102.

As with the application of Article 101 TFEU, it is therefore important in applying Article 102 to take a structured approach.

14.2.1 Undertakings

The term 'undertakings' has the same meaning as in Article 101 TFEU. Thus, with reference to Case C-41/90 *Höfner and Elser* [1991] ECR I-1979, it can be said that it has been interpreted widely and includes any legal or natural person engaged in some form of economic or commercial activity.

14.3 Dominant position

In Case 27/76 *United Brands Co v Commission ('Chiquita Bananas')* [1978] ECR 207, at para 65, the Court of Justice set out its classic definition of a dominant position as a 'position of economic strength enjoyed by an undertaking which enables it to prevent effective competition being maintained on the relevant market by giving it the power to behave to an appreciable extent independently of its competitors, customers and ultimately of its consumers'.

It is important to appreciate that the definition given in *Chiquita Bananas* draws attention to a number of things. First, it identifies the fact that the position of dominance may enable the undertaking to affect competition. This could be done by using short-term price cuts, for example, leading to competitors losing business and being forced out of business. It also identifies the fact that a dominant position may enable an undertaking to exploit customers, for example by linked sales or by charging unfair prices.

In addition to this, the definition in *Chiquita Bananas* makes it clear that dominance is assessed in relation to a relevant market. To simply talk of dominance in the abstract is meaningless, but by looking first for the relevant market and only then assessing an undertaking's dominance in relation to that market, a true picture of the dominance or otherwise of an undertaking can be found.

14.3.1 Relevant market

There are three aspects to the relevant market:

- the relevant product market (RPM);
- the relevant geographic market (RGM); and
- the relevant temporal (or seasonal) market (RTM).

The RPM and RGM will always be key considerations in determining the applicability or otherwise of Article 102 TFEU, but only rarely has an RTM been identified by the Court of Justice. However, this has not prevented undertakings from making the argument.

Of course, if dominance is assessed according to a relevant market, it seems clear that an undertaking will always seek to define it in the widest possible terms. In this way, the undertaking is less likely to be dominant and, in turn, dominance not having been established, its behaviour will not be further considered under Article 102 TFEU. However, the Commission will seek to define the relevant market in the narrowest terms such that dominance can be established and the undertaking's behaviour can be assessed against the Article 102 prohibition.

14.3.2 Relevant product market

How do we establish what product market a product actually falls into? It might at first seem to be a relatively straightforward question.

Take, for example, Poshchox, a (fictitious) manufacturer of high-quality chocolate products with a large market share. A potential competitor emerges that is rapidly increasing its own market share and Poshchox responds by slashing its prices below cost, with the intention of driving the competitor out of the market. Such behaviour would demand consideration under Article 102 TFEU, with the first factor to be established being the dominance or otherwise of Poshchox.

?! THINKING POINT

What do you think is the RPM of Poshchox?

If the relevant market is the high-quality chocolate market, Poshchox is likely to be dominant as it has a large market share of this market.

However, if it could be argued that the RPM is general chocolate products, the likelihood that Poshchox is dominant is reduced. Indeed, it may even be possible to argue that the relevant product market is general confectionary products. In this scenario, the likelihood of Poshchox being dominant is reduced further still.

REVIEW QUESTION

Why do you think such emphasis is placed upon the establishment of the RPM?

Answer: The RPM is likely to be the crucial factor in determining whether or not an undertaking is dominant. If there is no dominance, there is no breach of Article 102 TFEU.

Therefore, Poshchox is likely to argue that it is in the general confectionary market as the likelihood of it being dominant in this market is far less than if the RPM is the high-quality chocolate market.

14.3.2.1 Establishing the RPM

The Commission uses a consideration of product substitutability to determine the RPM. This comprises two distinct elements and an analysis of both is required. The first, demand substitutability, is concerned with the behaviour of customers, whilst the second is concerned with the behaviour of other suppliers.

14.3.2.2 Demand substitutability

Demand substitutability (often referred to as cross-elasticity of demand) requires a consideration of the extent to which a customer would be willing, and indeed able, to substitute the product in question for an alternative product—in other words, whether a customer would consider one product to be a substitute for another. Where two products are considered to be substitutable in this way, they can be seen to be in the same product market and the RPM will include both products.

Thus, considering Poshchox, would a consumer be willing to accept a candy bar as a substitute? If not, the products are in different product markets.

Case 27/76 *United Brands Co v Commission ('Chiquita Bananas')* [1978] ECR 207 is a useful case with which to illustrate demand substitutability. In this case, a Commission Decision had found United Brands, a banana producer, to have abused its dominant position contrary to Article 102 TFEU. United Brands sought annulment of the Decision and, in so doing, sought to define the RPM more widely as fresh fruit generally. The Commission argued, however, that the RPM was the narrower market for bananas.

Case 27/76 *United Brands Co v Commission ('Chiquita Bananas')* [1978] ECR 207

12. As far as the product market is concerned it is first of all necessary to ascertain whether, as the applicant maintains, bananas are an integral part of the fresh fruit market, because they are reasonably interchangeable by consumers with other kinds of fresh fruit such as apples, oranges, grapes, peaches, strawberries, etc. Or whether the relevant market consists solely of the banana market which includes both branded bananas and unlabelled bananas and is a market sufficiently homogeneous and distinct from the market of other fresh fruit.
13. The applicant submits in support of its argument that bananas compete with other fresh fruit in the same shops, on the same shelves, at prices which can be compared, satisfying the same needs: consumption as a dessert or between meals.
14. The statistics produced show that consumer expenditure on the purchase of bananas is at its lowest between June and December when there is a plentiful supply of domestic fresh fruit on the market.
15. Studies carried out by the Food and Agriculture Organization (FAO) (especially in 1975) confirm that banana prices are relatively weak during the summer months and that the price of apples for example has a statistically appreciable impact on the consumption of bananas in the Federal Republic of Germany.
16. Again according to these studies some easing of prices is noticeable at the end of the year during the 'orange season'.
17. The seasonal peak periods when there is a plentiful supply of other fresh fruit exert an influence not only on the prices but also on the volume of sales of bananas and consequently on the volume of imports thereof.
18. The applicant concludes from these findings that bananas and other fresh fruit form only one market and that [United Brands]'s operations should have been examined in this context for the purpose of any application of Article 86 of the Treaty [now Article 102 TFEU].
19. The Commission maintains that there is a demand for bananas which is distinct from the demand for other fresh fruit especially as the banana is a very important part of the diet of certain sections of the Community [now Union].

20. The specific qualities of the banana influence customer preference and induce him not to readily accept other fruits as a substitute.
21. The Commission draws the conclusion from the studies quoted by the applicant that the influence of the prices and availabilities of other types of fruit on the prices and availabilities of bananas on the relevant market is very ineffective and that these effects are too brief and too spasmodic for such other fruit to be regarded as forming part of the same market as bananas or as a substitute therefor.
22. For the banana to be regarded as forming a market which is sufficiently differentiated from other fruit markets it must be possible for it to be singled out by such special features distinguishing it from other fruits that it is only to a limited extent interchangeable with them and is only exposed to their competition in a way that is hardly perceptible.
23. The ripening of bananas takes place the whole year round without any season having to be taken into account.
24. Throughout the year production exceeds demand and can satisfy it at any time.
25. Owing to this particular feature the banana is a privileged fruit and its production and marketing can be adapted to the seasonal fluctuations of other fresh fruit which are known and can be computed.

[...]

31. The banana has certain characteristics, appearance, taste, softness, seedlessness, easy handling, a constant level of production which enable it to satisfy the constant needs of an important section of the population consisting of the very young, the old and the sick.

[...]

34. It follows from all these considerations that a very large number of consumers having a constant need for bananas are not noticeably or even appreciably enticed away from the consumption of this product by the arrival of other fresh fruit on the market and that even the personal peak periods only affect it for a limited period of time and to a very limited extent from the point of view of substitutability.
35. Consequently the banana market is a market which is sufficiently distinct from the other fresh fruit markets.

Thus, having considered product substitution and cross-elasticity of demand, the Court of Justice agreed with the Commission. It held that bananas are unique, that no other fruit are acceptable as substitutes, and that there is little cross-elasticity of demand. The RPM was therefore the banana market and the dominance of United Brands would be assessed in this particular market.

The consideration of the RPM in *Chiquita Bananas* was governed by the specific qualities of bananas, which meant that no perfect substitute existed. However, there are cases in which it is not the uniqueness of the product itself that has determined the RPM, but rather the specific use for which it is intended. Where a product has a very limited range of uses, it is likely that the RPM will be defined narrowly

14.3.2.3 The Commission's 1997 Notice on the definition of relevant market

The Commission's Notice on the definition of relevant market for the purposes of Community competition law, OJ 1997 C372/5, represents a more quantitative approach (evaluating numerical, measurable information) to product substitutability and the definition of the relevant market. The Commission's test, known as the small, but significant, non-transitory increase in price (SSNIP) test, considers the effect upon consumer choice following a small, but significant (5–10 per cent) permanent increase in the price of a product.

Commission Notice on the definition of relevant market for the purposes of Community competition law, OJ 1997 C372/5

13. Firms are subject to three main sources of competitive constraints: demand substitutability, supply substitutability and potential competition. From an economic point of view, for the definition of the relevant market, demand substitution constitutes the most immediate and effective disciplinary force on the suppliers of a given product, in particular in relation to their pricing decisions. A firm or a group of firms cannot have a significant impact on the prevailing conditions of sale, such as prices, if its customers are in a position to switch easily to available substitute products or to suppliers located elsewhere. Basically, the exercise of market definition consists in identifying the effective alternative sources of supply for the customers of the undertakings involved, in terms both of products/services and of geographic location of suppliers.

[...]

Demand substitution

15. The assessment of demand substitution entails a determination of the range of products which are viewed as substitutes by the consumer. One way of making this determination can be viewed as a speculative experiment, postulating a hypothetical small, lasting change in relative prices and evaluating the likely reactions of customers to that increase. The exercise of market definition focuses on prices for operational and practical purposes, and more precisely on demand substitution arising from small, permanent changes in relative prices. This concept can provide clear indications as to the evidence that is relevant in defining markets.
16. Conceptually, this approach means that, starting from the type of products that the undertakings involved sell and the area in which they sell them, additional products and areas will be included in, or excluded from, the market definition depending on whether competition from these other products and areas affect or restrain sufficiently the pricing of the parties' products in the short term.
17. The question to be answered is whether the parties' customers would switch to readily available substitutes or to suppliers located elsewhere in response to a hypothetical small

(in the range 5 per cent to 10 per cent) but permanent relative price increase in the products and areas being considered. If substitution were enough to make the price increase unprofitable because of the resulting loss of sales, additional substitutes and areas are included in the relevant market. This would be done until the set of products and geographical areas is such that small, permanent increases in relative prices would be profitable. The equivalent analysis is applicable in cases concerning the concentration of buying power, where the starting point would then be the supplier and the price test serves to identify the alternative distribution channels or outlets for the supplier's products. In the application of these principles, careful account should be taken of certain particular situations as described within paragraphs 56 and 58.

18. A practical example of this test can be provided by its application to a merger of, for instance, soft-drink bottlers. An issue to examine in such a case would be to decide whether different flavours of soft drinks belong to the same market. In practice, the question to address would be whether consumers of flavour A would switch to other flavours when confronted with a permanent price increase of 5 per cent to 10 per cent for flavour A. If a sufficient number of consumers would switch to, say, flavour B, to such an extent that the price increase for flavour A would not be profitable owing to the resulting loss of sales, then the market would comprise at least flavours A and B. The process would have to be extended in addition to other available flavours until a set of products is identified for which a price rise would not induce a sufficient substitution in demand.

Thus, if such a permanent, significant increase in relative price would result in customers substituting one product for another, the relevant market should be drawn to include both products. Conversely, if such an increase in price would not have these effects, the products are in separate markets and the RPM should be drawn accordingly.

?! THINKING POINT

Can you identify any problems with such an approach, given the potential for an already distorted market?

The limitations of the SSNIP test are clear when prices are already in excess of competitive prices. This will often be the case when dealing with an allegedly dominant undertaking that has been able to set its prices unaffected by competitive pressures. In such circumstances, to consider the effects of a yet further increase in price between 5–10 per cent may be to distort things considerably. Such an increase may have the result that it would cause customers to switch to a product that would not ordinarily be considered to be in the same product market. Such an argument is referred to by academics as the cellophane fallacy, after the famous US case of *United States v. El Du Pont de Nemours and Co.* 351 US 377 (1956), which involved a consideration of the RPM for cellophane products. However, the SSNIP test continues to be applied to Article 102 TFEU cases.

14.3.2.4 Intermediate markets

It is not necessarily the case that the RPM is considered to be the end product or service. Indeed, in Joined Cases 6 & 7/73 *Istituto Chemioterapico Italiano SpA and Commercial Solvents Corporation v Commission* [1974] ECR 223, Commercial Solvents argued that its refusal to supply aminobutanol—a raw material used in the production of certain anti-tuberculosis drugs—to an Italian pharmaceutical company did not fall within what is now Article 102 TFEU, as it was not dominant within the relevant market. Commercial Solvents argued that the RPM was the market for the drug supplied to the ultimate consumer (the end product) and not, as the Commission had found, the market for the supply of the raw material.

Joined Cases 6 & 7/73 *Istituto Chemioterapico Italiano SpA and Commercial Solvents Corporation v Commission* [1974] ECR 223

22. Contrary to the arguments of the applicants it is in fact possible to distinguish the market in raw material necessary for the manufacture of a product from the market on which the product is sold. An abuse of a dominant position on the market in raw materials may thus have effects restricting competition in the market on which the derivatives of the raw material are sold and these effects must be taken into account in considering the effects of an infringement, even if the market for the derivative does not constitute a self-contained market. The arguments of the applicants in this respect and in consequence their request that an expert's report on this subject be ordered are irrelevant and must be rejected.

The Court of Justice therefore held that the RPM was Commercial Solvent's raw material, aminobutanol. The decision can be seen as emphasizing the fact that the Court of Justice and the Commission will protect not only the end consumer, but also small and medium-sized enterprises (SMEs) at intermediate levels of the process.

14.3.2.5 Supply substitutability

Supply substitutability (often referred to as the cross-elasticity of supply) is concerned with the ability of manufacturers to switch production from one product to another in order to produce a substitutable product. Thus, if an undertaking can quickly and relatively inexpensively switch its production process to enter the product market in question, the RPM may include its product as well as that of the alleged dominant product.

The Commission's 1997 Notice on the definition of relevant market for the purposes of Community competition law, OJ 1997 C372/5, provides a useful explanation of this concept.

Commission Notice on the definition of relevant market for the purposes of Community competition law, OJ 1997 C372/5

20. Supply-side substitutability may also be taken into account when defining markets in those situations in which its effects are equivalent to those of demand substitution in terms of effectiveness and immediacy. This means that suppliers are able to switch production to the relevant products and market them in the short term without incurring significant additional costs or risks in response to small and permanent changes in relative prices. When these conditions are met, the additional production that is put on the market will have a disciplinary effect on the competitive behaviour of the companies involved. Such an impact in terms of effectiveness and immediacy is equivalent to the demand substitution effect.
21. These situations typically arise when companies market a wide range of qualities or grades of one product; even if, for a given final customer or group of consumers, the different qualities are not substitutable, the different qualities will be grouped into one product market, provided that most of the suppliers are able to offer and sell the various qualities immediately and without the significant increases in costs described above. In such cases, the relevant product market will encompass all products that are substitutable in demand and supply, and the current sales of those products will be aggregated so as to give the total value or volume of the market. The same reasoning may lead to group different geographic areas.
22. A practical example of the approach to supply-side substitutability when defining product markets is to be found in the case of paper. Paper is usually supplied in a range of different qualities, from standard writing paper to high quality papers to be used, for instance, to publish art books. From a demand point of view, different qualities of paper cannot be used for any given use, i.e. an art book or a high quality publication cannot be based on lower quality papers. However, paper plants are prepared to manufacture the different qualities, and production can be adjusted with negligible costs and in a short timeframe. In the absence of particular difficulties in distribution, paper manufacturers are able therefore, to compete for orders of the various qualities, in particular if orders are placed with sufficient lead time to allow for modification of production plans. Under such circumstances, the Commission would not define a separate market for each quality of paper and its respective use. The various qualities of paper are included in the relevant market, and their sales added up to estimate total market glut and volume.
23. When supply-side substitutability would entail the need to adjust significantly existing tangible and intangible assets, additional investments, strategic decisions or time delays, it will not be considered at the stage of market definition. Examples where supply-side substitution did not induce the Commission to enlarge the market are offered in the area of consumer products, in particular for branded beverages. Although bottling plants may in principle bottle different beverages, there are costs and lead times involved (in terms of advertising, product testing and distribution) before the products can actually be sold. In these cases, the effects of supply-side substitutability and other forms of potential competition would then be examined at a later stage.

In Case 6/72 *Europemballage Corp and Continental Can Co Inc v Commission* [1973] ECR 215, the Court of Justice found that when the Commission defined the RPM in its Decision against Continental Can, it had neglected to consider supply substitutability. Continental Can made light metal containers and lids for fruit and vegetables. The Commission, however, had not determined how difficult it would have been for potential competitors from other sectors of the market for light metal containers to enter this market by switching their production by simple adaptation to substitutes acceptable to the consumer.

In Commission Decision 2007/53/EC of 24 May 2004 relating to a proceeding pursuant to Article 82 of the EC Treaty and Article 54 of the EEA Agreement against Microsoft Corporation (Case COMP/C-3/37.792 – *Microsoft*), OJ 2004 L32/23, the Commission considered supply substitutability of client personal computer (PC) operating systems.

Commission Decision 2007/53/EC of 24 May 2004 relating to a proceeding pursuant to Article 82 of the EC Treaty and Article 54 of the EEA Agreement against Microsoft Corporation (Case COMP/C-3/37.792 – *Microsoft*), OJ 2004 L32/23

335. It should be highlighted that developing a new operating system is very costly and time consuming. This is because modern operating systems are very large and sophisticated software products. For example, Windows XP includes several tens of millions of lines of code. Any undertaking which might account for such supply-side substitutability needs to already have access to and the ability to modify the source code of an operating system in order to be able to switch production effectively and immediately to PC operating systems.

In this case, it was held that a new product would have to be substantially modified, entailing a development and testing process involving a large amount of time, expense, and commercial risk. As such, it was found that competitors could not easily enter the market and the RPM was defined accordingly by excluding such competitors.

14.3.3 Relevant geographic market (RGM)

In Case 27/76 *United Brands Co v Commission ('Chiquita Bananas')* [1978] ECR 207, at para 44, the Court of Justice gave consideration to the RGM and defined it as 'an area where the objective conditions of competition applying to the product in question must be the same for all traders'.

?! THINKING POINT

What is meant by the 'objective conditions of competition'?

Such conditions would include the cost and ease of transportation, purchasing behaviour, and preferences of consumers.

The RGM is normally the whole of the EU. For example, in Commission Decision 88/138/EEC of 22 December 1987 relating to a proceeding under Article 86 of the EEC Treaty (IV/30.787 and 31.488 – *Eurofix-Bauco v Hilti*), OJ 1988 L65/19, given that the goods (nails) could be easily and cheaply transported, the RGM was held to be the whole of the EU. However, the 'objective conditions of competition' can differ and the RGM is reduced accordingly.

In *Chiquita Bananas*, the RGM was judged to be all of the Member States except France, Italy, and the UK. It was decided that these Member States should be excluded because the effect of the national organization of these markets meant that United Brands' bananas did not compete on equal terms with the other bananas sold in these states.

The Commission's 1997 Notice on the definition of the relevant market provides useful guidance on the factors that the Commission takes into account.

Commission Notice on the definition of relevant market for the purposes of Community competition law, OJ 1997 C372/5

44. The type of evidence the Commission considers relevant to reach a conclusion as to the geographic market can be categorized as follows:
45. Past evidence of diversion of orders to other areas. In certain cases, evidence on changes in prices between different areas and consequent reactions by customers might be available. Generally, the same quantitative tests used for product market definition might as well be used in geographic market definition, bearing in mind that international comparisons of prices might be more complex due to a number of factors such as exchange rate movements, taxation and product differentiation.
46. Basic demand characteristics. The nature of demand for the relevant product may in itself determine the scope of the geographical market. Factors such as national preferences or preferences for national brands, language, culture and life style, and the need for a local presence have a strong potential to limit the geographic scope of competition.

In this regard, the *TV Listings* cases provide a useful example of an RGM being defined with reference to the area in which the goods or services are limited (Joined Cases C-241 & 242/91 P *RTE v Commission* (Case T-69/89); *BBC v Commission* (Case T-70/89); *ITP Ltd v Commission* (Case T-76/89); *Radio Telefis Eireann v Commission* (Joined Cases C-241 & 242/91 P) (Decisions upheld on appeal to the Court of Justice in *RTE & ITP v Commission*) [1995] ECR I-743).

Joined Cases C-241 & 242/91 P *RTE v Commission* (Case T-69/89); *BBC v Commission* (Case T-70/89); *ITP Ltd v Commission* (Case T-76/89); *Radio Telefis Eireann v Commission* (Joined Cases C-241 & 242/91 P) (Decisions upheld on appeal to the Court of Justice in *RTE & ITP v Commission*) ('*TV Listings*') [1995] ECR I-743

47. Views of customers and competitors. Where appropriate, the Commission will contact the main customers and competitors of the parties in its enquiries, to gather their views on the boundaries of the geographic market as well as most of the factual information it requires to reach a conclusion on the scope of the market when they are sufficiently backed by factual evidence.

48. Current geographic pattern of purchases. An examination of the customers' current geographic pattern of purchases provides useful evidence as to the possible scope of the geographic market. When customers purchase from companies located anywhere in the Community [now Union] or the EEA [European Economic Area] on similar terms, or they procure their supplies through effective tendering procedures in which companies from anywhere in the Community or the EEA submit bids, usually the geographic market will be considered to be Community-wide.

49. Trade flows/pattern of shipments. When the number of customers is so large that it is not possible to obtain through them a clear picture of geographic purchasing patterns, information on trade flows might be used alternatively, provided that the trade statistics are available with a sufficient degree of detail for the relevant products. Trade flows, and above all, the rationale behind trade flows provide useful insights and information for the purpose of establishing the scope of the geographic market but are not in themselves conclusive.

50. Barriers and switching costs associated to divert orders to companies located in other areas. The absence of trans-border purchases or trade flows, for instance, does not necessarily mean that the market is at most national in scope. Still, barriers isolating the national market have to be identified before it is concluded that the relevant geographic market in such a case is national. Perhaps the clearest obstacle for a customer to divert its orders to other areas is the impact of transport costs and transport restrictions arising from legislation or from the nature of the relevant products. The impact of transport costs will usually limit the scope of the geographic market for bulky, low-value products, bearing in mind that a transport disadvantage might also be compensated by a comparative advantage in other costs (labour costs or raw materials). Access to distribution in a given area, regulatory barriers still existing in certain sectors, quotas and custom tariffs might also constitute barriers isolating a geographic area from the competitive pressure of companies located outside that area. Significant switching costs in procuring supplies from companies located in other countries constitute additional sources of such barriers.

14.3.3.1 'Within the internal market or a substantial part of it'

Article 102 TFEU provides that abuse of dominance must be 'within the internal market or a substantial part of it'. However, although at first this may seem to be a considerable burden to satisfy, the case law of the Court of Justice has shown it to be less of a burden in practice. Thus, in Case 27/76 *United Brands Co v Commission ('Chiquita Bananas')* [1978] ECR 207, a number of Member States were held by the Court of Justice to satisfy the condition, whilst in Case 322/81 *Nederlandsche Banden-Industrie Michelin NV v Commission* [1983] ECR 3461 even a single Member State was deemed sufficient.

Michelin NV, the Netherlands subsidiary of the Michelin group, sought annulment of a Commission Decision finding that it had breached Article 102 TFEU by granting selective discounting arrangements and applying dissimilar conditions in respect of equivalent transactions in the market for new replacement tyres for heavy vehicles in the Netherlands. In considering the RGM, the Court of Justice stated as follows.

Case 322/81 *Nederlandsche Banden-Industrie Michelin NV v Commission* [1983] ECR 3461

26. The Commission's allegation concerns Michelin NV's conduct towards tyre dealers and more particularly its discount policy. In this regard the commercial policy of the various subsidiaries of the groups competing at the European or even the world level is generally adapted to the specific conditions existing on each market. In practice dealers established in the Netherlands obtain their supplies only from suppliers operating in the Netherlands. The Commission was therefore right to take the view that the competition facing Michelin NV is mainly on the Netherlands market and that it is at that level that the objective conditions of competition are alike for traders.
27. This finding is not related to the question whether in such circumstances factors relating to the position of the Michelin group and its competitors as a whole and to a much wider market may enter into consideration in the adoption of a Decision as to whether a dominant position exists on the relevant product market.
28. Hence the relevant substantial part of the common market in this case is the Netherlands and it is at the level of the Netherlands market that Michelin NV's position must be assessed.

The Court of Justice held that the RGM was the Netherlands and that this amounted to a substantial part of the internal market.

Perhaps more surprisingly still, there are cases in which single ports have been deemed to be the RGM and yet satisfy the requirement of being 'within the internal market or a substantial part of it'. In Case C-179/90 *Merci Convenzionali Porto di Genova* [1991] ECR I-5889, the Court of Justice drew attention to certain factors to be considered when determining whether a market may be regarded as constituting a substantial part of the internal market.

Case C-179/90 *Merci Convenzionali Porto di Genova* [1991] ECR I-5889

15. As regards the definition of the market in question, it may be seen from the order for reference that it is that of the organization on behalf of third persons of dock work relating to ordinary freight in the Port of Genoa and the performance of such work. Regard being had in particular to the volume of traffic in that port and its importance in relation to maritime import and export operations as a whole in the Member State concerned, that market may be regarded as constituting a substantial part of the common market.

14.3.4 Relevant temporal (or seasonal) market

The consideration of the existence of any RTM recognizes the fact that markets may change from time to time. However, in most cases, no such market exists and therefore it is not often raised before the Court of Justice.

The argument was advanced in Case 27/76 *United Brands Co v Commission ('Chiquita Bananas')* [1978] ECR 207 that demand for bananas was affected by the availability at certain times of the year of other seasonal fruit. Thus, in the summer, alternatives were plentiful and market power was therefore reduced. Had the argument been accepted, the dominance or otherwise of United Brands would have had to be considered in relation to each of the temporal markets proposed. The Commission and the Court of Justice, however, both identified a single temporal market.

Commission Decision 77/327/EEC of 19 April 1977 relating to a proceeding under Article 86 of the EEC Treaty (IV/28.841—*ABG/Oil companies operating in the Netherlands*), OJ 1977 L117/1, provides one of the few cases in which an RTM has been identified. In this Decision, the Commission identified a temporal market for oil at the time of the 1970s oil shortage.

14.4 Dominance

Having established the context in which dominance is to be assessed, consideration should be given to those factors that indicate a dominant position within the relevant market.

As was made clear in Case 85/76 *Hoffmann-La Roche & Co AG v Commission* [1979] ECR 461, at para 39: 'The existence of a dominant position may derive from several factors which, taken separately, are not necessarily determinative but among these factors a highly important one is the existence of very large market shares.'

Thus several factors may combine to indicate dominance, but market share is the primary indicator. Other relevant factors/barriers to entry include:

- market structure;
- duration of market share;
- financial and technological resources;

- vertical integration;
- intellectual property rights; and
- conduct.

?! **THINKING POINT**

The last of these factors has been considered to be controversial. In view of the other requirements of Article 102 TFEU, can you identify why?

14.4.1 Market share

Market share is perhaps the only factor taken by itself that could indicate dominance.

In practice, total monopoly situations (comprising a 100 per cent market share) are rare. An example of such was, however, identified in Case 226/84 *British Leyland plc v Commission* [1986] ECR 3263, in which a dispute arose as to the requirement of UK law that a person who wishes to register a vehicle for use on the roads must, unless they are importing the vehicle for personal use, produce a 'certificate of conformity' certifying that the vehicle conforms to a previously type-approved vehicle. The Court of Justice considered whether this amounted to an abuse of a dominant position, but first addressed the issue of dominance by reference to the market share.

Case 226/84 *British Leyland plc v Commission* [1986] ECR 3263

4. That certificate is issued by the manufacturer of the vehicle on the basis of the National Type Approval Certificate (NTA certificate) which it has obtained from the Department of Transport, or by the holder of a Primary Minister's Approval Certificate (PMAC), which can be obtained from the Department of Transport only if the manufacturer provides the necessary technical information.
5. In the light of those rules, the relevant market is not that of the sale of vehicles, as BL claims, but a separate, ancillary market, namely that of services which are in practice indispensable for dealers who wish to sell the vehicles manufactured by BL in a specific geographical area (see judgment of 13 November 1975, Case 26/75 *General Motors v Commission* (1975) ECR 1367, at p. 1378).

   [...]
7. In order to show that it does not occupy a dominant position in the market of the services described above, BL claims that private individuals may register vehicles purchased abroad in the United Kingdom without having to produce a certificate of conformity.
8. It appears from the British rules that that facility is exceptional and is reserved exclusively for private individuals. It is subject to strict conditions and accorded exclusively in respect of

personal use, and, although it has been used by certain dealers to obtain vehicles for their customers, it cannot be regarded as a regular procedure for registering cars imported commercially.

9. The British rules therefore confer on BL a form of administrative monopoly in the relevant market and, with regard to the issue of certificates of conformity, place the dealers in a position of economic dependence which is characteristic of a dominant position.

British Leyland had a statutory monopoly and was able to fix its own prices. This amounted to a dominant position within Article 102 TFEU.

In Case T-201/04 *Microsoft Corporation v Commission* [2007] ECR II-3601, Microsoft was found to have a market share of over 90 per cent of one of the identified markets. This was deemed by the European Commission to be clear evidence of dominance.

Case 85/76 *Hoffmann-La Roche & Co AG v Commission* [1979] ECR 461 related to an undertaking involved in the production of vitamins. The Court of Justice drew attention to market share, but also focused on the duration for which that market share had been held.

Case 85/76 *Hoffmann-La Roche & Co AG v Commission* [1979] ECR 461

41. An undertaking which has a very large market share and holds it for some time … is by virtue of that share in a position of strength which makes it an unavoidable trading partner and which, already because of this secures for it, at the very least during relatively long periods, that freedom of action which is the special feature of a dominant position.

In Case T-30/89 *Hilti AG v Commission* [1991] ECR II-1439, the Court of First Instance (now the General Court) considered Hilti's market share.

Case T-30/89 *Hilti AG v Commission* [1991] ECR II-1439

89. The Commission has proved that Hilti holds a market share of around 70 per cent to 80 per cent in the relevant market for nails …

[…]

91. With particular reference to market shares, the Court of Justice has held (*Hoffmann-La Roche* judgment [Case 85/76 *Hoffmann-La Roche & Co AG v Commission* [1979] ECR 461], paragraph 41) that very large shares are in themselves, and save in exceptional circumstances, evidence of a dominant position.

92. In this case it is established that Hilti holds a share of between 70 per cent and 80 per cent in the relevant market. Such a share is, in itself, a clear indication of the existence of a dominant position in the relevant market …

Thus a market share of between 70 and 80 per cent is, in itself, a clear indication of dominance.

14.4.2 Market structure

Market structure is an important factor that must be considered. The significance of market share varies from market to market, according to the structure of the market.

It is entirely possible that a relatively modest market share may lead to the expectation that the undertaking cannot possibly be dominant. However, in a fragmented market, when considered alongside the market share of the nearest and other competitors, the picture may be quite different from that initially painted.

The market structure of the banana market was analysed in Case 27/76 *United Brands Co v Commission ('Chiquita Bananas')* [1978] ECR 207, with the Court of Justice comparing the large, but not overwhelming, market share of United Brands to that of its nearest competitor, Castle and Cooke.

Case 27/76 *United Brands Co v Commission ('Chiquita Bananas')* [1978] ECR 207

107. A trader can only be in a dominant position on the market for a product if he has succeeded in winning a large part of this market.
108. Without going into a discussion about percentages, which when fixed are bound to be to some extent approximations, it can be considered to be an established fact that [United Brands]'s share of the relevant market is always more than 40 per cent and nearly 45 per cent.
109. This percentage does not however permit the conclusion that [United Brands] automatically controls the market.
110. It must be determined having regard to the strength and number of the competitors.
111. It is necessary first of all to establish that on the whole of the relevant market the said percentage represents *grosso modo* a share several times greater than that of its competitor Castle and Cooke which is the best placed of all the competitors, the others coming far behind.

Thus, given the structure of the banana market, the Court of Justice held that a market share of between 40 and 45 per cent was an indicator of dominance.

?! THINKING POINT

Do you think there is a minimum share beyond which it seems strange to define an undertaking as 'dominant'?

14.4.3 Financial and technological resources and intellectual property rights

It is important to appreciate that there is nothing inherently wrong in an undertaking having such resources, but that ownership of such does act as an indicator of dominance and undoubtedly acts as a barrier to entry for potential competitors. Such resources may be used to further invest in the undertaking such that its market position becomes entrenched, whilst intellectual property rights, such as copyright and patents, may be used to prevent competitors from reproducing information or making products that the rights protect.

Furthermore, such resources often enable a dominant undertaking to engage in the sort of behaviour that would be deemed to be an abuse of a dominant position.

Chiquita Bananas provides an example of the way in which such resources can act as barriers to entry.

Case 27/76 *United Brands Co v Commission ('Chiquita Bananas')* [1978] ECR 207

82. In the field of technical knowledge and as a result of continual research [United Brands] keeps on improving the productivity and yield of its plantations by improving the draining system, making good soil deficiencies and combating effectively plant disease.

83. It has perfected new ripening methods in which its technicians instruct the distributor/ripeners of the Chiquita banana.

84. That is another factor to be borne in mind when considering [United Brands]'s position since competing firms cannot develop research at a comparable level and are in this respect at a disadvantage compared with the applicant.

[…]

122. The particular barriers to competitors entering the market are the exceptionally large capital investments required for the creation and running of banana plantations, the need to increase sources of supply in order to avoid the effects of fruit diseases and bad weather (hurricanes, floods), the introduction of an essential system of logistics which the distribution of a very perishable product makes necessary, economies of scale from which newcomers to the market cannot derive any immediate benefit and the actual cost of entry made up inter alia of all the general expenses incurred in penetrating the market such as the setting up of an adequate commercial network, the mounting of very large-scale advertising campaigns, all those financial risks, the costs of which are irrecoverable if the attempt fails.

123. Thus, although, as [United Brands] has pointed out, it is true that competitors are able to use the same methods of production and distribution as the applicant, they come up against almost insuperable practical and financial obstacles.

124. That is another factor peculiar to a dominant position.

14.4.4 Vertical integration

Extensive vertical integration concerns the extent of control in the production and supply chain, and presents another barrier to entry. Simply stated, the greater the extent of vertical integration, the greater the likelihood of dominance in the relevant market. However, it is important once more to remember that vertical integration is merely an indicator of dominance and is not problematic in itself.

The Court of Justice subjected United Brands' operations to extensive analysis in terms of its integration.

Case 27/76 *United Brands Co v Commission ('Chiquita Bananas')* [1978] ECR 207

70. United Brands is an undertaking vertically integrated to a high degree.
71. This integration is evident at each of the stages from the plantation to the loading on wagons or lorries in the ports of delivery and after those stages, as far as ripening and sale prices are concerned, [United Brands] even extends its control to ripener/distributors and wholesalers by setting up a complete network of agents.
72. At the production stage [United Brands] owns large plantations in central and south America.
73. In so far as [United Brands'] own production does not meet its requirements it can obtain supplies without any difficulty from independent planters since it is an established fact that unless circumstances are exceptional there is a production surplus.
74. Furthermore several independent producers have links with [United Brands] through contracts for the growing of bananas which have caused them to grow the varieties of bananas which [United Brands] has advised them to adopt.
75. The effects of natural disasters which could jeopardize supplies are greatly reduced by the fact that the plantations are spread over a wide geographic area and by the selection of varieties not very susceptible to diseases.

[…]

78. At the stage of packaging and presentation on its premises [United Brands] has at its disposal factories, manpower, plant and material which enable it to handle the goods independently.
79. The bananas are carried from the place of production to the port of shipment by its own means of transport including railways.
80. At the carriage by sea stage it has been acknowledged that [United Brands] is the only undertaking of its kind which is capable of carrying two thirds of its exports by means of its own banana fleet.
81. Thus [United Brands] knows that it is able to transport regularly, without running the risk of its own ships not being used and whatever the market situation may be, two thirds of its average volume of sales and is alone able to ensure that three regular consignments reach Europe each week, and all this guarantees it commercial stability and well being.

Similarly, in Case 85/76 *Hoffmann-La Roche & Co AG v Commission* [1979] ECR 461, the Court of Justice recognized that the company's highly efficient sales network was a factor indicating a dominant position.

14.4.5 Conduct

Case 27/76 *United Brands Co v Commission ('Chiquita Bananas')* [1978] ECR 207 is an example of a case in which an undertaking's conduct has been deemed to be an indicator of a dominant position. Thus the charging of unfair prices based upon the ability of traders in a Member State to pay was evidence of United Brands' dominance in the banana market.

?! **THINKING POINT**

Can you appreciate why this indicator has often been argued to result in a circular argument?

The traditional view of Article 102 TFEU demands the establishment of dominance with reference to relevant markets, followed by a consideration of whether the behaviour of the undertaking concerned amounts to an abuse. The consideration of conduct or behaviour as another indicator of dominance is therefore controversial and has been criticized, as it presents a somewhat circular argument—that is, because an undertaking engages in abusive behaviour, it is therefore dominant and, because it is dominant, its behaviour amounts to an abuse under Article 102 TFEU. However, any undertaking engaging in abusive behaviour is, in itself, outside Article 102 TFEU. It is only when the undertaking is dominant that attention is paid to the abusive behaviour and therefore to say that the behaviour is an indicator of dominance is a challenging argument to accept. However, *Chiquita Bananas* provides clear authority for such a proposition.

14.4.6 Collective dominance

Whilst this chapter has focused on the more common position of single undertakings in a dominant position within a relevant market, Article 102 TFEU refers also to an abuse of a dominant position by one or *more* undertakings. The concept of *collective* dominance requires three conditions to be satisfied, as the Court of First Instance (now the General Court) set out in Case T-342/99 *Airtours/First Choice* [2002] ECR II-2585.

Case T-342/99 *Airtours/First Choice* [2002] ECR II-2585

62. [. . .]

- [F]irst, each member of the dominant oligopoly must have the ability to know how the other members are behaving in order to monitor whether or not they are adopting the common policy. In that regard, it is not enough for each member of the dominant oligopoly to be aware that interdependent market conduct is profitable for all of them but each member must also have a means of knowing whether the other operators are adopting the same strategy and whether they are maintaining it. There must, therefore, be sufficient market transparency for all members of the dominant oligopoly to be aware, sufficiently precisely and quickly, of the way in which the other members' market conduct is evolving;

- second, the situation of tacit coordination must be sustainable over time, that is to say, there must be an incentive not to depart from the common policy on the market. It is only if all the members of the dominant oligopoly maintain the parallel conduct that all can benefit. The notion of retaliation in respect of conduct deviating from the common policy is thus inherent in this condition. In that context, the Commission must not necessarily prove that there is a specific retaliation mechanism involving a degree of severity, but it must none the less establish that deterrents exist, which are such that it is not worth the while of any member of the dominant oligopoly to depart from the common course of conduct to the detriment of the other oligopolists. For a situation of collective dominance to be viable, there must be adequate deterrents to ensure that there is a long-term incentive in not departing from the common policy, which means that each member of the dominant oligopoly must be aware that highly competitive action on its part designed to increase its market share would provoke identical action by the others, so that it would derive no benefit from its initiative;
- third, it must also be established that the foreseeable reaction of current and future competitors, as well as of consumers, would not jeopardise the results expected from the common policy.

14.5 Abuse

Having identified the relevant market and determined dominance with reference to the indicators listed at 14.4, it is then necessary to consider what behaviour would amount to an abuse of such a position. It is important to note that, without such abuse, Article 102 TFEU will not be breached. Article 102 does not prohibit undertakings being successful in a marketplace and realizing a position of dominance. Indeed, it is almost inevitable that, in any given market, dominant undertakings will emerge. However, if a dominant undertaking abuses that position of dominance, Article 102 TFEU becomes relevant.

Abuse of such a position of dominance can take many forms. Article 102 TFEU sets out a non-exhaustive list of examples.

Article 102 TFEU

(a) directly or indirectly imposing unfair purchase or selling prices or other unfair trading conditions;

(b) limiting production, markets or technical development to the prejudice of consumers;

(c) applying dissimilar conditions to equivalent transactions with other trading parties, thereby placing them at a competitive disadvantage;

(d) making the conclusion of contracts subject to acceptance by the other parties of supplementary obligations which, by their nature or according to commercial usage, have no connection with the subject of such contracts.

exploitative abuses Exploitative abuses of a dominant position manipulate consumers.

anti-competitive abuses Anti-competitive abuses of a dominant position prevent or weaken competition or potential competition from other undertakings.

This list is not exhaustive, but merely gives examples of abusive behaviour. Often, abuses are classified into two categories: **exploitative abuses** and **anti-competitive abuses.**

It is often the case that abusive behaviour both exploits consumers *and* prevents or weakens competition.

?! THINKING POINT

In considering the following types of abuse, do you think they can be described as exploitative, anti-competitive, or both?

14.5.1 Unfair pricing

Charging unfair prices, at least where such prices are excessive, is a clear exploitative abuse. However, difficulty arises in determining exactly what a 'fair price' is. Any consideration of the fairness of a price has an inevitable element of subjectivity.

In Case 27/76 *United Brands Co v Commission ('Chiquita Bananas')* [1978] ECR 207, the issue of excessive prices was considered by the Court of Justice. In setting out an objective test upon which judgements of excessiveness of prices could be made, the Court of Justice clarified as follows.

Case 27/76 *United Brands Co v Commission ('Chiquita Bananas')* [1978] ECR 207

251. This excess could, inter alia, be determined objectively if it were possible for it to be calculated by making a comparison between the selling price of the product in question and its cost of production, which would disclose the amount of the profit margin; however the Commission has not done this since it has not analysed [United Brands]'s costs structure.

252. The questions therefore to be determined are whether the difference between the costs actually incurred and the price actually charged is excessive, and, if the answer to this question is in the affirmative, whether a price has been imposed which is either unfair in itself or when compared to competing products.

Thus the fairness of the price can be determined by comparing the price charged *less* both the costs (fixed and variable) of production.

Whilst the pricing policy of United Brands was found to be an exploitative abuse, abuses of this kind can also be anti-competitive abuses. Case 226/84 *British Leyland plc v Commission* [1986] ECR 3263 provides an example. In this case, British Leyland sought to discourage imports into the UK by charging unfair prices for the issue of approval certificates for imported left-hand-drive vehicles. In judging the price excessive in comparing the cost of the certificates with the service provided, the Court of Justice upheld the Commission's Decision finding of abuse.

Interestingly, pricing that is unnaturally low may also be deemed to be an abuse of a dominant position. Usually referred to as 'predatory pricing', such a scheme involves reducing prices below the costs of production to prevent potential competitors from gaining sufficient market share to present a competitive challenge. New undertakings are unlikely to have the resources to be able to compete on price for very long while making no profit or indeed actually making a loss. This anti-competitive abuse also has adverse impacts upon consumers and therefore can also be classified as an exploitative abuse. Once potential competitors have been driven out of the market, the dominant undertaking is then in a position to recoup its short-term losses. It has the market at its mercy and is ultimately able to charge whatever price the market will bear, free from the usual effects of competitive pressures.

Such predatory pricing was defined in Case C-62/86 *AKZO Chemie v Commission* [1991] ECR I-335, following the activity of AKZO in reacting to a potential competitor entering the market for organic peroxides for use in the plastics industry.

Case C-62/86 *AKZO Chemie v Commission* [1991] ECR I-335

71. Prices below average variable costs (that is to say, those which vary depending on the quantities produced) by means of which a dominant undertaking seeks to eliminate a competitor must be regarded as abusive. A dominant undertaking has no interest in applying such prices except that of eliminating competitors so as to enable it subsequently to raise its prices by taking advantage of its monopolistic position, since each sale generates a loss, namely the total amount of the fixed costs (that is to say, those which remain constant regardless of the quantities produced) and, at least, part of the variable costs relating to the unit produced.
72. Moreover, prices below average total costs, that is to say, fixed costs plus variable costs, but above average variable costs, must be regarded as abusive if they are determined as part of a plan for eliminating a competitor. Such prices can drive from the market undertakings which are perhaps as efficient as the dominant undertaking but which, because of their smaller financial resources, are incapable of withstanding the competition waged against them.

The Court of Justice held that prices were predatory and therefore an abuse of a dominant position if they were intended to eliminate competition. Such an intention is deemed to exist if prices are below average variable costs, whilst where prices are below average total costs, but above average variable costs, prices are abusive 'if determined as part of a plan for eliminating a competitor'.

In addition to charging excessive or unnaturally low prices, the act by a dominant undertaking of charging different prices to different customers for identical products can also amount to an abuse under Article 102 TFEU unless such differences are objectively justified.

In *Chiquita Bananas*, United Brands charged different prices to different traders in Member States dependent upon what the market could bear.

Case 27/76 *United Brands Co v Commission ('Chiquita Bananas')* [1978] ECR 207

208. The Commission blames the applicant for charging each week for the sale of its branded bananas—without objective justification—a selling price which differs appreciably according to the Member State where its customers are established.

209. This policy of charging differing prices according to the Member States for which the bananas are intended has been applied at least since 1971 in the case of customers of the Federal Republic of Germany, the Netherlands and the Bleu and was extended in January 1973 to customers in Denmark and in November 1973 to customers in Ireland.

[...]

212. The price customers in Belgium are asked to pay is on average 80 per cent higher than that paid by customers in Ireland.

213. The greatest difference in price is 138 per cent between the delivered Rotterdam price charged by [United Brands] to its customers in Ireland and the f.o.r Bremerhaven price charged by [United Brands] to its customers in Denmark, that is to say the price paid by Danish customers is 2.38 times the price paid by Irish customers.

214. The Commission treats these facts as an abuse of a dominant position in that [United Brands] has applied dissimilar conditions to equivalent transactions with the other trading parties, thereby placing them at a competitive disadvantage.

Objectively justifiable reasons, such as transport costs and labour costs, could potentially justify different pricing for different customers, but arguments of such will be subject to intense scrutiny, as the Court demonstrated in *Chiquita Bananas*.

Case 27/76 *United Brands Co v Commission ('Chiquita Bananas')* [1978] ECR 207

215. The applicant states that its prices are determined by market forces and cannot therefore be discriminatory.

216. Further the average difference in the price of 'Chiquita' bananas between the national markets in question was only 5 per cent in 1975.

217. The price in any given week is calculated so as to reflect as much as possible the anticipated yellow market price in the following week for each national market.

218. This price is fixed by the Rotterdam management after discussions and negotiations between the applicant's local representatives and the ripener/distributors must perforce take into account the different competitive context in which ripener/distributors in the different countries are operating.

219. It finds its objective justification in the average anticipated market price.

220. These price differences are in fact due to fluctuating market factors such as the weather, different availability of seasonal competing fruit, holidays, strikes, government measures, currency denominations.

221. In short the applicant has been asked by the Commission to take appropriate steps to establish a single banana market at a time when it has in fact been unable to do so.

222. According to the applicant as long as the Community institutions have not set up the machinery for a single banana market and the various markets remain national and respond to their individual supply/demand situations differences in prices between them cannot be prevented.

223. [United Brands'] answers to the Commission's requests for particulars (the letters of 14 May, 13 September, 10 and 11 December 1974 and 13 February 1975) show that [United Brands] charges its customers each week for its bananas sold under the Chiquita brand name a different selling price depending on the Member State where the latter carry on their business as ripener/distributors according to the ratios to which the Commission has drawn attention.

224. These price differences can reach 30 to 50 per cent in some weeks, even though products supplied under the transactions are equivalent (with the exception of the Scipio group, subject to this observation that the bananas from Scipio's ripening installations are sold at the same price as those sold by independent ripeners).

225. In fact the bananas sold by [United Brands] are all freighted in the same ships, are unloaded at the same cost in Rotterdam or Bremerhaven and the price differences relate to substantially similar quantities of bananas of the same variety, which have been brought to the same degree of ripening, are of similar quality and sold under the same 'Chiquita' brand name under the same conditions of sale and payment for loading on to the purchaser's own means of transport and the latter have to pay customs duties, taxes and transport costs from these ports.

226. This policy of discriminatory prices has been applied by [United Brands] since 1971 to customers of Germany, the Netherlands and the Bleu and was extended at the beginning of 1973 to customers in Denmark and in November 1973 to customers in Ireland.

227. Although the responsibility for establishing the single banana market does not lie with the applicant, it can only endeavour to take 'what the market can bear' provided that it complies with the rules for the Regulation and coordination of the market laid down by the Treaty.

228. Once it can be grasped that differences in transport costs, taxation, customs duties, the wages of the labour force, the conditions of marketing, the differences in the parity of currencies, the density of competition may eventually culminate in different retail selling price levels according to the Member States, then it follows those differences are factors which [United Brands] only has to take into account to a limited extent since it sells a product which is always the same and at the same place to ripener/distributors who—alone—bear the risks of the consumers' market.

229. The interplay of supply and demand should, owing to its nature, only be applied to each stage where it is really manifest.

230. The mechanisms of the market are adversely affected if the price is calculated by leaving out one stage of the market and taking into account the law of supply and demand as between the vendor and the ultimate consumer and not as between the vendor ([United Brands]) and the purchaser (the ripener/distributors).

231. Thus, by reason of its dominant position [United Brands], fed with information by its local representatives, was in fact able to impose its selling price on the intermediate purchaser. This price and also the 'weekly quota allocated' is only fixed and notified to the customer four days before the vessel carrying the bananas berths.

232. These discriminatory prices, which varied according to the circumstances of the Member States, were just so many obstacles to the free movement of goods and their effect was intensified by the clause forbidding the resale of bananas while still green and by reducing the deliveries of the quantities ordered.

233. A rigid partitioning of national markets was thus created at price levels, which were artificially different, placing certain distributor/ripeners at a competitive disadvantage, since compared with what it should have been competition had thereby been distorted.

234. Consequently the policy of differing prices enabling [United Brands] to apply dissimilar conditions to equivalent transactions with other trading parties, thereby placing them at a competitive disadvantage, was an abuse of a dominant position.

?! **THINKING POINT**

Can you think of any circumstances in which there may be a legitimate reason for charging different prices for the same product?

14.5.2 Discounting

Discounting is another price-based form of discrimination. It can be an exploitative abuse if customers may not benefit from the discounts introduced and it can be anti-competitive where discounts are offered to ensure that 'loyal' customers do not stray, thereby affecting the ability of potential competitors to penetrate the market. Of course, in many instances, it is both.

Discounts can take many different forms. The most often encountered are **quantity discounts**, **loyalty/fidelity discounts**, and **target discounts**.

quantity discounts
Quantity discounts are offered to customers who buy minimum quantities.

loyalty/fidelity discounts
Loyalty/fidelity discounts are offered to customers who agree to purchase all or most of their requirements from the supplier.

target discounts
Target discounts are offered to customers who reach specific sales targets.

The first of these, quantity discounts, are acceptable as long as they are available to all and justified by some objective ground. Thus, where a discount is offered to a customer in return for a large order, there may be objectively justifiable economies of scale to be enjoyed, involving a reduction in transport and administrative costs.

Fidelity discounts and target discounts, however, are likely to amount to abuse within Article 102 TFEU.

Case 85/76 *Hoffmann-La Roche & Co AG v Commission* [1979] ECR 461 concerned fidelity discounts.

Case 85/76 *Hoffmann-La Roche & Co AG v Commission* [1979] ECR 461

89. An undertaking which is in a dominant position on a market and ties purchasers—even if it does so at their request—by an obligation or promise on their part to obtain all or most of their requirements exclusively from the said undertaking abuses its dominant position within the meaning of Article 86 of the Treaty [now Article 102 TFEU], whether the obligation in question is stipulated without further qualification or whether it is undertaken in consideration of the grant of a rebate.

    The same applies if the said undertaking, without tying the purchasers by a formal obligation, applies, either under the terms of agreements concluded with these purchasers or unilaterally, a system of fidelity rebates, that is to say discounts conditional on the customer's obtaining all or most of its requirements—whether the quantity of its purchases be large or small—from the undertaking in a dominant position.

90. Obligations of this kind to obtain supplies exclusively from a particular undertaking, whether or not they are in consideration of rebates or of the granting of fidelity rebates intended to give the purchaser an incentive to obtain his supplies exclusively from the undertaking in a dominant position, are incompatible with the objective of undistorted competition within the common market, because—unless there are exceptional circumstances which may make an agreement between undertakings in the context of Article 85 [EC, now Article 101 TFEU] and in particular of paragraph (3) of that Article, permissible—they are not based on an economic transaction which justifies this burden or benefit but are designed to deprive the purchaser of or restrict his possible choices of sources of supply and to deny other producers access to the market.

    The fidelity rebate, unlike quantity rebates exclusively linked with the volume of purchases from the producer concerned, is designed through the grant of a financial advantage to prevent customers from obtaining their supplies from competing producers.

    Furthermore the effect of fidelity rebates is to apply dissimilar conditions to equivalent transactions with other trading parties in that two purchasers pay a different price for the same quantity of the same product depending on whether they obtain their supplies exclusively from the undertaking in a dominant position or have several sources of supply.

What the Court of Justice recognized in *Hoffmann* is that, in the absence of justification for an agreement under Article 101(3) TFEU, the only reason to offer fidelity discounts was to provide a financial incentive designed to prevent the natural effects of competition taking place. Such behaviour inevitably results in a reduction or restriction in choice for the consumer.

In addition to the fidelity discounts, all but five of the contracts in question contained an interesting clause, referred to as 'the English clause'.

Case 85/76 *Hoffmann-La Roche & Co AG v Commission* [1979] ECR 461

102. ... The customer, if he obtains from competitors offers at prices which are more favourable than those under the contracts at issue may ask Roche to adjust its prices to the said offers; if Roche does not comply with this request, the customer, in derogation from his undertaking to obtain his requirements exclusively from Roche, is entitled to get his supplies from the said competitor without for that reason losing the benefit of the fidelity rebates provided for in the contracts in respect of the other purchases already effected or still to be effected by him from Roche.

[...]

105. A number of contracts stipulate not only that the offer must come from important competitors but also from large competitors operating on the same scale as Roche or again provide that the offers must not only be comparable as to the quality of the product but also as to their continuity and such a condition, by eliminating a more favourable but occasional method of obtaining supplies, strengthens the exclusivity.

[...]

107. In fact the English clause under which Roche's customers are obliged to inform it of more favourable offers made by competitors together with the particulars above mentioned—so that it will be easy for Roche to identify the competitor—owing to its very nature, places at the disposal of the applicant information about market conditions and also about the alternatives open to, and the actions of, its competitors which is of great value for the carrying out of its market strategy.

The fact that an undertaking in a dominant position requires its customers or obtains their agreement under contract to notify it of its competitor's offers, whilst the said customers may have an obvious commercial interest in not disclosing them, is of such a kind as to aggravate the exploitation of the dominant position in an abusive way ...

The Court of Justice thus found that the company's practices were abusive.

14.5.3 Tie-ins

A tie-in is a clause within an agreement that requires or encourages a customer to buy other goods or services from the same supplier.

A modern example of tying in can be found in Case T-201/04 *Microsoft Corporation v Commission* [2007] ECR II-3601, in which the bundling of the Windows operating system and Windows Media Player was held to be an abuse of a dominant position.

The case is significant in its consideration of abuse as it focuses on the dominance of the operating system and the tying-in of a lesser product which was bundled without charge and, indeed, alternatives could be used. However, the existence of Windows Media Player as part of a package and the inability to purchase the Windows operating system without it amounted to an abuse of a dominant position.

14.5.4 Refusal to supply

In Case 27/76 *United Brands Co v Commission ('Chiquita Bananas')* [1978] ECR 207, United Brands refused to continue to supply green bananas to Olesen, a Danish ripener and distributor, because Olesen had taken part in an advertising campaign for one of United Brands' competitors. United Brands contended that even a dominant undertaking should be entitled to protect its interests. The Court of Justice's response was less than sympathetic to United Brands' plight.

Case 27/76 *United Brands Co v Commission ('Chiquita Bananas')* [1978] ECR 207

189. Although it is true, as the applicant points out, that the fact that an undertaking is in a dominant position cannot disentitle it from protecting its own commercial interests if they are attacked, and that such an undertaking must be conceded the right to take such reasonable steps as it deems appropriate to protect its said interests, such behaviour cannot be countenanced if its actual purpose is to strengthen this dominant position and abuse it.
190. Even if the possibility of a counter-attack is acceptable that attack must still be proportionate to the threat taking into account the economic strength of the undertakings confronting each other.
191. The sanction consisting of a refusal to supply by an undertaking in a dominant position was in excess of what might, if such a situation were to arise, reasonably be contemplated as a sanction for conduct similar to that for which [United Brands] blamed Olesen.
192. In fact [United Brands] could not be unaware of the fact that by acting in this way it would discourage its other ripener/distributors from supporting the advertising of other brand names and that the deterrent effect of the sanction imposed upon one of them would make its position of strength on the relevant market that much more effective.
193. Such a course of conduct amounts therefore to a serious interference with the independence of small and medium sized firms in their commercial relations with the undertaking in

a dominant position and this independence implies the right to give preference to competitors' goods.

194. In this case the adoption of such a course of conduct is designed to have a serious adverse effect on competition on the relevant banana market by only allowing firms dependent upon the dominant undertaking to stay in business.

Chiquita Bananas concerned a refusal to supply an existing customer. The *TV Listings* cases (Joined Cases C-241 & 242/91 P *RTE v Commission* (Case T-69/89); *BBC v Commission* (Case T-70/89); *ITP Ltd v Commission* (Case T-76/89); *Radio Telefis Eireann v Commission* (Joined Cases C-241 & 242/91 P) (Decisions upheld on appeal to the Court of Justice in *RTE & ITP v Commission*) [1995] ECR I-743) were concerned with a refusal to supply to new customers. The Commission found that three television companies had abused their dominant position on the market for weekly programme listings by relying on their copyright in those listings to prevent third parties from publishing complete weekly guides to the programmes broadcast by different television channels.

14.6 Effect on trade between Member States

Article 102 TFEU requires not only that a Member State has abused a dominant position, but also that the abuse 'may affect trade between Member States'. This has the same meaning as set out in Case 56/65 *Société Technique Minière v Maschinenbau Ulm GmbH* [1966] ECR 235 in relation to Article 101 TFEU. Thus the effect must be 'direct or indirect, actual or potential'. This final element of Article 102 TFEU is generally easy to satisfy since it is not dependent upon showing an actual effect. However, Case 22/78 *Hugin Kassaregister AB and Hugin Cash Registers Ltd v Commission* [1979] ECR 1869 provides an example of a case in which this element was not satisfied. The refusal of a Swedish company, at a time when Sweden was not a Member State of the EU, to supply a company in London that had the intention of extending its business beyond the very limited area within which it operated meant that no inter-State trade effect could be established.

14.6.1 The Commission's 2009 Guidance

In 2009, the European Commission published its Guidance on the Commission's enforcement priorities in applying Article 82 of the EC Treaty [now Article 102 TFEU] to abusive exclusionary conduct by dominant undertakings, OJ 2009 C45/7. The 2009 Guidance sets out the Commission's determination to prioritize those cases in which the exclusionary conduct of a dominant undertaking is liable to have harmful effects on consumers.

The main principles of the effects-based approach were articulated in the accompanying press release.

European Commission, 'Antitrust: consumer welfare at heart of Commission fight against abuses by dominant undertakings', Press release IP/08/1877, 3 December 2008

The main principles of the effects-based approach to Article 82 [now Article 102 TFEU] are the following:

- fair and undistorted competition is the best way to make markets work better for the benefit of EU business and consumers. Healthy competition, including by dominant undertakings, should be encouraged
- the focus of the Commission's enforcement policy should be on protecting consumers, on protecting the process of competition and not on protecting individual competitors
- the Commission does not need to establish that the dominant undertaking's conduct actually harmed competition, only that there is convincing evidence that harm is likely
- since the focus of the Commission's enforcement policy is on conduct that harms the competitive process rather than individual competitors, for pricing conduct the Commission examines whether the conduct is likely to prevent competitors that are as efficient as the dominant undertaking from expanding on or entering the market and that can be expected to be most relevant to consumer welfare
- since the focus of the Commission's enforcement policy is on the likely effects of a dominant undertaking's conduct on consumers, the Commission will examine claims put forward by dominant undertakings that their conduct is justified on efficiency grounds—as is already the case under Article 81 [now Article 101 TFEU] and for merger control.

SUMMARY

- Article 102 TFEU prohibits as incompatible with the internal market 'any abuse by one or more undertakings of a dominant position within the internal market or in a substantial part of it ... in so far as it may affect trade between Member States'.
- The term 'undertakings' has the same meaning as in Article 101 TFEU and includes any legal or natural person engaged in some form of economic or commercial activity.
- *Chiquita Bananas* provides a general definition of a 'dominant position' as a position of economic strength enjoyed by an undertaking, which enables it to prevent effective competition being maintained on the relevant market by giving it the power to behave to an appreciable extent independently of its competitors, customers, and, ultimately, of its consumers.

- More specifically, dominance requires a consideration of the relevant market, comprising the relevant product market (RPM), relevant geographic market (RGM), and relevant temporal market (RTM).
- The RPM is established with consideration of both demand and supply substitutability.
  - Demand substitutability concerns the willingness of a consumer to substitute the product in question for a different product.
  - Supply substitutability concerns the capability of other producers to supply.
- *RGM* was defined in *Chiquita Bananas* as an area in which the objective conditions of competition applying to the product in question must be the same for all traders.
- The RGM needs to be within the internal market or a substantial part of it.
- Dominance is assessed with reference to a number of indicators. These include market share, market structure, the length of time for which the undertaking has held its market share, its financial and technological resources, vertical integration, intellectual property rights, and behaviour.
- Dominance in itself is not prohibited. Having found a dominant position, consideration must then be given to examples of abuse of such a position.
- Abuses can be classified into two categories: exploitative and anti-competitive abuses. These include unfair prices, discriminatory pricing, certain discounting arrangements, tie-ins, predatory pricing, refusals to supply, and import/export bans.
- Finally, an effect on trade between Member States must be established. This rarely proves problematic.

FURTHER READING

Articles

S Baker and L Wu, 'Applying the Market Definition Guidelines of the EC Commission' (1998) 19(5) ECL Rev 273

An interesting look at the guidelines and, in particular, supply substitutability.

T Eilmansberger, 'How to Distinguish Good from Bad Competition under Article 82 EC: In Search of Clearer and More Coherent Standards for Anti-Competitive Abuses' (2005) 42 CML Rev 129

Consideration of guiding principles in relation to abuses under what is now Article 102 TFEU.

G Monti, 'The Scope of Collective Dominance under Article 82' (2001) 38 CML Rev 131

Further reading on collective dominance.

J Ysewyn and C Caffara, 'Two's Company, Three's a Crowd: The Future of Collective Dominance after the *Kali & Salz* Judgment' (1998) 19(7) ECL Rev 468

A detailed and progressive look at the collective dominance issue.

Books

C Graham, *EU and UK Competition Law* (London: Pearson, 2013)

A specialized competition law text, with substantive coverage of Article 102 TFEU and the EU/UK approach.

R Whish, *Competition Law*, 7th edn (Oxford: Oxford University Press, 2012)

A comprehensive account of all aspects of EU competition law.

QUESTION

LazyGurl plc (LazyGurl) is a UK manufacturer of high-quality TV viewing chairs combining massage facilities, built-in speakers, and a drinks refrigerator. LazyGurl supply the chairs across the EU. LazyGurl have been the best-selling high-quality chair producer for each of the last eight years, enjoying a 78 per cent market share.

However, a Belgian company, SuperChairz, has emerged as a competitive threat to LazyGurl. SuperChairz is rapidly increasing its market share by offering an equivalent quality, but cheaper, chair.

LazyGurl has embarked upon an EU-wide marketing campaign and has slashed prices in a special promotion. It has spoken to all of its retailers to offer discounts for bulk purchases and further discounts if they agree to buy chairs only from LazyGurl. Many retailers have been warned that if they stock the SuperChairz products, supplies of LazyGurl chairs will cease.

Advise SuperChairz.

To view an outline answer to this question plus further resources to support your EU law studies, visit the Online Resources for this book at **www.oup.com/uk/eulaw-complete4e**

15 Enforcement of EU competition law

KEY POINTS

By the end of this chapter, you should be able to:

- explain the enforcement regime of EU competition law;
- understand the system of cooperation between the Commission, national competition authorities (NCAs), and national courts; and
- understand the relevant provisions of the Treaty on the Functioning of the European Union (TFEU) and other relevant EU legislation (especially Regulation 1/2003).

INTRODUCTION

It is important to recognize that, in order to be effective, competition requires both that undertakings act independently of each other and that they are also subject to the competitive pressure exerted by each other. The EU legislation concerning competition law under Articles 101 and 102 TFEU addresses these issues and prohibits anti-competitive business practices. The European Commission, national competition authorities (NCAs), and national courts enforce Articles 101 and 102 TFEU in a system of cooperation under powers conferred by Article 105 TFEU and Council Regulation (EC) No 1/2003 of 16 December 2002 on the implementation of the rules on competition laid down in Articles 81 and 82 of the Treaty, OJ 2003 L1/1.

15.1 The enforcement regime

Article 105 TFEU provides as follows.

Article 105 TFEU

(1) … the Commission shall ensure the application of the principles laid down in Articles 101 and 102. On application by a Member State or on its own initiative, and in co-operation with the competent authorities in the Member State, which shall give it their assistance, the Commission shall investigate cases of suspected infringement of these principles. If it finds that there has been an infringement, it shall propose the appropriate measures to bring it to an end.

[…]

Article 105 therefore makes the Commission responsible for the enforcement of Articles 101 and 102 TFEU, subject to the concurrent jurisdiction of the Member States.

It is Regulation 1/2003 that provides the detail of the enforcement regime. The basis of this is a system of cooperation between the European Commission, national courts, and the NCAs. The European Commission and the NCAs are empowered to investigate alleged infringements of Articles 101 and 102 TFEU, issue decisions, and impose fines. Allocation and reallocation of cases is determined as set out in the Commission Notice on cooperation within the Network of Competition Authorities, OJ 2004 C101/43.

15.2 The burden of proof

It is clear from Regulation 1/2003 that, in any national or EU proceedings concerning application of Articles 101 and 102 TFEU, the burden of proving an infringement of EU competition law rests on the party or authority alleging the infringement (Article 2 of Regulation 1/2003).

15.3 The relationship between Articles 101 and 102 TFEU and national competition laws

Article 3 of the Regulation provides that where Member State NCAs or national courts apply national competition law to matters that would fall within Article 101 and/or 102 TFEU, they must also apply the relevant EU Treaty Article. Furthermore, national competition law may not prohibit agreements, decisions by associations of undertakings, or concerted practices that would not restrict competition within the meaning of Article 101(1) TFEU or which would be exempted under Article 101(3) TFEU. However, as regards Article 102 TFEU, Regulation 1/2003 does not preclude a Member State from adopting and applying stricter national law that prohibits or sanctions unilateral conduct engaged in by undertakings.

15.4 Cooperation with national authorities

To ensure consistency and effectiveness, Regulation 1/2003 requires close cooperation between the NCAs and the Commission, and between the NCAs themselves, including, for instance, the exchange of information. Details of this cooperation are set out in Articles 11 (cooperation) and 12 (exchange of information) of the Regulation.

Council Regulation (EC) No 1/2003 of 16 December 2002 on the implementation of the rules on competition laid down in Articles 81 and 82 of the Treaty, OJ 2003 L1/1

Article 11

[…]

2. The Commission shall transmit to the competition authorities of the Member States copies of the most important documents it has collected … At the request of the competition authority of a Member State, the Commission shall provide it with a copy of other existing documents necessary for the assessment of the case.
3. The competition authorities of the Member States shall, when acting under Article 81 or Article 82 [101 or 102 TFEU] of the Treaty, inform the Commission in writing before or without delay after commencing the first formal investigative measure. This information may also be made available to the competition authorities of the other Member States.
4. No later than 30 days before the adoption of a decision requiring that an infringement be brought to an end, accepting commitments or withdrawing the benefit of a block exemption Regulation, the competition authorities of the Member States shall inform the Commission. To that effect, they shall provide the Commission with a summary of the case, the envisaged decision or, in the absence thereof, any other document indicating the proposed course of action. This information may also be made available to the competition authorities of the other Member States. At the request of the Commission, the acting competition authority shall make available to the Commission other documents it holds which are necessary for the assessment of the case. The information supplied to the Commission may be made available to the competition authorities of the other Member States. National competition authorities may also exchange between themselves information necessary for the assessment of a case that they are dealing with under Article 81 or Article 82 [101 or 102] of the Treaty.
5. The competition authorities of the Member States may consult the Commission on any case involving the application of Community [Union] law.

Article 12

1. For the purpose of applying Articles 81 and 82 [101 and 102] of the Treaty the Commission and the competition authorities of the Member States shall have the power to provide one another with and use in evidence any matter of fact or of law, including confidential information.

   […]

15.5 Cooperation with national courts

Articles 101 and 102 TFEU are directly effective (see 4.1), and so they may be relied on in national proceedings. National courts can request information or advice from the Commission and may refer questions of interpretation to the Court of Justice under the preliminary rulings procedure (see 6.1). National court proceedings and Commission proceedings may run in parallel, and a national court may consider a case on which the Commission has already taken a decision. Regulation 1/2003 requires national courts to avoid judgments that conflict with Commission decisions.

15.6 The powers of the competition authorities of the Member States

Article 5 of Regulation 1/2003 provides that, acting on their own or following a complaint, NCAs may take decisions:

- requiring that an infringement is brought to an end;
- ordering interim measures;
- accepting commitments; and
- imposing fines, periodic penalty payments, or any other penalty provided for in their domestic law.

15.7 The European Commission's powers

The European Commission's powers are more extensive than those of the NCAs. Regulation 1/2003 empowers it to:

- investigate alleged infringements;
- require undertakings to terminate infringements;
- order interim measures; and
- impose fines and penalties where breaches are established.

Article 7 of Regulation 1/2003 provides that the Commission may, by Decision, impose behavioural remedies (which regulate future conduct) or structural remedies (which change the structure of the market, eg by way of asset transfer) that are proportionate to the infringement and necessary to bring the infringement effectively to an end. Examples of extensive behavioural remedies can be seen in the Commission's 2004 *Microsoft* Decision, concerning what was then the largest individual fine ever imposed on one undertaking in respect of a serious breach of Article 102 TFEU. The behavioural remedies awarded by the Court of Justice were as follows.

Commission Decision 2007/53/EC of 24 May 2004 relating to a proceeding pursuant to Article 82 of the EC Treaty and Article 54 of the EEA Agreement against Microsoft Corporation (Case COMP/C-3/37.792 – *Microsoft*), OJ 2004 L32/23

5. As regards the abuse referred to in Article 2(a) [refusing to supply interoperability information and allow its use for the purpose of developing and distributing work group server operating system products]:
   (a) Microsoft Corporation shall, within 120 days of the date of notification of this Decision, make the Interoperability Information available to any undertaking having an interest in developing and distributing work group server operating system products and shall, on reasonable and non-discriminatory terms, allow the use of the Interoperability Information by such undertakings for the purpose of developing and distributing work group server operating system products;
   (b) Microsoft Corporation shall ensure that the Interoperability Information made available is kept updated on an ongoing basis and in a Timely Manner;
   (c) Microsoft Corporation shall, within 120 days of the date of notification of this Decision, set up an evaluation mechanism that will give interested undertakings a workable possibility of informing themselves about the scope and terms of use of the Interoperability Information; as regards this evaluation mechanism, Microsoft Corporation may impose reasonable and non-discriminatory conditions to ensure that access to the Interoperability Information is granted for evaluation purposes only;
   (d) Microsoft Corporation shall, within 60 days of the date of notification of this Decision, communicate to the Commission all the measures that it intends to take under points (a), (b) and (c); that communication shall be sufficiently detailed to enable the Commission to make a preliminarily assessment as to whether the said measures will ensure effective compliance with the Decision; in particular, Microsoft Corporation shall outline in detail the terms under which it will allow the use of the Interoperability Information;
   (e) Microsoft Corporation shall, within 120 days of the date of notification of this Decision, communicate to the Commission all the measures that it has taken under points (a), (b) and (c).

Article 6

As regards the abuse referred to in Article 2 (b) [making the availability of the Windows Client PC Operating System conditional on the simultaneous acquisition of Windows Media Player]:

(a) Microsoft Corporation shall, within 90 days of the date of notification of this Decision, offer a full-functioning version of the Windows Client PC Operating System which does not incorporate Windows Media Player; Microsoft Corporation retains the right to offer a bundle of the Windows Client PC Operating System and Windows Media Player;
(b) Microsoft Corporation shall within 90 days of the date of notification of this Decision communicate to the Commission all the measures it has taken to implement point (a).

?! **THINKING POINT**

Why are behavioural remedies awarded in conjunction with, and indeed even in the absence of, financial penalties?

The power to impose structural remedies will be appropriate only in exceptional cases, such as where it is necessary to break up dominant undertakings under Article 102 TFEU.

Article 9 of Regulation 1/2003 allows the Commission to accept commitments from undertakings as to action to be taken by them to meet the Commission's concerns. The Commission may also, by Decision, make an undertaking's commitment binding such that it acts as a poised trigger should such action not be taken.

The Commission has (under Ch V of Regulation 1/2003) significant powers of investigation. These investigatory powers permit the Commission to request information from national governments and NCAs, to request or require undertakings to supply information, to interview individuals concerning its inquiries, and to inspect business premises. Inspections may be voluntary, conducted with an undertaking's agreement, or mandatory, the latter often being referred to as 'dawn raids'. Whilst the Commission has no power of forcible entry, it may require the necessary assistance from national authorities (Article 20(6) of Regulation 1/2003)—usually, the issue of a search warrant.

Council Regulation (EC) No 1/2003 of 16 December 2002 on the implementation of the rules on competition laid down in Articles 81 and 82 of the Treaty, OJ 2003 L1/1

Article 20

The Commission's powers of inspection

1. In order to carry out the duties assigned to it by this Regulation, the Commission may conduct all necessary inspections of undertakings and associations of undertakings.
2. The officials and other accompanying persons authorised by the Commission to conduct an inspection are empowered:
    (a) to enter any premises, land and means of transport of undertakings and associations of undertakings;
    (b) to examine the books and other records related to the business, irrespective of the medium on which they are stored;
    (c) to take or obtain in any form copies of or extracts from such books or records;
    (d) to seal any business premises and books or records for the period and to the extent necessary for the inspection;
    (e) to ask any representative or member of staff of the undertaking or association of undertakings for explanations on facts or documents relating to the subject-matter and purpose of the inspection and to record the answers.

3. The officials and other accompanying persons authorised by the Commission to conduct an inspection shall exercise their powers upon production of a written authorisation specifying the subject matter and purpose of the inspection and the penalties provided for in Article 23 in case the production of the required books or other records related to the business is incomplete or where the answers to questions asked under paragraph 2 of the present Article are incorrect or misleading. In good time before the inspection, the Commission shall give notice of the inspection to the competition authority of the Member State in whose territory it is to be conducted.
4. Undertakings and associations of undertakings are required to submit to inspections ordered by decision of the Commission. The decision shall specify the subject matter and purpose of the inspection, appoint the date on which it is to begin and indicate the penalties provided for in Articles 23 and 24 and the right to have the decision reviewed by the Court of Justice. The Commission shall take such decisions after consulting the competition authority of the Member State in whose territory the inspection is to be conducted.
5. Officials of as well as those authorised or appointed by the competition authority of the Member State in whose territory the inspection is to be conducted shall, at the request of that authority or of the Commission, actively assist the officials and other accompanying persons authorised by the Commission. To this end, they shall enjoy the powers specified in paragraph 2.
6. Where the officials and other accompanying persons authorised by the Commission find that an undertaking opposes an inspection ordered pursuant to this Article, the Member State concerned shall afford them the necessary assistance, requesting where appropriate the assistance of the police or of an equivalent enforcement authority, so as to enable them to conduct their inspection.
7. If the assistance provided for in paragraph 6 requires authorisation from a judicial authority according to national rules, such authorisation shall be applied for. Such authorisation may also be applied for as a precautionary measure.
8. Where authorisation as referred to in paragraph 7 is applied for, the national judicial authority shall control that the Commission decision is authentic and that the coercive measures envisaged are neither arbitrary nor excessive having regard to the subject matter of the inspection. In its control of the proportionality of the coercive measures, the national judicial authority may ask the Commission, directly or through the Member State competition authority, for detailed explanations in particular on the grounds the Commission has for suspecting infringement of Articles 81 and 82 [101 and 102] of the Treaty, as well as on the seriousness of the suspected infringement and on the nature of the involvement of the undertaking concerned. However, the national judicial authority may not call into question the necessity for the inspection nor demand that it be provided with the information in the Commission's file. The lawfulness of the Commission decision shall be subject to review only by the Court of Justice.

Article 21

Inspection of other premises

1. If a reasonable suspicion exists that books or other records related to the business and to the subject matter of the inspection, which may be relevant to prove a serious violation of Article 81 [101] or Article 82 [102] of the Treaty, are being kept in any other premises, land and means of transport, including the homes of directors, managers and other members of staff of the undertakings and associations of undertakings concerned, the Commission can by decision order an inspection to be conducted in such other premises, land and means of transport.
2. The decision shall specify the subject matter and purpose of the inspection, appoint the date on which it is to begin and indicate the right to have the decision reviewed by the Court of Justice. It shall in particular state the reasons that have led the Commission to conclude that a suspicion in the sense of paragraph 1 exists. The Commission shall take such decisions after consulting the competition authority of the Member State in whose territory the inspection is to be conducted.

As stated in the Commission's Press Release concerning Coca-Cola's alleged abuse of a dominant position in the market (Commission Press Release of 22 June 2005, IP/05/775), the Commission may levy substantial fines and daily penalties for infringements of Articles 101 and 102 TFEU (up to 10 per cent of the previous year's worldwide turnover *plus* daily penalties of up to 5 per cent of daily turnover for continuing infringements), for supplying incorrect or misleading information (up to 1 per cent of the previous year's turnover), or for failure to comply with a request for information (up to 5 per cent of the previous year's turnover).

On 5 December 2012, the European Commission imposed its largest ever fine of €1.47 billion on seven international producers in the cathode ray tubes sector concerning their involvement in either one or both of two distinct cartels over a ten-year period.

15.8 Safeguards for undertakings

There are a number of procedural safeguards in place. Information collected pursuant to Regulation 1/2003 may be used only for the purpose for which it was acquired and the Commission must have regard to the legitimate interests of undertakings in the protection of their business secrets, for instance when it publishes Decisions.

15.9 The Commission's 2006 Leniency Notice

The Commission Notice on immunity from fines and reduction of fines in cartel cases, OJ 2006 C298/11 ('2006 Leniency Notice'), provides incentives for undertakings involved in horizontal cartels contrary to Article 101(1) TFEU to come forward voluntarily to reveal information.

?! **THINKING POINT**

What is it about the very nature of a cartel that may require such a leniency notice to be in place to ensure that Article 101 TFEU can be upheld by the enforcement provisions?

The reasoning for the approach is clear from paras 3–5 of the 2006 Leniency Notice.

Commission Notice on immunity from fines and reduction of fines in cartel cases, OJ 2006 C298/11

(3) By their very nature, secret cartels are often difficult to detect and investigate without the cooperation of undertakings or individuals implicated in them. Therefore, the Commission considers that it is in the Community [Union] interest to reward undertakings involved in this type of illegal practices which are willing to put an end to their participation and co-operate in the Commission's investigation, independently of the rest of the undertakings involved in the cartel. The interests of consumers and citizens in ensuring that secret cartels are detected and punished outweigh the interest in fining those undertakings that enable the Commission to detect and prohibit such practices.

(4) The Commission considers that the collaboration of an undertaking in the detection of the existence of a cartel has an intrinsic value. A decisive contribution to the opening of an investigation or to the finding of an infringement may justify the granting of immunity from any fine to the undertaking in question, on condition that certain additional requirements are fulfilled.

(5) Moreover, co-operation by one or more undertakings may justify a reduction of a fine by the Commission. Any reduction of a fine must reflect an undertaking's actual contribution, in terms of quality and timing, to the Commission's establishment of the infringement. Reductions are to be limited to those undertakings that provide the Commission with evidence that adds significant value to that already in the Commission's possession.

Note that a distinction is drawn between acquiring immunity from fines and merely being in receipt of a reduction in a fine.

Commission Notice on immunity from fines and reduction of fines in cartel cases, OJ 2006 C298/11

II. IMMUNITY FROM FINES

A. Requirements to qualify for immunity from fines

(8) The Commission will grant immunity from any fine which would otherwise have been imposed to an undertaking disclosing its participation in an alleged cartel affecting the

Community [Union] if that undertaking is the first to submit information and evidence which in the Commission's view will enable it to:

(a) carry out a targeted inspection in connection with the alleged cartel; or

(b) find an infringement of Article 81 EC in connection with the alleged cartel.

Where an undertaking has taken steps to coerce others to join or remain in a cartel, it is ineligible for immunity but may still qualify for a reduction (para 13).

[...]

III. REDUCTION OF A FINE

A. Requirements to qualify for reduction of a fine

(23) Undertakings disclosing their participation in an alleged cartel affecting the Community [Union] that do not meet the conditions under section II above may be eligible to benefit from a reduction of any fine that would otherwise have been imposed.

(24) In order to qualify, an undertaking must provide the Commission with evidence of the alleged infringement which represents significant added value with respect to the evidence already in the Commission's possession and must meet the cumulative conditions set out in points (12)(a) to (12)(c) above.

(25) The concept of 'added value' refers to the extent to which the evidence provided strengthens, by its very nature and/or its level of detail, the Commission's ability to prove the alleged cartel. In this assessment, the Commission will generally consider written evidence originating from the period of time to which the facts pertain to have a greater value than evidence subsequently established. Incriminating evidence directly relevant to the facts in question will generally be considered to have a greater value than that with only indirect relevance. Similarly, the degree of corroboration from other sources required for the evidence submitted to be relied upon against other undertakings involved in the case will have an impact on the value of that evidence, so that compelling evidence will be attributed a greater value than evidence such as statements which require corroboration if contested.

15.10 Private enforcement

It should be noted that Articles 101 and 102 TFEU are directly effective, and can be relied upon by individuals in national courts. Indeed, there are a number of advantages should a complainant choose to pursue this course of action rather than an action before the Commission, as set out in para 16 of the Commission Notice on the handling of complaints by the Commission, OJ 2004 C101/05.

Commission Notice on the handling of complaints by the Commission, OJ 2004 C101/05

- National courts may award damages for loss suffered as a result of an infringement of Article 81 or 82 [EC, now Articles 101 or 102 TFEU].

- National courts may rule on claims for payment or contractual obligations based on an agreement that they examine under Article 81.

  It is for the national courts to apply the civil sanction of nullity of Article 81(2) [EC, now Article 101(2) TFEU] in contractual relationships between individuals. They can in particular assess, in the light of the applicable national law, the scope and consequences of the nullity of certain contractual provisions under Article 81(2), with particular regard to all the other matters covered by the agreement.
- National courts are usually better placed than the Commission to adopt interim measures.
- Before national courts, it is possible to combine a claim under Community [Union] competition law with other claims under national law.
- Courts normally have the power to award legal costs to the successful applicant. This is never possible in an administrative procedure before the Commission.

Case C-453/99 *Courage Ltd v Crehan* [2001] ECR I-6297 provides an example of such an action. Crehan was a tenant of two public houses under a standard lease that required him to purchase beer from Courage Ltd (known as a beer-tie clause) (see 4.3.2). Crehan alleged that the beer-tie clause was anti-competitive as it obliged tied tenants to purchase a fixed minimum quantity of beer at a set price from the landlord's (Courage Ltd's) choice of supplier. This therefore made it more difficult for other suppliers of beer to compete with Courage and also made it very difficult for tied tenants to compete with other publicans on price. The central question referred was whether it was possible for a party to an agreement, which breached Article 101 TFEU, to recover damages from another party to the agreement. The Court of Justice held as follows.

Case C-453/99 *Courage Ltd v Crehan* [2001] ECR I-6297

1. A party to a contract liable to restrict or distort competition within the meaning of Article 85 of the EC Treaty (now Article 81 EC) [now Article 101 TFEU] can rely on the breach of that provision to obtain relief from the other contracting party.
2. Article 85 of the Treaty precludes a rule of national law under which a party to a contract liable to restrict or distort competition within the meaning of that provision is barred from claiming damages for loss caused by performance of that contract on the sole ground that the claimant is a party to that contract.
3. Community [Union] law does not preclude a rule of national law barring a party to a contract liable to restrict or distort competition from relying on his own unlawful actions to obtain damages where it is established that that party bears significant responsibility for the distortion of competition.

Directive 2014/104/EU of the European Parliament and of the Council of 26 November 2014 on certain rules governing actions for damages under national law for infringements of the competition law provisions of the Member States and of the European Union, OJ 2014 L349/1, now makes it easier for private applicants, addressing, amongst other things, the national procedural obstacles that often stood in the way of successful claims for damages. Detailed consideration is outside the scope of this text.

SUMMARY

- Article 105 TFEU makes the Commission responsible for the enforcement of Articles 101 and 102 TFEU, subject to the concurrent jurisdiction of the Member States.
- Regulation 1/2003 provides the detail of the enforcement regime.
- The basis of this is a system of cooperation between the European Commission, the national courts, and the national competition authorities (NCAs).
- The European Commission and NCAs are empowered to investigate alleged infringements of Articles 101 and 102 TFEU, issue decisions, and impose fines.
- Article 5 of Regulation 1/2003 provides that, acting on their own or following a complaint, NCAs may take decisions requiring that an infringement is brought to an end, ordering interim measures, accepting commitments, and imposing fines, periodic penalty payments, or any other penalty provided for in domestic law.
- Regulation 1/2003 empowers the European Commission to investigate alleged infringements, to require undertakings to terminate infringements, to order interim measures, and to impose fines and penalties where breaches are established.
- The Commission has significant powers of investigation under Ch V of Regulation 1/2003.
- The Commission may levy substantial fines and daily penalties for infringements of Articles 101 and 102 TFEU.
- The 2006 Leniency Notice provides incentives for undertakings involved in horizontal cartels to come forward voluntarily to reveal information.
- Articles 101 and 102 TFEU are directly effective, and can be relied upon by individuals in national courts.

FURTHER READING

Articles

CS Kerse, 'The Complainant in Competition Cases: A Progress Report' (1997) 34 CML Rev 213

A useful summary of key case-law developments in this area.

A Komninoa, 'New Prospects for Private Enforcement of EC Competition Law' (2002) 39 CML Rev 447

Further analysis of *Courage v Crehan*.

B Rodger, 'Private Enforcement of Competition Law, the Hidden Story: Competition Litigation Settlements in the United Kingdom, 2000–2005' (2008) 29 ECL Rev 96

A consideration of private enforcement cases that never reached trial.

C Veljanovski, 'Cartel Fines in Europe' (2007) 30 World Competition 65

A consideration of Commission cartel fines and practice.

Books

C Graham, *EU and UK Competition Law*, 2nd edn (London: Pearson, 2013)

Specialist, but accessible, competition law text, covering both public and private enforcement.

L Ortiz Blanco, *EC Competition Procedure*, 3rd edn (Oxford: Oxford University Press, 2013)

Comprehensive work and key analytical commentary on EU competition procedures.

For further resources to support your EU law studies, visit the Online Resources for this book at www.oup.com/uk/eulaw-complete4e

Index